Fundamentals of Archaeology

Fundamentals
of Archaeology

Robert J. Sharer
UNIVERSITY OF PENNSYLVANIA

Wendy Ashmore
UNIVERSITY OF PENNSYLVANIA

The Benjamin/Cummings Publishing Company, Inc.
Menlo Park, California • Reading, Massachusetts
London • Amsterdam • Don Mills, Ontario • Sydney

Sponsoring editor: Larry J. Wilson
Production editor: Margaret Moore
Book designer: Pat Dunbar
Cover designer: John Edeen
Artists: Nova Young, Basil Wood

Cover photograph: Excavation of a middle formative platform (ca. 900–400 B.C.) at Las Tunas, Guatemala.

The quotes appearing on pages 148, 356, and 540 are reprinted by permission of Charles Scribner's Sons from *The Night Country* by Loren Eiseley. Copyright © Loren Eiseley.

Library of Congress Cataloging in Publication Data
Sharer, Robert J
    Fundamentals of archaeology.

    Bibliography: p.
    Includes index.
    1. Archaeology--Methodology. 2. Archaeology--History. I. Ashmore, Wendy, 1948- joint author. II. Title.
CC75.S47   930'.1'028   78-72311
ISBN 0-8053-8760-9

abcdefghij-HA-782109

The Benjamin/Cummings Publishing Company, Inc.
2727 Sand Hill Road
Menlo Park, California 94025

About the Authors

ROBERT J. SHARER received his B.A. from Michigan State University and his M.A. and Ph.D. from the University of Pennsylvania. He has taught archaeology at Beaver College, Pitzer College of the Claremont Graduate Colleges, and California State Polytechnic College. Sharer is currently Associate Curator, American Section, University Museum, and Associate Professor, Department of Anthropology, University of Pennsylvania. His main research area has been in Guatemala, particularly the Quiriguá Project for which he was Project Director (1971–1973) and Field Director (1973–present). He has published numerous research articles in various archaeological journals. Sharer is a Fellow of the American Anthropological Association and a member of the American Association for the Advancement of Science, the Royal Anthropological Institute, and the Society for American Archaeology.

WENDY ASHMORE received her B.A. from the University of California, Los Angeles, and is currently a Ph.D. candidate at the University of Pennsylvania where she is working on the Pre-Columbian settlement at Quiriguá, Guatemala. Ashmore is currently Research Assistant for the Quiriguá Project. From this and other research, she is developing papers on Pre-Columbian, Classic, Lowland, and Highland Mayan settlement patterns. She is a member of the American Anthropological Association, the American Association for the Advancement of Science, and the Archaeological Institute of America, among other professional organizations.

Foreword

Some time ago, a colleague, in the course of reviewing a book on the nature of archaeology, remarked that the volume in question, while all right in its way, was another "little" book about archaeology. What was needed, in that reviewer's opinion, was not still another such slender effort but a "big" book deserving of the title "Principles of Archaeology." I remember, at the time, thinking that this was a goal for only a very distant future. Archaeology still seemed too unformulated, too capricious, too undisciplined a discipline to be contained with such solidity. Then, in the intervening twenty years, archaeology entered into what has appeared as a period of upheaval, "agonizing reappraisal," and experimentation in many directions. This era of rapid growing pains is still with us. On the face of it the desired tome of rock-steady principles should be farther away than ever. And yet, paradoxically, this is not the case. This present book, *Fundamentals of Archaeology,* demonstrates that there is a body of method, technique, and even theory that, by quiet consensus, has been growing around us as a foundation for a true discipline of archaeology. Whether or not it comes up to the hoped for specifications of "bigness" that my colleague had in mind can be set aside for the moment. Its authors make no such claim for it; yet I think it is fair to say that it is the best attempt to date in that direction.

There have been other textbooks which set out to explain archaeology and to give it form as a discipline, and these have not been without merit; but most of them have been deflected from the central methodological target by trying to combine this aim with one of offering routine presentations of area or even worldwide prehistories. One senses in these, perhaps, the publisher's counsel to write a book that will be "all-purpose" and capture the widest audience. But academic archaeology is too far along for this now. Sharer and Ashmore have opted for the wiser course of confining themselves to the operational modes, the guiding strategies, and the theoretical orientations of archaeology. In so doing, they have written a book that is clear, concise, and compact. As a manual of instruction, it is well designed to lead the beginner into the field. To my mind their judgments and evaluations are well balanced. Even if one is of the opinion that there is no true objectivity, especially in archaeological matters, I think he or she must concede that the authors have opened the way for the student of archaeology to explore divergent opinion as one's sophistication in the subject builds to the level to do so intelligently.

The book does three things. First, it details archaeological research procedures: survey and excavation techniques; the processing and analyses of archaeological data; the building of chronologies; the explication of synchronic or inferred behavioral relationships; and theories and logic behind archaeological interpretations. While there is no attempt, as noted, at systematic presentation of substantive prehistory, all of this relating of procedures, both practical and theoretical, is well illustrated by specific archaeological field, laboratory, or general interpretive examples.

Second, the book provides the reader with an historical background to the pursuit of archaeology. This is done explicitly in an early chapter but more importantly, if implicitly, throughout. As examples, the explanations of the nature of stratigraphic excavation or of stylistic and artifact seriation are, in themselves, mini-histories of the development of these approaches over the past hundred years; and the same is true of the discussions of archaeological sampling or artifact classifications.

Third, this essentially historical perspective on the discipline of archaeology shows the additive nature of its growth. This last, I realize, is a controversial subject. To what extent has archaeology undergone, in the words of Thomas Kuhn, a "paradigmatic revolution?" Are the research outlooks and objectives of the past twenty years so utterly different from those that had gone before that a "new archaeology" of the present may be said to have no significant roots in the "traditional archaeology" of not so very long ago? Sharer and Ashmore deal with this question in the latter chapters of their book, as they discuss "culture historical" and "culture processual" approaches. They see a complementarity between them rather than an opposition.

Fundamentals of Archaeology is a testament on the part of its authors to their faith that the discipline has come of age. I share this faith. Perhaps it is a very early maturity, retaining some of the gangliness and lack of coordination of the adolescent; or perhaps we are wrong, and the ontogenetic estimate should be placed even further back. In any event, the discipline faces the future with the great expectations and high optimism of youth. This book is an excellent summation of where we have been and where we are now, and the future, as always, lies ahead.

Gordon R. Willey
Harvard University

Preface

Purpose and Focus of the Book

This textbook surveys the techniques, methods, and theoretical frameworks of contemporary prehistoric archaeology. In our presentation we view prehistoric archaeology as an integral part of the larger field of anthropology, conditioned by the historical development, concepts, and goals of its parent discipline. While we treat the evolving perspectives of archaeological method and theory, together with their implications for understanding the prehistoric past, the text is not a manifesto for any single doctrine or "school" within the field. Rather, it seeks to synthesize those aspects of both the "traditional" and "new" archaeology that have contributed significantly to the current status of prehistoric archaeology.

In writing this book, we have sought to emphasize two themes. The first is that the material remains providing a link with past societies are a finite resource and should not be disturbed or dug up simply for weekend entertainment—let alone for monetary profit. There is much knowledge to be gained from these remains, but only if they are handled with care. The second theme is that choices as to the ways one goes about studying archaeological remains depend on what one wants to know: selecting one site over another, or one field method over another, is always a decision that follows from the specified goals of the archaeologist in each particular situation.

The book is not intended to be a blueprint for digging. Rather, we hope it provides just what the title says—fundamentals of archaeology. It is a review of what archaeology is and has been and of the range of alternative methods and theoretical frameworks now used to glean information about past human societies from the materials they have left behind. We have tried to indicate which methods are suited to various kinds of field situations, offering some criteria for choosing between one approach and another. But there is much more to archaeology than digging and the reader should not expect simply to take the book in one hand, trowel in the other, and be ready to proceed. There is no way a textbook can substitute for active field participation, learning under the guidance of an experienced professional archaeologist.

Audience

The book was written to serve a number of overlapping audiences. It is intended primarily for introductory college courses in archaeological method and theory—courses lasting one term or a whole year. It should also be useful for introductory courses in accelerated high school programs and as a reference in introductory graduate-level method and theory courses. Field schools, too, could use this as a text to accompany the actual practice of field archaeology.

Flexible Usage

The text is flexible in its presentation. Throughout, it integrates explications of archaeological method and theory with case studies and examples selected to illustrate and amplify the points being covered. Rather than break the continuity of presentation with a large number of brief examples, we have elected to present fewer case studies, treating most in some detail and, when appropriate, re-introducing the same examples in later discussions.

The text's flexibility is also maintained by combining the basic subject matter with presentations of more detailed or advanced topics and examples at various points. These sections are designated by an asterisk and are designed for students with a good archaeological background or courses structured at an advanced level.

Depending on the particular course, this text can be complemented by books offering an outline of world prehistory and/or by selected readings amplifying discussion of the various topics. For the former, a number of texts are available, such as Lamberg-Karlovsky and Sabloff's *Ancient Civilizations: The Near East and Mesoamerica*. For additional readings in method and theory, several edited collections have been published. We have, in part, geared our bibliography to include selections from these standard readers to facilitate course organization as well as to make it easier for the student to locate supplementary materials.

Organization

Since the subject matter is archaeological method and theory, we have organized the text presentation to reflect the organization of actual archaeological research. That is, the first three chapters introduce the nature and history of the discipline, outlining what archaeology is and the intellectual forces that have fostered its development. Chapter 4 then gives an overview of the nature of archaeological research, emphasizing the importance of research design and planning. After this, individual chapters focus on particular aspects of the conduct of research—from data acquisition through analysis, synthesis, and interpretation—discussing each facet in the usual order it is accomplished. In so doing, we take the reader from the abstract—from formulation of an idea or problem that stimulates the research in the first place—to the more concrete steps of finding, manipulating, and describing the physical remains and, finally, back to the abstract again, the interpretation of the data in light of the original research questions and problems. The book closes with a chapter reminding the student of some of the challenges impinging on archaeological research, generated by the realities of modern life that, in our opinion, make archaeology an active and relevant discipline, rather than merely an "ivory tower" pursuit.

Bibliography

The bibliography is designed to introduce the newcomer to the archaeological literature, and thus provides a key into the huge library available to the reader. Since no bibliography can hope to be comprehensive, we have tended to favor recent works and, whenever possible, publications that explicitly review relevant antecedent literature. At the same time, we have tried to present varied points of view in theoretical debates. Bibliographic references are summarized topically by chapter in a suggestions for further reading section at the end of the book. These topical bibliographies are followed by a single, overall bibliography giving full citation information. We have also included a glossary of key terms that includes references to the chapter(s) where these concepts are discussed.

Acknowledgments

One never writes alone, and certainly we have been helped by many people in many ways during the three years this book has been in production. It originally grew out of the senior author's introductory archaeology method and theory course taught at the University of Pennsylvania. The students in this course were the first inspiration—as well as the first critics.

Larry J. Wilson, sponsoring editor at Benjamin/Cummings, became enthusiastic about the idea of converting the course to a textbook and has since given unflagging support and encouragement for our doing so. A number of friends and colleagues read and criticized the manuscript at various stages. Some remain anonymous, but we would like to thank them along with those whose names we do know, for their advice and helpful criticism; it may not always have been followed, but it was always considered and appreciated. We acknowledge specifically the comments and suggestions received from: Bruce Bevan, Elizabeth M. Christenson, John L. Cotter, Richard A. Diehl,

Don E. Dumond, Jeremiah F. Epstein, David A. Freidel, Virginia Greene, Norman Hammond, Alexandra Klymyshyn, C. C. Lamberg-Karlovsky, William A. Longacre, Ilene M. Nicholas, Robert L. Pallone, Vincent C. Pigott, William L. Rathje, Jeremy A. Sabloff, Izumi Shimada, and R. E. Taylor. We are especially pleased that our respected friend and colleague Gordon R. Willey has contributed the foreword.

Patricia A. Urban and Edward M. Schortman provided essential assistance in selecting, organizing, and obtaining rights to reproduce previously published illustrations. We thank them as well as the many people and institutions who have allowed us to reproduce their materials. For other illustrations, our working sketches were converted to admirable art by Nova Young and Basil Wood, and the maps were deftly prepared by Virginia Greene, Conservator of the University Museum, University of Pennsylvania. Unless otherwise noted, photographs are the work of the authors or, in Chapter 4, of other members of the Quiriguá Project. We would particularly like to thank several associates at the University Museum who went out of their way to provide many of the photographic materials: Bruce Bevan, Martin Biddle, William Coe, Caroline Dosker, Nicholas Hartmann, Ellen Kohler, Claudia Medoff, and Elizabeth Ralph, as well as the Museum photographers, William Clough and Fred Schoch, who prepared most of the prints. We are grateful to Clemency Coggins for help with two photographs for Chapter 15.

Ilene M. Nicholas compiled the core of the topical bibliographies, an exacting task ably accomplished and one for which we are very grateful. Tom McGarry also suggested several sources on reconnaissance and survey. Eleanor King supplied ideas on opening quotes for some chapters, and Catherine Santisteban helped with index entries.

Typing assistance was cheerfully provided by Jennifer Quick and Christine Pietrucha of the University Museum, and by Mary Emore, Jeanne Gallagher, Carol Morris, and Vanessa Fogler of the Department of Anthropology, University of Pennsylvania. Somehow, Philip C. Barnes, Julie C. Benyo, and Catherine Santisteban also kept smiling, through the endless proofreading, collating, list-making, xeroxing, and myriad other tasks asked of them.

As all these contributions were assembled, they were passed on to the capable hands of Margaret Moore, production editor at Benjamin/Cummings, who took charge of converting them to the book you now hold.

We would also like to thank our families—especially our spouses, Judith Kolm Sharer and Richard D. Ashmore, plus Daniel, Michael, and Lisa Sharer—for supporting us during all phases of this endeavor with love, patience, and good humor.

Despite a few low moments, this book *has* been rewarding to write. We argued often, seldom without benefit but always without rancor. Writing helped us think some things through more clearly than we had before; we hope the product will stimulate others to think more about the issues and choices we discuss in these pages.

The record of the human past is undeniably fascinating. But it is also very fragile. We dedicate this book to those readers who may learn to be committed to studying and protecting the past for the benefit of the future.

Robert J. Sharer
Wendy Ashmore
University of Pennsylvania

Brief Contents

Detailed Contents

PART

I

PART

II

Synthesis and Interpretation   451

PART

IV

Chapter 12: Analogy and Archaeological Interpretation   453

Chapter 13: The Cultural Historical Approach   477

Chapter 14: The Cultural Processual Approach   507

Fundamentals of Archaeology

Introduction

To introduce the subject of archaeology, we will consider its definition and meaning from several viewpoints, as well as its relationship to two larger fields, anthropology and history. Later in this section we will discuss the nature of archaeological evidence and outline the stages that constitute archaeological research. But let us begin by recalling one of the most dramatic archaeological discoveries of the twentieth century.

In November 1922, workers excavating in Egypt's Valley of the Kings for the British archaeologist Howard Carter and his patron, Lord Carnarvon, uncovered a rubble-clogged stone staircase leading down into the earth. When the rubble was cleared away, a plastered-over doorway was found at the foot of the stairs, bearing the hieroglyphs of a then little-known Pharaoh, Tut-ankh-amun. The doorway was then broken through; it led to a rubble-filled corridor some 25 feet long. Clearing this debris brought the excavators to a second doorway. Unfortunately, both doors had been broken open and resealed in ancient times. As a result, Carter was resigned to the fact that, though he had probably found a royal tomb, it must have been pillaged by tomb robbers long before his arrival. It would be empty, like almost every other Egyptian royal tomb discovered so far.

Despite these indications, Carter dared to hope that behind the second door he might find a tomb complete with the royal sarcophagus and the preserved remains of the Pharaoh himself, along with the everyday objects of Tut-ankh-amun's life and the funerary paraphernalia used in the rituals surrounding his death. It was thus with considerable anticipation that on November 26, 1922, Howard Carter removed several blocks from the plastered-over second doorway and, using the light from a lamp, peered into the dark chamber beyond. . . .

Dramatic archaeological discovery: Howard Carter and the tomb of Tut-ankh-amun

Cleared entrance passage to Tut-ankh-amun's tomb with security gate in place before removal of tomb contents. (Griffith Institute, Ashmolean Museum, Oxford.)

Introduction

For a moment—an eternity it must have seemed to the others standing by, I was struck dumb; then Lord Carnarvon inquired anxiously—"Can you see anything?"
  "Yes," I replied, . . . "wonderful things . . ."

> *(Howard Carter's narrative*
> *of the opening of the tomb of*
> *Pharaoh Tut-ankh-amun)*

A VIEW OF THE PAST

Archaeology holds a fascination for many people. The reasons for this attraction may be quite varied, but to most the life of the archaeologist conjures up a picture of adventurous travel to exotic places, together with the prospect of making dramatic discoveries of "lost" civilizations. Certainly the general public's image of archaeology is shaped by the reports of spectacular finds printed in newspapers or presented on television. Events such as Howard Carter's discovery of the tomb of Tut-ankh-amun (Fig. 1.1), or the more recent excavations of ancient royal tombs in China (Fig. 1.2), arouse tremendous public interest. In the United States, the fascination with Tut-ankh-amun's tomb, in particular, continues unabated some two generations after its discovery, as shown by the public enthusiasm for the

Figure 1.1 Howard Carter opening the doors of the second shrine, containing the remains of Tut-ankh-amun. (Griffith Institute, Ashmolean Museum, Oxford.)

Figure 1.2 Chinese archaeologists have discovered some 6000 life-size pottery figures guarding the 2200-year-old tomb of Emperor Ch'in, unifier of China. (Courtesy of Audrey Topping.)

recent traveling exhibit of objects from the tomb. Everywhere the exhibit traveled, thousands of people were willing to stand in line for four hours or more for just a few minutes' view of these ancient objects.

But a spectacular discovery such as the tomb of Tut-ankh-amun is obviously very rare in archaeology. Many archaeologists pursue their entire professional careers without finding anything that could be described as "spectacular." As we shall see, archaeologists are motivated not by the monetary or aesthetic value of their discoveries, but rather by the information these discoveries provide about the past. Yet the popular fascination with archaeology remains, so perhaps there is a deeper reason for it.

Many people are fascinated by the past. Archaeologists study every aspect of the human past, from its most remote and obscure glimmerings to its brightest glories. And they seek answers to fundamental questions that interest and concern most people: Where and when did human life originate on this planet? How and why did early human societies develop increasingly sophisticated cultures? How and why do civilizations rise and fall? Archaeologists even probe the crises faced by ancient societies to seek possible solutions to similar crises facing the present world.

When Howard Carter opened the door to the tomb of Pharaoh Tut-ankh-amun, he beheld a sight that left him speechless for several moments (see Fig. 1.1). He was overcome, not only by the splendor of what he saw, but by the realization that his were the first eyes to gaze upon that scene for more than 3000 years. And when he did attempt to describe what he saw, the "wonderful things" held him spellbound not only because of their beauty, but because they represented a moment suspended in time. Carter "saw" events that concerned a human life and death more than 3000 years ago, but that were so real and vivid that they might have happened the day before.

It would seem, therefore, that at a deeper level the fascination of archaeology is that in viewing the full range of the human past, archaeologists find answers to questions about their own society, and themselves. Howard Carter's experience of awe was something that all archaeologists feel in their day-to-day confrontation with the past. Archaeologists constantly confront the paradox of human mortality and immortality: though individual human life is finite, and though individual societies rise and fall, the cultural heritage of all humankind is continuous and immortal.

Whenever archaeologists reveal the remains of an ancient house or study the fragments of ancient pottery, they look into the past just as Carter did at the door of Tut-ankh-amun's tomb. Obviously, few of these views are as clear as Carter's, if only because they are based upon much less completely preserved remains. And sometimes deliberate destruction obscures the view. For instance, when the Spanish *conquistadores* led by Cortés entered the valley of Mexico in 1519, they were also spellbound by what they saw (Fig. 1.3):

Deliberate destruction of a civilization: Cortés and the Aztecs of Mexico

> . . . and when we saw so many cities and villages built in the water and other great towns on dry land and that straight and level Causeway going towards Mexico, we were amazed and said that it was like the enchantments they tell of in the legend of Amadis, on account of the great towers . . . and buildings rising from the water, and all built of masonry. And some of our soldiers even asked whether the things that we saw were not a dream. . . . I do not know how to describe it seeing things as we did that had never been heard of or seen before, not even dreamed about.
>
> (Diaz del Castillo
> 1956: 190–191; orig. 1632)

Yet that splendid scene was completely destroyed by these same Spanish in a brutal war of conquest that saw the cities of Mexico razed, thousands of people killed, and a whole way of life drastically altered. The *conquistadores* did more than wipe out an ongoing civ-

Figure 1.3 The Aztec capital of Tenochtitlán was situated on several is-lands in the middle of Lake Texcoco and could be reached only by causeways or canoe; this view shows the city rebuilt by the Spanish as it appeared in the early eighteenth century. (By permission of the British Library.)

ilization, however, for conquest included deliberate destruction of many of the buildings, tools, and records associated with Aztec life. As a result, the conquest also robbed future generations of much material crucial for understanding such a past civilization. Of course the destruction of archaeological evidence continues to the present day in the valley of Mexico, as it does everywhere in the world.

This brings up a darker side of the consequences of archaeological research—the fact that publicity about great discoveries may also give incentive to the looter who raids archaeological sites and sells the resulting plunder. For there are always individuals who view the remains of the past as a way to make money. Looting the past is nothing new: Egyptian tomb robbers were plying their secret trade during the time of the Pharaohs. The consequences of looting have even provided some unique archaeological discoveries, such as the discovery in 1881 of a cache of more than 40 mummies in a single chamber at Deir el-Bahri in Egypt. The mummies were brought in ancient times from their original tombs in the nearby Valley of the Kings to protect the dead rulers' remains from the depredations of tomb robbers in the royal burial grounds. The attempt was successful for more than 30 centuries, but when the chamber was finally rediscovered, its finders were none other than modern looters, heirs to an ancient and dishonorable tradition.

**Looting of the past:
The Deir el-Bahri
mummy cache**

**Looting of the past:
Commerce in Maya
artifacts**

Today the plundering of archaeological sites is proceeding far faster than the pace of archaeological research. The simple truth is that far more money is available to purchase ''art'' stolen from archaeological sites than to support archaeological research. As long as private collectors create the demand by buying ''art'' at inflated prices, the dealers and their agents who loot sites will reap the financial rewards. Even new laws that attempt to stem the destruction are often frustrated. For instance, until recently a single Maya sculpture from Mexico or Guatemala (often only a fragment sawed from a larger monument) brought as much as several hundred thousand dollars to enterprising dealers in Los Angeles or New York. But when U.S. customs laws were tightened to stop the flow of pre-Columbian antiquities, the market in Maya ''art'' shifted to polychrome painted vases which are more portable and easier to smuggle. As a result, the finest of these vases now bring prices nearly as high as those formerly paid for sculpture. And instead of several dozen sculptures being stolen each year from Central America, hundreds of these polychrome vessels are smuggled annually out of a single country such as Guatemala. Given the fact that Maya tombs, the source for these vases, usually contain only a single polychrome vase of the kind that the art market demands, and that the other contents of plundered tombs are usually broken, scattered, and abandoned, the loss to archaeology from this one portion of the ''art'' market alone is staggering.

Our final chapter will return to the specific problems of destruction of archaeological remains. But however much evidence remains intact for archaeologists to work with, their task is the same: to obtain as clear a view of the past as possible by reconstructing the behavior of individuals and the events of society. In reconstructing the past, archaeologists are not merely describing a series of detached and abstract events. The reconstructed past was composed of individual lives that shaped events both petty and important. And although both those individuals and their societies are dead and gone, their achievements and failures have shaped our present world. In an ultimate sense, then, the fascination of archaeology is that it bridges past and present. The past seen by archaeologists is nothing less than an imperfect reflection of life today.

ARCHAEOLOGY: A DEFINITION

Another popular image of the archaeologist is that of the single-minded (or absent-minded) scholar who spends a lifetime digging and studying the few fragmentary remains of some obscure civilization. This picture of a slightly befuddled, eccentric archaeologist abounds in popular films, novels, and even cartoons (Fig. 1.4). Of course, just as not all archaeologists happen to find tombs of Tut-ankh-amun, neither are all archaeologists befuddled scholars, entrenched for life in the pursuit of minutiae from the past. What, then, does the archaeologist do, and what is archaeology all about?

Method and Theory

First of all, the term *archaeology* is sometimes used to refer to a specific body of techniques used to recover evidence about the past, as in "doing archaeology." In this sense, archaeology often means excavating in the earth to recover the remains of the past. The term can also refer to information about the past gained primarily through excavation, as in the "archaeology of Mexico" or the "archaeology of Greece." However, the most basic and accepted meaning of archaeology refers to a field of inquiry, or discipline, that has grown during the last several hundred years from an amateur's pastime to an increasingly scientifically-based profession. Seen from this viewpoint, archaeology is the study of the social and cultural past through material remains—a study that seeks to order and describe the events of the past and to explain the meaning of those events.

In the broadest sense, then, a definition of archaeology incorporates the subject matter—the study of the past—and the techniques, which are the means to describe and explain the past. More specifically, in order to study the social and cultural past, archaeologists have developed a methodology or a series of techniques and procedures by which they discover, recover, preserve, describe, and

Figure 1.4 Popular view of the archaeologist, one fortunately not often confirmed by fact!

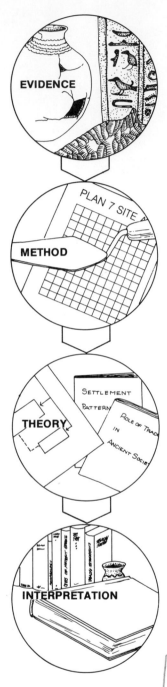

Figure 1.5 Archaeological reasoning relates evidence and interpretation by means of method and theory.

analyze the remains of the past (Fig. 1.5). In assessing the meaning of this evidence, archaeologists are guided by a body of theory. Ultimately, this body of theory provides the means to interpret archaeological evidence and allows the archaeologist both to describe and to explain the events of the past. This book will explore both the methods and the theory basic to modern archaeology.

We have said that archaeology seeks to describe and explain the events of the past. In order to do this, it has not only developed its own specialized methods and theory, but has benefited as well from the contributions of many other fields. In pursuing their goals, archaeologists often make use of the expertise of specialists trained in anthropology, geography, history, biology, astronomy, physics, geology, and computer technology, as well as other areas (Fig. 1.6). These fields contribute not only to the refinement of archaeological methods, but also to the development of a body of archaeological theory by which the evidence of the past is interpreted.

Goals of Archaeology

The archaeologist has three principal concerns in studying the past (Fig. 1.7). The first of these is the *form* of the past: the physical description and classification of the recovered archaeological evidence. Analysis of form allows the archaeologist to outline the distribution of the remains of past societies in both time and space. Second, the archaeologist is concerned with *function;* by analyzing the form and interrelationships of remains of the past the archaeologist attempts to determine what these remains were used for. The determination of function ultimately leads to the reconstruction of ancient customs, behavior, and beliefs. Finally, the archaeologist attempts to understand the *processes* of culture, using archaeological evidence to explain how and why ancient cultures changed. Here the full extent of the record of human existence may be used to understand better both the variations and the consistencies of the past.

ARCHAEOLOGY AS A DISCIPLINE

We have called archaeology a discipline. The term *discipline* implies a unified field of inquiry that recovers data by orderly methods and that interprets these data according to a body of theory. Archaeology is certainly unified, at least in that most archaeologists subscribe to the defined area of inquiry and goals that we outlined in the previous discussion. Yet when it comes to the actual application of archaeological method and theory to meet these goals, a great deal of diversity be-

(a) **(b)**

Figure 1.6 Archaeologists often rely on contributions from other fields such as physics (a), which has provided sensitive magnetometers and other devices for locating buried archaeological remains; or geology (b), in this case a geomorphologist (lower right) conducting soil analysis during an ongoing excavation.

comes apparent. The standards by which archaeological sites are excavated and the results recorded vary widely, as do the means by which the data are interpreted. In some cases the lack of standards results in an irreparable loss of information about the past, rather than a gain in knowledge. For example, Kent Flannery describes the following scene at a site in Mexico:

Destruction of archaeological evidence from substandard research

> Four stalks of river cane, stuck loosely in the ground, defined a quadrilateral (though not necessarily rectangular) area in which two *peones* [laborers] picked and shoveled to varying depths, heaving the dirt to one side. On the backdirt pile stood the archeologist himself, armed with his most delicate tool—a three-pronged garden cultivator of the type used by elderly British ladies to weed rhododendrons. Combing through every shovelful of dirt, he carefully picked out each figurine head and placed it in a brown paper shopping bag nearby—the only other bit of equipment in evidence. This individual was armed with an excavation permit that had been granted because, in the honest words of one official, "he appeared to be no better or worse than any other archeologist who had worked in the area." When questioned, our colleague descended from the backdirt pile and revealed that his underlying research goal was to define the nature of the

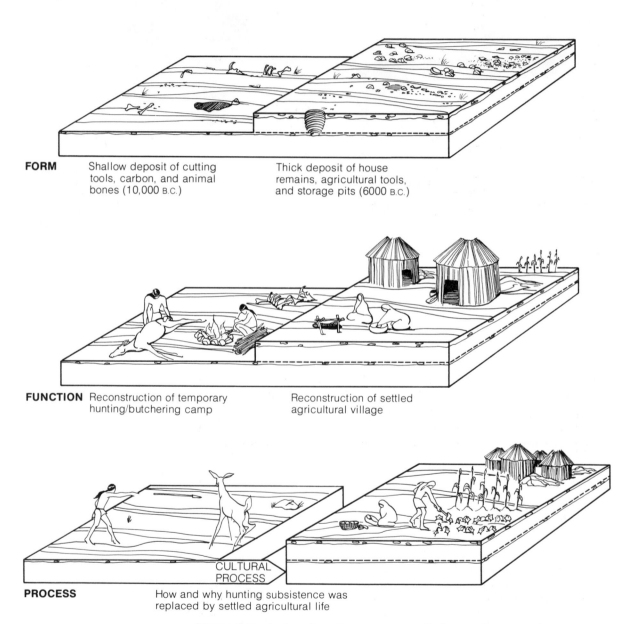

FORM   Shallow deposit of cutting   Thick deposit of house
                  tools, carbon, and animal   remains, agricultural tools,
                  bones (10,000 B.C.)   and storage pits (6000 B.C.)

FUNCTION   Reconstruction of temporary   Reconstruction of settled
                  hunting/butchering camp   agricultural village

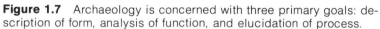

PROCESS   How and why hunting subsistence was
                  replaced by settled agricultural life

Figure 1.7 Archaeology is concerned with three primary goals: description of form, analysis of function, and elucidation of process.

"Olmec presence" in that particular drainage basin; his initial results, he said, predicted total success.

As [we] rattled back along the highway in our jeep, each of us in his own way sat marveling at the elegance of a research strategy in which one could define the nature of a foreign presence in a distant drainage basin from just seven fragmentary figurine heads in the bottom of a supermarket sack. . . .

(Flannery 1976:12)

At first this case strikes us as humorous, until we realize that it is based on an actual incident, and that unfortunately, similar situations continue to occur in the name of "archaeology" throughout the world.

While many archaeologists stress the unity of archaeology as a discipline, in fact it is only beginning to gain recognition as a distinct professional discipline. The field of archaeology is composed of individuals with diverse backgrounds and training and different interests and specialties. This diversity is reflected in the fact that in the United States alone, archaeologists have formed six major professional organizations: the Archaeological Institute of America (AIA), Society for American Archaeology (SAA), Association for Field Archaeology (AFA), American Society of Conservation Archaeologists (ASCA), Society for Historical Archaeology (SHA), and the Society of Professional Archeologists (SOPA).

overlap in membership

SOPA, founded in 1976, has attempted to define professional qualifications and standards for archaeologists. These include the following criteria of training and experience:

Society of Professional Archeologists defines standards for archaeologists

1. Education and Training
   a. A professional archaeologist must have received a graduate degree in archaeology, anthropology, history, classics, or another pertinent discipline with a specialization in archaeology;
   b. A professional archaeologist must have supervised experience in basic archaeological field research consisting of at least 12 weeks of field training and 4 weeks of laboratory analysis or curating;
   c. A professional archaeologist must have designed and executed archaeological research, as evidenced by a Master of Arts or Master of Science thesis or an equivalent research report.
2. Experience
   A professional archaeologist must have at least one year of experience in one or more of the following:
   a. Field and laboratory situations under supervision of a professional archaeologist, with a minimum of 6 months as a supervisor

b. Analytic study of archaeological collections
c. Theoretical, library, or archival research
d. Administration of archaeological research
e. Management of cultural resources
f. Museum work
g. Teaching
h. Marine survey archaeology

Yet even as it emerges as a fully developed professional discipline, archaeology remains linked to a vigorous amateur tradition. This connection is vital to public understanding and support of efforts to conserve and protect archaeological sites from destruction. For without a concerted effort to conserve the evidence of the past, archaeology stands to lose—*irretrievably*—its source of data.

We have described archaeology as being presently in a state of flux, as a professional discipline in the process of formation. In the next chapter we will explore the background and growth of the field to understand its present status more fully. But at this point we must consider two factors that are of importance to the present nature of the discipline. The first, which may be more apparent than real, involves the distinction between "academic" and "field" archaeology. The second factor has deeper historical roots, involving the differences between American and European archaeology.

In contrast to most disciplines, the teaching and training of archaeology cannot be carried out solely in an academic setting in colleges and universities. As the SOPA guidelines recognize, archaeological training must also include time spent in the field, so that what is learned in an academic setting can be put into practice. In most cases, archaeological field schools first expose students to the practical application of field methods. The classroom, then, introduces the student to archaeological method and theory, while the field school applies the techniques of data recovery and initial processing. After this training, the student returns to an academic setting for advanced work in methods of data analysis and in application of theory for archaeological interpretation.

Professional archaeologists usually participate in both the academic and the field aspects of research. Many archaeologists have academic appointments in universities or museums where they may teach archaeology as well as conduct field work. An increasing number of archaeologists, however, are employed by private or governmental agencies, such as the National Park Service, where they engage in full-time field research. Although most archaeologists participate in both academic and field situations at one time or another in their careers, some archaeologists recognize the duality of *roles* between field archaeologists and academic archaeologists. Unfortunately, they sometimes also imply that there are two categories of archaeologists. The "field archaeologist" emphasizes skills in method, while the academician deals more in developing archaeological theory. This book will hopefully make clear that no such division of knowledge or expertise should exist: every archaeologist needs an understanding of both method and theory to work with the remains of the past.

The second factor is a difference between the definition of professional archaeology in the United States and that in Europe. In North America, archaeology is still not considered a separate academic discipline. Rather, it is taught as a specialty within several academic fields, such as anthropology, classics, and history. Most archaeological training in the United States is offered within anthropology, and the resulting undergraduate degrees and most graduate degrees are in anthropology, not archaeology.

This contrasts with the situation prevailing in Europe, where archaeology is usually considered a distinct discipline. The European academic tradition considers archaeology to be more closely related to history than to anthropology. However, students can maintain a separate program of study culminating in a degree in archaeology. This difference in the academic status of archaeology highlights a difference in the emphasis placed upon the relationship between archaeology and the fields of anthropology and history. The reasons for this difference will be discussed in Chapter 2, but here we will consider the immediate consequences for the discipline of archaeology.

Archaeology and History

Archaeology is obviously related to the field of history in that both disciplines seek knowledge of the human past. The difference between the two disciplines begins with a distinction in *sources of information;* this leads to differences in methodology, the techniques by which the past is studied. History deals primarily with textual sources —written accounts from the past. Archaeology, on the other hand, deals primarily with the physical remains of the past.

Documents, of course, are "physical remains of the past" and can be studied as such. Clay tablets marked in cuneiform writing, Egyptian hieroglyphic texts on papyrus, and inscriptions carved on Maya stone stelae are just as much documents as are the books and records of Renaissance Europe. It should be obvious, then, that many ancient documents are discovered through archaeological research. The distinction is that, given a particular document, historians are concerned primarily with the written message it carries, while archaeologists deal with the document principally as a material object.

This is not to imply that archaeologists have no interest in what a document says. But whether or not a document can be read, archaeologists study it as an artifact—what it's made of, where it was found, and so on. For example, an ancient library may be identified and its use or ownership inferred from its location within an ancient settlement, even though the texts in the library may be in an undeciphered language. But for the historian, documents provide information principally by being read.

Distinctions between history and archaeology are made on other grounds as well. For one thing, history is traditionally particularizing in its research objectives. That is, historians seek and study the records of specific past events in order to compare them, judge their veracity, place them in chronological sequence, and interpret them in light of preceding, contemporary, and subsequent events. The results

Figure 1.8 Excavations at a historical site in Stenton Park, Philadelphia, revealing a brick pavement associated with a barn from about A.D. 1800. (Courtesy of the Museum Historic Research Center, University Museum, University of Pennsylvania.)

of such detailed studies are sometimes used to develop generalizations or descriptions of larger historical trends and processes. Studies such as those by Arnold Toynbee and Oswald Spengler represent generalizing approaches to the study of history, in that they seek to discover major trends or themes in the sequence of human events.

Nevertheless, the traditional subjects of history are the movers and shakers—the lives of great men and women and the destinies of their nations. Historical studies are, of course, dependent upon the available written record, which often does not include information about everyday people and events. Thus historical studies of major political, social, and economic processes seldom consider the role of family institutions, village life, and other similar local events. There are significant exceptions to this, of course: social historians often evince an interest in the lives of ordinary people and the cultural conditions under which they lived. For example, the famous diary of Samuel Pepys is a historical document offering a wealth of details about the way of life in seventeenth-century London.

Archaeology, on the other hand, studies the way of life of a broad cross-section of the ancient populace. Although it has been true until recently that archaeologists often emphasized spectacular remains—the tombs and palaces of kings, for instance, rather than the less impressive remains of farms and villages—they have attempted to look at the full range of human activities, not just the pivotal events on which history turned.

History and archaeology are closely allied in several established fields in which the methods of both disciplines are brought to bear upon the study of a particular era of the human past. For instance, the long-established field of classical archaeology combines the methods of archaeology with use of historical sources to document better the classical civilizations of Greece and Rome. Classical archaeology is also allied to the field of art history, which provides another route—the analysis of art styles and themes—to the understanding of the past. Several universities in Europe and North America offer separate training and degree programs in classical archaeology. Other, more specialized combined fields, such as medieval archaeology (spanning the tenth to fourteenth centuries in Europe), American historical archaeology (generally the seventeenth to nineteenth centuries in the United States), and industrial archaeology (the Industrial Revolution of the eighteenth and nineteenth centuries), have emerged in the past few decades (Fig. 1.8). Some universities offer courses and even degree programs in these related fields.

Most archaeologists, however, are concerned with aspects of the past that cannot be directly supplemented by historical studies. This is because history is limited to the relatively recent era of human development, encompassed by the invention and use of writing systems. This "historical era" extends at most only some 5000 years into the past, in the area with the earliest examples of writing, southwestern Asia. When compared with the total length of human cultural development, the era of history represents less than 1 percent of the overall span of far more than a million years (Fig. 1.9). Historical studies are even more limited outside of southwest Asia, and they are not possible in areas where writing systems never developed. In places where writing systems are present but remain only partially deciphered, such as in the New World, the era of history begins with discovery and colonization by other literate peoples (in the New World, by Europeans beginning in the sixteenth century). Other regions have remained unknown to the literate world—and thus not recorded—until quite recently, as late as the nineteenth or twentieth centuries for some remote areas of the Arctic or the Amazon basin. And the Tasaday people of the Philippines were not contacted until 1971.

Historical and Prehistoric Archaeology

It is often useful to distinguish archaeological studies on the basis of whether or not the subject society possessed a writing system. *Historical archaeology* refers to archaeological investigations carried out in conjunction with analyses of written records. *Prehistoric archaeology* studies societies and time periods that lack historical traditions. The latter area of archaeology seeks an understanding of the full sweep of human development on earth, from its earliest traces to its most remote variations. It is prehistoric archaeology, therefore, that is concerned with the bulk of our past, and that is the primary focus of this book. Although the methods and theoretical approaches discussed here may be applied to any archaeological research, including research directly combined with documentary sources, they are not *dependent* upon historical supplements.

Of course the distinction between prehistory and history is not always clear. Both historical and archaeological data are fragmentary in that they can never provide a complete reconstruction of the past. Thus even when historical records are available, archaeological information can add to our understanding of that past era. A famous example in which history was illuminated by archaeology is the excavation of Masada, in Israel. Descriptions by the first-century historian Josephus Flavius recount the construction and history of occupation of the fortress of Masada, where in A.D. 73 Jewish patriots chose suicide rather than surrender to the besieging Roman troops. But it was excavations in 1963 through 1965 that revealed the full length of occupation of the hilltop site, details of daily life there, and such information as the length of time—at least 40 years—the Roman garrison remained after the end of the siege.

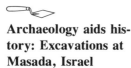

Archaeology aids history: Excavations at Masada, Israel

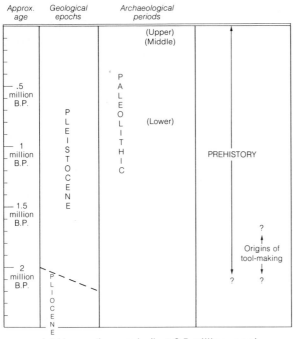

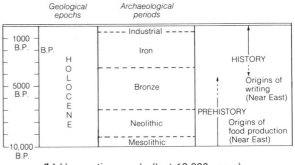

(b) Human time scale (last 10,000 years)

(a) Human time scale (last 2.5 million years)

Figure 1.9 The eras of human prehistory and history. Note that the historical era represents much less than 1% of the total span of known cultural development.

Other archaeological projects bridge the transition between prehistory and history—the period sometimes called *protohistory*. For instance, recent excavations at Winchester, England, directed by Martin Biddle over an eleven-year period, were not oriented to a particular period in the past. Rather, the goal was to study the origins and development of Winchester as a town, from its prehistoric roots through its Roman, Saxon, and Norman periods, right up to the present day. In this case, a research problem dealing with the phenomenon of urbanism was investigated using archaeological data during periods devoid of historical documents, and combined historical and archaeological data during times when records were available (Fig. 1.10).

On the other hand, some areas that were once known to us solely from the perspective of prehistoric archaeology are beginning to develop the possibility of a historical perspective. A case in point would be the Classic Maya civilization, which flourished between about A.D. 200 and 900 in what is now Mexico and Central America. The Maya developed a writing system to record political, religious, and astronomical events. But most of these records, sculpted on wood and stone as well as written in folding books, have yet to be

Bridging the transition between history and prehistory: Excavations at Winchester, England

Historical perspective emerges: Classic Maya civilization

22

Figure 1.10 Excavations at Winchester, England, at the site of the principal cathedral of the Anglo-Saxon kingdom of Wessex, located to the left (north) of the present cathedral built after the Norman Conquest. (Courtesy of Martin Biddle, © Winchester Excavations Committee.)

fully deciphered (Fig. 1.11). Thus, until recently, archaeological investigations of the Maya took place without the aid of historical interpretation. Recently, however, a true historical perspective of dynastic succession, political events, and social interaction has begun to emerge as the result of the gradual decipherment of Maya writing.

In dealing with most areas of the human past, however, archaeology lacks any sort of historical record to supplement its studies. In such cases, prehistoric archaeology has drawn upon the resources of several other fields, including anthropology and geography. Traditionally, prehistoric archaeology has allied itself most closely to anthropology. Through the concept of culture, anthropology provides a framework upon which prehistoric archaeology can build both to describe and to explain the past.

Archaeology, Anthropology, and Culture

In its broadest sense, anthropology is the comprehensive science of humankind—the study of human biological, social, and cultural form and variation in both time and space. In other words, anthropology seeks to study human beings both as biological organisms and as culture-bearing creatures. It also studies human society from two per-spectives: a *diachronic* view that stresses the developmental aspect through time, and a *synchronic* view that emphasizes the contempo-rary state of human societies with little or no time depth.

The field of anthropology is normally divided into a series of sub-disciplines (Fig. 1.12). The subdiscipline that studies the human spe-cies as a biological organism is usually called physical anthropology. The diachronic aspect of physical anthropology investigates our bio-logical evolution, while the synchronic perspective studies humanity's contemporary biological form and variation. The study of the human species as a cultural organism is usually referred to as cultural anthro-pology. The synchronic aspect of cultural anthropology includes two general approaches to the study of living cultures. The first, eth-nography, refers to particular studies of individual cultures or cultural systems—studies of a single society or of a segment of a complex so-ciety, such as a particular community. Ethnology, on the other hand, assumes a comparative and generalizing perspective, based on eth-nographic data, in order to attempt to understand the processes of culture. By comparing data from many societies, ethnology studies how and why contemporary cultural systems operate and change. In addition, some anthropologists specialize in the study of human social institutions (social anthropology), or languages (anthropological lin-guistics). Finally, from this perspective, prehistoric archaeology rep-resents that aspect of cultural anthropology that studies culture from a diachronic viewpoint—in other words, the study of our cultural and social past. In this sense prehistoric archaeology is sometimes re-ferred to as *paleoanthropology.*

The incorporation of physical anthropology and prehistoric archae-ology within a broad definition of anthropology is typical of North American universities. In Europe, these fields usually maintain a more separate existence. But even in Europe these subdisciplines of anthropology are by no means isolated or exclusive concerns. There is a great deal of overlap, and some of the most fruitful and significant research takes place in studies that combine the approaches and methods of several anthropological subdisciplines. For example, pre-historic archaeology and physical anthropology often combine to re-cover and study the fossil evidence of human biological and cultural evolution.

The foregoing description of anthropology is a simplified view of a very complex field. This situation should not be surprising, however, for the pursuits of anthropological research must be as diverse as the varieties of human behavior and the complexities of culture.

Despite its internal diversity, anthropology is unified by one com-mon factor, the concept of culture. The term *culture* has both a gen-eral and a specific connotation. In its general sense, culture refers to

Figure 1.11 Some ancient cultures, such as the Maya, formerly con-sidered prehistoric, emerge into history when their records are de-ciphered. The photograph shows a Maya calendric inscription in a tomb at Tikal, Guatemala. (The date is read as 9.1.1.10.10 4 0c, equiv-alent to March 18, A.D. 457.) (Courtesy of the Ti-kal Project, University Museum, University of Pennsylvania.)

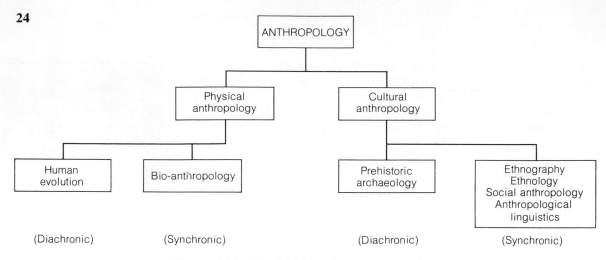

Figure 1.12 The field of anthropology may be divided into synchronic and diachronic aspects; in this view, prehistoric archaeology represents the diachronic part of cultural anthropology.

the uniquely human addition to the biological and social dimensions we share with other life forms. It is culture in this general sense that we will be concerned with, and it is this concept that we will attempt to define below. But we must also realize that the term *culture* may be used in a specific sense to refer to the particular and unique cultural systems of individual human societies, as when we speak of the "culture of the Samoan Islanders" or of "Korokoro culture," referring to a particular group in East Africa.

The concept of culture in the general sense is much too complex to define comprehensively in a few paragraphs, encompassing as it does well over a million years of human evolution, as well as hundreds of unique and varied contemporary societies throughout the world. Yet one of the most often cited definitions, written more than 100 years ago by Edward Tylor (1871) remains useful today:

> That complex whole which includes knowledge, belief, art, morals, law, custom, and any other capabilities and habits acquired by man as a member of society.

Today many prehistoric archaeologists prefer to emphasize culture as the primary means by which human societies adapt to their environment, in contrast to the genetic (biological) adaptations of other life forms. According to this view, culture comprises the cumulative resources of human societies, perpetuated by language, that provides the primary means for nongenetic adaptation to the environment by regulating behavior on three levels: the technological (relationships with the environment), the social (organizational systems), and the ideational (belief systems).

We will return to this concept in the next chapter when we discuss the various views of culture that have developed along with the field of anthropology.

ARCHAEOLOGY AND SCIENCE

We have called anthropology the "science of humankind," but what do we mean by the word *science*? Science is concerned with gaining knowledge about the natural world and therefore seeks an understanding of the world that can be observed. Science is not concerned with that which cannot be observed and tested; the latter remains the subject of theology, philosophy, and the occult. Obviously, by observing and experiencing the real world, everyone gains knowledge in the course of a lifetime. But is this "science"? No; science implies a disciplined search for knowledge, as when the description, ordering, and meaning of phenomena are pursued in a systematic manner. Science also implies a method of acquiring knowledge that is continuously self-correcting, because it involves the testing and refinement of the conclusions that result from accumulated research. The method used in the pursuit of knowledge is often conditioned by the circumstances of each branch of scientific study, being tailored to the specific goals of each kind of research. In other words, the methods used in astronomy to gain knowledge of our universe must differ from those used in biology to study life forms on earth. But all branches of science share a generally accepted set of procedures that have been found to be trustworthy methods for gaining and testing our knowledge of the real world. This set of procedures is generally called the *scientific method*.

The Scientific Method

Science discovers facts about the natural world by observing either objects or events. A scientist may draw conclusions by observing the real world, and then test those conclusions by seeing if they hold true in other circumstances or cases. That is, science proceeds by reasoning both *inductively* and *deductively*. Inductive reasoning starts from specific observations and proceeds to a generalization. Deductive reasoning goes in the other direction, proceeding from a generalization to specific implications.

In order to see how these reasoning processes work, let us examine an archaeological example in which both are explicitly used. Julian Steward, an anthropologist about whom we will say more in later chapters, conducted extensive ethnographic fieldwork in the Great Basin of the western United States in the 1920s and 1930s. From this

The scientific method in archaeology: Research in the Great Basin (Reese River Ecological Project)

Steward

Thomas

work, he *inductively* developed a generalization to describe the distribution of prehistoric Shoshonean Indian activities and campsites, relating their locations to the seasonal cycle of food procurement. That is, in synthesizing his data, Steward abstracted the patterns and regularities that he thought would describe and account for the data he had recorded. In the late 1960s, David Hurst Thomas took Steward's theory of Great Basin settlement patterns and *deductively* derived a series of propositions, or *hypotheses*. These concerned the distribution and density of artifacts discarded in the various ecological zones of the Great Basin: riverine zone, sagebrush flats, piñon-juniper zone, and upper sagebrush-grass zone. As Thomas phrased it, "if the late prehistoric Shoshoneans behaved in the fashion suggested by Steward, how would the artifacts have fallen on the ground?" If Steward's theory of shifting settlement and seasonal exploitation of differentially located food resources were true, then Thomas could expect to find the tools associated with specific activities in roughly predictable locations and densities. Hunting tools and butchering knives, for example, should be found more abundantly in the sagebrush zones, where hunting was argued to have been more important.

Thomas derived more than 100 predictions from Steward's theory; these were then tested by collection of relevant archaeological data from the Reese River Valley of central Nevada. In this test, more than 75 percent of the specific hypotheses were supported. As a result, Steward's theory could be refined and new hypotheses derived, including, for example, more precise predictions about campsite forms and locations. The 1971 field season of the Reese River Ecological Project provided new and independent data for testing the second round of hypotheses—which in turn allowed further refinement of the theory. This sequence of scientific hypothesis generation and testing could be continued indefinitely.

Are induction and deduction equally valid approaches for gaining knowledge? While recognizing the differences between these two approaches, most scientists today would answer "yes." Induction may at times be a less precise method of reasoning than deduction. This is because inductively arguing a general regularity from a set of particular instances involves some degree of insight or intuition. For this reason, some scientists dismiss induction as an untrustworthy method of gaining knowledge. In recent years, however, with the well-intentioned aim of making archaeology more scientific, some archaeologists have rejected induction altogether, opting exclusively for a research strategy based on deduction. The vast majority of scientists do not accept such a position, however, for the rejection of induction implies the rejection of all knowledge gained by this procedure.

On the other hand, in some cases the general principles used in the deductive method may also derive from intuition or accident: Although the story that a falling apple inspired Sir Isaac Newton to formulate the law of gravity may be only a myth, it does illustrate one means by which general ideas are discovered. In fact, as we saw in the example above, induction and deduction work together to produce a harmonious method for generating new hypotheses or principles from particulars and then testing those hypotheses.

We have used the term *hypothesis,* but what is a hypothesis and how is it tested? A hypothesis expresses a proposed relationship between two or more variables, based upon certain assumptions or "givens." In testing a hypothesis, one attempts to determine how well it actually accounts for the observed phenomena. One type of hypothesis tested in the Reese River Ecological Project, for example, related presence of sites (variable 1) to particular predictable kinds of locations (variable 2). The research team discovered 65 sites, of which all but 2 were in expected locales. They also found 11 "appropriate" locales that lacked sites, although the theory predicted that sites would be there. Even so, these results strongly support the relationship expressed by the hypothesis.

It is important to remember that a hypothesis must be tested by rigorous and efficient scientific procedures. It is generally agreed that to test any given hypothesis, one must perform the following steps:

1. Devise a series of alternative and mutually exclusive hypotheses.
2. Devise a test (usually an experiment) that will discriminate among the various hypotheses.
3. Perform the test or experiment (or gather the relevant data, as in the Reese River Valley reconnaissance).
4. Eliminate those hypotheses found not to be supported.

This procedure does not attempt to *prove* one hypothesis correct. Rather, the testing procedure seeks to eliminate those hypotheses that are apparently incorrect, in order to isolate the one hypothesis (or set of related hypotheses) that best fits the observed phenomena. We have already seen how this works in the Reese River Project, where the results of one round of hypothesis testing allowed reformulation of more refined hypotheses. The logical implication here is that, except for some fields of mathematics, there is no proof in science, only elimination or disproof of inadequate hypotheses. Science advances by disproof, proposing the most adequate explanations for the moment, knowing that new and better explanations will later be found. This continuous self-correcting feature is the key to the scientific method.

**Hypothesis testing:
Reese River Ecological
Project**

Is Archaeology a Science?

Many archaeologists, though they concede the contributions of science to archaeology (in the institution of systematic, rigorous research procedures and so forth), nonetheless deny that archaeology is a true science. This position maintains that since archaeology deals with phenomena outside the realm of physical science—that is, with the processes of social life, the vagaries of individual and group behavior, and a concept as diffuse as culture—the scientific procedures developed for disciplines such as chemistry and physics can never be successfully applied to archaeology. This view is consistent with archaeology's traditional link to history and with its humanistic perspective. And, since both history and anthropology, the parent disciplines of archaeology, have great difficulty in formulating laws of culture process, even from considerably more complete data, these archaeologists ask how archaeology can do more with only fragmentary evidence of past human behavior. Furthermore, the physical sciences rely upon the controlled experiment in order to test and retest the hypotheses that lead to, or bear upon, general theories. Obviously, archaeology cannot make use of the devised experiment to test its propositions but can only observe the remains that have survived the rigors of time. It is ironic that, in order to extract information about the past from an archaeological site, the archaeologist must usually excavate and thus destroy all, or at least portions, of that site. Thus, not only are archaeologists unable to conduct controlled experiments, once they have extracted their data from the earth, that portion of the record left from the past has been physically destroyed.

On the other hand, a growing number of archaeologists express the opposite view: archaeology must be a science because the scientific method is the only way to secure valid knowledge. They point out that not all science is based upon the repeatable experiment. For instance, astronomy, geology, and several other nonexperimental fields rely on fragmentary information, but that does not prevent these disciplines from making use of the scientific method. This point of view also holds that the available archaeological record is complete enough to allow archaeologists to interpret all aspects of ancient behavior—the task of the scientific archaeologist is to devise a way of gaining this information from the available record.

Thus, like any science, archaeology deals with a specified class of phenomena: the remains of past human activity. Also, like any science, archaeology attempts to isolate, classify, and explain the relationship among the variables of these phenomena—in this case, the variables are form, function, space, and time. Archaeology can observe the formal and spatial variables directly, but the functional and temporal variables must be inferred. Once these interrelationships are established, the archaeologist may then infer past human behavior and reconstruct past human society from these data. In this sense archaeology is both a behavioral science and a social science—it uses the scientific method to understand past human social behavior. Archaeologists may use their data to formulate and test alternative hypotheses to exclude all but the most acceptable.

Archaeology continues to grow and mature as a discipline; as a part of this process, it has become increasingly dependent upon the scientific method to reach its goals. As a result, the less-than-rigorous research done in the past is being replaced by the careful procedures of science. Most archaeologists now recognize that they must carefully state the assumptions under which they work and clearly formulate the questions they are asking of their data. Interpretations of archaeological data can no longer be haphazard or intuitive. Instead, along with their data, archaeologists must present their assumptions and hypotheses, and explain how these hypotheses were tested.

In general, however, the strength of archaeology stems from the diversity of its interests and its practitioners. This means that as archaeologists become increasingly scientific, the value of the traditional historical and humanistic perspectives should never be discarded.

SUMMARY

Our first chapter began by looking at some of the reasons for the popular fascination with archaeology, including the obvious appeal of exotic adventure and dramatic discoveries. However, we have argued that a deeper attraction is generated by the substance of archaeology itself—the study of the past—and by the realization that the reconstruction of the past mirrors the present. Beyond this, we examined various ways of defining archaeology: as a technique, a body of knowledge, and finally as a professional discipline. We then summarized the general goals of professional archaeology: to consider the *form* of archaeological evidence and its distribution in time and space, to determine past *function* and thereby reconstruct ancient behavior, and to delineate the *processes* of culture or determine how and why cultures change.

Next we traced the relationship of archaeology to allied disciplines and concepts. First, by contrasting archaeology and history we defined the principal subject of this book, *prehistoric archaeology*. Then a brief treatment of the field of anthropology allowed us to delineate the relationship of prehistoric archaeology to this broader discipline. We used a general definition of science, as a disciplined search for knowledge through a logical and consistent method, to place prehistoric archaeology within an evolving scientific context.

See p. 571 for "Suggestions for Further Reading."

Early twentieth-century excavations on Marajo Island, at the mouth of the Amazon, Brazil. (Courtesy of the University Museum, University of Pennsylvania.)

The Growth of Archaeology

*The city was desolate. No remnant of this race hangs round the ruins. . . .
It lay before us like a shattered bark in the midst of the ocean, her masts
gone, her name effaced, her crew perished, and none to tell whence she
came . . . perhaps, never to be known at all.*

*(Stephens and Catherwood
at the ruins of Copan,
Honduras, in 1839–40)*

THE GROWTH OF SCIENTIFIC DISCIPLINES

The growth of science is one of the hallmarks of Western civilization.
Although its development can be traced back several millennia to
roots in the classical Mediterranean civilizations, science and the scientific method have taken their modern form in the 500-year period
since the Renaissance. Of course, each branch of science has had its
own pace and trajectory of development; different branches have
seemed to take the lead in importance during different periods. Thus,
one can argue that the development of Western science began with
the astronomical discoveries made by Nicholas Copernicus and Gal-
ileo Galilei in the sixteenth century. Similarly, the middle and late
nineteenth century might be characterized as the Age of Evolutionary
Biology, because of the influential work of men such as Alfred Wallace, Charles Darwin, and Gregor Mendel. On the other hand, the
first half of the twentieth century was dominated by advances in nuclear physics. However, no branch of science has grown in isolation;
each has benefited from contemporary developments in other fields.
For example, the biological theory of evolution depended not only on
Darwin's observations of biological variety, but also—among other
things—on the concurrent development of certain principles in
geology.

In this growth process, archaeology is a relative infant. But it has
followed and is following a course of development similar to other scientific disciplines. It is worth outlining that course in order to understand how archaeology has reached its present state.

Collectors and Classifiers

It is instructive to note that most scientific fields, including archaeology, begin their development with amateur collectors. These individuals, often part-time hobbyists, pursue their various interests
because they value the objects they collect, often as things of beauty
or as curiosities. For instance, the modern science of biology has firm
roots in the European collectors of local plant and animal species,

such as the English country parsons and other gentlemen of leisure who flourished in the seventeenth and eighteenth centuries.

Amassing a collection leads naturally to attempts to bring order to the assembled material, resulting in the first efforts at *classification*. These early classifications are usually based upon a description of the most obvious criteria, primarily the form of the objects collected. The usual procedure in such studies is to isolate those traits deemed significant or "convenient," and to use these as the basis of the classification (grouping based upon shared traits). The oldest recorded biological classification, that of Aristotle, was based on form: it divided life forms into classes called species according to observable and describable physical and behavioral characteristics. As he observed in *History of Animals* (Book I, Chapter 1), "Animals differ from one another in their modes of subsistence, in their actions, in their habits, and in their parts. . . ." The most exhaustive biological classification system, the eighteenth-century Linnaean system still used today, was simply a refinement of this approach.

Classification by form: Aristotle's *History of Animals*

Attempts to classify often lead to the first questions concerning the meaning or significance of the phenomena being studied. The desire to know more about a collection leads to questions about the origins of a particular set of objects or about the relationship of one category in the classification to another. Why should these differences and regularities exist? Ultimately, collectors in most fields have sought the meaning behind the entire classification. Such questions were often answered with pure speculation, but at times with firmer conclusions based, at least in part, upon systematic observation. More often than not, the first answers to such questions have since been discarded. For example, in the development of biology, questions as to the origins of certain forms of life were answered by such "explanations" as the theory of spontaneous generation. This thesis held that mice were spawned from piles of dirty linen and flies from dead flesh. To quote Aristotle again: "So with Animals, some spring from parent animals according to their kind, whilst others grow spontaneously . . . some come from putrefying earth or vegetable matter, as is the case with a number of insects . . ." (*History of Animals,* Book V, Chapter 1). The ultimate "explanation" for the Aristotelean–Linnaean classification of life, "the Great Chain of Being," was theologically based—a static scheme of unchanging life forms created by God (Fig. 2.1).

Speculation from classification: Aristotle and the Great Chain of Being

Professional Disciplines

In time, amateur collectors began to give way to individuals who were committed to discovering the meaning behind the collected facts. First a range of forms was appreciated and broken down into

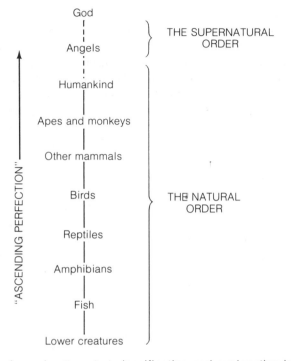
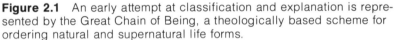

Figure 2.1 An early attempt at classification and explanation is represented by the Great Chain of Being, a theologically based scheme for ordering natural and supernatural life forms.

classes; then the classifiers could begin trying to ferret out the underlying principles of organization of the classification. In other words, concern with function and explanation replaced concern with form. With this step, in many branches of science, the first professionals can be discerned. The amateur never disappears completely, and often continues to make important discoveries that lead to scientific advances. But in every scientific discipline, true professionalism has meant the rise of full-time specialists interested in "understanding" rather than "collecting."

As attention shifted to questions of function and explanation, it became obvious that descriptive classifications based solely on lists of isolated traits could not provide sophisticated answers about the origins and significance of observable phenomena. In biology, for example, the interrelationship of organs and systems within individual life forms began to be studied. In other words, *structure* was studied to reveal how the individual organs functioned to maintain the total living individual. A pioneer in this regard, eighteenth-century French biologist Georges Cuvier, formulated the principle of functional interrelationships between organs on the basis of his thorough studies of comparative anatomy.

The final step toward understanding a set of phenomena is the attempt to comprehend the processes of its development—to explain the causes of change. Again using biology as an example, this step in the development of science is illustrated by the breakthrough made by Darwin and Wallace, the synthesis that produced the theory of evolution by natural selection.

ANTIQUARIANS AND THE ORIGINS OF ARCHAEOLOGY

These trends of scientific development are visible in the emergence of archaeology as a professional discipline. Archaeology did not spring forth fully developed, but emerged gradually from diverse origins. As with other disciplines, its roots lie in the work of amateur collectors and speculators, often called *antiquarians,* who in this case were the collectors of remains from the past. But archaeology did not begin to develop as a formal discipline until it went beyond collection and acquired the means to interpret cogently the materials being assembled.

In this section we will trace the growth of archaeology from its antiquarian roots to its emergence as a professional discipline. This development begins with the first attempts to classify the remains from the past and proceeds from purely speculative explanations of the past (often with only token reference to the actual remains) to efforts to use the archaeological evidence to infer what happened in the past. The means of archaeological interpretation, taken largely from history and anthropology, have been refined ultimately by the scientific method. It should be noted that refinements in methods of recovery (especially excavation) accompanied and aided the growth of interpretive schemes. But because of space limitations, we cannot trace both developments in detail here; and since the development of interpretive sophistication marks the growth of a science, we will treat this aspect of the history of archaeology most fully.

Early Archaeological Collectors and Classifiers

Innumerable individuals have doubtless encountered the remains of the past: some made accidental finds, others were treasure-seekers or looters who lacked recognition or appreciation of the meaning of their discoveries. Indeed, as we noted in Chapter 1, archaeology has always had to compete with the destructive looter, the individual who digs only in the hope of reaping a profit. However, as more and more discoveries were made, some individuals began to realize that the objects recovered from the earth were beyond price. These artifacts were, in fact, clues to the understanding of past lives and of entire societies that had long since disappeared.

**Early excavations:
Nabonidus, King of
Babylon**

One of the earliest examples of this kind of interest is provided by Nabonidus, the last king of Babylon. According to tradition, he conducted excavations at the city of Ur in the mid-sixth century B.C. in order to probe the ancient Sumerian culture, which was by then already 2500 years old. It is reported that Nabonidus even exhibited the artifacts from his excavations.

The classical civilizations of the Mediterranean do not appear to have used excavation to recover information about their past. But the Greek historian Herodotus wrote and speculated at length on the past, especially on the antiquity of Egyptian civilization. The interest in the past expressed by the Romans, on the other hand, is infamous. The Romans systematically looted many sites of the Mediterranean for sculpture and other works of ancient art, but they seemed to have little concern for using their finds to understand the past.

During the Dark Ages, the centuries following the collapse of the Roman Empire in A.D. 476, there was little interest in antiquities, classical or otherwise. However, one account that comes down to us from the succeeding Middle Ages holds a special interest because it represents one of the earliest examples of the use of excavation to discover a specific relic of the past for very practical purposes. (Alternatively, one might view it as one of the first attempts at archaeological forgery for financial gain.) It appears that in the twelfth century the monks of Glastonbury Abbey in England were interested

**Excavations at Glaston-
bury: King Arthur**

in discovering evidence for the existence of the already legendary King Arthur. At the very least, such a discovery would provide the monks with considerable financial benefit from pilgrimages to an Arthurian shrine. In a practical sense, such proceeds would be useful for rebuilding the Abbey, which had burned in 1183. According to the twelfth-century account, excavations in 1191 in an ancient cemetery south of the Abbey produced a lead cross with the following inscription (translated from the Latin): "Here lies buried the famous King Arthur in the Isle of Avalon." Beneath the cross, the excavators found a large oak log; inside the hollowed log were the remains of a human skeleton. The skeleton was reported to be that of a large male, and the conclusion seemed obvious: the excavators had found the remains of King Arthur. The story does not end there, however: archaeological excavations in 1962 in the area south of the Abbey revealed the remains of a large pit which had been opened and refilled sometime in the late twelfth century. It is thus possible that the medieval monks did indeed excavate and find an early burial at the Abbey; but there is, of course, no proof that they found Arthur. Unfortunately, neither the original inscribed cross nor the reputed remains of Arthur, subsequently reburied in Glastonbury Abbey, have survived the ravages of time (Fig. 2.2).

The period following the Middle Ages, the Renaissance of the fourteenth to seventeenth centuries, was an era of reawakened interest in

Figure 2.2 View of modern Glastonbury, on the "Isle of Avalon"; the abbey, where King Arthur's remains reputedly were found, is behind the hill to the right.

the arts, literature, and learning. It was also a time of renewed interest in the past, especially in the antiquities of the classical Mediterranean civilizations. For example, the work of Michelangelo clearly shows the influence of classical art. But interest was not confined to revival: excavation and direct recovery of antiquities also came into vogue. For example, at the turn of the sixteenth century, Pope Alexander VI sponsored excavations in various Roman ruins in a search for antiquities. Later, in 1594, excavations at a villa garden near Naples led to one of the most important discoveries of the period, that of the lost Roman city of Pompeii (Fig. 2.3). Excavations there continue to the present day. Activities such as these began a general frenzy of looting in Italy and other countries of Europe. The sixteenth, seventeenth, and eighteenth centuries were highlighted by "gentlemen of leisure" from countries such as England, France, and Germany who conducted expeditions to sites all over the classical world in order to recover sculpture and other remains from the past.

The term *antiquarian* began to be applied to those inquiring individuals who recovered ancient remains more to preserve the past than to realize economic gain. This is not to say that all antiquarians had the highest motives. On the contrary, the distinction between those who were trying to learn about the past and those who wished only to profit by the discovery and sale of long-lost treasures was sometimes impossible to make. And even the highest of motives did not guarantee that an overzealous digger would not destroy much precious evidence. This was the heyday of the antiquarian, but archaeology as we know it has at least some of its roots in this period. Despite the damage, some useful contributions to archaeology resulted. Knowledge of the past was gained, monuments were saved, and specific excavation techniques began to be developed; all these were contributions to the modern discipline of archaeology.

As the looting and destruction of antiquities continued in Europe and other areas of the world, some individuals began to stand out not only as collectors, but as people interested in learning about the past through their attempts to classify and interpret the remains. One of the earliest of these was an English gentleman named William Camden; in 1587, he produced *Britannia*, the first comprehensive directory of British antiquities. Camden's work is significant in that he compiled a descriptive listing of all archaeological sites and artifacts then known in England. Through his work interest in British prehistory had its start. Two other British antiquarians of the seventeenth and eighteenth centuries, John Aubrey and William

Early classifier of archaeological remains: William Camden in England

Figure 2.3 A street in the Roman city of Pompeii, Italy, after excavation and partial reconstruction. (Courtesy of Elizabeth K. Ralph.)

Stukeley, are important for their speculative attempts to use material remains to interpret the prehistoric past of England. Both men took an interest in the great stone enclosures of Avebury and Stonehenge (Fig. 2.4); they fostered the still persistent interpretation that these were Druid temples.

Elsewhere in Europe, people were similarly probing their prehistoric past. In sixteenth- and seventeenth-century Scandinavia, for example, royally commissioned antiquarians such as Ole Worm of Denmark and Johan Bure of Sweden were recording ancient runic inscriptions, excavating in burial sites, and compiling inventories of national antiquities. At the same time they were encouraged to connect their findings with the semilegendary accounts of national history (Fig. 2.5).

William Dugdale, a seventeenth-century prehistorian from Warwickshire, gathered and studied extensive collections of the stone hand-axes common throughout the English countryside. His interpretation of their origin and use was revolutionary for his time: "These are weapons used by the Britons before the art of making arms of brass or iron was known." This represents one of the first reported interpretations that credited prehistoric people with making these stone tools; the prevailing view at that time held that such artifacts were manufactured by elves or other mythical beings.

Speculative interpretation of the prehistoric past in Europe gradually gave way to more solidly based interpretations as evidence accumulated that demonstrated the association of human bones and tools

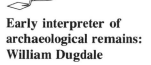

Early interpreter of archaeological remains: William Dugdale

Figure 2.4 The ancient function of Stonehenge, located on the Salisbury Plain of England, remains a subject of popular speculation—regardless of the archaeological evidence.

Figure 2.5 Runic inscriptions were used as early as the sixteenth and seventeenth centuries to aid archaeological investigation in Scandinavia. (By permission of the British Library.)

with the bones of animals known to be extinct. However, another two centuries would pass before the implications of these discoveries for human prehistory would be generally accepted. The initial reaction to these discoveries was to ignore or reject them, since they conflicted with the prevailing view, based on the version of creation given in the Old Testament, that human existence was confined to the 6000 years since the Flood of Noah.

Early Archaeological Issues

The early development of archaeology was intertwined with one central question: How long had the human race existed on earth? On the one hand, the theological position held to a literal interpretation of the Old Testament as to the length of human prehistory. On the other hand, a growing number of scholars accepted an increasing body of evidence implying that human prehistory extended much farther into the past than Biblical accounts indicated. Before archaeology could develop further, the issue of the duration of human prehistory had to be settled.

The Discovery of Old World Prehistory

This controversy was centered in the Old World, where accumulating archaeological discoveries pointed to the great antiquity of the human species. In London, in the year 1690, a man named Conyers discovered a series of stone axes that were apparently as old as the extinct elephant bones with which they were found. But critics dismissed this dramatic find with the speculation that Conyers had discovered the remains of an ancient Briton's attempt to defend his homeland against Roman elephants during the historical conquest of Emperor Claudius! More than a century later, in 1797, John Frere described the discovery of chipped flint in association with bones of extinct animals from Hoxne, a gravel pit also in England. These finds, from a depth of 12 feet below the modern surface, were sealed in place by three higher and therefore later deposits. Frere described the remains as belonging "to a very remote period indeed; even beyond that of the present world." In this case the discovery was simply ignored. Between 1824 and 1829 another excavator, Father MacEnery, discovered more stone tools associated with extinct animal bones, sealed by a stalagmite deposit in Kent's Cavern, Devon. One of the leading English geologists of the day, William Buckland, dismissed the Kent's Cavern finds as a mixture of ancient animal bones with relatively recent weapons; the latter were again assigned to the historical Britons.

Stone tools associated with extinct animals: John Frere, Father MacEnery, and Boucher de Perthes

Elsewhere in Europe, material evidence for human antiquity met similar reactions. In France in the 1830s, a customs inspector named Boucher de Perthes discovered an assemblage of crude hand-axes and extinct animal bones among the Somme River gravels. Convinced of the significance of his finds, he tried without much success to persuade his scientific contemporaries that the stone tools indeed represented *antediluvian* (before the Biblical Flood) human existence. And in 1856 some fossilized human bones were retrieved from the Neander Valley in Germany. These bones are now seen to be important fossils of Neanderthal man, but at the time, their "primitive" and possibly ancient anatomical attributes were explained away (as coming from a pathological modern individual) by Rudolph Virchow, the leading pathologist of the day.

The tide of scientific opinion finally turned, however; the year 1859 marked several important events in the change. In that year, two prestigious English scholars, Sir John Prestwich and Sir John Evans, announced to their fellow scientists that, as a result of their studies of Boucher de Perthes' finds, they concurred that the Somme River artifacts were indeed ancient. This influential assessment coincided with the vindication of MacEnery's earlier discoveries by the work of William Pengelly, who had conducted excavations in both Kent's Cavern and Windmill Hill Cave. And 1859 was the year of publication of Darwin's *The Origin of Species*. In sum, in the mid-nineteenth century the theory of evolution and the archaeological evidence combined to challenge successfully the theological opposition to prehistoric human development in the Old World.

The Discovery of New World Prehistory

As early as the sixteenth century, Europeans encountered and destroyed sophisticated urban civilizations in both Mexico and Peru. However, remains of earlier cultures—mounds, temples, sculptures, and burials—were often said to be the work of Old World peoples. Such speculative interpetations credited immigrant groups of ancient Egyptians, Hebrews, Babylonians, Phoenicians, Hindus, Chinese, and even the mythical inhabitants of Atlantis and Mu with building the lost cities of America. The living American Indians were believed incapable of such accomplishments. Even such a sober scientist as Benjamin Franklin attributed the construction of the mounds of the Mississippi Valley to the early Spanish explorer Hernando de Soto.

First recorded excavation in America: Thomas Jefferson in Virginia

Accumulating archaeological data eventually established rightful credit for the ancient New World monuments. One of the first contributors of such data was Thomas Jefferson. Soon after the American Revolution, Jefferson conducted the first recorded archaeological excavation in America: the subject was a 12-foot-high mound in the Rivanna River Valley, Virginia. Jefferson wrote: "I proceeded then to make a perpendicular cut through the body of the barrow, that I might examine its internal structure. . . ." Jefferson found the mound to be stratified, with several differentiated levels of earth containing human burials. He noted that the burials lower in the mound were less well preserved than those near the surface; this led him to interpret the mound as a place of burial that was used and reused over a long period of time. Beyond this, he credited the work of building the mound to American Indians. Jefferson's achievement is remarkable; besides being a pioneer in systematic excavation and accurate recording of results, he was one of the first individuals to use stratigraphy (see Chapter 7) to interpret his discoveries.

Neither Jefferson's attribution of burial mound construction to American Indians nor his admonitions for careful fieldwork were accepted by all. The battle lines had been drawn in the New World: during the first half of the nineteenth century, a great dispute raged between those who saw the American Indians as builders of the archaeological wonders of the Americas and those who thought one or another of the Old World civilizations was responsible. Speculation flourished in both camps. Eventually, as more excavations were conducted, evidence accumulated to give strong support to the thesis of indigenous origin. Although we cannot mention all the evidence that led to this conclusion, a few of the more important discoveries will illustrate its development.

Popular appeal of archaeological discovery: Stephens and Catherwood in Central America

In 1841 and 1843, John Lloyd Stephens and Frederick Catherwood published their account of the discovery of spectacular ruins of the lost Maya civilization in the jungles of Central America. Several ear-

Figure 2.6 Publication of drawings by Frederick Catherwood sparked public interest in ancient New World civilizations in the mid-nineteenth century. (From an original print, courtesy of the Museum Library, University Museum, University of Pennsylvania.)

lier accounts had been published of visits to various ruined Maya cities, such as Antonio del Rio's visit to the site of Palenque in 1786, but these had attracted little attention. Stephens and Catherwood's books, however, became best sellers, revealing the wonders of the ancient Maya civilization to the populace of England and America (Fig. 2.6). This publicity helped spur the often romantic and frenzied search for lost civilizations, not only in the New World but in Africa, Asia, and elsewhere. But Stephens' appraisal of the origin of the Maya civilization stands in marked contrast to the unfounded speculations popular at the time: "We are not warranted in going back to any ancient nation of the Old World for the builders of these cities. . . . There are strong reasons to believe them the creations of the same races who inhabited the country at the time of the Spanish Conquest, or of some not-very-distant progenitors. . . ."

In 1839, after studies of skeletal evidence, Dr. Samuel Morton of Philadelphia pronounced contemporary American Indians to be of one and the same population with the builders of the ancient mounds. Albert Gallatin, founder of the American Ethnological Society, noted in 1836 the similarities of form between the platform mounds of the Mississippi Valley and the pyramids of Mexico; on the basis of that likeness he postulated a gradual diffusion of cultural influences from Mexico to the United States. And he saw no reason to attribute construction of these monuments to other than native New World peoples.

Still the debate went on. In 1848, when E. G. Squier and E. H. Davis published the results of their research into the mounds of the Mississippi and Ohio valleys, they provided extensive and valuable descriptive data. They also devised one of the first classifications of

Early mound classification: Squier and Davis in the Mississippi Valley

Indigenous origin of mounds: Samuel Haven's *Archaeology of the United States*

mounds, distinguishing burial mounds, temple platforms, and effigy mounds and inferring that different types of mounds probably served different functions. But in trying to identify the builders of the mounds they lapsed into pure speculation, refusing to believe that the American Indians—or their ancestors—could be responsible. In contrast, Samuel F. Haven's sober appraisal of American Indian prehistory makes his study—*Archaeology of the United States,* published in 1856—a landmark in the development of archaeology. Haven used the available archaeological evidence to dismiss many fantastic theories about the origins of the American Indian; he concluded that the prehistoric monuments in the United States were built by the ancestors of known tribal groups. Although the controversy continued for another quarter century before it was finally settled by Cyrus Thomas, careful empirical work such as Haven's, rather than speculations like those of Squier and Davis, finally carried the day.

The works both of Haven and of Squier and Davis represent the culmination of antiquarian research in the New World. By midcentury, similar studies in Europe were already leading to the emergence of archaeology as a professional discipline. Archaeology was gaining recognition as a separate field of endeavor and a legitimate scholarly activity in its own right.

Looters and Prehistorians

In the nineteenth century, European and American colonial expansion into previously unexplored areas of Asia, Africa, and Latin America ushered in a new era of archaeological discoveries—and, unfortunately, a corresponding increase in archaeological looting. England, France, Germany, the United States, and other powers established control in areas such as Egypt, Mesopotamia, India, and China. Proprietary claims were staked over ruins in these areas, and archaeological sites were often mined like mineral deposits. For instance, from 1802 to 1821, Claudius Rich, a British consular agent in Baghdad, collected and removed thousands of antiquities and sent them home to England. In a similar manner, Henry Rawlinson collected clay tablets in Persia. The extraordinary Italian, Giovanni Belzoni, working for the English government, systematically looted Egyptian tombs; he even used battering rams to enter the ancient burial chambers. And Thomas Bruce, the seventh Earl of Elgin, spent several years at the beginning of the nineteenth century removing a series of sculptures, now called the Elgin Marbles, from the Parthenon in Athens to their present home in Britain.

These discoveries of ancient civilizations—even those made by plunderers—were sometimes used to supplement documentary history. This work was made easier by the decipherment of Egyptian hieroglyphs in 1822 by Jean Jacques Champollion, and of Mesopotamian cuneiform writing soon thereafter.

THE TRANSITION TO PROFESSIONAL ARCHAEOLOGY

By the late nineteenth century, the impact of the accumulating evidence of the human past was impressive. And the increase in finds was accompanied by a gradual refinement of recovery and classification methods that served to make the record even stronger. But what did all this new information mean? How could it be interpreted?

The Problem of Interpretation

The problem was immense. Depending upon the particular circumstance, archaeologists usually have only scattered remnants of past cultures to work with. One way to visualize the problem is to imagine what could survive from our own civilization for archaeologists to ponder some 5 or 10 thousand years from now. What could they reconstruct from our way of life on the basis of scattered soft-drink bottles, porcelain commodes, plastic containers, spark plugs, parking structures, fast-food restaurants, and other durable products of our civilization? In approaching the problem of interpreting the past, the archaeologist needs a framework to help in putting the puzzle together. As an analogy for this problem, imagine an incredibly complex three-dimensional jigsaw puzzle. If we knew nothing about its size, form, or subject matter, the puzzle would be impossible to reconstruct. But if we proposed a scheme that accounted for the puzzle's size, form, and subject, we could use this scheme to attempt to put it together. Thus, by proposing a hypothetical size, form, and subject matter for the puzzle, we might be able to reconstruct it. If one scheme failed to work, we could propose another in its stead, until we succeeded.

By the beginning of the nineteenth century, the rapidly accumulating body of archaeological materials, together with the inadequacy of the traditional theological interpretation of the past, made dedicated antiquarians realize that they needed some scheme to aid them in understanding and interpreting all the data about the past.

The solution to this problem came with the gradual definition of a new discipline—anthropology. The development of anthropology is beyond our scope here, but we can highlight the major themes that are important to both anthropology and archaeology.

*The Influence of Anthropological Ideas

Anthropology developed during the nineteenth century as a fusion of several diverse philosophical trends. These include the idea of biological evolution, the doctrine of social progress, and the idea of cultural evolution.

The Idea of Evolution

The concept that the forms of biological life are the result of gradual long-term transformation is an old one, long out of favor with theologians because it ran counter to the account given in the Book of Genesis. The theological view was that the history of the earth was relatively short and that all species of life were of fixed and unchanging form. But the theological position was gradually weakened by accumulating evidence that the earth was far older than the approximately 6000 years allowed by orthodox religious accounts. Eventually, the growing discrepancy between the religious interpretation and the geological and paleontological evidence led to the emergence of two schools of thought for interpreting this evidence.

The first school is generally known as *catastrophism*. Catastrophists held that during the history of the planet a series of geologic disasters took place that destroyed all life forms of their time. Each disaster was followed by a new creation. This view was often seen as a reconciliation of the geological and paleontological evidence with the theological position, since the creation recorded in Genesis could be interpreted as the creation after the most recent catastrophe, and the older forms of life revealed through fossils could represent earlier creations.

Competing with this interpretation was another view of the geological evidence, the theory of *uniformitarianism*. This theory saw the structure of the earth's crust as the result of a gradual, continuous interaction between processes of erosion and of deposition. The word *uniformitarianism* derives from the idea that a single uniform set of processes can account for both past and present geological forms. This position, supported by the stratigraphic evidence revealed by eighteenth-century geologists such as William Smith and James Hutton, implied that the earth was much older than the Biblical accounts would allow. Thus the uniformitarian point of view was often in conflict with the theological interpretation. The most influential geologist of the nineteenth century, Charles Lyell, developed the ideas of uniformitarianism in his classic work *Principles of Geology,* published in 1830–1833.

The uniformitarian theory—along with the fossil evidence that life on the planet was also much older than 6000 years and that it too had changed gradually over time—contributed directly to the formulation and, eventually, to the general acceptance of the concept of biological evolution. The grand synthesis of many ideas into a theory of biological evolution was put into print by Charles Darwin in 1859 in *The Origin of Species*. Darwin's evolutionary concept adopted the perspective of the long geologic history of the earth as interpreted by Lyell. Over this vast time span the gradual process of natural selection, in which better adapted forms produce more offspring and multiply, while less "fit" forms die out, operated to produce the incredible diversity of life forms on the earth.

The Ideas of Progress and Positivism

The idea of biological evolution which postulates that change rather than stability is the natural order, in turn gave support to the idea of social evolution. Like biological evolution, the idea that the forms of human society change and evolve is a relatively ancient view. An early form of it is evident in the ideas of the Roman philosopher Lucretius in the first century B.C. By the eighteenth century, many European philosophers were arguing that change—and progress—were a part of the natural human social order. In the nineteenth century a complementary theme was also current: that all natural and social phenomena could be understood by determining their causes. This philosophical position, called positivism, made natural selection seem as plausible a mechanism for social evolution as for biological evolution. And just as Darwin had used the diversity of modern species as evidence for biological evolution, so the diversity of human societies encountered by Europeans in the nineteenth century offered evidence for social evolution.

The Idea of Cultural Evolution

By the nineteenth century, European colonial expansion had brought Western society into contact with a tremendous variety of other human societies, many of whose people had diverse physical characteristics. Some of these human variations appeared to be so different from Europeans that one of the questions in the sixteenth century was whether or not these newly discovered peoples were human beings. The issue was settled by the Papal Bull of 1537, which declared that the inhabitants of the New World were indeed human! However, the question of the technological and cultural diversity of these alien peoples still remained. A major issue for European scholars in the nineteenth century was the explanation of the technological and cultural dominance of Europe over the rest of the world. In this context, anthropology developed in the nineteenth century as a discipline that attempted to gather and analyze information about non-Western societies, largely in order to create a universal theory of human cultural and social differences. That theory is often known today as the theory of *cultural evolution.*

During this period, some scholars were studying and writing about human origins, using the archaeological evidence then available. Others were interested in human culture, and how it developed, and how the diversity in human customs originated. These investigators combined current intellectual ideas with first-hand evidence from their own fieldwork and with previously recorded descriptions of primitive peoples such as missionary accounts. We now designate many of these researchers as "early anthropologists." Whatever we label them, these nineteenth-century scholars were, for the most part, generalists: people who attempted to use any and all of the somewhat limited data available to them to answer very broad questions. Their goal was to provide a history where none existed—to write a universal history of human culture.

Unilinear Evolutionary Anthropology

Typical of these nineteenth-century scholars was Herbert Spencer, a cultural evolutionary thinker as well as an apologist for colonialism; he coined the phrase "survival of the fittest." Spencer believed that the present human social order was imperfect, but that it was constantly adapting (progressing) to become more perfect. Spencer's explanation for the success of some cultures was simple: successful evolution was due to an innate superiority.

Social Darwinism

L. H. Morgan's unilinear evolutionary scheme

Lewis Henry Morgan, whose studies of the Iroquois are classics to this day, saw cultural evolution through a somewhat different concept, that of the *psychic unity of mankind.* By this concept, Morgan meant that the mental ability of all humans was essentially the same, since we all react to similar conditions in similar ways. Using this line of reasoning, Morgan concluded that all cultures move or evolve in a parallel fashion through formally defined stages he labeled "savagery," "barbarism," and, ultimately, "civilization." But some cultures move faster or progress further than others; Morgan considered those that are furthest advanced to be superior. The foremost English anthropologist in the nineteenth century, Edward Tylor, attempted to catalog all aspects of human culture, including their variations as well as their similarities. Tylor felt that European superiority in the nineteenth century could be explained by environmental factors, such as advantageous geographical position.

The universal theory of cultural evolution, as developed by these scholars and others, was based on comparisons of societies with one another. Data from any source—ethnographic, archaeological, or whatever—were acceptable in assessing a society's "evolutionary status." Above all, cultures were compared in order to determine relative positions on a single scale of development or success. This assumption that all human cultures develop along a single or *unilinear* path, perhaps best expressed by Morgan's evolutionary stages, stands out as the greatest weakness in nineteenth-century cultural evolutionary theory.

deductive but speculative

The errors of the unilinear evolutionists are readily apparent to us, with the benefit of more than 100 years of hindsight. In the nineteenth century, however, little thought was given to the possible effects of vast differences in time and space. Since all cultural evolution was thought to proceed along the same course, ancient societies were assumed to be directly comparable to contemporary societies. A definite bias is evident in the use of technological criteria for defining stages and for assigning a developmental status to a given culture. And many errors were committed in interpreting or evaluating the data used; sources were often not evaluated critically. Above all, these nineteenth-century evolutionists were *ethnocentric*—their assessment of the developmental stages of other societies was heavily biased by their assumption that nineteenth-century Western culture represented the *current* pinnacle of evolutionary achievement.

Today, the idea that human behavior does change and that societies and cultures do evolve remains an important aspect of modern anthropological theory; we shall return to the theme of evolution later. But by the turn of the twentieth century it was evident that the weaknesses of the case made for unilinear cultural evolution outweighed its strong points, and the attempt to write a universal history of human culture was cast aside or altered to remove its inherent weaknesses.

Franz Boas and Empirical Anthropology

The next stage in the emergence of modern anthropology and archaeology took place in America through the efforts of Franz Boas and his students during the early part of the twentieth century. In opposition to the unilinear evolutionists, Boas adopted a rigorous inductive approach for his study of human beings and their culture. Boas and his students challenged the methods and assumptions of the unilinear evolutionists, emphasizing field research to gather primary data which would eventually lead to viable theory and explanation. This was an understandable reaction to the deductive, but highly speculative, approach then current. Boas saw the need for accumulation of great quantities of well-controlled and documented empirical data. He felt that scholars could reconstruct the cultural history of a single given society only after rigorous collection of all kinds of data—archaeological and linguistic as well as ethnographic. Thus as part of his inductive approach Boas emphasized the importance of archaeology for

Inductive approach in archaeology: Franz Boas' use of archaeology

the gathering of prehistoric data. In fact, he even sponsored the first stratigraphic excavations in the Valley of Mexico, conducted by Manuel Gamio in 1911.

THE EMERGENCE OF MODERN ARCHAEOLOGY

Modern professional archaeology emerged when interpretive schemes began to be applied to the evidence of prehistory. Archaeologists and other scientists now generally refer to interpretive schemes as *models*. A model is essentially a form of hypothesis; it is constructed and tested according to the scientific method (see Chapter 1). Although various kinds of models have been devised, all are schemes or "templates" based upon a set of assumptions (or givens) that are compared with the available data and used to bring order to those data. As data are placed in order according to the model, two things can happen. Either the data "fit" or they do not. If the data agree with the model, then the two together form a basis for an adequate interpretation—subject, of course, to further testing. If the data do not fit the model, then the model might be revised or replaced and the new one tested. However, this method always contains potential sources of error: the data may be biased, for example, or our assumptions may be incorrect. As a result, even when a "fit" occurs, we cannot be sure we have found *the* solution; we have only found the best available under the circumstances. Thus, in keeping with the scientific method, we can reject a model, but we can never completely prove its applicability (Fig. 2.7).

The models used to interpret archaeological data are of two types: descriptive and explanatory. As the names imply, *descriptive models*

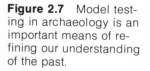

Figure 2.7 Model testing in archaeology is an important means of refining our understanding of the past.

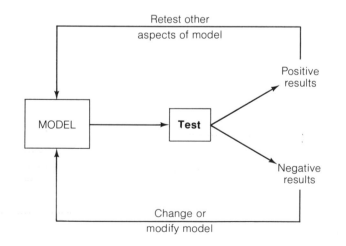

merely describe observable characteristics—the form and structure of phenomena—whereas *explanatory models* seek to determine the causes of these forms or structures. In archaeology, both kinds of models can be subdivided into synchronic and diachronic aspects. *Synchronic models* are static; they describe or explain phenomena at one point in time. *Diachronic models* are dynamic, describing or explaining phenomena through time. An example of a synchronic descriptive model would be the classical biological classification scheme of Linnaeus or "the Great Chain of Being" (Fig. 2.1). The diachronic descriptive model is exemplified by most chronological historical schemes, such as those commonly used in European history: Classical Period, Dark Ages, Medieval Period, Renaissance, and so forth. Sir Isaac Newton's explanation of the rotation of the moon about the earth is a synchronic explanatory model. Finally, the theory of evolution by means of natural selection is a diachronic explanatory model.

The earliest archaeological interpretations were based on historical models: typically these were diachronic descriptive schemes. The application of such historical models was especially prevalent in areas with documented historical traditions, such as Europe and the Near East. But early scholars also applied historically based schemes to prehistoric evidence. Later, models borrowed from anthropology, including evolutionary schemes that anthropology had in turn derived from biology, were used to interpret prehistoric data from both the Old and New Worlds.

The early models used to interpret archaeological data were not always formally defined, nor were the assumptions underlying the schemes made explicit. In fact, rather than rejecting a model when the data did not fit, investigators often forced facts to conform to their expectations. Explicit definitions of interpretive schemes and of the assumptions behind them, as well as the procedures for testing these schemes, had to await the further development of archaeology as a scientific discipline. But we can trace the beginnings of this trend even before the nineteenth century.

Historical Interpretations

The first historical scheme widely used in archaeological interpretation was the well-known *three-stage technological sequence* which held that prehistoric society developed progressively through ages of stone, bronze, and iron technology. The idea behind this theory can be traced to Greek concepts of the eighth century B.C. For instance, the philosopher Hesiod proposed five ages for human existence: the "Golden Age" or Age of Immortals; the "Silver Age," the Age of Degeneration; the "Bronze Age," the time when humanity arrived on the scene; a fourth age, or the "Age of Epic Heros"; and finally, the "Iron Age," the age of Hesiod and his contemporaries. This ancient Greek idea was later combined with the concept of linear progress to produce the notion of the technological advancement of human culture. One of the earliest proposals of a three-stage sequence for technological development in Europe was made by Johann von Eckart, a German historian of the early eighteenth century. Interpreting artifacts from burial mounds, Eckart asserted that the earliest materials came from an era prior to the invention of metal tools (Stone Age), and that this era was followed by a Bronze Age and finally an Age of Iron.

Three-age sequence in Europe: Thomsen and Worsaae in Denmark

Because Eckart's interpretation was generally ignored, credit for promulgating the three-stage sequence for European prehistory is generally given to two early nineteenth-century Danish scholars, Christian Thomsen and Jens Worsaae. Thomsen organized the collections in the Danish National Museum of Antiquities according to this scheme, not only as a convenience but also because it seemed to reflect chronological stages of human progress. The energetic Jens Worsaae, assisted by funds from the King of Denmark, conducted excavations in burial mounds to demonstrate the validity of the three-age sequence. Worsaae's excavations verified the earlier position of stone tools underlying those of bronze, which in turn underlay the later tools of iron. Worsaae went beyond chronological interpretation to conclude that bronze technology was brought to Denmark by a new population, because of the lack of gradual transition from stone to bronze tool forms. He also stressed the importance of careful excavation technique and of preserving all available evidence. For Worsaae, the goal of excavation was far more than simply to collect artifacts for museum display—it was to learn about the development of human culture.

The three-age scheme was refined by further excavations, including the famous investigations of Swiss "lake dwellings" in 1857. As time went on the sequence grew more detailed, beginning in 1865 with Sir John Lubbock's distinction between an earlier chipped-stone technology (paleolithic) and a later ground-stone technology (neolithic). In 1890, the Swedish archaeologist Oscar Montelius integrated most of Europe into a single chronology on the basis of a typological analysis of artifacts. In 1871 Heinrich Schliemann used quasi-historical sources—Homer's *Iliad*—to discover Troy, thereby initiating investigation of the predecessors to classical Greek civilization. Also in the nineteenth century, archaeological method was refined to near-modern precision by the work of the Englishman, General Pitt-Rivers.

Thus by the end of the nineteenth century, European archaeology was based on a well-developed historical chronological framework.

To this day, many European archaeologists regard their discipline as allied more closely to history than to any other field.

Anthropological Interpretations

At the dawn of the twentieth century, American archaeologists were borrowing the excavation methods developed largely in the Old World, but they were taking a rather different path from their Old World counterparts in their attempts to interpret the past. The difference was due largely to contrasting circumstances. For one thing, the New World, unlike many areas of the Old World, generally lacked an indigenous historical tradition. In addition, cultural development in the Americas did not have the time depth found in the Old World: the earliest migration in the New World appeared to be relatively recent, taking place during the last glacial epoch. This meant that the historical (or historically based) schemes used in the Old World could not be meaningfully applied in the New. Since the connection with history was not so immediately apparent in the New World, archaeologists began to turn to anthropology in order to interpret the remains that were being discovered. As a result, for New World archaeologists anthropology ultimately became the main source of interpretive models —in essence it replaced history. Indeed, many anthropologists of this period did archaeological as well as ethnographic and linguistic fieldwork.

In discussing this difference of emphasis, one cannot forget that European archaeologists were studying *their own prehistoric origins*. As a result it was perhaps inevitable that Old World archaeology was not always completely objective, but sometimes became a vehicle to further nationalistic or philosophical points of view. In the New World, on the other hand, there has been a traditional detachment about the study of prehistory, since archaeologists, almost invariably of European descent, were studying the origins and development of non-European cultures.

Ethnographic Links to the Past

The most obvious approach to interpreting ancient New World remains was to accept the conclusions of Gallatin, Morton, Haven, and their contemporaries that continuity existed from the past to contemporary Native American societies. If this was true, then the archaeologist could use ethnographic (anthropological) studies of living groups to interpret the past. This was done by comparing contemporary artifacts with those recovered archaeologically—working from the present back through time as far as possible. This method, often labeled the *direct historical approach* (something of a misnomer), was

**Use of ethnographic
data in archaeology:
Cyrus Thomas, F. H.
Cushing, and others**

pioneered by the investigations of the Bureau of American Ethnology established in 1879. Under the auspices of the Bureau, Cyrus Thomas, like his associates from several other institutions (the Peabody Museum of Harvard University, the American Museum of Natural History, the New York State Museum, and others), used this approach to study the history of the prehistoric mound builders of the American Midwest. And it was Thomas's 1894 report that finally removed any lingering doubts and established that native New World peoples built the splendid monuments in America.

In the southwestern states, F. H. Cushing, taking pottery as his key, used this same method in 1890 to trace the connections between the contemporary Pueblo peoples and their ancient forebears. And, much later, ethnographic studies of tribal groups on the Great Plains, such as the Cheyenne, were combined with archaeological research to trace the prehistoric origins of these tribes back to the Great Lakes region. We will discuss the direct historical approach in more detail in Chapters 12 and 13.

Although successful in certain cases, the direct historical approach has serious limitations. To use it one moves backward from artifacts and sites identified with a historically known group to similar but earlier archaeological materials. The method works, however, only so long as a given cluster of artifacts remains coherent—recognizably distinct from those of other prehistoric societies. Because these conditions are obviously not fulfilled in all cases, other means of interpreting the past were soon found to be necessary. Archaeologists needed a far more inclusive and flexible framework to guide their interpretations. This was provided by anthropology and its concept of culture. However, anthropology has developed several different cultural models or concepts that apply somewhat differently to archaeological interpretation. We shall briefly review the development of each of these concepts; Chapters 13 and 14 will consider in detail their use as the basis of archaeological interpretation.

The Normative Model of Culture

The first concept of culture to be applied to archaeology derived from the Boasian tradition of American anthropology. It is usually called the *normative* concept. As a model for interpretation, the normative concept of culture is descriptive rather than explanatory. Although it is based upon a synchronic analysis of culture, it is adaptable to a diachronic perspective, viewing culture through time.

All human behavior is patterned, and the form of the patterns is largely determined by culture. The normative concept of culture holds that, within a given society, behavior patterns are the result of adherence to a <u>set of rules or *norms*</u> for behavior. The rules are passed from one generation to the next—some within the family (parent to child), others within occupations (master to apprentice), still others in other contexts. Some behavior, of course, is idiosyncratic—unique to the individual—and is not passed on, but most behavior is regulated by norms.

In any given cultural system, however, a range of behaviors is tolerated; what the norms really specify are the ranges and their limits. Each such range represents only a portion of the potential behaviors possible in a given behavioral realm. For instance, one realm of behavior is location of the residence of newly married couples. The potential choices for such residence are many: a couple could reside with the bride's parents (called *matrilocal*), the groom's parents (*patrilocal*), or an uncle's family (*avunculocal*), or they could establish a new and separate residence (*neolocal*). In fact, however, all cultures restrict the choice. Individuals learn which residential behavior is considered correct within their culture. <u>Deviance</u> from the norm may be corrected in a variety of ways, such as subjecting an offender to social ostracism, gossip, or even threats of violence. The mere existence of these means for counteracting deviant behavior will lead most individuals to conform to the acceptable norm of behavior for their culture; by conforming, they gain a measure of security and well-being.

By observing actual human behavior in as many contexts as possible, anthropologists attempt to abstract the "rules" that describe and even predict forms of behavior. In the example cited above, residence behavior is often abstracted in *residence rules* that describe and predict where married couples will live under given circumstances. Anthropologists are thus able to discover regularities in human behavior and can describe and predict behavior by abstracting the underlying principles or norms within a given cultural system. This is analogous to the grammar (a set of abstracted rules) that describes and predicts the regularities within a language. Of course there are always discrepancies between the "ideal" of behavior and the observed behavior, but the norms should always predict the majority of actual, observed behavior.

Though the basic normative concept of culture is synchronic, it can be adapted to a diachronic perspective. In this view, cultures change through time as a result of shifts in the shared norms that regulate behavior. Changes in cultural norms can result from the arrival and acceptance of new ideas in the culture. Such interaction with other cultures is usually called *diffusion*. Ideas can also change over time through internal mechanisms such as *innovation* or *cultural drift* (chance variations in the inventory of shared ideas, analogous to the

Residence rules viewed as normative behavior

biological concept of genetic drift). In general, however, the normative view of culture has emphasized the regulatory and stabilizing aspects of culture rather than culture change. When change *is* considered, its causes have most frequently been attributed to nonspecific external causes such as diffusion.

Reconstruction of past behavior: Pottery as reflection of cultural norms

The archaeologist often makes use of this view of culture to reconstruct or describe the nature and sequence of past behavior. The remains of past cultures recovered by the archaeologist may be assumed to represent past behavioral norms. For instance, pottery, because of its durability, is often considered a useful indicator of past cultural behavior. According to the normative concept of culture, pottery can be viewed as a reflection of norms governing technological behavior. Although the methods for making and decorating pottery are potentially numerous, each culture uses only a few of these techniques. The behavior of potters, then, is controlled in much the same way as the behavior of married couples selecting a new residence. The potter is bound by the manufacturing techniques learned from the older generation; departures from these standards may be discouraged by both social and economic sanctions. The archaeologist can infer the ancient "rules" governing pottery making by studying the pattern of similarities and variations in the surviving pottery, just as the anthropologist discovers the "rule of residence" by studying actual behavior.

Thus the normative view sees culture as the set of rules that regulate, maintain, and perpetuate appropriate behavior within society. Because such behavior is patterned and to a degree predictable, archaeologists can infer past cultural norms from surviving products of a culture. The patterns and variations apparent in this evidence enable archaeologists to reconstruct variation and changes in behavioral norms in both space and time.

Under the influence of such men as Franz Boas and Alfred V. Kidder, the normative model of culture dominated anthropological archaeology during the first half of the twentieth century. The bulk of prehistoric archaeological interpretation, especially in the New World, has been based on the normative concept either implicitly or explicitly. Until quite recently, the general procedures followed by most prehistoric archaeologists have reflected not only the normative cultural concept, but a general inductive research strategy based upon Boasian anthropology. Refinements in excavation and classification methods and construction of site and regional chronologies were the most common concerns of normative archaeologists in the first half of the twentieth century. Such an inductive archaeological approach has been an efficient and appropriate means of gaining an integrated data base for the prehistoric past from most areas of the world. This emphasis has been quite successful in providing a descriptive outline of the prehistory for vast expanses of time and space. However, normative archaeology tended to address only one of the three fundamental concerns of archaeology. Only the first goal, that of outlining the distribution in time and space of the material forms from the past, was being pursued. The remaining goals—reconstruction of past behavior and the delineation of culture process—were not usually addressed by use of a normative cultural framework. Different views of culture were necessary in order to focus on these concerns.

The Functional Model of Culture

While the normative view of culture is usually associated with American (Boasian) anthropology, the functional concept developed primarily within French and British social anthropology, under the name of *functionalism*. We cannot fully describe the development of the traditional functional school or the important roles of such scholars as Emile Durkheim and A. R. Radcliffe-Brown, but we shall briefly outline one of the most refined versions of this concept—that presented by Bronislaw Malinowski (Fig. 2.8).

Culture, for Malinowski, consists of "inherited artifacts, goods, technical processes, ideas, habits, and values." In literal definition, this idea is not too different from preceding ones. But Malinowski goes further, asserting that each cultural whole consists of a set of inseparably interrelated aspects, each serving the dual function of main-

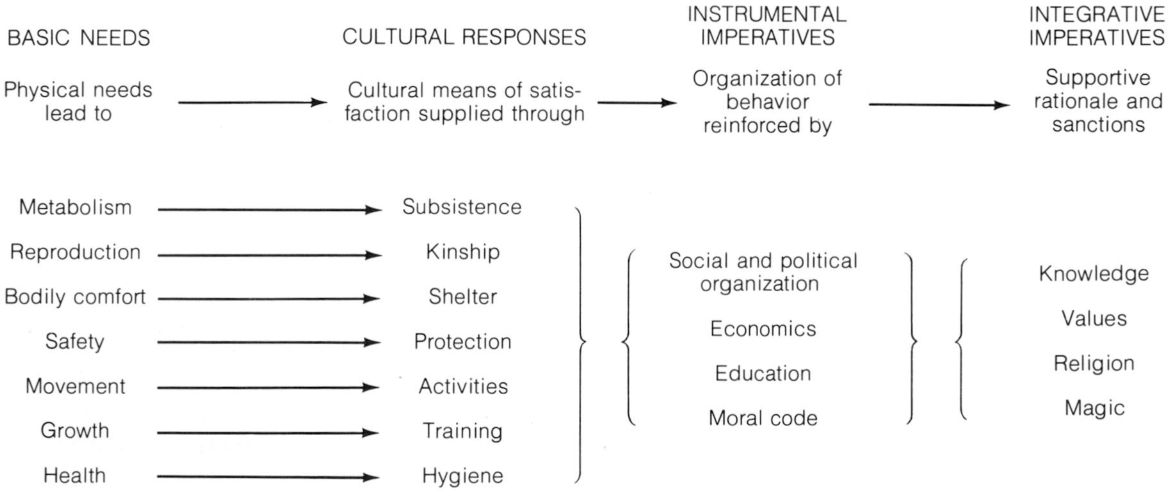

Functional relationships within culture: Bronislaw Malinowski's view

BASIC NEEDS	CULTURAL RESPONSES	INSTRUMENTAL IMPERATIVES	INTEGRATIVE IMPERATIVES
Physical needs lead to	Cultural means of satisfaction supplied through	Organization of behavior reinforced by	Supportive rationale and sanctions
Metabolism → Subsistence			
Reproduction → Kinship			
Bodily comfort → Shelter		Social and political organization	Knowledge
Safety → Protection		Economics	Values
Movement → Activities		Education	Religion
Growth → Training		Moral code	Magic
Health → Hygiene			

Figure 2.8 A functional view of culture as presented by Bronislaw Malinowski.

taining the whole and of fulfilling the society's (and the individual's) basic needs for survival. More specifically, Malinowski begins with a list of universal biological needs—metabolism, reproduction, health, and so on. Culture, then, is fundamentally the human means of fulfilling these basic needs, permitting both the individual and the society *physically* to survive. At the same time, for humans as *social* beings to survive, a secondary set of "derived" needs must be met, such as the need for social control (through law) and for education. A third level of needs, which Malinowski calls "integrative," involve the symbols—norms, art, religion, and so on—by which the above solutions could be codified and communicated. The forms of a given culture can be understood as the totality of that culture's particular solutions to the hierarchy of needs. These solutions are interrelated so that the proper functioning of each aspect (the family, economic activities, magic, and so on) is dependent on and contributes to the functioning of all other aspects. This network of relationships constituted the *structure* of the society or culture.

In this way, according to the functionalist view, cultural systems provide for the various needs of the members of society both individually and collectively. Each component of the cultural system has a *function* (its contribution to the maintenance of the system) and is related to the remainder of the system through a *structure* (network of relationships).

Residence rules viewed via functional relationships

We can illustrate this view of culture by returning to the example discussed previously. Instead of viewing residence choices of newly married couples within a normative range of behavior, the functional approach examines the relationship of this trait to other aspects of the society (structure) and its consequences within the total cultural system (function). Thus a particular pattern of residence (such as matrilocality) may be linked directly to other traits (such as marriage patterns, power and authority figures, inheritance, and parent-child relationships). Furthermore, this residence pattern may contribute to the continuity of economic and political responsibilities held by women (since daughters continue to reside with their mothers after marriage), thus maintaining social stability and minimizing disruption between female generations. Residence patterning does not affect the survival of the society directly (as do most technological aspects of culture), but it has an indirect role in maintaining the social system by facilitating the orderly transferral of responsibility and authority between generations, reducing tension and conflict, and providing the circumstances for effective cooperation and interaction in the matrilocal residence group.

The functional approach provides a synchronic view of culture; it tends to picture society as a constantly adjusting, yet stable, internally regulated system. Does such a view of culture have any application to archaeology and its primary concern with diachronic processes in culture? The answer is yes; though its synchronic perspective has restricted the role of functionalism in archaeology, researchers have increasingly realized that its advantages should not be overlooked. With a functional approach each archaeological trait can be seen, not in isolation, but as part of a network of interrelated traits, each with functions contributing to the maintenance of a larger system.

Although functionalism has never gained widespread application in prehistoric archaeology, recently used cultural ecological models also view culture as a constantly adjusting, stabilizing system. The principal difference is that cultural ecology regards cultural systems as being externally regulated by means of their adaptation to their environment.

A recent refinement of the functional approach for archaeology has been made by Lewis Binford, who classifies archaeological materials into three categories according to function. *Technofacts* are those artifacts that function directly to maintain the survival of society by providing food, shelter, and defense. *Sociofacts* function to maintain social order and integration. *Ideofacts* function to furnish psychological security, well-being, and explanations for the unknown.

Functionalism in archaeology: Lewis Binford's scheme

This is not to say that each artifact must be assigned to only a single category, or that each artifact has only a single function. On the contrary, each artifact will have at least one function, but many will have more than one. For instance, one of the most common archaeological materials, pottery, can obviously be assigned to the category of technofact. Most pottery vessels function directly for the acquisition, transport, storage, or preparation of food or water. Thus many characteristics of pottery (the kind of clay used, the way it is made, its shape and size, and so on) are directly related to or dependent upon its function as part of the food acquisition system. However, the same vessel may also have attributes that relate to social functions and may thus be a sociofact: for example, the vessel's decoration may signify social status or affiliation with specialized groups such as family or lineage. These characteristics of a pottery vessel function as symbols of membership and social solidarity. Other attributes, such as special shapes and decorative traits, may have ideological functions, making the vessel an ideofact as well.

A striking ethnographic example of the multiplicity of functions served by some artifacts is provided in a description by Lauriston Sharp of the Yir Yoront Aborigines of Australia. A group of missionaries contacted the Yir Yoront and, full of the best intentions, started distributing abundant steel axes to replace the less efficient, less

Multiple functions of artifacts: The Yir Yoront of Australia

numerous stone axes. What the missionaries did not realize was that their action affected more than the technological realm: the stone axes also served as sociofacts and ideofacts for the Yir Yoront. As sociofacts they symbolized the social order, for the owners were all senior men; women and junior men had to defer to the authority of these men every time they needed to borrow an axe. Trade in stone axes was also a major reason for annual gatherings of multiple Yir Yoront bands. As ideofacts, the stone axes were sacred possessions with clear symbolic status in the traditional cosmology. The unrestricted introduction of steel axes disrupted the social order, both by threatening the established patterns of dependency and subordination and by decreasing interest in and need for annual gatherings. It also undermined the traditional belief system by forcing the Yir Yoront to question a cosmology that could not easily account for the steel tools. Even the technological realm had not been clearly "improved": Sharp suspects that whatever time was saved may have been used for extra sleep! In his words, "the steel axe . . . is not only replacing the stone axe physically, but is hacking at the supports of the entire cultural system." Although the missionaries had hoped to "protect" the Yir Yoront from the intrusion of Western society, their misunderstanding of the many roles of the stone axe had effects rather opposite to their goals.

Using an approach of this kind, a study of the patterns of the various characteristics of artifacts and of their interrelationships as technofacts, sociofacts, and ideofacts may lead to conclusions not only about ancient technology (kinds of food used, methods of acquisition, transportation, and preparation, and so on), but also about the social organization and (perhaps) the belief system. Furthermore, changes in the various kinds of attributes may come about independently. That is, changes in the attributes that reflect use as sociofacts or ideofacts probably result from processes different from those that affect technofacts. Therefore, changes in social institutions, status relationships, or even belief systems might result in changes in certain attributes of pottery, without affecting those attributes that derive from the function of the vessels as technofacts.

Processual Models of Culture

As we have seen, the normative view of culture is based upon form and has both synchronic and diachronic aspects; the functional model of culture is based on the functions of components within a system (structure) and is synchronic. We shall now consider models of culture that seek an understanding of culture process—that is, identification of the factors responsible for the direction and nature of change within cultural systems.

Obviously, cultural models that seek an understanding of process must be diachronic in nature. They attempt to identify and interrelate the causes of culture change through time. We will consider two models—one based upon cultural ecology, the other upon multilinear cultural evolution. The first is more specific in its view, attempting to delineate individual cases of culture process. The second is concerned with the broad processes and trends of cultural evolution. Both models view technology as the primary factor in change, determining to a varying degree the nature and relative rapidity of culture change. And both consider the roles of the other two aspects of culture—the social-organizational and ideational factors that may be involved in culture change—and attempt to demonstrate the linkages among all three of these components.

The two approaches derive from the work of cultural anthropologists, notably Leslie White and Julian Steward. But archaeologists, from V. Gordon Childe to Lewis Binford, have also contributed to these conceptual frameworks. We shall discuss each model briefly here; they will be treated in more detail in Chapter 14.

The Ecological Model of Culture. The ecological model is based on the adaptive aspects of culture. It views culture, and especially its technology, as the primary means by which human societies adapt (with varying degrees of efficiency) to their environment. Change—and, ultimately, cultural evolution—stems from changes within this adaptive relationship between culture and environment. For instance, if the environment changes the technology will make an adaptive adjustment, leading in turn to further changes in the total cultural system as components of both the organizational and the ideational aspects adjust to the technological change.

This model is analogous to biological evolution, which views each species as adapting to a particular set of conditions that define its environment. If the environment changes, the species will adjust (adapt new modes of behavior, migrate, or whatever) or perish. Thus each species is continually adjusting or adapting to the selective pressures of the environment. Evolution is the sum of all such adjustments or changes through time.

The analogy generally holds when we turn to the relationship of human societies with their environment, but some significant differences must also be considered. The environment that animal species adapt to consists of two components: the physical environment (geography, climate, and so on) and the biological environment (other species of plant and animal life). Human societies adapt to these components of the environment, but they must also adapt to a third component— other cultural systems (neighboring groups or societies). More important, in strictly biological evolution the mechanism responsible for variations in form or behavior within a species is genetic inheritance. Therefore the ability of a species to respond or adapt biologically to environmental change is, in the short run, relatively limited and inflexible. As a result, the pace of adaptive change—evolution—is limited by the length of a generation. This means that biological evolution is very gradual and can be perceived only over a span of many generations. On the other hand, human societies have an additional mechanism for variation that is not genetically controlled: culture. To a large degree human behavior is determined by culture (see the discussion of the normative model of culture on p. 54). And because culture is transmitted socially, changes need not wait for a new generation before they spread. Thus human societies can respond to environmental change rapidly and flexibly. As a result, cultural evolution is often rapid and perceptible over short periods of time.

It must be stressed that cultural ecology does not imply that the environment *determines* the nature of culture. On the contrary, through the course of cultural evolution even the physical and biological components of the environment have become increasingly determined by human culture. We need only look at our own environment to see the changes our culture has wrought—altering the landscape and the very composition of the water we drink, the food we eat, and the air we breathe.

Cultural ecology: Successive adaptations in the Great Plains

Every human society exploits and changes its environment in some way. And each society's technology basically determines which portions of the total environment will be utilized. For example, the Great Plains region of the United States has supported a succession of different cultures, each exploiting a different aspect of its resources. The earliest hunters and gatherers on the Plains were limited in their mobility; they exploited a wide variety of subsistence alternatives (hunting small game, occasionally hunting large game, gathering wild plant foods, and so on) in small, localized groups. A dramatic change in the biological environment—the arrival of herds of horses introduced by the Spanish—presented a new subsistence choice. Some groups adapted to the changed environment by creating a new technology focused on the horse, and thereby gained an increased mobility that enabled them to specialize in the hunting of large game animals (bison). But because of their specialization, these same groups proved vulnerable to outside invaders who had a different technology. The latter technology included the repeating rifle which was used to decimate the herds of bison and thereby destroy the subsistence base of the mobile Plains societies. The same technology included the plow, which allowed the invading settlers to harness a previously unexploited portion of the environment for extensive agriculture. Of course in the twentieth century a still newer technology has led to the exploitation of yet another portion of this same environment—the vast deposits of fossil fuel located beneath the surface of the Plains.

The environment has not determined each of these successive ways of life it has supported; it has merely provided the opportunities for human technological exploitation. Each technology exploits a different niche in the environment, thereby redefining the effective environment. And, since each technology is different, the organizational and ideological aspects of each culture, which follow the technological adaptation, will obviously be unique.

Although the choices each environment offers to human exploitation are not preordained, some environments offer more alternatives—and more lucrative alternatives—than others. In another parallel with biological evolution, those societies that are less specialized in their environmental adaptations tend to be less vulnerable to changes in their environment than are more specialized societies. Just as the nineteenth-century Plains Indians were vulnerable because of their heavy dependence upon bison, so the twentieth-century United States is vulnerable because of its dependence on fossil fuels. When environmental conditions change, societies either change their cultural adaptations or face extinction.

But we must remember that not all culture change results from environmental change. And environmental change can stem from specific shifts in the physical, biological, or cultural realms. The arrival of the horse altered the biological environment of the Plains. But the changes stemming from the use of plow agriculture resulted from a technological innovation, not from a shift in the environment. This technological change altered the effective environment of the Great Plains. The link between culture and environment goes two ways: a change in either one will cause a change in the other.

Archaeologists who use the ecological model of culture seek to identify as many components as possible of the ancient interactive system. It is usually possible to distinguish among the physical, biological, and cultural aspects of ancient environments, and to identify segments of the technology adapted to each; for instance, classes of technofacts such as digging sticks or baskets relate to exploitation of plant life. It may be possible to identify at least some of the sociofacts and/or ideofacts associated with each of these technofacts. For example, digging sticks and baskets may be found associated with individual houses, but in an area separate from artifacts that represent hunting activities. This situation enables the archaeologist to reconstruct at least a portion of an ancient cultural system. The division just described might be interpreted as reflecting an ancient division of labor and suggesting what parts of the environment were exploited by each side. If the system can be reconstructed, and if a change in one of its components can be identified, then the consequences of that change for other components can be traced. For instance, the introduction of metal tips for digging sticks may lead to increased horticultural production, a decrease in reliance upon food gathering, and perhaps a change in settlement pattern (such as a more concentrated grouping of houses). This change may result in shifts in the organizational system (residence rules, kinship, and so on) and, eventually, changes in the belief system (such as increased importance of agricultural deities). By viewing the archaeological record from this perspective, the archaeologist may be able to discover the cause and consequences of change instead of merely describing the changes in form (new artifacts, new settlement pattern, and so on) and shifts in proportions of various artifacts. In other words, rather than merely describing what has changed, the archaeologist begins to unravel the process of change.

Multilinear Cultural Evolution.   When viewed over the long expanse of time, each individual culture manifests change resulting from the accumulation of its specific behavioral-adaptive responses. The process of adaptation and change is called cultural evolution. Unlike the nineteenth-century unilinear evolutionary theorists, however, the proponents of current cultural evolutionary theory do not rely on speculation or implied causes for evolution. Instead, the contemporary concept of cultural evolution is based on objective data, gathered and tested (for the most part) by the scientific method. Most importantly, the modern evolutionary concept is *multilinear:* it conceives of each society as pursuing an individual evolutionary career rather than changing in a predestined unilinear course. Although the origins of cultural evolution, as applied by archaeologists, lie in the writings of nineteenth-century social evolutionists such as Lewis Henry Morgan and Karl Marx, the model has been refined for its modern applications; for example, documentation from individual anthropological studies has replaced the pure speculation that handicapped the nineteenth-century theory.

The multilinear evolutionary model: Stability vs. growth in cultural development

The multilinear evolutionary model, like cultural ecology, is based upon the assumption that each human society adapts to its environment primarily via its technology, and secondarily through its organizational and ideational subsystems. But the evolutionary model goes beyond considering the particular instances of adaptation and change stressed by the ecological model, and emphasizes the degree of success or efficiency each system manifests in its development. According to the model, the efficiency of cultural development can be measured by two criteria: *survival* and *growth*. A particular society may be well adapted to its environment so that it achieves a stable balance or *equilibrium*. In this case adaptation involves refinements in the existing technology, as well as in the organizational and ideational aspects of culture, but no profound change in the overall culture. In such cases survival is the measure of adaptation efficiency. Societies such as that of the Eskimo have achieved this kind of stable adaptation, which results in survival without growth. Human societies in many other environments have also achieved similarly stable adaptations. This fact suggests that there are some optimum organizational and ideational systems for given technologies within certain environments.

In other cases, human societies become involved in growth cycles. Changes originating either from the environment or from within the society trigger changes in the technological system (and in some cases, in the organizational and ideational systems as well). If these technological changes result in increases in food production, and if the organizational and ideational changes allow for increases in population size, a process of growth may begin. Continued growth will eventually place new strains upon the technology (amount of food produced), the organization (control of people), and the ideology (belief system). This pressure may trigger further changes in the society —technological innovations to increase food production further or new forms of social and political organization to mobilize the population. At some point every society reaches its limit of growth; every specific environment and particular technology has an upper limit on the number of people it can support. Obviously, some environments have greater potential and some technologies are more efficient in this growth process than others. Fertile temperate zones populated by peoples who practice plow agriculture can produce more food and thereby support larger populations than desert zones occupied by hunters and gatherers. In the same way, certain organizational systems are more efficient than others at mobilizing and harnessing human resources. Specialized labor under centralized control is generally more efficient than nonspecialized individual enterprise. Finally, ideational systems may also differ in the degree of efficiency they produce. A belief system that provides sanctions for centralized organization and gives its adherents security and confidence will have an advantage over a system without clear-cut sanctions or one that instills fear and insecurity in the population.

Why do some societies appear to seek a stable equilibrium with their environments, while others maintain growth cycles? Under certain circumstances, adaptive changes appear to trigger "chain reaction" growth. In such cases, emphasis is placed on technological innovation leading to continual increases in food supplies and population. This growth spiral is evident in the archaeological record of the development of the world's complex civilizations in both the Old and New Worlds.

Today's sophisticated concepts of culture, including those based on cultural ecology and multilinear evolution, allow prehistoric archaeologists to explore the dynamics of growth within human societies. In this way, archaeologists attempt to document the causal mechanisms for both the development and the downfall of complex civilizations.

SUMMARY

This chapter has traced the origins and growth of the discipline of archaeology. Like other branches of science, archaeology has its roots in the work of amateur collectors. As collections of antiquities grew, attempts were made to bring order to them by classification. Some individuals tried to understand the meaning of their collections—what they were and what they could tell us about the prehistoric human past—but early "explanations" were largely speculative. All too often, the evidence from the past was misconstrued to fit inflexible theories. Growing dissatisfaction with this approach was illustrated by the study of human antiquity in both the Old and New Worlds. Ultimately, empirically based works of such scholars as Boucher de Perthes and Haven broke the hold of speculative theories.

The emergence of archaeology as a professional, scientific discipline was marked by the rise of full-time specialists committed to understanding the meaning behind the physical remains of the past. This commitment to meaning implied the adoption of one or more interpretive frameworks or models which could be tested against the evidence. Models developed in the Old World, such as the three-age system, have derived primarily from history. In the New World, where the aboriginal cultures lacked a historical tradition, archaeology became allied with the new field of anthropology and adopted a variety of cultural frameworks in order to interpret the past.

Since the beginning of the alliance between archaeology and anthropology at the end of the nineteenth century, archaeology has developed interpretive power and sophistication as it proceeded, in concert with anthropology, to develop and use a series of successively more useful models of culture. The normative concept of culture, arising from the work of Franz Boas and his students, focused both synchronically and diachronically on the form of cultural attributes. The functional concept of culture stressed synchronic study of the function of traits within the overall structure of a culture. With the re-emergence of evolutionary models of culture, the emphasis has centered on change and the delineation of cultural process. These models view human culture as a means of adaptation, changing in response to changes in its physical, biological, and cultural environment; they regard technology as the primary mediating link. A cultural ecological approach to culture emphasizes specific interactions within particular systems of culture and environment. Multilinear cultural evolution, on the other hand, attempts to establish general cross-cultural trends of human prehistory, often arguing that the technological realm of culture has played the leading role in cultural evolution.

The growth of archaeological interpretation—and therefore of archaeology—has emphasized, in successive periods, each of its major goals. It has progressed from a collector's concern with form to early speculative attempts at understanding what these forms meant. With the rejection of wholly speculative explanations and the emergence of professional archaeology, came a return to interest in specific forms now collected by rigorously inductive procedures. In the 1930s and 1940s, concern grew over function and structure in the overall context of a given culture. More recently, concern with understanding the evident changes in form and function has placed emphasis on process and explanation. This sequence of interpretive emphasis was not preordained, nor has the development of interpretive sophistication ceased. But with the benefit of hindsight we can observe that this course of development shows a logical progression from the most concrete (form) to the most abstract and inclusive (process) (Fig. 2.9).

The attempt to understand culture process, of course, involves further study of form and function, but this analysis uses a deductive, hypothesis-testing strategy. This recent trend in archaeology, however, is built on the foundation laid by the inductively-oriented archaeologists who were concerned with form and function. Science is concerned with *meaning behind form,* and the growth of archaeology as a scientific discipline is marked by increased attention to explanations of both function and process.

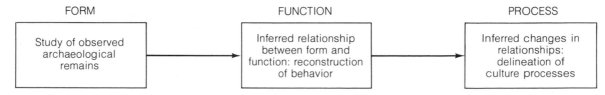

Figure 2.9   The growth of archaeology as a discipline has involved changing emphases, beginning with Form, from this to Function, leading to the present concern for Process.

See p. 571 for "Suggestions for Further Reading."

The basic archaeological concepts of *provenience, association,* and *context* are illustrated by the tomb of a Maya ruler from Tikal, Guatemala. (Courtesy of the Tikal Project, the University Museum, University of Pennsylvania.)

The Nature of Archaeological Data

Too often we dig up mere things unrepentantly forgetful that our proper aim is to dig up people.

> (Sir Mortimer Wheeler,
> Archaeology from the Earth,
> *1954)*

. . . data relevant to most, if not all, the components of past sociocultural systems are preserved in the archeological record. . . . Our task, then, is to devise means for extracting this information. . . .

> (Lewis R. Binford,
> An Archaeological Perspective,
> *1972)*

In this chapter we will consider the kinds of information archaeologists work with and the ways this material is acquired. Most people are familiar with the commonest kinds of archaeological evidence; they have probably read about archaeologists "piecing together the past" by studying ancient pottery, "arrowheads," or other tools found by excavation. However, tools represent only one of several kinds of evidence that archaeologists study, and excavation is only one of several means of collecting information about the past. The many and varied kinds of information, together with the ways they are recovered, are all crucial to archaeologists' efforts at understanding what happened in the past. In this chapter we will examine the characteristics of the evidence archaeologists seek. But first we will consider the basic forms of archaeological data.

THE FORMS OF ARCHAEOLOGICAL DATA

The material remains of past human activity, from the smallest stone-chipping debris to the most massive architectural construction, become *data* when the archaeologist recognizes their significance as evidence from the past and collects and records them. The collection and recording of remains of the past constitutes the acquisition of archaeological data. We will occasionally use the term *evidence* to refer in a general way to past material remains ("potential data"). Later, in Chapters 5 through 7, we will discuss the various methods by which archaeologists acquire data. Here we are concerned with the three basic classes of archaeological data: artifacts, features and ecofacts.

Artifacts

Artifacts are discrete entities whose characteristics of form result wholly or partially from human activity (Fig. 3.1). Objects such as a

Figure 3.1 Artifacts are discrete objects whose form results all or in part from human behavior, here represented by both the figurine head being recovered and the pottery vessel in the background. (Courtesy of the Tikal Project, the University Museum, University of Pennsylvania.)

stone hammer or a fired clay vessel are artifacts because they are either natural objects modified for or by human use (such as the stone hammer), or new objects formed completely by human action (such as a vessel made of clay). The shape and other characteristics of artifacts are not altered by removal from the surroundings in which they are discovered: a stone axe and a pottery vessel both retain their appearance after the archaeologist takes them from the ground. Thus, an artifact is any discrete portable object whose form is modified or wholly created by human activity.

Features

Features are nonportable artifacts; that is, they are artifacts that cannot be recovered from their matrix (Fig. 3.2). Position and arrangement are key aspects of features; for this reason they cannot be removed after their discovery without either altering or destroying their original form. They may, however, be reconstructed after removal, as in a museum display. Some common examples of archaeological features are hearths, burials, storage pits, and roads. It is often useful to distinguish between simple features such as these and composite features such as the remains of buildings. Structures (houses, storage buildings, temples, palaces, and so on) are usually revealed archaeologically by the patterned arrangements of floors, post holes, walls and doorways, as well as by associated simple features such as hearths, refuse pits, and the like.

Figure 3.2 Features are artifacts that cannot be recovered intact, here represented by a partially excavated cremation burial pit.

Figure 3.3 Ecofacts are nonartifactual remains that have cultural relevance. This photograph records a volcanic deposit which has buried and preserved the impression of maize (corn) plants, indicated by the white markers, along with the cultivated ridges of the field (associated features). From the size of the plants, the excavators concluded that the ash fell in late May. (Courtesy of Payson D. Sheets.)

Ecofacts

Ecofacts are nonartifactual material remains that nonetheless have cultural relevance (Fig. 3.3). Although not directly created or modified by human activity, ecofacts do provide significant information about past human behavior. Examples of ecofacts include remnants of both wild and domesticated animal and plant species (bones, pollen granules, and so forth). Such material contributes to our understanding of past human behavior by indicating the environmental conditions and the kinds of food and other resources used.

Sites

An archaeological site can be defined as a spatial clustering of artifacts, features, and/or ecofacts (Fig. 3.4). Some sites may consist solely of one form of data—a surface scatter of artifacts, for example, such as flint scrapers and cutting tools. Or they may consist of any combination of the three different forms of archaeological data. The boundaries of archaeological sites are sometimes well defined, especially if features such as walls or moats are present. Usually, however, a decline in density or frequency of the material remains is all that marks the limits of a site. In some cases the archaeologist may be unable to detect clear boundaries and may have to assign arbitrary limits for convenience of research; examples include extensive sites in dense rainforest cover and sites partially buried by flood deposits or volcanic ash. However boundaries are defined, the archaeological

Figure 3.4 Sites are spatial clusterings of archaeological remains. In this case, Stonehenge provides an example of a site with well-defined boundaries. (British Crown Copyright — reproduced with permission of the Controller of Her Brittanic Majesty's Stationery Office.)

site is usually a basic working unit of archaeological investigation.

Sites can be described and categorized in a variety of ways, depending on the dimensions of difference one wants to note. For instance, location—sites in open valley positions, cave sites, coastal sites, mountaintop sites, and so forth—may reflect past environmental conditions, concern for defense, or relative values placed on natural resources located in different areas. Sites may be distinguished by the single or multiple functions they are believed to have served in the past. For example, one can speak of habitation sites, trading centers, hunting (or kill) sites, quarry sites, ceremonial centers, burial areas, and so on. Sites may also be described in terms of their age and/or cultural affiliation. For example, a Near Eastern site may be described as belonging to the Bronze Age or a Mexican site may be termed "Aztec."

The nature and depth of cultural deposits at a site can reveal the time span of activities—whether overall occupation was short-term or covered a long period of time (Fig. 3.5). At some sites occupation (and deposition of artifacts) may have been continuous; others may have had multiple occupations, with the interspersed periods of abandonment marked by naturally deposited (nonartifactual or "sterile") layers. Depth of accumulation is not an infallible or automatic indicator of length of occupation; at one spot a great deal of material can be deposited very rapidly, while elsewhere a relatively thin deposit of trash might represent strata laid down intermittently over hundreds or thousands of years.

74

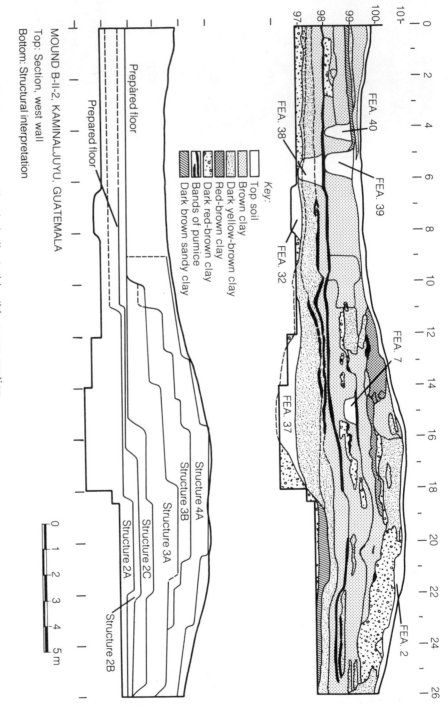

Figure 3.5 Continuous occupation is indicated by this cross-section drawing of superimposed earthen platforms. (After Austin, in Sanders and Michels 1969.)

Top: Section, west wall
Bottom: Structural interpretation

MOUND B-II-2, KAMINALJUYU, GUATEMALA

Key:
Top soil
Brown clay
Dark yellow-brown clay
Red-brown clay
Dark red-brown clay
Bands of pumice
Dark brown sandy clay

FEA. 40
FEA. 39
FEA. 38
FEA. 32
FEA. 7
FEA. 37
FEA. 2

Prepared floor
Prepared floor

Structure 4A
Structure 3B
Structure 3A
Structure 2C
Structure 2A
Structure 2B

0 1 2 3 4 5 m

It is still true, however, that "surface" sites—those with no appreciable depth of deposition—are usually the result of short-term, erratic, or temporary human activity such as in hunting and gathering camps. Examples include some of the seasonal camps studied by David Hurst Thomas in the Great Basin of the U.S. (see Chapter 1), where ancient stone tools and bone fragments still litter the ground. Most archaeological sites, however, have both surface and depth components. Surface manifestations may be apparent at such sites, but a considerable accumulation may also be hidden beneath the surface. These sites, more typical of permanent stations of past activity, may range in composition from simple shell middens, common on coast and shore lines, to large and complex urban centers such as Teotihuacán in Mexico or Uruk in Iraq.

A third kind of site may exist completely beneath the surface of the ground. In this case the surface gives no indications of the presence of such a site—all evidence of previous human activity has been buried by forces of deposition such as wind-blown sand or volcanic ash or water-laid alluvium (Fig. 3.6). Detection of buried sites presents special problems to the archaeologist; these will be discussed in Chapter 5.

Some "buried" sites lie not underground but underwater. Not surprisingly, the most common underwater sites are sunken ships. However, sites that were once on dry land may also become submerged because of changes in water level (sometimes resulting from human activity such as dam building) or land subsidence. A famous example of the latter is Port Royal, Jamaica, a coastal city that sank beneath the sea after an earthquake in 1692. In some cases human activity may intentionally submerge artifactual material, as when refuse is dumped into lakes or oceans or when ritual offerings are thrown into sacred bodies of water, such as the famous sacred *cenote* at Chichén Itzá in Mexico. The Gallo-Roman sanctuary of Sequana, at the source of the Seine River, has yielded 190 carved wooden figures; whether they were originally left as trash or as ritual offerings, these fragile figures owe their unusually long survival to their 2000 years of submersion.

We will return to the issue of the definition of archaeological sites later in this chapter in discussing the ways archaeological data are structured. But next we consider the ways archaeological data may be distributed beyond the level of individual sites.

Regions

Archaeologists generally seek to understand the prehistory of much larger areas than a single site. However, this task has often proved to

Surface sites: David Hurst Thomas in the Great Basin

Figure 3.6 Completely buried sites, in this case a structure covered by flood silts, pose special problems of detection.

be difficult, since most archaeological studies have taken the individual site as their primary investigative unit. During the past few decades, however, an increasing number of archaeological investigations have turned to a more comprehensive research unit, the archaeological *region*. The region is basically a geographic concept: a definable area bounded by topographic features such as mountains and bodies of water. But the definition of an archaeological region may also consider ecological and cultural factors. For instance, a region may be defined as the sustaining area used by a prehistoric population to provide its food and water. Most archaeologists appear to follow Doxiadis and his definition of an "ekistic" region: a geographically defined area that contains a series of interrelated human communities sharing a single cultural-ecological system (Fig. 3.7).

Obviously, the nature and scope of an archaeological region varies according to the degree of complexity of the prehistoric society and the kind of subsistence system it used. Part of the archaeologist's task is to identify the factors that define a particular region under study, as well as to show how these factors changed through time. In other

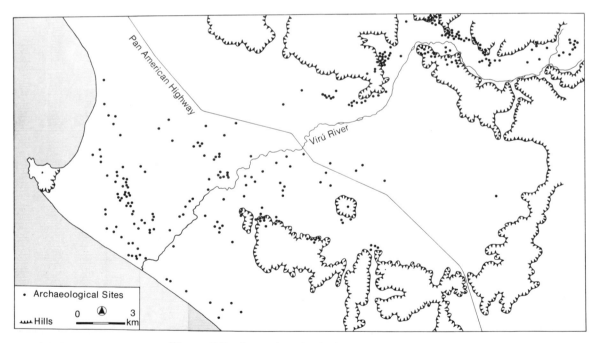

Figure 3.7 An archaeological region is often defined by topographic features; in this case, mountain ranges and sea coast define the limits of the Virú Valley, Peru. (After Willey 1953.)

words, the archaeologist usually works with a convenient natural region defined beforehand by geographical boundaries, and then seeks to determine that region's ancient ecological and cultural boundaries as well.

The Regional Approach

By emphasizing the region as the basic spatial unit for archaeological research, several scholars have defined a new approach to prehistory. Lewis Binford is often cited as the first North American archaeologist to call explicitly for a regional approach; he was followed shortly by Stuart Struever. At this time—in the mid-1960s—other archaeologists, such as MacNeish in his investigation of the Tehuacán Valley in Mexico (see Chapter 5), had already shown tangible evidence of the value of this approach. And Gordon Willey had pioneered regionally oriented research in his famous study of the Virú Valley in Peru in the 1940s (see Fig. 3.7). Only within the past decade, however, has research begun to adopt a regional orientation to any marked degree.

Regional archaeology: Gordon Willey, Richard MacNeish, Lewis Binford, and Stuart Struever

The regional approach orients prehistoric archaeology to a larger geographic unit. Traditionally, archaeologists have tended to consider the site as their investigative unit. Conclusions about larger areas were based on comparisons *between* sites. In other words, the prehistory of geographical spaces between sites was "filled in" from what was known about a few specific points, the sites. But the regional approach frees archaeological investigations from restriction to a single site or even to all the identified sites within a region. Intersite areas or vacant terrain may also be sampled to provide useful archaeological data that may be hidden from view or otherwise ignored. Overall, the regional approach stresses a research strategy aimed at sampling an entire region; the data thus gathered will enable the archaeologist to reconstruct aspects of prehistoric society that may not be well represented by a single site. Of prime importance here is the reconstruction of ancient subsistence and social organizational systems. Of course, beyond gathering better data bearing upon these specific concerns, regional archaeology remains oriented to meeting the overall objectives of all prehistoric archaeology (see Chapter 1).

How does the regional approach meet its objectives? Obviously, translating any fragmentary remains left by past peoples into a reconstruction of ancient society is a difficult task. Some of the ways archaeologists do this will be discussed in Chapter 11. Here we shall consider how past human behavior is transformed into archaeological evidence and how the characteristics and distribution of these remains become the basis for archaeological interpretation.

MANUFACTURE

USE

DEPOSITION

Figure 3.8 Archaeological data represent at least one behavioral cycle of manufacture, use, and deposition.

THE DETERMINANTS OF ARCHAEOLOGICAL DATA

Now that we have defined the various forms of archaeological data, we can describe the processes responsible for creating evidence of past human behavior and the ways the archaeologist detects these processes in order to reconstruct that behavior. The archaeologist responsible for the most thorough discussions of these processes is Michael Schiffer.

Behavioral and Transformational Processes

Archaeological data are the result of two factors: behavioral processes and transformational processes. We will describe these in the order in which they act on the data.

All archaeological sites, from the smallest temporary overnight hunting camp to the largest, longest-occupied urban center, represent the products of human activity. Of course not all human activity or behavior produces tangible remains. Entire unwritten languages as well as philosophical concepts and belief systems that existed in the past may be completely lost, since they leave little or no direct evidence. Most kinds of human behavior, however, do modify the natural environment to some degree; every society affects its surroundings in some way. Forests are felled, animals hunted, plants gathered, rivers diverted, and minerals extracted, all to satisfy the needs of human societies. The material products of this behavior—the tools, food, roads, buildings, and so forth—are the artifacts, ecofacts, and features that the archaeologist recovers. And the activities that affect the environment to produce tangible remains (later recovered as archaeological data) are what we call ancient *behavioral processes*.

In recovering these data, the archaeologist attempts to determine what specific kinds of ancient behavior they reflect. All archaeological data represent three ideally consecutive stages of behavior: manufacture, use, and deposition (Fig. 3.8). Of course, some items are eventually modified for new uses or recycled, involving new manufacturing and use activity. Artifacts such as tools are made, used for one or more specific purposes, and then discarded when broken or worn. Features such as houses are constructed and then occupied; when they are no longer habitable or needed, they may be abandoned, torn down, or burned. Ecofacts, such as animals used for food, pass through similar stages: the animal may be hunted, butchered, and cooked (manufacture), eaten (use), and both the digested and undigested waste products discarded (deposition). The aggregate of these activities at a site delineate the same three stages in the life

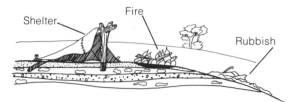

2000 B.P.: Hunting camp (manufacture, use, and deposition behavior)

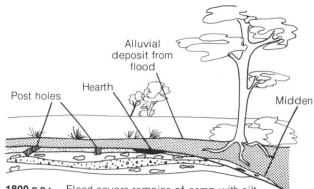

1800 B.P.: Flood covers remains of camp with silt.

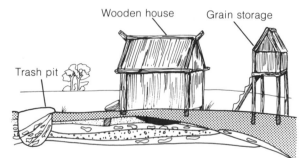

1500 B.P.: Farming village built on silt (new cycle of manufacture, use, and deposition behavior)

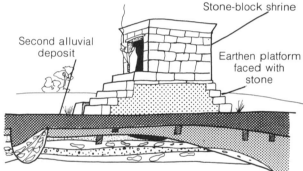

1000 B.P.: New flood destroys farming village; stone shrine built on new ground surface (new cycles of manufacture, use, and deposition behavior)

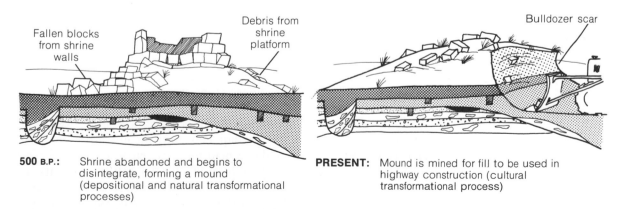

500 B.P.: Shrine abandoned and begins to disintegrate, forming a mound (depositional and natural transformational processes)

PRESENT: Mound is mined for fill to be used in highway construction (cultural transformational process)

Figure 3.9 The characteristics of archaeological data and their deposition reflect both behavioral and transformational processes.

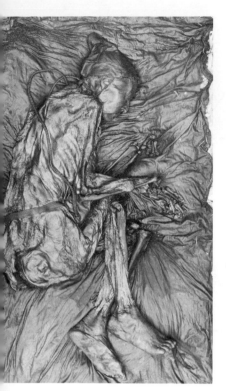

Figure 3.10 Tollund Man, a corpse preserved for some 2000 years in a Danish bog. (Reprinted from P. V. Glob: *The Bog People: Iron-Age Man Preserved*. This translation copyright © Faber & Faber, Ltd., 1969. Copyright © P. V. Glob 1965. Used by permission of the publisher, Cornell University Press.)

Transformation processes: Thera

span of the site as a whole: setting up areas or structures to house activities (shelter, work, ritual, and so forth), use of these areas for the various activities, and, ultimately, destruction or abandonment of the site.

Thus the archaeologist can use all forms of archaeological data, individually and together, to reconstruct the manufacture, use, and deposition stages of ancient behavior. Clues to all three kinds of ancient behavior may be found in characteristics of the data themselves and in the circumstances of their deposition (Fig. 3.9). In Chapters 9 to 11 we will discuss how the archaeologist reconstructs past behavior from data analysis; and later in this chapter we will see how the archaeologist can determine aspects of ancient behavior from the circumstances under which data are found.

These behavioral processes represent the first stage in the formation of archaeological data. The second step consists of *transformational processes*. These processes include all conditions and events that affect archaeological data from the cessation of ancient use (that is, from deposition) to the time the archaeologist recognizes and acquires them.

The tangible products of ancient human behavior are never completely indestructible. But some survive better than others. As a result, the data recovered by the archaeologist always present a picture of the past that is selected or biased by the effects of transformational processes (see Fig. 3.9). To know in what ways the recovered data may be biased, it is crucial to determine the nature of the processes that have been at work in each archaeological situation. Both natural and human events act either to accelerate or to retard destruction. Natural agents of transformation include climatic factors, which are usually the basic influence acting on the preservation of archaeological evidence. Temperature and humidity are generally the most critical climatic factors, although others may be important. Extremely dry, wet, or cold conditions act to preserve fragile organic materials, such as textiles and wooden tools, as well as bulkier perishable items such as human corpses (Fig. 3.10). Organic remains have been preserved under these circumstances along the dry coast of Peru, in the wet bogs of Scandinavia, and in the frozen steppes of Siberia.

Natural destructive processes (such as oxidation and decay) and catastrophic events (such as earthquakes and volcanic eruptions) also have profound effects on the remains of the past. Underwater remains may be broken up and scattered by tidal action, currents, or waves. Catastrophes such as volcanic eruptions may either preserve or destroy archaeological sites; often the same event may have a multitude of effects. For example, sometime around 1500 B.C. both an earthquake and a volcanic eruption struck the island of Thera, at the

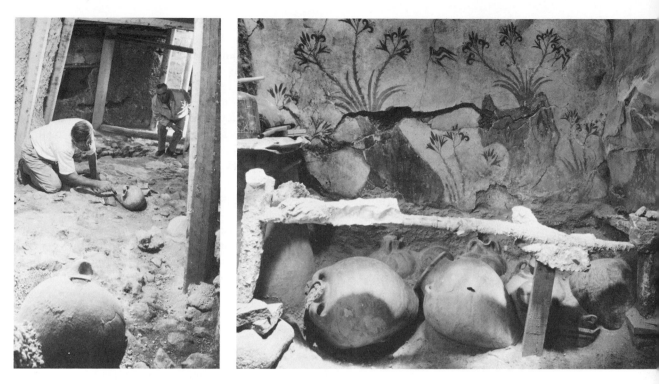

Figure 3.11 Excavations on Thera, where a blanket of volcanic ash has sealed and preserved the remains of a large Bronze Age settlement. (Otis Imboden, © National Geographic Society.)

southern end of the Cyclades (Fig. 3.11). Part of the island blew up; another part collapsed inward and was filled by the inrushing Aegean Sea; and still other areas were immediately buried under a blanket of ash. The local population abandoned the island, but the remains of its settlements were sealed beneath the ash. Recent excavations have disclosed well-preserved buildings, some intact to the third story—a rarity in more exposed sites—as well as beautiful wall paintings. Such fragile artifacts as baskets have also been found, thoroughly disintegrated but recoverable by application of a hardening agent to "stains" left in the ash.

One of the most decisive factors in the transformation process is subsequent human activity. Reoccupation of an archaeological site by a later people may destroy all traces of previous occupation. Earlier buildings are often levelled to make way for new construction or to provide construction materials. In other cases, however, later activity may preserve older sites by building over and thus sealing the earlier remains (Fig. 3.12). Of course, large-scale human events such as war, conquest, and mass migration usually have destructive consequences for archaeological preservation. Finally, economic conditions that support a flourishing market in antiquities have a profound negative effect by encouraging the looting and consequent destruction of archaeological sites.

Thus the archaeologist must carefully evaluate the preservation status of data gathered, in order to determine what conditions and events have acted to transform the materials originally deposited by past human behavior. The most fundamental distinction to be made is between natural and human agents of transformation. Obviously the transformation processes that have modified the data are specific to each site, so each archaeological situation must be evaluated individually.

As we have seen, the form of archaeological data is the result of sequential behavioral and transformational processes. In order to derive as much information as possible from the available data, the archaeologist must understand both sets of processes. How is this done? We will see that the archaeologist begins to reconstruct these processes from the circumstances under which the data are recovered, including their matrix, provenience, and association.

Matrix, Provenience, and Association

All archaeological material, from the smallest arrowhead to the grandest temple complex, has a provenience within or relative to a matrix.

Figure 3.12 Structure E-VII sub at the Maya site of Uaxactún, Guatemala, preserved by a later overlying construction completely removed in 1928: (a) view before reclearing and restoration in 1974; (b) restoration completed, 1974. (Courtesy of Edwin M. Shook.)

(a)

(b)

The term *matrix* refers to the physical medium that surrounds, holds, and supports the archaeological material (Fig. 3.13). Most frequently this medium consists of various kinds of earthen substances, such as humus, sand, silt, gravel, and pumice. The nature of a matrix is usually an important clue to understanding the artifacts, features, or ecofacts it contains. For instance, artifacts recovered from an alluvial matrix (deposited by running water) may have been deposited by natural action of a river or stream. A matrix may also be the product of human activity such as the deposition of immense amounts of soil in order to construct an earthen platform. In this case, the soil is not only a feature (the construction), but also an ecofact (the soil), and a matrix for any artifacts contained within it and for other features constructed upon it.

Provenience simply refers to a three-dimensional location—the horizontal and vertical position on or within the matrix—at which the archaeologist finds data. Horizontal provenience is usually determined and recorded relative to a geographical grid system using known reference points. Vertical provenience is usually determined and recorded as elevation above or below sea level, also using known reference points. Chapter 7 will discuss the actual methods used to determine provenience; here we wish only to stress that determination and recording of provenience for all kinds of archaeological data are always necessary if that information is to be useful. Provenience information allows the archaeologist to record (and later to reconstruct)

Figure 3.13 In this photograph, a human burial has been excavated from most of its matrix, but the relationship of the remains to the matrix remains readily apparent. (Courtesy of the Ban Chiang Project, Thai Fine Arts Department/University Museum.)

Importance of provenience, association, and context: The archaeologist vs. the looter

association and *context*. An artifact is associated with other, adjacent artifacts, ecofacts, and features that occur in the same matrix (Fig. 3.14). The associations of various kinds of data may be crucial to the interpretation of past events. Context is the interpretation of the significance of an artifact's deposition in terms of its matrix, provenience, and association—that is, where it is and how it got there.

One point of sharp contrast between the archaeologist and the looter is that when the looter finds "buried treasures"—let us say, two beautifully painted pottery bowls within a tomb chamber—he does not bother to record either provenience or association. Being interested only in the money to be gained from selling the vessels, he does not care that archaeologists might know the age of one of the kinds of vessels he discovered but not of the other. If archaeologists knew the provenience, association, and matrix of these two vessels— that is, if they knew that the two were discovered in association on the floor of an ancient tomb—they would probably infer that the two were deposited at the same time and had remained undisturbed until their discovery. The unknown vessel could then be assigned the same date as the known one. Because the information was unrecorded, however, these insights are forever lost. Although the vessels themselves were recovered and preserved, their significance as sources of information about past human behavior was destroyed.

As another example of the importance of context, discoveries of

Figure 3.14   A group of pottery vessels found in association.

stone projectile points in clear association with the bones of extinct prey animals have been important keys to the reconstruction of early human occupation of the Western Hemisphere. In the mid-1920s, finds at Folsom, New Mexico, revealed such points in undisturbed context, associated with bones of a species of bison that had been extinct for 10,000 years or more. Similar finds at other sites, such as Lindenmeier, Colorado, established firmly that bison hunters lived and stalked their prey in North America at least 10,000 years ago. The dates were supplied by paleontological study, but archaeological association and contextual interpretation were critical in establishing the cultural significance of the finds.

Reconstruction of early human occupation of the Western Hemisphere: Folsom, New Mexico

The point is that any kind of excavation, by archaeologists or anyone else, *destroys* matrix, association, and context. The only way to preserve the information these factors convey is in drawings, photographs, and written records. Such records will be discussed in Chapter 7; here we wish only to underscore the importance of *keeping* accurate records of archaeological work. Without them, even the most painstakingly controlled excavation is no more justifiable or useful than a looter's pit.

Context

The archaeologist uses the products of past behavior—archaeological data—to reconstruct both the behavior and the cultural systems by which they were produced. As the first step in linking the data to a past cultural system, the archaeologist must assess the effects on the data of the processes we have discussed in this chapter: the kinds of ancient behavior—manufacture, use, and deposition—that originally produced the evidence (the behavioral processes), and the natural or human events that have affected these data from the time of their deposition to the moment of archaeological recovery (the processes of transformation).

Understanding these sets of formative processes begins with evaluation of the context of archaeological data. Context refers to the characteristics of archaeological data that result both from their original behavioral associations and from their postdepositional transformation history (Fig. 3.15). Context is evaluated at the data acquisition stage (see Chapter 4) by careful observation and recording of the matrix, provenience, and association of all data.

Archaeological contexts are of two basic kinds: primary and secondary contexts. Each of these may be divided into two categories to produce four kinds of context. We shall first define each of the four kinds and then examine a series of brief examples to clarify the relationships among these context categories.

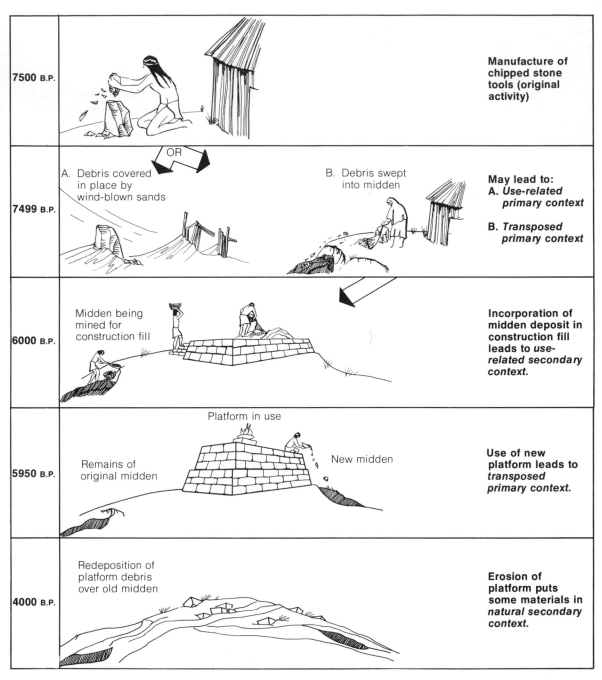

7500 B.P.	**Manufacture of chipped stone tools (original activity)**
7499 B.P.	A. Debris covered in place by wind-blown sands OR B. Debris swept into midden	**May lead to:** **A.** *Use-related primary context* **B.** *Transposed primary context*
6000 B.P.	Midden being mined for construction fill	**Incorporation of midden deposit in construction fill leads to *use-related secondary context*.**
5950 B.P.	Platform in use Remains of original midden New midden	**Use of new platform leads to *transposed primary context*.**
4000 B.P.	Redeposition of platform debris over old midden	**Erosion of platform puts some materials in *natural secondary context*.**

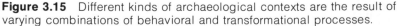

Figure 3.15 Different kinds of archaeological contexts are the result of varying combinations of behavioral and transformational processes.

Primary context refers to conditions in which both provenience and matrix have been undisturbed since original deposition by the manufacturers or users of the artifact or ecofact. Intact archaeological features are always in primary context, although later disturbance can remove components of such features from primary context.

There are two kinds of primary contexts. *Use-related primary context* results from deposition in the location where the artifact was made or used. The occurrence of two or more associated artifacts in use-related primary context usually means that they were used and deposited at the same time. Furthermore, such an occurrence allows the reconstruction of the ancient activity of which the artifacts were a part. *Transposed primary context* results from behavior not related to the manufacture or use of artifacts—that is, from specialized behavior concerned with disposing of refuse (formation of trash deposits or *middens*). The association of two or more artifacts in transposed primary context does not help the archaeologist to reconstruct ancient manufacture or use behavior from the circumstances of their deposition. However, their association in transposed primary context does support the inference that they were made and used during the same period.

Secondary context refers to a condition in which both provenience and matrix have been wholly or partially altered by processes of transformation. *Use-related secondary context* refers to disturbance caused by subsequent human behavior. The archaeologist may be able to determine the chronological position of the disturbance, and the nature of the secondary context may allow identification of the kinds of activity that caused the disturbance. This may or may not be archaeologically significant, depending on what it reveals about otherwise unknown past behavior. For instance, evidence of warfare, construction, or looting may indicate "significant" past disturbances when these were ancient activities. The same kinds of evidence related to recent and otherwise well known time frames—a World War II bombing, 1960s housing construction, or modern plundering— would probably not be thought archaeologically significant in themselves, but they would be important nonetheless in their effect on the earlier remains. *Natural secondary context* results from disturbance caused by nonhuman agents, such as animal burrowing, tree roots, or natural events (earthquakes, volcanism, erosion).

The following discussion illustrates both the differences among types of archaeological context and the significance of the determination of context. Any artifact may be used over an extensive period of time; furthermore, it may be modified to be reused for different kinds of activity throughout its use span. Thus a single pottery vessel may be manufactured to be used for water transport, food storage, and meal preparation, as well as to serve when inverted, as a mold for the shaping of new pottery vessels. If this particular vessel were abandoned during, or immediately after, any of these activities—say during its use as a mold for the manufacture of other pottery—and if it remained within an undisturbed matrix together with its associated artifacts, ecofacts, and features, then its archaeological context upon discovery would be *primary* (undisturbed) and *use-related* (representing an ancient human behavior pattern). Knowing the provenience, association, matrix, and context, in this case reflected in the find of an inverted vessel surrounded by other vessels in various stages of manufacture along with clay-shaping tools and so forth, the archaeologist would be able to reconstruct not only a kind of manufacturing behavior (pottery making) but many of the specific details of the process of pottery making. Determination that a context is primary and use-related allows the direct reconstruction of ancient behavior.

The survival of use-related primary contexts depends on transformation processes that act to preserve rather than to destroy. Many kinds of subsequent activity can disturb or erase use-related primary contexts. In some cases, however, subsequent human activity can preserve them—as in the building of a new structure over a recently abandoned potter's workshop. In other cases, the manner of original deposition may tend to secure use-related primary contexts from disturbance. One of the best examples of such deposition is provided by the preparation of burials and tombs. In many areas of the world, elaborate funerary customs developed in the past; the resultant tombs, when undisturbed, provide opportunities to reconstruct ancient ritual activity and belief systems. A good illustration of this is the Royal Tombs of Ur, excavated by Sir Leonard Woolley in the late 1920s (Fig. 3.16).

The Royal Tombs of Ur: Use-related primary context

The burials of King A-bar-gi and Queen Shub-ad were accompanied by interment of more than 80 other people. The actual chamber in which A-bar-gi lay had been plundered in ancient times—perhaps, as Woolley argues, when an adjacent chamber was prepared somewhat later for the queen. But the original entry pits and ramps of both tombs were undisturbed; excavation gradually disclosed an incredible retinue, including soldiers with gold- and silver-headed spears, female attendants wearing headdresses of lapis, carnelian, and gold, a decorated chariot accompanied by asses and their grooms, and an array of spectacularly beautiful artifacts such as gaming boards and harps. Recovery was slow and painstaking: because of the quantity and in many cases the fragility of the remains, the overall area was divided into squares. Finds in each square were cleared and removed before work on the next square was begun. As a result of the

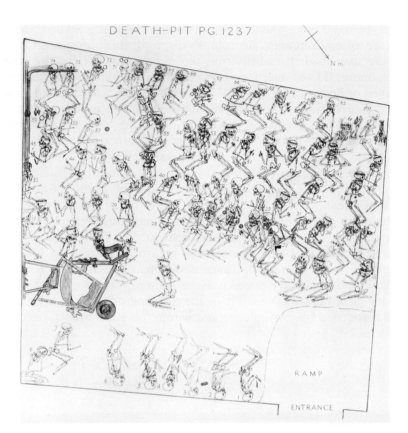

Figure 3.16 This plan shows positions of bodies in the "Great Death-Pit" adjacent to the royal tombs at Ur. (From Woolley 1934; by permission of the University Museum, University of Pennsylvania.)

careful recording of provenience and of relationships between artifacts, a nearly complete funerary scene could later be reconstructed by combining information from each square. From reconstruction, Woolley was able to infer a great deal about royal Chaldean funerary customs generally as well as about specific details such as court costume. Only the chamber of A-bar-gi, which had been looted, could not be reconstructed; the rest had been protected and preserved by interment.

Other examples of use-related primary context have been preserved by natural events. The deposition of soil by wind and water has buried countless sites under deep layers of earth; a famous example of a dramatically buried site is the ancient Roman city of Pompeii, which was covered by volcanic ash from the eruption of Mount Vesuvius in A.D. 79 (Fig. 2.3).

But not all primary contexts are use-related. People in most societies discard items after they are damaged, broken, or no longer

Archaeological middens: Transposed primary context

useful. In some cases this disposal activity produces a *midden*. Middens are specialized areas for rubbish disposal; they contain artifacts that are usually undisturbed from the moment of their deposition. Furthermore, if used over long periods of time, middens may become stratified or layered (see Chapter 7), with each layer corresponding to a period of rubbish deposition. Middens are thus in primary context, but because of the nature of their deposition, the only past behavior directly reflected by this context is the general practice of rubbish accumulation and disposal. For this reason, material recovered from middens is in *transposed primary context*. If rubbish is not transported to specialized areas but is discarded haphazardly within occupation areas (often in association with living floors), then a combination of evidence may result, with some in use-related primary context, some in transposed primary context, and even some in secondary context. The use or function of an artifact cannot be inferred directly from associations in transposed primary context. Of course, in either kind of primary context, association can be used to establish chronological contemporaneity: in the absence of later disturbance, items associated by provenience and within the same matrix are con-

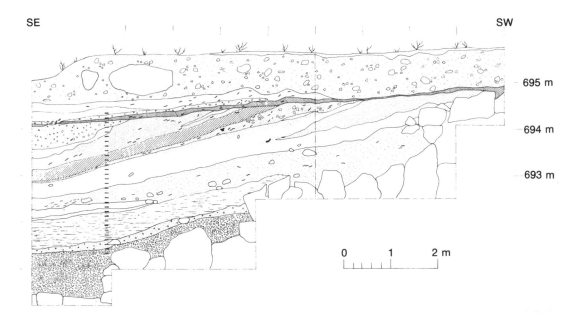

Figure 3.17 Cross-section drawing of a stratified midden representing nearly 2000 years of accumulation.

temporary. If a midden is used over a long period of time, then relative position within the deposit (or within a particular stratum of the midden) can be used to assess relative chronological position (see Fig. 3.17).

With regard to secondary (disturbed) context, the identification of *use-related secondary* context can often aid the archaeologist in understanding how artifacts came to be associated. On the other hand, if the disturbed context is not recognized as such, chaotic and erroneous interpretation can result (Fig. 3.18). For example, the contents of a heavily disturbed tomb might include not only some portion of the original furnishings, but also material such as tools and containers that were brought in and left behind by the looters. During the

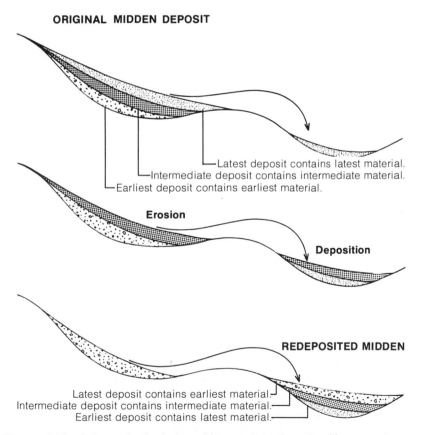

ORIGINAL MIDDEN DEPOSIT

Latest deposit contains latest material.
Intermediate deposit contains intermediate material.
Earliest deposit contains earliest material.

Erosion

Deposition

REDEPOSITED MIDDEN

Latest deposit contains earliest material.
Intermediate deposit contains intermediate material.
Earliest deposit contains latest material.

Figure 3.18 Schematic depiction of inverted stratigraphy. Uppermost (latest) material in the original deposit erodes first, and is redeposited as the lowermost layer downstream, resulting in natural secondary context.

Recognition of use-related secondary context: The tomb of Tut-ankh-amun

Recognition of natural secondary context: Ban Chiang, Thailand

excavation of the tomb of the Egyptian Pharaoh Tut-ankh-amun, ancient looting was recognized by evidence of two openings and reclosings of the entry; the final sealings of the disturbed areas were marked by different motifs from those on the undisturbed portions. If the disturbance had not been recognized, the associations and arrangements of recovered artifacts might be wrongly interpreted as representing burial ritual behavior. As another example, suppose construction material used to build a series of superimposed earth platforms has been mined from several abandoned middens. Then chronological interpretations could appear to defy logic: the artifacts contained in the latest construction, the top layer (whose fill derived from an early midden deposit) might be of an earlier date than artifacts in older, lower construction levels, whose fill matrix derived from a late midden deposit.

Natural secondary context, which might occur when burrowing animals have placed later artifacts in apparent association with earlier features, can also make interpretation difficult. For example, at Ban Chiang, a site in northern Thailand, a series of ancient burials are juxtaposed in a very complex fashion, with later pits intruding into and/or overlapping earlier ones. But the job of segregating aboriginally distinct units was made even more difficult by the numerous animal burrows, including those of worms, crisscrossing the units, so that tracing pit lines and other surfaces was exacting and intricate work.

Archaeologists, then, must not only record carefully the associations, provenience, and matrix they are working with, but they must use this information with great care to determine the context of their data. For unless they do so, the significance of the data will be diminished or even destroyed.

*THE STRUCTURE OF ARCHAEOLOGICAL DATA

We shall now examine the structure of the basic forms of archaeological data—artifacts, ecofacts, and features. This structure is usually apparent to the archaeologist from the distribution of the data as they are revealed. Such structure, conditioned by the behavioral and transformational processes discussed above, provides the basis for reconstructing prehistoric behavior and culture. This discussion assumes determination of *primary context;* for all practical purposes this is limited to use-related primary context.

The structure of archaeological data allows the archaeologist to infer certain kinds of ancient activity. This structure, together with the kinds of inferred activities (behavior) is summarized in Figure 3.19.

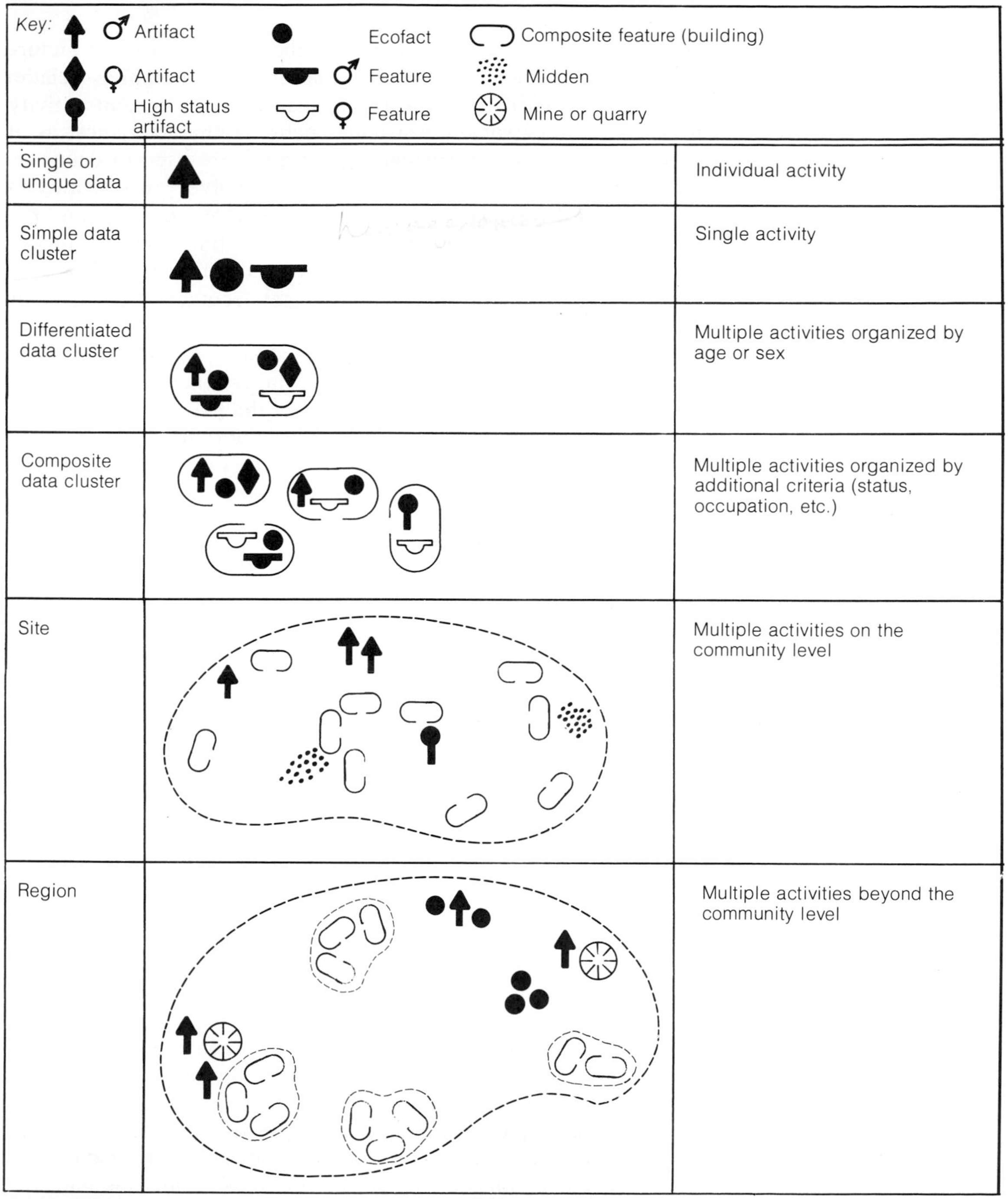

Key:	↑ ♂ Artifact	● Ecofact	◗ Composite feature (building)
	◆ ♀ Artifact	⬬ ♂ Feature	⦂⦂ Midden
	⬩ High status artifact	⬭ ♀ Feature	⊛ Mine or quarry

Single or unique data		Individual activity
Simple data cluster		Single activity
Differentiated data cluster		Multiple activities organized by age or sex
Composite data cluster		Multiple activities organized by additional criteria (status, occupation, etc.)
Site		Multiple activities on the community level
Region		Multiple activities beyond the community level

Figure 3.19 The hierarchical structuring of archaeological data based on use-related primary context.

The inference of prehistoric behavior relies upon two basic factors: clustering and patterning. Data units that are recovered in association (clustering) are used to define the spatial areas of ancient activity. Clusters that show some consistent functional characteristics, as either homogeneous or heterogeneous patterns, are used to define the kinds of ancient activity. The latter step involves an inference of function from the available data units. Consistent clustering and patterning of similar data tends to reinforce such functional inferences. For example, the discovery of cutting tools (artifacts) in association with disarticulated and broken animal bones (ecofacts) allows the archaeologist to infer ancient butchering activity.

Obviously archaeologists will often encounter isolated artifacts of other kinds of data units, or clusters of data, that lack distinguishable patterning. Although such finds may reflect the past activities of individuals or groups, the lack of clustering or patterning prevents the archaeologist from making the kinds of inferences regarding prehistoric behavior that we are discussing. For convenience, we can refer to data of this kind as *isolated data* or *unpatterned data clusters*.

Setting aside these exceptions, at the most basic level of structuring the archaeologist may encounter data clusters that are internally homogeneous in regard to a single function. For example, the discovery of several projectile points together with animal remains is consistent with the reconstruction of ancient hunting activity. Similarly, clusters of obsidian chipping debris, broken obsidian tools, and antler ''punches,'' or of clusters of raw clay, polishing stones, molds, and burned areas are both indicative of ancient manufacturing activity (obsidian tools and pottery, respectively). Homogeneous data clusters indicative of single activities may be termed *simple data clusters*. Simple data clusters may consist of any combination of artifacts, ecofacts, and features. However, since composite features such as buildings are usually associated with multiple functions, they are probably less likely to be associated with simple data clusters.

At the next level (see Fig. 3.19), data clusters may be heterogeneous but are consistently patterned. These clusters may be interpreted as indicating two or more distinct activities that are often spatially segregated, reflective of age or sex differences. Since all known human societies manifest at least some behavioral distinctions between males and females and between adults and children, some reflection of these distinctions can be expected in the archaeological record. For example, a composite feature such as house remains (consisting of foundation, floors, walls, and so on) may contain a hearth associated with cooking utensils and food residues in one area, along with hunting tools and weapons in another area. This kind of patterned heterogeneity is inferred to be reflective of female versus male activity areas within a household. Child-size utensils and toys similarly reflect nonadult activities. These sex and age distinctions define *differentiated data clusters*, which are usually associated with residences housing nuclear families or larger kin groups.

Beyond the level of the differentiated data cluster, the archaeologist may find heterogeneous data clusters that indicate multiple activities based on other social distinctions besides age and sex. Such behavioral distinctions include those founded in occupational specialization, wealth or status distinctions, and class or caste differences. For example, a cluster of several composite features representing residences may contain the patterning of artifacts, ecofacts, and features reflective of the male/female activity distinction discussed above. In addition to this patterning, one of the residences may be associated with such distinct artifacts as unusually decorated pottery, imported articles of adornment, and so forth; these may be indicative of higher status or greater wealth. Other buildings may differ in their size, shape, or decoration and be associated with distinct clusters of artifacts, ecofacts, or features. Depending upon such criteria, these clusters may reflect civic activities, ceremonialism, markets, and so forth. Heterogeneous data clusters that embody distinctions beyond age and sex may be termed *composite data clusters*.

By viewing archaeological data according to a hierarchical structure based on cluster, pattern, and inferred functions, we may define more precisely two concepts discussed earlier in this chapter: site and region. Although the archaeological site remains a convenient unit for investigation, it can be defined as a contiguous concentration of the kinds of data clusters we have just discussed. Thus a site may be composed of one or more of any single kind of data cluster, or any combination of such data clusters. The archaeological region, which remains the preferred means of defining the limits to archaeological research, may be defined as a coherent geographical area containing two or more related sites.

APPROACHES
TO ARCHAEOLOGICAL DATA ACQUISITION

Now that we have defined the forms of archaeological data, discussed their determinants, and examined the way this evidence is structured, we will consider the basic approaches to data recovery. The archaeologist is concerned with gathering evidence of past human behavior as a first step toward understanding that ancient behavior and toward meeting both the specific objectives of the research and the general goals of archaeology (see Chapter 1). Realization of these objectives requires discovery of as much as possible about the characteristics of the data. Ideally, the archaeologist seeks to recover the full range of variation in the archaeological data relevant to his research questions. What was the range of activities carried on at a site? What was the range of places chosen for location and settlement? What was the range of forms and styles of pottery? To the extent that such variation existed but is not known, the research findings are incomplete and conclusions based on them may be misleading or wrong. This means that the archaeologist must do everything possible to avoid acquiring an unrepresentative set of data—evidence that reflects only a part of the variation in the archaeological record. In a sense, archaeological data are always unrepresentative: not all behavior produces tangible evidence, and even for that which does, not all the remains will survive. So the ideal goal is seldom realized. But to some extent the unevenness in the availability of data can be compensated for by understanding the processes that affected the production and preservation of the evidence. At this point we need to consider how the archaeologist chooses data acquisition strategies in order to maximize the usefulness of the evidence that *is* available.

Data Universe and Sample Units

The first step in data acquisition is defining the boundaries of the region being investigated in order to place a practical limit on the amount of evidence to be collected. A bounded area of investigation may be referred to as a *data universe*. An archaeological data universe (which is not the same as a statistical universe) is bounded both in geographical space and in time. Thus an investigator may define a data universe to correspond to a single site, or even to a portion of a site. In the regional approach the investigation extends over a much larger universe, such as an entire valley or mountain range containing many individual sites. The archaeologist must also draw temporal boundaries—the data sought are those from a specific time interval. Thus one investigator may seek to acquire data corresponding to a relatively short period of time, such as the Late Classic era of Mesoamerica (ca. A.D. 700–900); another archaeologist might be interested in a much longer time span, such as a period of several thousand years corresponding to the most recent interglacial period at the end of the Pleistocene.

Once defined, the archaeological data universe is subdivided into *sample units*. A sample unit is the unit of investigation; it may be defined by either arbitrary or nonarbitrary criteria. *Nonarbitrarily* defined sample units correspond either to natural areas, such as microenvironments, or to cultural entities, such as various data clusters

Figure 3.20 Universe with nonarbitrary units, in this case, rooms in a prehistoric Southwestern pueblo; the shaded rooms were the ones excavated. (By permission from *Broken K Pueblo, Prehistoric Social Organization in the American Southwest,* by James N. Hill, University of Arizona Anthropological Paper #18, Tucson: University of Arizona Press, copyright 1970.)

(in rooms, houses or sites) (Fig. 3.20). *Arbitrarily* defined units, on the other hand, are spatial divisions with no inherent natural or cultural relevance (Fig. 3.21). Examples of the latter include sample units defined by a grid system (equal-size squares, called quadrats), by geographical coordinates (point locations, called spots), or by axes (linear corridors of equal width, called transects). In general, larger numbers of smaller-size arbitrary sample units are preferable to fewer units of larger size. *Sample units should not be confused with data:* If an archaeologist is looking for sites, the sample units will be geographical areas where sites might be located. If sites are the sample units, the information (data) to be gathered will be the constituent data clusters (artifacts, ecofacts, and features) within the site.

The choice between arbitrary and nonarbitrary sample units is made by the investigator; it reflects the specific objectives of the study (see Chapter 4). But in any case all sample units are (or are assumed to be) comparable. That is, nonarbitrarily defined units are assumed to yield similar or complementary information about ancient behavior. For example, if sites are the sample units, one "cemetery" site will give information similar to that from another cemetery site and complementary to information from "habitation" sites and other sample units within the data population. Arbitrarily defined units, on the other hand, are comparable because they are always regular in size and/or shape.

Sample units, whether arbitrary or nonarbitrary, can be described and manipulated according to their location in both time and space, their distribution within the universe, their form or characteristics, their frequency, and their structure or the pattern of relationships among units. We will discuss these and other specific uses for sample units in Chapters 5 through 7 when we consider methods of data acquisition.

The aggregate of all sample units is the *population,* which is not necessarily the same as the universe. If the universe is a region and the sample units are defined as known sites, for instance, the population will not include unknown sites or locations in the region that are not sites, even though these areas are part of the universe. Nevertheless, conclusions drawn about the population are often inferred to be "true" of the universe as well.

The archaeological *data pool* is the evidence available to the archaeologist within a given area of study (the data universe), conditioned by both behavioral and transformational selective forces. Note that the data pool is the total potential evidence, while the population is the sum of the sample units. The amount of material actually recovered from a given archaeological data pool depends upon the acquisition methods used.

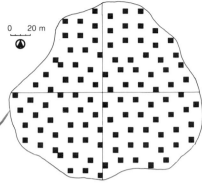

Figure 3.21 Universe with arbitrary units; the shaded areas were the units investigated. (After Redman and Watson, reproduced by permission of The Society for American Archaeology, adapted from *American Antiquity* 35:281–282, 1970.)

Total Data Acquisition

Total data acquisition involves investigation of all the units in the population. The archaeologist never succeeds in gathering every shred of evidence from a given data universe: new techniques of recovery and analysis (such as flotation or archaeomagnetic dating, discussed in later chapters) are constantly being developed which broaden the definition of data. A change in the definition of a research problem also alters the definition of what observed materials and relationships are data. It is nonetheless important to distinguish between investigations that attempt to collect all available archaeological evidence (by investigation of all sample units) and those that set out to collect only a portion of the available data. Something approaching total data acquisition, in this sense, is often attempted in salvage situations (Chapter 15), as when a site or region is threatened with imminent destruction by construction of a new road or dam.

Sample Data Acquisition

In most cases, however, only a portion or sample of the data can be collected from a given archaeological data pool. The limits to the sample recovered are often partly dictated by economic realities—the archaeologist seldom has the funds to study all potential units. Nor is research time unlimited: factors such as seasonal weather conditions (periods of heavy rains, extreme cold, or other inclement conditions), scheduling commitments (such as teaching or research duties at the investigator's home university or museum), and other constraints often limit the time available to gather data. Access to archaeological data may be restricted: portions of a single site or some sites within a region may be closed to the investigator because of inability to secure adequate permissions from governmental agencies or private property owners. In other cases, access may be hampered by natural barriers or by lack of roads or trails. Even in the absence of these limiting factors, in most cases it would still be desirable to collect only a part of the available archaeological evidence. Except in such cases as a site or area under threat of immediate destruction, most archaeologists recommend that a portion of every archaeological site be left untouched to allow future scientists, using more sophisticated techniques and methods than those in use today, a chance to work with intact sources of archaeological data. In this way future investigations can check and refine the results obtained using present techniques.

*Probabilistic and Nonprobabilistic Sampling

Since most archaeological situations demand that only a part of the available data be collected, we need to consider the methods used to determine which units will actually be investigated. Two approaches are available for the selection of data samples: *probabilistic* and *non-probabilistic* sampling methods.

Nonprobabilistic sampling uses informal criteria or personal judgment in the selection of data samples. Such sampling techniques have been used since the early days of archaeology; until recently, they were by far the most common means for choosing data sources. In this approach, samples are selected by informal criteria such as prominence and accessibility. This usually means that data are acquired from the most obvious and/or most easily investigated available archaeological remains. In many cases such archaeological investigations are guided by precedent, intuition, or guesswork. This is not to say that such uncontrolled sampling methods are wrong; no archaeologist should *ignore* prominent or obvious remains. And no one can deny the ability of skilled investigators to locate archaeological evidence, whether on the basis of experience, intuition, or some "sixth sense." It is also true, however, that nonprobabilistic sampling has often been accompanied by disregard for defining the units being sampled, as well as little attention to defining the population or the data universe. Unless these definitions are precisely made, and unless the researcher can state in what ways the defined entities are related, no one can judge the likelihood that the acquired sample is representative of the overall population and universe. Suppose that Structure X, located at Site Y, is studied. Is it to be taken as representative of *all* structures within Site Y, as representative only of structures with like form and size (within this site or within some larger region of which Site Y is a part), or as representative of some other, unspecified population? Why was Structure X chosen for investigation?

Nonprobabilistic sampling can lead to significant and/or spectacular discoveries, and it is often useful as a probing device when the area of investigation is completely unknown. It is also the appropriate choice when something specific is sought, such as a ritual "cache" whose contents may be used to date a construction. In this case, data are being acquired for a specialized purpose, and the unit is not chosen as an example of all units of its kind. But if a sample is supposed to be a substitute for total data acquisition and is therefore intended to represent some larger population in microcosm, nonprobabilistic sampling techniques are not the best ones to use.

The field of statistics offers a range of sampling techniques, all based on probability theory, in which the resultant samples are related in mathematically specified ways to the population. The application of sampling theory—and statistics generally—to archaeological situations has been a fairly recent phenomenon. Early reactions to such applications tended to be polarized: some archaeologists wrote off statistics as cumbersome and unnecessary, as "creating truth" by fancy manipulation of numbers; others hailed the new development as solving all the problems an archaeologist had ever faced. As light began to predominate over the heat of debate, archaeologists began to see that statistics, properly applied, could indeed improve both the quality of data collection and analysis and the power and reliability of the conclusions reached. On the other hand, statistics did not apply to every question or problem and could never be a "cure" for poorly conceived questions or sloppily collected data. With regard to sampling, statistical procedures never ensure that a sample is fully representative; they do, however, maximize that probability. They also indicate the assumptions made about the relation of the sample to the population.

How are probabilistic samples taken in archaeological situations? Because of the need to adapt statistical designs to the specialized demands of archaeology, the designation of techniques appropriate to various situations is still being refined. There is no single or easy answer here: choice of sampling technique is dependent on the kind of population and what is already known about it, on the goals of the investigation, and on the characteristics of the various techniques. Our discussion will outline some of the more common and useful sampling principles and procedures used thus far in archaeology, but the criteria for choosing among them for a given application are beyond the scope of this book.

Once the universe, sample unit, and population have been defined, the archaeologist proceeds with probabilistic sampling by deciding whether to draw a sample of individual sample units or of statistical clusters. (The statistical clusters discussed here should not be confused with the archaeological data clusters described earlier.) *Clusters* are groups of spatially proximate units whose internal variability is believed to be similar to that present in the overall population. In one sense, what are archaeological data *units* at one level are *clustered* data at another—sites are clusters of artifacts, artifacts are clusters of attributes, and so on—and in that sense all archaeological sampling will involve cluster sampling. That is one reason why definition of the sample unit is important. But once the sample unit is defined, the archaeologist must decide whether to collect probabilistic samples of individual units or of clusters. Selection of cluster sampling over elemental unit sampling is primarily a question of economy: it enables the archaeologist to draw a sample more rapidly. In a reconnaissance of a large area, cluster sampling would mean reconnoitering groups of adjacent sampling-unit areas (see Fig. 3.22); in artifact analysis, it could mean drawing a sample of provenience units and studying all artifacts within them, rather than drawing a sample of individual artifacts directly. In return for the economy of cluster sampling, the ar-

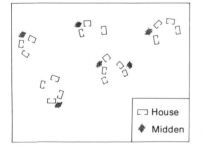

Figure 3.22 Universe with clustered units, in this case, houses with adjacent middens. A cluster sample would entail investigating several parts of a single cluster rather than more limited tests spread across the sampling universe.

☐ House
✳ Midden

chaeologist gives up some degree of power to predict from the sample to the population, because the assumption that the clusters are representative is less than certain.

The next step in probabilistic sampling is to label all the units (or clusters) and convert them to a list. This list is the *sampling frame,* from which a number of units will be drawn. The total number of units drawn, called the *sample size,* may also be expressed as a percentage, called the *sampling fraction,* of the total population size. Sample size may be set statistically, but just as archaeologists are still testing which sampling schemes are appropriate to which kinds of situations, they are also assessing appropriate sample sizes for specified kinds of research. In practice, sample size is usually greatly influenced—if not altogether dictated—by limits of time and funds. Of course, the closer one gets to a sample size of 100% (total data acquisition), the more closely the characteristics of the sample can be expected to reflect those of the population. But the absolute size of the sample and the population are also very important. In a population of 10, for example, 20 percent is 2 units and each unit represents 10 percent of the population. In a population of 1000, however, a 20 percent sample contains 200 units, and each unit accounts for only 0.1 percent of the total. As the sample and population sizes increase, the probable importance of any one unit decreases; at the same time, the "risk" of missing an example of important variation by excluding any one unit declines. That is one reason why samples based on very large populations—such as national opinion polls—can often use relatively small sampling fractions. In the United States, a sample of less than 1 percent of the total population would still include over 2 million respondents. Archaeological populations and samples are seldom so large: regional populations of site units are typically totals on the order of 10s and 100s, but potsherd populations (excavated collections) may have 10,000 to more than a million (sherd) units.

There are three basic probabilistic sampling schemes—simple random, systematic, and stratified.

Simple Random Sampling

Simple random sampling is the most basic method of probabilistic sampling. Random sampling does *not* mean haphazard, hit-or-miss sampling; rather it means that each unit in the frame has a statistically equal chance for selection. Once the sample units have been defined, totalled (N) and listed in a frame, they are designated by a series of consecutive numbers (1 through $N,$ inclusive). After the sample size is determined, the required number of units is selected in a random manner from the frame. One common means of randomizing the selection procedure is to match the numerical designations of the sample units to a table of random numbers until the required quantity of units has been selected. But any selection procedure that allows each sample unit an equal probability of being chosen may be used. Investigators have selected samples by drawing from a deck of cards or by picking slips of paper out of a hat. Whatever the selection procedure, once the sample units have been chosen, the archaeologist proceeds to investigate them. If any unit of those chosen cannot remain in the sample—as when permission to investigate is not obtained or when an artifact to be analyzed is lost—the sample is no longer random. One "solution" to this problem is to resolve all questions of accessibility before drawing the sample and to exclude inaccessible units from the frame; in that case the sample will be random, but the definition of the population will have been changed to include only accessible units.

In general, simple random sampling is used only when practically nothing is known about a population. It treats all sample units as equivalent, ignores any known dimensions of variability—such as location of some sites on hilltops as opposed to others on the valley floor. An archaeologist who has knowledge about a population beforehand should take that information into account in designing a sampling strategy.

Systematic Sampling

The first unit of a *systematic sample* is selected at random (by a random number table or some other randomizing technique); once the initial unit is established, all other units in the sample are selected at predetermined intervals from the first until the total sample size is reached. The size of the interval is a function of the sample size: if the population is 800 units and the desired sample size is 200 units (a sampling fraction of 25 percent), the sampling interval would be 4 (800/200 or the reciprocal of the sampling fraction, which is 25/100 or ¼).

Systematic sampling can be used to ensure equal intervals—spatial or otherwise—between sample units. This method thus eliminates one potential problem encountered in simple random sampling: the latter may yield heavy concentrations of sample units in some areas of the population, with little or no coverage in other areas. At the same time, systematic sampling involves the assumption that there is no regular pattern or *periodicity* in the distribution of characteristics of the sample units. For instance, suppose rooms within a structure are used as sampling units; if, unbeknownst to the archaeologist, every fifth room had been used for storage, systematic sampling with an interval of five would hit only storage rooms—*or*, with a different starting point, would hit no storage rooms at all (see Fig. 3.23).

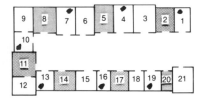

☐ Systematic sample of rooms excavated

● Hearth

Figure 3.23 Periodicity: Note that hearths (not visible without excavation) occur in every third room; a systematic sample with an interval of 3 would encounter either all or none of these features.

Stratified Sampling

In many archaeological situations, it is obvious from the onset of investigation that the data units are not uniform. When the nature of this variation is believed (or known) to be important to the research, a *stratified sampling* method may be used to ensure that sample units are drawn from each area of observed variation within the population. In this method, the sample units are divided into two or more groups (sampling strata) which correspond to each kind of observed variation within the population. For example, in a valley to be studied by reconnaissance, strata could correspond to ecological zones. Strata can be defined by multiple criteria; in analysis of chipped stone artifacts, for example, strata could correspond to artifact types and to stone used. A division into blades and non-blades and into obsidian and flint would yield four strata: obsidian blades, obsidian nonblades, flint blades, and flint nonblades. Once the strata are defined, simple random or systematic samples may be chosen within each. The sample size is determined for the total sample; samples sizes for the separate strata may be *proportional* or *disproportional*. In proportional sampling of the strata, the number of sample units chosen in each stratum has the same ratio to overall sample size that the total number of units in the stratum has to overall population size (see Table 3.1).

Table 3.1

PROPORTIONAL AND DISPROPORTIONAL STRATIFIED SAMPLING

Strata	*Total units*	*Ratio of units to population*	*Sample size* *Proportional*	*Disproportional*
Obsidian blades	40	40/200	8	10
Obsidian nonblades	25	25/200	5	10
Flint blades	72	72/200	14 (rounded)	10
Flint nonblades	63	63/200	13 (rounded)	10
Total	200		40	40

Other, more complex sampling techniques have been devised, but these are the basic ones. The criteria for choosing among them in a given situation are quite involved; a thorough grounding in statistics is necessary to make the best choice, but so is a thorough consideration of the particular archaeological situation. Archaeologists who are not well trained in statistics should at least know how to consult a statistician in order to get help. It is crucial to consult the statistician *be-*

fore the sampling (unit selection *or* data collection) begins. This is because many statistical techniques of data analysis are valid only if the sample data were selected by probabilistic sampling; if difficulties in sampling occurred, the statistician will not be able to cure them. Just as it is far better to consult a lawyer before signing a contract than to try to "fix" the situation later, so the archaeologist should consult the statistician before becoming committed to working with a specified set of data. In both instances it may be difficult—if not impossible—to get out of a bad deal.

As general rules, we may note two final points on choice of sampling techniques. First, the more the archaeologist knows beforehand about the population to be sampled, the more sophisticated the sampling procedures may be. Political pollsters—who are among the best-known users of sampling techniques—are able to make the predictions they do because of the quality and detail of the census data they use to stratify their population. In archaeology, we know much less about the populations we seek to study. At the present time, much of the attention being paid to sampling in archaeology concerns the selection of techniques appropriate in various situations. A number of experimental studies have taken "known" populations and sampled them hypothetically by computer simulation of a number of different sampling techniques with varying sample units and sample sizes. The results of the "samples" (for example, the number, location, and types of "sites" that would have been discovered in a valley) generated by each technique are then projected to predict the characteristics of the total population. Those results that differ least from the actual population indicate the technique, unit, and sample size most appropriate to that kind of research. One of the consistent conclusions drawn from these experiments is that there are no simple rules for deciding on sampling procedure.

The second point is that sampling techniques (and sample size) should be appropriate to the scale of the archaeologist's research and the quality of the data. There is no point in working out a complicated sampling design when the sample is so small that, for example, each stratum will be represented by only one or two numbers. Nor will complicated sampling designs be very useful with "poor" data pools, such as sites that have been nearly obliterated or artifacts whose original form is undefinable. This kind of methodological overkill wastes time, energy, and funds.

The application of probabilistic sampling is of great benefit to archaeological data acquisition. However, no single method can anticipate all the normal complexities of archaeological data. Archaeologists cannot allow their methods to rigidly restrict their research; the means by which they acquire data must remain flexible.

If, for instance, an archaeologist encounters a new and unique site within the defined universe after drawing a stratified random sample of different-size sites, the fact that the new site is outside the chosen sample does not mean that it should be ignored. Instead the investigator collects data from the new site and uses that information to shed light on the variation in the overall sample. Because it was not chosen by probabilistic sampling techniques, the new site cannot be included in statistical analyses that assume such selection procedures, but to avoid all consideration of relevant data because of this is to lose potentially vital insights.

Thus, in many cases, probabilistic and nonprobabilistic sampling methods are both used, to yield the most representative overall sample possible. These approaches to sampling are used in archaeology not only for site location and field data acquisition—including the surface surveys and excavations to be discussed in the next few chapters —but also in later analysis of the data. This is true for any category of data, from the analysis of artifacts such as ceramics or stone tools to the analysis of entire sites and of settlement patterns. Whenever possible, from the onset of the investigation to its conclusion, the archaeologist chooses sampling methods that maximize the chance that the samples are actually representative of the populations from which they were drawn.

SUMMARY

In this chapter we have discussed the characteristics of archaeological data. Beginning with the forms of data—artifacts, features, and ecofacts and their distributions within sites and regions—we described what these kinds of data are and how they are related. We defined the fundamental determining factors of matrix, provenience, and association. We then saw how these determinations lead the archaeologist to evaluate context. The understanding of archaeological context (or more specifically, the discrimination among various kinds of context) is the crucial link that allows the investigator to evaluate the significance of data—that is, to reconstruct the kinds of behavior that the data represent.

Archaeologists can never recover data representing all kinds of past behavior. Some behavior leaves no tangible evidence. The evidence of other kinds of ancient behavior may be transformed through time by a variety of processes, both human and natural in origin. These processes often act selectively to preserve or destroy archaeological evidence. Thus the data available to the archaeologist constitute a sample determined first by ancient activity (behavioral processes) and then by human and natural forces acting after the evidence is deposited (transformation processes). Assuming primary context, the archaeologist can infer various kinds of ancient behavior directly, by the ways the data are clustered and patterned. We have, therefore, defined five levels in this data structure (beyond that of unpatterned or isolated data): the simple data cluster, the differentiated data cluster, the composite data cluster, the site, and the region.

The resulting archaeological data form the base that the investigator attempts to recover, either totally (by collection of all available evidence) or by sampling methods. Whatever methods are used, the archaeologist attempts to acquire data that represent, insofar as possible, the full range of human behavior.

Except in certain cases such as salvage situations, it is generally practical and desirable to collect only a sample of the data base (as defined by a bounded data universe). The methods used to acquire data samples may be either probabilistic or nonprobabilistic, but only probabilistic samples allow reliable projections concerning the nature of the overall data base. In the past, archaeologists often collected samples in a manner that was biased toward discovering the most prominent and spectacular remains of the past. Today, however, specific research goals and field conditions call for a flexible mix of sampling schemes to enable the archaeologist to learn as much as possible about the past.

See p. 572 for "Suggestions for Further Reading."

Archaeological research design is illustrated in this chapter by a discussion of the Quiriguá Project; here we see part of a wall decorated by the image of the Maya sun god, *Kinich Ahau,* discovered by that project in 1975.

Archaeological Research

. . . the research design must be directed by a well-trained anthropologist capable of making interpretations and decisions in terms of the widest possible factual and theoretical knowledge of general anthropology. . . .

(Lewis R. Binford, *"A Consideration of Archaeological Research Design,"* 1964)

. . . the excavator without an intelligent policy may be described as an archaeological food-gatherer, master of a skill, perhaps, but not creative in the wider terms of constructive science.

(*Sir Mortimer Wheeler,* Archaeology from the Earth, *1954)*

Today's archaeologist is primarily a scientific researcher. Most archaeologists in all nations either work for research institutions, including museums or governmental agencies (such as the U.S. National Park Service, the Mexican National Institute of Anthropology and History, and the Archaeological Survey of India), or have academic appointments in universities. Although archaeologists employed by governmental agencies may devote virtually all their professional energies to field research, some museums and most universities require the archaeologist to teach as well. In any case, the conduct of good archaeological research requires teaching skills: the professional archaeologist must train and supervise the individuals working on a project, whether they are students, volunteers, or day laborers.

This chapter will examine the nature of archaeological research from various points of view. We will begin by considering the complexity of modern archaeology and the archaeologist's consequent need for the aid of specialists from a variety of other disciplines. Next we will discuss archaeological projects, and the design of archaeological research. We close with a detailed case study as an illustration of the way modern archaeological research is conducted.

ARCHAEOLOGY AS INTERDISCIPLINARY RESEARCH

Proper scientific archaeology demands a broad range of expertise. Today's archaeologist must be a theoretical scientist, a methodologist, a technician, an administrator, and more. Although the archaeologist must be able to perform all of these functions, in reality it is nearly impossible for one individual to do everything necessary for a particular project; usually the archaeologist must bring together specialists from a wide variety of disciplines. Doing so requires an interdisciplinary approach—coordinating the efforts of many scientists, each of whom focuses upon a particular aspect of the research. Only by depending on others can the archaeologist ensure that the data collected are utilized to the maximum degree possible. Thus one extremely important skill the archaeologist must have is to recognize which is the proper specialist and when this individual should be consulted. We can see some of the intricacies of modern archaeological research by examining the research functions the individual archaeologist is required to assume.

As a theoretical scientist, the archaeologist should be able to define appropriate research problems based on a thorough knowledge of current problems and relevant research already completed or being conducted. These problems are usually broadly delimited areas, such as the origin and development of food production (When? Where? Under what conditions?). The definition of a research problem involves specification of the general and specific goals to be met and the hypotheses to be tested by the proposed project. The theoretical scientist must be able to evaluate and synthesize the results of research and, finally, to interpret those results in light of the goals originally set forth.

The archaeologist as a methodologist plans the approaches (methods) to be used in the research in order to meet the theoretical goals. This task includes choosing tactics of data collection and analysis. The analysis of data in modern archaeology almost invariably involves consultation with a variety of specialists from allied disciplines. If the archaeologist is a well-trained anthropologist, the need for ethnographers to provide contemporary material or for physical anthropologists to analyze skeletal remains may be limited. However, most archaeologists find it necessary at one time or another to consult with geologists or geomorphologists, ecologists, botanists, zoologists, geographers, paleontologists, and other specialists. In addition, statisticians, computer programmers, and other individuals may be called in to facilitate the processing and analysis of data.

The archaeologist as a technician is concerned with the collection of archaeological data by various means. In order to gather the data needed, the archaeologist may have to assume or employ others to assume the roles of explorer, surveyor or cartographer, photo interpreter, architect, and geologist, as well as excavator. Recording and processing data may require other abilities, such as skills at drafting scaled records, photography, and conservation of recovered material.

The final function of the archaeologist is that of administrator. In order to carry on archaeological research effectively, an archaeologist must be an executive able to keep all phases of the research process on schedule. Furthermore, the archaeologist must have—or furnish through specialists—the other skills necessary for administering an archaeological project. These include an agent or troubleshooter for arranging permits and the like, an accountant, a secretary, and—when the research reaches the publication stage—an editor.

The effectiveness of a research organization depends on the archaeologist's application of overall management skills to integrate the four functions just discussed. In some cases the archaeologist may find most of the required support specialists housed under one roof, as in the larger museums and research institutions in many parts of the world. In the United States, the Smithsonian Institution provides one of the most complete support facilities for archaeology. Many university museums, through their laboratories and other facilities, provide more than adequate support for their research archaeologists. However, no single institution can furnish all the specialists and facilities that today's archaeologist requires. Thus, at one time or another, all archaeologists must seek outside assistance in order to complete their research successfully.

ARCHAEOLOGICAL RESEARCH PROJECTS

The size and duration of archaeological research projects depend upon the scale of the problems being investigated. A few months of a single individual's work may sometimes be all that is required to plan and conduct the data-gathering stages of research. But even the single individual will need some form of assistance from outside specialists in processing and analyzing the results. On the other hand, archaeological research concerned with complex civilizations, such as research at large urban sites in the Near East and Mexico, usually calls for a large archaeological staff and a huge labor force (Fig. 4.1). For decades, projects in these and similar areas have employed teams of on-site specialists such as architects, conservators, and epigraphers. Furthermore, projects such as these may extend over many years or even decades. The Tikal Project, one of the largest research efforts ever conducted in the New World, has been operating since 1956 in the jungle rain forests of northern Guatemala. For its first 15 years, this project was sponsored by the University Museum of the University of Pennsylvania. But since 1970 work at Tikal has been under the sole auspices of the Guatemalan government.

The difficulties in recovering and analyzing many kinds of archaeological data, as well as increasing restrictions on the export of recovered material to other nations, have resulted in the emergence of multidisciplinary archaeological projects. Scientific teams, usually led by an archaeologist but including botanists, ecologists, geologists, and

Large-scale project: Tikal, Guatemala

Figure 4.1 Modern large-scale archaeological excavations at Quiriguá, Guatemala.

other specialists, are often created in order to conduct thorough field research bearing upon a specific question. The Tehuacán Archaeological-Botanical Project (discussed in Chapter 5), an investigation that carried out four seasons of research into the origins of maize (corn) domestication in the New World, involved the contributions and expertise of more than 35 specialists and consultants.

Like most activities, archaeological research is limited by the availability of time and money. In some cases, when nationalistic and economic priorities favor archaeological study, governments may spend millions of dollars on such work. But many archaeologists have considerable difficulty in securing enough research funds—and enough time away from their other duties—to undertake their own research projects. A far greater problem, however, is one that threatens the very existence of archaeological research: the increasing pace of destruction wrought by our rapidly expanding world. The destruction

Interdisciplinary project: Tehuacán, Mexico

of archaeological remains has reached such proportions that we may well ask, "Does the past have a future?" We will consider the problem of the destruction of archaeological sites in the final chapter of this book.

ARCHAEOLOGICAL RESEARCH DESIGN

Traditionally, most archaeological research has been "site-oriented": the major or sole objective was to excavate a particular site and, often, to collect spectacular material. Research was conducted by choosing a prominent site, forming an expedition, excavating the site, and transporting the recovered artifacts to a museum storeroom or other facility. In many cases the full results of such investigations were never published.

With the emergence of archaeology as a scientific discipline, more systematic approaches to research have become the rule. Among the

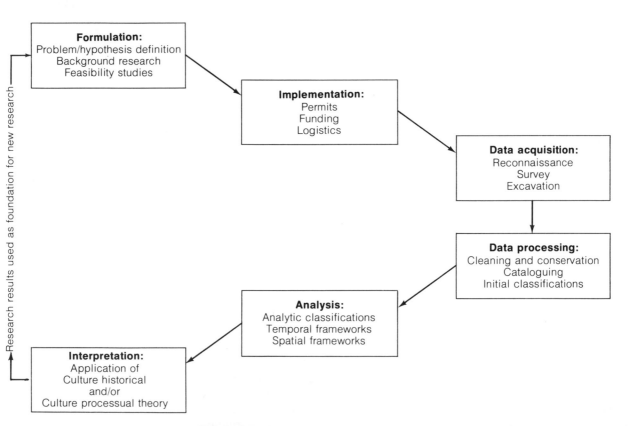

Figure 4.2 Diagram of stages of archaeological research.

first to call explicitly for systematic research design in archaeology were Walter Taylor and Lewis Binford. Binford's appeal for scientific research design in archaeology emphasized regional "problem-oriented" research projects. Today, in some areas at least, such research programs are increasingly replacing site-oriented investigations. Regional problem-oriented research aims at solving specific problems or testing one or more hypotheses by using controlled and representative samples of data from a particular region. Because of its complexity, research of this kind demands a thorough, systematic plan or design to coordinate all its facets successfully. Problem-oriented research begins with the definition of the research problem and the geographical or cultural region to be investigated. The selection of the actual sites within the region is often secondary; it is usually based on evaluation of their potential for producing data bearing on the research problem.

Systematic research design involves a formal process that guides the conduct of the investigation, both to ensure the validity of research results and to maximize the efficiency with which time, money, and effort are utilized. The design is systematic and formal because it divides the research process into a series of steps or stages, each with specific functions (Fig. 4.2). Each functionally distinct research stage forms a part of an overall sequence of investigation that extends from origin (formulation stage) to conclusion (publication stage). We will discuss each of these stages in sequence below. Note, however, that the clear-cut sequence we will outline is an idealization. In most actual cases, aspects of two or more stages take place simultaneously, and some stages may be delayed or postponed until later than "normal" in the research sequence.

Furthermore, since each specific archaeological situation is unique, this research design must be flexible enough to adapt to a wide variety of individual needs. Thus the following design, while outlining broadly the stages of archaeological research, does not attempt to specify the actual ways in which research is conducted at any particular stage in the process. Later chapters discuss the various specific procedures used to discover, gather, process, analyze, and interpret archaeological data.

The first stage in archaeological research begins long before field-work commences; it involves formulation of a specific problem or area of interest on which the investigation will focus. Background research is conducted to refine the problem further and to define research goals. These goals usually include testing of one or more specific research hypotheses. Background investigation often includes a feasibility study—a trip into the field to evaluate the site (or sites) and local working conditions. The second stage involves making the necessary arrangements to enable the archaeologist to conduct the planned investigations in the field. The third stage includes the actual collection of archaeological data. If not already completed by previous archaeologists or as part of the feasibility study, archaeological reconnaissance to locate and identify sites and archaeological survey to collect surface data may take place in this stage. Excavations, however, are usually the principal means for data collection. In the fourth stage, the data are processed and initially classified in the field. The fifth research stage involves detailed data analysis that may be carried out by specialists, either in the field or at permanent laboratories or other facilities. The archaeologist uses the results of analysis in the sixth or interpretation stage. And the final step in the archaeological research design is publication and dissemination of the results of the program.

Formulation of Research

Archaeological research begins with a decision regarding the geographical area or problem of interest. This decision both limits and guides further investigation. Once that choice is made, the archaeologist conducts background research, locating and studying previous work that may be relevant to the investigation. Previous archaeological research in the same region or even within the same site would obviously be crucial, but investigations that covered adjacent regions or concerned similar problems are important as well. Useful background information includes geographical, geological, climatological, ecological, and anthropological studies, if available. Gaining access to such background data often presents difficulties. Some information may be readily available in published form in any good research library. In many cases, however, such data are not published and must be pursued in archives, laboratories, and storerooms of various kinds. Consultations and interviews with individual experts may be necessary and advisable. Because archaeological research customarily requires fieldwork, a feasibility study involving a trip to the region or sites to be investigated is usually advisable. The objective of this trip is evaluation of the archaeological situation and of local conditions such as accessibility, availability of labor force, and so on. If the area under study has never been investigated archaeologically, or if previous work has been inadequate, archaeological reconnaissance (see Chapter 5) is usually advisable in order to identify and locate archaeological remains.

Thorough background investigations facilitate the actual archaeological research by refining the problem under investigation and defining specific research goals. The goals of most archaeological research include testing of one or more specific hypotheses. Some hypotheses may derive from previously proposed models; others may arise during the formulation of the research problem. As the research progresses, of course, new hypotheses will be generated and tested. It is important to remember, however, that the initial formulation of research problem(s) is what leads the archaeologist to look for particular kinds of data. One theory about the change from food gathering to food production, for example, might predict that the transition took place in a mountain valley setting; another theory might predict a seaside locale. In either case, the archaeologist would need to define not only where to look, but also what kinds of data to look for: the specific artifacts, ecofacts, and features believed to be evidence for and against the changes being documented. Data collection will certainly include more than just these materials, but the formulation stage of research must include definition of the kinds of data necessary to test adequately and fairly the hypotheses set forth.

Implementation of Research

Once the research goals have been formulated, the next step is to plan and make arrangements for the proposed fieldwork. These arrangements may be complex, especially if the research is to be carried out in a foreign country. The first step, in any case, is to secure the necessary permissions for conducting field research. Most countries have special government agencies charged with overseeing archaeological activities; official permission must be secured from these agencies. Furthermore, since archaeological research often requires access to wide areas of land, and involves a measure of disturbance of this property through excavation, the owners of the land on which the work is to take place must also grant permission before investigations can proceed. In many nations, private landowners do not have ownership rights to archaeological sites or artifacts on their property. But in most cases, landowners can still refuse to allow their land to be disturbed by archaeological investigations. Since the laws governing access to and investigations of archaeological sites vary from country to country, the archaeologist must be aware of the relevant laws and customs within the country where the project is to take place. Crossing international boundaries also requires special arrangements for the import and export of research equipment, research funds, and other materials. Import and export permits must therefore be secured from the appropriate government agencies.

Once permissions have been secured, the archaeologist must attempt to raise the necessary funds to finance the research. Most funding agencies will not accept research proposals until the work has been given permission to proceed. In some cases funds may be available from the inception of the research, but more often the archaeologist must submit a research proposal to either private or governmental institutions that fund archaeological investigations. In the United States, one of the most active governmental funding agencies for archaeological research has been the National Science Foundation. The National Park Service and other agencies also underwrite a great deal of work within sites located on government lands. And a variety of private foundations are active in supporting archaeological work in the United States and abroad.

When the research is funded, the archaeologist must then turn to logistic arrangements. Research equipment and supplies must be purchased; alternatively, some expensive equipment might be rented, lent, or donated to the project. Field facilities must be rented or built for the safekeeping of this equipment and for processing and storage of artifacts and research records. Large-scale projects require a supervisory staff that must be recruited, transported, and housed. If international boundaries are to be crossed, additional difficulties arising from the foreign residence of staff members must be resolved. Although short-term projects often house staff in temporary quarters such as tents, long-term projects may find it more efficient to use permanent facilities that may be rented for, donated to, or even built by the project. Major items of equipment, such as vehicles, should be insured; staff members should carry health and accident coverage (most projects require that all members obtain their own insurance). Many projects rely on trained local labor forces for moving the massive amounts of earth required by large-scale excavations. In such cases, the workers must be hired, trained, supervised, and in some cases housed. Other projects make use of volunteer nonprofessional or student labor for excavation, but these work forces still must be recruited, transported, supervised, and often housed.

Acquisition of Archaeological Data

Archaeological data collection involves three basic procedures: reconnaissance, survey, and excavation. Probabilistic sampling techniques can be used with all three to maximize the likelihood that the data collected are representative of the total data pool. At this point we will discuss these procedures only briefly, since they will be treated in depth in subsequent chapters.

Archaeological reconnaissance is the means for location and identification of archaeological sites. This may be done by actual inspection of the region being covered (by foot, mule, or jeep) or by remote sensors such as aerial or satellite photography, radar, or other instrumentation (see Chapter 5). Archaeological survey (see Chapter 6) is undertaken to record as much as possible about archaeological sites without excavation. Recording often includes photography (aerial or ground-level), mapping, and sampling by subsurface probes such as remote sensors and mechanical devices. Most commonly, samples of artifacts are collected from the ground surface of sites. Excavation is undertaken to reveal the subsurface configuration of archaeological sites. The archaeologist uses a variety of techniques both to retrieve and to record excavation data; these will be treated in Chapter 7.

Data Processing

Once archaeological evidence has been collected, it must be processed in the field. This processing involves manipulation of both raw data (artifacts and ecofacts) and recorded data (photos, drawings, descriptions and so forth). Portable data—artifacts and ecofacts—are usually processed in a field laboratory or museum, undergoing several steps to insure that they are preserved and stored so as to be easily retrievable. Artifactual data are often transformed into recorded data in the lab, using card or log registration systems and photography. Nonportable data (features) are always transformed into recorded data in the field via notes, photography, scale drawings, and similar records. These recorded data are normally not further processed in the laboratory, but must be stored for easy retrieval and later use. Sorting involves division of the data into classes, both as the initial step in classification and as an aid to later manipulation during analysis. Both raw and recorded data are usually sorted and stored in the field laboratory. Data processing is described in detail in Chapter 8.

Analysis of Archaeological Data

The purpose of data analysis is to provide information useful for archaeological interpretation. Analyses are of various kinds, including typological classifications, chronometric analyses (determination of age), and various technical analyses, such as identification of what the artifact is made of and how it was made. Some analyses, such as classification, can be done in the field laboratory. However, the more technical kinds of analysis are usually undertaken at specified permanent laboratory facilities. When the quantity of data precludes analysis of the entire collection, the archaeologist may study a controlled sample as representative of the total collection. Chapters 9 through 11 consider the analysis of archaeological data.

Interpretation of Archaeological Data

The use of scientific procedures in interpreting data is what differentiates the professional archaeologist from his amateur counterparts. Interpretation involves the synthesis of all results of data collection, processing, classification, and analysis in an attempt to answer the original research questions. In most cases, historical and anthropological models provide the most consistent reconstructions and explanations of the past. Chapters 12 through 14 discuss data interpretation.

Publication of Results

Once all stages of research are completed, the professional archaeologist must publish both the data and the results of the data analysis and interpretation as soon as feasible. Publication makes the research accessible so that its results can be used and retested by fellow archaeologists, other scholars, and indeed by any interested individual. In this way the research furthers the broadest objectives of archaeology and of science in general. Too often archaeologists have failed to match the scale of their data acquisition effort with the scale of their publication effort; but data acquisition is justified only if the information is later made public.

*A CASE STUDY IN RESEARCH DESIGN: THE QUIRIGUA PROJECT

In order to illustrate the research design outlined above, we will devote the balance of this chapter to a case study of an actual research project. The Quiriguá Project, an archaeological investigation focusing on the Classic Maya site of Quiriguá, Guatemala, was chosen for this case study because, in addition to being familiar to the authors, it is representative in size and scope of many archaeological projects. It is certainly not so massive in scale as some investigations, but it is larger than many others. As such, the project offers a useful illustration of the steps required to plan, prepare, organize, and conduct archaeological research using an interdisciplinary perspective to accomplish scientific objectives, while dealing with the political, economic and social realities of the contemporary world.

Formulation

The formulation work of the Quiriguá Project stretched over more than three years (1970–1973). The general area of research interest was established by deciding that investigations would center upon a major lowland Classic Maya site and its immediate surrounding region. This limitation reduced the geographic area of interest to an already defined zone within Mexico and northern Central America. The choice of sites was further limited by additional criteria: the region to be investigated had to be relatively unknown archaeologically, yet it had to have the potential of yielding data bearing upon important unresolved questions concerning ancient Maya civilization. On the basis of these criteria, seven potential sites were evaluated. The choice was then narrowed to two sites that fulfilled all requirements. Initial feasibility studies subsequently eliminated one of these sites, since the projected archaeological research did not coincide with the requirements of the nation in which the site was located. The remaining site, Quiriguá, located near the Caribbean coast of Guatemala, was selected. The feasibility study of this site indicated that, despite past sporadic archaeological work there, practically no published archaeological data were available from Quiriguá or its surrounding region. Furthermore, Quiriguá's location—within a region defined by the fertile flood plain of a major river—and its partially known dynastic history, as derived from the hieroglyphic inscriptions at the site, indicated that a research program could produce data relevant to several unresolved problems. These included the structure of political organization, especially dynastic relationships among Maya centers; the economic foundations of Quiriguá and its region; and the reasons for the ultimate collapse and abandonment of Maya sites. Finally, despite the lack of archaeological data from Quiriguá, scholars had proposed several models to account for the location and function of this site. These models could be refined and tested against actual archaeological data.

Once Quiriguá was selected for investigation, background research began, both to document relevant previous archaeological work in the region and to collect information bearing on the research (local geology, climate, geography, anthropology, history, and so forth). Previous archaeological work at Quiriguá had been largely exploratory, involving clearing of surface debris and restoration of at least one masonry structure. Few excavations had actually cut into the structures at the site. None of the artifacts collected from this early work had been classified or analyzed; most had apparently disappeared. Archives were combed, and copies were made of all reports, field notes, and photographs; the assembled file of background information was taken to the field for easy reference.

As a result of this background investigation, several specific research goals were formulated to guide investigations at Quiriguá. The first of these was to define spatially both the site of Quiriguá itself and its sustaining valley region. The second goal was to derive a chronology for past activity at the site and within the region, including attention to the timing of abandonment in relation to the time of the general "collapse" of Maya civilization in about the ninth century A.D. The third goal was to determine the specific activities carried on at the site of Quiriguá and at the other sites within the valley region. The fourth goal was to refine the historical and dynastic record at Quiriguá. The final goal was to refine and test specific hypotheses or models, some of which had been previously advanced, concerning Quiriguá's location and ancient function(s) in the Motagua valley region.

Briefly, these models concerned the following possible roles for Quiriguá:

1. As a colony for the larger Maya center of Copán, 50 km to the south (suggested by prior hieroglyphic and sculptural evidence).
2. As an administrative center for a plantation system geared to the production of an economically valuable crop, such as cacao or oil palm (suggested by documents from the Spanish conquest period on cacao production and by knowledge of the appropriate soil and climate conditions in the area).
3. As a trading center for control of commercial traffic along the Motagua River (suggested by the site's location relative to the locations of sources and destinations for such trade goods as jade and obsidian).

Note that the models are generalized and not mutually exclusive: the objective was to determine which—if any—of these roles the site fulfilled.

These goals mandated the collection of particular kinds of data; in many cases the same data were applicable to more than one question. To test the Colony model, the Project needed first to establish a chronological framework: were Quiriguá and Copán both founded at the same time, or was Quiriguá established well after the occupation of Copán? The latter condition would support the Colony theory; the former would refute it. Furthermore, data would be sought to demonstrate either links or barriers between the two sites, such as similarities or differences in artifactual, architectural, and sculptural styles. And finally, decipherment and interpretation of relevant hieroglyphic texts from both sites would certainly be pertinent to this question.

The Plantation model could be tested by environmental and ecofact evidence indicating the existence of ancient cash crops. And study of the density and nature of settlement remains in the immediate area of the site would both define the spatial limits of the site and indicate whether or not sufficient space was available for a plantation of cacao trees or other similar crops.

Testing the Trade Center model would depend on evidence of actual nonperishable trade items such as jade and obsidian, of their processing or manufacture at the site, and of facilities for storage and transshipment. Indirect evidence for trade might lie in measures of wealth, power, and prestige accruing to the leaders of the ancient community.

In the course of collecting and analyzing these and other data, the Project would need to draw upon the skills of several specialists. Included among these were a geophysicist, a geomorphologist, a botanist, an epigrapher, and an architect.

In conjunction with the archaeological activities, steps were to be taken to halt the processes of erosion and decay that were threatening the site and to preserve Quiriguá for future generations: the sculptured monuments were to be secured against further damage, and the structures at the site were to be consolidated and preserved. The latter work would be conducted while the Quiriguá Project was in operation, under the auspices of and with the support of the Guatemalan government.

Implementation

Implementation of research began as soon as the site of Quiriguá was selected for investigation. Early in 1973, a formal feasibility study was conducted in Guatemala, and Quiriguá was visited to determine the scope and priorities for research. A proposal was written and submitted to both governmental and private agencies in Guatemala to determine local interest in and support for the project. The proposed research required this support and cooperation because funds to preserve the site of Quiriguá were to come from the government of Guatemala. Since this cooperative venture was unprecedented in Guatemala, various governmental agencies were also consulted for their advice as to how such an arrangement could be made. On the basis of these recommendations a formal legal contract was drawn up between the research institution (the University Museum of the University of Pennsylvania) and the appropriate agency of the Guatemalan government (the Ministry of Education), creating the Quiriguá Project as a joint undertaking of the Museum and the Guatemalan Institute of Anthropology and History (IDAEH).

The contract defined the rights and duties of the Project, including permission to conduct investigations both at the site of Quiriguá and in the surrounding valley region over a five-year period (1974–1978). The responsibilities of both the University Museum and IDAEH were specified. The contract also granted duty-free status for short-term importation of archaeological equipment and reaffirmed

Table 4.1

QUIRIGUA PROJECT CONTRACT BUDGET

Year	Restoration (Guatemalan Government)	Research (University of Pennsylvania)	Total
1973	$3,000	$2,900	$5,900
1974	13,762	45,025	58,787
1975	12,575	43,025	55,600
1976	17,700	54,350	72,050
1977	17,700	54,350	72,050
1978	15,637	43,737	59,374
1979		20,000*	20,000
Totals:	$80,374	$263,387	$343,761

*Projected preparation costs for final report.

Guatemalan ownership of all archaeological materials recovered during the course of the investigation. Since the owners of the land containing the site of Quiriguá (an American fruit-growing company) wished to donate the entire tract to the government of Guatemala, another provision of the contract specified that the area be made a national park. Finally, the contract outlined the operating budget both for research and for preservation of the ruins of Quiriguá (Table 4.1). This contract was signed by both parties and ratified by the President of Guatemala and his Ministers at the end of 1973. Unfortunately, the government's portion of Project funds did not become available in time for the scheduled onset of research in 1974. As a result, only reconnaissance and survey within the valley region could begin in 1974; large-scale work at Quiriguá did not begin until January 1975. The research plan for excavations at Quiriguá was modified to span four seasons (January through May, 1975 through 1978) instead of the originally proposed five seasons.

Meanwhile, research funds for the project were raised by appropriations from the University Museum and through proposals submitted to outside agencies (the National Geographic Society and the National Science Foundation). Research equipment and supplies were purchased both in the United States and in Guatemala, and shipped to Quiriguá. Facilities constructed at the site by the Guatemalan government included a field laboratory and storage area for both artifacts and research records; a storage facility for equipment and supplies; shops for a mechanic and a carpenter; and living quarters for the supervisors of both the site and the labor force. These structures were built so they could be converted into a permanent on-site museum and storage facility upon completion of the research. A search was made for facilities to house the 10 to 12 individuals who would make up the archaeological staff. Since no facility large enough to accommodate the staff was found, a permanent camp was specially constructed in a nearby town. This was done with the understanding that once the project terminated, the buildings could be sold and the proceeds used to help fund publication of the research findings. The camp was equipped with kitchen facilities; a live-in cook and laundress were hired, along with a caretaker to oversee the facility in the off season. Three vehicles were purchased in Guatemala, two of which were for research use and for transportation of the staff from the camp to the site. The third was purchased by the government for the site preservation program. Arrangements were made with another archaeological project (the Tikal Project) for the loan of a dump truck and other excavation supplies, while additional research equipment was borrowed from a Maya highland investigation (the Verapaz Project).

The project staff included a Project Director, a Field Director, an Administrative Director, and directors or supervisors for each of the major research or support areas (site-core program, site-periphery program, valley program, laboratory, and labor). Field assistants, mostly graduate students from the United States and Latin America, were recruited to conduct and supervise each research operation. A Guatemalan citizen with expert archaeological experience was hired to supervise the local labor force, and a mechanic and a carpenter were recruited. Six archaeological laborers, experienced in excavating Maya sites, served as the initial nucleus of the work force; they trained most of the inexperienced local workers during the 1975 season. At its peak during the 1977 season, the total work force numbered in excess of 80.

The arrangements for undertaking this research took nearly two years to accomplish—from early 1973 through 1974. The Project Director and the Field Director did the overall planning, the writing of research proposals, the feasibility studies, and the original negotiations in Guatemala. However, the burden of implementing the project was carried largely by the project's Administrative Director, a resident of Guatemala, who had constantly to be present and ready to act to ensure that the necessary arrangements were completed. As a result he spent much time in the capital city overseeing the various stages of contract approval, land transfer and creation of a park, and appropriation of government funds. His presence was also required at the site, some 200 km away, to oversee construction of the project camp, lab, and storage facilities and to supervise the hiring of the work force.

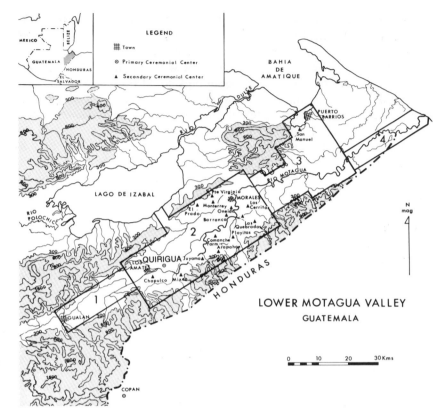

Figure 4.3 Map of the Lower Motagua Valley universe, showing division into districts, within which reconnaissance, survey, and excavation were carried out.

Acquisition of Data

All three methods of data acquisition—reconnaissance, surface survey and excavation—were used in the Quiriguá Project. In most cases these research activities were carried out simultaneously but under separate programs of the Project.

Reconnaissance

The site of Quiriguá did not require discovery; rather, reconnaissance research was directed to the surrounding Motagua valley region in order to locate undocumented areas of prehistoric activity. In fact, two separate reconnaissance programs were conducted. The first had begun in 1972 as an independent investigation; after creation of the Quiriguá Project in 1973, it continued under the Project's auspices as the Valley Program. In its initial phase, this reconnaissance was carried out by its graduate student director, assisted by other graduate students provided by the Quiriguá Project in 1973 and 1974. The work was designed to identify, locate, and map sites within a universe cor-

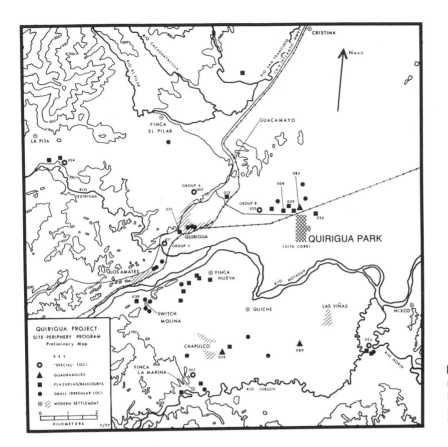

Figure 4.4 Map of the universe of the Quiriguá Periphery Program, showing sites with surface features.

responding to the entire lower Motagua Valley (ca. 2125 km²), except for the region immediately surrounding Quiriguá itself, an area of nearly 100 km². Obviously, total coverage of such a vast area was nearly impossible. Instead, sample areas of the valley were examined by ground reconnaissance. To facilitate the search, the entire universe was divided into four districts, and portions of each were covered (Fig. 4.3). The sample was not probabilistic; areas covered were determined largely by accessibility via roads or the fruit company's plantation rail networks. Aerial photographs and accurate maps at various scales (1:50,000 to 1:250,000) were used to control the reconnaissance and to plot the location of identified sites. This reconnaissance program identified and located some 50 sites. A later phase, in which another graduate student resumed the reconnaissance, tested the locational patterns suggested by the first phase.

The second reconnaissance program, which was the first phase of the Quiriguá Project Site-Periphery Program, was directed by a graduate student member of the Project staff. It required three seasons

(1975, 1976, and 1978) to complete. The data universe for this program was defined to cover an area of 95 km², roughly quadrilateral in shape and centered on the site-core of Quiriguá (Fig. 4.4). This universe was divided into three segments, each of which was examined in turn for evidence of prehistoric activity. Because areas of the universe were not equally accessible, sampling was not probabilistic. Rather, an attempt was made at "representative" (but nonprobabilistic) sampling by investigating widely separated areas within and cutting across the different ecozones represented by the three segments of the survey universe. In addition, a zone extending 1 km in all directions from the site was reconnoitered with virtually total coverage.

Most of the ground reconnaissance was conducted by one or two students, accompanied by one or more local workers who also served as guides. Peripheral sites were identified by obvious features (mounds and terraces) and concentrations of surface artifacts (generally potsherds); they were plotted on maps scaled at 1:10,000 and 1:50,000.

As sites were identified and located, it soon became obvious that they were not distributed randomly across the universe. Except for the concentration of remains immediately north of the site-core, sites were found to occur in certain locations that shared several characteristics. All were on ground raised above the general level of the flood plain, adjacent to good agricultural land and sources of water, and on or near natural communication routes or trails that were still in use. A few larger sites were spaced fairly evenly across the southern flood plain. After these patterns were recognized, reconnaissance was concentrated in areas possessing these characteristics. But to test the hypothesis that other zones were truly empty of prehistoric sites, some areas that lacked the stated characteristics were also examined; no sites were found. Subsequent aerial reconnaissance, including both direct observation and a variety of recording formats, supported the reliability of the ground-based findings.

Since there was every indication that some prehistoric remains on the flood plain were buried by as much as a meter of alluvial soils, it was possible that a number of sites, including low structures, might be hidden from direct surface detection. Aerial observation and photography failed to reveal crop marks in pasture areas with low grass cover, although a number of mound sites were readily detectable by those methods. Accordingly, a ground-based remote sensor—a cesium magnetometer—was used during the 1976 season in an attempt to locate buried features. The magnetometer probed several test areas adjacent to the site of Quiriguá, and did detect several subsurface features, subsequently verified by excavation. These tests demonstrated the local usefulness of the magnetometer, but only when buried features incorporated highly magnetic stone rubble in their construction fill. After one month of testing, the magnetometer work was discontinued because of its high cost in time and money.

The Project's plan called for a systematic coring and test-pitting program in the 1978 season to look for remains buried in the flood plain. The fruit company, however, had decided to renew its local plantation efforts at this time, and as part of the preparation, dug a series of regularly spaced drainage ditches, each about 2 m deep, around the site-core. These ditches, spaced 76 m apart, provided a systematic sample of flood plain remains that was much larger than the Project could have afforded to uncover (Fig. 4.5).

As a result of the site-periphery reconnaissance, more than 150 sites were discovered within the 95 km² universe around Quiriguá. These sites were initially classified by size, form, and complexity into four provisional groups, ranging from sites lacking visible architectural features—basically artifact surface scatters—to complex, if still relatively small, architectural groups.

1. *Nonarchitectural sites:* Surface scatters of artifacts, with or without ecofacts; no visible construction features, but may represent destroyed or buried construction.
2. *Single structures and small structure-groups:* Mounds or mound groups, less than 2 m high, usually arranged around a central court or patio.
3. *Quadrangles:* Mound groups containing mounds 2 m high or higher, with at least one courtyard group with restricted entry at two or more corners of the court.
4. *Complex sites:* Mound groups of varying and complex form, often including plain or sculptured monuments.

These sites constituted sample units, stratified by type, in the sample frame used to select sites for later excavation.

Surface Survey

A surface survey was carried out in conjunction with, and simultaneous with, both reconnaissance efforts. In the Valley Program, 16 of the 50 located sites were mapped, several by transit but most by compass and tape. Artifacts—primarily potsherds—were collected from surface scatters, and a few initial test excavations were conducted to facilitate later chronological assessment of the sites.

In the Quiriguá site-periphery, all sites with observable construction features were mapped; several methods were used, including transit, plane table and alidade, and Brunton compass and tape (Fig.

Figure 4.5 View of a drainage ditch in the Quiriguá Periphery. Note the cobblestones in the foreground, representing the dislodged construction fill of one of the cut pre-Columbian Maya house platforms. (Compare another cut platform, visible in Fig. 1.6(b).)

4.6). All visible surface artifacts (again, mostly sherds) were collected from each identified site within the 95 km² universe. These collections were used in an attempt to assess both chronological position and (where excavation was not undertaken) function of sites. In many cases, however, the sherds were few in number and too eroded to be of much use for chronological determination. Evaluations of vessel form were often more successful; these data could be used to give some indication of ancient activities and functional associations. Most of the functional associations thus revealed were prehistoric domestic activities, indicated by cooking and storage pottery forms. By this means, several sites of ancient residence were identified for possible later excavation; several midden deposits were identified as well.

Within the site-core of Quiriguá, survey activity entailed compilation of a detailed contour map of the site (Fig. 4.7). The map was prepared during the 1975 and 1976 seasons at a scale of 1:1000 (published at 1:2000), using a plane table and alidade. A primary benchmark, established at a marked point in the concrete floor of the laboratory, provided elevation (vertical provenience) control for all

Figure 4.6 Oblique aerial photograph of a site within the Quiriguá Periphery universe that was mapped by transit and surface-collected. (This is Group A in Fig. 4.4).

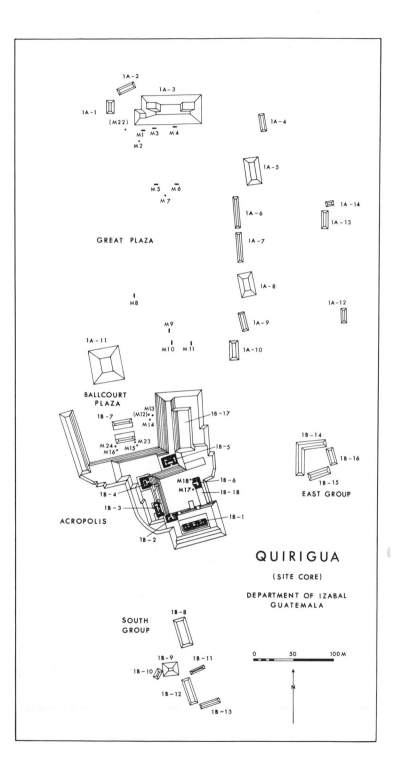

QUIRIGUA

(SITE CORE)

DEPARTMENT OF IZABAL
GUATEMALA

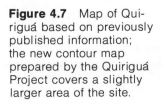

Figure 4.7 Map of Quiriguá based on previously published information; the new contour map prepared by the Quiriguá Project covers a slightly larger area of the site.

further work in and adjacent to the site core. The elevation was assumed to be 70 m above sea level, on the basis of the 1:50,000 government topographic map. A north-south baseline bisecting the site was used to establish horizontal control and to extend vertical control from the benchmark. The baseline consisted of regularly spaced stakes, each with a known elevation. This baseline was the basic referent for mapping, for recording excavations, and for measuring provenience data of artifacts, ecofacts, and features encountered. Using this baseline, a grid system was laid out using squares each 500 m on a side. The squares were labeled to provide a designation system for all structures at the site (see Fig. 4.7); the system was expandable, so that it could eventually be used to designate peripheral structures as well.

Excavation

Excavations were conducted in all three Project investigations, the Site-Core Program, the Site-Periphery Program, and the Valley Program. Since we have already mentioned the structure of the ex-

Figure 4.8   Excavation of a masonry house platform in the Quiriguá Periphery. The man standing at left is on the center of the front step of the house.

Figure 4.9   North-south trench in the Great Plaza of Quiriguá, revealing the original cobbled plaza surface.

cavation sample in the Site-Periphery Program, we will describe this effort first.

Not counting structures and features simply recorded in the drainage ditches, planned excavations were conducted at 17 sites, distributed disproportionally across the four preliminary form classes. Teams averaging four to six laborers were supervised by a student field assistant at each excavated site. The goal of these excavations was to determine the chronology of construction and the nature of other ancient activities carried on at each site. Each sample unit (i.e., each site) was probed by an initial test pit, with extensions into trenches or wider clearing excavations when possible.

The activity areas revealed by these excavations were, for the most part, low stone platforms that once supported structures of pole and thatch or other perishable materials (Fig. 4.8). Several of these platforms were associated with data in use-related primary context (subfloor burials with associated artifacts, domestic pottery, and so forth). Other identified areas included ceremonial constructions—one a mound containing an apparent tomb chamber—and middens yielding sherds and other artifacts in transposed primary context.

The principal excavation effort of the Quiriguá Project was in the core of the site. Here excavations were conducted in the three main architectural areas: the expansive "plaza" areas supporting sculptured monuments (Fig. 4.9); separated structures flanking the plazas (raised platforms and one "pyramid," all apparently once supporting perishable buildings); and the most impressive construction at the site, the centrally located Acropolis (a 200 by 200 m quadrangle of high platforms, supporting six masonry buildings surrounding a central court) (Fig. 4.10). Overall excavations in the site core were carried out by as many as 60 laborers. Each individual excavation (or operation) was supervised by one or more student field assistants. The largest of these operations, employing an average of 30 laborers, was the excavation in the Acropolis. This work was supervised at all times by a member of the directorial staff.

In the Site-Core Program, excavation sampling was non-probabilistic since each potential excavation locus (plazas, separate structures, and Acropolis) was unique in form (on the basis of pre-excavation appearance) and possibly in function (this was to be determined through excavation). Accordingly, the basic research objectives dictated the choice of excavation locations. In addition, once excavation of a structure began, it almost invariably revealed a complex sequence of construction stages: buried floors and walls of earlier buildings, additions, renovations, and so forth. Full documentation of these data required subsequent expansions that could not be foreseen when excavation units were originally marked off.

Figure 4.10 Oblique aerial photograph of excavations in progress in the Quiriguá Acropolis (looking northwest).

The basic objective of the site-core excavations was to gain an understanding of the chronological and functional range of ancient activity at Quiriguá. The more basic aspect of this dual objective—documentation of the sequence of construction—could be directly observed and evaluated through excavations that revealed both the extent and depth of construction. This was done through use of two different kinds of excavations: deep cross-sectional trenches and extensive lateral clearing. The initial effort in most cases used deep cross-sectional trenches that cut through the axis of a particular construction to document the full vertical sequence of building activity, from the earliest (lowermost) to the latest (uppermost). In the Acropolis, for instance, the first trenches laid out and excavated in 1975 and 1976 consisted of two axial cuts, one bisecting the Acropolis platforms in an east-west direction, and the other in a north-south direction. The vertical sections provided by these trenches were the keys to the sequence of a multitude of superimposed constructions: plaza floors, staircases, platforms, and buildings lying one on top of another (Fig. 4.11). During later seasons, extensive lateral trenches (along with secondary deep cross-sectional probes) were laid out from these axial cuts to reach the corners of the Acropolis and to peel back sample portions of each construction layer. These lateral excavations were used to document the three-dimensional extent of each con-

Figure 4.11 Beginning lateral clearing excavations in the Acropolis (Structure 1B–5, view towards the north).

struction layer and to show how each was related to the others. Ultimately these excavations revealed four major periods of constructional activity in the Acropolis.

Excavations in the Quiriguá Acropolis frequently encountered disturbed areas on or near the uppermost construction levels. Most of these were apparently recent, the result of the shallow excavations made by several past archaeological investigations. Unfortunately, most of this previous work at the site was not well recorded, so it was impossible to determine the extent or significance of the evidence that may have been discovered. It could only be assumed that this earlier work had destroyed both remains in primary contexts and constructional evidence. When artifacts were encountered in these disturbed areas, they were known to be from secondary contexts and thus were not used for analytical purposes that required primary context.

On the other hand, the data gained from the bulk of the site-core excavations, including artifacts and ecofacts that survived in both kinds of primary contexts as well as in use-related secondary context, were used to infer ancient activities. These activities, in turn, reflect the past functions of individual structures and plaza areas, as well as those of the site as a whole. In this way ancient functions such as elite residential occupation, ritual and ceremonial activity, and (less certainly) economic and political activity have been inferred.

Outside the immediate vicinity of Quiriguá, the Valley Program began to investigate a series of sites within the Lower Motagua Valley region in 1977. In 1978 major research began with test excavation programs in two of the largest sites in the valley, Las Quebradas and Choco (Fig. 4.12). The former site contained more than 300 mapped structures, including two major quadrangle complexes, and the latter had more than 100 mapped structures and one large quadrangle complex. The objective of these excavations was to gather a sample of both chronologically and functionally relevant data. Although the data acquisition stage of the Quiriguá Project formally ended in April 1978, an extension of the research permit allowed further excavation in 1979 in several additional valley sites of varied forms and sizes.

Other Data Acquisition Programs

Another important part of the overall research, the Monument Recording Program, was designed to record all the sculptured stones at Quiriguá, especially those with Maya hieroglyphic inscriptions. The latter epigraphic data complemented the excavated data and provided invaluable documentation concerning political activities, dynastic succession, and other historical events at Quiriguá. The basic record was assembled from two sources. The first source derives from records collected during the past century by other investigators; it includes photographs, drawings, and casts of the sculptured monuments. Most of these materials are scattered in museums and archives in England and the United States. These data are invaluable since many recorded portions of inscriptions have since been damaged or destroyed. These sources were supplemented by a new record assembled by the Project, based upon scaled photography supplemented by casts and rubbings.

Another aspect of the project that was not strictly relevant to the data acquisition process, was the simultaneous program to preserve the site of Quiriguá. The site preservation effort, directed by the Institute of Anthropology and History of Guatemala, included work to secure the sculptured monuments from encrustations of lichens and other growths and to strengthen the stone against further erosion damage. The most extensive effort involved consolidation and renovation of selected masonry structures at the site on the basis of architectural data gained from the site-core excavations (Fig. 4.13). This work was financed by the Guatemalan government.

The Processing of the Quiriguá Data

Both raw and recorded data from the Quiriguá Project were processed in the field laboratory located adjacent to the site (Fig. 4.14). All facets of this processing were supervised by the laboratory direc-

Figure 4.12 Platform stairway cleared and partially excavated at one of the outlying Motagua Valley sites, as part of the Valley Program of the Quiriguá Project.

Figure 4.13 Restoration of Structure 1B–1 in the Quiriguá Acropolis, conducted under supervision of the Guatemalan government.

tor, who was assisted by hired laboratory helpers and by members of the field research staff. Following the various stages of processing, data were placed in orderly storage within the laboratory building to facilitate retrieval for analysis.

The field investigations produced two forms of raw data processed in the field laboratory: artifacts and ecofacts. The research also generated four forms of recorded data: a card system, field notes, scale drawings, and photographs. The heart of the entire data record is the 5-by-8-inch card system, which is easily manipulated and stored. Field investigators filled out two kinds of cards. The "operation card" recorded the location, definition, and objectives of each excavation or surface collection. The "lot card" defined each provenience unit, giving its location, matrix, associations, context evaluation, and contents (features, artifacts, and ecofacts). More detailed information was reported by each supervisor in a field notebook, which formed a running chronicle of the progress of the research season. Scale drawings (plans and sections) were used to record features, especially architectural units, accurately in their horizontal and vertical dimensions. Black-and-white photographs served to document and supplement all the other record forms. Color slides were also taken as auxiliary illustrations.

Laboratory processing of the recorded field data was minimal. The field cards provided the key to the provenience of all artifacts and ecofacts brought to the laboratory for processing; the cards were maintained in a file for ready reference. At the close of each season,

Figure 4.14 Processing of pottery from excavations at Quiriguá in the field laboratory.

all recorded data were transported to the United States, where copies were made of both the cards and the field notes. At this time photographs were also processed: negatives were developed and catalogued, and proof or contact prints were made. At the close of the Project the complete duplicate set of records, together with duplicates of all background information, was turned over to IDAEH in Guatemala.

The laboratory processing of the raw field data was more complex. The process consisted of a series of steps, culminating in recording by both photography and the card system. Artifacts were brought to the laboratory at the close of each day, bagged by provenience units (lots). First the artifacts were washed, dried, and, if necessary, preserved or repaired. Immediately afterward, artifacts were labeled with the proper provenience code, sorted into categories on the basis of substance and technology, and then inventoried. At this stage the most numerous and redundant categories of artifacts—mostly pottery sherds—were bagged and placed in storage to await later analysis. The other, more varied and less numerous artifacts were individually catalogued. Cataloguing involved assigning to each artifact a catalogue number, and recording on a catalogue card a detailed description, including measurements and drawings. The catalogued artifacts were then photographed. Like operation and lot cards, catalogue cards were duplicated after each field season, cross-referenced, and integrated into the separate files maintained in the field and at the University Museum. The artifacts were then placed in storage in the laboratory building, pending analysis. Ecofacts underwent a similar process, but special care was taken to preserve these more delicate remains. Most ecofacts were later transported to the United States, under permit from the Guatemalan government, for analysis.

Analysis of the Quiriguá Data

The first data analysis undertaken involved classification of several kinds of artifacts and features recovered by the Quiriguá investigations. The artifact industries defined at this stage were pottery, chipped stone, ground stone, pottery "censerware," figurines, and metal objects. After this preliminary analysis, samples of artifactual and ecofactual data were shipped to the United States for more detailed studies. These included radiocarbon age assessments of carbonized remains, constituent analysis of the composition of various artifacts, including copper ornaments, and technological analysis to determine manufacture-behavior as reflected in certain artifacts such as chipped stone tools. However, we will here describe only some of the initial analysis, conducted in the field laboratory, of some of the pottery recovered at Quiriguá.

The pottery classification had two objectives—to provide a chronological framework based on a typological analysis and to create a functional framework based upon vessel form analysis. The typological analysis began by dividing the pottery collection into a series of categories ("types") primarily on the basis of differences in surface characteristics of style and technology (color, hardness, texture, decoration, and so forth). These types were then assessed as to relative age; that is, determinations were made as to which categories were manufactured and used in earlier periods at Quiriguá, and which were manufactured and used in later times. This chronological evaluation relied on the proveniences, associations, and context of the pottery itself, as well as on cross-checks with similar pottery dated from other Maya sites. As a result, the Quiriguá pottery types were ordered from earliest to latest in a pottery sequence.

The form analysis also divided the pottery collection into categories, in this case based on the shape of the original vessel as determined by evaluating the three basic form components of each (rim, body, and base). More than 20 overall vessel forms were eventually defined. The most fundamental functional distinction, based upon form, was between "domestic pottery"—vessels used for subsistence activities, usually as part of household duties such as carrying and storing water, preparing and storing food, and so on—and "nondomestic pottery" used for nonsubsistence activities such as rituals, burials, and so forth. These functional determinations were also based on provenience, association, and context, as well as cross-checks with related pottery from other sites. Eventually, more precise functional distinctions could be made to provide more detailed information on this aspect of ancient use-behavior at Quiriguá.

Both of these analyses were carried out in the field laboratory, beginning with experimental sortings during the 1975 season. In the course of the 1976 season, pottery analysis received major emphasis: two staff members defined more than 50 typological units and 14 form categories. These classifications, expanded and refined during subsequent seasons, provided the basic frameworks for preliminary chronological and functional evaluations of artifacts, features, and sites associated with pottery remains. However, other classes of data, such as chipped stone and ground stone artifacts, were also subjected to similar chronological and functional analyses in order to cross-check the evaluations based on pottery analysis. Other approaches to analysis, including technological studies, added important information bearing upon ancient manufacturing behavior as well as on resource acquisition and distribution at Quiriguá.

Interpretation of the Quiriguá Data

The interpretation stage of the Quiriguá Project has only begun. However, aspects of interpretation relevant to all the original goals have been completed in a preliminary sense. These interpretations include temporal and spatial frameworks, ancient activity definitions, and a refined dynastic record; they are preliminary in that they still await verification or refutation from other programs of the Project. A further consideration is that as the Quiriguá Project's research program was ending, a new archaeological investigation began at the nearby site of Copán. The results of this research, when available, may add a great deal to our understanding of ancient Quiriguá, especially with regard to economic and political ties between the two centers. With this in mind, for illustrative purposes we shall briefly examine some of the preliminary findings relevant to the testing of the three models outlined on page 122.

In general, the available evidence acquired by the Quiriguá Project seems to refute the Colony model. In the first place, chronological data provided by pottery analysis and calendrical inscriptions indicate that Quiriguá may have been founded at about the same time as Copán. If further analysis bears out this finding, it might be concluded that both Quiriguá and Copán were founded by colonists from another region, perhaps to the north. This possibility is supported by sculptural stylistic links to one or more Maya sites located to the north in present-day Belize. However, it is still possible that in its early years Quiriguá was politically subordinate to the larger site of Copán to the south. Quiriguá hieroglyphic inscriptions contain repeated references to Copán; this fact was one of the original reasons for development of the Colony model. But recently, the meaning of these inscriptions has been reinterpreted. They are now thought to refer to an event in A.D. 738 in which Quiriguá triumphed over Copán; the event was either military conflict or the ritualistic capture of Copán's ruler. The archaeological evidence, including that from constructional activity, indicates that immediately after this date Quiriguá was transformed into a major independent power center. Finally, contrary to the expectations derived from the Colony model, the artifactual material excavated at Quiriguá—especially highly diagnostic pottery types—demonstrates a striking lack of interaction with Copán.

Evidence bearing on the Plantation model is less clear-cut. On the one hand, no direct ecofactual data were recovered at Quiriguá that indicate an ancient cash-crop economy. However, this lack of evidence must be evaluated in light of the botanical conclusion that there is little likelihood of the survival in soils around Quiriguá of pollen from one of the prime potential cash crops, cacao. On the other hand, indirect evidence to support the model was found in the form of several ceramic cacao pod effigies. The settlement data, indicating that Quiriguá was a small but rather densely nucleated center with a rapid decline in structure frequency within 1 km of the site core, also support the plantation model. The agricultural lands surrounding Quiriguá appear to have been relatively vacant, allowing for intensive agricultural activities. Unfortunately, this evidence does not favor the Plantation model exclusively, since this kind of settlement pattern is not inconsistent with other site functions, such as a trading center.

Little direct evidence pertinent to Quiriguá's role as an ancient trade center was recovered. No specialized features such as storage structures or transshipment facilities were discovered. However, evidence of two distinct obsidian tool manufacturing technologies at the site may reflect Quiriguá's ancient economic system. One technology represents a large-scale production of obsidian blade tools from cores imported from one or more highland sources. Tools of this type were highly favored throughout Mesoamerica, and thus they represent a potentially valuable trade item. The second technology is less sophisticated, involving flake tools struck from obsidian cobbles recovered in the Motagua river gravels near the site. These tools were apparently produced solely for the use of local inhabitants. Other indirect support of the Trade Center model comes from Quiriguá's geographical position astride natural east-west and north-south communication routes, and from the location of secondary administrative centers, controlled by Quiriguá, that monitor these routes into and out of the valley. Finally, the rapid growth in wealth and power at Quiriguá, inferred from evidence of a rapid increase in building activity and the acquisition of stone construction materials from increasingly distant sources, is consistent with the thesis that after A.D. 738 Quiriguá was free to exploit the wealth from trade without interference from other centers, including Copán.

On the basis of presently available evidence resulting from the investigations of the Quiriguá Project, then, it does not seem likely that Quiriguá was founded as a colony from the larger site of Copán to the south. On the other hand, Quiriguá very probably did function as a major center for the trade in obsidian—perhaps importing "blank" cores and manufacturing them into finished blades for export—as well as other commodities. As a trade center, Quiriguá controlled one of the most important routes leading from the Maya highlands to the Caribbean coast. In addition, Quiriguá's role as a production center for certain cash crops remains a viable model; cacao is still one of the most likely crops.

Publication of the Quiriguá Data

The final stage of the Quiriguá Project, the publication of the research results, is already under way. Obviously, the final report cannot be prepared until all previous stages are completed. However, a plan has been established to coordinate all facets of publication. According to this plan, the publication of the Quiriguá research will be completed in three formats: a preliminary series of reports released during the course of the Project, professional journal publications released both during and after the research program, and a set of final reports to synthesize the results of all research stages once they are completed.

The first of these formats, the preliminary reports, was inaugurated in 1978 with the creation of the *Quiriguá Reports* series. Each of the initial volumes contains a series of papers—including both summaries of general progress to date and reports of particular facets of research as they are completed—that are of interest primarily to professional archaeologists. For instance, the first volume contains five papers; three are progress reports covering the formulation and implementation stages and the research seasons of 1974, 1975, and 1976. A fourth paper describes the epigraphic analysis of a single sculptured monument from Quiriguá, and the fifth is a progress report on efforts to control the destructive growth of microflora on the Quiriguá monuments. The site-core map is also included in this volume.

The second publication format—the release of articles in professional journals—is an outlet for research results with a wider range of appeal, including not only fellow archaeologists but also other anthropologists and the interested lay public. For example, an article published in the *Journal of Field Archaeology* gives an overview of the research conducted at Quiriguá during the first three seasons at the site. Other articles of this kind are planned or in progress.

The third format, now in the planning phase, is the final report of all research carried out by the Quiriguá Project. These studies, which will comprise the final volumes of the *Quiriguá Reports,* will emphasize the overall research results. Coverage will include a full description of the data acquired, the results of the data analysis, and synthesis and interpretation in light of the research objectives of the Quiriguá Project.

With the completion of the final report, the archaeological research process of the Quiriguá Project will come to an end. Of course, the publication and documentation of the results should provide the groundwork for further research both at Quiriguá and at other sites.

SUMMARY

This chapter has shown why archaeologists need to call upon the expertise of many specialists in the conduct of their research. It has also outlined a generalized design for the conduct of scientific archaeological research. In order that the results be scientifically useful, it is essential that all archaeological inquiry be conducted in a systematic manner. The research design described in the chapter was illustrated by a detailed description of one archaeological research program, the Quiriguá Project.

The research design format described in this chapter will provide the basic organization of the remaining chapters of the book. The formulation and implementation stages have been discussed in this chapter, as has the final stage, publication. Subsequent chapters will describe the identification of archaeological sites (Chapter 5), acquisition of data by surface survey and excavation (Chapters 6 and 7), processing and analysis of data (Chapters 8 through 11), and interpretation (Chapters 12 through 14). Finally, in Chapter 15 we will offer a discussion of some important challenges to the future of archaeological research.

See p. 572 for "Suggestions for Further Reading."

Data Acquisition

With a well-designed research program in hand, the next consideration is the collection of archaeological data. Archaeologists use three means of collecting evidence about the past: archaeological reconnaissance, surface survey, and excavation. Although excavation dominates the popular image of what archaeologists do, both reconnaissance and surface survey play crucial roles in acquiring data, as the following three chapters will show.

Ground reconnaissance is the most traditional and still the most widely used means of searching for archaeological sites.

Archaeological Reconnaissance

One's ears are filled with chatter about assorted magnetometers and how they are used to pick up the traces of buried objects and no one has to guess at all. They unearth the city, or find the buried skull . . . then everyone concerned is famous overnight.

(Loren C. Eiseley, The Night Country, *New York: Scribner's, 1971)*

OBJECTIVES OF RECONNAISSANCE

Time transforms the sites of past human activity in a variety of ways. Some sites such as Stonehenge may be well preserved and remain obvious to any observer. Others may be nearly destroyed or completely buried under tons of overburden; in such cases the task of identification may be extremely difficult. The systematic attempt to identify archaeological sites is called *archaeological reconnaissance*. By identification, we mean both the discovery and the location (determination of geographical position) of sites. This identification process must often be distinguished from what is usually termed archaeological survey. Archaeological survey (see Chapter 6) involves the initial data gathering at and evaluation of identified archaeological sites. Obviously, it may be more efficient in many instances to combine identification and data gathering, but the functions remain distinct. In fact, because reconnaissance is an initial step in the research process, it is sometimes more profitable to limit research at this point to discovery and location. The information thus gained—through repeatable and nondestructive procedures—can be used to formulate or refine hypotheses to be tested through surface survey or excavation. This is especially true when the reconnaissance is taking place in geographical areas with no prior archaeological information or as part of a feasibility study for a larger overall project.

Archaeological reconnaissance yields data concerning the range in form (size and internal arrangement) of sites as well as their total number and spatial distribution within a region. The distribution data may reveal patterns in the placement of sites, relative both to each other and to variables of the natural environment, such as topography, biotic and mineral resources, and water. Sometimes these findings may be used to define the region for later, more intensive study: at Teotihuacán, Mexico, the perimeter of the zone to be covered by intensive survey and mapping was established by reconnaissance location of the limits of continuous surface (archaeological) debris. For the Tehuacán Project, one phase of reconnaissance helped to define the study region by indicating the correlation between limits of the arid Tehuacán Valley (Fig. 5.1) and distribution limits of two pottery styles.

Uses such as these for archaeological reconnaissance also emphasize the need for ecological studies of the region, either prior to actual archaeological reconnaissance (as part of background research) or in conjunction with the site identification process. Defining ecological zones within a study area can guide the archaeologist in searching for sites if site distribution can be correlated with distribution of different environmental variables. The archaeologist may thereby gain an initial understanding of possible ecological relationships between past peoples and their environment.

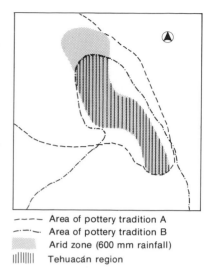

---- Area of pottery tradition A
-·-·-·- Area of pottery tradition B
▓▓▓ Arid zone (600 mm rainfall)
||||||| Tehuacán region

Figure 5.1 Definition of the Tehuacán Region was based on both cultural and ecological criteria. (After MacNeish, et al. 1972.)

LITERATURE, LUCK, AND LEGENDS

Not all sites are located through general reconnaissance. To begin with, some archaeological sites are never lost to history: in areas with long literate traditions, such as the Mediterranean basin, the locations and identities of many archaeological sites are well documented. Obviously the locations of Athens, imperial Rome, and many other sites in the ancient world have never been forgotten. Most sites, however —even many documented by history—have not fared so well. Many once recorded sites have been lost, razed by later conquerors or ravaged by natural processes of collapse and decay. Ancient Carthage, for example, was systematically destroyed by its Roman conquerors in 146 B.C.; it has only recently been rediscovered near Tunis. Similarly, the Greek colony of Sybaris, still remembered for its luxurious and dissolute ("sybaritic") way of life, was lost for centuries.

Sometimes histories and even legends provide the clues that lead to the relocation of "lost" cities. Literary references were valuable in the case of Sybaris. But the most famous quest of this sort was Heinrich Schliemann's successful search for the legendary city of Troy (Fig. 5.2). As a child, Schliemann became fascinated with the story of Troy and decided that someday he would find that lost city. By age 30 he had become a successful international merchant and had amassed the fortune he needed to pursue his archaeological goals. He had, at the same time, learned more than half a dozen languages and had quickened his appetite for Troy by reading Homer's tales of the Trojan War in the original Greek. Study of textual descriptions of the location of the ancient city convinced him that it was to be found at Hissarlik in western Turkey. Accordingly, in 1870, he began excavations that ultimately demonstrated the physical existence of

The discovery of Troy: Heinrich Schliemann

Figure 5.2 A contemporary view of Heinrich Schliemann's excavations at Troy. (From Schliemann 1881.)

Priam's legendary city. Later it was found that the burned remains Schliemann had called Troy were really an earlier settlement, and that he had cut right through the Trojan layers in his determined digging! Nonetheless, Schliemann is credited with the discovery of Troy, and his successful persistence there and later in Greece at Mycenae and Tiryns gave great impetus to the search for the origins of Greek civilization.

Many archaeological sites are observed and recorded incidentally by mapmakers. In areas of the world covered by accurate maps, archaeologists may be able to rely on distributional information provided by cartographers. In England, for instance, the excellent coverage provided by the Ordnance Survey Maps, made mostly from ground survey, includes identification of many archaeological sites. Similar coverage exists for the United States (U.S. Geological Survey maps) and many other countries. Since World War II, much of the world has been mapped by methods using aerial photography. One of the most useful series of maps produced by this method is that made by the U.S. Army Map Service at a standard scale of 1:50,000. These maps often note the location of identifiable archaeological sites. Even though pre-existing maps may be used to locate archaeological remains, these sources must always be field checked to test their accuracy.

Perhaps more archaeological sites come to light by accident than by any other means. The forces of nature—wind and water erosion, natural catastrophes, and so forth—have uncovered many long-buried sites. The exposed faces of Tanzania's Olduvai Gorge (Fig. 5.3), from which Louis and Mary Leakey have retrieved so many "early man" finds, are the product of millennia of riverine bed-cutting ac-

Figure 5.3 This oblique aerial photograph of Olduvai Gorge, Tanzania, amply illustrates the erosional forces which exposed evidence of human physical and cultural development. (Emory Kristof, © National Geographic Society.)

tion. And the famous Neolithic lake dwellings of Switzerland were discovered when extremely low water levels during the dry winter of 1853–54 exposed the preserved remains of the wooden pilings that once supported houses.

Chance discoveries of ancient sites continue to occur all the time. For example, it was French schoolboys who in 1940 first happened on the Paleolithic paintings of Lascaux cave: the boys' dog fell through an opening into the cave, and when they went after their pet, they discovered the cavern walls covered with ancient paintings. As the world's population increases and the pace of new construction accelerates, more and more ancient remains are uncovered. Unfortunately, many are destroyed before the archaeologist has a chance to observe and record them. An important discovery in the highland Maya site of Kaminaljuyú, however, provides one example in which archaeologists were notified.

In 1935, members of a soccer club in Guatemala City decided to lengthen their playing field. To do this, they began to cut away sections of the two mounds at the ends of the field; in the process they exposed long-buried Maya structures. Archaeologists were called in and the structures were excavated, revealing not only well-preserved ancient architecture, but a series of tombs containing an undisturbed assortment of ancient artifacts. Since that time, Kaminaljuyú has been fruitfully excavated by two separate large-scale archaeological projects. Much of the overall site had been destroyed before 1935, and the expanding city continues to demolish and engulf what remains (Fig. 5.4). But the soccer players' disclosure brought to the attention of archaeologists a long-ignored site that is now known to have played a critical role in Maya prehistory.

Maya structures at Kaminaljuyú exposed by local soccer club

Figure 5.4 Recent view of the ruins of Kaminaljuyú, Guatemala; the expansion of Guatemala City (visible in upper right) continues to destroy the site.

Construction of Mexico City subway uncovers buried Aztec ruins

Similar incidents occur constantly throughout the world, but only a very small proportion of such discoveries gain the attention of archaeologists. Nonetheless, many archaeologists, such as those working for governmental agencies, are kept busy salvaging archaeological sites discovered during construction projects or similar activities. All archaeologists, especially those working in the field, must be alert to reports of accidental discovery and be able to react quickly in order to save and record as much as possible. In many countries, laws require building contractors to stop work immediately when they encounter archaeological materials. In most cases, work cannot resume until archaeologists, whose work is funded either by government agencies or by the contractors themselves, can excavate and remove the material. More and more frequently, in cases in which modern construction will be likely to come across ancient remains, archaeologists work hand in hand with builders to minimize both the destruction of the past and delays in construction. When Mexico City's Metro subway system was being built in the 1960s, archaeologists worked in the tunnels to recover artifacts from the Aztec capital of Tenochtitlán, now buried beneath the modern city. Occasionally they encountered complex features, including portions of buildings and a small temple dedicated to Ehecatl, the Aztec god of the wind. This temple has been preserved as it was found; it may be seen today at the Pino Suárez Metro Station underneath the modern streets of Mexico City.

Many sources, then, provide the archaeologist with information concerning the location of archaeological sites. But identification of sites by these means must always be verified by archaeological investigation. Too often researchers have assumed the location of archaeological sites without rigorous checking. For instance, historical records based on Aztec and Spanish accounts identified the ancient Toltec capital of Tollán with the famous ruins of Teotihuacán near

Mexico City. But subsequent archaeological work at a much smaller site near Tula, Hidalgo, about 50 miles north of Mexico City has established that this city was Tollán and that the historical accounts were wrong.

METHODS OF RECONNAISSANCE

Despite the great numbers of known archaeological sites, the bulk of sites of ancient activity and settlement have never been discovered. Many sites have been destroyed, and more are being destroyed every day. To identify those that have survived, the archaeologist must begin with a systematic search for sites of ancient activity.

Archaeological reconnaissance can begin during background investigation using documents, records, maps, previous reports, local informants and other sources in order to learn as much as possible about the area to be studied before going into the field. Reconnaissance at this stage is often part of a feasibility study to determine the practicability of pursuing the planned research. Preliminary reconnaissance can also indicate the best areas (or even the only possible areas) in which to test a given hypothesis. For example, by the late 1950s New World archaeologists had documented much of the sequence of human occupation from the earliest settlers of the New World to the time of European conquest. However, very little information had been obtained about one particular era of crucial importance: the transition from societies subsisting by hunting and gathering to sedentary, agriculture-based societies. As a result, a team of archaeologists and paleobotanists led by Richard MacNeish planned a research project specifically to locate and investigate archaeological sites spanning this critical period.

Previous research—much of it done by MacNeish—indicated that the most important agricultural species, corn (*Zea mays*), had been domesticated prior to 3000 B.C., probably somewhere between the Valley of Mexico and the Mexican state of Chiapas. Within this general area, the research location selected would have to combine two environmental characteristics: first, it would have to be in the highlands where the wild ancestor of corn would have been likely to grow; and second, it would have to contain dry caves in which ancient and continuous stratified deposits with well-preserved organic remains could have accumulated. Preliminary reconnaissance in the areas meeting the first requirement allowed MacNeish to eliminate those that did not also meet the second. Government permit in hand (and military protection in tow), he scouted out a series of rock shelters or caves on his own, but the most promising sites were those shown to him by local inhabitants in the Tehuacán Valley, located in the state

Reconnaissance defines area of Tehuacán project

of Puebla. In this case, the feasibility study was capped by a week of exciting and fruitful test excavations in one rock shelter, Ajuereado cave. This initial reconnaissance and test-pitting led to the formation of the Tehuacán Archaeological-Botanical Project (1961–1964), which has become a standard for systematic and productive archaeological research.

Reconnaissance may be conducted in many ways, but the actual techniques and procedures used often depend on the kinds of archaeological sites being sought. The methods used to locate surface sites differ greatly from those intended to discover deeply buried sites. Likewise, a small, poorly preserved seasonal hunting camp requires a different means of detection from that used to locate a large, well-preserved urban center. In most cases, limitations of time and money prevent the archaeologist from covering every square meter of the research area in attempting to identify sites. Accordingly, carefully selected sampling procedures should be used in order to maximize the chance that the number and location of sites in the areas actually searched are representative of the universe under study. In some cases, a systematic sample may be taken by dividing the reconnaissance universe into squares (quadrats) and covering as many squares as time and money will allow. In other cases, knowledge about the area may enable the archaeologist to use a stratified random sampling procedure. For instance, previous accounts might indicate that archaeological sites are found in only two ecological zones—along coasts and on hilltops. The research area could then be

(a)   (b)

Figure 5.5 Present environmental conditions have a great influence on reconnaissance: (a) tropical rainforest greatly reduces visibility while (b) arid landscapes are often conducive to detection of surface sites. (Courtesy of the Tikal and Gordion Projects, the University Museum, University of Pennsylvania.)

stratified into these zones and sample areas within each zone selected and searched. In such a case it would be advisable to test the posited distribution by also reconnoitering sample areas of the other ecological zones to verify that, in fact, no sites are located in these areas. Such a procedure was used in the reconnaissance conducted at Quiriguá.

Finally, it is worth noting that some environments are simply more conducive to reconnaissance than others. Dry climates and sparse vegetation offer near ideal conditions for both visual detection of archaeological sites and ease of movement across reconnoitered terrain (Fig. 5.5). Such environments have greatly aided archaeologists in discovering sites in the Near East, coastal Peru, highland Mexico, the southwestern United States, and similar areas.

Good quality maps are essential for reconnaissance; they may be supplemented in some cases by aerial photos. Maps are used first to plot the grid squares or other boundaries for sample units, and then to plot the location of new archaeological sites discovered. Plotting of sample unit boundaries enables the archaeologist to indicate which areas have been covered and which have not, so that sampling adequacy can be assessed and possible distributions in nonreconnoitered areas can be posited. Plotting of new sites is necessary for distributional studies within the sampled area—and, of course, for returning to the sites later. Techniques for making and using maps will be discussed later in this chapter and in Chapter 6.

There are three basic methods used to conduct archaeological reconnaissance: ground reconnaissance, aerial reconnaissance, and subsurface detection. Each requires specialized techniques, and each is effective in identifying sites under different conditions.

Ground Reconnaissance

The oldest and most common reconnaissance method is to search the study area by visual inspection at ground level. Ground reconnaissance has been used since the days of antiquarian interest, when exploration by such men as William Camden in England or Stephens and Catherwood in Central America led to the discovery of countless sites. Today, well-defined sample areas such as transects or quadrats are covered systematically by moving back and forth or across in sweeps (see Fig. 5.6). Most ground reconnaissance is still conducted by walking—the slowest method, but also the most thorough. Often the efficiency of reconnaissance on foot may be increased by using teams of archaeologists (or an archaeologist and several trained assistants) to sweep through designated areas. Many archaeologists increase the speed of ground reconnaissance by use of horses, mules, or motorized transport (four-wheel-drive vehicles are

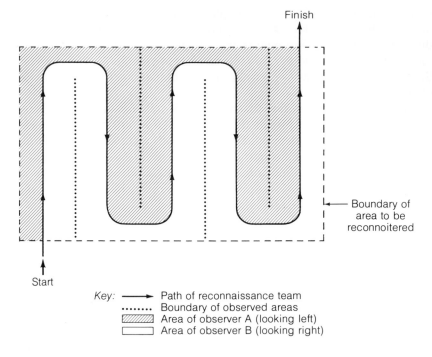

Figure 5.6 A schematic illustration of one efficient technique of conducting ground reconnaissance. (After Mueller, reproduced by permission of The Society for American Archaeology, adapted from *American Antiquity* 39 (2, part 2, Memoir 28):10, 1974.)

Finish

Boundary of area to be reconnoitered

Start

Key: ———▶ Path of reconnaissance team
      ‥‥‥‥‥ Boundary of observed areas
      ▨▨▨ Area of observer A (looking left)
      ▢▢▢ Area of observer B (looking right)

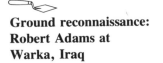

Ground reconnaissance: Robert Adams at Warka, Iraq

frequently necessary). Combinations of these methods are very commonly used: jeeps or horses may transport archaeologists initially from a base camp to areas that are then reconnoitered on foot. Such an approach was used, for example, by Robert Adams in the Warka (ancient Uruk) area of Iraq, where some 2800 km² were covered during a period of 4½ months.

Ground reconnaissance can be greatly aided by the cooperation and assistance of local inhabitants. Being on friendly terms with the resident population is always desirable. But in addition to allowing the archaeologist freedom of movement, local people may also serve as guides and indicate the location of sites. Of course, the site sample gained from local informants will not be a random one, but in some cases it is the most feasible one. For example, in the dense rain forest of the department of Peten, Guatemala, an inexperienced traveler can easily become lost and, during the dry season, literally die of thirst (among other things). Explorers and archaeologists, from the nineteenth century to the present day, have wisely and profitably employed local *chicleros*—men who gather the resin from the *chicozapote* tree and sell it to be processed into chewing gum—to lead them through the rain forest, to ruins as well as water holes (see Fig. 5.5).

How does the archaeologist recognize archaeological sites on the ground? Many sites, of course, are identified by their prominence. Some sites of ancient settlement in the Near East are called *tell* or *tepe*—both of which mean "hill"—because they stand out as large mounds against a relatively flat plain. In other cases, only a slight difference in elevation or a rise or fall in the landscape that appears unnatural may indicate a buried ancient wall or other feature. Semisubterranean Eskimo dwellings, for example, appear as slight depressions after their roofs have collapsed. In other cases, construction features such as building walls, earthen platforms, or paved roadways are sufficiently well preserved to be easily recognizable. Many sites are identified by concentrations of surface artifacts such as pottery sherds and stone tools. Shahr-i Sokhta in eastern Iran was recognized as a site because of its densely littered surface. Because of its richness, this artifactual layer was long thought to be the sole remnant of a thoroughly wind-eroded hilltop settlement; as it turned out, the "hill" was the buried—and beautifully preserved—site!

Surface debris identifies site at Shahr-i Sokhta, Iran

Not all sites are easily detectable; some leave no surface indications. Recent exposures of underlying material, such as road cuts, eroded stream banks, or newly plowed fields, provide access to subsurface possibilities (see Fig. 3.6). Although buried sites are often missed by ground reconnaissance, under some circumstances they may leave clues to their location. Low-growing vegetation, such as grass, grain and other ground covers, is often sensitive to subsurface conditions. Many plants grow higher and more luxuriant where ancient human activity, such as the construction of canals, deposition of middens, or interment of burials, has improved soil moisture and fertility. For example, at the Salmon Ruin of New Mexico the large *kiva* subterranean chamber was clearly distinguishable in 1973, without excavation, as a circular patch of green amid the drier, browner surrounding vegetation. In contrast, solid construction features such as walls or roads immediately below the surface will often impede vegetation growth. For example, at certain times of day differential absorption of salt made the tops of the buried mud-brick walls at Shahr-i Sokhta stand out as white against the rest of the surface of the mound (Fig. 5.7). Patterned differences in the distribution of plant species may also indicate archaeological sites. In the dense jungle of lowland Central America, early explorers were aided in locating Maya sites by looking for concentrations of a large tree known as the *ramon* (breadnut tree). It now appears that the association of *ramon* with Maya sites is due to ancient cultivation of these trees, for their edible fruit, in gardens around the houses. Although the sites are long abandoned, the stands of *ramon* have continued to propagate in the same locale.

Vegetation contrast identifies feature at Salmon Ruin of New Mexico

Ramon trees as indicators of lowland Maya sites

Figure 5.7 Traces of a building visible on the surface of Shahr-i Sokhta. (Courtesy of Centro Studi e Scavi Archeologici in Asia of IsMEO, Rome.)

However, in most cases these and other differences in soil and vegetation conditions are invisible to the ground observer; this brings us to the next means of reconnaissance—*remote sensing*. Remote sensing approaches to site discovery involve a number of techniques in which the observer is not in direct contact with the archaeological remains. These techniques may be divided into two major categories: reconnaissance from the air and subsurface reconnaissance from ground level.

Remote Sensing: Aerial Reconnaissance

The development of *aerial reconnaissance* is an outgrowth of military necessity. Somewhat ironically, the techniques designed to improve the destructive capabilities of modern warfare have also been of great benefit to archaeologists in their efforts to record and preserve past human achievements. The same techniques of aerial observation that gather information for the world's armies, by permitting observers to see large-scale spatial distributions and patterns, aid archaeologists in identifying ancient sites.

Aerial reconnaissance includes a variety of established and developing techniques. Direct observation from an airplane, helicopter, or even balloon, although sometimes useful, is usually inefficient without some method of simultaneously recording that which is observed. Aerial photography provides the most common means of recording. Aerial photos are of two types: vertical coverage, in which the ground is photographed from directly above, with the camera pointed straight down, and oblique coverage, in which the ground is photographed at an angle, as in viewing from an airplane window. Vertical aerial photography is generally the most versatile. Because the scale is constant throughout the photo, patterns in ground features can be seen without distortion. In addition, plan measurements can be drawn directly from the photo. With oblique shots, the scale varies throughout the photograph, and because of distortion the location of reference points on the ground may be difficult to determine. On the other hand, oblique views reveal more area per photo, and since the perspective is from the side, slight changes in elevation—including some archaeological features—are often easier to see.

Aerial photography is useful to the archaeologist in a number of ways. First, it provides data for preliminary analysis of the local environment and its resources. Second, it yields information on site location. Although aerial photography can reveal sites from their surface characteristics or prominence, one of its most useful applications is in detecting buried sites. The same phenomena of differential vegetation growth that are useful to ground reconnaissance are often vividly revealed in aerial photography (Fig. 5.8). The best circumstance for such detection is a uniform, low-growing plant cover, such as may be found in grassy plains, savannahs, or croplands. Areas of luxuriant growth are usually darker than contrasting poor-growth areas. As we have seen, under some circumstances ancient activity produces areas that promote growth; other archaeological features retard the growth of overlying vegetation.

Aerial reconnaissance is not always helpful in locating archaeological sites. For one thing, in low-altitude work—the kind most archaeologists do—the coverage area must be relatively free of dense vegetation. Thus, with some exceptions, the technique is seldom useful in heavily forested regions. Another difficulty is that differences in elevation that are obvious to the ground observer may be imperceptible in aerial photography. Elevation differences can best be seen in photographs through shadows; for this reason, aerial photos are often most useful if taken under bright, sunlit conditions when shadows are longest, either early in the morning or late in the afternoon. Differences in elevation can also be detected by use of stereo photography. The principle of stereo photography is the same as that of stereoscopic vision; it is occasionally used commercially, as in 3-D movies. Aerial stereo cameras are programmed to take vertical photographs with overlapping coverage (usually 60 percent of each frame overlaps the area covered by the previous photo). By placing any two adjacent frames under an instrument called a stereoscope, an observer can see the area of overlap in three dimensions. Stereo photography can reveal slopes and heights even when the sun's shadows do not indicate their relief. By using sophisticated equipment, cartographers employ stereo coverage to make contour maps.

Because vertical air photos are so useful for mapmaking, extensive coverage already exists for many areas. Depending on the range in altitude of the aircraft and in the type of camera used, coverage may be available at one or more of a variety of scales. As a general rule, scales from 1:4000 to 1:10,000 are most useful for locating ancient archaeological sites. But some smaller scales (up to 1:50,000) may be useful as well, for such purposes as plotting the regional distribution of sites relative to environmental resources. Most existing vertical photos are available from government agencies or from private cartographic companies. They are usually easy to obtain and relatively inexpensive.

The equipment necessary for taking aerial photographs consists of a camera, film, and a means of getting these (and either the photographer or a remote shutter-tripping mechanism) aloft. A wide variety of specific equipment is available in all three categories; the choice depends on the coverage desired and the funds available.

Common cameras appropriate to aerial photography include single and double lens reflex models and military surplus cameras, such as

(a)

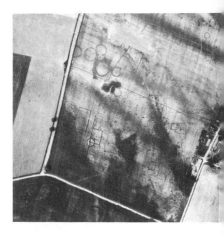

(b)

Figure 5.8 A pair of vertical aerial photographs in which detection of buried archaeological features has been greatly enhanced with the maturation of the barley growing in the field: (a) taken June 4, 1970; (b) taken June 19, 1970. (Courtesy of the Museum Applied Science Center for Archaeology, University Museum, University of Pennsylvania.)

Figure 5.9 Vertical aerial photograph, shot by remote control, from a balloon moored over the site of Sarepta, Lebanon. (Photo by Julian Whittlesey.)

Aerial Reconnaissance: Cauca Valley, Colombia and Quiriguá, Guatemala

the K-20, which uses 4-by-5-inch film; any camera that has a rapid enough shutter speed and is not too cumbersome will do.

Black-and-white panchromatic film is generally used, because it is more economical than color. Black-and-white photography also has better resolution—it can better be enlarged to show detail—and it is better for recording contrasts in the brightness and texture of ground features. Other film types, however, such as infrared, are useful for specific goals such as increasing contrast among some types of trees. In addition, special filters can sometimes enhance detection capabilities. Just as oblique and vertical images serve complementary purposes, so multiple coverage using more than one type of film (or filter or camera) allows the advantages of the various types to complement, rather than substitute for, one another. But because flight time is expensive, it is worthwhile to combine coverages to maximize the number of photographs taken in a given flight. For his reconnaissance in the Cauca Valley of Colombia, Thomas Schorr rigged up a mounting device that enabled him to handle two cameras at once, taking synchronized photos with black-and-white and infrared film. At Quiriguá, Guatemala, aerial coverage was increased by taking four passengers and equipping each with one or more cameras. In about 5 total hours flying time, approximately 300 photographs were exposed, using black-and-white, color, and infrared film in twin-lens reflex (120 film), single-lens reflex (135 film), and K-20 cameras.

The most common approach to aerial photography is use of a small airplane. Balloons and helicopters have also been used, as have kites equipped with remote-controlled cameras (Fig. 5.9). But airplanes are the best-known and most flexible means of getting aloft. For vertical photographs, the camera is mounted through the bottom of the aircraft. For oblique coverage, a light single-engine craft with high wings and a removable passenger door gives maximum visibility and minimum obstruction.

As with data from all remote sensing techniques, aerial reconnaissance data require knowledge of the corresponding *ground*

truth for reliable interpretation. One must determine, by some degree of surface investigation, what the various contrasting patterns and features present on a photograph represent on the ground. Features such as rivers and towns may be self-evident. But even familiar things such as modern golf courses can sometimes go unrecognized by an individual who is not acquainted with the area photographed or experienced in reading aerial photographs. After doing some ground checking, one may be able to pick out the distribution of specific crops or the like. Local inhabitants can be of great help in this work. In general, successful interpretation of aerial photography depends on first-hand investigation of a sample of covered areas on the ground.

Aerial reconnaissance data can also be recorded by a variety of nonphotographic—and usually much more expensive—devices. Infrared or heat radiation can be detected and recorded by thermal sensors (*thermography*). The resulting image, which can be stored on videotape or regular film, indicates the differential retention/radiation of heat. Thermography has been used to locate such archaeological features as buried ditches and prehistoric fields. Note that infrared photographic film detects reflected radiation from the sun, while thermography (infrared thermal sensing) detects heat emitted from the object being examined.

Radar images, such as *side-looking airborne radar* (SLAR), which provides an oblique image of the ground surface, have also been used for archaeological purposes. Radar is effective in penetrating cloud cover, and to a certain extent it will "see through" dense vegetation (as in a rain forest) to record abrupt changes in topography or large manmade features (Fig. 5.10).

Figure 5.10 A SLAR image taken through extensive cloud cover from 35,000 feet over the rainforest of northern Guatemala. The darker zones in the center to lower right corner are probably areas of standing water; the regular outline of this area is of interest since this may represent agricultural modifications made by the ancient Maya (the visible straight lines are from 3 to 5 km long; scale ca 1:50,000). (SLAR image courtesy of NASA-Jet Propulsion Laboratory.)

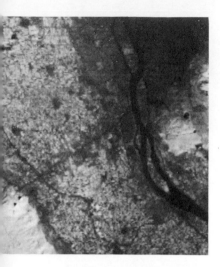

Figure 5.11 LANDSAT image of a portion of the Nile Valley in Egypt, with the Great Pyramids visible on the desert margin at lower left. (Produced by John Quann, Goddard Space Flight Center, from LANDSAT photo E–1165–08002, Band 7.)

Exploration of the potential archaeological utility of satellite sensing is just beginning. The nonmilitary Earth Resources Technology Satellites—now called LANDSAT 1 and 2—have multispectral scanners that record the intensity of reflected light and infrared radiation. The minimum units recorded are called *pixels* (a word coined from "picture elements"); each pixel covers about ½ hectare (a little more than an acre). Efforts are being made to further reduce the size of the minimum area recorded. The data for these pixels are converted electronically to photographic images which can be built up, in a mosaic, to form a very accurate map (Fig. 5.11). The resolution of the images, however, is low; study units must normally exceed 10 acres for the method to be useful. These images are frequently distributed at a scale of 1:1,000,000, at which scale such massive features as the great pyramids of Egypt are barely visible. For archaeologists, this immediately suggests that studies involving regional or interregional distributions are the ones most likely to make use of satellite data. For example, in reconnaissance work with computerized image-processing equipment, one might usefully search for new sites in unexplored pixel areas that are similar to pixel areas containing known sites. One problem, however, is that latitude and longitude data are seldom precise enough to allow determination of which pixel(s) represent a given site, and the site itself may well not be visible.

Remote Sensing: Subsurface Detection

Not all buried sites are detectable by either ground or aerial reconnaissance. Furthermore, sites that are identified on the surface by either of these means may have unknown subsurface components. It is often necessary, therefore, to use methods of *subsurface detection* in order to identify buried remains. Various methods of this type have been developed, ranging from the rather simple and commonplace to those requiring exotic and expensive equipment. Most of the procedures we will discuss have been adapted or modified from geology, where they were originally developed for petroleum and mineral prospecting. Most of these techniques provide limited coverage and are time-consuming and expensive. For these reasons they are used primarily for subsurface identification within archaeological sites; but, as we shall see, they may sometimes be used to locate entire sites.

The simplest and most straightforward approach is often called *bowsing;* it involves thumping the earth's surface with a heavy bat or mallet. Using this technique—analogous to tapping walls to find studs for hanging pictures—a practiced ear can successfully detect some subsurface features such as buried walls and chambers by differences in the sound produced by striking the earth. Several sophisticated electronic elaborations of this idea have been tested. All are based upon differential reflection or transmission of seismic waves by buried features—the same principle used in submarine sonar detection. Unfortunately, few of these experiments have enjoyed success.

Another simple technique, designed to be used in earth matrices, is *augering* or coring. An auger is a large drill run by human or machine power. It is valuable in ascertaining the depth of deposits such as topsoil or middens. *Corers* are hollow tubes that are driven into the ground. When removed, they yield a narrow column or core of the subsurface material. Depending upon the depth of the site or deposit involved, cores can provide a quick and relatively inexpensive cross-section of subsurface layers or construction. A specialized subsurface probe called a *Lerici periscope* uses either a camera or a periscope equipped with a light source; it has been used to examine the contents of subterranean chambers (Fig. 5.12). The best-known application of this technique is in the examination of underground Etruscan tombs that have been previously identified by aerial photography. The probes are placed through a small opening drilled in the top of the tomb to determine whether the contents are undisturbed (in primary context) or have been looted by grave robbers. Since only the undisturbed tombs are worth excavating, the technique saves the archaeologist time and money.

The *magnetometer* is an instrument that discerns minor variations in the magnetism present in many materials. Unlike the compass, which measures the direction of the earth's magnetic field, magnetometers measure the intensity of the magnetic field. These instruments have been successfully applied to archaeological re-

**Lerici Periscope:
Etruscan tombs in Italy**

Figure 5.12 Conventional photograph of the interior of a recently discovered Etruscan tomb; such tombs are often discovered by subsurface probes. (Courtesy of Ellen Kohler.)

Figure 5.13 Magnetometers are important aids in subsurface detection: (a) the person in the foreground carries the detector while the two in the background (b) read and record the magnetic values. (© Nicholas Hartmann, MASCA, University Museum, University of Pennsylvania.)

(a)   **(b)**

connaissance because some remains create anomalies in the magnetic field. For example, iron tools and ceramic kilns are especially easily found. Such buried features as walls made of volcanic stone, ditches filled with humus, and even burned surfaces may all be detected by the magnetometer (Fig. 5.13). Its primary use, then, is to locate features within a site. To use the magnetometer, magnetic readings are usually taken by the instrument at regular intervals, often 1 meter, and the numbers are recorded on graph paper (see Fig. 5.14); some machines, however, give continuous magnetic readings. The readings are then converted into a magnetic contour map by connecting areas of equal magnetism. Areas of high magnetism stand out on the map as "peaks"; areas of low magnetism form "valleys."

Areas with steep gradients of magnetic intensity may indicate archaeological features. Sometimes the shape of an anomaly suggests what lies buried (such as a wall), but the source of the anomaly is not always a cultural feature. To distinguish "signals" from "noise," the anomalies must be tested by excavation. The function of the magnetometer is to tell the archaeologist where to dig.

Cesium magnetometer locates Sybaris in Italy

The cesium magnetometer was first applied archaeologically in the search for the Greek colonial city of Sybaris mentioned earlier in this chapter. Sybaris had a history and a reputation but no tangible existence. It was founded in 710 B.C. and became notorious for the self-indulgent way of life of its inhabitants; in 520 B.C. it was destroyed by its neighbors from the city of Croton. It was known to be located somewhere in or on the plain of the River Crati in the instep of Italy's boot; beyond this, all attempts at locating the ancient city had been unsuccessful. But in the 1960s, a multi-season, joint Italian–American expedition succeeded in locating Sybaris (Fig. 5.15). The investigators used a variety of approaches, including coring and resistivity

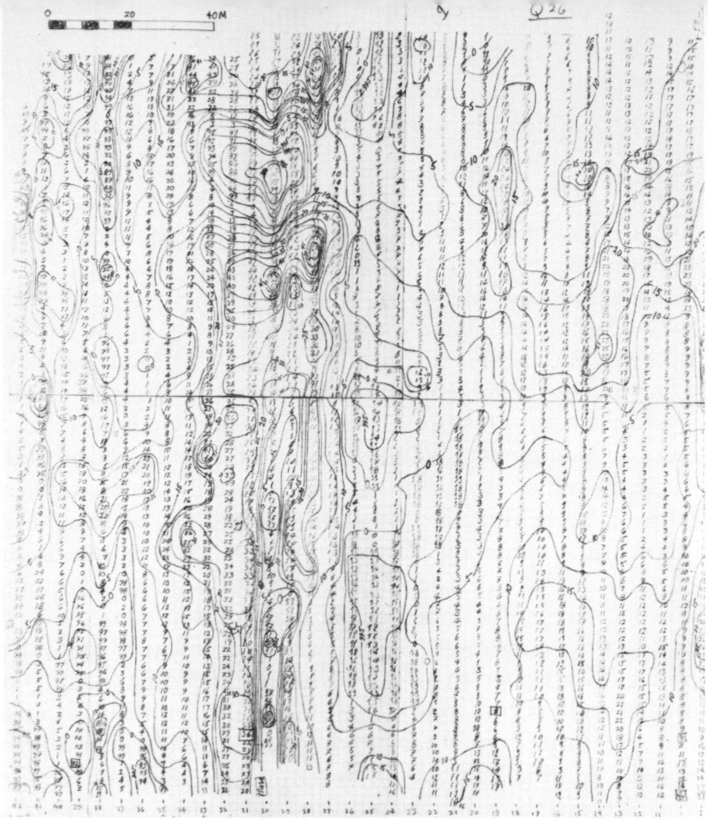

Figure 5.14 Field plot of magnetic values with contours superimposed, revealing a pronounced linear anomaly (top-to-bottom in the figure) later found to correspond to a buried wall. (Courtesy of Museum Applied Science Center for Archaeology, University Museum, University of Pennsylvania.)

Figure 5.15 Excavations at Sybaris, following reconnaissance by magnetometer, expose Roman construction superimposed on the remains of the earlier Greek colony. (Courtesy of the Museum Applied Science Center for Archaeology, University Museum, University of Pennsylvania.)

techniques (see below), but the center of attention was the magnetometer. A proton magnetometer was first brought in, but it did not have sufficient sensitivity. A version using rubidium as the active element proved more sensitive but too cumbersome for adequate field maneuverability. Finally, the cesium magnetometer was found to combine enough sensitivity with enough portability to trace the outlines of part of the buried remains. There were problems, to be sure, and the extent of "ground truth" testing was limited by the depth of the remains (5 meters or more below the present plain surface) and the high water table (only 2 meters below the surface). Still, the magnetometer work was the key to the final location and mapping of this elusive site.

Another instrument, the *resistivity detector*, measures differences in the ability of subsurface features to conduct electrical current. Again, features within sites are those most often sought. Moisture content gives most soils a low resistance to the passage of electrical current, while solid features such as walls or floors have a higher resistance. The most common method of resistivity detection is to place four probes along a line and to pass a current through the outer pair of probes (Fig. 5.16). The resistivity is determined from the voltage as measured at the inner pair of probes. When the results are plotted, the resulting pattern of high and low resistances reveals resistivity anomalies. Again, only excavation will reveal which represent buried cultural features. In general, archaeologists have found resistivity devices more time-consuming and less successful than magnetometers.

The search for new means of remote reconnaissance continues. One newly adapted technique uses *radar pulses* to locate buried features. Like seismic techniques, ground-penetrating radar sends waves into the earth, to be reflected back as "echoes" by subsurface discontinuities—construction features, artifacts, or soil changes (Fig. 5.17). The detection equipment includes an automatic recorder that produces a radar profile, representing a vertical cross-section below the path of the radar equipment. To gain a horizontal representation or plan of the buried "anomaly" like that obtained by contour plotting in magnetic and resistivity reconnaissance, one builds a composite "plot" on the basis of a series of parallel, aligned profiles. This is a complex and time-consuming task. On the other hand, the individual radar profiles are richer than the results of the other techniques in vertical data such as the approximate depths of both the top and the bottom of a feature. Like other approaches, ground-penetrating radar is not applicable in all situations; in particular, the general nature of the subsurface matrix is important. And, of course, interpretation of profile data is always dependent on "ground truth" excavation. At present, archaeological applications of this technique emphasize its experimental status: by testing areas in which subsurface ground truth is already known, such as the "reconnaissance" of backfilled excavations in Chaco Canyon, New Mexico, the range of sensitivity of the apparatus can be explored relative to known features. One cannot yet cite a long list of radar "discoveries," but the technique seems to hold promise for future usefulness.

Pulse radar experiments: Chaco Canyon, New Mexico

Figure 5.16 Subsurface detection by resistivity at an historical American site. (Courtesy of the Museum Applied Science Center for Archaeology, University Museum, University of Pennsylvania.)

APPROACHES TO RECONNAISSANCE

Total Coverage

Archaeological reconnaissance may aim for total coverage of the data universe. Because reconnaissance, unlike survey and excavation, does not involve the actual removal of archaeological evidence, total reconnaissance coverage does not raise the issue of leaving a portion of data intact for future investigators. In fact it is usually preferable to cover an entire study area whenever possible, especially when prior knowledge of the area is limited. The practicality of complete coverage depends in part on the methods to be used; for example, aerial reconnaissance can often cover vast areas quickly for the detection of sites. In other cases, total or near-total coverage has been achieved by combining ground-based and air-based techniques. For instance, once the archaeologist has done enough general local ground reconnaissance to be able to read local air photos accurately, sample areas that are not accessible on the ground may be covered by searching the photographs for evidence of sites. Ground checking is always advisable, but it is not always possible.

Sample Coverage

Total reconnaissance of a given universe may not be feasible for any of several reasons. The reconnaissance method chosen may preclude total coverage. For instance, the use of ground-based remote sensors is extremely time-consuming and expensive and thus can cover only very restricted areas. In other cases, the data universe may be too vast to undertake any kind of total coverage in a reasonable length of time. The highland valleys of central Mexico have been subjected to

(a)

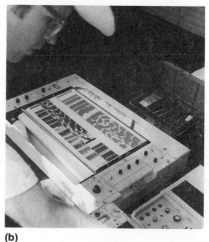

(b)

Figure 5.17 Ground-penetrating pulse radar may be used to locate subsurface remains: (a) the portable radar transmitter yields the cross-section of subsurface strata seen in (b). (© Nicholas Hartmann, MASCA, University Museum, University of Pennsylvania.)

intensive and extensive reconnaissance work by scores of researchers over decades of time—and there are still gaps. Finally, in many areas of the world unsuitable environmental and political conditions may preclude complete reconnaissance. Local guerrilla warfare is at least as discouraging to research as dense vegetation. In circumstances such as these, sample coverage is the only alternative; and both probabilistic and nonprobabilistic methods have been applied to select the samples.

*Nonprobabilistic Sampling

Nonprobabilistic sampling: Reconnaissance in the Maya lowlands

As an example of the reconnaissance difficulties imposed by environmental conditions, we shall consider the case of the ancient Maya of Mesoamerica. For years, the tropical environmental conditions that harbored one of the New World's most brilliant civilizations have hampered dozens of reconnaissance attempts that have sought to discover pre-Columbian Maya sites. Until recently, the vast, almost impenetrable lowland rain forest of the Petén, centered in what is now northern Guatemala, had made travel for any purpose—let alone archaeological reconnaissance—nearly impossible. As a result, nonprobabilistic sampling has forcibly governed most reconnaissance undertaken in this region. Ground reconnaissance has been largely restricted to the system of narrow trails kept open by *chicleros*. During the past decade, access to the Petén has been improved by the opening of a network of unpaved roads and a few landing strips. Nevertheless, ground reconnaissance has remained difficult because the thick jungle growth restricts visibility to a few feet on either side of the trail or road. Numerous tales are told of travelers and explorers who have passed completely through the ruins of large Maya centers, unaware of their existence. Even trained archaeologists have failed to observe large pyramids and other structures hidden in the dense vegetation.

These difficulties made the Maya lowlands the focus of some of the pioneer attempts at aerial reconnaissance. In 1929, Dr. A. V. Kidder of the Carnegie Institution of Washington flew with Charles Lindbergh over the central and eastern parts of the Yucatan Peninsula; in the process he discovered more than half a dozen new sites. In the following year Percy Madeira led an aerial expedition over a somewhat wider area, recording several new sites as well as a number of unmapped lakes. On the other hand, one well-known and precisely located large site—Yaxchilán—could not be detected, even from as close as 150 feet! To this day, however, large Maya sites continue to be discovered by airline and private pilots flying over the area. Air reconnaissance has also been useful more recently in searching for differential tree-growth patterns that may indicate such extensive

Figure 5.18 Although Mirador (arrows) is known to be a large and imposing site, it barely disturbs the rainforest canopy, illustrating the difficulty of finding sites in such a forested environment. (© University of Pennsylvania Museum—Fairchild Aerial Surveys Photo.)

features as causeways and canals. The recent discoveries of remains of intensive agriculture (raised fields and terracing) that have altered previous conceptions of the tropical environmental adaptations of the Maya have been largely due to aerial photography.

As a result of several centuries of sporadic exploration and perhaps a century of serious archaeological reconnaissance, hundreds of Maya sites have been identified and located. However, as one might expect with basically nonprobabilistic sampling, most of these are large sites located within traveled areas, and they were discovered because of their prominence and accessibility. There is little doubt that more Maya sites remain undiscovered in the areas of Petén that are most inaccessible. The case of Mirador illustrates the problem; one of the largest of all Maya sites, it is located in an almost unknown region of northern Petén. Mirador was first reported by the Madeira air reconnaissance expedition of 1930 (Fig. 5.18). But because of the site's inaccessibility, few archaeologists and explorers visited it in succeeding years, and even the ones who tried could not always locate it. On the other hand, it is probable that the vast majority of the smaller Maya sites—representing the villages and farmsteads of the ancient population that once sustained the larger elite centers—have not been documented. We know of their existence primarily because in a few cases fairly large areas of the jungle have been deliberately cleared to locate such sites. For instance, during the archaeological research at Tikal, the largest known Maya site, a series of four transects, roughly cardinally oriented and about 500 m wide, were searched for a distance of up to 12 km from the site core to document the distribution of Maya occupation. Numerous sites were found as a result, representing individual houses, house clusters (compounds), hamlets, and even small specialized centers that perhaps once served as markets or religious areas. Although this reconnaissance still represents a non-probabilistic sample—the areas sampled were not selected by probabilistic procedures—it does indicate the amount and variety of archaeological remains that previous attempts at reconnaissance have missed.

*Probabilistic Sampling

Probabilistic sampling attempted in Maya lowland reconnaissance

We may conclude from the above example that if future reconnaissance in the Maya lowlands were based upon attempts to secure controlled samples, the results would yield a more representative picture of Maya sites, exposing the full range from the largest to the smallest. The work of Don Rice, involving randomly placed transects of equal length radiating from Lakes Yaxhá and Sacnab, is the most promising research in this direction to date. The results of such studies allow the investigators to project not only the total number of sites in the study area, but also such things as the proper proportion of smaller (satellite) sites to the larger centers. Thus, for example, a 20 percent controlled sample within a given universe (perhaps a single drainage basin in the Petén) that identified 10 sites (9 satellites and 1 larger center) would allow the archaeologist to project a total data pool of 50 sites (45 satellites and 5 larger centers) within their study area. Of course, statistical manipulations such as these are based upon probability theory and are accurate only within certain tolerance limits or ranges of error.

In Chapter 3 we noted that archaeologists are still testing the relative efficacy of various schemes of probabilistic sampling. Reconnaissance sampling is one of the most common areas for such testing. In this process, archaeologists take a universe that has been reconnoitered with total coverage and subject it to a series of simulated reconnaissance forays in order to assess which sampling techniques are the most accurate and economical. In one such experiment, James Mueller compared the information gained from 326 simulated reconnaissance surveys with actual 1967–68 research on the Paria Plateau of northern Arizona. In the actual research, an area of 85¼ mi² was covered and 498 sites recorded. The probabilistic sampling schemes Mueller used were simple random, stratified, systematic, cluster, and *vector;* the vector pattern is a random transect sample comparable to the path of a ball on a billiard table. He tested these against several nonprobabilistic schemes. He also varied the size and shape of the sample unit (1 mi² versus ¼ mi² quadrats with some limited use of the transect, in the vector scheme) and the sampling fraction. Although cluster sampling was argued to be the most economical, stratified proportional sampling gave the most accurate

Probabilistic sampling experiments: James Mueller on the Paria Plateau, Arizona; Stephen Plog in Oaxaca, Mexico

results; a sampling fraction of 0.4 was found to be the optimal size and the 1 mi² quadrat the best sample unit.

At about the same time, Stephen Plog was comparing simulated reconnaissance with actual work in the Oaxaca Valley in Mexico. Here the overall population, in 3 survey blocks, was 71 sites in 127 km². Plog too used simple random, stratified, and systematic sampling, as well as *stratified systematic unaligned* sampling, in which the position of the sample unit within the interval is varied to avoid the problem of periodicity. Both transects and quadrats were tested, but sampling fraction was consistently 0.1. For nearly all conditions, 100 tests were run on the computer—a total of more than 3200 simulated surveys. The results showed, again, that stratified sampling was the most consistently efficient in locating a sample of sites (although its superiority was not statistically significant); in Plog's research optimum results were gained using relatively small transects as sampling units.

On the other hand, Mueller and Plog were testing different specific hypotheses, and details of their results suggest interesting problem areas. Also, as Flannery notes in an addendum to Plog's paper, local conditions sometimes override these considerations altogether: for example, transect sampling may be the only choice in a jungle situation. Both authors conclude that probabilistic sampling is worthwhile, but that no simple rules for it exist.

PLOTTING THE LOCATION
OF ARCHAEOLOGICAL SITES

Discovery is only half the task of reconnaissance. The other half is recording the location of the sites encountered. The central objective of recording is to relate the new finds to their spatial setting, to place the previously unknown within the realm of the known. Usually, but not always, this involves plotting on preexisting maps or aerial photographs. Sometimes base maps may be specially drawn up for reconnaissance purposes; but since most reconnaissance uses preexisting maps, we shall confine discussion here to that circumstance. Techniques for mapmaking will be discussed in Chapter 6.

Some circumstances may occur under which location cannot be recorded on maps. Verbal descriptions of location and means of access can be an adequate record, but they inevitably lack the graphic explicitness afforded by map plots. A picture *is* worth a thousand words in relating the distribution of archaeological remains to the distribution of other features of the natural and cultural environment. Nonetheless, in cases in which maps do not exist or cannot be taken along during reconnaissance, verbal descriptions can be used. Even when maps are used, supplemental verbal data—notes on road conditions, local friendliness or hostility, and so on—can be handy in regaining access. As a minimum, the description should relate the discovered remains to known, permanent features that are easy to locate. Rivers, towns, roads, and—where available—surveyors' benchmarks are examples of reference points. The archaeologist should bear in mind, however, that landscapes change; sites have been "lost" when their verbal reference points were destroyed. "East of and adjacent to Highway 66, three miles north of the sawmill" is a useful (if imprecise) description only so long as Highway 66 and the sawmill continue to exist or to be remembered. Even formal benchmarks may be removed: local inhabitants have been known to dig these up in order to "salvage" the steel spikes or other materials involved. And benchmarks are, of course, subject to the same erosion or burial processes as any archaeological feature or site. As a general rule, the more locational data supplied, the greater the chance that the site can be found again.

In addition to the reference points, one must give the distance and direction from them to the archaeological remains, specifying how these measurements were made. It is possible to determine latitude and longitude during reconnaissance, but the procedures involved are technical and often not within the competence of archaeologists. (We do not mean to discourage archaeologists from learning to make the appropriate observations, but since maps with such information are usually available, we shall not describe them here.)

Location is most commonly recorded by plotting on maps or aerial photos. Aerial photos with vertical coverage and maps made from them are frequently available for the area of interest. Sometimes archaeological sites may already be indicated on the maps or be visible on the photos. This lessens the archaeologist's work somewhat, but it is not a substitute for checking the "ground truth" of the marked features. The date of the base map or photo can be important here: since that date, new roads may have been built or old ones overgrown, sites may have been obliterated, cultivated crops may have changed. In addition, magnetic north is constantly changing; the rate and direction is usually marked on the map, but any location system that uses magnetic bearings must take this factor into account. Since ground-pattern clues, reference points, and even the archaeological data might have been altered since publication of a map or photo, it is wise to be aware of the recent—as well as the long-term—history of the study area. The corollary to this observation, of course, is that the more numerous the maps and photos the archaeologist has available, and the more varied the dates they represent, the larger the fund of potential information or clues they will give about the study area.

The scale of maps used for plotting is usually between 1:5000 and 1:25,000, but, depending on the thoroughness of reconnaissance and the scale of the remains sought, it can be much smaller. The Diyala Basin Archaeological Project in Iraq, for example, used both air photos and maps at a scale of 1:50,000; in seven months, during 1958–59, more than 850 sites were examined in a region of approximately 8000 km². To be useful during reconnaissance, map sheets are often cut to a portable size and mounted on a board or similar hard surface. Alternatively, they can be stiffened with starch or paste and made foldable for ease in field manipulation. A plastic covering can provide protection from rain or dirt. When an archaeological site is encountered, its position is plotted—with a hard pencil, to lessen smearing but allow erasure—by noting its distance and direction from one or (preferably) more reference points. Bearings to reference points are usually determined from a compass. More accurate instruments, such as a surveyor's transit, may be used, but these are bulky. Distance from a single reference point can be taped, paced, estimated or determined by a range finder. If at least two reference points are used, such as hilltops, and if they are far enough from the site and from each other, triangulation will give the site's location exactly. To determine location by triangulation, the bearings of the compass readings to the reference points are plotted on the map; they will intersect at the point of observation—that is, at the location of the site. The accuracy of these procedures, of course, depends upon the accuracy of the base map, the compass, and the compass readings as well as the separation and distance of the reference points involved. At Quiriguá, for instance, both the built-in error of the base map and the small size of the reconnaissance zone precluded use of this system for site plotting. In the Virú Valley Project in Peru, a pioneer effort to locate and map all sites within a single valley, air photo sheets were mounted on the lowered windshield of the project's jeep. This procedure not only provided a stable plotting surface, it was also a help against getting lost: the jeep could be aligned with the ''north'' of the photos and photo reference points sought by looking in line with their position on the car hood. The match between base map and ''ground truth'' was so vivid in this case that one of the workmen claimed he could watch the jeep move across the photo as reconnaissance progressed!

At the end of each day's or week's work, the field plots should be transferred to a base map, usually located at the project's field headquarters. The latter copy provides a complete record of the reconnaissance as well as insurance against loss of the field plots. Also, the base-camp copy often represents a larger area—either a large, uncut original map, or a mosaic of smaller original sheets—on which overall progress can be gauged and emergent distributional patterns examined.

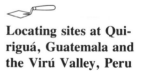

Locating sites at Quiriguá, Guatemala and the Virú Valley, Peru

Along with plotting its location, the archaeologist must give each site a label. Numbers are easiest; they may run in a single consecutive series or be subdivided and coded to indicate location; for example, each grid square or map sheet might have an independent series. Letters alone are less satisfactory labels, since they are exhausted very quickly and one must then resort to double letters ("AA") or different alphabets (such as Greek) or the like. Names can be descriptive and easy to remember, but they also tend to be more cumbersome than numbers for data analysis. The whole point of labelling is to tie the locational data to other information—physical descriptions of the remains, surface collections taken, drawings, maps, and photographs made, later excavations conducted, and so forth. Much of this information may be recorded at the same time as the reconnaissance activity. But reconnaissance, as defined at the beginning of this chapter, is essentially the discovery and location of archaeological sites. The collection of other kinds of data falls under other headings—survey and excavation—and will be discussed in later chapters.

SUMMARY

In this chapter we have outlined methods and techniques for discovering and locating archaeological sites. Each approach has its own set of advantages and disadvantages. Ground reconnaissance is the oldest and the most thorough way to identify sites that have surface manifestations, but it is often slow and in most cases cannot detect buried sites. Aerial reconnaissance provides rapid coverage of wide areas; in addition it is perhaps the best way of detecting buried sites, provided some surface indications exist. However, aerial reconnaissance may not detect all sites, and it may fail to distinguish smaller ones. Subsurface detection is perhaps the slowest and most cumbersome means of site identification; its coverage area is the most limited. Nonetheless, it may be the only choice in situations where deeply buried sites exist. No single technique can guarantee success, but by learning as much as possible about the search area prior to reconnaissance, the archaeologist can design a program that combines methods to provide the highest probability of success. If total coverage of the reconnaissance universe is impractical, the archaeologist should choose sampling techniques that will maximize the extent to which data from the actual reconnaissance may be generalized. No matter what discovery or sampling techniques are used, the spatial location of the archaeological remains must be recorded. Other information may be recorded at the same time, but discovery and geographical location are the essential aspects of reconnaissance.

See p. 572 for "Suggestions for Further Reading."

An important aspect of surface survey is the collection and recording of surface artifacts.

Surface Survey

Of the three of us, Vay (Sylvanus G. Morley) was the only one who knew what an archaeological survey was all about. It should, he said, be a stocktaking of all the remains in an area and their description in the form of notes, plans, and photographs in as full detail as possible without excavation.

(From A. V. Kidder's journal written during E. G. Hewett's Colorado Plateau expedition, 1907)

Now that we have described the way archaeological sites are identified and located, we shall consider the specific methods used to acquire archaeological data. Two basic methods are used for the acquisition of archaeological data: surface survey and excavation. We will describe the first of these methods in this chapter, and consider excavation in Chapter 7.

OBJECTIVES OF SURFACE SURVEY

Surface survey refers to a variety of methods used by archaeologists to acquire data from sites without excavation. The overall objective of surface survey is to determine as much as possible about a given site or area from observable remains and from what can be detected beneath the ground without excavation. The archaeologist uses surface survey methods to gather data that represent as much as possible of the full range of variation present in the data universe.

The next section will describe the specific methods used by the archaeologist to conduct surface surveys. And later in the chapter we will discuss the problems inherent in this kind of research, including the question of the reliability of surface-acquired data. But first we will consider the specific kinds of data sought in surface surveys.

The way surface survey is conducted in a given situation depends on the nature of the site or area involved and on the kind of data being gathered. To begin with, in surface surveys archaeologists attempt to detect and record surface features at their location. Many substantial archaeological features, such as the remains of ancient buildings, walls, roads, and canals, exist on the present ground surface where they can be detected by direct observation. Features so preserved are recorded in surface survey by mapping; the techniques used will be described later in this chapter. On the other hand, buried archaeological features may not be directly detectable from the surface. In some cases these buried remains can be located and mapped by one or more of the remote sensing methods described in Chapter 5. For example, the mapping of Sybaris was done in this manner.

Surface surveys also include detection and recording of artifacts and ecofacts. When these kinds of archaeological remains are found on the surface, their provenience is recorded and then, because they are portable, they are usually collected and taken to a field laboratory for processing and later analysis. Like features, artifacts and ecofacts are sometimes buried beneath the surface; unlike features, they cannot usually be detected by remote sensors. In some cases mechanical probes, such as the augers and corers discussed in Chapter 5, can be used to determine whether or not artifacts or ecofacts are present below ground. But such probes were not primarily designed to recover this kind of evidence; they yield only limited samples of small items. As a rule, recovery of buried artifacts and ecofacts in useful quantities must await archaeological excavation.

A surface survey may be conducted at the same time as archaeological reconnaissance. In some cases the objectives of both can be met most efficiently by combining reconnaissance and survey into a single operation. This is especially true if the same sample units can be used for site identification and for the acquisition of surface data. But in other situations these objectives may have to be pursued separately. For instance, a particular investigation may undertake total coverage of its data universe to identify and locate sites, but only have the resources to cover a sample of the universe for the gathering of surface data.

Whether or not it is combined with reconnaissance, surface survey is, in most research situations, an essential complement to subsequent excavation. It *is* possible to conduct archaeological research by gathering data solely by surface survey methods. These methods may be the only alternative when research time and money are limited, especially when relatively small-scale projects investigate large regions or complex sites. In other cases, difficulties in securing the necessary permissions may preclude excavation as a means of acquiring data. Whatever the reasons, productive archaeological research can be conducted by relying on surface survey for data gathering. As an example, let us consider the Teotihuacán Mapping Project of the University of Rochester, which was designed to emphasize surface investigations.

Surface survey at Teotihuacán, Mexico

Famous among tourists as well as archaeologists, Teotihuacán is a complex pre-Columbian urban site located in a semiarid side valley of the Valley of Mexico, northeast of modern Mexico City. The population of Teotihuacán reached its peak in the period A.D. 0–700, when 150,000 or more people lived there. In part because of the overall size of the ancient city, no comprehensive, detailed map of the site had ever been made. Yet such a map should be a prerequisite for studies of the city's growth and decline and of the distribution of the presumably numerous activities carried on there. Fortunately, Teotihuacán

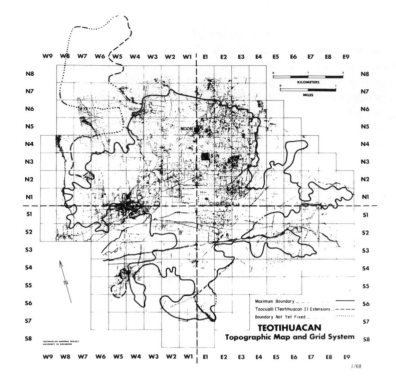

Figure 6.1 Overall
archaeological map of
Teotihuacán, Mexico,
originally published
at 1:10,000. (From
*Urbanization at
Teotihuacán, Mexico,*
vol. 1, *The Teotihuacán
Map,* copyright © 1973
by René Millon,
all rights reserved.)

lends itself well to surface inquiry, for archaeological materials tend to be at or near surface level, and, in contrast to the *tells* and *tepes* of the Near East, the discrete structures and courts that make up the city remain individually perceptible. With all these factors in mind, René Millon and his associates designed a program that coordinated mapping and surface collections to record the pre-Columbian metropolis. Archaeological reconnaissance was the first step, covering an area of about 53 km² with aerial photographs and maps (Fig. 6.1) as guides. The reconnaissance operation defined the limits of the aboriginal city (Fig. 6.1); the 20 km² within these limits then became the principal focus of intensive mapping and surface collections. More than 5000 structural units and activity areas were recorded. Some excavations were conducted to test survey-derived interpretations, but the primary thrust of research was toward surface survey. The resulting published maps (Fig. 6.2) and accompanying verbal descriptions contain a wealth of archaeological data that will be mined by archaeologists for decades to come.

Despite such research efforts, surface survey remains most commonly a valuable and necessary prelude to excavation. Surface survey methods are used to gather data that can guide subsequent archaeological research; whether this information is necessarily reliable is a question we shall examine later.

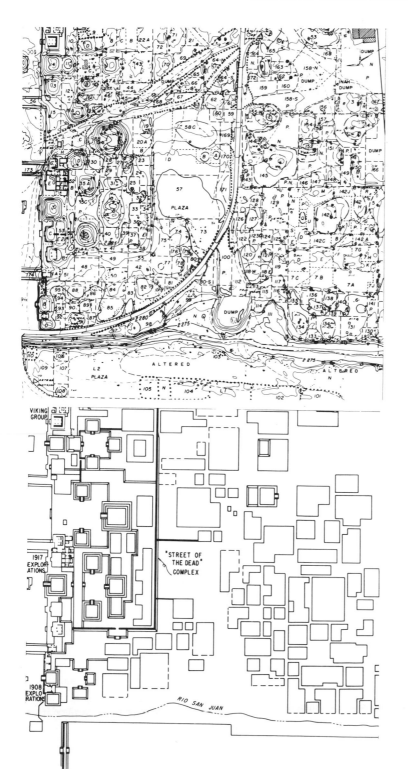

Figure 6.2 Detailed pair of archaeological maps (originally published at 1:2000) representing one grid square of the map in Fig. 6.1: (a) records topographic and archaeological information and (b) provides the archaeological interpretation of that information. (From *Urbanization at Teotihuacán, Mexico,* vol. 1, *The Teotihuacán Map,* copyright © 1973 by René Millon, all rights reserved.)

METHODS OF SURFACE SURVEY

The following discussion of surface survey considers two basic methods: ground survey and remote sensing. Each of these methods involves several different techniques.

Ground Survey

Ground survey encompasses techniques of direct observation used to gather archaeological data present on the ground surface. By "direct observation" we mean walking the site or sites under investigation in order to detect and record whatever surface artifacts, ecofacts, and features may be present. Archaeologists use one body of survey techniques to record surface features and another for surface artifacts. The first set consists of mapping techniques; the second involves surface collections. Insofar as the spatial *arrangement* of artifacts and ecofacts can be considered a feature (being non-portable) it too is subject to mapping; surface features, however, are by definition *not* subject to collection.

Recording Surface Features: Maps

A map is a scaled symbolic representation of a segment of the earth's surface as viewed from above; it is a two-dimensional rendering of a three-dimensional reality. Archaeologists use two basic kinds of maps: planimetric maps and topographic maps (Fig. 6.3). Archaeological *planimetric maps* depict archaeological features (buildings, walls, tombs, or whatever) without indicating relief or other topo-

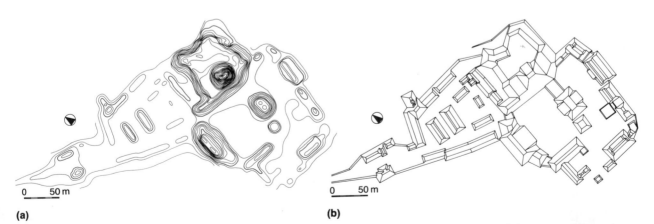

0   50 m

(a)

0   50 m

(b)

Figure 6.3 Comparison of information conveyed by (a) topographic and (b) planimetric archaeological maps of the same site, Nohmul, Belize. (Courtesy of Norman Hammond.)

graphic data. *Topographic maps,* on the other hand, show not only archaeological remains but also the three-dimensional aspects of land forms, using conventionalized symbols such as contour lines or hachures. In addition to depicting relief, topographic maps usually contain symbols for vegetation, for hydrographic features such as rivers, springs, and lakes, and for modern cultural features such as roads and buildings.

Both kinds of maps must contain a scale, expressed either as a numerical ratio (such as 1:200) or in graphic representation (see Fig. 6.3). Although most topographic maps give scales in both the metric and English systems, nearly all archaeological work is now done in the metric system. The English system remains particularly useful for work at sites such as those of British colonial North America, where the original inhabitants measured in yards, feet, and inches. In most situations, however, archaeologists use the metric system, for purposes of standardization and comparability of recording.

Maps also indicate orientation information—often an arrow pointing north—and usually include the survey date and magnetic declination information.

Functions of Maps.   The archaeologist uses maps in a variety of ways, from working data sheets in reconnaissance work to finished summaries of settlement and structural patterns in published reports. They are a compact and effective means of storing a great deal of archaeological data. But the function and utility of a particular map for the archaeologist depends both on the kind of information the map presents and on the scale to which it is drawn. The map scale is critical, since it determines the amount and detail of data that can be presented on a map. Our discussion of map functions will consider three broad uses, each defined in part by ranges of scale.

Regional Maps.   Regional maps are designed to depict archaeological sites within their local environmental setting (region). They are especially important in presenting the relationship of the site to hydrographic and physiographic features. The optimum scale for the map depends, of course, on the numbers and sizes of sites being depicted, but regional maps are generally small in scale (1:10,000 to 1:50,000). Because of their function, they do not attempt to depict individual archaeological sites or features in any detail. Sites are usually just indicated by triangles, circles, or other simple symbols. It is normally beyond the means of most archaeologists to prepare regional maps "from scratch" because they cover such extensive areas; however, existing topographic maps can usually be adapted for this purpose (see Fig. 3.7, an example of a regional map).

Site Maps. Site maps depict archaeological sites in detail. They normally serve as the basic record of all surface archaeological features, as well as of relevant physiographic and hydrographic data, as these things appear at the beginning of investigation. Site maps also indicate the site grid system used to designate and record archaeological features and other data. Limits to areas investigated, such as sample areas for surface collections or areas excavated, are often marked on site maps. Scales vary according to individual cases, but they range from about 1:1000 to 1:5000. Site maps may be purely topographic, with both natural and archaeological features indicated by the same conventionalized symbols, such as contours or hachures (Fig. 6.3a). On the other hand, a distinction may be made, with only the natural relief shown by contours or hachures and archaeological features depicted in distinct symbols (see Fig. 6.3b).

Site Plans. Site plans are used to show details of site components, usually archaeological features such as buildings, tombs, walls, and so forth. They are almost always planimetric, emphasizing only the relevant feature and its constituent parts (Fig. 6.4). Because they show great detail, these are relatively large-scale maps, generally 1:250 or larger. In many cases site plans are used to present the results of excavation, by first presenting a plan of the feature before excavation, then depicting the same feature after excavation. This is especially useful in cases of superimposed construction; often a complex sequence of constructional activity can be clearly recorded only by a series of plans, each corresponding to a single stage in construction. Site plans will be discussed in Chapter 7 when we consider the recording of excavation data.

Preparing Archaeological Maps. For regional maps the archaeologist can often use available topographic maps at suitable scales as base maps. A regional map can be prepared simply by adding the relevant archaeological data. But seldom, if ever, will the archaeologist find pre-existing maps of suitable quality and adequate scale to serve as site maps. And because scientific standards change and objectives differ, even archaeologists who re-investigate a site that has already been mapped may find previous maps inadequate for their needs. In other cases, good-quality, large-scale maps are available, as for an archaeological site located within or adjacent to a modern town or city that is itself well mapped. But even if these maps contain accurate data, such as contour information, that make them useful as base maps, they seldom contain sufficient archaeological detail. In such cases the archaeologist can use the existing map as a base map, simply plotting the location of archaeological features on it.

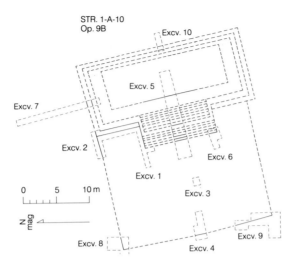

STR. 1-A-10
Op. 9B

Excv. 10

Excv. 5

Excv. 7

Excv. 2

Excv. 6

Excv. 1

0   5   10 m

Excv. 3

N mag

Excv. 8

Excv. 9

Excv. 4

Figure 6.4 Plan of a masonry structure. Solid lines indicate walls and platforms revealed in excavations or visible on the surface; broken lines represent extensions from known architecture to complete the stucture. Excavation limits are also shown. (Drawing by Diane Z. Chase.)

Preparation of a site map is the first field priority in any archaeological investigation, for the map will serve as the basic spatial control in all records of provenience. In addition to both archaeological and topographic features, the site map must indicate the location of source areas of surface collections and the limits to all excavations. In many cases the site map will control the selection of probabilistic samples, with units based on either archaeological criteria (such as features) or arbitrary criteria (grid systems).

Because archaeologists usually must create their own site maps, we shall describe the basic steps in the process, beginning with the determination of a site datum and grid.

Site Datum Points and Grids. The first step in making a site map is to establish a control point or *site datum*. The site datum is a well-marked, permanent feature with known location and elevation. It is often the highest point in the area, but it certainly cannot be a point that subsequent excavation will remove. A pre-existing datum point, such as a surveyor's benchmark, may be used if available. If no such known control point is convenient to the site, a permanent feature such as a rock outcrop or a solid concrete building foundation can be marked or engraved to serve as a site datum. Alternatively, a non-magnetic (bronze) rod may be set in the ground and encased in concrete. In selecting a site datum, the archaeologist should keep in mind that work will be simplified if the control point has clear lines of sight in all directions. If the location and elevation of the site datum are not known, they must be determined as accurately as possible. This is usually done by triangulation (see Chapter 5) using a surveyor's transit, which is set up over the site datum and used to take bearings on at

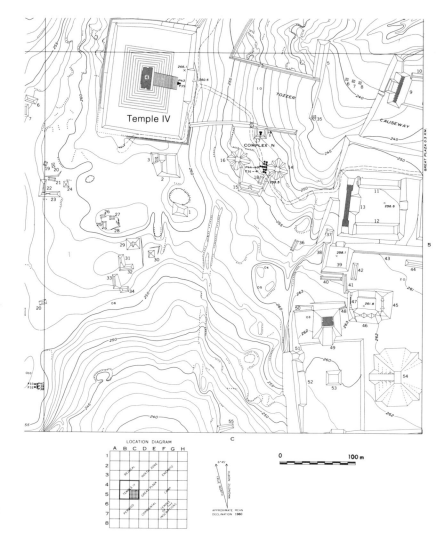

Figure 6.5 Grid square 5C from the Tikal, Guatemala site map, a planimetric and topographic map originally published at 1:2000. The center point of Temple IV is located 130 m east and 40 m south from the northwest corner of the grid. This grid square is located within the overall map in the diagram below. (From Carr and Hazard 1961.)

least two known points such as distant benchmarks or geographic features. Elevation can also be determined by the transit from a known elevation point.

Once established, the site datum is used to lay out a site grid. The site grid is a coordinate system for recording the precise location of any point. It is a simplified, small-scale version of the geographic coordinate system—degrees, minutes, and seconds of longitude and latitude—used to locate points on the earth's surface. In an archaeological site grid, lines running north-south (meridians) and east-west (base lines) are laid out at regular intervals. Each grid square receives a designation. Thus any point within a square can be located by recording the distance in meters or centimeters north (or south) of the base line and east (or west) of the meridian (see Fig. 6.5).

It is usually most convenient to use magnetic north as an orientation for the site grid, and for all future surveying, so that compass readings made in the field will need no correction. Some researchers prefer to use true north, which can be determined from the local declination angle and its annual rate of change; this information may be printed on the regional base maps or available from other sources. If true north is to be the standard, all surveying instruments with compasses must be set to the same declination. In either case, the map and all other appropriate records must clearly indicate the kind of north reference being used for mapping. Sometimes cardinal orientation of the site grid is not practical: in a narrow cave site, for example, the grid is often aligned to the axis of the cave.

The site grid is laid out by setting up the transit over the site datum, or, if this is not convenient, over an alternate known point. The meridian line is established by shooting a north (0°) bearing to a point beyond the limits of the site (if possible). This point is marked, usually with a heavy stake. Similar stakes are placed at regular intervals along the meridian; each of these corresponds to the intersection of an east-west grid line. Thus, if the site is being divided into grid squares 10 meters on a side, a stake can be placed every 10 meters along the north meridian and permanently marked (N10, N20, N30, etc.). These distances must be accurately determined; it is best to measure each interval with a steel tape. Once the north meridian is established, the transit's telescopic sight is flipped over so that it is aligned 180° from the first bearing, and a south line is staked in the same manner. Once the north-south meridian has been laid out, the transit base plate and telescope are turned exactly 90° to either east or west, and the procedure is repeated to lay out and stake the east-west base line. If the research objectives and the data acquisition methods require it, these procedures can be repeated to locate and stake out each meridian and base line until each grid intersection point is marked with a stake designated as to its location (N10E10, N10E20, etc.). A site must usually be completely staked when the grid system is used to define sample units, such as surface collection areas.

With the establishment of the site grid, a designation system must be selected. Several kinds of grid designations are commonly used by archaeologists, but the basic choice is between a two-component system (letter/number symbols, as in "A3") and a four-component system (cardinal direction/number symbols, as in "N1E4"). The two-component system is simpler—an advantage when the grid designation system is used to record the provenience of every feature and artifact. Since only half as many symbols need be written on each item, they are easier to fit on small items and misrecording is less likely. On the other hand, the four-component system records the grid's cardinal location, so that a given designation immediately gives an approximate location within the site.

If the limits of the site are known to the archaeologist, a finite grid can be used. As Figure 6.5 shows, a two-component designation can be used with a finite grid, with each east-west line corresponding to a letter and each north-south line corresponding to a number. Thus the grid square adjacent to the site datum is designated "A/1." A point within this grid square may be located as "(A)4.6/(1)2.7", which means 4.6 m north of the "A" base line and 2.7 m east of the "1" meridian line. The same finite grid could receive a four-component designation in which the grid square adjacent to the site datum point would be designated "N1/E1." Location of any point within the square can be determined and recorded as before: (N1)4.6/(E1)2.7. Note that a finite grid can be expanded away from the datum point in only two directions. For this reason, a finite grid should be used only when site limits are firmly established, since the system has no capacity for expansion if the site boundaries are later found to extend beyond the original grid.

In most archaeological situations the limits of a site are not known prior to investigation. For this reason an infinite grid designation system is usually preferable. The most common form of an infinite grid is the *union grid,* an expansion in all four cardinal directions of the four-component designation system just described (see Figs. 6.1 and 6.2). A two-component infinite grid can be created by alternating the letters and numbers designating each meridian and base line, as shown in Fig. 6.6.

Mapmaking Methods. There are four basic methods for making archaeological maps; we will discuss each of these. The intent is not to present a step-by-step manual on mapmaking, but rather to evaluate the usefulness of each method to the archaeologist.

Sketch Maps. The simplest maps, and the quickest ones to make, are sketch maps (Fig. 6.7). Sketch maps are impressionistic renderings made without instruments. They are often made during feasibility studies or archaeological reconnaissance efforts in order to record graphically the general characteristics of a site. In this role sketch maps can be valuable supplements to written descriptions and photographs. However, sketch maps do not have a uniform scale, do not depict the topography, and cannot accurately delineate the forms or relationships of archaeological features; for these reasons their use-

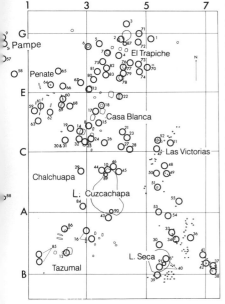

Figure 6.6 Two-component infinite-grid map, showing surface features (light outlines) and surface-survey locations (numbered circles). (From Sharer 1978.)

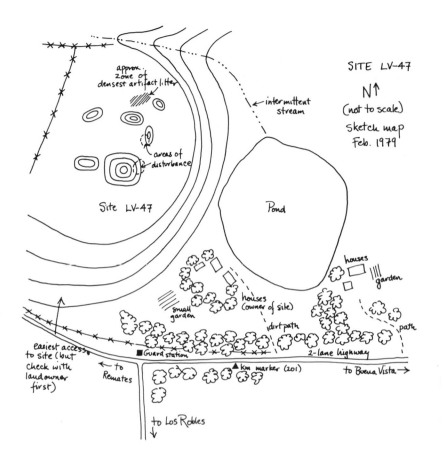

SITE LV-47

N↑
(not to scale)

Sketch map
Feb. 1979

approx.
zone of
densest artifact litter

← intermittent
stream

areas of
disturbance

Site LV-47

Pond

houses

garden

houses
(owner of site)

small
garden

dirt path

path

2-lane highway

■ Guard station

▲ km marker (201)

easiest access
to site (but
check with
landowner
first)

← to
Remates

to Buena Vista →

to Los Robles
↓

Figure 6.7 Sketch map, made without instruments, recording both surface features and other useful information.

fulness is limited. They represent a preliminary record, but they should always be replaced by more accurate mapping as research progresses.

Compass Maps. The use of surveying instruments allows the archaeologist to make much more accurate maps. The most basic instrument usually available to the archaeologist is a good quality magnetic compass. A lensatic compass (such as military surplus types) is adequate for direction-finding and for taking reasonably accurate bearings in order to locate sites. The best compass for all-around use, including mapmaking, is the Brunton pocket transit. This compass can be adapted to a tripod mount, allowing it to be used as a stable and accurate instrument for taking bearings.

The first step in making a compass map is to choose mapping stations—one or more points with clear lines of sight to as many parts of the site as possible. These stations are first located by taking bearings

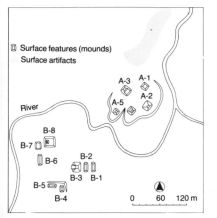

⊡ Surface features (mounds)
Surface artifacts

Figure 6.8 Compass map, accurately recording planimetric information without depicting topographic relief. (After Sedat and Sharer 1972.)

Mapmaking at Tikal, Guatemala

to known points (triangulation) and then plotted on scaled metric graph paper. If the site grid has been staked, the staked points may be used as mapping stations or reference points. Once the first mapping station is located and plotted, compass bearings are taken to the various features that are to be mapped, and the distance from the mapping station to each of these points is determined—either by pacing or, more accurately, by measurement with a steel tape. To plot the points, the bearings are marked with a protractor and the distances measured with a scaled straightedge.

The use of compass and tape is the fastest method of making a reasonably accurate planimetric map (Fig. 6.8). However, this method is not as efficient or accurate for measuring differences in elevation, so it is usually not preferred for making topographic maps. Although instruments such as the Brunton compass are indispensable to the archaeologist, they should be used for mapmaking only when more accurate instruments are not available. Realistically, there will always be cases in which lack of time or money precludes the use of accurate mapmaking instruments such as the alidade or transit. Such instruments are also much more cumbersome to transport on a foot survey, and they take longer to set up at each station. Therefore good quality compasses, especially the tripod-mounted Brunton, remain valuable alternative devices for mapping. In some cases compass-and-tape methods have been used to extend the coverage provided by more accurate instrument mapping. At the huge site of Tikal, Guatemala, the central area—9 km²—was mapped by plane table and alidade over a period of four field seasons. Another 7 km² surrounding the central area, a set of 28 squares each 500 m on a side, was mapped by compass and tape during the fourth season.

Aerial Photographic Maps.   A common means for producing a reasonably accurate planimetric map is to trace ground features directly from an aerial photograph. Of course the usefulness of such a map depends on the scale of the photograph; many aerial photographs are at too small a scale to be useful for site maps. On the other hand, photographic traces are often of great help as base maps in reconnaissance efforts and surveys that cover wide areas. Other factors besides scale also affect the quality of this kind of map, including the accurate identification of ground features on aerial photographs and the quality of the photographs themselves. Every camera lens produces distortions, which increase toward the edges of the photograph; thus features traced from the edges of an aerial photograph will always be less accurately rendered than those traced from the photograph's center. In addition, in many situations archaeological features are not detectable on aerial photographs. And finally, these traced maps are always planimetric rather than topographic.

Of course, aerial photographs can be used to produce accurate contour information; most modern topographic maps are made from aerial photos. This method, using stereo photographs of the ground surface, requires sophisticated cartographic equipment that is beyond the reach of most archaeologists. In some cases, however, larger archaeological projects have been able to secure professional cartographic assistance to produce topographic site maps from aerial photographs. One example of this is provided by the Teotihuacán Mapping Project, discussed at the beginning of this chapter (see Fig. 6.1). This case illustrates the fact that with very large and complex archaeological sites, aerial photography is often the most efficient means of making topographic site maps, provided the extra cost is not an insurmountable obstacle. Of course, if this method is to be useful archaeologically, the aerial coverage must be at a sufficiently large scale and the site in question must be clear of obscuring vegetation. Furthermore, the features to be mapped must be readily detectable on aerial photographs. At Tikal, the size and complexity of the site led to an attempt to supplement ground-based instrument mapping by use of aerial photographs. In this case, however, the dense jungle growth covering most of the site made the method ineffectual.

Mapping with Surveyors' Instruments.   The preferred method for making archaeological maps involves either or both of two basic kinds of surveyors' instruments: the *transit,* or *theodolite,* or the *plane table and alidade.* Generally speaking, the transit or theodolite is the more accurate instrument for taking bearings and measuring angles; for this reason it is often preferred for making planimetric maps and site plans. On the other hand, the plane table and alidade are much more efficient in measuring and recording both elevations and distances, and are therefore preferred for making topographic maps, especially site maps. Whatever instrument is chosen, the archaeologist must have some basic surveying equipment and supplies. A smooth drawing surface is essential. The plane table provides a portable drafting surface for the map, which is usually drawn on a transparent plastic film such as Mylar. If a transit is used, the map is usually plotted, from data recorded in the surveyor's book, on gridded metric paper, either in the field on a portable drawing board or back at the field laboratory on a drafting table. To produce precise, unsmudged lines, the map is drawn with a straightedge, an accurate metric scale, and a mechanical or wooden pencil with a hard, sharp lead point. Other equipment needs vary with the method used; they may include a good quality protractor, a drawing triangle, and a steel metric tape.

The surveyors' transit (Fig. 6.9) consists of a telescope that can be elevated or depressed, fixed to a baseplate and compass that can be rotated 360°. The baseplate is graduated so that any angle can be mea-

Figure 6.9 Field recording of planimetric and topographic information by surveyor's transit.

sured in degrees and minutes. The instrument is mounted on a rotating head attached to a tripod; with the aid of a plumb bob or sighting device, the transit can be positioned directly over a known point. Once firmly positioned and leveled (some instruments are now automatic), the transit can be used to sight and record precise bearings to distant points by centering the vertical cross-hair of the telescope on a rod or plumb line held by an assistant. The telescope also contains horizontal stadia hairs for determining distance using the marked intervals on a stadia rod. When the transit is used in combination with a stadia rod, the central horizontal sighting hair can be used to determine the elevation of a distant point. This is determined by recording the difference between the elevation of the instrument scope and the height of the stadia rod's base (see Fig. 7.21); combining this difference with the instrument's elevation yields the elevation of the sighted point. Thus the transit can determine the bearing, distance, and elevation of any given point. These data are recorded in a surveyor's notebook according to a standard format. Because data obtained by transit survey must later be translated from the record book to map paper, transit mapping is a slow process, especially if elevation data are being recorded. Thus the transit, though more accurate for planimetric work, is less efficient than the plane table and alidade for preparation of contour maps.

The plane table is a stable drawing board mounted on a tripod with a universal swivel head. A map sheet—usually plastic drafting film such as Mylar—is fixed to the plane table. The alidade, like the transit, consists of a telescope fitted with both crosshairs and stadia hairs. But in contrast to the transit, the alidade is not fixed to a tripod: the telescope is mounted on a plate with a straightedge, and the whole rests on the plane table and is free to move across its surface. Once the plane table is level, a line is drawn bisecting the map sheet. The blade or straightedge of the alidade is then set against this bisecting line and the plane table rotated until the alidade's compass (and with it, the alidade blade and map line) aligns with magnetic north. Next, the instrument station is marked on the map. With the alidade straightedge bisected by this point, the telescope is then used to sight a stadia rod placed at a distant point. The bearing and distance to the point can be plotted directly on the plane-table map: once the stadia rod is sighted, a line is drawn along the alidade straightedge to record the bearing. The distance to the point is determined by the stadia intervals; a scaled ruler is used to mark off the distance along the line just drawn on the map (Fig. 6.10). For example, if the map is being made at a scale of 1:1000 and the point is 75 m away, then a distance of 7.5 cm is measured along the bearing line from the marked mapping station to locate the sighted point on the map. The stadia rod is then moved to another point and the process repeated.

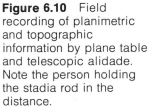

Figure 6.10 Field recording of planimetric and topographic information by plane table and telescopic alidade. Note the person holding the stadia rod in the distance.

Elevations are determined with the plane table and alidade in the same manner as with a transit; each elevation figure is usually recorded in small numerals next to the appropriate point. The plane-table map is, then, drawn in the field by plotting and recording the location and elevation of all visible archaeological features, as well as of spot locations that will be used in constructing contour lines. This method is thus more efficient than the transit method for checking accuracy as one proceeds.

Normally, if architectural features are present and can be mapped, they are drawn planimetrically, often according to conventions or symbols that have become established in the particular region. For instance, architectural features such as platforms, pyramids, staircases, and structures are often plotted by locating their corners, and then depicted according to conventionalized symbols (see Fig. 6.11). In other cases, especially if standing masonry architecture is not apparent, all archaeological information may be depicted by contouring (compare Fig. 6.3).

When enough points of known elevation are plotted to indicate the general characteristics of the local topography, contours can be drawn. The map should show areas or points of maximum and minimum elevation; differences in gradient and patterns of drainage should also be made clear by the contours. A contour map is made by drawing continuous lines connecting areas of equal elevation, interpolating between points of known elevation (Fig. 6.12). Note that the goal is not to locate points of equal elevation, but rather to indicate the overall topographic pattern. Equal elevation is inferred from the

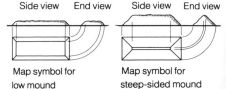

Side view   End view   Side view   End view

Map symbol for   Map symbol for
low mound   steep-sided mound

6.11 Conventionalized symbols used to depict construction for planimetric maps. (After Carr and Hazard 1961.)

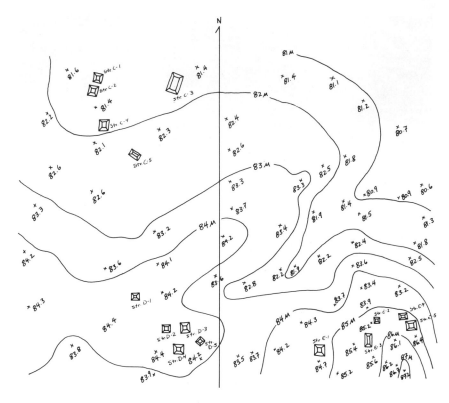

Figure 6.12 Portion of a plane table field record, showing recorded elevation points and interpolated contour lines along with structures rendered planimetrically.

spot elevations. Contour maps can be made with the transit, but work proceeds more quickly with the alidade. The latter method has the additional advantage of immediate feedback—the surveyor can see while drawing whether or not the interpolated contours make sense and agree with the actual topography.

Contour lines should be smooth and continuous; widely spaced lines indicate gradual slopes and closely spaced ones represent steep gradients. Except in the case of a vertical overhang, the lines should never cross. Depending on the scale of the map, contours may be drawn at various intervals. The most common contour interval in site maps is one contour for every 1 meter of change in elevation, with a heavier line called an index contour at every fifth meter. But contour intervals of ½ m may be used on very large-scale maps, or if there is little relative relief over the site. And wider intervals may be necessary on small-scale maps, especially if there are great changes in elevation.

Recording Surface Artifacts and Ecofacts: Surface Collection

The collection of surface artifacts and ecofacts remains the most common and effective surface survey technique. At one time or another, almost every archaeologist has used artifactual data from surface proveniences to provide at least a preliminary evaluation of a site under study. In most areas of the world, many archaeological sites are recognized by surface scatters of durable artifacts such as stone tools and pottery sherds. The recovery of artifacts such as these often provides an immediate clue to the age and even the function of the sites.

Surface remains may be collected from archaeological sites in a variety of ways. Some archaeologists prefer to select their collection by choosing only the diagnostic artifacts from the surface. *Diagnostic,* in this case, refers to those artifacts that are significant to the particular research problem under investigation. In order to determine the probable occupation period of a site littered with surface pottery, for example, the archaeologist may collect only decorated sherds, because they may be the best chronological indicators. Alternatively, an archaeologist interested in ancient function might collect only sherds from the rims of vessels, because they may be the best functional indicators. The remaining sherds and all other artifacts would be left behind as "undiagnostic." Other archaeologists prefer to collect all available surface remains, allowing later laboratory analysis to evaluate which artifacts are significant and which are not. Of course the collection of every kind of surface artifact is especially important in areas with little previous archaeological knowledge. In most cases collection of all kinds of surface artifacts is probably best: sometimes the most uninteresting lump proves significant once it has been washed in the laboratory.

Artifacts and ecofacts may be collected with or without first plotting (mapping) their surface location. The choice of whether or not to map surface provenience usually depends on two factors—the context and the amount or extent of the remains. If the surface artifacts or ecofacts appear to be in secondary context, badly disturbed by human or natural events, plotting individual locations may not be necessary or useful. However, if the surface material appears to be in primary context, it is usually advisable to plot the provenience of each artifact accurately. Whether or not this is feasible may depend upon how many artifacts are present and how large an area they cover. It may be possible to map accurately the location of each of several dozen chipped stone tools and animal bones lying on the surface of a site that covers only several hundred square meters. In such a case, the provenience of each artifact is recorded by plotting its location on a

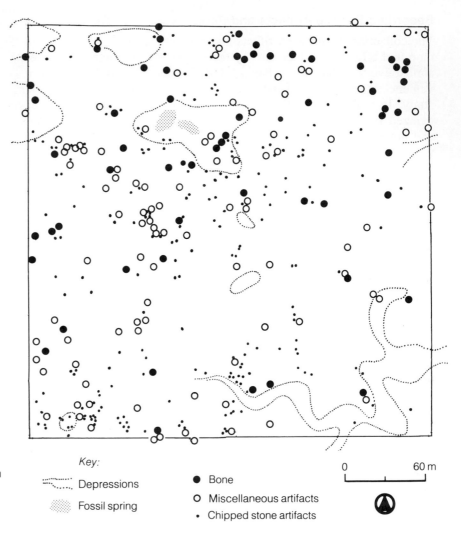

Figure 6.13 Detailed plot of surface finds at China Lake, California. (After Davis 1975, reproduced by permission of The Society for American Archaeology, adapted from *American Antiquity* 40:51, 1975.)

Key:

⋯⋯ Depressions

░░ Fossil spring

● Bone

○ Miscellaneous artifacts

· Chipped stone artifacts

0   60 m

Individual plotting at China Lake, California

site map or plan and then numbering each item as it is collected, keying the same number to the artifact symbol on the map or plan. To study association patterns at the exposed sites of China Lake Valley, California, individual artifacts and ecofacts were plotted for a number of squares, each about 300 m on a side (Fig. 6.13).

But when the archaeologist is confronted with several hundred thousand pottery sherds scattered across an ancient village site covering several thousand square meters, plotting the location of each artifact may not be possible. In such a situation, the surface area of the site is usually divided into small provenience units called *lots*. These units can be defined either arbitrarily, as by grid squares, or nonarbitrarily, as when archaeological features are used to subdivide a site. For instance, artifacts can be collected and provenience keyed to their association with structures, rooms, and so forth. In either case, each artifact's provenience is recorded as part of a lot, but not by its precise individual location. Thus the provenience of any single artifact—say a particular sherd—will indicate that it was found on the surface of grid square D-3 or on the surface of structure 4E, in either case along with dozens of other artifacts from the same lot.

Remote Sensing

Archaeologists have applied a variety of remote sensing techniques to the task of detecting and recording both features and artifacts. The actual techniques are the same as those used in archaeological reconnaissance: air-based sensors such as cameras and radar instruments and ground-based sensors such as magnetometers, resistivity instruments, and pulse radar, as well as mechanical devices such as augers and corers. All of these were discussed in Chapter 5 and need not be described again. Although the remote sensing techniques are the same, their objectives are different when they are used in surface survey. Instead of being used to identify previously unrecorded archaeological sites, in surface survey these techniques are used to detect and record components of sites as part of a data acquisition process. They are used to collect information about features, artifacts, and even ecofacts without resorting to excavation. Thus aerial photography may assist in the mapping of features such as buildings and roads, whether these are present on the ground surface or are buried and detectable by crop markings, to more fully reveal the range in the form and extent of such features prior to the excavation of a site. And ground-based sensors such as magnetometers and resistivity instruments may be used to estimate the form and extent of buried features prior to excavation. The buried site of Sybaris, discussed in Chapter 5, is a case in point.

Remote sensing instruments often cannot detect anything as small as individual buried artifacts or ecofacts, unless they are deposited in rather dense clusters and can therefore be detected in aggregates. The presence of buried artifacts and ecofacts may be more easily detected by mechanical augers or corers. For example, by recovering sherds as well as soil layers, an augering program on a flood plain in central Italy helped to outline the effects on local settlement of the flooding of the Treia river from about 250 B.C. to the present. At best, however, both remote sensors and mechanical probes can only determine whether artifacts are present or absent beneath the surface. Neither can recover adequate data samples for broad evaluation and analysis; this must be accomplished by excavation.

Augering along the Treia River, Italy

Preliminary Site Definition

A well-executed surface survey using one or more of the methods de-scribed above provides the archaeologist with a preliminary definition of the study universe, whether it consists of a single site or a region containing many sites. This preliminary definition should also include data bearing upon the *form, density,* and *structure* of archaeological remains within the study universe. The range in the forms of various classes of features may be assessed by both ground survey (mapping) and remote sensing. The range in the forms of artifacts and ecofacts may be assessed by surface collecting. Surface survey information may then be used to determine the relative density of each kind of data, together with their interrelationships (structure). Thus by plot-ting the spatial distribution of one artifact class, say grinding stones, the investigator may find areas in which these artifacts cluster. Fur-thermore, it may be possible to relate these relative densities to the distribution of other classes of artifacts, as well as of ecofacts and fea-tures. Surface survey data of this kind are often transformed into maps to show the distribution and density of artifacts, ecofacts, and features within a site. By evaluating such results, the archaeologist may be able to formulate working hypotheses to account for the sur-face data distributions and patterns. For example, in the China Lake Valley of California, artifact/ecofact distributions were used to infer

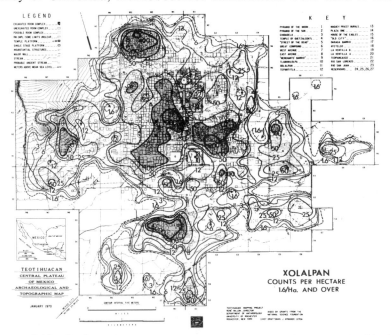

Figure 6.14   Surface densities of recovered pottery at Teotihuacán, Mexico ca. A.D. 450–650. (After Cowgill 1974.)

that two different stone tool types represented different parts of one tool kit rather than different populations. At Teotihuacán, George Cowgill has plotted surface potsherd density for different time periods to study growth and decline of population (Fig. 6.14). In surface-oriented research, these insights are an ''end product'' of the investigation. In most cases, however, such survey results are preliminary findings; they guide the archaeologist in choosing where to excavate in order to explore promising areas and test specific hypotheses.

APPROACHES TO SURFACE SURVEY

The archaeologist may choose various approaches to the conduct of surface surveys. Basically, the alternatives are the same as those discussed in Chapter 5—whether the data universe will be subjected to total or sample coverage.

Total Coverage

When surface features are being identified and recorded by mapping, total coverage of a given data universe is preferred. The only reason to use a sampling strategy in mapping would be excessive size or inaccessibility of the study universe. If, on the other hand, the surface survey includes actual collection of surface remains (artifacts and ecofacts), the need to leave some data intact for future investigations favors a sampling strategy. In archaeological salvage situations, however, total coverage remains the preferable approach to surface collecting.

Surface surveys conducted for total coverage involve two kinds of investigation, depending on the nature of the data universe. If the universe is defined to correspond to a single site, then total coverage implies surface survey (by any method) of the entire extent of that site. If the survey is being pursued by collecting surface artifacts, for example, then total coverage means that every square meter of the site will be traversed and examined for the presence of artifacts on the surface. If, on the other hand, the universe is defined to correspond to an archaeological region containing more than one site, then total coverage implies surface survey of the entire extent of every site in the universe.

As an example of total survey coverage, let us consider the investigation of Hatchery West. This is one of a set of sites on a terrace overlooking the Kaskaskia River just east of Carlyle, Illinois. A grid of 6-m squares was laid out over the whole Hatchery site zone, covering almost 15,000 m² in the Hatchery West area alone. Once all the observed artifacts and ecofacts were collected and recorded as to

**Total survey coverage:
Lewis Binford at
Hatchery West, Illinois**

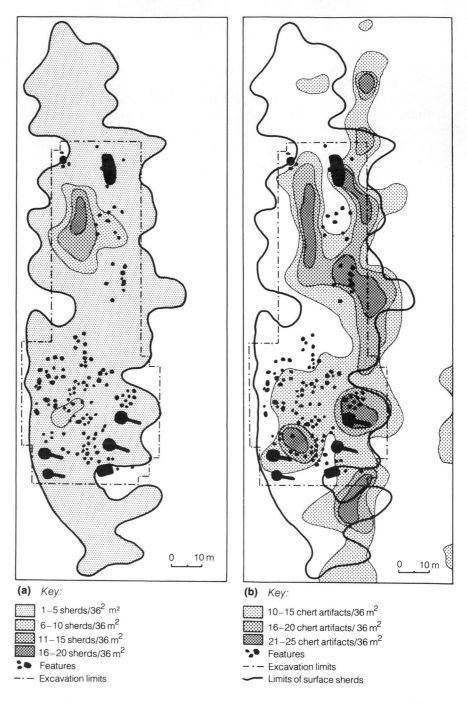

(a) *Key:*

- 1–5 sherds/36^2 m²
- 6–10 sherds/36 m²
- 11–15 sherds/36 m²
- 16–20 sherds/36 m²
- Features
- Excavation limits

(b) *Key:*

- 10–15 chert artifacts/36 m²
- 16–20 chert artifacts/ 36 m²
- 21–25 chert artifacts/36 m²
- Features
- Excavation limits
- Limits of surface sherds

Figure 6.15 Surface densities of (a) pottery and (b) chipped stone at Hatchery West, Illinois. (After Binford et al. 1970, reproduced by permission of The Society for American Archaeology, adapted from *American Antiquity,* "Archaeology at Hatchery West" (memoir of The Society for American Archaeology) 24: Figs. 5 and 10, 1970.)

grid-square provenience, contour maps were prepared showing distribution density of five artifact/ecofact categories—ceramics, cracked cobbles, chipped stone debris, chipped stone artifacts, and ground stone artifacts (see Fig. 6.15). Each category showed different distribution limits and different areas of concentration, but the fourteen identified concentration areas could be grouped into eight types by their content. Using only this surface-derived information, Lewis Binford and his associates formulated a number of preliminary postulates. For one thing, the site was posited to include several distinct occupations, separable both temporally and functionally. The excavators were able to use this surface survey information to place key excavation units so as to test the hypotheses generated from surface data. (See below concerning some of the excavation results.) They also noted that a representative picture of this variability in time and activities could not have been gained by surface collections from one area alone or by attending to only one of the artifact categories. At Hatchery West the archaeologists had the opportunity to make complete survey coverage; when total coverage is not possible, however, the Hatchery West example should serve as a reminder that uncontrolled samples may be less than adequate clues to the makeup of a site.

Sample Coverage

As we have said, surface surveys using surface collecting should usually gather data on a sample basis. But even in cases in which total coverage is preferable, limitations on research time and money may dictate less than total coverage. Surface surveys using remote sensors are virtually always forced to adopt a sampling design because of limitations of time and money.

Surface surveys using sample coverage also include two kinds of investigations, again depending on the nature of the data universe. When the universe is defined to correspond to a single site, sample coverage implies a surface survey of only a portion of that site. If the survey is being pursued by magnetometer probes, for example, then sample coverage means that only designated portions of the site will be subjected to the magnetometer survey. On the other hand, if the universe is defined to correspond to a region containing two or more sites, then sample coverage implies surface survey of only a portion of the sites in the universe, *and/or* survey of only a portion of each selected site.

In many cases, when archaeologists are working with multiple-site universes, it may be preferable to combine sample coverage with total coverage. This would mean conducting a surface survey of portions of every site in the universe (total coverage of sites combined with sample coverage of individual sites), or, alternatively, conducting a surface survey of the entire extent of a portion of sites in the universe (sample coverage of sites combined with total coverage at each individual site).

*Nonprobabilistic Sampling

In this as in other sampling situations, the first question the archaeologist faces is whether to select the data samples by probabilistic or nonprobabilistic means. Surface surveys using nonprobabilistic samples have dominated archaeological research until recently. Thus surface collections have usually been gathered from the most prominent or accessible archaeological sites, or from portions of such sites. This kind of nonprobabilistic sampling has certain advantages: it is often the fastest and easiest means of conducting surface surveys. Speed and ease, in turn, usually result in less expenditure of research funds. However, as we have seen before, nonprobabilistic sampling has certain serious disadvantages, the chief among these being the inability of the archaeologist to judge the reliability of the data.

*Probabilistic Sampling

Although surface surveys using probabilistic sampling schemes may be more time-consuming and expensive, they produce data that stand a better chance of being representative of the total data pool. For this reason, such controlled sampling methods are preferable for the conduct of most surface surveys. This is especially true for research that involves surface collection of artifacts and ecofacts. In such cases, most of the specific sampling designs discussed in Chapter 3, such as stratified random sampling, can be of great benefit to the archaeologist. After the data universe is defined, either arbitrary or nonarbitrary sample units are selected to control the acquisition of surface data. Three forms of arbitrarily defined sample units—quadrats, transects, and spots—have been used successfully by archaeologists to secure representative collections of surface artifacts.

To conduct a surface collection using quadrats, the data universe must be surveyed to define the grid (sample units) on the ground. This is usually done by placing stakes at grid line intersections. The examination and collection of surface material then proceeds within each of the quadrats selected by the sampling design being used. Quadrat-based samples have become increasingly widely used; examples include the work of Redman and Watson at Çayönü, Turkey, and that of Schiffer and Hanson at the Joint Site of Arizona.

For recording purposes, each quadrat may correspond to a single provenience unit (lot), or it may be subdivided into several smaller lots. Of course, if the conditions are appropriate, the individual location of each artifact may be mapped before it is collected. In addition to their use in defining sample units for surface collections, quadrats are often used to control remote sensor surveys, such as magnetometer surveys, searching for buried features. Similar means may be used to define transects and to collect surface data from a designated sample of this kind of sample unit.

Spot sample units are usually defined by the intersection of grid lines or coordinates, but they may be defined by nonarbitrary criteria such as surface features. In this method of collecting surface material, each spot (usually located on the ground by a stake) becomes the center point of a uniform circular sample unit. This circular area is defined by a given radius, such as 10 meters; the surface collections within the area are controlled by attaching a string or a tape measure of appropriate radial length to each center-point stake. This is called the "dog leash" method of defining sample units for surface collection. Definition of spot sample units is also the most useful procedure for controlling mechanical subsurface probes such as augers and corers.

Nonarbitrary sample units may also be used to control surface collections. This means is best suited to situations characterized by well-defined archaeological features, such as individual structures or rooms within structures, or by natural divisions, such as ecozones. At Teotihuacán, surface collections were controllled by constructionally defined areas—buildings, courts, and so on—although these entities were also sometimes subdivided arbitrarily.

Even with probabilistic sampling schemes, the archaeologist should remain flexible enough to include new areas of unexpected finds if the need arises. At Çayönü, Turkey, for example, when the randomly selected quadrats left some large areas untested, other units from the latter areas were added to the sample for spatial balance (Fig. 6.16). Evidence from such additional units cannot be included in later statistical analyses that presume random sample selection, but it may still yield valuable information.

Combined probabilistic and nonprobabilistic survey: Redman and Watson at Çayönü, Turkey

RELIABILITY OF SURFACE COLLECTIONS

How reliable are surface-collected data for archaeological interpretation? In this section we will consider the degree to which surface artifacts and ecofacts are representative of subsurface remains. This question is of fundamental importance because of the popularity of surface collections for data acquisition. Surface collection is a quick and relatively nondestructive means of gathering information over large areas, and in some cases such collection has been relied on as the primary data source for chronological, functional and processual

Figure 6.16 Map of sampled areas at Çayönü, Turkey: stippled quadrats represent original probabilistic sample, while open quadrats are nonprobabilistically selected sample areas added for more uniform spatial coverage of the site. (After Redman and Watson 1970, reproduced by permission of The Society for American Archaeology, adapted from *American Antiquity* 35:281–282, 1970.)

0 _____ 20 m

■ Surface collected areas:
   Random sample
□ Added (nonprobabalistic) areas

interpretations. In the case of Teotihuacán, among many others, archaeologists have assumed that surface remains accurately reflect both the temporal and the functional range of materials lying beneath the surface. On the basis of this assumption, investigators have used surface collections to form their conclusions. At Teotihuacán test excavations supported the assumption, but is it a valid one in all cases? We shall examine the merits of this assumption by looking at several cases in which surface collections were followed by excavations in order to test the reliability of the survey findings. In so doing, we will also have a chance to see how archaeologists use various approaches to surface survey.

Case Studies

Surface collection reliability: Hatchery West, Illinois

Our first test of the reliability of surface collections comes from the investigations at Hatchery West, described earlier in this chapter. This Woodland period site, located in Illinois, was surface-collected over its entire extent of nearly 15,000 m² using 6-by-6-meter grid squares as provenience units. Contour maps were prepared showing the relative surface density and distribution of various kinds of artifacts. After the excavations at the site were completed, the results of the surface work were compared with results revealed from excavation. The excavations first demonstrated that Hatchery West was a shallow site: the depth of archaeological materials averaged only about 45 cm beneath the ground surface. The excavations also revealed the remains of Woodland period houses; interestingly, these features were generally in site areas with the lowest surface densities of pottery sherds. The areas of highest surface sherd densities were found upon excavation to correspond to middens. Evidence of occupation from pre-Woodland periods was found to correlate with areas with the highest surface concentrations of cracked rock. In general, then, the Hatchery West findings indicate that the distribution and density of surface artifacts were directly (if sometimes negatively) related to presence of subsurface features, involving in this case at least two kinds of use-related primary contexts (houses and occupation areas) and one kind of transposed primary context (middens).

For our second test of surface collection reliability, let us look at some results of an extensive nonprobabilistic sample of surface materials from the site of Chalchuapa, El Salvador. The surface samples at Chalchuapa were nonprobabilistic because surface collections could be made only in limited portions of the site zone. The remainder was inaccessible because of modern cultivation (coffee trees were the biggest obstacle) and, in a few cases, property owners who refused to open their land to the survey. In addition, the modern town of Chalchuapa covers the western portion of the site, making it inaccessible. Most of the remaining area, some 2.5 km², was examined by ground survey, including surface collection. Areas showing high concentrations of surface artifacts were subsequently excavated on a priority basis. Three areas with unusually high concentrations of surface artifacts, especially pottery sherds, were predicted to represent middens. All three areas were excavated, and all three were revealed to be middens (Fig. 6.17). However, none of the surface collections indicated the full time-depth of the middens as revealed by excavation; only the uppermost levels of the middens were represented in the surface collections.

Also at Chalchuapa, the excavations of eroded adobe platforms (mounds) were always preceded by surface collections. The surface materials here, though frequently badly weathered, generally *did* reflect the range of artifacts recovered from the subsequent excavations, even though some of the latter materials came from 3 to 4 meters below the mound surface. However, excavations also revealed that the artifactual material associated with these adobe platforms was almost exclusively from use-related secondary contexts. The artifacts were in a matrix of construction fill that had been mined from previous structures, middens, and so forth, resulting in a uniform mixture of cultural debris from a variety of time periods. The artifacts collected from the surface of the mounds had reached the surface through processes of transformation, specifically the erosion of the earthen construction fill and its artifactual contents caused by rainwater and modern agricultural activity.

Surface collection reliability: Chalchuapa, El Salvador

Figure 6.17 Excavation of a stratified midden at Chalchuapa, El Salvador; materials from the lower levels seen here were not represented on the surface.

**Surface collection
reliability: Joint Site,
Arizona**

At the Joint Site in east-central Arizona, a 6400 m² area was divided into 1 m squares which were grouped into larger squares 20 m on a side (Fig. 6.18). Within each of the larger units, smaller units (4 m squares or 2 m strips) were selected randomly to a total of 36 percent coverage of the area (a proportional stratified random sample). Then archaeologists chose locations for test excavations in order to test the surface-subsurface relationship: a stratified random sample of units was drawn, with the strata defined by different densities of surface materials. The result was a *lack* of correspondence: surface densities, whether high or low, were not reliable predictors of buried deposits. Going beyond this observation, however, the researchers showed how surface distributions could have been combined with an understanding of transformational processes such as wind and rain erosion patterns to yield more accurate predictions. As an obvious example, surface materials on a slope may be wind-blown or washed downhill from their original location. Chapter 3 discussed the fundamental importance of considering the effects of postdepositional transformations; the Joint Site example points up as well that surface debris alone do not necessarily indicate what lies underground.

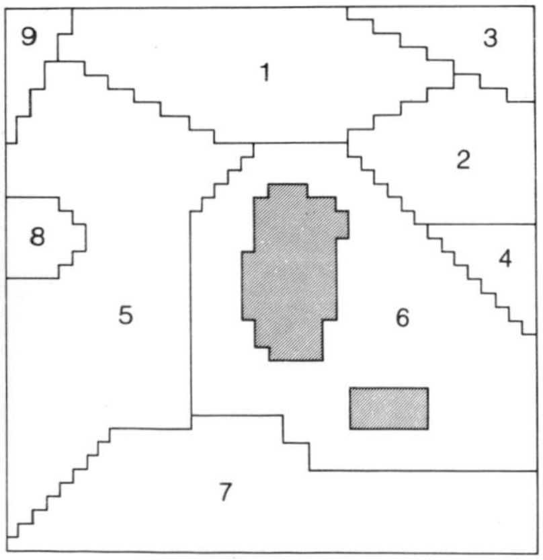

The Surface-Subsurface Relationship

Figure 6.18 Schematic representation of sampling strata based on density of surface collections at the Joint Site, Arizona; shaded areas contain architectural remains and were sampled separately. (After Schiffer 1976.)

These examples, along with other studies not summarized here, show that the relationship between surface artifacts and ecofacts on the one hand and subsurface archaeological evidence on the other is both complex and highly variable. In some cases there may be a good correspondence, but in others, there may be little or no direct relationship. Obviously the relationship between the surface and subsurface configurations depends both on the nature of the site and on the transformation processes that have either preserved or altered the surface evidence of occupation.

As an example of the former variable, consider a site that is deeply stratified, with ancient remains extending to a great depth beneath the surface. Then under normal circumstances only the uppermost levels of the site will be represented on the surface. This effect was noticeable in the case of the middens at Chalchuapa, where only the artifacts from the uppermost levels were represented in surface collections. In these cases, later excavation revealed pottery and other artifacts in the lower levels of the middens that was more than 1000 years older than the materials from the surface collections. The degree of correspondence between surface remains and subsurface evidence exposed by excavation at Hatchery West or at Teotihuacán appears to result primarily from the fact that the occupation levels are close to the surface and not very thick.

The other major factor responsible for the distribution of surface materials is the combined forces of transformation. These transformation processes were discussed in detail in Chapter 3, but it may be useful to review them here to indicate specifically how they affect the surface-subsurface relationship.

Natural agents of transformation include wind and water; we saw in Chapter 5 how river-laid soils had completely buried the site of Sybaris. The study at the Joint Site, however, showed that wind and water are also erosive, displacing surface remains from their original positions. Flannery reports a similar case from the Valley of Oaxaca, Mexico. There, at an unnamed preceramic site, the results of a total-coverage surface collection were plotted on a distribution map, revealing that projectile points tended to be distributed in a ring around the edges of the site. It soon became apparent, however, that since the site was elevated in the center, this curious pattern resulted from water erosion.

Transformation of surface remains: Valley of Oaxaca, Mexico

+ plowing

Plants and animals also affect surface remains. Tree roots may dislodge buried artifacts, sometimes pulling them to the surface when the tree falls. And animal burrows can either unearth buried artifacts or allow surface materials to be displaced into subsurface positions. Grazing animals may cause some lateral displacement of surface remains; heavy animals such as cattle may even pulverize cultural debris such as sherds.

Human agents of transformation are also important to the nature of surface-subsurface relationships. At Chalchuapa, erosion had exposed artifacts from disturbed and uniformly mixed construction fill (use-related secondary context) of earthen mounds; in this case, surface samples usually reflected excavated materials regardless of their depth. In another area of Chalchuapa, surface collections produced a baffling variety of artifacts and ecofacts, including prehistoric pottery from several time periods, human bones, bits of rusted iron, several lead bullets, and at least one brass button. The significance of these finds was revealed with the discovery of a historical account that described a decisive battle fought at Chalchuapa in 1885 between an invading Guatemalan army and a defending Salvadorean force. The historical account related that the major action was fought among a group of ''low hills'' northwest of the town. The only ''low hills'' northwest of the town of Chalchuapa are the several dozen mounds that represent the remains of pre-Columbian platforms. At least part of the battle, then, was fought in this part of the archaeological site. Further examination of the area from which the puzzling surface materials originated indicated that the collections were from what appeared to be the remains of defensive earthworks from this battle.

Transformation of surface remains: Chalchuapa, El Salvador

The nineteenth-century soldiers who dug trenches and built earthworks probably brought pre-Columbian artifacts to the surface; the bullets and the button were evidence of the battle itself; and the human bones may testify to the usual results of warfare. However, examination of the area, including several subsequent test excavations, indicated that the area had also been badly disturbed by recent coffee cultivation and by looters' pits. The result of all this activity, from the battle in 1885 to the time of the archaeological investigations, was a badly disturbed array of both prehistoric and historic artifacts lying mixed and scattered on the present ground surface.

Other earth-moving activities frequently figure in the surface-subsurface relationship. Discards from looting excavations provide an example; the effect of plowing is a more common one. When confronted by surface disturbance from plowing, the archaeologist must try to estimate the degree of displacement, both lateral and horizontal, that has been introduced. Sometimes, when site areas are known to have been plowed previously but have since become recompacted, archaeologists have resorted to replowing before collection. This loosens the already disturbed materials, in effect *re*-establishing a surface component. Such an approach was used, for example, at the Hatchery West site.

It is obvious, then, that surface artifacts and ecofacts can provide information about the archaeological site being investigated. But the archaeologist must be aware of the depth and contextual status of the site, as well as of the processes of transformation that have acted to stabilize or rearrange the surface materials. No archaeologist should assume that the data collected from a site's surface can be used to predict what lies beneath *without testing by excavation*. The distribution and density of surface materials can indicate promising areas of ancient activity, but these leads must be followed by excavation to document the archaeologist's findings.

SUMMARY

This chapter has discussed the basic objectives and methods archaeologists use in conducting surface surveys. Surface surveys are designed to yield representative data from archaeological sites without resorting to excavation. In some cases, data acquired in this way are the primary or sole basis upon which the archaeologist formulates reconstructions of the past. More often, however, the acquisition of data through surface survey is a prelude to the next stage of research, excavation. Surface data thus aid in selecting areas to excavate, as well as in providing specific problems or hypotheses for the archaeologist to test by excavation.

Most surface surveys consist of ground surveys. Ground surveys acquire data by mapping the surface characteristics of sites, including features such as surviving remains of buildings, walls, roads, canals, and so forth, as well as relevant topographic and environmental information. Ground surveys usually rely heavily on the collection of surface artifacts and ecofacts. Surface surveys also use remote sensors (either aerial or ground-based) to map the form and extent of obscure or buried features. Remote sensors and mechanical devices may be used to determine whether artifacts or ecofacts are present beneath the surface. Together, ground surveys and remote sensors are used to produce site maps and maps showing the distribution and density of surface artifacts and ecofacts.

Whatever method is used, surface surveys may aim for total coverage of the study universe, whether the latter is defined as a single site or as an area containing two or more sites. Alternatively, many surface surveys use either probabilistic or nonprobabilistic samples of the study universe. As in the case of archaeological reconnaissance, probabilistic sampling designs are preferable under most circumstances. However, all sampling should be flexible enough to include unexpected discoveries that may add to the investigator's knowledge of the full range of data present within the study universe.

The reliability of data collected from the surface of sites is a matter of concern to archaeologists. As several studies concerned with this question show, it may be dangerous simply to assume that surface data are a direct reflection of the evidence beneath the ground. Instead, the archaeologist should couple the surface evidence with inferences about the probable transformations that have acted upon it in selecting promising areas for excavation. Not only are subsequent excavations guided spatially by the results of surface survey, but they may also be used to test specific functional questions and hypotheses generated by the distribution and density patterns of surface data. At the same time, the inferences about transformational processes should also be tested by excavation.

See p. 572 for "Suggestions for Further Reading."

Excavation must be accompanied by the careful recording of archaeological data. (Courtesy of the Tikal Project, the University Museum,
University of Pennsylvania.)

Excavation

. . . there must always be an element of chance and of opportunism in an excavation, however carefully planned. But scientific digging is not on that account a gamble . . .

(Sir Mortimer Wheeler,
Archaeology from the Earth,
1954)

Excavation is the principal means by which the archaeologist gathers data about the past, being used both to discover and to retrieve data from beneath the ground surface. As we have seen in Chapter 6, surface survey is often an essential prelude to excavation. Collections of artifacts and ecofacts from the surface often provide clues as to what may lie beneath the ground, guiding the archaeologist in planning excavations. In addition, as Chapter 5 pointed out, remote sensors such as magnetometers or pulse radar equipment may detect the existence of buried archaeological features. But the only way to verify the presence and nature of subsurface data is through excavation.

Data retrieved through excavation are especially important for the archaeologist since subsurface data are usually the best preserved and the least disturbed. Surface artifacts and ecofacts are seldom in primary context and are usually poorly preserved. Surface features such as ancient walls or roads, though generally still in primary context, are often less well preserved than similar features buried—and therefore protected—below the surface. Excavation increases the archaeologist's chances of finding well-preserved data of all kinds. Most importantly, excavation often reveals *associations* of artifacts, ecofacts, and features in primary contexts. As we have seen, this kind of data is the most useful to the archaeologist for inferring ancient function and behavior.

The two basic goals of excavation are first to reveal the three-dimensional patterning or *physical structure* in the deposition of artifacts, ecofacts, and features, and second to assess the functional and temporal significance of this patterning. Where were stone tools, pottery vessels, and animal bones found, relative to each other and to house remains or other areas in which they were used? Determination of this three-dimensional patterning depends on establishing provenience and associations of the individual artifacts, ecofacts, and features, with respect both to each other and to their surrounding matrix. At the same time, evaluation of provenience and association allows the assessment of context. As Chapter 3 pointed out, it is attention to these relationships—to the links among the elements of archaeological data, as established by records of provenience, association, and context—that differentiates the archaeologist from the antiquarian and the looter. Only by knowing which of these elements were found together (provenience and association) and by inferring how they got there (association and context) can the archaeologist reconstruct ancient behavior. So proper records of an excavation are just as crucial to its interpretation as proper methods of actual excavation. Of course, behavioral reconstruction also depends on analysis of what the individual artifacts, ecofacts, and features were used for; this analysis, in turn, is based partly on their provenience and association, but also on form and other attributes of each artifact, ecofact, and feature. Such analysis of individual elements will be discussed in Chapters 8 through 11.

If we consider the three-dimensional structure of an archaeological deposit, what do the three dimensions represent? We must draw a fundamental distinction between the single vertical dimension (depth) and the two horizontal ones (lateral extent). The combined horizontal dimensions represent, in an idealized situation, the associated remains of a *single point in time*. The case of Pompeii, where a whole community was buried and preserved as if in suspended animation, provides an extreme illustration. The point is that artifacts and features on the same horizontal surface ideally represent use or discard that is approximately contemporaneous (Fig. 7.1). Over time, new surfaces are created, usually by levelling and covering over the old; repetition of this process creates a vertical dimension (Fig. 7.2). Thus

Figure 7.1 Recovery of evidence representing a single moment in time at Ceren in El Salvador. Excavations have exposed the remains of an adobe house and adjacent cornfield (seen in Fig. 3.3), buried by a local volcanic eruption which collapsed and carbonized the roof beams and thatch. Later eruptions are represented by the upper deposits of ash. (Courtesy of Payson D. Sheets.)

Figure 7.2 This view of a modern village in Iran shows that occupation at a single point in time does not always mean occupation of a single level ground surface. The different elevations of the houses shown here are the product of accumulation of occupation debris, not hilly topography. (Courtesy of Ilene M. Nicholas.)

the vertical dimension in an archaeological deposit represents *accumulation through time*. This distinction and its implications are crucial in excavation. Before turning to excavation methods, then, we shall discuss the structure of archaeological deposits in more detail.

ARCHAEOLOGICAL STRATIFICATION AND STRATIGRAPHY

Archaeological *stratification* refers to the observed layering of matrices and features. These layers or *strata* may be sloping or roughly horizontal; they may be thick or thin. In some cases they are well-defined by contrasts in color, texture, composition, or other characteristics, but in others their boundaries may be difficult or even impossible to discern; one apparent stratum may simply grade into another. Whatever the specific characteristics, the layering of stratified deposits reflects the geological law of superposition: the sequence of observable strata, from bottom to top, reflects the order of deposition, from earliest to latest. Lower layers were deposited before upper layers. The individual strata of an archaeological deposit may represent formal occupation surfaces, as in the example of Pompeii, or they may be the result of other acts of deposition, such as accumulated layers of trash in a midden. Strata may also be deposited naturally, as when floods cover an area with a layer of alluvium.

Note, however, that the law of superposition refers to the *sequence of deposition,* not to the *age* of the materials in the strata. Although in most cases the depositional sequence of the material found in stratified matrices does reflect its relative age, there are exceptions. For example, some stratified matrices may be formed of redeposited material, as when water erosion removes soil from a location up-stream and redeposits it in a new location downstream. If this soil contains cultural material, chronologically late artifacts could quite possibly be removed and redeposited first, to be followed by rede-position of chronologically earlier artifacts (see Fig. 3.18). Thus the redeposited matrix contains later artifacts in its lower strata and ear-lier artifacts in its upper strata. Note, however, that even in this case of "reversed stratification," the law of superposition holds: the lower layers were redeposited first, followed by the upper layers. The same reversal effect can result from human activity, as when stratified deposits are mined for construction fill.

Another reason superposition may not directly reflect age is be-cause of intrusive strata. Pits or burrows, dug either by humans or by animals, may insert later materials into lower levels (see Chapter 3).

The interpreted significance of stratification is called *stratigraphy*. That is, stratigraphy refers to the archaeological evaluation of the temporal and depositional meaning of the observed strata. In strati-graphic analysis, the archaeologist combines use of the law of super-position with a consideration of context. Since intact archaeological features are invariably in primary context, problems of temporal determination usually arise with portable data—artifacts and ecofacts. In essence, the archaeologist must judge whether the artifacts and ecofacts associated with stratified deposits are the undisturbed result of human activity (primary context) or whether they have been trans-ported and redeposited by either human agents or natural events (sec-ondary context). If the archaeologist can demonstrate primary context with reasonable assurance—that is, if there is no evidence of redeposition disturbance—then the temporal sequence of the archae-ological materials within the deposit may be assumed to follow that of the strata. In this way, a stratigraphic sequence is established.

Let us consider some examples of stratigraphy. In the Lindenmeier Valley of northern Colorado, bison hunters some 11,000 years ago camped in the area now called the Lindenmeier site. The hunting groups left evidence of their presence in the form of stone tools, tool-making debris, hearths, and the bones of prey animals. Although each individual group probably spent only a brief time camped at Lin-denmeier, repeated use of the campsite over time led to a gradual ac-cumulation of occupation debris. During this time period, whose exact limits we do not know, the level of the ground surface was be-ing raised by natural processes: small depressions would flood with water from a nearby stream, after which plants would grow in the wet areas and eventually die and decay. The humic soil from the decayed plants would fill the old depressions, and the stream overflow would

Stratigraphy: Lindenmeier, Colorado

begin the process in another low area. The new, raised surfaces created by such filling-in were used as camping stations, and older debris would be buried and sealed in place when a given locale was flooded. In this way, the combined effects of geological buildup and repeated reoccupation produced a stratified deposit in which the matrix accumulation resulted from natural causes but included (and preserved) evidence of human occupation. At Lindenmeier the law of superposition is relatively unaffected by disturbing factors: the basic stratigraphy is simply vertical accumulation upward through time, and the relative age of artifactual remains correlates well with stratigraphic position.

When people live in permanent communities, the stratigraphic record usually becomes more complicated. For example, individual houses in a village are built, occupied, and abandoned, but the village as a whole continues to be occupied. In time, a given house may collapse and become a dumping area for nearby residences. Eventually this debris area may be chosen as the location for a new house; the area will be levelled somewhat, but the debris will not be totally removed. The new house may therefore have its base at a somewhat higher level than those of its neighbors (Fig. 7.3; compare Fig. 7.2).

Two contemporary houses at same ground level

One house is abandoned, collapses, and is used as a rubbish dump.

Figure 7.3 An example of one means by which differential accumulation of occupational debris results in complex stratigraphy.

Resulting mound is leveled and a new house is built on its summit, which is now contemporary (although at a higher level) with still-occupied house at right.

The primary accumulation represented by this sequence is, again, upward with time, but the correspondence between deposition sequence and age of use of materials may be disrupted. For example, in the period during which the house was used as a dump, materials of *later* use would be placed within the walls of this *earlier* structure; then, when the area was leveled for the new construction, the old walls might be knocked down, releasing artifacts from within the walls and partly covering the trash deposits. In this way later materials would *underlie* earlier materials, so that superposition would not indicate age.

Intrusions cause other disruptions of stratigraphy. In an area used as a cemetery over long periods, later burials may be intruded into earlier ones. Sometimes the walls of earlier burial pits are broken by later pits so many times that their outlines are difficult to trace. Later

Figure 7.4 Excavators at Ban Chiang, in northeastern Thailand, were confronted with a complex stratigraphy of multiple intrusive pits. The light surface at left and in the background is an occupation surface, through which the later pits, some of them human graves, were excavated, and sometimes the pits intruded on each other. Note that the lower leg of the skeleton in the right foreground has been cut by the pit of the later grave in the left foreground. (Courtesy of the Ban Chiang Project, Thai Fine Arts Department/University Museum.)

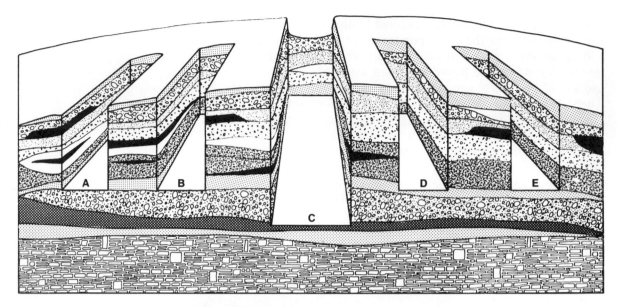

Figure 7.5 An example of complex stratigraphy revealed and coordinated from multiple excavations.

pits may also be dug deeper than earlier ones; thus, when dealing with pits, the archaeologist must tie the *top* of each one into the overall stratigraphy. In other words, one establishes what level the pit was dug down *from* (Fig. 7.4). At Ban Chiang and other village sites in northeastern Thailand, the intrusive pit problem is further aggravated by—of all things—the repeated burrowing of insects, riddling pit walls and other stratification levels with holes that may be as large as tennis balls.

Once the stratigraphic sequences have been evaluated for each separate excavation unit, the archaeologist attempts to correlate these individual sequences to form a master sequence for the entire site (Fig. 7.5). In some cases this process may be facilitated by physically linking excavation units—removing barriers between adjacent test pits and trenches—to create a continuous cross-section of the stratified deposit. This enables the investigator to observe directly the connections between the strata revealed in each excavation. Some individual strata or features, such as tamped-earth floors, may be very limited in extent, while others may extend over the entire site. These spatial variations must be considered in determining the site sequence. The problem is more difficult in large or complex sites in which linking of excavation units is impossible or impractical. In such cases, the characteristics of each individual layer—its thickness, color, composition, apparent extent, and relative position with respect to other strata—

must be carefully defined to avoid mismatching similar features in the sequence. Photography can be an important aid in this process; ultraviolet film, for example, may pick up subtle differences that are not otherwise visible. Or direct comparisons may be made by taking physical samples of each stratum and either visually comparing them or, if necessary, submitting them to soil laboratories for analysis. A useful method for taking a sample of an entire stratified deposit is to apply a vertical strip of adhesive—such as rubber cement reinforced with cloth backing—from top to bottom of the excavation wall. When dry, the strip can be peeled from the wall; a continuous sample of the stratified column will adhere to it. Comparing strata from each excavation may enable the archaeologist to create a full composite stratigraphic sequence for the entire site.

The functional dimension of stratigraphy involves distinguishing evidence of natural activity from that of cultural activity. In essence, the archaeologist attempts to determine which layers in the stratified deposit are "features" and which are naturally laid soils. For some deposits, evidence of past human activity is obvious: burials, house foundations, refuse deposits, and so on. In the absence of such clear indicators, however, determining whether or not a given stratum was produced by human agents may be more difficult. Clues to human occupation include the presence of unusually high concentrations of organic remains, which may give occupation layers a dark, "greasy" appearance, and the presence of pollen from domesticated plants.

Once the archaeologist has distinguished cultural strata from natural strata, a further functional distinction may be made between architectural and nonarchitectural features. Nonarchitectural features include middens, burials, tamped-earth floors, hearths, quarries, and so forth. Architectural features include walls, prepared or plastered floors, platforms, staircases, roadways, and the like. Of course, nonarchitectural features such as hearths and burials are often associated with architectural units. The analysis of features will be discussed further in Chapter 9.

Stratigraphic evaluation, then, incorporates both temporal and functional aspects. Combining the law of superposition with assessments of context, the archaeologist interprets the depositional history of the physical matrix. Functional interpretation begins with a distinction between those parts of the sequence that are natural strata and those that are cultural features. On the basis of these evaluations, the archaeologist establishes first a stratigraphic sequence for each excavation and then, by comparing stratigraphy between excavations, an overall (composite) stratigraphic sequence for the entire site. This stratigraphic sequence forms the underlying framework on which all further interpretation is founded.

Stratigraphy thus emphasizes sequence and accumulation over time; it is primarily related to the vertical dimension of archaeological deposits. Distribution in the two lateral dimensions—that is, the spread of features and artifacts through a given horizontal layer—associates these data with one another in a single point or span of time. Because horizontally associated materials within a stratum are ideally the remains of behavior from a single unit of time, these lateral distributions fill in the functional picture and provide data to reconstruct the range of activities carried on simultaneously. Taken together, stratigraphy and association—the vertical and the horizontal—constitute the three-dimensional physical structure that excavation attempts to reveal. We now turn to the means used to reveal these three dimensions.

APPROACHES TO EXCAVATION

The Importance of Surface Survey

Surface information, such as maps of distributions of features or collections of surface artifacts, is indispensable in choosing the location of excavations. As Chapter 6 showed, this kind of data may define the approximate limits of sites and even suggest the probable location, nature, and function of subsurface activity areas. For instance, distribution patterns of surface artifacts often suggest hypotheses concerning the nature and function of buried activity areas that can be tested only by excavation. A concentration of surface pottery debris may indicate the location of a midden, or surface scatters of grinding stones might signal the presence of buried house remains. The formulation of such working hypotheses is useful in guiding subsequent excavations, for excavation provides the means to *test* the hypotheses—in these examples, to document the presence or absence of a midden or of house remains. Of course, surface data can be gathered in a cursory manner, just prior to actual excavation, by walking over the site and making a subjective assessment of surface distributions. But the time and thought involved in an organized and detailed surface survey is a worthwhile investment: the more that is known about surface remains, the better the archaeologist can estimate the variability excavation may encounter. This estimate may be inexact, of course, for surface configurations do not always reflect subsurface ones. But the potential guiding capacity of surface data should be exploited—and, indeed, if the surface-subsurface configurations do *not* match, disconformities (such as the nineteenth-century buttons and bullets at pre-Columbian Chalchuapa) should be explained (see Chapter 6).

Total Coverage

Once the surface variability of a site or area has been analyzed, the archaeologist must decide how much of the site to examine further by excavation. Total excavation, either of all sites in a region or of the whole of a single site, is extremely rare. Most archaeological projects have neither the time nor the funds for such an undertaking; in addition, archaeologists usually try to leave some undisturbed areas for potential future investigations. In salvage situations, however, where the remains will later be destroyed by nonarchaeological means anyway, total coverage may be chosen. At Hatchery West, for example, after removing the disturbed plow layer from the entire area of the site, Binford and his associates excavated every feature they encountered—a total of 8 structures, 109 pits, and 7 human burials.

Total coverage: Hatchery West, Illinois

Sample Coverage

In most situations, total coverage is not appropriate. Selection of the sites, features, or areas to be excavated may be determined by either probabilistic or nonprobabilistic sampling procedures; often the two means are combined. When the sampling units—whether grid squares, structures, sites, or whatever—appear similar in surface characteristics, probabilistic sampling maximizes the extent to which data from the sample can be generalized to the overall population. But generalization is not always the archaeologist's goal: if a number of apparently unique units call for investigation, or if a particular kind of information is required and the archaeologist can predict, from past experience, where to find it, then a nonprobabilistic sampling scheme is preferable.

To illustrate the use of a nonprobabilistic sample in excavation, let us consider work in the Salamá Valley of highland Guatemala in 1972. Preliminary reconnaissance indicated that a site called El Portón was the largest and apparently the focal site of the valley. The principal structure at the site, and the largest in the valley, was an earthen "pyramid" some 15 m high. Within the overall research goals of this archaeological project, a prime concern was establishment of the date and probable function of this unique and presumably important structure. But the project had neither the time nor the funds necessary to undertake extensive excavations, and the excavators did not want to devote all efforts to this single structure. From past experience, however, they knew that the ancient builders often placed dedicatory offerings or "caches" along the center or axial line of the structure, in front of or beneath the staircase leading to the summit. Caches such as these often contained pottery vessels that could be dated to a time span as short as 100 to 200 years. Furthermore, since

Nonprobabilistic sampling: Test excavations in the Salamá Valley, Guatemala

caches were usually associated with ceremonial structures ("temples") and not with other kinds of buildings, the mere presence of such a deposit would be an indication of ancient function.

Location of the front of the structure—the side containing the staircase—was made difficult by the badly eroded state of the pyramid's surface. But the east face was considered the best candidate, both because it faced the center of the site and because it showed a slight bulge that might have been the remnants of the staircase. The midline of the east face was calculated and located on the ground. A small test excavation was then made along this line, some 10 m in front of the pyramid, at the point where the slope angle of the mound surface led the archaeologists to expect that the buried base of the staircase should be (Fig. 7.6). After several days of excavation, they discovered the bottom step and balustrade of a plastered adobe staircase about 2 m beneath the present ground surface. Carefully digging under the bottom stair and the ancient plaza surface in front of the staircase, the archaeologists found the predicted cache, containing some sixty pottery vessels, two elaborate jaguar-effigy incense burners, obsidian knife blades, and remnants of burned materials. The pottery vessels were characteristic of the end of the Preclassic era of Maya

Figure 7.6 Dedicatory deposit at El Portón, Guatemala, found beneath the base of a buried staircase (remains of which are visible above).

prehistory, corresponding to about 200 B.C.–A.D. 0 in our calendar. This information enabled the archaeologists to make a reasonable chronological and functional evaluation of this large structure by means of a small and simple excavation, at the expenditure of only two weeks time and a few hundred dollars in project funds.

On the other hand, when the archaeologist encounters a series of potential activity loci, all possessing similar surface characteristics, probabilistic sampling is most useful in selecting excavation locations. In the initial stages of the Sustaining Area Project around the Maya lowland site of Tikal, hundreds of small mounds or mound groups were encountered and mapped on four strips, each 500 m wide and extending in the four cardinal directions approximately 10 km from the site core (Fig. 7.7). To investigate the distribution in time of the occupation represented by these constructions, a test-pitting program was instituted for gathering datable samples of excavated ceramics. Total coverage was out of the question; to achieve maximum representation, a proportional stratified random sampling scheme (see Chapter 3) was used. The universe was defined to coincide with the north and south survey strips, and the population included all mound clusters within those strips. The individual mound cluster was then

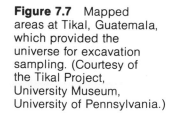

**Probabilistic sampling:
Test excavations at
Tikal, Guatemala**

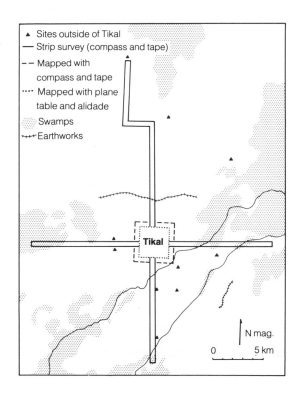

Figure 7.7 Mapped areas at Tikal, Guatemala, which provided the universe for excavation sampling. (Courtesy of the Tikal Project, University Museum, University of Pennsylvania.)

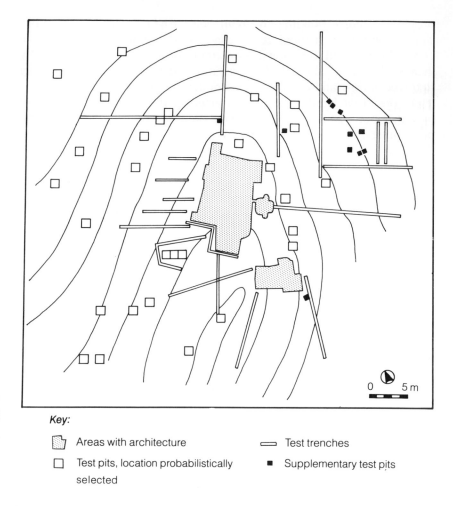

Figure 7.8 Map of nonarchitectural excavations at the Joint Site, Arizona, showing original test pits selected by probabilistic sampling of the strata defined in Fig. 6.18, along with later nonprobabilistically located excavations. (After Schiffer 1976.)

Key:

▨ Areas with architecture

▢ Test pits, location probabilistically selected

▭ Test trenches

■ Supplementary test pits

Probabilistic sampling: Test excavations at the Joint Site, Arizona

the sampling unit. Sampling strata—sets of sampling units—were defined by segmenting the strips; one-third of the units in each stratum were then selected randomly for excavation. In this way, about 100 construction units were tested.

Probabilistic sampling may also be used to select specific locations for individual excavations within a single site. As an example, we will describe some of the excavations at the Joint Site in Arizona (Chapter 6 discussed surface survey at this site). For the selection of the excavation sample, sampling units were defined by a grid of 2-by-2-meter squares (a total of 1506 squares), excluding areas of visible architecture. Because one of the project's goals was to test the relation of surface remains to those recovered by excavation, the population of grid squares was divided into nine sampling strata, each with a dif-

Table 7.1

PROPORTIONAL STRATIFIED RANDOM SAMPLE OF
TEST PITS (JOINT SITE, ARIZONA)

Sampling Stratum	Stratum Size (Number of 2 × 2m squares)	Sample size (excavated)
1	216	4
2	113	2
3	56	1
4	36	1
5	369	7
6	378	8
7	278	6
8	30	1
9	30	1
Total sample size		31

SOURCE: after Schiffer 1976, Table 7.2.

ferent density of surface artifacts (Fig. 6.18). Then a 2 percent proportional stratified random sample was drawn: using a table of random numbers, 2 percent of the units in each stratum were chosen for
excavation (Table 7.1 and Fig. 7.8). (For strata containing less than
50 sample units *total,* the ''2 percent samples'' drawn were rounded
off to a single whole unit.) In this case, as in survey at Çayönü, Turkey (discussed in Chapter 6), supplementary excavations *not* located
probabilistically were added to fill in spatial gaps; also as at Çayönü,
data from these additional units could not be used in statistical analyses based on random samples, but they provided checks as to the
areal representatives of the sampled units. This sampling strategy
maximized the efficiency and statistical reliability of an investigation
over a large area with a limited amount of actual excavation.

EXCAVATION METHODOLOGY

An archaeological excavation is usually a complicated, painstaking process. The aim of an excavation program is the acquisition of as much three-dimensional data relevant to its research objectives as possible, given the available resources. The success of any particular program depends upon a variety of factors, the most important of which is the overall organization or strategy of the excavations. This strategy guides the archaeologist in choosing the locations, extent, timing, and kinds of excavation to meet the research goals with maximum efficiency.

Many of the factors involved in organizational and strategic decisions are unique to each research situation, such as the kind of problems being investigated, the nature of the site or sites, and the availability of resources. But the range of choices among which the archaeologist must decide is limited. At this point decisions concerning the conduct of reconnaissance and survey will already have been made. In the process of choosing an excavation sampling scheme to fit the objectives and scale of the excavation program, the archaeologist completes the excavation strategy by choosing particular excavation methods. To make the best decisions for a given project, the researcher should be thoroughly familiar with all the alternatives and the ends they are best suited to accomplish.

We shall now consider four aspects of excavation methods: first, the kinds of archaeological excavations and the relationship of each kind to a general data acquisition strategy; second, the various techniques used to carry out excavations; third, the ways to control provenience of excavated data; and finally, the recording of excavated data.

Kinds of Excavations

The two basic kinds of excavations mirror the two kinds of dimensions in archaeological site formation. *Penetrating excavations* are primarily deep probes of subsurface deposits: their main thrust is vertical, and their principal objective is to reveal, in cross-section, the depth, sequencing, and composition of archaeological remains. They cut through sequential or adjacent deposits. *Clearing excavations,* on the other hand, aim primarily at horizontal investigation of deposits: their main thrust is outward or across, and their principal objective is to reveal, in plan view, both the horizontal extent and the arrangement of an archaeological deposit. Clearing excavations emphasize tracing continuities of single surfaces or deposits.

Penetrating Excavations

The most basic kind of penetrating excavation is the *test pit*. Test pits are extensive only in the vertical dimension; that is, they can probe the full depth of a deposit but not its horizontal extent. Test pits are essentially excavations in only one dimension (the vertical dimension); their horizontal extent is limited to that necessary to accommodate one excavator (about 1 m square) or two excavators (about 2 m square). Even more restricted test pits may be excavated by using post hole diggers or augers. Because they are so small and reach such limited depths, however, these probes are usually restricted to survey testing.

The objectives of test pits are to sample subsurface artifacts and ecofacts and to gain a limited cross-sectional view of the site's depositional history. For this reason, test pits are often the first excavations placed within a site. Some archaeologists prefer to place their initial test excavation outside the main areas of known or suspected archaeological interest. This kind of test pit, often called a sounding pit (*sondage*), is used to preview what lies beneath the ground, either to reveal natural strata to better distinguish these from cultural deposits, or to probe the full vertical extent of cultural deposits. In the latter case sounding pits are usually excavated down to the natural soils beneath the lowest cultural layers, so that the cross-section shown on the walls of the pit represents a complete stratigraphic record. In view of their uses, sounding pits are usually considered entirely exploratory and are not intended to acquire large samples of artifacts or other kinds of archaeological data.

Test pits may also be excavated within specific surface features such as mounds to evaluate composition and, if possible, temporal position and function. The excavation at El Portón discussed earlier in this chapter is an example of this kind of test pit. The archaeologist may then evaluate the results of test-pit excavations in order to determine whether more extensive excavations within the feature are justified. In other words, test pits are often a prelude to more elaborate vertical and horizontal excavations.

The archaeologist may use sets of test pits to gain information about the large-scale distribution of data in, and the overall composition of, an archaeological site. This is done by excavating a number of test pits in various locations in a site. Such extensive coverage may be achieved by using the site grid system, with each test pit corresponding to a given grid square. This kind of test-pit program is well suited to a probabilistic sampling design (Fig. 7.9); Schiffer's test-pitting at the Joint Site has already been described as an example. In other cases, preselected intervals, such as alternate squares of a grid, may be used to acquire extensive site coverage.

Figure 7.9 A systematic line of test-pits, located at regular 15-m intervals and aligned with the site grid.

The chief limitation of test pits is their lack of a horizontal dimension. Their deliberate emphasis on depth yields much evidence on sequence or accumulation over time, but very little information on the materials associated with any one time. A compromise solution to this problem is the *trench*. A trench is a narrow linear excavation used to expose both the full vertical extent of a deposit and its horizontal extent in one direction. Trenches, then, are essentially excavations in two dimensions (the vertical dimension and one horizontal dimension). They resemble extended test pits, often 1 to 2 meters wide but as long as necessary to cut through the feature or area being probed. Thus trenches explore both vertical accumulation and horizontal association. A trench often begins as a single test pit within a conspicuous feature, becoming a trench by extension of one axis of the pit to provide a fuller cross-section of the feature. Alternatively, a line of individual test pits may provide a nearly continuous cross-section; if a fully continuous view is required, the balks (remaining matrix) separating the pits may be removed. Like test pits, trenches cut through deposits and often serve as a prelude to more extensive lateral excavations.

Figure 7.10 View of an earthen structure revealed by a trench; a second, smaller trench has now penetrated this structure and its supporting platform.

Trenching excavations can be used in many ways. One of their most familiar uses is in probing individual surface features such as mounds (Fig. 7.10). Burial mounds, ruined earthen platforms, and the like are usually examined either by a single trench or by two perpendicular cross-cutting trenches. Similarly, when a whole site consists of a single mound—as in the *tells* and *tepes* of the Near East or the town and village sites of Thailand—trenches may reveal the overall stratigraphy of the site. Trenches for these purposes may be aligned with the axes of the mound being excavated or with cardinal directions. The archaeologist may follow trench penetration with lateral clearing excavations designed to expose discovered features— floors, burials, hearths, and so on—in plan view. Of course, deeply buried features are often difficult to expose fully. When the deposits being cut are very deep, the excavation may take the form of a step-trench (Fig. 7.11) so that greater depths may be reached with less risk of the trench walls collapsing for lack of support.

Occasionally the location of trench operations may be guided by probabilistic sampling methods. In most cases, however, the means are nonprobabilistic: the archaeologist uses trenches to cut into areas of some particular interest for some specified reason. For example, a trench may be cut on the axis of a structure in order to reveal the stratigraphic relationships between successive renovations of the building and floors or pavements that might lie adjacent to it. Or a trench into the end of a single-mound site could be used to determine whether the site boundary at surface level was the same as that below the surface.

Figure 7.11 Step-trench used to probe a large (23-m-high) mound.

One final kind of excavation may be mentioned in this section—the *tunnel*. Archaeological tunnels resemble test pits that have been rotated to a horizontal plane. Like test pits, tunnels are essentially one-dimensional excavations, but that dimension is a horizontal one. Unless supplemented by test pits or trenches, tunnels do not reveal the vertical dimension of a feature or deposit. They may still yield information on temporal sequence, however, as when they cut into successively renovated constructions (see Fig. 7.12). But, like test pits and trenches, single tunnels give little data on horizontal associations at any one level.

Tunnels are best suited for testing within features or site areas that are too deeply buried to be reached by other means of excavation. They are an efficient means of exploring such areas because they reach deeply buried areas with less expenditure of time and money. However, this efficiency factor must be weighed against the fact that tunnels provide only a one-dimensional view, as compared to the fuller two-dimensional view provided by a trench. Even more important, tunnels are potentially dangerous enterprises which should be undertaken only after the matrix has been evaluated for stability.

Clearing Excavations

The primary objective of clearing excavations is to expose in plan view the nature and extent of subsurface archaeological data. Clearing excavations are not usually initiated until penetrating operations (usually test pits and/or trenches) have revealed the basic stratigraphic relationships of the site and its components. With this information in hand, the archaeologist can expose as much as possible of the three-dimensional patterns and relationships of features, artifacts, and other data within the site (Fig. 7.13).

Figure 7.12 Tunnel used to probe the center of a large earthen mound.

Area excavations are used to expose the horizontal extent of data, with the vertical stratigraphic record preserved in balks, or unexcavated divisions between excavations. Area excavations usually consist of squares, often 5 or 10 m on a side, which resemble large test pits, but their information yield is much different. Vertical penetration takes place more slowly because a much larger horizontal area is being investigated at one time. In this situation the archaeologist usually places a small *sondage* or control pit, within the excavation to preview the stratigraphy. Clearing to a given stratigraphic level is then done across the square by peeling away the overburden to reveal the full horizontal distribution of remains within the square at that stratigraphic level, including remains of architecture as well as other features and artifacts. Once recorded, all the features and artifacts at this level are removed, and the next lower level is exposed. Excavation of multiple squares within a site allows the archaeologist to assemble a series of successive site plans. An analogous "composite clearing" situation concerning the excavation of the royal burials of Ur was described in Chapter 3. With area excavations, the balks, or matrix left standing between adjacent squares, provide a record of the stratigraphic position of each layer within the square after its remains within the square boundaries have been removed. Area excavation techniques have been the primary excavation approach at such varied sites as Hasanlu in Iran, Taxila in Pakistan, Ban Chiang in Thailand, and the Abri Pataud rock shelter in France.

Stripping excavations are used to clear large areas of overburden to reveal uninterrupted spatial distributions of data, such as the foundations of large buildings, remnants of entire settlements, and other extensive remains (Fig. 7.14). Stripping excavations do not leave balks

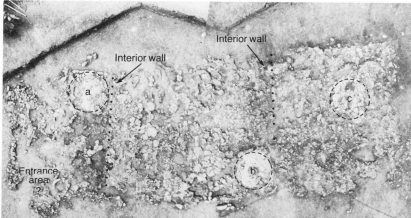 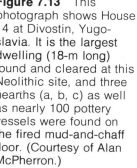

Figure 7.13 This photograph shows House 14 at Divostin, Yugoslavia. It is the largest dwelling (18-m long) found and cleared at this Neolithic site, and three hearths (a, b, c) as well as nearly 100 pottery vessels were found on the fired mud-and-chaff floor. (Courtesy of Alan McPherron.)

Figure 7.14 Large area stripped of overburden by mechanical earth movers and cleaned by hand, revealing circle of cremation pits.

to preserve stratigraphic relationships. Mechanical equipment is sometimes used to strip vast extents of overburden from a buried site. But this can only be done after the depth of the overburden is first established by penetrating excavations. The same basic strategy—first penetrating vertically to discover the nature and depth of subsurface situations, and then clearing laterally to expose their horizontal extent —can also be applied to archaeological situations that do not involve formal occupation surfaces. For instance, middens are usually probed by test pits or trenches to determine the nature and depth of the deposit. Once the midden has been tested in the vertical dimension, a lateral excavation may be initiated at the face of the vertical cut to follow the surface of the uppermost stratified layer and discover its limits. By this method, each layer in turn can be "peeled back" to expose the extent of the next. In such transposed primary contexts, especially if the deposit is extensive, the main objective of clearing excavation is often to acquire a larger sample of artifactual and ecofactual data from each layer rather than to define its exact horizontal extent. In such situations, the vertical excavations may be used to isolate a block or column of the midden. The column is then peeled back one layer at a time and the artifacts and ecofacts are collected from each level.

Variants and Combinations

Clearly, most excavation projects will involve both penetration and clearing operations. Each type has its advantages (Fig. 7.15); as always, specific choices among alternative techniques depend on the nature of the deposits and the goals and resources of the project.

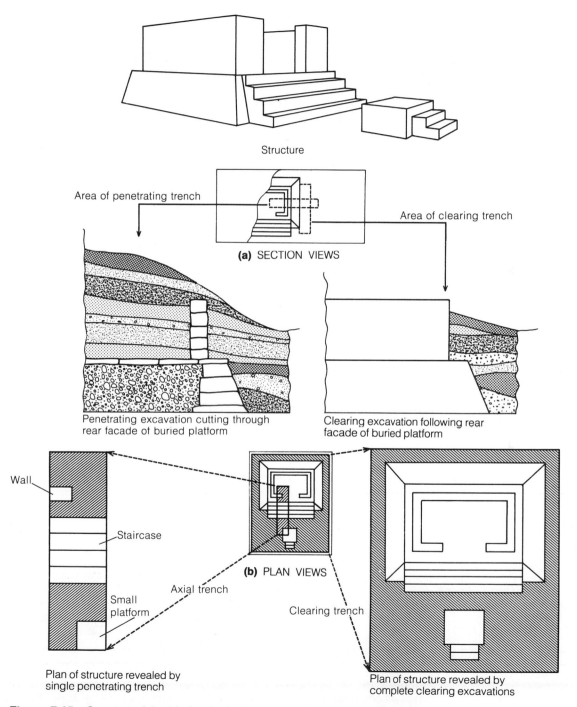

Structure

Area of penetrating trench

Area of clearing trench

(a) SECTION VIEWS

Penetrating excavation cutting through
rear facade of buried platform

Clearing excavation following rear
facade of buried platform

Wall

Staircase

Axial trench

(b) PLAN VIEWS

Clearing trench

Small
platform

Plan of structure revealed by
single penetrating trench

Plan of structure revealed by
complete clearing excavations

Figure 7.15 Contrast of the kinds of information provided by penetrating
and clearing excavations of the same hypothetical feature.

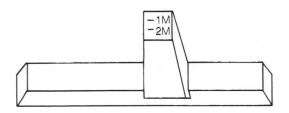

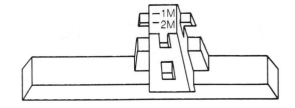

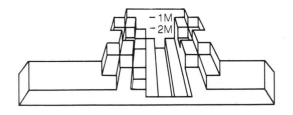

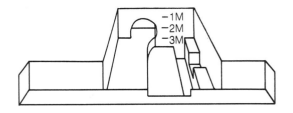

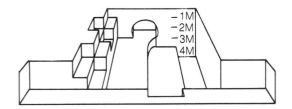

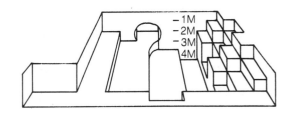

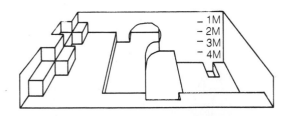

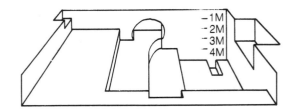

Figure 7.16 An example of combined penetrating and clearing excavations applied to stratified deposits in Purron Cave in the Tehuacán Valley, Mexico. (After MacNeish 1972.)

In the Tehuacán Valley, Mexico, during a project described at length in Chapter 5, excavation of each site began with a trench through the apparently deepest part of the deposit. Along with evaluation of the stratigraphy of each trench, Richard MacNeish and his colleagues assessed the time span represented by the deposit and the range of materials being recovered from it. They were especially interested in the recovery of organic remains, over a long time span, that would bear on the question of the development of domesticated plants. On the basis of these evaluations, the archaeologists selected 11 of the 39 tested sites, most of which were caves, for more extensive excavation. These excavations proceeded by peeling horizontal strata, moving away from the trench wall, in alternate small "squares" (or descending columns) of 1 m in width (Fig. 7.16). Eventually the intervening 1-m balk columns were removed, and horizontal clearing continued via these small discrete vertical segments away from the trench face. In this way each stratum was traced, little by little, yielding information on horizontal arrangements (and thus on possible use-related associations) as well as larger numbers of remains. A similar approach was used by Hole, Flannery, and Neely at Ali Kosh in the Deh Luran plain of Iran to facilitate detailed control in a finely layered deposit.

A different combination, stressing clearing, was used in the Abri Pataud site of the Dordogne region of France. The rock shelter was occupied between about 34,000 and 20,000 years ago, and the 14 strata of habitation surfaces and debris accumulated during this time formed a deposit some 9.25 m deep. The excavations, directed by Hallam L. Movius, Jr., were organized by a 2-m grid system. Instead of a central trench as at Tehuacán, a set of 1-m test trenches bordering a central area 4 m wide served as control pits for previewing stratigraphy. With these test trenches as stratigraphic guides, individual layers were cleared across the larger gridded area, exposing broad living areas including hearths and associated evidence of human occupation.

A striking contrast to the Abri Pataud in site and research goals is provided at Tikal, Guatemala. The North Acropolis of this Maya site covers an area of about 1 hectare or 2½ acres. Its uppermost plaza level, 10 m above limestone bedrock, represents the accumulation of more than a millennium of construction, beginning about 600 B.C. The primary goal of investigations here, as directed by William R. Coe, was to understand the constructional development of the architectural complex; as a result penetration excavations were emphasized. A huge trench was cut through the overall feature; myriad small, secondary clearing excavations and radiating tunnels linked component features—buildings, tombs, and so on—located outside the main trench to the master constructional sequence (Fig. 7.17). Some of the

Excavation methods at Tehuacán, Mexico

Excavation methods at the Abri Pataud, France

Excavation methods at Tikal, Guatemala

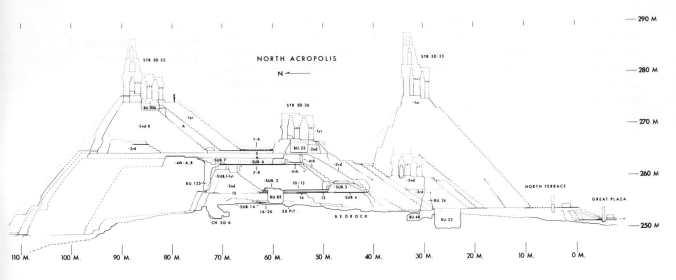

Figure 7.17 Simplified section of some 1000 years of superimposed construction at the North Acropolis of Tikal, Guatemala. (Courtesy of the Tikal Project, the University Museum, University of Pennsylvania.)

tunnels are still accessible, allowing visitors today to appreciate directly the way the ancient Maya builders encased earlier constructions in later ones.

Clearly, many strategies are possible for excavating an archaeological site. More than one archaeologist has compared the excavation task to solving a three-dimensional jigsaw puzzle. Of course, excavation does not attempt to put the pieces together; rather it takes them apart. The archaeologist "reassembles" them later, on paper, by section and plan drawings. In order to reassemble the pieces, the investigator must not only use care in taking them apart (excavating) but must also observe and record precisely how they originally fit together. In the following sections we will consider the techniques for conducting and recording excavations—techniques that, when properly executed, enable the archaeologist later to reconstruct and interpret the original three-dimensional site.

Excavation Tools and Techniques

A variety of time-tested procedures are used in conducting the kinds of excavations we have discussed. New techniques and equipment are continually being developed to improve the rate and quality of archaeological data recovery. We can reflect on the cumulative refinements made in the past, which have led over time to more detailed and precise observation. But we can also see all too clearly the mistakes and omissions of past investigators, and the consequential loss of irreplaceable information about the past. To keep things in perspective, of course, we must consider that future archaeologists will undoubtedly look with criticism, if not with amusement, upon the ways in which we acquire data today. The point is that each archaeologist has a responsibility to use the most refined techniques and equipment available.

Archaeological excavation begins with selection of tools. The alternatives range from the largest mechanical earthmovers, such as front-end loaders and backhoes, to the finest hand-held brushes and dental picks. Obviously, the scale of equipment used to move earth depends on the particular excavation situation, and reflects the relative requirements of the situation for precision and attention to detail versus speed and capacity for earth removal.

If great quantities of sterile overburden or badly disturbed debris cover a site or a feature, removal of this material with heavy-duty equipment may be expedient. At some sites, such as deeply buried Sybaris, mechanical earthmovers are the only feasible way to reach the necessary depths. In other cases, one or more test pits may be placed to gauge the depth of the overburden, to guide its removal by mechanical means.

In many excavation situations, pick-and-shovel crews usually provide the appropriate combination of precision and speed, especially for removal of overburden and penetration of materials in secondary context, such as construction fill. When intact features are encountered or artifacts are found in apparent primary context, archaeologists resort to finer tools to remove surrounding matrix. The sharpened mason's pointing trowel is one of the most valuable tools in such situations because its shape is well suited for such tasks as clearing and following plastered floors or masonry walls. With careful trowel scraping, tamped-earth floors can be distinguished from overlying soils by changes in texture and hardness. The edges of "negative" features such as post molds, pits, drainage ditches, and the like can also be detected and traced by trowelling, through noting changes in color and texture (Fig. 7.18). Excavations at Sutton Hoo in Suffolk, England, are an example of painstaking recovery of negative evidence—in this case the impression of a wooden ship used to house a seventh-century Saxon burial. Virtually all traces of the wood itself were gone, but the undisturbed array of nails and the excavated

**Precision excavation:
Sutton Hoo, England**

Figure 7.18 Casts of victims of the Vesuvius eruption of A.D. 79, recovered at Pompeii when careful excavation revealed voids in the ash which were then filled with plaster. (Courtesy of the University Museum, University of Pennsylvania.)

Table 7.2

INVENTORY OF INDIVIDUAL EXCAVATOR'S "DIG KIT"

1 2¼ × 2¼ format camera and film
1 mason's trowel
1 Brunton compass
1 small palette knife
1 Swiss army knife
1 wooden 2-meter folding rule (English and metric units)
1 steel 3-meter tape
1 steel 15-meter tape
Nylon line
2 line levels
Assorted dental picks
Assorted small paintbrushes
1 plumb bob
1 plastic metric ruler
Ball-point pens
Assorted drawing pencils (with erasers and sharpener)
String tags (provenience labels)
1 marking pen (waterproof ink)
Assorted cloth artifact bags
Assorted plastic ecofact bags
Notebook and extra note paper
Graph paper (8½ × 11 inches)
1 Clipboard
1 Canvas "dig kit" bag

(a)

(b)

Figure 7.19 Excavation of a burial mound showing initial exposure of
(a) the principal stone-lined tomb chamber and (b) an accompanying burial
(the outline of the burial pit can be seen above the label).

''mold'' of the ship's hull give a good picture of the vessel's appearance.

When very small or fragile materials are encountered, the finest excavation instruments are used to free them from their matrix. Small
brushes of assorted sizes, along with dental picks and air blowers, are
very useful in clearing remains such as plaster or stucco sculpture,
bones, burials, and other organic items (Fig. 7.19). When such finds
are poorly preserved, as in the case of crumbling bones, they must be
treated in the field for strengthening and protection before removal to
a laboratory for further conservation.

The full inventory of archaeological equipment is quite extensive. It
includes not only excavation tools but also survey and drafting instruments (some of which were discussed in Chapter 6), cameras,
notebooks, and so on. Table 7.2 lists the items in a standard archaeological ''field kit'' as used by members of one research project.

Using appropriate excavation tools, the archaeologist proceeds to isolate archaeological materials and clear away their encasing matrix. The manner in which matrix is removed is extremely important. There are essentially two ways to remove matrix in the course of excavation: one approach is to remove the matrix in *arbitrary levels;* the other is to work in units corresponding to visible strata or *natural levels*. Most archaeologists strongly favor the stratigraphic method, excavating each visible layer as a discrete unit before proceeding to the next. We have already mentioned the basic method for this procedure: use of a preliminary sounding pit to give the archaeologist a general indication of the sequence of strata to be encountered in other excavations, of the relative thickness and composition of each stratum, and of any special precautions or attention that should be given to particular strata.

In some cases, however, the matrix may be devoid of visible strata. In these situations, rather than excavating the entire deposit as a single unit, the archaeologist may subdivide it into uniform blocks of arbitrary thickness—usually 5, 10, or 20 cm thick—and remove each arbitrary level in turn. Such a procedure is preferable to excavation in larger units for two reasons. First, by dislodging smaller volumes at any one time, one maximizes control of provenience of artifacts and ecofacts encountered. Second, even in matrices lacking visible stratification, temporal distinctions in deposition may exist. By removing material in relatively small units, the archaeologist may preserve at least an approximation of the original stratigraphic relationships. For the same reason, many archaeologists recommend subdividing observed strata—especially when these are relatively thick—into several arbitrary levels, both to facilitate excavation and to maintain any depositional distinctions that may later be suggested, in laboratory analysis, for artifacts recovered from the same gross stratum.

Once features, artifacts, or ecofacts are located and isolated within their matrix, their provenience must be determined and recorded. Provenience control allows the archaeologist to determine data associations—the three-dimensional relationships among features, artifacts, and ecofacts. Since these variables are crucial ingredients in the evaluation of context, determination of provenience is a basic task for all forms of archaeological data and in every excavation situation.

*Provenience Control: Units and Labels

Controlling provenience in excavation, like that for surface collections, begins with labeling of the excavation operations. If the source of an item is to be recorded, that source must have a label. If excavation areas are located according to a site grid system, it is usually most convenient to designate each data collection operation by the grid square in which it is located. For example, an excavation in grid square N1/E3 would take this designation as its operation label. If, however, more than one operation—including excavations and/or surface collections—take place within the same grid square, the label should so indicate. For example, a surface collection in square N1/E3 could be operation N1/E3(A), and two test pits within the square might be labeled operations N1/E3(B) and N1/E3(C).

The usefulness of grid designations as operation labels is obvious, especially in the case of surface collections. Such a system is also useful in test-pitting programs. This approach may prove cumbersome or confusing, however, when operations focus on features that extend across two or more grid squares. In this case work pertaining to a single feature might require several different labels. Thus an archaeologist who is likely to encounter extensive features may find it more efficient to label operations according to the features they explore. But in that case a separate designation system would be required for investigating areas that lacked visible features.

One way to avoid these problems is to designate operations and suboperations by a system that is independent of both grid squares and features. This system defines an "operation" as data collection in some particular, specified area or in different areas for a single specified purpose. For example, in the archaeological research at Quiriguá, Operation 2 was defined as all data collection related to Structure 1A-3. Operation 3, on the other hand, was a set of test pits, located in various parts of the site, which were used to seek and investigate middens or other nonarchitectural deposits. Within these operation categories, suboperation labels indicated particular investigations: at Quiriguá, Suboperation 2B was an axial trench into the rear of Structure 1A-3, and Suboperation 3F was a specific test pit near the project laboratory. Since labeling of each operation and suboperation is independent of any grid or map of the site, all locations must be accurately plotted to tie provenience within the operations to the site provenience system.

Beyond designation of operation, precise control of provenience is based on determination of physical location in both horizontal and vertical dimensions. Horizontal location is determined with reference to the site grid (see Chapter 6). No matter what system of operation labeling is used, all operations must be accurately plotted with respect to the site grid. Within each operation, then, the location of artifacts and features discovered can be related to the grid system, either by direct reference to specific grid coordinates or by location within the

Provenience control: Quiriguá, Guatemala

limits of the excavation (Fig. 7.20). These determinations may be made by instruments such as the surveyor's transit, by measuring angle and distance from a known reference point such as a grid-intersection stake. Or location can be measured directly by means of a steel measuring tape; however, this must be done precisely, maintaining right angles with respect to reference points.

Vertical location is determined with respect to a known elevation; this may be done with surveyors' instruments or by direct measurement. An instrument such as a level or transit may be used to measure relative elevation with reference to a known elevation datum (see Chapter 6), or elevation relative to that of some known point nearby may be measured with a line level, steel tape, and plumb bob (Fig. 7.21).

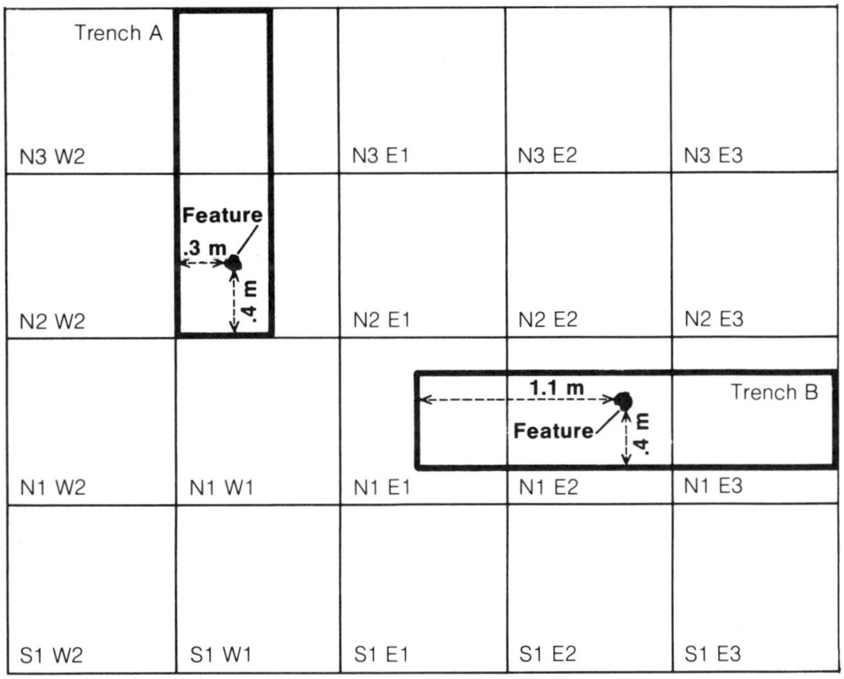

Figure 7.20   A site grid (in this case, a four-component infinite grid) may be used to designate the horizontal provenience of excavated features, as in Trench A, where measurements are made north and east of the N2W1 stake, to record the provenience as "(N2)40 cm/(W1)30 cm." In Trench B, horizontal provenience is measured from the excavation limits, as "110 cm east of west wall, 40 cm north of south wall." The latter is convertible to a site grid designation as long as the location of the trench walls is known in respect to the grid.

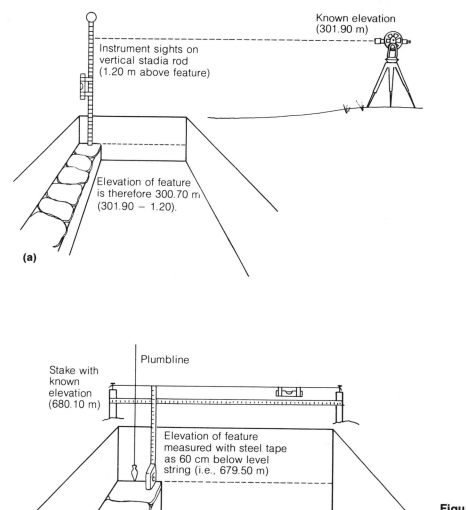

Known elevation
(301.90 m)

Instrument sights on
vertical stadia rod
(1.20 m above feature)

Elevation of feature
is therefore 300.70 m
(301.90 − 1.20).

(a)

Stake with
known
elevation
(680.10 m)

Plumbline

Elevation of feature
measured with steel tape
as 60 cm below level
string (i.e., 679.50 m)

(b)

Figure 7.21 Two ways of determining vertical provenience: In (a), an instrument of known elevation is used in conjunction with a stadia rod; in (b), an elevation is measured along a plumb line intersecting a level string of known elevation.

**Provenience control:
Abri Pataud, France**

In an innovative adaptation to a rock-shelter setting, Movius used an elevated grid as a provenience control system for the Abri Pataud site in France. He set up a frame of pipes to form a grid of 2-m squares over the excavation area. Plumb bobs suspended from the frame defined the grid on the surface of the excavation, thus providing horizontal referents; measurements down from the pipes defined vertical provenience (Fig. 7.22). A similar pipe grid has been used to control horizontal provenience in underwater sites (Fig. 7.23). In open sites—mounds, mound groups, or whatever—provenience controls are usually set at a horizontal rather than a vertical distance from the excavations. But the principle of establishing a permanent, accessible set of horizontal and vertical reference points is the same.

Provenience designations also include labels for matrix units, both stratigraphic layers and cultural features. These may simply be numbered in a running series within each operation: if 23 features were encountered within Operation 2 at Quiriguá, for example, they would be designated F-1 through F-23. A similar but independent series could be developed for observed soil strata (S-1 through S-n). Features may be further specified, as by segregating a series of burials or designating component parts of complex architectural constructions.

In situations of complex stratigraphy or construction, there is an advantage to delaying numerical designation of features until after excavation is completed, in order to evaluate the nature and interrelationships of features before placing them in any order. For example, suppose an excavator begins by defining three construction phases called I, II, and III, and then finds later that there is a fourth, located between phases II and III. Is the latter phase "IIA," or perhaps "II/III"? The same potential difficulty exists for soil strata. A solution that has proved useful in such widely varying excavation situations as Tikal, Guatemala and Dun Aileen, Ireland, is the field use

Figure 7.22 During excavation of a Paleolithic shelter at Abri Pataud, France, provenience control was maintained by a pipe grid suspended over the site. (By permission of the Peabody Museum, Harvard University, and Hallam L. Movius, Jr.)

of temporary "nonsense" word labels that imply neither order nor any other relationship. "MIT floor" may serve as a perfectly good interim label without implying any relation in time or space to "BOT floor" or "YIL wall."

The same caution should be used in applying functional labels early in an investigation. If a feature designated upon discovery as a "post hole" and so described in lists of construction features is later determined to be a pit for a cremation burial, the whole designation scheme may be thrown into chaos. This is precisely why neutral terms such as *stratum* or *feature,* are useful to the archaeologist: noncommittal labels may be applied first, with segregation into functional classes taking place after analysis.

Thus far we have considered how the archaeologist can refer to and control provenience for data acquisition operations and for the features and noncultural matrix units discovered by these operations. It is now time to consider provenience control for the most common kind of archaeological evidence—the artifact—along with its companion in portability, the ecofact.

Provenience control for such data is often complicated by their frequently small size and their usual abundance. When artifacts are relatively rare, or when they are being encountered in apparently primary context, each item discovered may be individually and precisely plotted. The same means for determining provenience positions that have already been discussed can be used for artifacts; means for graphic recording, such as photographs and plans, will be considered below. After they are recorded, artifacts are removed from their matrix and placed in a bag or other container to be taken to the field laboratory for processing. From this point on, they must always carry a label relating them to their provenience.

Figure 7.23 Note the pipe grid used to control provenience during the underwater excavation of the Roman shipwreck at Yassi Ada, off the coast of Turkey. (© National Geographic Society.)

A number that refers to a finds registry or object catalogue provides one kind of label. For example, provenience and other data for object #347 may be found by looking through a numerically ordered log. But many artifacts such as potsherds, are too numerous to be registered. What labels should they receive? Alternatively, precise, individual provenience information (N143.26/E16.21/V70.18) can serve. But obviously this system becomes cumbersome to deal with in the actual labelling of the finds; it also implies that, to have a label, every artifact must have such precise provenience information.

One system that contains some provenience information, but also provides for differentiation between bulk and "special" artifacts, uses the provenience concept of the *lot*. A lot is a minimum provenience unit within an operation. Lots may be used to control surface collections, as in grouping artifacts from a specific area or concentration. Within an excavation, each level recognized to have internal uniformity may be defined to correspond to a lot. For instance, if the archaeologist is excavating a test pit by arbitrary 20-cm levels, each level may be defined as a lot as long as the matrix within it appears homogeneous. If a change occurs in the observable characteristics of the matrix, such as the appearance of a new texture or color, the excavator closes the previous lot and defines a new one to incorporate material recovered from this distinct stratum. Of course, if an excavation is proceeding by natural levels, each observed stratum would be defined as a distinct lot. Any other kind of discrete deposit encountered, from a pocket of outwashed debris to a burial pit, should be segregated and defined as a distinct lot. A lot is, therefore, a general kind of unit; the size, form, location, and composition of each actual lot must be defined specifically. Exact horizontal and vertical limits of lots may be determined by either tape or instrument, using the same provenience techniques already discussed for operations and features.

Labels for lot units should indicate the operation and suboperation of which they are a part. For example, Lot 3F/4 would be the fourth lot defined for Suboperation F of Operation 3; at Quiriguá, this particular lot happened to be the fourth 20-cm level below the surface in the test pit in the project laboratory compound.

All artifacts and ecofacts must carry their lot designation as a label. But at this point a further distinction may be made between bulk artifacts, such as most potsherds, and items that deserve special note, such as whole vessels, other unusual objects, and objects found in use-related primary contexts. The bulk items would simply receive the lot label: the sherds from the lot described in the last paragraph were all labeled "3F/4." But if a whole vessel were encountered within that lot, it would receive an additional designation keying it to the catalogue or finds registry. This can be a number in a separate, running registry series; the designation of this vessel would then be "3F/4" *and* "467." Alternatively, the catalogue could be organized and ordered by the operation system, so that catalogue designations would incorporate operation and lot (and therefore provenience) information; in this case, the vessel might be designated "3F/4-1," indicating that it was the first catalogued find from lot 3F/4. As a third option, the lot label can be entered in the registry, with the artifact itself bearing only the catalogue running-series number, such as "467." Cataloguing procedures will be discussed in detail in Chapter 8.

Use of a lot label provides a general provenience designation for items too small or plentiful to be plotted individually. This in turn encourages controlled recovery of more of these items through bulk processing of matrix units. The most common means of recovering artifacts and ecofacts under bulk conditions is by screening. Matrix may be shoveled directly into a screening box (Fig. 7.24) adjacent to the excavation or transported by wheelbarrow or basket to a central screening area. Of course, it is crucial in all cases to maintain carefully the separation of material from distinct lots. Once the matrix has passed through the screen, the recovered artifacts and ecofacts are removed from the screen surface and bagged. At this point, the lot label is attached to the bag, which is then securely closed to prevent losses and mixups. (Most archaeologists prefer cloth bags that can be tied shut with a drawstring.)

Flotation or water separation is another method of bulk processing that has been of special benefit for recovery of organic materials. When matrix is submerged in water, lighter organic materials such as seeds and bone will sink more slowly than soil, stones, and burned

Figure 7.24 Screening provides a means of recovering small artifacts and ecofacts which might otherwise be missed during excavation. (Courtesy of the Peabody Museum of Harvard University and Gordon R. Willey.)

Figure 7.25 Flotation is used to recover organic remains from matrix, here being collected in a fine-mesh screen. (Photo by Susan Luebbermann, Arizona State Museum.)

clay; the lighter material can then be skimmed off, dried, and bagged (Fig. 7.25). (Plastic bags, sealed and labeled by lot, are the preferred field containers for most organic remains.) In some cases, chemicals such as sodium silicate or zinc chloride may be added to water used for flotation (sometimes in a second stage of flotation) to increase its specific gravity and hence its ability to segregate bone from plant remains. Water separation techniques have proven so valuable for recovery of organic remains that, in arid environments such as the southwestern United States, archaeologists have adapted the approach so as to "float" as much matrix as possible while using a minimum of water.

Because each excavation situation is unique, each will pose somewhat different problems for data recovery; the archaeologist must be ready to improvise in order to recover as much data as possible. For instance, archaeologists excavating within construction fill of earth mounds of the Salamá Valley, Guatemala, noted that screening of the earth matrix failed to segregate very fine fragments of jade that appeared to be redeposited workshop debris. In order to recover—efficiently—at least a sample of this material for identification, several lots of matrix were passed through a makeshift sluicing system, constructed of wood and using running water from a nearby irrigation canal. As a result, the archaeologists recovered a full range of jade particles, from small chips and flakes to sand-size grains, that indicated ancient jade-working activities in the vicinity.

All artifacts and ecofacts, once removed from their matrix, are transported in labeled containers to the laboratory. There the provenience label and/or catalogue label will be applied directly to each object; this and other aspects of laboratory processing will be discussed in detail in Chapter 8. At this point we return to the excavation, to discuss how other records besides provenience labels are made.

*Recording the Acquisition of Archaeological Data

Apart from artifacts and other samples physically removed and preserved by research operations, all data retrieved by the archaeologist are in the form of photographs or verbal or graphic descriptions. Furthermore, any portion of a site that is excavated is thereby destroyed. Thus the only record of the original matrix, proveniences, associations, and contexts of archaeological data is the set of field notes, drawings, and photographs produced by the investigator. The manner by which archaeological research is recorded is therefore of prime importance.

There are many specific ways to record data; we will discuss some of the most useful means later in this section. No matter which methods are used, however, all data records should have certain common characteristics. First, they must be permanent: the paper used to record data should be of high quality and have a long life span. Inks should not be water soluble or subject to rapid fading. Whenever possible, copies of all records should be made as protection against loss. Some archaeologists prefer to make carbon copies of written notes in the field; in other cases photocopies of all notes, drawings, and other records are made as soon as possible after leaving the field. If the research takes place over a long period of time, one set of records should be maintained in the field laboratory or headquarters, and another at the home base or institution.

Records should be prepared clearly enough that anyone could understand them. If symbols are used, they should be standardized, and a key must be provided, as must definitions for all specialized terms and notations. Above all, records must be kept up to date. Excavators should never allow themselves to fall behind in recording data in the field. A useful—if somewhat grisly—way to think about this point is the "hit-by-a-truck" consideration. Each investigator should continually ponder whether, if he or she were dispatched by a truck tomorrow, a successor would find the data record usable and current.

One way to increase recording accuracy and speed is to use standardized forms for at least a part of the data record. Such forms usually assure that comparable information is gathered about all examples of a particular kind of archaeological data, regardless of who compiles and completes the form. Forms are especially useful, therefore, in large-scale research programs involving large numbers of investigators. For example, use of a standardized burial form (Fig. 7.26) results in acquisition of the same categories of data for all burials. Standardized forms can also provide a link between field recording and computerized storage of recorded data. It is important, however, that forms such as these retain enough flexibility to assure that the data are not being distorted, or that other information is not being ignored simply because the form makes no specific provision for it. Open-ended sections for miscellaneous comments and observations may help to prevent such difficulties.

The data acquisition record must be well integrated with other aspects of research. Surface survey and excavation records should be linked to data generated later in laboratory processing and analysis (see Chapter 8). It is especially important, therefore, that all records be labelled for easy cross-referencing and indexing. In a well-integrated recording system, a researcher can begin at any point—for instance, with a particular burial—and follow cross-references to locate easily all other records pertaining to that burial.

SGS ARCHAEOLOGICAL PROJECT
Human Burial Form

Context: ☐ Primary*   Site:

       ☐ Simple burial   Operation/Lot(s):
       ☐ Prepared chamber   Excavator:

   ☐ Secondary   Date(s):

      Give circumstances: Cross-references:

                       Notebooks:
_____

                       Drawings:
_____

                       Photos:
_____

*Dimensions of grave or chamber: DESCRIPTION OF SKELETAL REMAINS:

Length: _____ cm   Completeness or Number
                                                     (left)   (right)
Width: _____ cm   Skull   _____

Orientation: Vertebrae   _____
                                 Sternum   _____
Position of principal skeleton: Sacrum   _____
                                 Innominates _____
    ☐ Supine   Scapula   _____ _____
                                 Ribs   _____ _____
    ☐ Prone   Humerus   _____ _____
                                 Radius   _____ _____
    ☐ On side (☐ left/ ☐ right) Ulna   _____ _____
                                 Carpus   _____ _____
    ☐ Flexed   Metacarpals _____ _____
                                 Phalanges   _____ _____
    ☐ Extended   Femur   _____ _____
                                 Tibia   _____ _____
Orientation: Patella   _____ _____
                                 Tarsus   _____ _____
Main axis of body   Metatarsals _____ _____
                                 Phalanges   _____ _____
With head to: Clavicle   _____ _____

Face to:
                                 Note any obvious pathologies:_____
Estimated age:
                                 _____
    ☐ Fetus   ☐ Child
                                 _____
    ☐ Young adult
                                 _____
    ☐ Mature adult
                                 Preservatives used, if any: _____
Sex: ☐ Male

    ☐ Female   _____

    ☐ Indeterminate

Cross-reference to other skeletons
  if this is a multiple burial:

Associated artifacts/samples	Field no.	Provenience	Cross-references

THIS FORM MUST BE ACCOMPANIED BY SCALED 1:10 PLAN AND SECTION DRAWINGS.

Figure 7.26 An example of a standardized form for recording burial data.

Forms of Data Records

Field data records are of four basic kinds: field notes, scaled drawings, photographs, and standardized record forms. These records are used in all kinds of data collection operations, but they are generally more detailed and elaborate when used to record archaeological excavations than when used in surface survey or reconnaissance.

Field notes are usually the fundamental record of any archaeological research project. They normally consist of a running chronicle of the progress of research, most commonly divided into individual daily entries. When completed, a record of this kind provides a thorough history of the investigations. The chronicle often begins during the preliminary phases of research; it should include all information acquired during background and feasibility studies as well as logistic matters, budget information, preliminary research objectives, and so forth. Since no one can anticipate what kind of information will be useful or even crucial at a later date, it is better to record as much potentially relevant information as possible in the field notes, rather than to regret later that some useful fact or insight was omitted.

The core of field notes is the day-to-day description of the progress of excavation or surface operations. Each excavator should keep an individual notebook to describe his or her research responsibilities. Some archaeologists prefer to create a standard form for field notes; others write in regular notebooks with no set format. In the latter case, each excavator should be guided to record at least a standard body of information, the specifics of which depend partly on the project's objectives. The minimum required information usually includes daily observations of the weather and other working conditions, methods of data acquisition, short-range and long-range objectives, and so forth. For instance, a daily record in the progress of a particular excavation might include the number of people actually at work (excavating, screening, removing back dirt, etc.); descriptions of matrix and stratigraphy; provenience and association information about each artifact or ecofact encountered (or definitions of each provenience lot, if that system is being used); descriptions of features; and preliminary assessments of context. In addition, the researcher should use the field notes to orient or focus thoughts on larger issues raised by the investigations—defining working hypotheses, proposing tests for hypotheses, stating priorities of research, and so on.

Scaled drawings are always essential data records, but they are much more detailed and elaborate for excavations than for most surface operations. Plan and cross-section views are normally required to record, respectively, the horizontal and vertical aspects of observed strata, features, and artifact/ecofact distributions encountered during excavation. Some archaeologists prefer the convenience of

Figure 7.27 This excavator is using a line level, on a taut string, and a tape measure to draw a scaled section of the test pit.

graph paper kept in the field notebook for doing scaled drawings; surveyors' notebooks often provide alternating pages of plain and gridded paper to facilitate both kinds of recording. One should check the kind of scaled grid to be used, however, since metric ruled is the preferred international standard for all scientific research. In many cases, scaled drawings must be rendered on sheets larger than notebook size. Metric gridded paper for this purpose is available in a variety of sizes, including large rolls, to accommodate even the largest archaeological plans and sections.

As a normal rule, the walls of all types of excavations should be recorded by scaled *section drawings* as well as by photography. If, however, all walls of a given excavation show the same stratification, then recording one north-south wall and one east-west wall is usually sufficient. Before recording, excavation walls must be plumbed to be vertical and cleaned and scraped smooth with a trowel or similar tool. This is done to assure the most accurate and detailed scale recording possible by reducing scale distortions from sloping or uneven surfaces. Under some circumstances, brushing or spraying the walls with water may help to define the stratum boundaries and features more clearly. And some archaeologists use a trowel to incise the upper and lower limits of each stratum so that they are easier to record. If this is to be done, photographs should be taken first in order to have an "unbiased" record of the excavation.

One of the easiest ways to produce a scaled section drawing is to impose a horizontally level string on the excavation wall (using a line level), securing it with nails or line pins. Vertical measurements can then be taken, using a tape and plumb line, on the excavation wall from the horizontal string to the features being recorded; these can then be converted to the scaled drawing sheet (Fig. 7.27). Some archaeologists have used scaled photographs, shot at precise right angles to the excavation wall, that can be traced later in the laboratory to prepare scaled section drawings. Whatever technique is used, a convenient scale for most sections is about 1:20 (one cm on the drawing represents 20 cm on the excavation wall).

Different symbols may be used to represent distinct strata or features. The degree of detail or "realism" to be shown is up to the archaeologist, but it is usually standardized for all sections produced in a given project (Fig. 7.28). In all cases, cultural features—architectural and otherwise—should be distinguished from naturally deposited layers, and each stratum should be labeled. Other information to be given on every section drawing includes horizontal location of the section (by operation and/or grid provenience), cardinal orientation (north-south, east-west, or otherwise), vertical elevations portrayed, scale, lots located (with their boundaries indicated), and data as to when and by whom the section was drawn.

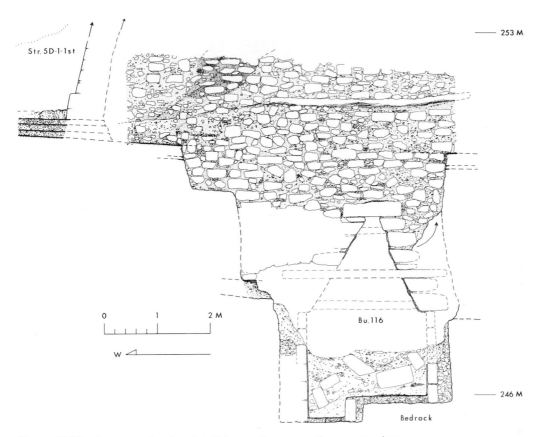

253 M.

Str. 5D-1-1st

0   1   2 M

W

Bu. 116

246 M

Bedrock

Figure 7.28 An example of a detail from a larger section, portraying excavated matrix and construction in a realistic manner. (Drawing by William R. Coe. Courtesy of the Tikal Project, the University Museum, University of Pennsylvania.)

Some archaeologists prefer to wait until a given excavation is completed before drawing the scaled sections. But most prefer to draw the section as the excavation progresses, adding new features and other information as it is encountered. In most cases, especially when excavating in complex architectural or stratified situations, it is necessary to avoid falling behind in data recording by drawing as excavation proceeds. Also, stratification may sometimes be better defined when freshly excavated: once the excavated surface dries out, stratum boundaries may disappear. Thus, delaying the section drawing may result in a loss of information.

Scaled *plan drawings* are used to record the horizontal relationships of features and associated artifacts or other materials. The scale of plans may vary according to the size of the area being depicted, although most researchers adopt a set of standard scales for specific

Figure 7.29 Preparing balloon and radio-controlled camera for early morning flight to record excavations at Sarepta, Lebanon. (Courtesy of the Museum Applied Science Center for Archaeology, University Museum, University of Pennsylvania.)

categories of plans. For instance, detailed plans of features such as burials may be rendered at 1:10, plans of larger features such as buildings may be 1:50, and composite plans depicting groups of structures may be done at 1:100. If an excavation encounters superimposed features—such as sequent living floors, each with associated artifacts and debris—a separate plan will be required to document each individual floor. The crowded superimposition on a single plan of data from different excavation levels should be avoided.

For extensive plans, the mapmaking techniques described in Chapter 6 may be used. In most cases the surveyor's transit should be used to assure accuracy. Less extensive plans can be drawn easily and accurately by superimposing a horizontal string grid, the grid aligned using compass bearings, on the cleared and cleaned area that is to be recorded. Measurements are then taken in the same manner as in preparing a section drawing with a level string. Photographs, of course, are used to supplement the recording of plan data. Gridded site areas may also be recorded by scaled vertical photographs taken from overhead platforms or scaffolding or from balloons (Fig. 7.29); scaled plan drawings can be traced directly from the photographs. Most plans of underwater sites, such as ancient shipwrecks, are recorded in this manner.

As with sections, the degrees of ''realism'' chosen for recording plans may vary. Some differences in detail depend on the scale of the drawing; others involve rectification conventions, such as the degree

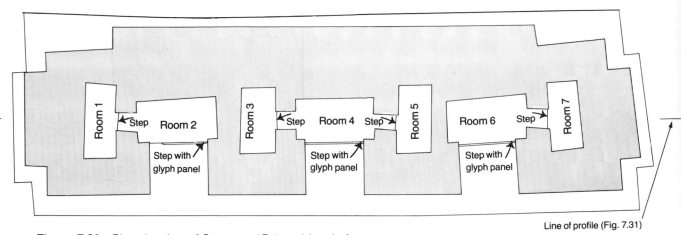

Line of profile (Fig. 7.31)

Figure 7.30   Plan drawing of Structure 1B-1 and its platform at Quiriguá, Guatemala (walls are symbolized by shaded area). (Based on a drawing by Kevin D. Gray.)

to which a slumping masonry wall is drawn as a ''straight'' line. All plans must indicate location and orientation, scale, lots (if appropriate), and by whom and on what date the plan was drafted (Fig. 7.30).

Other kinds of drawings supplement plans and sections when the need arises. *Profiles* are like silhouettes: they portray the outline of a feature without showing its internal composition (Fig. 7.31). Profile data are therefore included within section drawings, but not the other way around. Profiles are useful to show the exposed form of an unpenetrated feature or an unpenetrated part of a feature. *Elevations* are straight-on views of exposed feature surfaces, such as the façade of a building (Fig. 7.32). An *isometric drawing* is often a reconstructed interpretation of field data, showing what the feature is believed to have looked like when in use, rendered in a three-dimensional perspective (Fig. 7.33).

We have already mentioned the use of photography in connection with the recording of excavation sections and plans, but photography is an indispensable aid to the recording of all facets of archaeological

Figure 7.31   Longitudinal profile of Quiriguá Structure 1B-1 along the line indicated in Fig. 7.30.

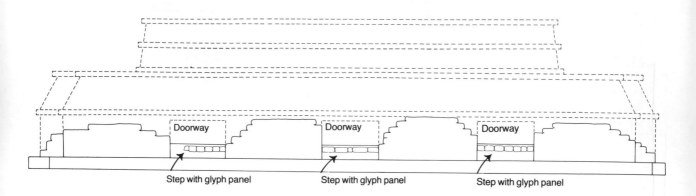

Figure 7.32 Front elevation drawing of Quiriguá Structure 1B-1. Solid line indicates platform and walls standing in 1977; broken line shows restoration based on work in 1912 when building was more complete.

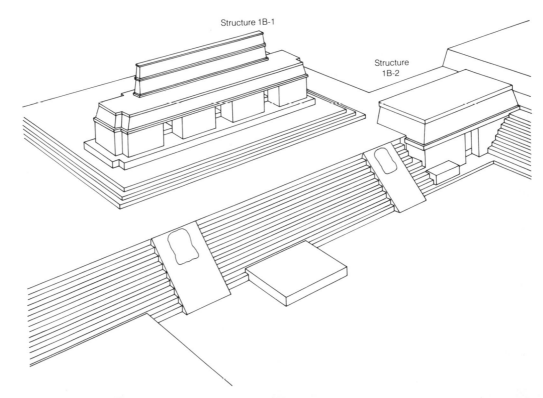

Figure 7.33 Isometric reconstruction of Structure 1B-1 and adjacent construction in the Quiriguá Acropolis. (After Morley 1937–38.)

data acquisition. Archaeological sites and site areas should be thoroughly photographed before, during, and after the research process. Pre-excavation photos are important to document the appearance of sites and features before excavation disturbs them. Once excavation is under way, a continuous series of photographs should be taken of each excavation unit as a chronicle parallel to that contained in the field notes (Fig. 7.34). Important features—burials, building foundations, and the like—should also be photographed from a variety of perspectives.

(a)

(b)

(c)

(d)

Figure 7.34 Near vertical views of successive stages (a through d) in the excavation of the Church of St. Mary, Winchester, England. Foundations visible in (a) date from ca. A.D. 1150; those exposed in (d) represent an earlier building dated at ca. A.D. 1000. (Courtesy of Martin Biddle, © Winchester Excavations Committee.)

Each photograph must contain an easy-to-read scale (usually a boldly painted metric ruler); it may also include information concerning the orientation and identification of the excavation and/or feature being recorded. The latter information may be written on a slate or letterboard and placed so that it will appear in one corner of the photograph. Alternatively, to avoid cluttering the photograph, this information may be entered in a separate photographic record notebook. In all cases, the photo notebook is a necessary supplement to the photographic record: for each photograph, the record should contain all the above information as well as the date, the name of the photographer, and—optionally—the film and camera type and exposure setting.

Most archaeological photography is done in black and white. Given the quantity of film necessary to record most research programs, color film would be prohibitively expensive. Color film may be used in special instances, such as recording stratified deposits in which soil color changes or differences are significant. Ultraviolet or infrared film may similarly be useful for particular "detection" needs. Regardless of the film type, it is usually preferable to use cameras designed for 120 film or larger, such as a twin-lens reflex or similar models. This film format is large enough to withstand considerable enlargement without significant loss of quality (film type is also important, of course). In addition, contact (unenlarged) prints from 120 film are large enough to be readable for day-to-day reference purposes. For these reasons, smaller film formats, such as the popular 135 size, are less desirable for most archaeological recording purposes (Fig. 7.35).

Figure 7.35 This pair of contact prints illustrates the practical advantage of larger format cameras: (a) 135 film, (b) 120 film (actual size).

As mentioned previously, archaeologists often include one or more standardized recording forms in their record system. Such forms may be made in a size compatible with storage in field notebooks, or they may be printed on smaller cards. Card systems are often more convenient for physical manipulation, as within a card file or punch-card system. Any standardization in recording aids conversion to computerized data storage. Of course, standardized information entered on notebook forms may later be transferred to a card system for easier manipulation.

Examples of standardized data records include forms for reconnaissance, surface survey, and excavations, all designed to record basic information on each data acquisition operation and to gain specific data for each provenience lot. Similar standardized forms may be used to record features and to catalogue artifacts and ecofacts. Special forms are often valuable to record the complex archaeological and skeletal data acquired from human burials. Samples gathered for special studies such as pollen, soil, and radiocarbon analyses should be accompanied by standardized information. Figure 7.36 shows examples of these and other data recording forms.

As we mentioned earlier, all forms of data records must be cross-referenced in order to be useful during later stages of study. To make cross-referencing and indexing possible, records must be labeled for identification. Each standardized record form can be identified by its subject matter—for example, the form for "Burial 3" or for "Pollen Sample 24." Other forms of data records—such as field notes, drawings, and photographs—may be more efficiently controlled by subdividing into smaller groups. One convenient code for this purpose specifies the site, the year, and the person doing the recording, as well as the kind and number of the record. For example, the label "L71-3-P17" might refer to the Lanning site ("L"), the 1971 excavation season ("71"), recorded by excavator number 3, and finally, page 17 of the field notebook (the notebook, then, is designated as L71-3). "L71-3-N301" would refer to the same site, season, and person, but specifies negative ("N") 301; and "L71-3-D9" would refer to drawing 9 by that person. These reference codes should be placed on all forms of the data record at or before the close of the season; cross-referenchng then "L71-3-P17" might refer to the Lanning site ("L"), the 1971 excavation season the page(s) discussing the excavation of Burial 3, the researcher would add references to the drawings, photographs, and feature (or, specifically, burial) forms pertaining to this item. The burial form would, in turn, include references to the notebook pages and the other records.

SITE: *L-27*　　　OPERATION: *13*　　　SUB-OPERATION: *P*

DESCRIPTION: *Excavation of structure* encountered in sub-op G via stripping of overburden between trench G and K*
　　　　　　　*3C-11

OBJECTIVE: *To reveal full horizontal extent of Structure 3C-11 together with possible associated occupation debris for both chronological position and functional assessment.*

EXCAVATOR: *4*
DATE: *2/26/73*

　　　　　　　　　　　　　　　　　　　　OP. CARD

OPERATION: *13P*　　LOT: *7*　　DATES: *3/16/73*　EXCAVATOR: *4*　　SITE: *L-27*

PROVENIENCE: *Occupation debris adjacent to feature 7 (probable hearth)*

DEPOSITIONAL SIGNIFICANCE: *Primary context - refuse*
(Fill, midden, burial, etc.)

PRELIMINARY TEMPORAL ASSESSMENT: *Late or terminal occupation of Structure 3C-11; probable equivalent to late Lerma Ceramic Phase*

CROSS-REFERENCES: *Notebook:*
(Notebooks,　　*73-4-109-113; 115; (see also 126)*
photos, etc.)　*Photo:*
　　　　　　　73-4-171-174

CONTENTS:
Fragments of at least 3 pottery vessels
1 partial grinding stone
16 pcs burned animal bone
2 pcs carbonized wood (carbon sample 73-4-4)
14 fragments chipped-stone (obsidian)
misc pottery sherds

　　　　　　　　　　　　　Object Lot Card
　　　　　　　　　　　　　Complete this side at excavation

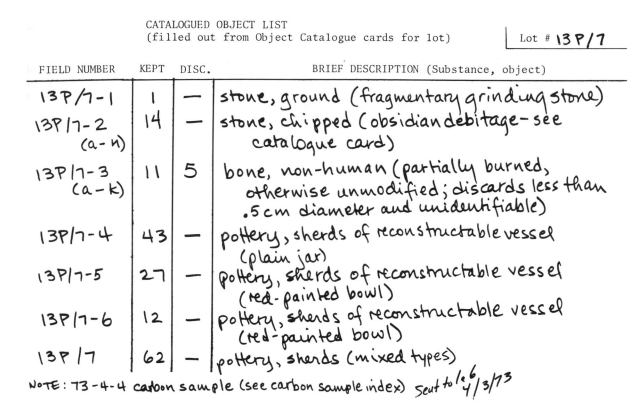

CATALOGUED OBJECT LIST
(filled out from Object Catalogue cards for lot)

Lot # 13P/7

FIELD NUMBER	KEPT	DISC.	BRIEF DESCRIPTION (Substance, object)
13P/7-1	1	—	stone, ground (fragmentary grinding stone)
13P/7-2 (a-n)	14	—	stone, chipped (obsidian debitage—see catalogue card)
13P/7-3 (a-k)	11	5	bone, non-human (partially burned, otherwise unmodified; discards less than .5 cm diameter and unidentifiable)
13P/7-4	43	—	pottery, sherds of reconstructable vessel (plain jar)
13P/7-5	27	—	pottery, sherds of reconstructable vessel (red-painted bowl)
13P/7-6	12	—	pottery, sherds of reconstructable vessel (red-painted bowl)
13P/7	62	—	pottery, sherds (mixed types)

NOTE: 73-4-4 carbon sample (see carbon sample index) sent to l.c.b. 4/3/73

Figure 7.36 Examples of standardized forms for recording excavation, inventory, and cataloguing information.

SUMMARY

In this chapter we have discussed how excavations are conducted. The objectives of excavation are to investigate the three-dimensional structure of buried archaeological remains and to understand the temporal and functional significance of this structure. In combination, the three dimensions of an archaeological deposit represent the processes of site formation: occupation at any one time was distributed horizontally in space; and through time, new occupation surfaces and accumulations of occupation debris buried older remains, giving the site a vertical (depth) dimension. The archaeologist therefore investigates stratigraphy—the interpreted sequence of deposition—and examines the remains within individual stratigraphic layers for evidence of activities carried on during single periods within the sequence.

A program of excavation begins with an assessment of the surface variability within the site or area under investigation, as determined by surface survey. Once this is done, the archaeologist must decide how much of the total to examine further by excavation. Part of this decision is a choice first between total and sample coverage and then, if sample coverage is selected, between probabilistic and nonprobabilistic sampling schemes.

Excavations are of basically two kinds. Penetrating excavations cut through deposits to reveal depth, sequence, and composition of archaeological sites. Clearing excavations are aimed at revealing horizontal extent and arrangement of remains within a single stratigraphic layer. Most excavation projects use some combination of the two approaches, in order to investigate fully the complementary vertical and horizontal dimensions of site structure.

Excavation begins with the selection of appropriate tools. A full inventory of excavation equipment includes a wide range of alternatives, from front-end loaders and backhoes to shovels, trowels, and even dental picks and air blowers. The factors that determine specific choices are the relative requirements of a particular excavation for precision and attention to detail, on the one hand, versus speed and quantity of earth removal on the other.

In actually removing archaeological matrix, the archaeologist must decide whether to extract units that correspond to observed stratigraphic layers or blocks, or to define the excavation units arbitrarily. It is preferable to follow observed stratigraphy whenever possible, thereby removing archaeological matrix and materials by the same units in which they were deposited, although in reverse order. Exceptions are cases in which different stratigraphic layers cannot be distinguished, or where observed strata are very thick and subdivision provides for more controlled removal.

Provenience control is crucial: in order to reconstruct later how the site was formed, the archaeologist must be able to re-establish the precise locations where all the discovered materials were found. All data collection operations—excavations or surface collections—are given distinctive labels and plotted with reference to the site grid and vertical elevation system. Features and stratigraphic deposits can then be located either by direct reference to the grid/elevation system or, indirectly, by reference to the operation in which they were discovered. Portable remains—artifacts and ecofacts—may be individually plotted, but because of their usual great quantity they are often more conveniently and efficiently handled in bulk provenience units called lots. All artifacts and ecofacts are then labeled as to their lot provenience before they leave the excavation area; particular artifacts and ecofacts may be further identified or more precisely plotted when their unusual nature or their location within a significant context so requires.

Because excavation destroys a site, detailed records are essential to all later reconstruction and analysis. The four kinds of recorded data from field operations are field notes, scaled drawings, photographs, and standardized forms. Each type contributes indispensably to the record of an archaeological excavation; for maximum utility, the four should be cross-referenced so that all records pertaining to a given excavation or a given feature can be readily located.

With this set of cross-referenced records, data recording in the field is complete. At this point the work emphasis shifts to the field laboratory, and data processing in the field laboratory is the subject of Chapter 8.

See p. 573 for "Suggestions for Further Reading."

Data Processing and Analysis

Once archaeological data are collected and recorded in the field, the archaeologist faces two essential tasks. First, the recovered materials and records must be physically organized. These data must be processed so they will be preserved, secure, and easily available for study. Although this step is not often consciously considered part of the research program, it is an essential prerequisite to any further work. Just imagine trying to do research in a library in which all the books are simply piled on the floor as they arrive—that may suggest the importance of *orderly processing* of archaeological data, described in Chapter 8.

The other essential organizational task is *analysis* of the recovered data. Analysis means the study of a material in order to understand both its constituent elements and their relationships. In Chapter 9 we will see how archaeological data are identified and classified to describe their form and attributes in a detailed, systematic way. In Chapters 10 and 11 the focus shifts: although we are still examining individual categories of data, we emphasize the *relations* among these categories, looking for structure in the archaeological data as a first step in fitting the pieces of the archaeological puzzle back together.

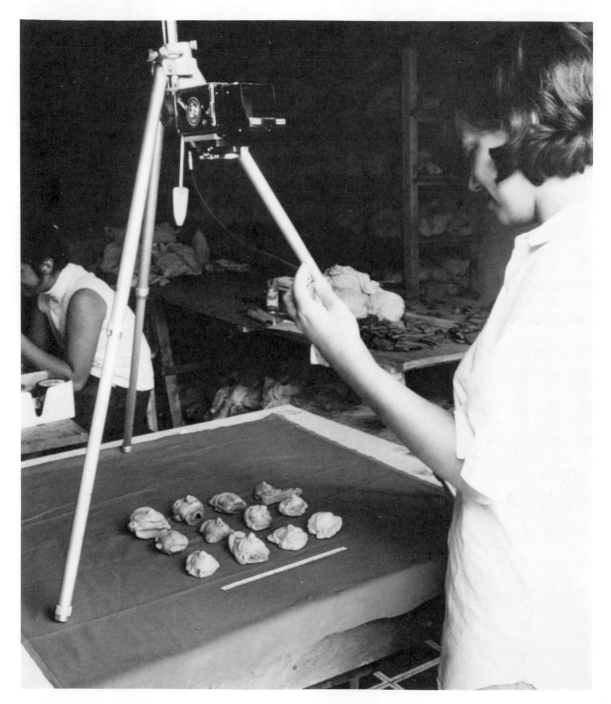

The photographic recording of artifacts is an essential task carried out in the archaeological laboratory.

Data Processing and Classification

Classification, like statistics, is not an end in itself but a technique . . . to attain specific objectives, and so it must be varied with the objective.

> *(Irving Rouse, "The Classification of Artifacts in Archaeology," 1960)*

Next time, be sure, you will have more success, when you have learned how to reduce and classify all by its use.

> *(Johann Wolfgang von Goethe,* Faust)

This chapter will consider the initial manipulations of archaeological data that follow the acquisition processes already described. These procedures, usually consisting of data processing and classification, are often undertaken in the field as data are being gathered. All forms of archaeological data are processed in some way—cleaned, labeled, sorted, and so on—to prepare them for later analysis. In addition, some forms of data may be classified or broken down into groups as a preparation for further study. Preparation and organization are thus the basic goals of the initial stages of analysis.

It is important that this processing and classification be done while fieldwork is still going on, usually in a field laboratory. In this way the archaeologist can evaluate the data as they are recovered and can formulate and modify working hypotheses which can then be tested through new or continuing acquisition strategies. For example, if the archaeologist recognizes that evidence being recovered in a given operation suggests occupation during a little-known period, excavation efforts in that locale (site, mound, trench, or whatever) can be expanded by adding new excavations or enlarging old ones. If, however, processing and classification of data are postponed until active fieldwork has ended, the archaeologist loses the chance to use such evaluations to guide continuing data acquisition.

DATA PROCESSING

Of all the types of archaeological data, artifacts usually undergo the most complex and thorough processing. They are nearly always classified in some way in the field, before being subjected to more detailed analysis. Ecofacts are generally handled more simply in the field laboratory, and features, because they are not portable, are not "processed" at all beyond field recording. (Of course, the constituent elements of some features—such as the bones and mortuary goods in a burial—*are* processed, but they are treated as artifacts and ecofacts, not as "parts of features.") Recorded data such as notebooks, drawings, and standardized forms also pass through the laboratory system. However, artifacts receive the most attention in the field laboratory. Accordingly, we will deal primarily with artifactual data in this chapter, but the processing of other data forms will be discussed when appropriate.

We will begin by considering the field laboratory itself. Once we have described the physical and organizational setting, we will outline the flow of artifacts through the stages of laboratory handling. The remainder of the chapter will be concerned with the final step in field processing, which is also the first in analysis—classification.

The Field Laboratory

Most archaeological projects have a specialized facility or field laboratory in which to carry out processing, initial classification, and storage of archaeological data. Although the same building may also be used to store excavation tools, most excavation programs use a separate shed for storage of excavation equipment and heavy machinery. The size and complexity of the field laboratory depend upon the kind and amount of data being collected. Tents or other portable structures are sometimes used, especially for short-term seasonal projects. Most archaeologists, however, prefer to house the field laboratory in a permanent building in order to provide for the security of the collected data. Whatever its form, the field laboratory should be close enough to the site or sites under investigation to facilitate the day-to-day transport of artifacts, ecofacts, records, and equipment. If the project involves many sites within a broad area, a central location for the field laboratory has obvious advantages. Figure 8.1 shows a schematic plan of one archaeological field laboratory.

Portable data—artifacts and ecofacts—should be brought to the field laboratory for processing at the close of each work day. Field records—notebooks, standardized forms, and drawings—are usually stored in the laboratory when not in use in the field. Laboratory storage of all kinds of data and equipment must therefore be systematic and orderly, so that any item can be quickly retrieved. Distinct, clearly labeled areas for each category of data make retrieval much easier (Fig. 8.1).

The field laboratory is staffed according to the needs of the project. If research is being conducted by a single person, the same individual may undertake both data collection and laboratory processing. At the other end of the continuum, large-scale projects often require a specialized staff of laboratory workers, supervised by a full-time laboratory director. Regardless of the project's size, the laboratory must have sufficient staff that archaeological data can be processed as soon

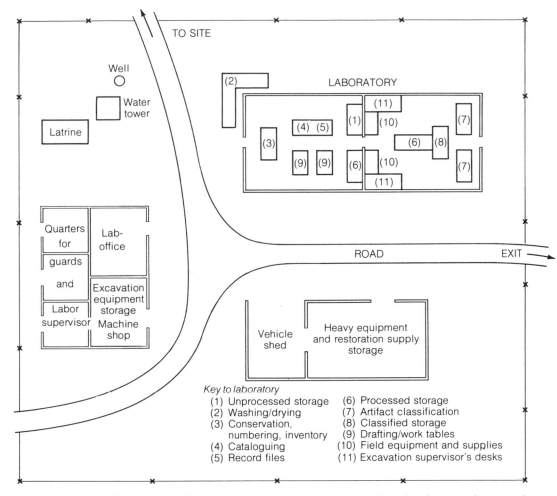

Figure 8.1 Plan of a laboratory compound designed to house a large and self-sufficient archaeological project.

as possible after they are collected. This promptness is important both to guard against errors, such as loss of labels on artifacts or lot bags, and to allow quick evaluation of the data as a guide for ongoing research.

Data Processing

Artifacts are usually processed in five stages: cleaning, conservation or repair, labeling, inventory, and cataloguing. These stages are diagramed in Fig. 8.2. Newly arrived bags of artifacts in the laboratory should be placed in a distinct storage area as they await processing

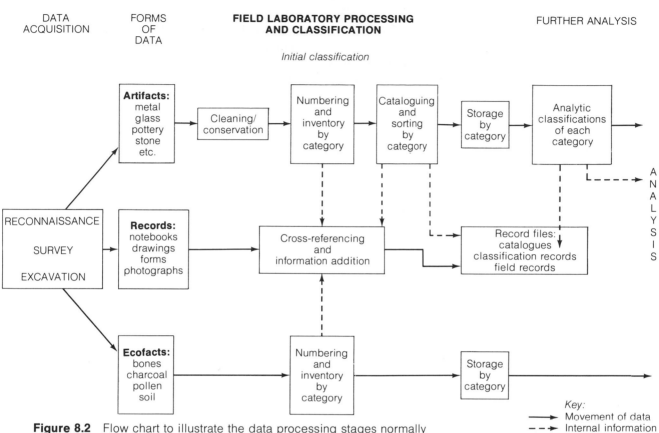

Figure 8.2 Flow chart to illustrate the data processing stages normally undertaken in a field laboratory.

(see Fig. 8.1). To avoid losses or mixups, a tally sheet may be kept to record each artifact bag as it is received in the laboratory, and to monitor its progress through each stage of processing. Of course, each artifact bag must be accompanied by a tag to identify its provenience and, where these are used, the appropriate standardized form (lot card, burial form, or whatever). Many archaeologists recommend that, to guard against loss of provenience information, each bag of artifacts be accompanied by two provenience tags: one goes inside the bag, and the other is tied to the outside.

Processing begins with cleaning. Most pottery and stone artifacts must be washed in water to remove any earth that remains on them. It should be stressed that washing of even such durable pieces is a delicate process, to be entrusted only to trained individuals, since improper treatment can damage or even destroy the artifact. As a general rule, washing can be done with soft brushes, as long as they do not erode or scratch the surface of the artifact (Fig. 8.3). Artifacts that require special treatment must be segregated by the archaeologist prior to washing. For instance, pottery vessels that contain remains of ancient food or other substances must be handled specially: they may be washed and the wash water saved for analysis, or they may be left unwashed and reserved for later treatment to identify their contents.

Other artifacts may be too fragile to wash and may need preservatives. Conservation and repair of artifacts can be undertaken at any point, but it normally begins as soon as possible after the artifact arrives in the field laboratory. Conservation may entail consolidation or strengthening of weak substances, as in the gradual application of a solution of plastic to crumbling bone. As the liquid in the solution evaporates, the plastic—such as polyvinyl acetate (PVA)—remains, holding the bone together. In other cases, when positive conservation measures are unnecessary or impossible in the field, treatment may involve no more than careful protective packing, as for fragile textile or basketry materials. Repair of artifacts includes such common activities as gluing together smashed pots or broken projectile points.

Conservation requirements vary from one project to another. If recovery of fragile remains is expected, it is best to call in a professional conservator. An extreme example is given by Ozette, a site in northwestern Washington excavated by Richard Daugherty. There, a wealth of fragile organic materials, including cedar house planks,

Conservation situations: Ozette, Washington and Vindolanda, England

Figure 8.3 Washing artifacts in the field. Note the compartmentalized drying tray and attached provenience labels.

wooden bowls, baskets, and dried foods, were preserved by the waterlogged (anaerobic) surroundings; it was necessary to work out a number of on-the-spot treatment schemes to cope with the abundance of perishable remains. Similarly, Vindolanda, in England, has yielded such incredible finds as leather shoes, woolen textiles, thin wooden documents, insects, tanners' combs (complete with cattle hair), and uncorroded metal, all from a 1900-year-old Roman garrison settlement near Hadrian's wall. Most sites do not promise such riches— or such headaches—but it is well to be prepared. If the field laboratory staff will not include a professional conservator, the archaeologist is well advised to consult such a person before fieldwork begins, in order to anticipate and plan for problem situations that may arise.

At the moment artifacts are removed from their bag for washing and/or conservation, they become separated from the containers that carry their provenience identification. Great care must therefore be taken to ensure that provenience information is not lost during these stages: until each item is individually labeled, it can be identified only by its proximity to the field tag for its provenience unit (lot). For this reason, artifacts are washed in groups corresponding to separate lots and then removed to distinct areas for drying. Portable drying trays, such as screens with wooden frames, are usually used (Fig. 8.3). The provenience tag can be pinned to each tray to identify its contents, or a piece of chalkboard can be affixed to the end of the tray and the lot label changed with each use.

The best way to avoid loss of provenience information is to place a permanent label on each artifact as soon as possible after cleaning. If drying trays are used, each tray, with its identification tag attached, can be passed to this next stage for numbering. Artifact labeling is a simple task, but care is necessary to avoid errors that can destroy the usefulness of the data. Permanent ink, such as black India ink, is most often used; white ink may be necessary for dark artifacts. A coating of clear nail polish will usually seal the ink for further security; the same substance may be applied before labeling to provide a better surface for marking. Each artifact must receive a provenience code for identification; the simplest and easiest method is to transcribe the field provenience code (such as "5C/7") onto the artifact. The number should be placed in an inconspicuous spot, and *not* upon any surface that may be important in later analysis, such as the cutting edges of tools or decorated surfaces of pottery.

Once an artifact bears a permanent provenience label, it need no longer remain grouped or bagged with its original lot. At this point it is usually convenient to classify artifacts initially into gross categories that provide the basis for inventory and detailed description. These

Table 8.1

REPRESENTATIVE ARTIFACT INDUSTRIES

Lithic Industries	Ceramic Industries	Metal Industries	Organic Industries
Chipped stone	Pottery	Copper	Bone
Ground stone	Figurines	Bronze	Ivory
	Musical	Iron	Horn
	instruments	Gold	Wood
	Beads	Silver	Shell
		Tin	Hide
			Basketry
			Textiles

categories (Table 8.1) are defined both by substance—the raw material used to make the artifact—and by the general technique by which the artifact was manufactured. The combined criteria of substance and technology yield convenient categories called *industries,* such as a chipped stone industry or a ground stone industry.

Inventory consists simply of counting and recording the quantity of artifacts within each industry. These counts are usually recorded on an appropriate standardized form. If a lot system is being used, for instance, the numerical totals of each industrial category within each lot

Table 8.2

ILLUSTRATION OF DIFFERENCES IN LOT CONTENTS FROM CONTRASTING
PROVENIENCES

	Transposed Primary Context (midden)	Use-Related Secondary Context (construction fill)
Chipped stone	282*	141
	(6.4%)**	(56.0%)
Ground stone	7	—
	(0.1%)	(—)
Pottery (sherds)	3957	110
	(89.5%)	(43.6%)
Figurines	57	1
	(1.3%)	(0.4%)
Other clay artifacts	111	—
	(2.5%)	(—)
Ecofacts	8	—
	(0.2%)	(—)
Total:	4422	252
	(100.0%)	(100.0%)

*Number of artifacts of this industry in the lot.
**Percent of total artifacts in the lot represented by this industry.

are entered on the card or form for that lot. Record forms of other "special" provenience units, such as burials, receive the same treatment. This quantitative information can be valuable in interpretive assessments of the data. For example, the relative amounts and proportions of artifact categories found in secondary contexts such as construction fill may be constant, in contrast to the amounts and proportions of artifacts found in primary contexts (Table 8.2). Recognition of such a pattern is an aid to future identification of secondary or primary contexts within the immediate excavations. Such evaluations of artifactual data can emerge very quickly, as long as the field laboratory is continuously processing material from the field; we see again how initial laboratory results can aid and guide further research.

After inventory has taken place, many artifacts are described and recorded in detail. This individualized description constitutes cataloguing. Standardized forms are used for cataloguing; the format may be a notebook, a bound registry log, or a card system (Fig. 8.4). The catalogue format may be designed for entry on computer cards or tapes; occasionally direct computer recording facilities such as keypunch machines are available in the field. Catalogue information usually includes a record of substance, color, and form (description of overall shape and measurements of length, width, and thickness) as well as provenience information and the catalogue number. The description of the artifact's form is often supplemented by a scaled drawing. In all cases, each catalogued artifact should be photographed and the appropriate negative number cited on the catalogue

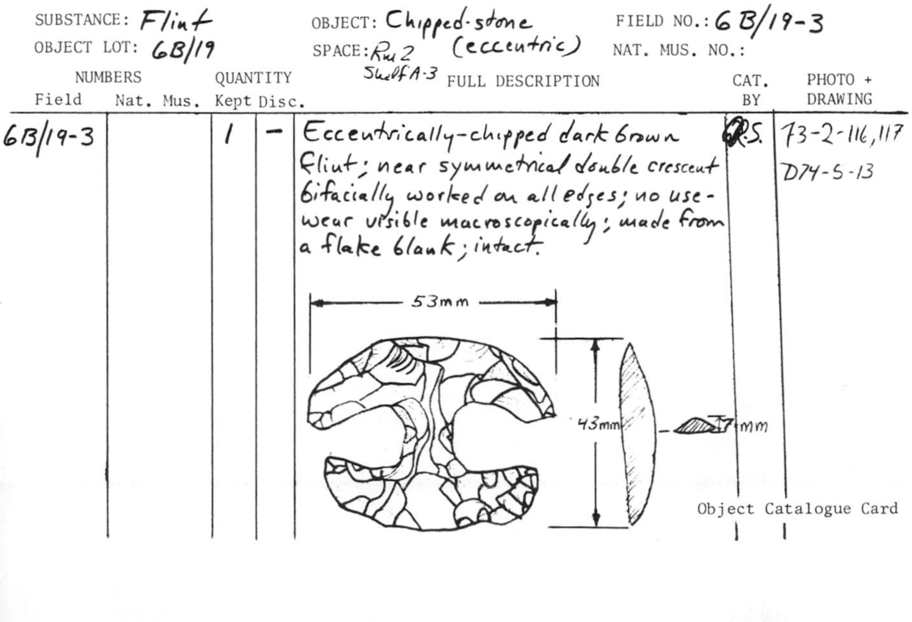
SUBSTANCE: Flint
OBJECT LOT: 6B/19
OBJECT: Chipped-stone (eccentric)
SPACE: Rm 2 Shelf A-3
FIELD NO.: 6B/19-3
NAT. MUS. NO.:

NUMBERS Field	Nat. Mus.	QUANTITY Kept	Disc.	FULL DESCRIPTION	CAT. BY	PHOTO + DRAWING
6B/19-3		1	—	Eccentrically-chipped dark brown flint; near symmetrical double crescent bifacially worked on all edges; no use-wear visible macroscopically; made from a flake blank; intact.	R.S.	73-2-116, 117 D74-5-13

Object Catalogue Card

Figure 8.4 Cataloguing: an example of a completed artifact catalogue card.

form. Once each artifact is described, a catalogue number is usually added to the provenience label, both in the catalogue and *on* the artifact, to identify each individual item. As discussed in Chapter 7, the catalogue numbers may form a running series for the whole project, or separate series may be set up within each excavation or lot.

Cataloguing is a time-consuming process. For this reason, many archaeological programs that produce large quantities of artifacts cannot afford to catalogue each individual item recovered. In such cases, the most plentiful artifact categories—such as pottery fragments—are usually not catalogued. Exceptions may be made—in particular it may be advisable to catalogue whole vessels as well as fragments derived from use-related primary contexts (occupation floors, burials, and so forth). But most often, bulk items are simply given bulk provenience labels and then counted.

With cataloguing, the basic sequence of artifact processing is completed. At this point, processed artifacts are either placed in storage or moved on to the preliminary step in analysis, classification.

CLASSIFICATION

In all branches of science, classification provides the working basis for further study. Before any investigator can analyze and interpret collected data, these materials must be arranged and ordered. To do this, the researcher must determine what units arc to be studied—chipped stone tools, for instance—and by what characteristics they are to be compared. As Chapter 2 discussed, much of the work of early archaeologists was devoted to the description and classification of objects from the past. Although classification is no longer the archaeologist's sole or principal concern, it remains a fundamental analytical step toward interpretation of the past.

Classification is the process of ordering or arranging objects into groups on the basis of the sharing of particular characteristics. These characteristics are termed *attributes*. Ordering of phenomena based on directly observable attributes comprises primary classification. Objects can also be classified on the basis of inferred characteristics. or of attributes measurable only by tests more complicated than simple visual inspection. Such tests include microscopic inspection, chemical analysis, and the like. Ordering of phenomena based upon inferred or analytic attributes constitutes secondary classification. Secondary classifications are less often carried out in the field, since they usually require specialized laboratory facilities and technicians—either archaeologists with specialized training or outside consultants.

In this chapter we will discuss the objectives and bases of the two kinds of classification. Specific applications of both kinds of classifications will be presented in the next chapters.

Objectives of Classification

All classifications serve a variety of purposes. First and most fundamentally, classifications create order from apparent chaos by dividing a mass of undifferentiated data into groups (classes). Classification thus allows the scientist to organize vast arrays of data into manageable units. As a very basic example, "artifacts" are distinguished from "ecofacts" and "features" in terms of their collection and processing requirements. Artifacts are often further subdivided into gross categories or industries such as chipped stone, pottery, or metalwork. These classes may then be subjected to detailed primary and secondary classification, breaking them down into kinds of chipped stone artifacts, kinds of pottery, and kinds of metalwork.

The second purpose of classification is to allow the researcher to summarize the characteristics of many individual objects by listing only their shared attributes. Most archaeological classifications result in definition of *types*. Types represent clusters of attributes that occur together repeatedly in the same artifacts. For example, the potsherds and whole vessels in a given pottery type will share attributes such as color and hardness of the fired clay; but other attributes, such as evidence of ancient vessel repair or of ritual vessel breakage, may not be defining traits of the type class. Thus, reference to types enables the archaeologist to describe large numbers of artifacts more economically, ignoring for the moment the attributes that differentiate among members of a single type.

Third, by ordering and describing classes and types, the scientist suggests a series of relationships among classes. The nature and degree of these relationships should generate hypotheses that stimulate further questions and research. For instance, the most obvious kind of question that may emerge from a classification concerns the meaning of the classification: how did the order originate and what is its significance? As we saw in Chapter 2, in biology, the descriptive classification of plant and animal species and the questions it generated gradually led to the theory of biological evolution as an attempt to account for the origin of the described order and to ascribe meaning to the hierarchical relationships among the classes. In classifications of artifacts, the described order and relationships among categories or types represent aspects of the artifacts' raw materials, techniques of manufacture, use (function), and decorative style.

From a broader philosophical viewpoint, questions about the meaning of classification plunge scientists into debate as to whether classifications reflect the *discovery* of a "natural" order inherent in the data, or on the other hand an *imposition* by the scientist of an "artificial" order. In archaeology, this debate has a long and colorful tradition of its own. Without becoming immersed in the debate, we shall briefly review the basic positions involved, since they lie at the root of all assumptions about the significance of classification in archaeology. The debate in archaeology focuses on whether classifications and types represent an ancient cultural order (the "natural order" position) or whether they are categories imposed by the archaeologist (the "artificial order" position).

Most archaeologists agree that members of all cultural systems, past and present, organize and categorize the world they observe and live in. For example, animals may be categorized by whether they walk or fly, whether or not they are edible, or whether or not they are good beasts of burden. People may be ordered by age, sex, occupation, status, wealth, and so on. Pottery vessels may be viewed from many perspectives: as well or poorly suited for storage, as variably valuable in terms of prestige, as purchased or homemade, and so on. And human activities can be differentiated into such categories as food preparation, tool manufacturing, and disposal of the dead. Thus all societies maintain a kind of cultural classification or "cognitive structure," and different societies structure their world in different ways. It follows that human activities—including those forms that produce material evidence recovered by archaeologists—should reflect the cognitive structure of the people who perform them. The debate, then, concerns whether or not (or to what degree) archaeologists can rediscover aspects of such an ancient cultural order by (re)classifying the material remains of past behavior.

Archaeologists such as Krieger, Spaulding, Deetz, and Gifford maintain that this *can* be done. They argue that by carefully considering the distribution of specific characteristics within any given category of artifact, the archaeologist can pick out clusters of attributes that co-occur regularly. Traditionally, most observations of co-occurrence have been made impressionistically, but today these "impressions" are increasingly being replaced by statistical tests of co-occurrence, such as the Chi-Square test. By whatever means they are isolated, the resulting attribute clusters are called types. Then, the proponents reason, since the clustered attributes occur together more than chance would predict, the clustering must represent selection and grouping by the ancient makers and users of the artifacts. Therefore the "types" represent the ancient cognitive structure.

The opposite position is taken by scholars such as Brew, Rouse, and Ford, who hold that cognitive structure or cultural classification

Figure 8.5 One difficulty in classifying archaeological materials is illustrated by this hypothetical example. Note that the complex variation in house forms makes it difficult to define a single classification based upon all observable attributes. (After Ford 1954.)

is too complex to be captured in a single typology. They argue that artifacts have so many attributes that, depending on which attributes one considers, a number of cross-cutting classifications could result, each of them an arbitrary breakdown of the total array (Fig. 8.5). And types grade into each other, so that some artifacts could as justifiably be put in one type as another (Fig. 8.6). The proponents of this point of view do not suggest that classification be abandoned; they do insist, however, that it be recognized as an arbitrary categorization. Indeed, what these archaeologists suggest is *more* classifications, using differing attributes to define the classes; they suggest choosing the different attributes with a view toward studying different kinds of variation, such as use, manufacture, or decorative treatment. Rouse has argued also for the study of distributions of isolated attributes themselves (see below).

This debate remains unresolved, but we can see that the question as to whether or not archaeological classifications correspond to ancient cognitive structures may be too complex for a simple answer. A

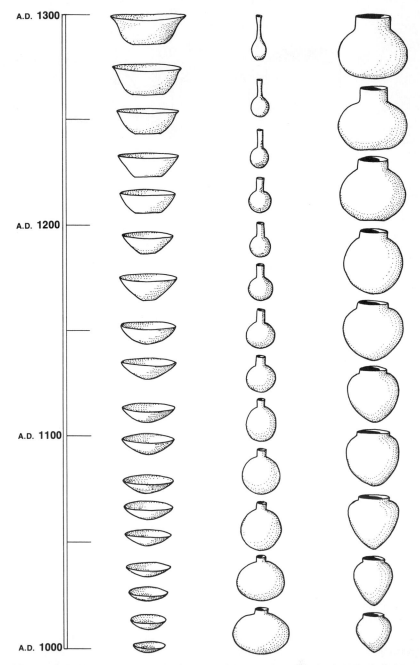

Figure 8.6 Another difficulty in classifying archaeological materials is illustrated in this example of gradual change in three pottery forms through time. (After Ford 1962.)

given set of statistically demonstrated attribute clusters or types may well represent "discovered" aboriginal decisions and groupings, but selection of different attributes for attention may produce different, cross-cutting types that are equally "real." The point is that classification is a convenient ordering *tool,* organizing artifacts or other archaeological data into manageable groups. The significance of the types in terms of ancient human behavior is a question that must be answered for each classification.

Kinds of Classification

As we stated above, archaeological classifications are based upon attributes. An attribute is any observable individual characteristic that can be isolated or defined. Three basic categories of attributes apply to archaeological data: stylistic attributes, form attributes, and technological attributes. *Stylistic attributes* usually involve the most obvious descriptive characteristics of an artifact—its color, texture, decoration, secondary alterations, and other similar characteristics. *Form attributes* include the three-dimensional shape of the artifact as a whole as well as the forms of various components or parts of the artifact; they include measurable dimensions such as length, width, and thickness ("metric attributes"). *Technological attributes* include characteristics of the raw materials used to manufacture artifacts ("constituent attributes") and any characteristics that reflect the way the artifact was manufactured.

To be meaningful, an attribute must potentially have two or more alternative states. Some attributes may be expressed qualitatively: a grinding stone either has leg supports or it does not (presence/absence), and it takes one of a number of forms (basin, trough, and so on). Other attributes may be expressed quantitatively, such as angle of the working edge of a chipped stone tool. Attributes in all three categories may be expressed either qualitatively or quantitatively. For example, the surface attributes of a pottery vessel can be qualitatively described as being "red, well-smoothed, and moderately hard" or quantitatively described according to a standardized color scale, such as the Munsell system ("5YR 4/6"), and a hardness scale, such as the Mohs system ("5.1"). Further examples of pottery attributes are listed in Fig. 8.7.

In order to classify any given category of artifacts, the archaeologist identifies the attributes to be considered and defines their variable states. The classification itself can proceed either by manipulating and physically grouping the artifacts according to their attributes (hand-sorting) or by coding attributes and recording them

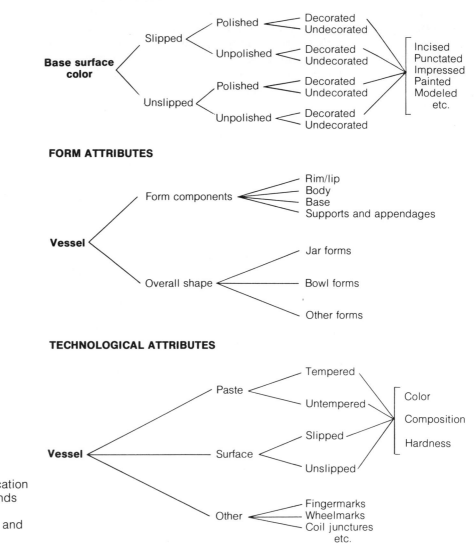

STYLISTIC ATTRIBUTES

FORM ATTRIBUTES

TECHNOLOGICAL ATTRIBUTES

Figure 8.7 Classification of pottery: a list of kinds of attributes used to define stylistic, form, and technological types.

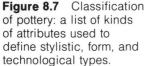

Definition of attribute clusters: James Sackett and Aurignacian end-scrapers

on punch cards or computer cards to establish attribute clusters statistically. For example, in most pottery classifications, the potsherds are hand-sorted into groups by similarity of appearance—color, smoothness, thickness of vessel wall, decorative techniques and motifs, and so on. The other approach may be exemplified by the work of James Sackett, who studied a collection of a traditional category of tool called an Aurignacian end-scraper (Fig. 8.8) to define the attribute clusters represented. Sackett isolated a set of nine attributes and

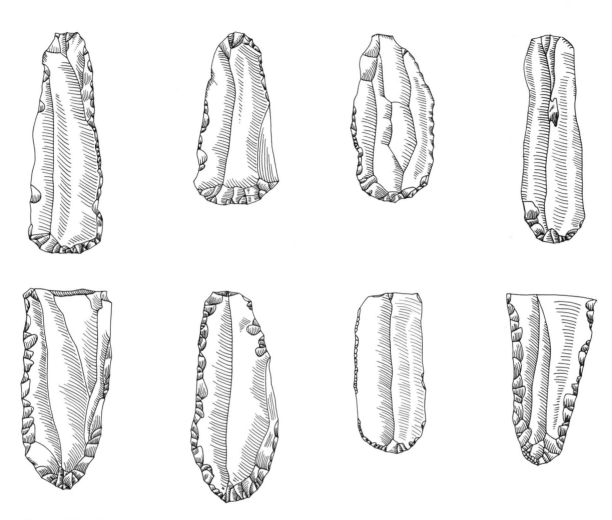

Figure 8.8 Examples of Aurignacian end-scrapers showing variation of form within this artifact category. (After Sackett 1966.)

their potential alternative states (Fig. 8.9); by a statistical cluster analysis, he was able to divide the collection of end-scrapers into three attribute-cluster categories:

1. Those that were retouched and any two of the following: rounded front contour; narrow piece width; convergent body contour.
2. Those attribute combinations not included in Classes 1 and 3.
3. Those that were unretouched and any two of the following: medium shallow front contour; wide piece width; parallel body contour.

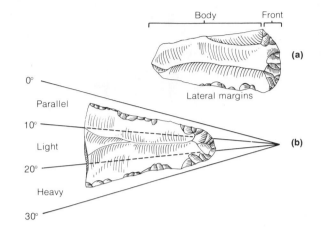

Figure 8.9 The systematic definition of attributes for Aurignacian end-scrapers may be based upon (a) the extent and location of retouch and (b) angle of lateral margins. (After Sackett 1966.)

Another related distinction can be made in classificatory procedures—namely, whether one considers all attributes to be equally important, or whether some are more important than others in defining types. Obviously, the mere selection of an attribute for consideration in a classification implies that it is more important than those which were not selected. But within the set chosen as the basis for classification, the archaeologist may choose whether or not to weight the various attributes equally. *Paradigmatic* techniques are those that build inclusive types from individual attributes, isolating attribute clusters. These techniques weight all attributes equally. Sackett's study of Aurignacian end-scrapers illustrates this approach; indeed, most statistically derived typologies have tended to be of this kind. Figure 8.10 gives a diagram of paradigmatic classification. The other approach, a hierarchical or *taxonomic* approach, involves a series of decisions that break the larger collection of artifacts into ever smaller groupings; the divisions at each decision point are based on the alternative states of one or several attributes. Different "types" result from considering the same attributes in a different order. The taxonomic approach has been used in pottery typologies, and it can

Figure 8.10 An example of a paradigmatic classification. Note that the definition of each type is *independent* of the order in which the attributes are considered.

	TEMPER ATTRIBUTES			
	Shell-tempered		Sand-tempered	
Unslipped	Bowls	Jars	Bowls	Jars
Slipped without decoration	Bowls	Jars	Bowls	Jars
Slipped with decoration	Bowls	Jars	Bowls	Jars

DECORATIVE ATTRIBUTES

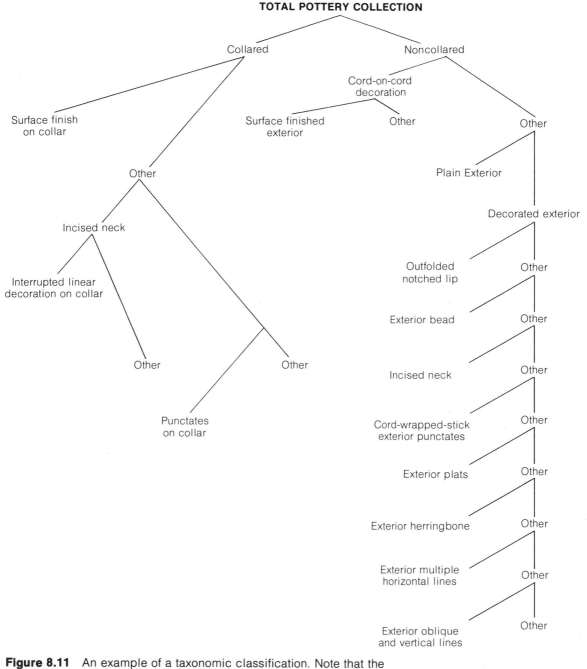

Figure 8.11 An example of a taxonomic classification. Note that the definition of each type is *dependent* upon the order in which the attributes are considered. (After Whallon, reproduced by permission of The Society for American Archaeology, adapted from *American Antiquity* 37:17, 1972.)

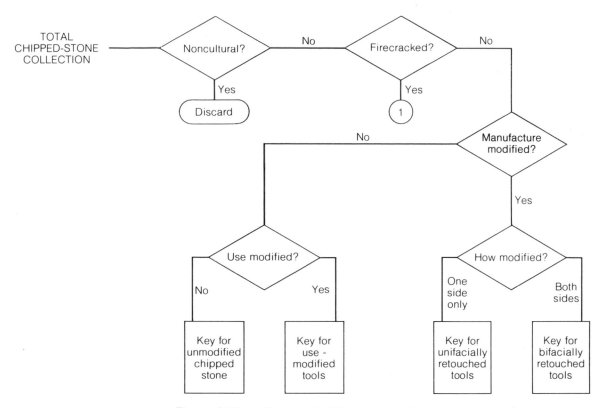

Figure 8.12 A flow chart of the process of decision making involved in taxonomic classification. (After Schiffer 1976.)

be illustrated graphically for a North American pottery typology (Fig. 8.11) as well as for Schiffer's classification of chipped stone artifacts from the Joint Site (Fig. 8.12).

Attributes that define types and distinguish between them are called modes. Irving Rouse, who originally advanced the term *mode,* argues that these should be studied along with types. Although some modes are recognized as important because they cluster to form types, others occur across types as markers of a particular time period or a restricted area. For example, use of iridescent paint on pottery in southern Mesoamerica is a stylistic mode found on a very early time level—about 1500–1200 B.C.—regardless of the other attributes or the "type" of the vessel or sherd on which it is found. There are also, of course, technological modes, such as wheel-made pottery, and form modes, such as restricted mouths on vessels. Modal analysis allows the archaeologist to study particular aspects of technology, form, and surface treatment apart from the way the modes were combined within the artifacts. For example, one may study the distribution in time and space of resist painting as a decorative technique, or of effigy feet as pottery supports, separately from the study of the pottery types on which they occur.

The kind of attributes selected will, of course, determine the kind of archaeological typology or modal analysis that results. Depending upon the nature of the artifacts and the objectives of the study, the archaeologist may be able to define *technological types, form types,* or *stylistic types*. Technological types may be based on one or both of the major groups of technological attributes—constituent attributes and manufacturing attributes. For example, in Near Eastern metal artifacts, different copper alloys may be distinguished by their constituents, such as brass (copper and zinc) or bronze (copper and arsenic *or* copper and tin). And drilled beads may be classified according to whether their holes were drilled from one direction only or from both sides, with the two drill holes connecting in the middle.

Form types are based upon component shape attributes, metric attributes, or both. Component shape attributes, such as body shape, are especially important in classifying fragmentary artifacts, such as pottery sherds; metric attributes such as vessel height are usually more useful in working with largely intact specimens. An example of form types is the common classification of hand-held grinding stones by their cross-sectional shape (round, subrectangular, and so forth).

Stylistic types are generally based on color, surface finish, and decorative attributes. Pottery classification systems usually emphasize surface attributes, such as the presence or absence of painted decoration and, if decoration is present, the number of paint colors involved.

Unfortunately, the archaeological literature is crowded with references to a multitude of confusing labels for kinds of typologies. For instance, terms such as "natural" or "cultural" types and "arbitrary" types make reference to the controversy mentioned earlier in this chapter; actually, these terms are evaluations of typologies, not descriptive labels. In the past, archaeologists also used categories called "functional" types that were based upon the assumption that form can be used directly to infer ancient function. As a result of this assumption, the archaeological literature contains a series of labels such as "scrapers," "batons," "gravers," and so on. Some of these labels may be accurate; more often than not, however, these functional labels were applied without any contextual evidence to support them. To avoid further misunderstandings, most archaeologists today avoid applying functional labels to classifications, preferring to use neutral terms instead.

Given the great variety of potential ways of classifying artifacts, how does the archaeologist make a choice? The answer lies both in the objectives of the classification to be undertaken and in the nature of the data. The archaeologist selects a classification that is suitable to the artifacts under study and that will meet the particular objectives of the investigation.

Uses of Archaeological Classifications

Archaeologists often use types to reconstruct ancient human behavior; they do this by correlating hierarchical classifications with various levels of behavior. The most widely cited example of such behavioral reconstruction is that outlined by James Deetz (Fig. 8.13). According to this scheme, the individual creators of artifact *types* (archaeologically defined by consistent patterning of attributes) adhere to culturally defined standards. Patterned *sets* of artifacts used by occupational *groups* (archaeologically classified by criteria of form and function), such as the various tools used by hunters or farmers, are called *sub-assemblages*. Patterned sets of sub-assemblages, representing the sum of social activities, define the *assemblage* of the ancient *community*. At the highest level, patterned sets of assemblages are used by archaeologists to define *archaeological cultures*.

It should be made clear, however, that behavioral reconstructions of this kind are built upon artifactual classifications, not on the context and associations of archaeological data. The validity of such behavioral reconstructions, often based on style and form types as in the example described above, relies upon the validity of the assumption that archaeological classifications reflect ancient cognitive structure. We will consider an alternative basis for the reconstruction of ancient behavior, founded on contextual patterning, in Chapter 11. At this point we shall simply stress that the classification of archaeological data is undertaken to meet a variety of objectives. The actual approaches vary according to the kind of data being classified.

In the next chapter we will discuss the analytic procedures commonly used for artifacts, ecofacts, and features. Chapters 10 and 11 will examine the objectives of data analysis by considering the ways the archaeologist structures data according to temporal and spatial frameworks, with the aim of reconstructing ancient behavior.

Figure 8.13   Behavioral reconstruction based upon hierarchical   ⟶
classification, independent of archaeological context (compare with Fig. 3.19). (After Deetz 1967.)

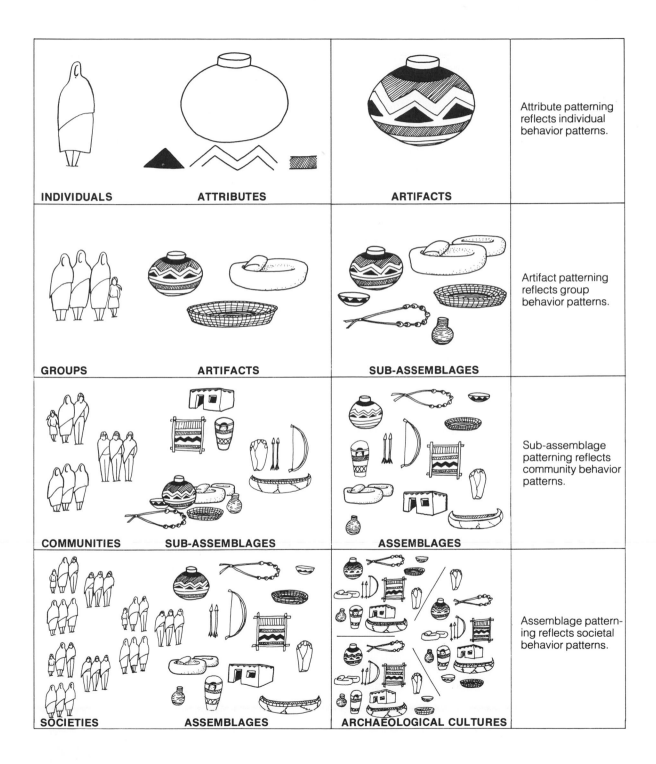

INDIVIDUALS   ATTRIBUTES   ARTIFACTS

Attribute patterning reflects individual behavior patterns.

GROUPS   ARTIFACTS   SUB-ASSEMBLAGES

Artifact patterning reflects group behavior patterns.

COMMUNITIES   SUB-ASSEMBLAGES   ASSEMBLAGES

Sub-assemblage patterning reflects community behavior patterns.

SOCIETIES   ASSEMBLAGES   ARCHAEOLOGICAL CULTURES

Assemblage patterning reflects societal behavior patterns.

SUMMARY

In this chapter we have discussed what happens to archaeological data, primarily artifacts, when they are brought from the field.

In the field laboratory, specimens are cleaned, conserved (when necessary), and labeled. Bulk items are then tallied by industry for each provenience unit; some items receive detailed individual descriptions through cataloguing. The field laboratory also provides space for storage of archaeological data, both processed and unprocessed, as well as storage of data records and some excavation equipment. Once archaeological materials have passed through the stages of laboratory processing, they are available for analysis.

Analysis begins with classification. The objective of classification is to organize the mass of undifferentiated data into manageable units. Such organization also suggests relationships among sets of data—the type classes of the classification. Whether or not these categories would have been meaningful to the makers and users of the artifacts, they are useful tools for the archaeologist, providing a starting point for analysis and interpretation of the collected data.

Classification is based on attributes or descriptive characteristics of the artifacts. The classes may consist of single attributes (modes) or clusters of attributes (types). There are three basic kinds of attributes—stylistic, form, and technological attributes; selection of different kinds of attributes results in correspondingly different classifications (stylistic, form, and technological types). Finally, classifications may be used as the basis for the analyses of each kind of archaeological data, according to a variety of specific objectives; these will be discussed in the next three chapters.

See p. 573 for "Suggestions for Further Reading."

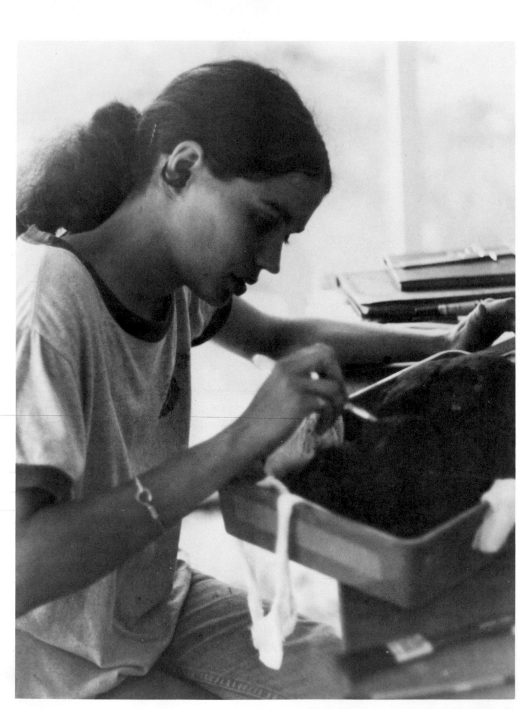

Excavating and analyzing a child burial in the laboratory. Because bone material is often the consistency of cheese in the ground, the burial is taken to the laboratory encased in earth, hardened for several weeks, then excavated, mapped, and analyzed. (Courtesy of David A. Freidel.)

Analysis of Archaeological Data

CHAPTER

9

The classification of the constituents of a chaos, nothing less is here essayed. Listen to what the best and latest authorities have laid down.

(*Herman Melville,* Moby Dick)

In this chapter we will examine the various kinds of studies archaeologists commonly use to analyze each of the categories of archaeological data: artifacts, ecofacts, and features. Since each of these broad categories encompasses a wide variety of archaeological remains, our discussion will emphasize the forms of data most commonly encountered by archaeologists. For example, under the heading of artifacts we will examine lithic tools and pottery in some detail, but will only briefly discuss other forms of artifactual data, such as those composed of metal and various organic substances.

In discussing each kind of archaeological data, our principal goal will be to examine the most important kinds of studies appropriate to that data type and to consider the uses the archaeologist may have for the results of these analyses. We will emphasize the characteristics of each kind of data that differentiate it from the others, in order to show the ways each type of data can most effectively contribute to an understanding of past behavior.

By organizing the present chapter according to categories of data, we do *not* intend to imply that either the data categories or the resulting analyses are determining factors in guiding archaeological research. On the contrary, throughout this book we have stressed the importance of the *research problem* as the most important factor determining the course of archaeological research. Thus, in a given instance, the recovered quantities and relative importance of artifacts, ecofacts, and features are usually determined by the specific research problem and the research design chosen to investigate that problem. In the same way, the choice of classification method and the uses to which classification is put also depend on the research objectives. In other words, problem-oriented archaeology seeks both to define relevant data and to indicate appropriate data analysis procedures in order to reach conclusions relevant to the original research objectives.

THE ANALYSIS OF ARTIFACTS

In this section we will consider the analytic methods most appropriate to each of the major artifactual industries. As discussed in Chapter 8, these industries are defined according to both substance and manufacturing techniques. This discussion will emphasize the lithic and pottery industries, but it will also briefly treat the most important classification methods and uses appropriate to remaining industries.

Lithic Artifacts

Lithic technology refers to the manufacture of tools from stone. Stone tools were undoubtedly among the earliest used by human societies; in fact, their use predates the evolution of modern *Homo sapiens* by more than a million years. The first stone tools used by the ancestors of modern humans were probably unmodified rocks or cobbles, used only once for tasks such as hammering or pounding. But lithic technology has its roots in the first attempts to *modify* and *shape* stone in order to make tools.

There are two basic kinds of lithic technology: one involves the fracturing or flaking of stone (chipped stone industry); the other is based on the pecking and grinding or polishing of stone (ground stone industry). Because chipped stone is the oldest preserved form of culture and technology, archaeologists have used it to name the earliest period of cultural development, the Paleolithic ("Old Stone") period. In this traditional scheme, the later development of a stone technology involving grinding signals the advent of the second developmental age, the Neolithic or "New Stone" Age. Ground stone tools did not, of course, replace chipped stone; rather, the two technologies coexisted for several thousand years in both the Old and New Worlds. Of the two, chipped stone is usually more commonly encountered by the prehistoric archaeologist, and it will be emphasized in the following section.

Resumé of Lithic Technology

Lithic technology involves exploitation of the inherent physical properties of certain classes of stone. Chipped stone technology takes advantage of the characteristics of several hard, nonresilient, and homogeneous minerals. When struck, these materials fracture in a uniform manner and not according to any natural planes of cleavage in the rock. The most commonly exploited stone types possessing these characteristics include flint or chert and obsidian (a natural volcanic glass). When the surface of one of these materials is struck a sharp blow—usually from another, harder stone—the shock waves spread through the struck stone or *core* in a cone-shaped pattern, producing a conchoidal fracture that detaches a fragment called a *flake*. The flake can be recognized by its *bulb of percussion* on the inside or bulbar surface (see Fig. 9.1). Below the bulb of percussion, one can usually detect faint concentric rings or ripples marking the path of the radiating shock waves from the blow that produced the flake. The core will show a corresponding concave surface or *flake scar* marking the site of the flake's detachment, including a small depression or *negative bulb of percussion* immediately below the point at which the

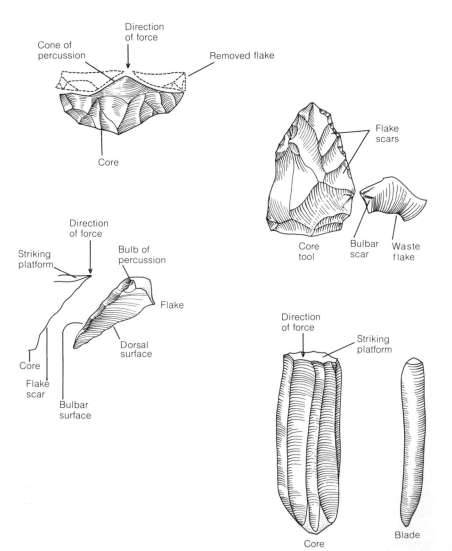

Figure 9.1 Terminology used in describing lithic core and flake tools. (After Oakley 1956.)

blow was struck. Chipped stone tools are produced either by re-moving flakes to give a sharp edge to the core (core tools), or by uti-lizing one or more of the detached flakes (flake or blade tools).

Chipped stone tools may be made by a variety of techniques. Some of these have been inferred from traces left on the tools themselves, others from ethnographic observations of peoples still manufacturing stone tools, and still others through archaeologists' experiments in duplicating the ancient forms. Some of these techniques are as old as the origins of stone tools; others represent later refinements during the long development of lithic technology. We shall briefly summarize some of the more important techniques.

The shape and size of the flake detached from a core depend both on the physical characteristics of the stone itself and on the angle and force of the blow being struck. Short, rather thick flakes are produced by striking the core with a hammerstone or by striking the core against a fixed stone called an anvil. The earliest recognizable stone tools, manufactured during the lower (earliest) part of the Paleolithic period more than a million years ago, were produced by these meth-ods. To increase the manufacturer's (or *knapper's*) control over the flaking process, the core may be "prepared" by shaping the *striking platform* or surface to be struck. This is done by splitting the core or by removing a *lateral flake*—one at a substantial angle to the other flakes to be detached. This preparation gives the striking platform a relatively flat and smooth surface, allowing the knapper to strike off longer and thinner flakes than would be possible from an unprepared core. One of the most sophisticated technological developments of the Paleolithic was the *Levalloisian technique,* involving the careful preshaping of cores such that when a single, large flake was removed it had a predetermined, well-controlled shape (Fig. 9.2).

A basic refinement of the percussion technique used in forming both core and flake tools is the *indirect percussion* technique, which involves placing a punch made of bone or wood between the core and the hammerstone. The punch softens the resultant blow (see Fig. 9.3), producing a longer, narrower cone of percussion and, therefore, longer and thinner flakes. A further refinement makes its appearance in the Upper Paleolithic. This technique is *pressure flaking:* instead of either direct or indirect percussion, it uses steady pressure exerted on a punch to detach flakes from the core. The usual result of either indi-rect percussion or pressure flaking is a series of long, thin, parallel-sided flakes called *blades*. True blades produced from prepared cylin-drical cores are typical of the Upper Paleolithic in the Old World and of much of the pre-Columbian era in the New World.

Once a flake or blade tool has been detached, it may be ready for use as a cutting or scraping tool (as in Levalloisian flakes or blades).

SIDE VIEWS   **TOP VIEWS**

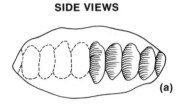
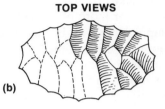

(a)   (b)

(c)

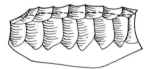
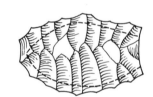

(d)

FLAKE

(e)

CORE

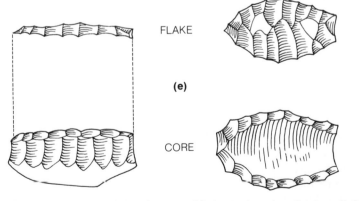
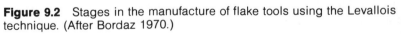

Figure 9.2 Stages in the manufacture of flake tools using the Levallois technique. (After Bordaz 1970.)

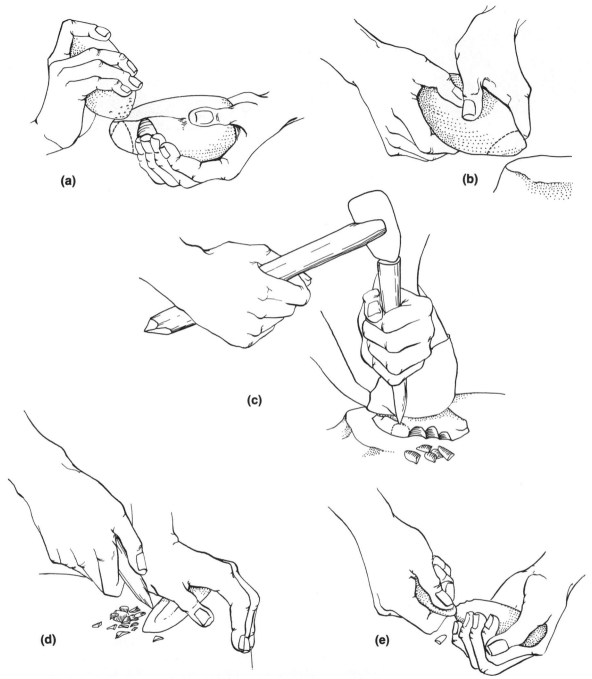

Figure 9.3 Manufacturing techniques for chipped stone tools: (a) direct percussion using a hammer stone, (b) direct percussion against an anvil stone, (c) indirect percussion using a wooden punch and mallet, (d) pressure flaking using a punch, and (e) pressure flaking with a stone tool.

Figure 9.4 Chipped flint effigy produced by skillful pressure flaking (Late Classic Maya). (Photo by José Lopez, courtesy of Administración del Patrimonio Cultural de El Salvador.)

In other cases, the tool must be further modified for particular use. For example, edges too sharp to be held in the hand were often dulled by battering with stone hammers. Edges that required strength and durability rather than sharpness, such as those on scrapers (see Fig. 8.8), were usually *retouched* or secondarily flaked by pressure techniques to remove small, steep flakes. Skillful pressure flaking can sometimes completely alter the shape of a flake, as in production of barbed or notched *projectile points* and miniature forms (microliths). One of the high points of pressure-flaking skill is represented by the so-called "eccentric" flints and obsidians produced by Classic Maya craftsmen (Fig. 9.4).

Archaeologists have traced the development of chipped stone technology through a span of more than a million years. During that time, new techniques and forms gradually emerged that increased both the efficiency of tool production and the available inventory of tool forms. By the Upper Paleolithic period, however, a new lithic technology was also being developed—the shaping of harder, more durable stone by pecking and grinding against abrasives such as sandstone. These tools, which took the form of axes and adzes, had much more durable edges than their chipped counterparts and were thus more efficient for such tasks as cutting trees and splitting lumber. Ground stone techniques were also used to shape large basins (*querns* or *metates*) used for grinding grain and other tasks.

Analysis of Lithic Artifacts

Traditionally, most analysis of lithic artifacts involved a classification based upon form, often using direct or implied functional labels such as "scrapers," "spokeshaves," and so on. The overall shape of stone artifacts usually provided form types that could be described by their outline, profile, and dimensions. The earliest and best-known classifications of this sort, made in Europe during the nineteenth and early twentieth centuries, still serve as the basic reference classifications for the assemblage of Paleolithic chipped stone tools. Particular forms, such as the Acheulian handaxe and the Levallois core and flake, were isolated as "type fossils" or *fossiles directeurs* of specific time periods and cultures. More recently, François Bordes, Denise de Sonneville-Bordes, and James R. Sackett have been among the leaders in refining form classification, specifying more precisely the sets of criteria that distinguish among form types.

In Europe and elsewhere, inferred function was often a primary criterion for lithic classifications; one common distinction was between supposedly "utilitarian" objects (those with domestic or household uses) and "ceremonial" objects having ritual or nondomestic uses.

This division could sometimes be validated when applied to artifacts from secure contexts, such as tools from household living floors versus those from burials. But the distinction was often misused: many analysts succumbed to the temptation to associate elaborate forms with "ceremonial" uses and those of simpler shapes with "utilitarian," even in the absence of good contextual data. Most modern archaeologists recognize that even artifacts from secure "ceremonial" contexts, such as burials, may once have served multiple functions, including "utilitarian" ones, prior to their final deposition in a burial or cache.

A. V. Kidder, one of the pioneers in the systematic analysis of New World chipped stone artifacts, used this functional dichotomy as the basis of his 1947 classification of chipped stone tools from the Maya lowland site of Uaxactún. After segregating the Uaxactún collection into presumed "ceremonial" and "utilitarian" categories, Kidder subdivided artifacts in each class further according to raw material (obsidian versus chert) and, finally, form. Kidder's earlier study (1932) of lithic artifacts from the Pecos site in the Southwestern United States ignored this functional entanglement. The Pecos study, based uniformly upon kind or degree of flaking and form, is usually regarded as the first systematic (or "modern") classification of chipped stone artifacts in the New World.

To a large extent, lithic typologies based on overall form have given way to more sophisticated attribute analyses based on criteria selected as indicators either of manufacturing technology (technological types) or of actual use (functional types). Stone tools are particularly well suited to such analyses and classifications because stone working and use are progressively *subtractive* actions: each step in the shaping and use of stone tools permanently removes more of the stone. At least for chipped stone artifacts, clues to most steps in ancient manufacturing and use processes are preserved—and can be detected—in flake scars, striking platforms, and other identifiable attributes. For instance, the length-to-thickness ratio of flakes (or of flake scars on a core) may indicate whether the piece was formed by direct percussion, indirect percussion, or pressure flaking. Even manufacturing mistakes are preserved: *hinge fractures,* for example, indicate that the flake removal process was incorrectly carried out or that a flaw in the stone caused the flake to snap off abruptly. By analyzing the full range of lithic material, both artifacts and workshop debris, the archaeologist can reconstruct most or all of the steps in tool manufacture.

Significantly, the workshop debris—nontool byproducts of chipping, called *debitage*—was usually ignored by traditional classifications that focused only on the forms of finished tools.

Early classification of chipped-stone artifacts: A. V. Kidder at Uaxactún and Pecos

Technological classification of chipped-stone artifacts: P. D. Sheets at Chalchuapa, El Salvador

Experimental lithic technology: François Bordes and Don Crabtree

Pioneering petrological analysis: Herbert Thomas at Stonehenge

Debitage, however, can include a wide range of technologically informative materials, from primary flakes that were hammered away to remove the outer weathered layer of the stone, to trimming flakes removed in preparing the form of the core for production of uniform flakes or blades, to the tiny secondary flakes that are the byproducts of retouching a blade or flake. In analyzing the chipped stone artifacts from Chalchuapa, El Salvador, Payson D. Sheets used technological criteria as his basis for classification. By attending to the technological "clues" preserved in the full range of chipped stone materials, he was able to reconstruct the chain of manufacturing steps used by pre-Columbian lithic craftsmen during a span of some 2000 years (see Fig. 9.5). Michael Schiffer has performed a similar "behavior chain" analysis on chipped stone from the Joint Site in Arizona.

In order to test and refine reconstructions of ancient tool manufacture, lithic specialists such as François Bordes and Don Crabtree have attempted experimental duplication of ancient chipped stone technology. Through these experiments, and through their training of other archaeologists in the techniques used to manufacture stone tools, lithic specialists have increased the sensitivity with which ancient manufacturing practices can be analyzed, as well as proposing alternative methods that may have been used in the past.

Petrological examinations of thin-sections of stone are sometimes useful in establishing the source of the raw material. Petrology is the scientific study of rock, and a *thin-section* is a specially prepared slice of a stone. When first cut, the section is a few millimeters thick, but after it is fixed to a glass slide, its thickness is reduced to about 0.03 mm, at which point most of the minerals in the rock are transparent. By examining the thin-section through a special microscope, the analyst can describe the size, shape, and other characteristics of the minerals in the stone. Comparing quarry samples with artifact samples, petrologists can sometimes identify distinctive quarry "signatures"— particular patterns of constituent minerals that come from one source alone. Some sources do not have distinctive signatures, however; a petrological study of flint axes in England, for example, has been unable to distinguish among different flint bed sources, although the same study defined more than 20 source-groups for axes made of stone other than flint. And in one of the early archaeological applications of petrological analysis, Herbert Thomas demonstrated in 1923 that the bluestones of Stonehenge had been brought from the Prescelly Mountains of Wales, a straight-line distance of about 130 miles, but actually some 240 miles by a feasible transport route.

Another analytic procedure that has been successfully applied to chipped stone artifacts is examination of attributes related to ancient tool function. This technique examines characteristics of form, such as angle of the cutting edge, as well as attributes of wear resulting

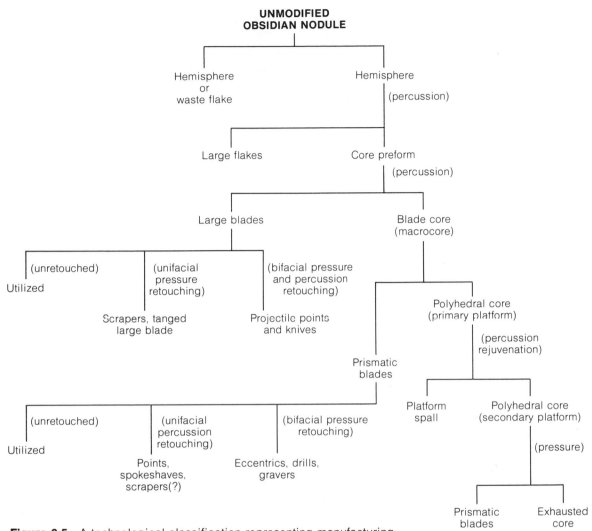

Figure 9.5 A technological classification representing manufacturing steps used in production of chipped stone artifacts at Chalchuapa, El Salvador. (Courtesy of Payson D. Sheets.)

from use—microscopic fractures, pitting, or erosion of the edge—in order to establish the range of tasks once performed by lithic artifacts.

The interpretation of *what* function these attributes indicate is, as we shall argue in Chapter 12, based on analogy—comparison of the attributes of the archaeological materials with those of modern forms whose function is known. Some of the analogs—the sources for interpretation—are drawn from ethnographically observed stone tools: for example, ancient projectile points, including "arrowheads" and spear points, are identified by the similarity of archaeological forms with modern forms used as projectile points. In other cases, analogs are provided by imitative experiments in which archaeologists make stone tools and use them to chop, scrape, slice, whittle, or saw various materials such as meat, bone, wood, and so on. After such an experimental tool is used, its edges can be examined microscopically to detect the pattern of wear resulting from each kind of use. Distinctive wear "signatures" can be identified in some cases; these can be used to infer ancient tool uses when archaeological specimens show similar wear patterns. For example, in studying Upper Paleolithic end-scrapers (see Fig. 8.8), S. A. Semenov found scratches and luster along the edges that had been retouched to a steep angle. The consistent direction and shape of the scratches or striations indicated the direction in which the tool had been moved, while the luster suggested that it had been used on relatively soft organic materials. From these inferences, Semenov reconstructed that the tools had indeed been used as scrapers, specifically for cleaning animal skins (Fig. 9.6).

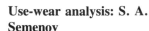

Use-wear analysis: S. A. Semenov

In some cases, residues left on working edges also provide clues to ancient function. A well-known example is the interpretation of silica residue as an indicator that an artifact was used as a sickle to cut grain or other plants containing silica. The presence of such a silica sheen has been sought as evidence of crop harvesting for sites believed to have been occupied during early stages of the development of grain agriculture.

Ground stone tools can also preserve clues to manufacture and use, but when both of these processes involve grinding, many of the traces necessarily get "erased." Whether because of this decreased information potential, or simply because chipped stone is more common, ground stone has traditionally received less analytic attention—a situation that will hopefully change. One analysis that is often fruitful is examination of residues, to see what was cut with or ground on the implement in question. For example, a quern or mortar could have been used to grind food or, alternatively, to grind pigment materials; only analysis of residues or wear will tell.

Ceramic Artifacts

The generalized term, *ceramics,* is a blanket term that covers all industries in which artifacts are modeled or molded from clay and then rendered durable by firing. In addition to pottery, this overall category includes production of ceramic figurines (three-dimensional representations of animals, humans, or other forms), musical instruments

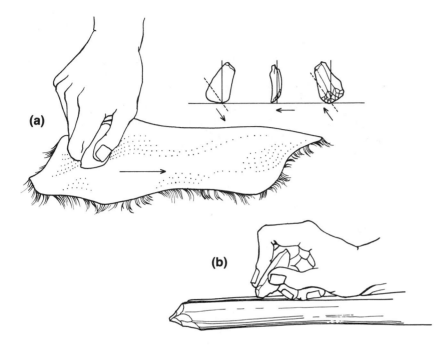

Figure 9.6 Determination of function of chipped stone endscrapers: (a) traditional speculated use as an engraver for bone or wood; (b) inferred use as a scraper based on comparison of wear patterns with those resulting from experimental use. (After Semenov 1964.)

(such as flutes or pipes), articles of adornment (such as beads), hunting or fishing implements (such as clay pellets and fish-line weights), and spindle whorls (used for spinning thread or yarn). Although clay figurines—such as the ''Venus'' figurines of the Upper Paleolithic in Europe—appear to be the earliest known form of ceramic technology, pottery is undoubtedly the most abundant and widespread kind of ceramics.

Pottery can be defined as a separate ceramic industry because of its unique body of manufacturing techniques as well as its specialized function: providing containers for a wide range of solid and liquid substances. Archaeological evidence throughout the world indicates that pottery originated with humanity's first attempts at settled life, usually associated with new subsistence adaptations such as coastal fishing and gathering or, inland, experiments with agriculture. In the Near East, Southeast Asia, and South America, pottery appears very early in the record of settled communities; it developed as part of a more complex, expanding technology that was fostered by the relative stability of settled village life. Pottery was and still is used to transport, cook, and store a wide range of solid and liquid foods, as well as to contain other supplies. But as societies became increasingly complex, pottery also assumed other, specialized functions, including such ritual uses as burial urns and incense burners.

Compared with the age of the chipped stone industry, pottery's 8000-year history seems short. But pottery vessels have been used by most of the world's settled communities, and this widespread and common occurrence, combined with extreme durability and capacity for great variety in form and decoration, make pottery one of the most commonly analyzed and useful kinds of artifacts available to archaeologists. The traditional importance of the "infamous potsherd" in archaeological research can hardly be overstressed; at least one unabridged dictionary even gives as its *definition* of potsherd "a broken pottery fragment, esp. one of archaeological value."

Resumé of Pottery Technology

Pottery, like other ceramic artifacts, may be made from a wide variety of clays. *Clay* is a general term for any fine-grained earth that develops plasticity when mixed with water. Clays are often water-laid soils; they vary in their consistency according to grain size, degree of sorting, and chemical composition. The finest-quality clays contain *kaolinite* (hydrated aluminum silicate), whose particles are as small as 0.05 microns (0.00005 mm) in diameter.

Pottery is manufactured in a variety of ways throughout the world, ranging from simple household hand-production to modern factory mass-production methods. Because the bulk of prehistoric pottery encountered by the archaeologist was produced by rather simple means, we will briefly describe the general manufacturing process as it is carried out by small, family production units in many parts of the world to this day.

First, the potter must acquire the proper clay, either by mining it or by purchasing it from a supplier. Then the potter processes and prepares the clay to assure its purity and uniformity. Because clay is often collected dry or allowed to dry out, it must be pulverized and mixed with water until it reaches the proper consistency for forming vessels. The moist clay must then be thoroughly kneaded or wedged to drive out air bubbles and create a uniform, plastic mass. *Plasticity* refers to the capacity to be molded and shaped; the plasticity of moist clay is what gives it practical value. But another property of clay is that, as it loses water during drying and firing, it shrinks and is subject to cracking or breaking. As part of the clay processing, then, nonplastic substances that retain their shape and size—called *temper*—may be added to reduce shrinkage and thus lessen the chance that the completed vessel will break during drying or firing. Common tempering agents include sand, ground shell, volcanic ash, mica, ground pottery sherds, and organic materials. Some clays already contain these or similar substances, and thus do not require the addition of temper.

Once processed, the clay is ready for forming. There are three basic techniques for making pottery from clay: hand forming, mold forming, and wheel forming. These techniques may be used separately or combined. Hand-forming methods undoubtedly represent the oldest kind of pottery technology; they are usually associated with small-scale production by part-time specialists for immediate household uses, or sometimes for limited markets outside the family. Mold- and wheel-forming techniques, because of their potential for mass production, are often associated with full-time specialist potters who manufacture their vessels for widespread market distribution.

Hand-forming pottery involves modeling a vessel either from a clay core or by adding coils or segments and welding the junctures with a thin solution of clay and water (Fig. 9.7). Mold-forming is commonly used not only to make pottery, but also to mass-produce small clay artifacts such as figurines and spindle whorls. Pottery molds may be *concave,* with the clay pressed inside the mold and the mold supporting and giving shape to the vessel's exterior; or they may be *convex,* with the clay pressed over the outside of the mold, which then shapes the vessel's interior. Some molds have both concave and convex aspects. For simple forms, such as open bowls, molds may serve to form the entire vessel; with more complex pottery shapes, such as jars, molds can be used for one part, such as the rounded base, while the upper portion is hand-formed.

Wheel forming is the most common means of mass-producing pottery vessels. A relatively recent invention—appearing sometime before 3000 B.C. in the Near East—this technique is the most common throughout the world today. The true *potter's wheel* is used to form the vessel by manipulating a rapidly rotating clay core centered on a vertically mounted wheel, powered by the potter's hands or feet or by auxiliary sources. The forming process is similar to the turning of wooden or metal forms on a lathe, except that the principal tools used in forming pottery are the potter's hands. A similar technique, often called the *slow wheel,* uses a concave basal mold that is allowed to rotate freely upon a flat platform, somewhat like a toy top. However, the slow wheel is not fixed to an axle as is the true potter's wheel, so it cannot be rotated fast enough or with enough stability to produce the "lathing" effect of the potter's wheel.

Once the vessel is formed by any of these methods, its surface is usually smoothed with a wet cloth, a sponge, or the palm of the hand to create a uniform, slick surface. An overall coating with a thin clay solution or *slip* may be applied, by dipping or brushing, to give the surface a uniform texture and color. Special clays are often used for slipping because of their ability to impart a particular color upon firing. Other slips or paints may be used to decorate the vessel in a

Figure 9.7 Selected steps in pottery manufacture: (a) hand-forming vessels (Chinautla, Guatemala); (b) applying a slip (Senegal); (c) decorating vessel shoulder by incising with a shell (Senegal); (d) firing pottery in an open kiln (Chinautla). [Photos (b) and (c), courtesy of Olga F. Linares.]

variety of painted patterns and colors. Specialized slips that vitrify during high-temperature firing are called *glazes*. The vessel may also be further modified or decorated by modeling, either adding clay (welding appliqués) or subtracting clay (incising, carving, cutting, and so on). As the clay begins to dry, it loses its plasticity. When it cannot be further modeled but is still somewhat moist to the touch, the clay is described as being *leather hard*. Leather-hard clay can still be carved, incised or punctated. At this stage the vessel's surface may be polished by rubbing with a smooth hard object such as a beach pebble. The effect of polishing is to compact the surface and give it a lustrous gloss.

After decorating and drying, the pottery vessel is ready for firing. Firing transforms clay from its natural plastic state to a permanent nonplastic one. During the firing process, clay may pass through as many as three stages: dehydration or loss of water occurs at temperatures up to about 600° C; oxidation of carbon and iron compounds in the clay takes place at temperatures up to about 900° C; and finally, *vitrification*—a complex process in which glass and other new minerals are formed in the clay—occurs at temperatures above about 1000° C. Vitrification fuses the clay so that the vessel walls lose their porosity and become waterproof. The earliest and simplest method of firing is to place the vessels in an open fire, specially prepared to ensure the proper and even temperatures required by pottery. Open kilns can usually attain temperatures within the oxidation range, but they cannot reach the threshold point of vitrification. Closed kilns, which are usually specially constructed ovens, are necessary to vitrify pottery. Glazed pottery is actually fired twice in closed kilns: the first process, bisque firing, dehydrates and oxidizes the clay; then, after the vessel cools and glazes are applied, it is fired again to vitrify the glaze. The earliest glazed pottery appears to have been produced in China by 1500 B.C.

Analysis of Pottery

The archaeologist uses a variety of approaches to analyze pottery; the methods used in any given study depend on the objectives of that study. We will consider each of the three broad approaches discussed earlier—studies based upon stylistic attributes, form attributes, and technological attributes—and discuss the major applications of each.

Analysis of Pottery Style. Traditionally, stylistic analyses of pottery have received the greatest emphasis by archaeologists (Fig. 9.8). This is because pottery lends itself to such a variety of stylistic and decorative treatments—painting, appliqué, incising, and so on—that have no effect on the vessel's usefulness as a container. This underlying "freedom of choice" in pottery style leads archaeologists to assume

Figure 9.8 Pottery style classification: vessels from the Southwestern United States representing four different pottery types defined by painted decoration. (After Carlson 1970.)

that stylistic regularities represent culturally guided choices rather than technological or functional limitations. Pottery styles have been used to trace ancient social and cultural links in time and space, and stylistic classification remains one of the most important methods of analyzing ancient pottery collections.

In many cases, pottery collections have been classified into types on the basis of the most readily observable style characteristics, usually color. However, such classifications tend to provide only very broad and general type categories, such as "red ware" and "gray ware," and to lack precision in defining the criteria used to separate one type from another. Most unfortunately, for many years and in many parts of the world, pottery analysts made no attempt to standardize the procedures, nomenclature, or criteria used in defining pottery types on the basis of stylistic attributes; instead, each pottery analyst worked independently. The lack of comparability among analyses greatly reduced their usefulness for making fine temporal distinctions, intersite comparisons, area syntheses, reconstruction of trade networks, and other higher-level generalizations. The situation was similar to that in other early scientific attempts to classify complex phenomena, such as the beginnings of biological classification: individualistic classification schemes tended only to compound a chaotic situation, until agreement upon a single set of procedures emerged.

In several areas of the world, archaeologists have begun to standardize their approaches to defining stylistic types. One example of this process is the development and spread of a particular classification method known as type-variety-mode analysis. This method originated in classification systems based on *types* and *varieties,* developed in both the southwestern and southeastern United States. However, in its modern application the method combines those considerations with use of the *mode* concept developed by Irving Rouse, an approach that is often used as a separate means of classification in some geographical areas. The type-variety method was eventually extended into the Maya area of Mesoamerica as a solution to the classificatory chaos that prevailed in that region.

Type-variety analysis is based on the definition of minimal attributes and the determination of the way sets of attributes combine to form a hierarchy of typological units called modes, varieties, types, and groups (see Fig. 9.9). Definition of the attributes within a given pottery collection, as well as the eventual definition of typological units, is based on visual and tactile examination of each sherd or vessel in the sample. Although the type-variety method emphasizes stylistic attributes as those most readily recognized and manipulated by

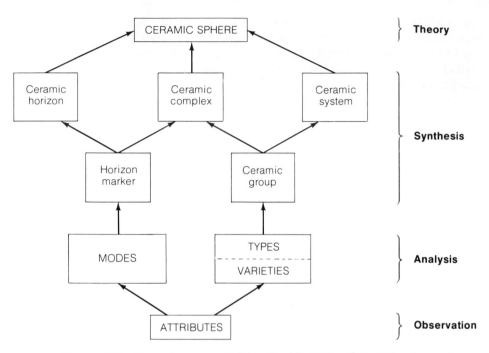

Figure 9.9   Flow chart summarizing the hierarchy of classification units defined in type-variety-mode analysis. (After Gifford 1976.)

the ancient potter, form and technological attributes may be used as secondary criteria to help in the definition of types.

This hierarchical classification, from modes to varieties, types, and groups reflecting different degrees of variability in attribute clustering, is presumed to reflect the ancient potter's social system. That is, the minimal cluster of attributes—the variety—may represent the work of individual potters or small groups of potters closely related in time (a family of potters descending over several generations) or space (a family of potters during a short time interval). The type corresponds to the next level of social organization, usually a group of family units such as a neighborhood, settlement, or village. Finally, the ceramic group reflects a larger social unit, such as an area of several villages, a town, or even an entire region. The kinds of organizational units vary from one society to another, but the general hypothesis is the same: that the levels of pottery classification correspond to the appropriate levels of ancient social organization in each situation. Moreover, characteristics of the pottery classification provide insights into the nature of the ancient social and political system. For instance, a great profusion of varieties for each type may indicate considerable freedom of expression for individual potters, the result of a noncoercive sociopolitical system. On the other hand, more restricted types—each with few varieties—might reflect a more rigid and tightly controlled system. On the basis of these assumptions, the most outstanding proponent of this sytem, James Gifford, used his analysis of pottery to derive rather broad conclusions as to the nature of ancient lowland Maya society and the way its characteristics changed through time. For example, Gifford contrasted the great local diversity of early lowland pottery of the Middle Preclassic period (800–300 B.C.), the Mamom Ceramic Complex, to the widespread distribution of uniform types characteristic of the Late Preclassic period (300 B.C. to A.D. 250), in the Chicanel Ceramic Complex. From this pattern Gifford postulated a consolidation from a series of small, vigorous, independent communities to a single society operating with a consistent system of values as well as unifying social, economic, and political systems.

Type-variety-mode pottery analysis: James Gifford and lowland Maya pottery

As an analytic tool, the type-variety-mode method has been most effective in encouraging consistency in classification and description of pottery collections in areas in which it is in use. The validity of the specific behavioral assumptions that underlie the method has yet to be thoroughly tested by long-range studies of contemporary pottery-producing communities. Gifford's interpretation, though logical and intuitively attractive, remains undemonstrated, and it should not be assumed to be the only possible interpretation. The point is rather that by encouraging production of comparable type descriptions, type-variety-mode analysis has facilitated recognition of time-space patterns in pottery, such as the contrast between the Mamom and Chicanel complexes. The behavioral interpretation of such patterns is a separate question, which will be discussed in Chapter 12.

Analysis of Pottery Form and Function.   The analysis of pottery on the basis of vessel form is perhaps not as common as that based on stylistic attributes. However, form attributes may be combined with stylistic classifications (such as those in the type-variety method) to assist in the definition of types. And because of the capacity of clay to take a very wide variety of shapes, differences in form among pottery vessels should represent the potter's choices rather than technological limits, although constrained by functional considerations.

Initial classifications of vessel form are usually based on the consistent clustering of overall vessel shapes or on clustering of component shape attributes such as form of vessel lip, neck, shoulder, base, and so on (Fig. 9.10). When possible, classification based on overall vessel form may make use of comparisons with vessel shapes still used in the area under archaeological study. These classifications often produce rather broad categories or form types, such as bowls,

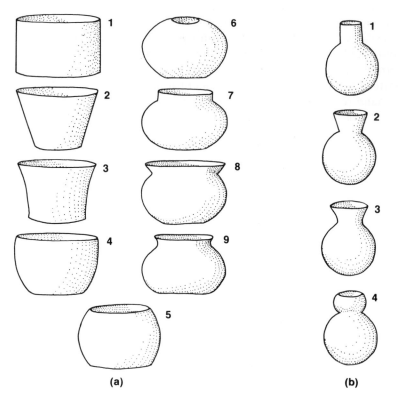

Figure 9.10   An example of pottery form classification: (a) nine defined bowl categories, (b) four defined jar categories. (After Sabloff 1975.)

platters, or jars. On the other hand, detailed studies of each component attribute of vessel form often produce finer, more narrowly defined categories. The broader classification has greater utility in proposing relationships between vessel form and function, while the more detailed approach is often better for defining spatial relationships and temporal distinctions. Since we have already discussed spatial and temporal applications under stylistic classifications, we will restrict our discussion here to the question of functional implications. The discussion will also include other means of assessing vessel function.

Ancient vessel function may be determined in several ways. The archaeologist may recover direct evidence of function in association with the pottery. In such cases, skill in excavation and use of analogy in interpretation may enable the archaeologist to reconstruct a great deal about ancient patterns of pottery usage. In most instances, however, direct evidence of function is not present, and ancient use must be inferred from analysis based on vessel form.

Archaeologists commonly argue that a strong correspondence exists between a vessel's shape and its function; they base their arguments upon a variety of general contemporary analogs. However, we must remember that although function is an important determinant of form, other factors such as technological limitations, properties of the clay being modeled, and cultural value orientations all influence vessel shape. The use of general shape-function analogs is common in archaeological studies. For instance, vessels with necks are assumed to have been used for storing and dispensing liquids, as they are today in most areas of the world without running water; the restrictive neck helps to control spillage and thus to reduce waste. Smaller jars with narrow necks are usually intepreted as vessels for carrying liquids, while larger, wider-mouthed vessels are usually seen as stationary water storage jars.

A functional distinction is commonly drawn between utilitarian (domestic) and ceremonial pottery; this distinction may be based on direct evidence from vessel provenience and from associated residues, or it may be inferred from vessel form. Such categorizations involve the assumption that an ancient distinction existed among vessel forms, so that certain shapes were associated with ceremonial uses and others with domestic tasks. Some of these classifications, involving the degree of vessel elaboration or decoration, assume that more elaborate pottery forms were associated with ceremonial or higher-status activities, while simpler pottery was used for lower-status and domestic activities. As we noted in discussing lithic analysis, such an equation of form elaboration with ritual use is not always justified, and it should be made only when other evidence, such as association of particular elaborate forms with ritual contexts, so indicates.

Analysis of vessel function also includes examination of remnants or residues that resulted from use. Such remnants may be present in visible quantities or may be discovered through microscopic analysis. For example, cooking vessels may have interior residues that can be identified. In such cases, the archaeologist can not only infer vessel function but also reconstruct ancient cooking practices and food preferences. Vessels that lack food residues but have burned and blackened exteriors may still be identified as cooking containers. Conversely, pottery that has interior food residues but lacks exterior burning may be interpreted as cooking vessels utilizing internal heat sources such as heated stones. Other residues, such as incense resins, grain pollen, or unfired clay can also help in identification of function —for example, as incense burners, storage jars, or potter's equipment.

The archaeological provenience of the pottery may also allow the investigator to determine past uses. Vessels found in tombs or associated with burials are usually regarded as ritual paraphernalia used in funerary rites. Other ritual uses include constructional offerings or caches found in ancient structures; these are analogous to the cornerstones of modern buildings. In pre-Columbian Mesoamerican sites, for instance, pottery is often found as apparent dedicatory offerings or as containers for offerings placed within a building platform; an example of such a dedicatory cache from the site of El Portón in Guatemala was described in Chapter 7. In some cases, however, the archaeologist must be cautious in assigning single functions for pottery vessels. For instance, funerary vessels often show traces of prior use, indicating that they served different purposes before being assigned their final ritual function. Determination of multiple uses and recycling of pottery vessels is often not possible, but this complicating factor should be kept in mind in interpreting vessel functions.

Analysis of Pottery Technology.   The manufacture of pottery involves a complex technology consisting of a series of operations performed by the potter. This technology includes the acquisition and preparation of raw materials (clays, tempers, pigments, wood for firing, and so forth), the shaping and decoration of the vessels, preparation for firing, and the actual firing process. An analysis of ancient pottery remains may reveal clues as to the actual manufacturing methods used. But in contrast to a subtractive technology such as the manufacture of stone tools by chipping and flaking, pottery involves a plastic, additive technology. Manipulation of the clay in the later stages of manufacture may thus obliterate the diagnostic markings and features left by earlier stages. For this reason, archaeologists usually cannot completely reconstruct the manufacturing process solely on the basis of examination of the traces provided by the archaeological record. The only way to overcome this difficulty is to use analogy with documented instances of pottery production today. In this way, new clues may be recognized by observing actual production procedures and matching these with similar features on ancient pottery. In addition, manufacturing steps that leave no trace may be proposed or inferred for a better understanding of ancient technology.

Unfortunately, only a relatively few technological studies of pottery have been completed; more research of this kind is needed. One of the most common technological studies done by archaeologists involves analysis of firing conditions. Ancient firing procedures may be inferred from observable characteristics of the finished product. If the vessel surfaces are vitrified or glazed, for example, the pottery was fired at a temperature in excess of ca. 900° C., probably in an enclosed kiln. Open-kiln methods may produce hard, fully oxidized pottery; that is, they can provide sufficient time and temperature to burn off all organic substances from the clay. But at these lower temperatures, the pottery remains unvitrified and permeable to water. Complete oxidation may be diagnosed from a uniform color in the interior clay (paste): if the paste has a dark core (usually dark gray or black), chances are that the firing was insufficient to fully oxidize the vessel. Blotchy surface discolorations on the vessel, called *fire clouds,* are also typical of open firing methods. The overall color of the vessel may also be affected by firing conditions: for instance, insufficient oxygen can produce *smudging* or blackened surfaces.

The outstanding pioneering work in archaeological pottery technology was done by Anna Shepard. She conducted studies of the manufacturing processes used in several pre-Columbian wares by detailed analyses of sherd pastes. These efforts included the definitive study of plumbate ware, the only prehistoric vitrified pottery produced in the New World. In most areas of the world, technological analysis is made more difficult by the paucity of reported discoveries and systematic excavations of ancient manufacturing and kiln sites. Unfortunately, physical evidence of pottery manufacturing activity is often difficult to find. Open kiln sites may vanish or be difficult to distinguish from hearths or other burned areas. Evidence of ancient production can occasionally be inferred from the discovery of tools and materials used in pottery manufacture. For example, the excavations at Chalchuapa, El Salvador, revealed an array of indirect evidence for pre-Columbian pottery production, including lumps of unfired clay, small stone palettes for grinding pigments, pieces of unprocessed hematite pigments, and small polishing stones. However, the inherent difficulties of reconstructing ancient pottery technology reinforce the need for thorough ethnographic treatments of contemporary production that can be used as analogs for archaeological interpretation.

Technological analysis of pottery: Anna Shepard and plumbate ware

Indirect evidence of pottery manufacture: Chalchuapa, El Salvador

Metal Artifacts

The complex technology involved in the extraction of metal from ores and the production of metal artifacts is called *metallurgy*. The earliest traces of this technology are found in the Old World—specifically in the Near East—where between 8000 and 9500 years ago people began to shape copper into simple tools and ornaments. These first metal artifacts were *cold hammered,* probably with stone tools. However, within several millennia copper was being extracted from ores by the use of heat and cast into a variety of forms. Since that time, metallurgy has developed and spread throughout the world, almost completely replacing lithic technology. Today, of course, our sophisticated metal technology has become an essential part of our complex civilization.

Resumë of Metal Technology

Prehistoric metallurgy was based on three hard metals—copper, tin, and iron—and, to a lesser degree, on two rare or precious metals, silver and gold. Because the development of metallurgical technology followed a fairly regular sequence, gradually replacing the two established lithic technologies in the Old World, nineteenth-century archaeologists found it convenient to classify the "progress" of Old World civilization with labels referring to the appropriate successive "ages of metal." Thus, the first metal to be utilized gave its name to the "Copper Age," or Chalcolithic. The alloy of copper and tin that was produced in later times gave its name to the "Bronze Age," which was followed ultimately by the "Iron Age."

Since the nineteenth century, archaeologists have learned a great deal more about the origin and development of prehistoric metallurgy. As a result, the course of technological innovation can now be traced not only in the Near East but elsewhere—in Southeast Asia, China, Africa, and the New World. The picture is by no means complete; for instance, recent discoveries at Non Nok Tha and Ban Chiang in Thailand have generated new—if controversial—support for the hypothesis that tin-bronze metallurgy developed as early in Southeast Asia as in its traditionally assigned home, the Near East.

The sequence of metallurgical development is still best known for the Near East, however. In that area, the first uses of metal, sometime before 7000 B.C., involved cold hammering of native copper. (The term *native copper* refers to the metal's occurrence in an uncombined form, so that relatively pure supplies can be collected or extracted simply.) Copper is malleable enough to be shaped by hammering, but the progressive pounding cracks and weakens the metal. Annealing—heating and slow cooling—"heals" the cracks and stresses produced by hammering, thus providing renewed strength to the metal tool.

Before 4000 B.C., copper was being melted and cast in molds into a growing variety of desired shapes, from axe heads to spearpoints, swords, and ornaments. At the same time, intense heat was used to *smelt* copper from ores, thereby greatly expanding the range of sources for the raw material. At first only weathered, surface (oxidized) ores were mined, but by about 2500 B.C., deeper-lying and harder-to-reach sulfide ore deposits were also being used; their ex-

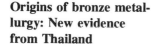

Origins of bronze metallurgy: New evidence from Thailand

ploitation indicates the increased importance of copper technology and copper artifacts.

Another significant advance involved deliberate production of metal *alloys*. Most scholars believe that experimental attempts to remove impurities from copper led to the discovery or realization that some of the "impurities" were beneficial. Most notably, inclusion of small quantities of tin or arsenic in copper forms a new metal combination or alloy, *bronze*. Bronze has several advantages over copper: not only is its melting point lower, but it also cools into a harder metal capable of retaining a sharper, more durable edge. Further hammering, after cooling, hardens it further. Other copper alloys can be made, but many are brittle, and tin bronze is not. The problem is that tin is relatively scarce. There are no verified major sources of tin in the Near East, and a major archaeological controversy has arisen over the origin of the tin exploited by Near Eastern metallurgists. But bronze was certainly being produced in the Near East by about 3000 B.C. As noted above, Southeast Asia has recently yielded some very early bronze artifacts, including daggers and axe heads, which may date to 3500 B.C. And Southeast Asia is known to be rich in tin ores. Whether the two postulated "homes" for bronze metallurgy represent independent inventions, or, if not, which developed the technology originally, remains an intriguing research question. Whatever its origins, bronze metallurgy spread swiftly (Fig. 9.11). Some of the most sophisticated products of bronze casting were created in China during the Shang Dynasty, extending from about 1500 to 1027 B.C..

Figure 9.11 A grouping of bronze vessels from the first millennium B.C. as found in a tomb chamber at Gordion, Turkey. (Courtesy of the Gordion Project, the University Museum, University of Pennsylvania.)

Iron metallurgy was the next major development in metallurgical technology. Meteoric iron was known and used during the Bronze Age, but in the later part of the second millenium B.C., ironworking displaced bronze casting as the principal metallurgical means of tool production. The change was more than one of material; ironworking is also a more complicated technology. Iron melts at 1537° C.: Chinese and possibly South Asian metallurgists were able to melt iron during the first millenium B.C. but there is no evidence for *cast iron* production in the ancient Near East. The principal iron output of the Near Eastern furnaces was a spongy mass called a *bloom,* which was then reheated in a forge and hammered by a blacksmith to shape the tool, increase the metal's strength, and drive out impurities. Even so, forged iron is relatively soft. Use of a charcoal fire for the forge, however, introduces carbon and strengthens the iron, producing carburized iron or *steel,* a much harder and more durable metal. By the end of the second millenium B.C., Near Eastern blacksmiths were making "steeled" iron tools, and the Iron Age was under way. Further technological advances increased the strength of the steel even more: for example, *quenching*—rapid cooling of the carburized iron by immersion in water—adds strength but increases brittleness. But as metallurgists discovered by the beginning of the fourth century B.C., *tempering*—reheating the iron to a temperature below 727° C.—offered a solution to the brittleness introduced by quenching.

Analysis of Metal Artifacts

Metal artifacts have been found in archaeological contexts from the Near East to Southeast Asia, and in Europe, Africa, and the Americas (Fig. 9.12). Archaeological analyses have varied with the geographical area, in accord with differing research priorities. Because metal—especially molten metal—is a plastic, malleable material, it, like pottery, should be particularly well suited to stylistic analyses and classifications. Such studies have been done; one example is the classification of bronze *fibulae* or "safety-pin brooches" from La Tène sites of Iron Age Europe (Fig. 9.13). Other studies have focused on the form of metal artifacts and on functional attributions based on formal variation, similar to studies done for stone and ceramic artifacts.

But a general focus in studies of metal artifacts is on analyses that aid in reconstructing ancient technology. Classifications divide the metal industry into subindustries according to the metal being worked. More technical analyses are then performed, including constituent analysis and microscopic examination of the metal structure; these studies help the archaeologist to understand the range of technology involved in production of the pieces, from procurement of raw

Figure 9.12 New World metallurgy: Pre-Columbian gold breast plate from Ecuador. (Courtesy of the University Museum, University of Pennsylvania.)

materials to formation and refinement of the final product. Constituent analysis, for example, can not only identify the metals and non-metallic materials present, but may allow specification of the metal sources. Examination of the microstructure of an artifact may yield clues as to the precise techniques used in its production—hammering, annealing, quenching, and so on.

A complicating factor in these analyses is that metallurgy, like pottery, is an additive and correcting process in which mistakes can to some extent be covered and "smoothed away" by subsequent treatment. Unlike pottery, however, in which firing permanently alters the raw material, metal artifacts can also be melted down and the "raw material" reclaimed and reused. Such recycling may, for example, account for a relative lack of bronze artifacts early in the Iron Age: the expected number of pieces may actually have been produced, but if their material was reclaimed, it entered the archaeological record only after its recycling ended, an unknown period of time after the original smelting.

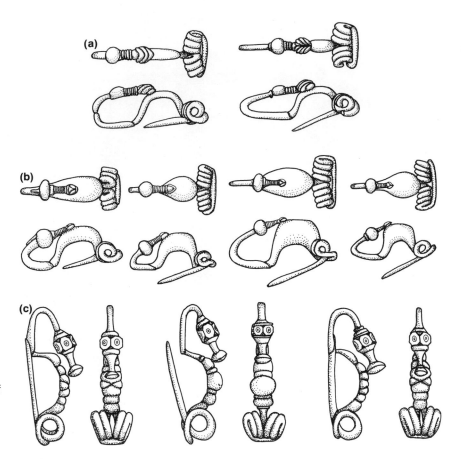

Figure 9.13 Three potential stylistic types of bronze fibulae from an Iron Age grave at Münsingen, Germany. (After Hodson 1968.)

Artifacts from Organic Materials

A variety of artifacts are made from organic materials such as wood, bone, antler, ivory, and shell. Although such items are known to be important or even numerically dominant in the tool assemblages of some modern societies, such as the Eskimo, they are quite susceptible to decay processes and thus are encountered by archaeologists only under special conditions.

Other kinds of organic materials have also been used to produce artifacts, of course: paper, leather, gourds, plant fibers, and many more have been exploited, and many have special technologies associated with their production and use. However, we shall restrict discussion here to the most frequently encountered artifact categories: bone and related materials (such as antler and ivory), wood, and shell.

Technologies

Animal skeletons have been proposed as the raw material for the earliest known tools. Raymond Dart, one of the discoverers of the early hominid form *Australopithecus,* has hypothesized that the tools used by this relative of modern man were made from the long bones and jaws of gazelles, antelopes, and wild boars. This so-called *osteodontokeratic* ("bone-tooth-horn") technology remains controversial, despite the dramatic portrayal in the film *2001;* Dart's principal body of evidence is the material found with the Australopithecine remains in Makapansgat cave, in the Transvaal of South Africa. Other scholars have proposed that the assemblage could be accounted for by factors other than toolmaking and discard behavior. Specifically, archaeologists such as Richard Klein, Lewis Binford, C. K. Brain, Catherine Read-Martin, and Dwight Read provide counterarguments that the Makapansgat remains need represent nothing more than a food-refuse deposit, accumulated by carnivores such as hyenas or leopards as well as (or even instead of) hominids. However, Dart reports some specific pieces that seem to represent deliberate shaping (Fig. 9.14), and the Leakeys have reported several apparent bone scrapers from the early Paleolithic levels at Olduvai Gorge, Tanzania. This evidence, together with elementary logic, argues for some use of bone tools by the early hominid relatives of modern humans.

Despite the controversy over the origins of bone tools, there is no doubt that by the Upper Paleolithic, people were making artifacts from a variety of animal parts. In both the Old and New Worlds, bone was split and carved with stone tools to form projectile points, fishhooks, and other tools (Fig. 9.15). It was also used to make articles of adornment, such as beads. Antler, usually from deer, was split or carved to make projectile points, especially barbed points for spears or harpoons. In the Arctic, the prehistoric tradition of carving ivory with stone to make harpoons and other artifacts has survived into historic times (Fig. 9.15).

The technology involved in the production of bone, antler, and ivory tools is subtractive like stoneworking. Technologically, the simplest such tools were those that involved *no* form modification, as when an animal bone would be used as a club. The next technological level would be breaking the bone to produce a sharp or jagged edge. Many forms, however, involved working with other tools. The earliest finds suggest that such working was first confined to chipping and cracking, but by the Upper Paleolithic, the production of controlled forms of bone, antler, and ivory tools shows great variety and sophistication; some forms even have engraved decoration. This devel-

Bone-tooth-horn technology: Raymond Dart at Makapansgat, South Africa

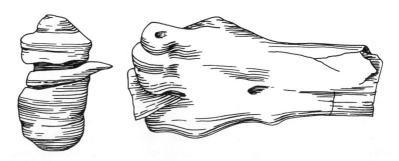

Figure 9.14 Controversial osteodontokeratic technology represented by finds from Makapansgat, South Africa. (After Sampson 1974.)

opment corresponds with the Upper Paleolithic proliferation of functionally more specialized stone tools, such as gravers and burins, as well as with the beginnings of art and—according to Alexander Marshack—of symbolic notation.

Like those made of bone, antler, and ivory, wooden artifacts are highly perishable; thus the origins and antiquity of woodworking are obscured by lack of preserved evidence. Lower Paleolithic wooden tools have been reported from waterlogged sites in Africa, however, and spear points from sites at Clacton, England, and Lehringer, Germany, testify that woodworking technology existed by the Middle Paleolithic in Europe. Woodworking, too, is a subtractive industry, involving achievement of the desired artifact shape by scraping, engraving, breaking, and so on. Indirect evidence of woodworking is preserved more often than the wood itself, in the form of certain stone tools—such as scrapers, spokeshaves, and gravers—that could have been used to manufacture wooden tools. Fire, too, may be used in the production of wooden tools, as in hardening the points of digging sticks by controlled exposure to fire.

Shell artifacts have been found the world over, including Neolithic Egypt, where they served as the raw material for some fishhooks. Certain kinds of shells are appropriate for use as cups or spoons, and, in areas where stone is scarce, they have occasionally been used as adze blades or other such tools. Shells are also used for adornment; in cultures such as the Hohokam of the American Southwest, the technology of shellworking includes the knowledge of etching designs into the surface of the shell by delicate application of a corrosive agent to eat away selected areas, leaving others in relief to form a decorative design (Fig. 9.16).

Analysis of Organic Artifacts

A fundamental kind of analysis performed on organic artifacts is identification of the material—including biological species from which it was made. Such analysis yields information on the range of biotic resources exploited by an ancient society and may give clues to communication links with other areas, as when shell artifacts at an inland site are found to be marine (saltwater) species. We will consider the "ecofactual" aspects of organic artifacts in more detail in the section on ecofacts.

Most classifications of organic artifacts are based on criteria of form (Fig. 9.17). Sometimes these form taxonomies have stylistic overtones, but more often they involve functional inferences, and the types may be labeled with direct or implied functional names. For example, the well-known artifact assemblages of the European Upper Paleolithic, especially the Magdalenian, include a great variety of

Figure 9.15 Bone harpoon heads from Alaska, with flint inserts, illustrate one kind of artifact fashioned from organic materials. (Courtesy of the University Museum, University of Pennsylvania.)

Figure 9.16 An example of a Hohokam etched shell from Arizona. The design was rendered by acid from a saguaro cactus (ca. A.D. 800–1200). (Arizona State Museum Collections, University of Arizona.)

barbed bone projectile points, almost always referred to as "harpoons." The dangers of such *a priori* functional labeling have already been noted: it provides convenient names—and easy ways to remember—the formal types, but it does not establish the actual function of these artifacts.

*Artifacts and Sampling

Artifactual studies can involve sampling strategies at two points: data collection and data analysis. Sampling in data collection procedures has been discussed in previous chapters, but we shall note again here that excavation planning can be organized to facilitate artifact studies. For example, if one wished to investigate the range of pottery forms used by an ancient community, one would want to maximize the variety of functional contexts investigated: different vessel forms might well be found in burials as opposed to domestic situations, and excavation of midden deposits would increase the quantity of material available for analysis.

Whether the archaeologist analyzes all or only part of the artifact collection obtained depends on two factors—the size of the artifact collection and the expense, in time and/or money, of the analysis. Generally speaking, the closer to total sampling one can get, the more confidence one has that the results of the analysis can be generalized to the whole collection.

Some artifact categories contain so few items that examination of all pieces is both desirable and easily feasible. Such a situation is more often associated with organic artifacts than with stone, ce-

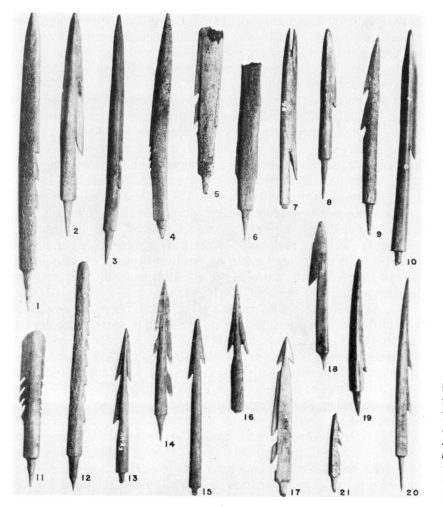

Figure 9.17 Classification of bone projectiles from Cape Denbigh, Alaska. (From *The Archeology of Cape Denbigh* by J. L. Giddings, Brown University Press, © 1964 Brown University.)

ramics, or metal, since the organic remains are least likely to survive. The reverse situation—more artifacts than can possibly be studied—is most often true for stone and ceramic collections; for instance, Kidder calculated that more than 1,000,000 sherds were recovered during his excavations at the highland Guatemalan site of Kaminaljuyú. In such cases consideration of sampling in artifact analysis comes into play.

The fundamental question in designing a sampling program concerns the question of representation: Of what is the analyzed sample to be representative? Randomized sample selection increases the probability that the sample is representative of the population from which it is drawn. But how are the sample units defined? One can choose individual artifacts, but George Cowgill suggests using provenience units—lots—as sampling units, and then analyzing all artifacts within the selected lots. Laboratory processing deals with the materials in provenience groups, so using these as sampling units makes drawing the sample easier.

As we noted in Chapter 3, the more one knows about the population in question, the more one can structure the random sample; *simple* random sampling is seldom the best sampling design to follow. If the artifact sample drawn for analysis is to be representative of the artifact collection as a whole, and if lots are to be the sampling units, then the most straightforward way to structure the sample is to *stratify* by the range of provenience types. For example, a balance may be struck among various functional contexts, such as burials, house floors and middens, as well as among different locations, such as "site core" versus "periphery." Variability through time can be handled by such stratifying factors as position in deep excavations. In general, it is better to control at the outset as many dimensions of potential variability as possible.

Sample size need not be set as a particular fraction. As Cowgill argues, it is less important that the sample include some particular percentage of the overall collection than that it be large enough in absolute numbers of pieces. For classificatory analysis based on observable characteristics—such as a pottery classification—thousands of pieces (in this case, sherds) can easily be handled.

Drawing samples for technical laboratory analyses is somewhat different. If the analyses require consultant experts and specialized laboratory equipment, expense usually places strict limits on sample size. For example, thin-sections, radiocarbon analyses, and neutron-activation analyses are so expensive that more than a few dozen such analyses per project are seldom feasible. The sampling unit for such studies is usually the individual artifact, and random sampling is less often possible or appropriate. For example, valuable whole artifacts might not be included in the range of potential candidates for any destructive analysis; and for some procedures, such as radiocarbon dating, sample pieces must have a certain minimum size. The objectives of research may also dictate the choice: if the analysis seeks to indicate the range of raw material sources anciently exploited, the sample units should be selected by characteristics—such as visible differences in stone type—that seem to reflect maximum variability. The point here, as in all questions of sampling, is to know what the sample is meant to represent, and then to structure the sampling design so as to make the sample as representative of the target population as possible.

THE ANALYSIS OF ECOFACTS

As defined in Chapter 3, ecofacts are archaeological data that do *not* owe their form to human behavior. Examples include plant and animal remains and soils found in archaeological deposits. One could argue that because domesticated plants and animals—corn, wheat, horses, turkeys, and so forth—owe their form to long-term human manipulation of reproduction, remains of these plants and animals are "artifacts" rather than ecofacts. However, it is more useful to draw the distinction between plants and animals as ecofacts or "natural" objects, and items *made from* plants and animals as artifacts. Examples of the latter would include bone scrapers and wooden spears.

Because they are "natural," unaltered objects, ecofacts do not yield direct information about human technology. They do, however, give us indirect information about past human societies. For example, at the Olsen-Chubbuck site in southeastern Colorado, a series of bison skeletons was revealed in association with some stone tools, all strewn along the base of a ravine (Fig. 9.18). The site represents the remains of human food-procurement behavior some 8500 years ago. The location and arrangement of both ecofacts and artifacts have been used to infer a good deal about hunting strategy (how and from

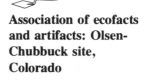

Association of ecofacts and artifacts: Olsen-Chubbuck site, Colorado

Figure 9.18 Remains of bison killed and butchered by hunters some 8500 years ago, excavated at the Olsen-Chubbuck site, Colorado. (Reproduced by permission of the Colorado State Museum and the Society for American Archaeology, from *Memoirs of the Society for American Archaeology* 26: ix, 1972.)

what direction the animals were driven over the ravine edge, including which way the wind may have been blowing), butchering techniques (how the carcasses were dismembered, which bones were stripped of meat on the spot and which were carried off to the presumed "camp" site) and yield (how much meat and byproducts would have been available from the kill).

Ecofacts can also tell us about noneconomic activities such as ritual. Analysis of the heavy concentration of pollen found scattered over Burial IV in Shanidar cave, northern Iraq, indicates that when this Neanderthal man was buried some 60,000 years ago, his survivors covered him with flowers, including daisies, cornflowers, and hollyhocks. Further, because such flowers now bloom locally in May and June, one can infer that the burial probably took place at that time of year.

Most frequently, however, ecofacts are used to reconstruct the environment in which past societies lived and the range of resources they exploited. Analysis by Clark and his co-workers of pollen samples from Star Carr, a 10,000-year-old Mesolithic site in northern England, indicate that the surrounding area was largely covered by forest of birch and pine; the presence of pollen from plants that thrive in open areas points to localized clearings, one of which was the site of Star Carr. By examining the abundantly recovered antlers of red deer, roe deer, and elk, the investigators could establish the time of year the site had been occupied. This was done by comparing the distribution of antlers broken from the animals' skulls with those that had simply been collected after being shed naturally, and correlating these data with the known seasonal cycles of deer antler growth and shedding (Fig. 9.19). The work at Star Carr was a landmark, showing the wealth of interpretation that could be gained from ecofactual data.

As with artifacts, the first step in analysis of ecofacts is classification. Artifacts may be classified in a number of ways—all of them involving effects of human behavior on the artifact. Clearly, the classification of ecofacts must use different criteria. Classification of ecofacts begins with sorting into gross categories: organic (plants and animals) and inorganic (sediments). Specimens are then further identified usually by specialists, within classificatory schemes borrowed from botany, zoology, and geology. Once these preliminary steps are completed, ecofacts may be classified in many specific ways, some of which will be discussed below, according to properties that might relate them to past human societies. For example, some plants and animals are available for harvesting only at limited times of the year; these, as the Shanidar and Star Carr cases indicate, may be used to determine seasonality of exploitation. Animals can also be

Ritual behavior: Ralph Solecki at Shanidar cave, Iraq

Pioneering environmental reconstruction: Grahame Clark at Star Carr, England

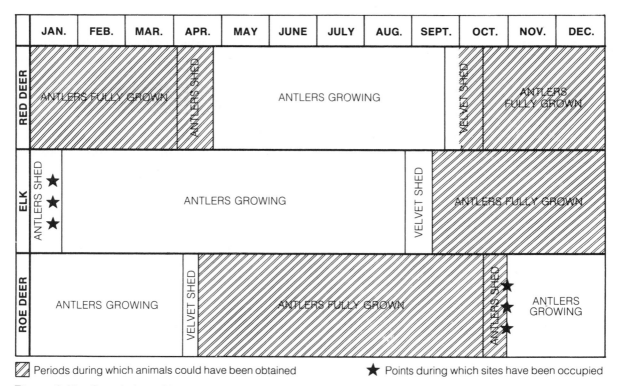

	JAN.	FEB.	MAR.	APR.	MAY	JUNE	JULY	AUG.	SEPT.	OCT.	NOV.	DEC.
RED DEER	ANTLERS FULLY GROWN			ANTLERS SHED	ANTLERS GROWING					VELVET SHED	ANTLERS FULLY GROWN	
ELK	ANTLERS SHED ★ ★★ ★	ANTLERS GROWING							VELVET SHED	ANTLERS FULLY GROWN		
ROE DEER	ANTLERS GROWING			VELVET SHED	ANTLERS FULLY GROWN					ANTLERS SHED ★ ★ ★	ANTLERS GROWING	

▨ Periods during which animals could have been obtained ★ Points during which sites have been occupied

Figure 9.19 Correlation of known antler growth cycles with antlers found at Mesolithic Star Carr indicate the seasons during which the site was occupied. (Courtesy of J. G. D. Clark *Star Carr: A Case Study in Bioarchaeology,* copyright © 1972 by Addison-Wesley Publishing Company, Inc. Philippines copyright 1972 by Addison-Wesley Publishing Company, Inc.)

studied in terms of the amounts of meat they would yield and therefore the size of the human population they could support. Similarly, soils may be classified as to their relative potential fertility under given kinds of agricultural exploitation.

Organic Remains: Flora

Plant remains in archaeological contexts comprise two basic categories: microspecimens (pollen) and macrospecimens (seeds, leaves, casts or impressions, and so forth). Indirect evidence of plant use can also be gleaned from such sources as pictorial representation—Egyptian murals illustrating growing wheat or brewing beer are examples. But here we wish to deal with archaeological plant remains and how they are studied.

Species Identification

Pollen samples are identified by specialists, either consulting botanists or botanically (palynologically) trained archaeologists. Pollen specimens are packed in sealed containers in the field to prevent contamination, and later sent to the specialist for microscopic examination. Macrospecimens are also identified in detail by trained botanical experts, although many items, such as maize cobs, can be identified in a preliminary way in the field. Some illustrated manuals give the range of species known in a given area, but the archaeologist may find it useful to collect and identify seeds, leaves, and flowers of forms currently present in the locality, as a direct comparative collection for the specific region being investigated.

As part of the identification process, many plants (and animals) are categorized as wild or domesticated. The domestication of plants and animals in the Old and New Worlds was a significant cultural development, giving people more direct control over the quantity and quality of their food supply. Accordingly, a good deal of study has been done on when, where, and how the domestication process was carried out. Critical to such study, of course, is the ability to identify wild and domesticated forms. Since domestication is a gradual effect of repeated selection for desired traits—as when larger or quicker-growing strains are deliberately replanted and nurtured—there is no single "original" domesticated maize cob or wheat kernel. Rather, one can discern trends in form from "fully wild" to "fully domesticated." In the Old World, for example, wild forms of wheat were characterized by a brittle *rachis* and a tough *glume* (Fig. 9.20). The rachis holds the seed and, if brittle, allows the mature plant to spread its seed easily to produce the next generation. A brittle rachis is unfavorable to human gathering, however, for it breaks when the plant is jarred by being harvested, and the seed is lost. Similarly, a tough glume protects the wheat kernel until it germinates, but it also makes the wheat more difficult to thresh, to yield the kernels for human consumption. It is not surprising, then, that in the course of wheat domestication, the brittle rachis and tough glume were selected *against;* selection favored forms that were easier both to harvest and to thresh. Other examples include the trend in New World maize domestication to larger size—more and longer rows of kernels (Fig. 9.21)—and, in avocadoes, to an increased ratio of edible pulp mass to seed. The list goes on for various plants domesticated in different parts of the world. The important point for this discussion is that the domestication changes in many plants have been studied and can be identified.

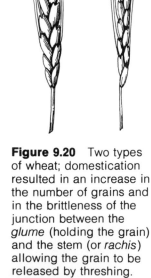

Figure 9.20 Two types of wheat; domestication resulted in an increase in the number of grains and in the brittleness of the junction between the *glume* (holding the grain) and the stem (or *rachis*) allowing the grain to be released by threshing.

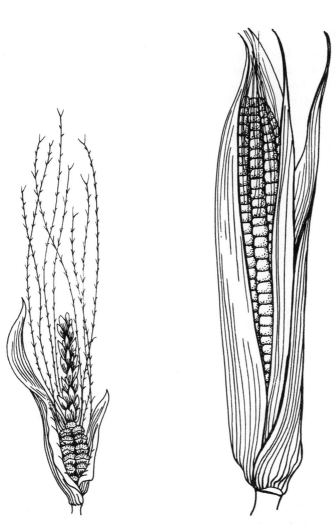

Figure 9.21 Comparison between a reconstructed view of wild maize (now extinct) on the left, and domesticated maize on the right.

Once the botanical identification of genus, species, and domestication status has been made, the specimens can be further classified or grouped in a number of ways. We shall not present an exhaustive inventory of floral analyses, and we shall present only analyses that require no special laboratory procedures. Basically the kinds of analyses we will discuss fall into three categories: what forms are present, what special traits these forms possess, and in what contexts they were found.

Floral Analysis

Simple tallies of presence/absence and relative abundance of the various forms represented at a site (or other archaeological unit) can be suggestive. For example, the relative abundance of wild versus domesticated plant forms may indicate relative reliance on food-collection as opposed to food-production strategies. The parts of the plants represented, such as macrospecimens versus microspecimens, may sometimes be important: pollen is windborne and may be introduced to an archaeological deposit accidentally without signifying deliberate ancient exploitation of the species represented. Macrospecimens, on the other hand, are more likely to represent human exploitation. Yet caution in interpreting such tallies is always necessary, since observed presence and absence or relative abundance figures are always affected by sampling design and differential preservation. For example, cacao pollen is most unlikely to be preserved in the tropical soils in which this tree is grown.

Beyond identification of the remains that are present, one can compare what is known of special growing requirements or other characteristics of the plants found. Some plants reflect very specific climatic conditions; others indicate specific conditions of open or forested vegetation cover. Mention has been made of the use of the latter factor at Star Carr to reconstruct the environmental surroundings of the site. More broadly speaking, palynological studies have used such properties to reconstruct climatic changes in temperate Europe for the millenia following the final retreat of the glaciers, and to trace (by evidence of large-scale deforestation) the advent of land-clearing practices and cultivation (Fig. 9.22). Other specific plant characteristics can also provide clues as to whether and how the plants were used. For example, plants have various effects on the human body when ingested: certain plants are known to be edible, others poisonous, hallucinogenic, or medicinal. Solecki has suggested that because many of the flowers found with Shanidar Burial IV are used medicinally today, such properties may have been appreciated anciently. He speculates that the flowers may indicate that the dead man was a shaman or curer.

Another dimension in the study of floral ecofacts is the context in which they are found. The Shanidar IV context is one of ideological or symbolic use of plants. On the other hand, the only sure indication that a plant was a food resource is contextual—occurrences in the gastrointenstinal tracts of mummies or bog corpses, or in human *coprolites* (preserved feces). Food remains and residues may also be found adhering to the interiors of food storage vessels or to preparation surfaces such as grinding stones. The archaeologist can look for this kind of evidence by removing macroscopic specimens and by

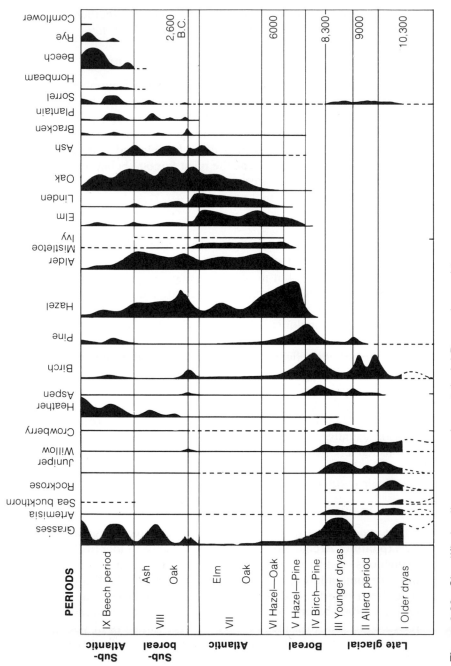

Figure 9.22 Simplified pollen sequence in postglacial Denmark, used to reconstruct climatic as well as vegetative changes. (After Dimbleby 1970.)

washing the relevant artifacts carefully and reserving the wash water in a sealed container for later pollen analysis. Of course, vegetal food remains may occur in other contexts, but in such cases their interpretation as "food" depends less on context than on whether the item is a known or probable food item, such as maize or barley.

Organic Remains: Nonhuman Fauna

Animal remains in archaeological contexts take a number of forms, from whole specimens, such as mummies, to partial ones, such as bones or coprolites. Bones and teeth, the most commonly recovered forms, have received the most attention. As with use of plants, human exploitation of animals may often be inferred from indirect archaeological evidence—perhaps the most famous being the Paleolithic cave murals of western Europe. But we shall confine discussion here to physical remains of actual animals.

Species Identification

As with plant materials, again the first step in analysis is classification. Detailed identifications are best referred to zoologists or zooarchaeologists, but most archaeologists can learn to distinguish the bones and teeth of common animals such as dogs and deer. Illustrated taxonomic manuals have been prepared for bone identification in specific areas, including Europe and North America, but more are needed, especially for animals other than large mammals. The best aid to species identification is a good comparative collection. However, such collections require much time and work to assemble, as well as a sizable and secure area as storage and study space. It may also be difficult, impossible, or ethically undesirable to obtain skeletons of rare, protected, or extinct species. For these reasons archaeologists usually rely on specialized experts who have access to established comparative collections. Once identified, the animal remains can be examined in terms of their inferred impact on the archaeological situation under study.

Faunal Analysis

A basic question of faunal studies is, What kinds of animals were being exploited? Archaeologists attempt not only to identify the species distinctions, but to establish the proportions of adult versus juvenile and, for some adult animals, male versus female. Tallies of this kind have been used as evidence for the very beginning of animal domestication, before bone changes due to selective breeding can be detected. In this case the presence of large numbers of young animal remains may indicate direct access to and control of a herd, or selective culling before breeding age to "weed out" certain characteristics.

In other cases the presence of young animals may point to use of the site in the season when the young animals would have been available.

A comparison of faunal species represented in Beds I and II of Olduvai Gorge, Tanzania, with those killed by modern Bushmen hunters revealed marked similarity in the two tallies, both in specific kinds of animals and in proportional amounts of each species found in each sample. In fact, a closer look at the Olduvai data led John Speth and Dave Davis to suggest not only that the prey taken by early hominid hunters of 1 to almost 2 million years ago was like that of modern Bushmen, but that faunal tallies from individual excavation levels could be further described as fitting seasonal aspects of the Bushmen hunting pattern. Specifically, they have used the analogy with modern Bushmen to contrast rainy-season occupations with dry-season sites (Fig. 9.23).

Archaeologists can also examine the parts of animals present at a site. At Star Carr, the occurrence of stag frontlets as well as detached antlers gave evidence not only of season of occupation of the site, but also of the range of antler "raw materials" that were desired by or acceptable to the site's occupants. At Olsen-Chubbuck, study of presence/absence of various skeletal elements led to inferences about aspects of butchering techniques by indicating which parts of the animals were taken back to the residence area for more leisurely utiliza-

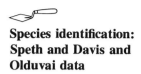

Species identification: Speth and Davis and Olduvai data

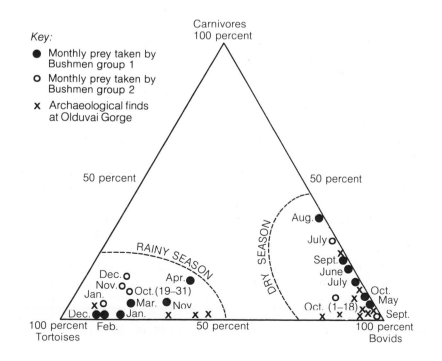

Figure 9.23 Proportions of tortoise, carnivore, and bovid prey taken each month by two groups of modern Bushmen hunters suggest that bones of the same kinds of animals found in Beds I and II at Olduvai Gorge (see Fig. 5.3) mark seasonal sites, most of them dry-season occupations. (After Speth and Davis, from *Science*, vol. 192, pp. 441–445, fig. 2. Copyright 1976 by the American Association for the Advancement of Science.)

tion. And at Tikal, Guatemala, the accumulation of layers of bat guano in buildings indicates intervals of human abandonment of those buildings.

One very basic manipulation in the analysis of animal remains is the calculation of *minimum number of individuals* (MNI) represented. Bones are categorized by species and *element* (skeletal part), such as all left bison ulnae, as well as age and sex if identifiable. The element category represented by the largest number of remains indicates the minimum number of individuals of that species that could be represented by the collection. That is, if for (adult) bison there are five right mandibles, one left calcaneus, and three left ulnae, the bones had to come from at least five bison. The MNI does not tell how many animals were ever present or exploited, but, it does indicate that *at least* a certain number must be represented. The MNI is important in the weighting of species representations: if all individual bones were simply tallied, a complete skeleton of a single animal of one species would grossly overrepresent that species relative to another that was represented by one or two bones each from several animals.

Special characteristics of particular animals may lead to specific interpretations. Some small animals, such as snails, are very sensitive to climate and thus can serve as indicators of local climatic change or stability. And an increase in white-tailed deer could, for example, signal an increase in cleared areas or a decrease in local forest cover. Presence of large mammals as prey often indicates organized group hunting practices, and herd animals require different tactics from solitary animals. Ideological interpretations may also be made from faunal evidence. For example, the swift fox (*Vulpes velox*) has a rich pelt that was ethnographically known to be prized by the Fox society of Skidi Pawnee of Nebraska. As B. Miles Gilbert has suggested, the presence of the bones of this fox in archaeological sites of that region might suggest that the ideological association of these pelts was present in prehistoric times as well.

Contextual associations can be related to various kinds of human-animal relations. For example, the occurrence of mummified cats in ancient Egypt and jaguar remains in elite Maya burials reflect the recognized high symbolic status enjoyed by those animals in the two societies. Bones found in middens, on the other hand, are usually interpreted as remains of food animals and/or scavengers.

As part of the consideration of context, the archaeologist must be careful to distinguish, as far as possible, which animals are related to human presence and exploitation and which are not. For example, burrowing animals such as gophers or opossums found in graves may have gotten there on their own, independent of the ancient burial.

Ideological behavior reconstruction: B. Miles Gilbert's analysis of fox remains

Other animals may simply take advantage of the shelter provided by occupation areas, such as bats roosting in abandoned Maya temples. As an example of how critical such a determination can be, consider the debate over Makapansgat, cited earlier in this chapter. Raymond Dart has used the pattern of occurrence of the nonhominid bones—how they were broken, what elements were present, and how they were deposited—to argue that these bones were tools used by the Australopithecines more than a million years ago. Other scholars, however, argue that the patterns fit those observed for bones accumulated by carnivores such as hyenas, and that the site does not represent a deposit of tools.

Organic Remains: Human

One entire branch of anthropology—physical anthropology—is concerned with study of the biological nature of human beings. Some physical anthropologists study the observable biological characteristics of living people; others study human remains preserved in the archaeological record. We obviously cannot here review the field of physical anthropology nor discuss the course of human biological evolution, although the physical remains that give direct evidence for this evolution are recovered by archaeological techniques. All archaeologists should have some classroom and laboratory training in these subjects. Here we shall simply review some of the ways in which human remains from an archaeological context may further the understanding of the extinct society being investigated. Forms of human remains include mummies, fragmentary bones and teeth, and coprolites. Bones and teeth are most often preserved, and they will receive most attention.

Analysis of human remains begins with identification of the particular elements (bones, teeth) present and of the number of individuals represented. Since people are often buried in individual graves, this may not be a difficult task, but mass graves or reused ones present special problems. All archaeologists should learn to identify human skeletal elements; illustrated manuals are available as field aids, but laboratory practice with skeletal collections is indispensable. Once the elements are identified, an assessment should be made of each individual's sex and age at death. Some skeletal elements are more reliable or easier to interpret in these assessments. For example, sex can be most readily judged from the pelvis, especially from the form of the sciatic notch. But other elements, including teeth, can be used when necessary. Because sexual differences do not appear in the skeleton until puberty, children's bones cannot be differentiated as to sex.

Age can be assessed by a variety of means, including eruption sequence and degree of wear on teeth, fusion of the sutures between bones of the skull, and fusion of the ends (epiphyses) to the shafts (diaphyses) of limb bones. In some cases, correlation of these rates and sequences with specific ages depends on the population involved. For instance, children's tooth eruption sequences are broadly predictable, whereas tooth wear patterns depend on age and diet, since gritty foods wear teeth down faster than do other foods.

Once age and sex identifications are made, a number of other studies may be done. Paleodemographic analyses seek to understand the structure of the ancient population under investigation, including determination of the sex ratio and life expectancy (Fig. 9.24). Great difficulties are involved in trying to characterize a whole human population on the basis of the remains of a relatively few individuals who may have lived at different times in the history of an archaeological site. The necessary assumptions and concomitant pitfalls are presented in some of the writings listed in the Suggestions for Further Reading at the end of the book. As one example, suppose that a large number of young men were killed in battle and buried away from home; they would not be represented in their home burial population, so that even if archaeologically excavated burials accurately represented the range of burials at the occupation site, they would not accurately represent the original overall population. Nevertheless, efforts at constructing life tables for archaeological populations have begun to reward paleodemographers by suggesting ways in which these populations may have been either similar to or different from modern populations. For instance, both Edward Deevey and Kenneth Weiss have attempted "histories" of human life expectancy; they find less difference among preindustrial populations than between them as a group and industrial populations—indicating that the cultural changes associated with industrialization had more effect on human longevity than did those associated with the advent of agriculture.

Human remains also yield information on the health of the population under study. Not all diseases or injuries affect the skeleton, but many do. Obvious examples are bone fractures and tooth caries; other maladies, including arthritis, yaws, and periodontal disease, leave tangible marks. (Of course, if mummified bodies are available for study, analysis can be much more complete, akin to a regular autopsy.) Nutritional problems may be detected in such forms as enamel hypoplasia, incomplete formation of tooth enamel during growth (Fig. 9.25). William Haviland has attributed differences in male stature at the Maya site of Tikal, Guatemala, to social class and concomitant wealth differences. The taller males, found in richer tomb burials, were probably also richer in life and thus able to secure

Human skeletal analysis: William Haviland at Tikal, Guatemala

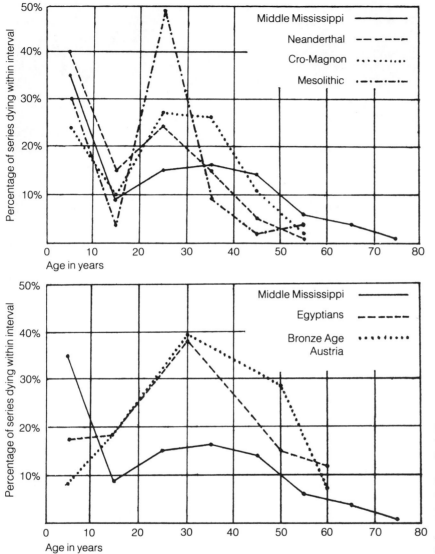

Figure 9.24 Comparative mortality profiles from selected ancient populations in both the Old and New World. (From Blakely 1971; courtesy of Robert L. Blakeley and the *American Journal of Physical Anthropology*.)

better food supplies than could their shorter counterparts buried in less well-made and well-furnished interments.

Some cultural practices also leave their mark on skeletal remains. One example is cranial deformation, practiced in pre-Columbian times in North, Central, and South America; according to this custom the head is tightly bound until it takes the desired form (Fig. 9.26); the Chinese practice of binding girls' feet to make them smaller is comparable.

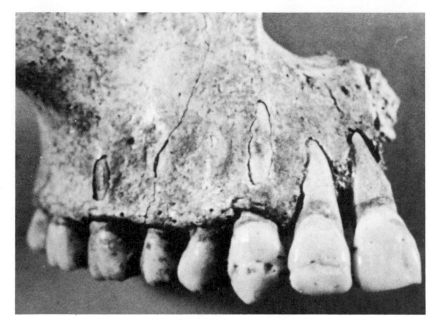

Figure 9.25 Right upper jaw of a young adult female with incomplete enamel formation that is especially visible on the second and third teeth from the right. This condition indicates malnutrition or other severe illness during growth, in this case, probably at about 3 to 4 years of age. (Courtesy of Dr. Frank P. Saul, Medical College of Ohio.)

Inorganic Remains

The most important inorganic ecofacts are the various soils uncovered by excavation. The soil in an archaeological deposit is more than just a matrix in which culturally relevant materials may be embedded. It is only in the last quarter century or so, however, that the importance of archaeological soils has begun to be recognized. Two principal aspects of soils should be examined: how the soil was deposited and of what it is composed. For both of these considerations a *pedologist* or *geomorphologist* is the expert to consult. The archaeologist should be able to make basic field distinctions, such as recognizing various soil types (sand, clay, loam, and so on), and should know enough about the potentials of sediment analysis to be able to frame questions for the geomorphologist to answer.

The deposition of soil layers can result from human activities or from natural geological processes. One of the more easily identifiable distinctions, for example, is between water-laid silts, which are fine-grained and evenly deposited by flooding, and deliberately packed construction fills. In other cases, depositional "cause" is not so easy to determine. For example, natural deposits such as black manganese dioxide can sometimes resemble hearth lines; chemical tests of the soil can often resolve these questions.

It is basic to stratigraphic evaluation to distinguish between natural and cultural origins for all deposits encountered. But in some cases

Soil analysis: Thera and vulcanism

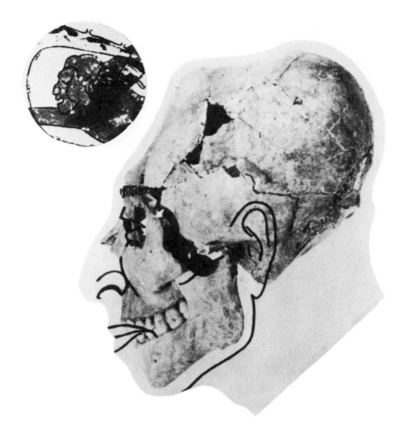

Figure 9.26 This photograph shows an artificially deformed skull from the Classic Maya site of Altar de Sacrificios, Guatemala, with a superimposed reconstruction of the individual's profile in life. The inset shows an individual with a similarly deformed skull as painted on a pottery vessel from the same site. (Courtesy of Dr. Frank P. Saul, Medical College of Ohio.)

the soils have a particularly dramatic story to tell. For example, on the island of Thera (now called Santorini) in the Aegean an earthquake destroyed the town of Acrotiri. In Chapter 3, we discussed the explosion of the volcano on that island, in about 1500 B.C., and the way this event completely disrupted local human occupation. However, excavations at Acrotiri have established that a considerable time elapsed between the earthquake and the volcanic explosion, since a thin humus layer (the result of natural, gradual soil formation processes) was found between the remains of the fallen abandoned buildings and the ejecta from the volcano. Indeed, two distinguishable eruptions apparently took place—a small one followed by the catastrophic destruction. The "warning" provided by the smaller eruption probably allowed most of the residents of Thera to leave: the remains excavated at Thera are relatively lacking in human remains—compared, for instance, to Pompeii, where the residents had no time to flee before the eruption of Vesuvius in A.D. 79 (see Figs. 3.11 and 7.18).

Sediment analysis should also include consideration of the basic structure and properties of the soil. For example, soil pH, a measure of alkalinity or acidity, is a critical factor in determining whether organic materials are likely to be preserved: the absence of visible organic remains may result from lack of preservation rather than lack of deposition. Soil structure is important in such practical ways as indicating how deep excavations may safely proceed before trench walls are likely to collapse; step-trenching, discussed in Chapter 7, is one solution to this problem for trenches that must penetrate to great depths.

Soil characteristics were observed by ancient inhabitants as well as modern investigators. Soil surveys in many areas of the world have indicated that, for example, occupation by agriculturalists correlates well with the distribution of well-drained and fertile areas. Fertility potentials must be tested, however, and not simply assumed. For example, volcanic ash is generally a fertile parent material for agricultural soils. But the ash fall from the eruption around A.D. 200 of Ilopango, traced by Sheets and his associates in what is now El Salvador, blanketed the area with an infertile layer that would have *decreased* local agricultural production capacities for as long as several centuries.

*Ecofacts and Sampling

Sampling strategies in ecofact analysis can be considered in two senses: the sample recovered and that actually studied. Because pollen is small and often windborne, it can be recovered from most locations in a site. A systematic sample of pollen cores can be designed to give a broad picture of horizontal (spatial) or vertical (temporal) distribution and variability in the pollen species. Collection of supplementary samples, as from grinding-stone surfaces or from abdominal areas of human burials, can help answer specific questions regarding use of plant materials. Soil, like pollen, can be sampled systematically from most parts of a site. Plant macrospecimens, animal and human remains, and other inorganic remains (stone, minerals, and so on) are usually less continuously distributed within a site, so their collection or observation tends to be dependent on what areas of the site are excavated. Sometimes the archaeologist tries to predict their occurrence, as, for example, by excavating a likely or known trash dump in an attempt to enlarge the sample of bone and plant remains. As we noted in Chapter 5, MacNeish's excavations in the Tehuacán Valley of Mexico were oriented to sites in which the perishable remains required for documentation of the development of food domestication were most likely to be preserved. In many situations, however, recovery patterns for ecofacts are the same as those for artifacts, and how representative—statistically or otherwise—the sample is depends on how representative the excavation units are relative to the site as a whole.

Once the ecofactual remains are found, a second sampling decision must be made concerning what portion will actually be studied. Again, pollen and soil samples differ from other kinds of data. Lack of funds may preclude study of all such samples taken. Decisions on "subsampling" in such cases depend on the research questions being asked. What is the sample supposed to represent? For instance, to reconstruct the sequence of climate and vegetal environment in a long-occupied site, a sequence of cores from a single deep, stratified excavation unit may be studied. These samples will be further "sampled" in the process of analysis: only a small fraction will actually be put under the analyst's microscope for a count of pollen grains and species represented.

Sampling of other organic ecofacts, on the other hand, usually involves inspection of all recovered items; in most cases only unidentifiable fragments are discarded in further work.

THE ANALYSIS OF FEATURES

Features, like artifacts, owe their form to human intervention, so it is not surprising that analysis of features is similar to that for artifacts. Formal, stylistic, and technological analyses are all appropriate approaches to the study of features. But artifacts can be moved, whereas features are fixed and thus are destroyed by removal. Two particular characteristics of features are important in analysis: location and arrangement. For example, when a multistory house collapses, features from the upper floors, such as hearths or mealing bins (Fig. 9.27), may still be inferred from their disarrayed component parts. But the original form, placement, and arrangement of the feature can only be estimated.

As in the case of an artifact, the archaeologist attempting to understand the significance of a particular feature makes use of provenience, association, and context. The difference is that intact features directly indicate the original makers' and users' intentional placement, while the locational aspects of artifacts are used to infer (by determination of context) whether a use-related placement has been preserved. Features are most valuable in understanding the distribution and organization of human activities, for they represent the facilities—the space and often some stationary equipment—with which these activities were carried out.

(a)   (b)

Figure 9.27 Features may sometimes be identified, even after disturbance: (a) an intact mealing bin, where stones were set for grinding grain, in a prehistoric pueblo from the American Southwest; (b) a feature presumed to be a collapsed mealing bin, the disturbance seemingly resulting from destruction of the building's roof or upper story. (Photo (b), by R. G. Vivian, Arizona State Museum, University of Arizona.)

Unfortunately, no single comprehensive system has been developed for categorizing features for study. The "industry" categories of artifacts or the species classifications of ecofacts have no analogs in feature analysis. Most studies isolate particular kinds of features, such as hearths, burials, or houses, but do not consider the entire range of forms or functions that features may take. With the growth of settlement pattern studies (see Chapter 11), a wider range of feature types is being considered, but there is still a tendency to focus on one or a small number of specific form-functional types.

In Chapter 3 we distinguished between simple features and composite ones. Here we shall divide features into two somewhat different categories that have possible behavioral implications: constructed features and cumulative features. *Constructed features* are those that were deliberately built to house or facilitate some activity or set of activities. They may provide an enclosed shelter, such as a house, or they may simply define or create an area appropriate to specified activities, as in the case of agricultural terraces or a boat-docking pier. *Cumulative features* include entities that do not seem to have a preplanned structure to them. They may grow by accretion, as middens or workshops do, or—in cases such as quarries—by subtraction.

Constructed Features

Constructed features were built to provide space for some activity or set of activities. Examples range from simple windbreaks to elaborate houses and temples, from burials and tombs to roadways and fortification walls, and from artificial reservoirs and stone-lined hearths to agricultural terraces and irrigation canals. The important criterion is that there is some construction that formally channels the ongoing use of space.

Classification and analysis of constructed features may examine attributes of form, style, technology, location, or some combination of these attributes. Technological analyses include consideration of the materials used in the construction and the ways these were put together. When complex architecture is involved, as in the construction of imposing features such as the Egyptian pyramids, analysis may require intricate study. The technological analysis of such features usually yields data not only about the physical act of construction, such as the use of particular materials and the sequence of their incorporation in the growing structure, but also about related social aspects of the construction process. At Quiriguá, Guatemala, for example, as the elite center grew in size and grandeur, so did the variety of stone resources its residents drew upon as construction materials. In the earliest constructions, soils and cobbles from the flood plain and the adjacent river were predominant. Subsequent use of successively more distant resources, including rhyolite, sandstone, schist, and marble from sources 2 to 7 kilometers away or more, suggests growing wealth and power in the hands of those who were commissioning the construction projects. And in some sites of the Moche Valley in Peru, the adobe brick construction was found to consist of discernibly discrete fill units; each multibrick unit bore distinctive labels which Moseley has inferred to represent maker's marks. Each work force responsible for supplying a certain number of bricks could thus verify that its proper contribution had indeed been made.

Even unimposing and partially perishable structures can yield complex data about construction methods and materials. For example, Christopher Donnan has analyzed and described in detail the construction and collapse of a small house at Chilca, Peru. And remains of one of the earliest known structures, revealed at the site of Terra Amata in Nice, France, indicated some of the constructional considerations of its builders of 300,000 years ago. For example, although the structure was a temporary, seasonal shelter, its builders showed concern for its stability and strength by bracing the stake walls with stones (Fig. 9.28). In addition, some protection from prevailing winds was provided by location of the entry and by provision of a windbreak for the hearth.

Changes in construction materials: Quiriguá, Guatemala

Evidence of task groups: Moche Valley, Peru

Construction techniques: Chilca, Peru, and Terra Amata, France

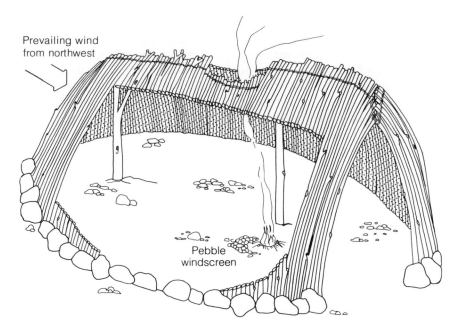

Figure 9.28 Reconstructed Paleolithic hut built of stakes braced by an outside ring of stones as found at Terra Amata, France, represents one of the earliest-known constructed features thus far discovered. (After de Lumley 1969.)

Solutions to construction problems: Swiss lake dwellings and Mohenjo-daro, Pakistan

Functional association of structures: James Hill at Broken K, Arizona, and Hallam Movius at the Abri Pataud, France

Different builders choose different technological solutions in response to similar constructional or engineering problems. This can be illustrated by comparing, for example, Neolithic lake dwellings in Switzerland with urban constructions of the late third and early second millennia B.C. at Mohenjo-daro in the Indus valley. Ignoring rather gross differences in construction scale, building materials, and precise setting, we can note that in both cases structures were set on saturated, unconsolidated, and ultimately unstable land. The builders of the lakeside dwellings enhanced the stability of their structures by driving support pilings into the ground beforehand (Fig. 9.29) to keep load-bearing elements from sinking uncontrollably into the ground. At Mohenjo-daro, on the other hand, the strategy—or perhaps the *post hoc* solution—seems rather to have been periodic levelling, repair, and renovation rather than prevention (Fig. 9.30).

Studies of form usually pertain to particular categories of features, such as rooms, structures, hearths, or burials. Formal attributes that have been studied include size, shape, arrangement of constituent parts, and so forth. For example, James Hill has argued that at least two gross categories of room size are distinguishable at Broken K, a thirteenth-century Pueblo site in east-central Arizona. Using associated artifacts for each room type, he asserts that larger rooms were for habitation and domestic activities, while smaller rooms were used

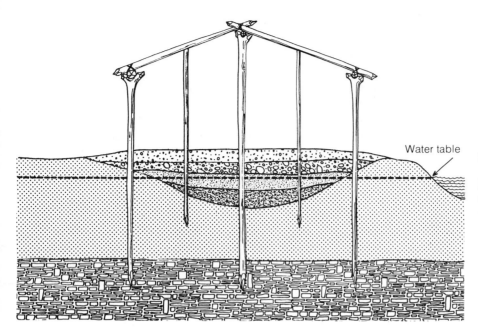

Figure 9.29 Traditionally it was thought that Neolithic Swiss lake settlements were built over water, supported by pilings; more recent evidence indicates that long pilings, shown here in a reconstructed dwelling, were used to stabilize buildings on saturated shoreline soils. (After Müller-Beck 1961.)

Figure 9.30 At Mohenjo-daro, the remedy for slumping construction caused by water-saturated soils was to level the old wall and build over it. (Courtesy of George F. Dales.)

as storage facilities (see Fig. 3.20). For the Abri Pataud, a rock shelter in southern France that has yielded cultural remains from about 32,000 to about 18,000 years ago, Hallam Movius has studied changes through time in the size, shape, and number of hearths within the shelter. He has used his analyses to suggest that marked differences existed from one period to another in the size and composition of resident social groups. Specifically, he would associate larger hearth areas with larger, more communally organized living units, while smaller, more numerous hearths were taken to imply a similarly smaller-scale social group as residential units.

Archaeoastronomy: Stonehenge

Internal arrangement, elaboration, and orientation of features may also be important attributes. The best example of this is the range of features now being studied as astronomical observatories. Gerald Hawkins has published a number of essays describing his analyses of the astronomical alignments found in the component parts of Stonehenge, interpreting the range of observations that could have been and probably were made from this Bronze Age station. Inspired at least in part by Hawkins' work, other scholars are examining other monuments to see if their arrangements suggest similar use. The kinds of features under investigation range from other "henge" sites in the British Isles, to the Big Horn Medicine Wheel in northern Wyoming, to Classic Maya sites with a particular plan known as the "E-Group."

Arrangement, elaboration, and location have also been fruitfully examined for other types of constructed features, such as burials. For example, both the location of a burial and elaboration of its contents may be taken as indicators of wealth, social status, and sometimes the occupation of the deceased. Earlier in this chapter, we mentioned the instance of Shanidar cave, where a Neanderthal was buried with flowers. Frequently, the analysis of an assemblage of contemporary burials will indicate marked differences in the variety and quality of goods included with the interments. The Royal Tombs of Ur and the tomb of Emperor Ch'in, the unifier of China, are obvious illustrations of formidable wealth and power distinctions; the latter tomb even contains a full, life-size army modelled in clay (Fig. 1.2).

Location of constructed features can be relevant to particular research questions. For example, location of burials in special mortuary structures or elite areas, such as the North Acropolis of Tikal, Guatemala, or the Great Pyramids of Egypt, may indicate special social status and privilege. Study of locations of these or other particular kinds of features may suggest factors involved in siting or placement decisions, such as preference for elevated ground or proximity to water sources in locations of houses. With the increased use of quantitative methods and with the adoption of analytic techniques from fields such as geography, archaeologists are beginning to study locational attributes more thoroughly and to specify more rigorously whether the locational choices observed are due, in fact, to human preferences and decisions or to chance. We shall discuss this topic further in Chapter 11.

Finally, constructed features may be analyzed by attributes of style or decoration. The idea of architectural style comes readily to mind in this regard. Archaeologists working with remains of Classical Greek and Roman civilizations have paid more attention to architectural style than have archaeologists working in most other areas. But stylistic analyses have been made elsewhere, such as the recent studies by George Andrews and by David Potter in the Maya area, or distinctions among styles in the ancient pueblos of the southwestern United States.

Cumulative Features

Cumulative features are those that are formed by accretion rather than by a preplanned or designed construction of an activity area or facility. Examples of such features include middens, quarries (which "grow" by subtraction of the exploited resource, sometimes accompanied by an accumulation of extracting tools), workshop areas, and so on.

Although stylistic analysis is clearly inappropriate here, cumulative features can be analyzed according to attributes of form, location, and sometimes technology. Formal attributes include, for example, size and content. Because we are dealing with accumulated entities, size can indicate either the duration or the intensity of use. For example, a trash deposit will be larger if it is used longer, but also if it is used more frequently. It is not always possible to distinguish the relative importance of these two factors in cumulative features; but when distinctions are possible, long-term stratified middens are particularly valuable to the archaeologist because they yield evidence concerning the temporal span of occupation at a site.

Analysis of the location of cumulative features may give information on the distribution of ancient activities. For example, distribution of quarry sites relative to living sites might indicate how far people were willing to travel to obtain stone raw materials, and the location of workshop areas reveals the distribution of manufacturing activities within or among settlements. Locational questions will be discussed in more detail in Chapter 11.

Cumulative features, because they are unplanned accretions of artifacts and other materials, have different technological attributes from constructed features. That is, cumulative features weren't "built," but they may still yield technological information. For example, quarries may preserve extraction scars as well as abandoned mining tools; these may indicate how the materials were removed. And, as noted earlier, study of the debris from stone-chipping stations may help in reconstructing the knapping technology. Similarly, artifacts from a midden—molds, bowl sherds containing unfired clay or pigments, and so on—may indicate the nearby presence of a pottery production area and aid in outlining the technology involved in its use.

*Features and Sampling

Two kinds of sampling are involved in the study of features: one governing data collection, the other for data analysis. In most cases all recovered features are analyzed, because their numbers are small enough that consideration of all examples is possible as well as desirable.

In planning a data recovery strategy, it is sometimes possible to anticipate roughly the number and variety of features that will be recorded. For example, in the southwestern United States, the preservation of pueblo sites (such as Broken K, mentioned earlier) is such that wall lines are usually visible on the surface. The archaeologist can then design sampling strategies that stratify along known dimensions of formal or locational variation, such as room size and shape or location in one or another part of the overall site. At Hatchery West, Lewis Binford and his colleagues wanted to maximize feature recovery, so they peeled away the plow-disturbed zone over the whole "site area" (see Chapter 6) and proceeded to record all features revealed.

In many situations, however, the number and range of features that will be recovered is impossible to predict. At deeply stratified Near Eastern *tell* sites, for example, surface remains may provide clues to the uppermost features but not to those in earlier, deeper levels. In such circumstances, the archaeologist may attempt to recover a variety of features by excavating in a varied set of locations within the site.

Once again, the paramount concern in sampling is the goal of the sample: What is it to represent? Once this has been decided, the archaeologist can design a sampling procedure accordingly.

SUMMARY

In this chapter we have reviewed in some detail three categories of archaeological data—artifacts, ecofacts, and features. For each category we have indicated some of the more common approaches to data analysis, and we have specified the characteristics of each kind of data that make it suitable to particular analyses.

Artifacts are portable items whose form is wholly or partially the result of human activities. Archaeologists first categorize artifacts into a number of separate industries according to the raw materials and manufacturing procedures used. Our discussion summarized manufacturing technologies for lithic, ceramic, metal, and organic tool-production industries. We also considered a range of analytic techniques, involving stylistic, formal and technological approaches, and discussed the ways the raw materials and production techniques of each industry suited it to analysis by the different approaches.

Ecofacts are unmodified natural items that are nonetheless relevant to the interpretation of past human behavior. We discussed various categories of ecofacts—plant, animal, human, and inorganic remains—and some of the ways these can be analyzed to yield culturally meaningful information.

Finally, we discussed features—nonportable artifacts that preserve in their form and location a record of the spatial distribution of past human activities. Some features are deliberately constructed to house certain activities, whereas others simply represent the accumulation of occupational debris. Because features owe their form to human behavior, they can be analyzed in somewhat the same ways as artifacts. But in addition, they provide information on the ways ancient societies organized the use of space.

In this chapter we have explored the kinds of information that can most appropriately be sought from each class of archaeological data. In the next two chapters we will change our perspective to consider how combining analyses of different kinds of data can reveal structure and meaning in the archaeological record.

See p. 573 for ''Suggestions for Further Reading.''

The bristlecone pine, found in the White Mountains of California, is the longest-living tree species known and is the key to increasing the accuracy of age determinations using the radiocarbon method. (Photo by Henry N. Michael, courtesy of the Museum Applied Science Center for Archaeology, University Museum, University of Pennsylvania.)

Temporal Frameworks and Chronology

It is possible to refine the sense of time until an old shoe in the bunch grass or a pile of nineteenth-century beer bottles in an abandoned mining town tolls in one's head like a hall clock. This is the price one pays for learning to read time from surfaces other than an illuminated dial.

(Loren C. Eiseley, **The Night Country,** *New York: Scribner's, 1971)*

In the previous chapter we surveyed the basic ways in which archaeological data are analyzed. We were principally concerned with identification and classification—with the orderly description of the materials recovered. In this chapter we will begin to describe the ways the identified and sorted data are organized to make them as useful as possible in the final step in archaeological research—the process of synthesis and interpretation. Just as analysis means breaking down the data into essential elements and their relations, so synthesis means putting these elements back together to form a meaningful whole.

Of course there is no definite line between analysis and synthesis: as we noted in discussing research design in Chapter 4, collection and analysis of archaeological materials often overlap in time, and the archaeologist is always operating within the framework of the questions formulated when the research was initiated. So even in examining the most minute attributes of the data—such as the decorative motif of a painted sherd—the archaeologist works with an eye to how this particular bit of evidence may bear on the larger questions the research seeks to answer. Chapter 9 indicated this orientation by describing not only the kinds of classificatory analysis archaeologists do, but also the kinds of questions each is most useful for answering.

In this chapter we turn explicitly from the aspect of analysis that breaks things down into their smallest elements to the aspect that examines relations among the elements. In earlier chapters we have noted some kinds of structure in archaeological remains: we have discussed the physical relationships among artifacts, ecofacts, and features, described in terms of provenience, association, and context and with reference to the vertical and horizontal dimensions of archaeological deposits. These are aspects of observed *physical structure,* and the record of such physical relationships is a crucial part of the evidence archaeologists use to reconstruct past behavior. But now we wish to begin to actually reconstruct ancient behavior; we do this by inferring the *systemic structure* in the archaeological record.

The systemic structure of archaeological data has three dimensions: time, space, and behavior. A goal in archaeology is always to infer and understand past behavior. But to do so one must first control the other two dimensions. For example, in order to trace the development of specialized production and the rise of craftsmen and artisans in a particular area, the archaeologist must be able not only to identify the material remains that represent craft production, but also to indicate when such materials first appeared in the area and where and how quickly their occurrence spread. Or, to reconstruct ancient political and economic systems, an archaeologist must first be able to specify which sites were occupied at the same time, before discussing the relations between their inhabitants.

In this chapter and the next we will discuss the reconstruction of systemic structure. First, in this chapter, we shall review the ways archaeologists control the temporal dimension—that is, ways to establish which remains are from the same period and which are from different periods. In succeeding chapters we shall proceed to examine inferred behavior systems at single points in time and the ways these systems change through time.

As we said in Chapter 2, archaeologists have been preoccupied, during most of the discipline's history, with establishing dates and sequence for their materials. Consequently, a sizable variety of methods have been developed for analyzing the age of archaeological materials. This traditional emphasis, combined with recent advances in such fields as chemistry and nuclear physics, has produced a wide —and still growing—assortment of methods for temporal analysis. In fact, probably the single most important implication of the wealth of new dating techniques is that they have freed archaeologists from their traditional concern with dating. The "radiocarbon revolution" of the 1950s has been followed by the development of a series of other dating techniques, all of which allow the archaeologist to focus research on behavior-oriented studies rather than chronological ones. The archaeologist must still understand the basis for the dating techniques to be used; the difference is that today a range of relatively reliable techniques can more easily relate one researcher's data temporally to that of other scholars.

Before we discuss specific techniques, however, we must consider a few basic definitions. First, age determination may be direct or indirect. *Direct* age determination involves analysis of the artifact, ecofact, or feature *itself* in order to arrive at a chronological evaluation. *Indirect* age determination involves analysis of material *associated with* the data under study, in order to derive a chronological evaluation. For example, an obsidian blade found in a cache might be dated directly by obsidian hydration analysis (see below); other materials in the cache and the cache feature itself can then be dated indirectly by assigning them the same age as the obsidian with which they were associated. Of course, the reliability of age determination by indirect means depends completely upon the security of the contextual association—in this case, the evidence that the obsidian and other materials were deposited at the same time.

The second distinction to be considered is that between *relative* and *absolute* age determinations. The first term refers to methods that evaluate the age of one piece of data relative to other data: for example, artifact A is older than artifact B. The second term refers to methods that place the age of the material on an absolute time scale, usually a calendrical system (artifact A was manufactured in 123 B.C.), or years before present (B.P.), and therefore assign an age in years. Absolute methods are seldom absolutely precise, however—it is often not possible to fix the age of a given artifact to an exact calendrical position. Instead, most absolute methods assign an age expressed as a time span or range, such as A.D. 150–275; they often include a statement of the degree of statistical certainty that the "true" age of the piece falls within that range.

An exception to this rule is provided by certain artifacts or features inscribed with calendrical notations, even if these refer to a calendrical system different from the one we use today. For instance, most coins minted during the Roman Empire carry at least one reference to a specific year in the reign of a particular emperor. And most stelae carved by the Maya of the Classic Period are inscribed with one or more dates in the Maya calendrical system. If the ancient calendars involved can be correlated with our own, the notations on these artifacts can be assigned to a precise position in time—in the case of the Maya system, even to the month and day. Such materials can thus be dated both directly and absolutely; they can then be used to provide indirect absolute dates for associated remains.

Absolute dates answer one of the two questions about the temporal dimension: How old is it? But relative dates—those that indicate whether A is older than B—usually have broader and more comprehensive significance, for they lead to definition of chronological sequence. By determining the age of a multitude of data sets *relative to each other,* and arranging these in chronological order, the archaeologist defines a sequential framework that can be used to organize all subsequent data. Finding out the individual *absolute* ages of the data sets is one—but only one—of many ways of determining their *relative* ages. Establishing chronological sequences has been one of the prime objectives of prehistoric archaeology, since those sequences provide a basic framework for reconstructing the order in which ancient

Absolute dating by notations on Roman coins and Maya stelae

events took place. In many areas of the world these basic sequences are well defined, and newly discovered data can simply be placed in the existing scheme. In other areas, however, the basic chronological sequences have yet to be defined or tested; in such areas the process of establishing the sequence of prehistoric data is still of prime concern.

In this chapter we will briefly discuss the most important methods used by archaeologists and other specialists to determine age and chronological sequence. In order to present these methods in a meaningful manner, we have categorized them according to their basis of age determination: archaeological methods, geological methods, floral and faunal methods, radiometric methods, magnetic methods, and calendrical methods.

AGE DETERMINATION BY ARCHAEOLOGICAL CLASSIFICATIONS

Patterns of human behavior change continually; and as the behavior changes, so do its material products, including the various kinds of data recovered by archaeologists. We have all observed how changes through time in design and style alter familiar products in our own society, such as clothing and automobiles. Furthermore, most of us can identify the trends of change in these and other artifacts, so that we can place any particular example in its proper position in the time sequence. For instance, when shown several automobiles of varying ages, many people in our society can arrange them at least roughly in order of their age (Fig. 10.1); similar sequential changes are noticeable in clothing, furniture, jewelry, and so on.

The artifacts and features studied by archaeologists are no different, and the archaeologist, by observing and studying various attributes, can usually determine trends of change through time. Changes in manufacturing methods, function, style, and decoration all result in shifts of corresponding attributes. By determining which attributes are most sensitive to changes through time—that is, which traits change most rapidly—the archaeologist can use these characteristics to form a classification that will best record changes through time. This classification may be either a typology or a modal study (see Chapter 8). In most cases, stylistic attributes—especially those of surface decoration—change most rapidly and most freely; they thus tend to be the best indicators of time change. This is because stylistic attributes are least affected by functional or technological requirements. For example, a water storage vessel may be of any color and bear any (or *no*) decorative design, but it must be deep enough to hold

1900

1910

1920

1930

1940

1950

1960

1970

Figure 10.1 Gradual changes in design are clearly evidenced in familiar aspects of our own culture, such as automobiles.

360

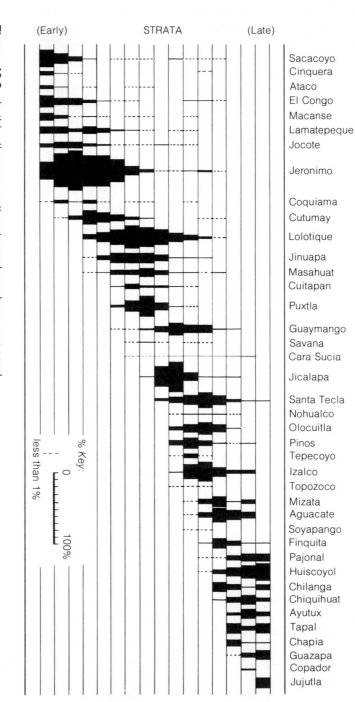

Figure 10.2 In this diagram, pottery types have been arranged chronologically by their stratigraphic order in a midden. Charting the gradual increases and decreases in the occurrence of each type through time creates the lens-like pattern called "battleship-shaped curves."

(Early)   STRATA   (Late)

POTTERY CLASSES

Sacacoyo
Cinquera
Ataco
El Congo
Macanse
Lamatepeque
Jocote
Jeronimo
Coquiama
Cutumay
Lolotique
Jinuapa
Masahuat
Cuitapan
Puxtla
Guaymango
Savana
Cara Sucia
Jicalapa
Santa Tecla
Nohualco
Olocuitla
Pinos
Tepecoyo
Izalco
Topozoco
Mizata
Aguacate
Soyapango
Finquita
Pajonal
Huiscoyol
Chilanga
Chiquihuat
Ayutux
Tapal
Chapia
Guazapa
Copador
Jujutla

% Key:
less than 1%
0
100%

water, and preferably it should have a restricted mouth to lessen spilling. Similarly, artifacts made from such plastic or malleable materials as clay or metal are usually good sources for deriving temporal sequences, because they are amenable to surface-treatment manipulation. It is not surprising, then, that in most areas of the world, pottery—the infamous potsherd—is the archaeologist's principal gauge of temporal change.

Stratigraphy

In discussing stratification as a geological concept in Chapter 7, we pointed out that *stratigraphy* refers to the archaeological interpretation of the significance of stratification. We have also seen how archaeological stratigraphy may result from both behavioral and natural transformation processes (as in a midden composed of alternating strata of materials in primary context and redeposited alluvium). As long as the context—and, therefore, the temporal order—of a stratified deposit is clear, the archaeologist can use stratigraphy to determine the proper sequence of artifact classes from the deposit.

Accordingly, an archaeologist who is fortunate enough to be dealing with artifacts excavated from a long-term, undisturbed stratified midden deposit will be able to determine the temporal sequence of the types or modes from the order of deposition. Thus once a given category of artifacts, such as pottery, has been classified, the classes can be placed in a time sequence by plotting their distribution according to their provenience within the stratified deposit (Fig. 10.2). In this situation, the temporal ordering of artifact classes is clearly based upon the accurate recording of provenience and determination of context.

Seriation

Seriation refers to a variety of techniques that seek to order artifacts "in a series" such that adjacent members in the series are more similar to each other than to members further away in the series. Seriation has two basic applications: stylistic seriation and frequency seriation.

Stylistic seriation refers to a technique through which artifacts and attributes are ordered according to similarity in style (Fig. 10.3). Here the variation observed may be ascribable to either temporal change or areal differences. It is therefore up to the archaeologist to intepret which dimension is represented in each situation. Generally, the more limited the source area of the artifacts—such as a small valley or a single site, as opposed to an area such as "southern France"—the more reliably the seriation relates to time changes. Such temporal seriation depends on observable trends—such as decreasing size—in the

ARBITRARY SEQUENCE
DATES

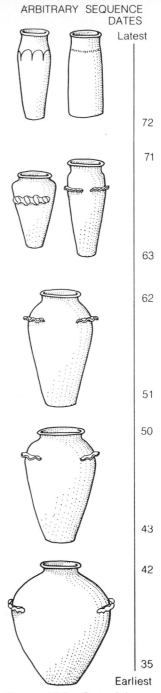

Latest

72

71

63

62

51

50

43

42

35

Earliest

Figure 10.3 One of the earliest applications of stylistic seriation was Petrie's chronological ordering of tombs at Diospolis Parva based on changes in associated pottery vessels. (After Petrie 1901.)

gradual change of attributes or artifacts; it also involves the assumption that such trends do not change direction capriciously. Our ability to place familiar artifacts from our own culture—such as cars or clothes—into approximate chronological order is based on our knowledge of this kind of gradual change, and is comparable to what the archaeologist attempts to accomplish by seriation.

Stylistic seriation: Sir Flinders Petrie

One of the first studies to use stylistic seriation successfully was the Diospolis Parva sequence done by Sir Flinders Petrie at the close of the nineteenth century. Petrie was faced with a series of predynastic Egyptian tombs that were not linked stratigraphically, but each had yielded sets of funerary pottery. To organize the pottery and its source tombs chronologically, he developed what he called a *sequence dating* technique. He ordered the pottery by its shape (Fig. 10.3) and assigned a series of sequence-date numbers to the seriated pots. The "dates," of course, did not relate to a calendar of years, but indicated instead the relative age of the materials within the series. Nonetheless, the sequence-dating technique allowed Petrie to organize the pottery chronologically and, by association, to order the tombs as well.

Petrie's study also provides evidence that the archaeologist cannot assume that the trend of change is always from simple to complex or that it implies "progress" as our own culture defines that term. In the Diospolis Parva sequence, the vessel handles began as functional attributes and ended as decorative lines "mimicking" the handles. Thus, for a sequence to be valid, the archaeologist must ensure that it is free from presumptions of "progress," increasing complexity, or other ethnocentric biases.

Frequency seriation is a method that is more strictly oriented to chronological ordering. It involves determining a sequence of sites or deposits by studying the relative frequencies of certain artifact types they contain. These seriation studies are based on the assumption that the frequency of each artifact type or mode follows a predictable career, from the time of its origin to an expanding popularity and finally to total disuse. Of course, the length of time and the degree of popularity (frequency) varies with each type or mode, but when presented diagramatically, most examples form one or more lenslike patterns known as *battleship-shaped curves* (Fig. 10.2). The validity of this pattern has been verified by plotting the frequencies of artifact types from long-term stratified deposits and by testing historically documented examples. The best-known historical test is that by James Deetz and Edwin N. Dethlefsen, involving dated tombstones from the eighteenth and early nineteenth centuries in New England. This study demonstrated that the popularity of various decorative motifs on the headstones did indeed show battleship-shaped distribution curves over time (Fig. 10.4).

Frequency seriation: Deetz and Dethlefsen

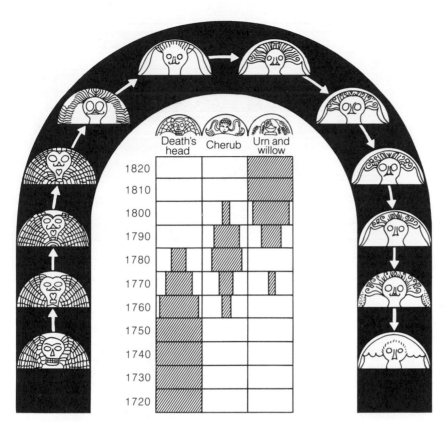

Figure 10.4 A study of dated New England tombstones shows that the changes in popularity of particular styles is aptly described by battleship-shaped curves, and it supports assumptions used in both stylistic seriation and frequency seriation. (After Deetz and Dethlefsen 1967.)

To seriate an artifact collection—let us say a set of surface sherd collections from a number of different sites in a valley—one can construct a battleship-shaped curve diagram using a technique described by James Ford. On a sheet of **graph paper**, one designates vertical lines or positions as representing the types in the collections, and horizontal rows or positions as representing individual collections from the various sites, each containing one or several of the range of types (Fig. 10.5). For each horizontal row, one marks a bar for each type represented; the horizontal extent of the bar indicates the percentage of that collection accounted for by that type. When all collections have been tallied for all types, the paper is cut into horizontal strips. The strips—each standing for a different collection, or, in this case, a different site—are then physically ordered and reordered by hand until the order is found that best approximates battleship patterns. Of course, one must also have some idea of which end of the resulting seriation is "up"—that is, which is the earlier end and which is the later. In most cases, comparisons with established sequences will provide this information.

Frequency seriation method: James Ford

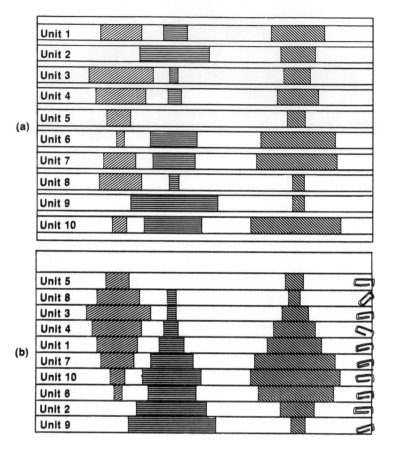

Figure 10.5 One can seriate an artifact collection by taking strips of paper which graphically record type frequencies for each provenience unit and by finding the arrangement that yields a set of battleship-shaped curves. (After Ford 1962.)

Frequency seriation method: Brainerd and Robinson

Another technique for frequency seriation was developed by George Brainerd and W. S. Robinson. Tables 10.1 through 10.5 present a very simple illustration of the principles involved. Using pottery assemblages from various excavation units as their study material, Brainerd and Robinson first calculated the percentages of each pottery type in each assemblage (Table 10.1). Then they determined a coefficient, or measure, of similarity for each pair of assemblages. These coefficients are calculated by taking the difference in percentage between assemblages for each pottery type, summing these differences, and subtracting the total from 200 (Table 10.2). The number 200 was chosen because it represents the maximum contrast between two assemblages—the case in which each is composed of completely different pottery types (Table 10.3).

Next, the coefficients are put into table form (Table 10.4), with the assemblages listed in the same order in the rows (top to bottom) as

Table 10.1

		Assemblages			
		A	B	C	D
	I	32	57	43	26
Pottery types	II	61	22	38	70
	III	7	21	19	4
		100%	100%	100%	100%

Table 10.2

CALCULATING COEFFICIENTS OF AGREEMENT/SIMILARITY

	To compare Assemblage A with Assemblage B:	Coefficients
Pottery types	I: $57 - 32 = 25$	A–B: 122
	II: $61 - 22 = 39$	A–C: 156
	III: $21 - 7 = 14$	A–D: 182
	78	B–C: 168
		B–D: 104
	$200 - 78 = 122$	C–D: 136

Table 10.3

MAXIMUM DIFFERENCE BETWEEN ASSEMBLAGES

		Assemblage		
		X	Y	Comparison
Pottery types	I	100	0	I: $100 - 0 = 100$
	II	0	100	II: $100 - 0 = 100$
		100%	100%	200
		Coefficient of similarity = 0		

they are in the columns (left to right). Since the coefficients along the diagonal represent comparisons between each assemblage and itself, and since such "comparisons" necessarily indicate perfect similarity, these diagonal values are the highest in the table—always 200. When the rows and columns of the table are arranged in proper order of similarity, the size of the coefficients will increase consistently as one moves toward the diagonal of the table; hence the researcher changes the order of rows and columns in the table until that arrangement is achieved (compare Tables 10.4 and 10.5). (Note that each table presents a mirror image on either side of the diagonal. For this reason, only half of the table need be printed.)

Table 10.4

ASSEMBLAGES

	A	B	C	D
A	200	122	156	182
B	122	200	168	104
C	156	168	200	136
D	182	104	136	200

Table 10.5

ASSEMBLAGES

	B	C	A	D
B	200	168	122	104
C	168	200	156	136
A	122	156	200	182
D	104	136	182	200

As the number of seriated units increases, however, the number of potential arrangements rises dramatically. As a result, hand manipulation of the Brainerd-Robinson tables rapidly becomes unmanageable. To alleviate this problem, computer programs have been developed to facilitate the search for the best arrangement. Indeed, several computer-based seriation techniques have been worked out; reference sources are listed in the bibliography at the end of the book. Remember, however, that all seriation techniques require some additional information to indicate which end is "early" and which is "late."

Sequence Comparison

If seriation is not feasible, the archaeologist has another recourse in order to construct a temporal sequence. If other well-documented artifact sequences exist in the geographical area being investigated, the artifact classes in question may be compared to those already defined from nearby sites, and placed into a temporal order corresponding to those already established. This comparative method, however, makes the assumption that some past cultural connections, such as trade, did exist and that the resemblances are therefore not accidental. Furthermore, even if connections can be documented, two similar types or modes may not be exactly contemporaneous. The work of Deetz and Dethlefsen, for example, showed that even among colonial communities as close together as Plymouth, Concord, and Cambridge,

Massachusetts, the temporal limits to the occurrence of tombstone motifs were rather variable (Fig. 10.4). Because of these difficulties, the comparative method is usually the weakest means for inferring a local chronological sequence; it should be used only when other means are impossible.

Sequence comparison is very useful, however, for building broad areal chronologies. By matching sequences already established for individual sites or regions, archaeologists produce the time-space grids important to cultural-historical interpretation, as discussed in Chapter 13. These time-space grids allow identification of trends and regularities in cultural change and stability across broad expanses of space and time. Recent summaries of comparative chronologies are available in volumes edited by Robert Ehrich (Old World) and R. E. Taylor and Clement Meighan (New World).

GEOLOGICAL AND GEOCHEMICAL AGE DETERMINATION

The age of archaeological materials can sometimes be assessed by their association with geological deposits or formations. Often these assessments are relative, as in cases based upon the rule of superposition, which states that materials in lower strata are older than those higher up. But in other instances, geologists have determined the age of geological formations using radiometric or other techniques; these allow the archaeologist to assign an approximate date to artifacts found with such deposits. Geological dating of archaeological materials is thus often indirect, requiring valid association in primary contexts.

Geochronology

The effects of long-term geological processes such as glacial advance and retreat or fluctuations in land and sea levels can sometimes be useful in dating archaeological remains. If the chronology of the geological events is known, then the associated archaeological materials can be fit into that scheme.

For instance, changes in sea level related to the cyclical advance and retreat of glaciers during the Pleistocene (Ice Age) had marked effects on the action of rivers on their beds. In general, as sea levels fall (or land levels rise), rivers increase their downcutting action; on the other hand, a rise in sea level would encourage deposition or terrace building. Sequences of erosion and deposition have been worked out for a number of river valleys, especially in Europe, and in some

Geochronology: Dating the Heidelberg jaw (Germany)

cases archaeological materials or fossil human remains can be dated by their association with geological features of known position within a sequence. The "Heidelberg jaw," for example, a complete *Homo erectus* mandible (lower jaw) found by German gravel-pit workers in 1907, has been dated by its location in the "Mauer sands," a known feature of the sequence of Rhine river terraces. The Mauer sands, in turn, were fixed in time—during the interglacial period of ca. 500,000 years ago—by both faunal and radiometric dating techniques.

The dating of archaeological remains by association with a particular geological deposit or formation, as in the Heidelberg case, is most commonly done with extremely old sites. For example, archaeologists and physical anthropologists interested in the remains of early hominids are working closely with geologists and others in reconstructing the environment and prehistory of the past several million years in the Rift Valley of East Africa. The latter group of scholars are basically the "producers" of the chronology for this work, while the archaeologists and physical anthropologists are the "consumers." As the subject of study moves closer to the present, archaeologists turn increasingly to other means of dating. In fact, Frederick Zeuner notes that for later periods, especially after 3000 B.C. or so, the producer/consumer roles may sometimes be reversed: geological features may be assigned dates for their association with "known" archaeological materials!

Even in attempting to date relatively recent remains, however, the archaeologist will find an understanding of geological processes very useful. For example, the successive formation of post-Pleistocene shorelines at Cape Krusenstern, Alaska, provided J. Louis Giddings with a means of chronologically ordering sites. As the beach expanded seaward through time, people continued to locate their camps near its high-water limit or crest. In this progression, the younger beaches—and, through association with them, the more recent sites—are those located closer to the current beach front. Today, more than 100 old beach lines are discernible at Cape Krusenstern, representing some 5000 years of accumulation (Fig. 10.6). Through this beach sequence—which some have called *horizontal stratigraphy*—Giddings arranged the sites in temporal order. By applying other dating techniques, he then converted the relative dating to an absolute scheme.

Geochronology: Sequence of beaches at Cape Krusenstern, Alaska

Varve Accumulation

In the case of the Cape Krusenstern beaches, accumulation of new land surfaces has proceeded at varying rates through time. It is sometimes possible, however, to find geological processes that follow a calculable rate. Such is the case with *varves,* the paired layers of outwash deposited in glacial lakes by retreating ice sheets. The first to

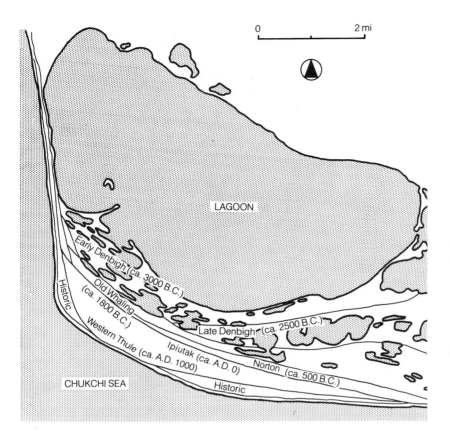

0   2 mi

LAGOON

Early Denbigh (Ca. 3000 B.C.)

Old Whaling (ca. 1800 B.C.)

Historic

Western Thule (ca. A.D. 1000)

Late Denbigh (ca. 2500 B.C.)

Ipiutak (ca. A.D. 0)

Norton (ca. 500 B.C.)

CHUKCHI SEA

Historic

Figure 10.6 This map of Cape Krusenstern, Alaska, emphasizes some of the series of ancient beach ridges which have been related to particular periods of occupation during the last 5000 years. (Redrawn from *Ancient Men of the Sea* by J. Louis Giddings. © estate of J. Louis Giddings, New York: Alfred A. Knopf, Inc., 1967.)

recognize that this phenomenon could be used for assessing age was a Swedish researcher, Baron Gerard de Geer, in the late 1870s. De Geer noted a regular alternation between coarser silts, deposited by glacial melt water in the summer, and finer clays, deposited as suspended particles settled during the winter months when the lakes were covered with ice. The recurring pattern of coarse and fine sediments could be read as a yearly record of glacial discharge (Fig. 10.7), and by moving back in time from a recent layer of known age, one could establish an absolutely dated sequence of varves. The thickness of the varve pairs varies from year to year, depending on the amount of glacial melting; this gives the sequence recognizable landmarks and allows sequences from different bodies of water to be linked. Through such links, the varve record in Scandinavia has been extended back some 12,000 years and has been used to chart sea-level changes in the Baltic region. By providing dates for some ancient shorelines, the varve sequence has also indirectly yielded dates for sites associated with those shorelines. For example, sites of the Ertebölle culture in

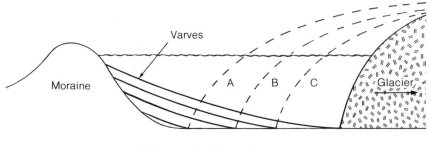

(a) Formation of annual varves

Figure 10.7 Varves are sediment layers deposited by melting glaciers. In (a), when the ice had retreated to position A, the sediments contained in the melted waters settled to form the lowermost varves. In successive years, more sediments were deposited, each varve extending horizontally to the point where that winter halted the glacier's thaw and representing in thickness the amount of glacial discharge. When varves from several glacial lakes have been recorded, they can be correlated (b), to create a master sequence for an area. (After Zeuner 1958.)

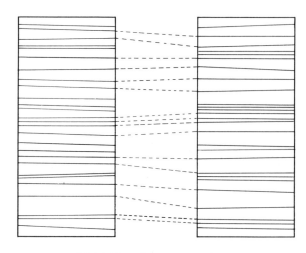

(b) Linking of two varve columns

Varve dating: Ertebölle sites in Finland

Finland are found only at or above a shoreline dating to about 5000 B.C. (see Fig. 10.8). After this time the waterline dropped, but Ertebölle sites are not found on this newly exposed land. Varve sequences have also been established for other parts of the world, including North America, South America, and East Africa; however, these are much shorter than the Scandinavian sequence.

Patination and Obsidian Hydration

It has long been observed that the surfaces of many geological materials undergo chemical alteration through time. These weathering reactions create a visibly distinct surface layer or *patina*. Among stones that are subject to such changes are flint and obsidian, common raw materials for prehistoric stone tools. Because the amount or degree of patination has been assumed to be a function of time, some archaeologists have used the observed patina as a rough guide to the relative age of stone artifacts. However, we now know that patina formation

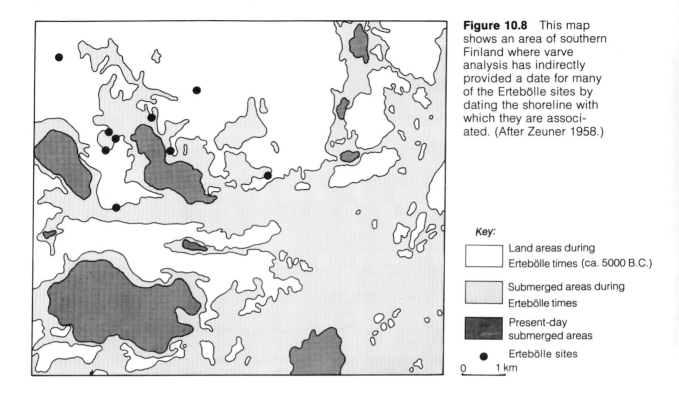

Figure 10.8 This map shows an area of southern Finland where varve analysis has indirectly provided a date for many of the Ertebölle sites by dating the shoreline with which they are associated. (After Zeuner 1958.)

Key:

Land areas during Ertebölle times (ca. 5000 B.C.)

Submerged areas during Ertebölle times

Present-day submerged areas

● Ertebölle sites

0   1 km

is a complex process that seems to follow no consistent rate of accretion. In fact, even as a clue to relative age, the amount of visible patina is not a reliable indicator.

Another kind of change also affects the surface of obsidian, however, and this one *can* be related to a time scale. In 1960, Irving Friedman and Robert L. Smith announced a new age-determination technique based on the cumulative *hydration,* or absorption of water, by obsidian. Over time, the water forms a hydration layer at the surface of the obsidian (see Fig. 10.9). This layer is measured in microns ($1\mu = 0.001$ mm) and is detectable microscopically. Since the hydration layer penetrates deeper into the surface through time, the thickness of this layer can be used to determine the amount of time that the surface has been exposed. In other words, the age of manufacture or use—either of which could fracture the obsidian, exposing a new surface for hydration—can be calculated if the rate of hydration (expressed as μ^2 per unit of time) is known. Once this rate is established, the thickness of the hydration layer from a given obsidian sample can be compared to a chronological conversion table and the sample's age determined.

Interior of
obsidian
specimen

Hydration
zone

Figure 10.9 In this
magnified view, the
3μ-wide hydration zone
appears as a wide band
at the edge of the
obsidian. (From Michels
1973; by permission of
the author and Seminar
Press.)

Unfortunately, since the method was originally applied, problems
have emerged that have somewhat diminished its early promise.
First, we now know that the hydration rate varies with the composition of the obsidian. Since each obsidian deposit was formed
under slightly different conditions, it has slightly different characteristics. Therefore, this method of age determination can only be
applied to a given sample if the source of the sample can be identified
and if its particular hydration rate is known. And the calculation of
hydration rates is difficult: they must be worked out by measuring the
hydration of a series of known-age samples, such as obsidian artifacts
whose age has been determined indirectly by association with radio-
carbon-dated materials. This means not only that we lack a single,
globally applicable hydration rate, but also that archaeologists cannot
assume, as they did initially, that all obsidian from a single archaeological site can be dated by using a single rate. Many sites contain
obsidian brought in from several different obsidian sources, and these
will absorb water at different rates.

A more complicated problem has emerged with the realization that
the hydration rate also changes through time, in response to variations in the temperature conditions to which the obsidian has been
subjected. Unless these rate fluctuations are known, accurate age determination by obsidian hydration is difficult at best. For some areas,
correction factors have been worked out on the basis of a long sequence of known-age samples. But since such sequences of known-
age samples are difficult to accumulate, most areas of the world do
not yet have a reliable means to assess hydration rates accurately.

Obsidian hydration still holds great promise as an accurate, simple,
and inexpensive means to determine the age of obsidian artifacts directly. However, its potential can be realized only when the variations due to composition and environmental conditions are fully
controlled.

FAUNAL AND FLORAL AGE DETERMINATION

Archaeological dating methods involving floral and faunal material fall
into two categories. One of these involves application of analytic
techniques designed to indicate when an *individual organism* died or
how long it has been in the ground. We will discuss several of these
techniques, such as dendrochronology and fluorine dating.

The other general category involves dating simply by identification
of the *species* present. Many plants and animals have (or had) a
rather restricted existence in time and space. Faunal remains of vari-

ous species, from insects to elephants, have been used as markers for particular time periods. For example, the sequence of elephant species in Europe has been used to divide the Pleistocene into three periods:

Elephas primigenius	Upper Pleistocene (ca. 200,000 to 20,000 B.C.)
Elephas antiquus	Middle Pleistocene (ca. 700,000 to 200,000 B.C.)
Elephas meridionalis	Lower Pleistocene (ca. 2,000,000 to 700,000 B.C.)

In the New World, too, such faunal associations are sometimes important. One notable case was the 1926 discovery near Folsom, New Mexico, of stone projectile points in association with the bones of an extinct bison. Human presence in the New World was then widely believed to be restricted to the last 3000 to 4000 years. But since the type of bison found in the Folsom site had died out by 8000 B.C., its association with these manmade artifacts was clear evidence that people had been in the New World for at least 10,000 years.

Presence of particular floral species is more often an indication of past local climatic conditions than, directly speaking, of dates. Particular plant species are often sensitive indicators of temperature and humidity conditions, as well as of whether an area was covered by forest or grassland. Stratified palynological (pollen) data have been used to reconstruct climate and general environmental sequences in a number of places, especially in Europe; in those areas, pollen recovered from an archaeological site can indicate the site's position in the climate sequence, thereby indirectly placing it in time.

The dating inferences in the preceding examples rely on the occurrence of particular faunal or floral species in an archaeological deposit. Let us now consider several dating techniques that involve direct technical analyses of the *individual* faunal or floral specimens encountered in an archaeological context.

Dendrochronology

The best-known method of directly determining absolute age for floral materials is *dendrochronology,* an approach based on counting the annual growth rings observable in the cross-sections of cut trees. This means of determining the age of a tree has been known for centuries; it was even used fairly commonly in the nineteenth century to date archaeological features. In 1848, for instance, Squier and Davis reasoned that the minimum age of mounds in the Mississippi valley could

Dating by faunal associations: Folsom, New Mexico

Early dating technique: Squier and Davis (Mississippi valley mounds)

be ascertained by learning the age of the oldest trees growing on the ruins. Assuming that trees would not be allowed to grow on mounds before abandonment of the site, one could say that, if the oldest tree growing on a site were 300 years old, the site itself could be no more recent than that age.

The modern method of dendrochronology involves a refinement of such tree-ring counts. The basic refinement is the cross-linkage of ring-growth patterns among trees to extend a sequence of growth cycles into the past, far beyond the lifetime of a single tree (Fig. 10.10). The compilation of a long-term sequence of tree-ring growth patterns is analogous to the development of the varve sequence; it was first established by an astronomer, A. E. Douglass, working in the southwestern United States in the first decades of the twentieth century. Douglass's original research was aimed at relating past climatic cycles—as reflected in cycles of wider and narrower tree-ring growth—to sunspot cycles. Although variations in tree-ring growth do provide valuable clues to past climatic cycles, the additional usefulness of this method in establishing an absolute chronological sequence was soon

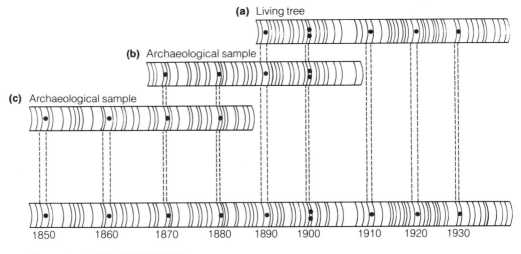

Reconstructed master sequence

Figure 10.10 As with varve sequences, a master dendrochronological sequence is built by linking successively older specimens, often beginning with living trees (a) that overlap with archaeological samples (b), (c). Provided the sequence is long enough, specimens of unknown age can be dated by comparison with the master sequence. (After Bannister 1969.)

realized. By counting back from a known starting point, the tree-ring sequence could be projected back for thousands of years; a given tree segment could be dated by matching to a part of the known sequence. In the case of the bristlecone pine in southeastern California, the record spans more than 8000 years. As we shall see, the bristlecone pine has been archaeologically important in the refinement of radiocarbon dating; it is not, however, generally found in archaeological sites. Other species, such as the Ponderosa pine, do not provide so long a total record as the bristlecone pine but are more often found in archaeological contexts, and so are more often useful for dendrochronological dating of these deposits.

This method has been of prime importance for establishing a chronological sequence in the southwestern United States. Although it would seem potentially useful anywhere in the world where trees were used by prehistoric peoples, dendrochronology has in fact been applied in only a few parts of the world: the southwestern U.S., Alaska, northern Mexico, Germany, Norway, Great Britain, and Switzerland. The method has found only limited use because it depends upon the presence of four conditions that cannot everywhere be met. First, the proper kind of tree must be present: the species must produce well-defined annual rings and be sensitive to minute variations in climatic cycles. Many species of trees produce roughly uniform rings regardless of small changes in climate. Second, the ring-growth variation must depend primarily upon one environmental factor, such as temperature or soil humidity. Third, the prehistoric population must have made extensive use of wood, especially in construction. Finally, cultural and environmental conditions must allow for good archaeological preservation of tree segments.

Dendrochronology determines the age of a tree by placing its last or outermost growth ring within a local sequence. This date represents the time when the tree was cut; if the outermost ring is missing from the tree sample, the cutting date cannot be certainly assessed. But even if a tree can be assigned a cutting date, that may or may not be related to the time when the tree was used. The validity of an archaeological date based on dendrochronology also depends on correct assessment of the archaeological context and association of the wood. Wood specimens that form parts of construction features—and that are therefore in primary context—are more reliable. Even so, Bryant Bannister has listed four types of errors in interpreting tree-ring dates, three of them involving wood used as a construction element.

1. The wood may be re-used and therefore *older* in date than the construction in which it was used.

2. Use of the construction feature—house or whatever—may have extended well beyond its construction date, so that the wood is *older* than this use date.
3. Replacement of old, weakened beams by newer, stronger ones may result in the wood being *younger* than the original construction.
4. Wooden artifacts or ecofacts found within a construction feature—such as furniture or charcoal in a house—may be *younger or older* than the building date for the feature.

To help offset these problems, the archaeologist should try to recover multiple samples for dendrochronological analysis. The dates from the various specimens can then be used to check each other: good agreement among several samples relating to the same feature creates a strong presumption that the date is correct.

Dendrochronology offers the archaeologist the rare opportunity of specifying a date that is accurate to the year or sometimes even to the season. If used correctly and with appropriate caution, it is indeed a precise and valuable dating tool.

Bone Age Determination

A variety of techniques are available for determining the age of bone specimens. These techniques can be used to date bone ecofacts, including human skeletal material, as well as bone artifacts. Some of the techniques yield relative dates, but absolute determinations can be made by aspartic acid racemization or by radiocarbon dating of bone collagen.

The relative age determinations enable the archaeologist to determine whether bones found in the same matrix were indeed deposited together. The fundamental premise involved is that a given bone will lose organic components, principally nitrogen, and gain inorganic components, such as fluorine and uranium, at the same rate as other bones buried at the same time in the same deposit. Nitrogen is a component in bone collagen that begins to be depleted when the organism dies; fluorine and uranium, on the other hand, are absorbed by the bone from groundwater through a process of chemical substitution. Within a single deposit, then, a bone with more nitrogen, less fluorine, and less uranium will be younger than a bone with less nitrogen, more fluorine, and more uranium. Since the rates of nitrogen depletion and fluorine accretion vary on the basis of such local environmental conditions as temperature and humidity, the rates are not the same for separate deposits. Thus the method cannot be used to establish absolute dates. Two bones from different sites but with the same relative amounts of nitrogen and fluorine *cannot* be assumed to be of the same age, since the depletion and accumulation rates will not have been the same. Nitrogen and fluorine measurements are, however, useful for distinguishing whether any of the bones in a single deposit are younger (intrusive) or older (redeposited) than the rest.

The classic demonstrations of the usefulness of these relative dating techniques concerned evaluations of some human skeletal remains of disputed antiquity. The first was the Galley Hill skeleton, first reported in 1888; it was said to have come from the Swanscombe gravels of the Thames River, from an undisturbed context that had also produced Lower Paleolithic tools and fossil bones of extinct mammals. The importance of the Galley Hill skeleton was that it seemed to indicate that anatomically modern humans already existed very early in the Pleistocene, thereby contradicting the evolutionary evidence of the rest of the human fossil record. Fluorine measurements made in 1948 by Kenneth Oakley finally settled the 60-year-old controversy by demonstrating that the Galley Hill bones contained far too little fluorine to be contemporary with the fossil animal bones (Table 10.6). The same tests indicated, however, that the Swanscombe skull, an anatomically "earlier" hominid from the same gravel deposit, did have fluorine and nitrogen contents appropriately equivalent to those of the extinct mammals, thus confirming its position in the evolutionary record.

The great Piltdown hoax was unmasked by the same methods. The Piltdown finds, unearthed between 1911 and 1915, revealed an apelike jawbone apparently paired with a modern-looking human cranium. Overall, the two were anatomically mismatched, but the geological evidence, combined with the uniformly discolored appearance of age in all the bones and some hominid characters in the otherwise apelike jaw, soon convinced all but a few disbelievers that "Piltdown Man" represented a significant new discovery that altered conceptions about the course of human evolution. The skeptics held out, however, and finally prevailed. In 1950, Oakley tested the bones for

Bone age-determination: Galley Hill and Swanscombe, England

Piltdown hoax exposed by bone age-determinations

Table 10.6

FLUORINE AND NITROGEN CONTENTS OF THE GALLEY HILL SKELETON
AND THE SWANSCOMBE SKULL

	Fluorine, %	Nitrogen, %
Neolithic skull, Coldrum, Kent	0.3	1.9
Galley Hill skeleton	0.5	1.6
Swanscombe skull	1.7	traces
Bones of fossil mammals from Swanscombe gravels	1.5	traces

SOURCE: after Oakley 1970, Table A, p. 38.

Table 10.7

FLUORINE AND NITROGEN CONTENTS OF PILTDOWN AND RELATED MATERIALS

	Fluorine, %	Nitrogen, %	Uranium parts per million
Fresh bone	0.03	4.0	0
Piltdown fossil elephant molar	2.7	—	610
Piltdown cranium	0.1	1.4	1
Piltdown jaw	0.03	3.9	0

SOURCE: after Oakley 1970, Table B, p. 41.

fluorine content and later for nitrogen; he found that the jaw was markedly younger than the cranium (see Table 10.7). Uranium tests reinforced these findings. Upon further examination, the "hominid" aspects of the jaw were shown to be due to deliberate alteration of a modern chimpanzee jaw. The whole forgery was publicly unravelled in 1953 by Oakley, J. S. Weiner, and Sir Wilfred E. LeGros Clark.

Aspartic Acid Racemization

Jeffrey L. Bada has recently adapted for archaeology a new technique for determining the absolute age of bone. This technique depends on cumulative changes in amino acids in the bone after the animal has died. Of the 20 or so kinds of amino acids in modern bone, all but one can exist in two mirror-image forms. While an organism is alive, the amino acid molecules are all of the "left-handed" or L-isomer form, but at death they begin to change to distinct "right-handed" forms, or D-isomers. The process of change is called *racemization,* and the principle behind the dating technique is that if one knows the racemization rate and can measure the extent of racemization in a particular sample, one should be able to calculate the date the organism died.

Since amino acids racemize at different rates, Bada chose to focus on one of them, *aspartic acid,* which has the most potential for measuring ages in the range between about 5000 and 100,000 years. As the demonstration case for the dating technique, Bada and his associates analyzed some human bones from southern California, which by their geological context were suspected of being among the oldest human remains in the New World. No one today seriously disputes the idea that the principal peopling of the New World took place via what is now the Bering Strait, during a part of the Pleistocene Ice Age when sea levels were lower and the area of the Bering Strait was a land bridge between Siberia and Alaska. What is not settled, however, is the question of *when* people arrived in the New World. The generally prevailing view has been that the migration began at some

Aspartic acid racemization: Southern California samples

time during the last 20,000 years. But the results of the racemization analyses indicated that several of the southern California samples were older than that date; indeed, one specimen—SDM 16704 or "Del Mar Man"—was assigned an age of 48,000 years!

Needless to say, the racemization dates met with some skepticism. Not only was the technique a new one, it was also providing controversial results. Of course, there are problems with aspartic acid racemization dating, as Bada and his associates recognize. Chief among their concerns has been the fact that the racemization rate depends on the temperature of the bone. Like obsidian hydration rates, racemization rates are area-specific and depend on local climate conditions. To correct for this, Bada and his coworkers had "calibrated" their aspartic acid analyses by relating them to a bone sample dated by other means. Using a female human skull from Laguna, California, which had been dated by radiocarbon analysis to $17,150 \pm 1470$ years, they had determined a local correction factor for the general aspartic acid racemization equation. When they tested the corrected equation against another bone sample from the same general area and climate, the radiocarbon method indicated that the bone was older than 23,600 years, and the aspartic acid analyses agreed, indicating an age of 26,000 years. Since these initial tests, good agreement has also been found between radiocarbon and racemization dates for bone samples from Arizona, Turkey, and parts of South and East Africa.

Aspartic acid racemization is still an experimental dating technique. Other problems do exist, such as determining whether the bone has lain in a deposit subject to leaching. But, for a number of reasons, its potential utility is very great. First, it is a direct dating technique and thus does not rely on establishing the association of the bone with other datable material. Also, although the analysis is destructive, only a few grams of bone need be analyzed, much less than is required for bone-collagen radiocarbon analyses.

RADIOMETRIC AGE DETERMINATION

A variety of age determination techniques exploit the principle of radioactive decay—transformation of unstable radioactive isotopes into stable elements. These methods are all usually termed *radiometric* techniques. Although they can sometimes be used to date archaeological materials directly, they more frequently provide indirect age determinations. The radiometric technique most commonly used by archaeologists is *radiocarbon dating;* the following discussion will emphasize this particular technique. Most other radiometric techniques are applicable to extremely long time spans (Table 10.8), usu-

Table 10.8

HALF-LIVES AND UTILITY RANGES OF RADIOACTIVE ISOTOPES

	Half-Life (in years)	Limits of Usefulness for Archaeological Dating
$^{14}C \rightarrow {}^{14}N$ (Radiocarbon) (Cambridge half-life)	$5,730\pm40$	normally 50,000 years and younger
$^{40}K \rightarrow {}^{40}Ar$ (Potassium–Argon)	$1,300,000,000\pm40,000,000$ $(.04 \times 10^9)$	100,000 years and older
$^{235}U \rightarrow {}^{207}Pb$ (U-235–Lead)	ca. 700,000,000	—
$^{238}U \rightarrow {}^{206}Pb$ (U-238–Lead)	ca. 4,500,000,000	—
$^{232}Th \rightarrow {}^{208}Pb$ (Thorium–Lead)	ca. 14,000,000,000	—
$^{87}Rb \rightarrow {}^{87}Sr$ (Rubidium–Strontium)	ca. 50,000,000,000	Too slow to be of archaeological value

ally beyond the time range of human existence. They are used mainly by geologists to determine the age of geological formations.

The physical properties of radioactive decay can only be used for dating purposes if three facts are known: 1) the original amount of the radioactive isotope present at the onset of decay; 2) the amount now present; and 3) the rate of radioactive decay. In most cases the first factor cannot be directly determined, but it can be computed as the sum of the radioactive material now present plus the amount of the daughter isotope—the stable residue of the decay process. The amount of the radioactive isotope now present is "counted" directly, using different methods according to the isotope being measured. The decay of any unstable isotope is a random process, so (except for directly counted radiocarbon) there is really no strictly determinable rate; it is possible, however, to calculate the statistical probability that a certain proportion of the isotope will disintegrate within a given time (Fig. 10.11). This disintegration rate is usually expressed as the *half-life* of the isotope—the period required for one half of the unstable atoms to disintegrate and form the stable daughter isotope. It is important to remember that the half-life of any radioactive isotope does not represent an absolute rate, but rather a statistical average with a range of error that can be specified.

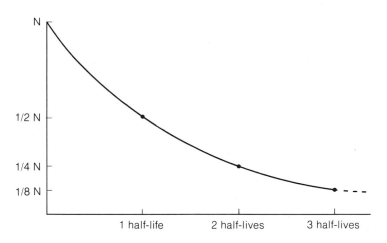

Figure 10.11 The decay rate of a radioactive isotope is expressed by its half-life, or the period after which half of the radioactive isotopes will have decayed into more stable forms. After two half-lives, only ¼ of the original amount of radioactive isotopes will remain, and by the end of the third half-life, only ⅛ (½ × ½ × ½) will remain radioactive.

Radiocarbon Age Determination

One of the effects of the bombardment of the earth's atmosphere by cosmic rays is the production of ^{14}C, the radioactive isotope of carbon:

$$^{14}N + n \longrightarrow {}^{14}C + {}^{1}H$$

This heavy, radioactive isotope of carbon (radiocarbon) is, however, unstable. It decays by releasing a beta particle to return to the stable ^{14}N form:

$$^{14}C \longrightarrow \beta^- + {}^{14}N$$

The extremely small quantities of ^{14}C distribute evenly through the atmosphere, and they combine with oxygen in the same way as normal carbon to form carbon dioxide. Through photosynthesis, carbon dioxide enters the chemistry of plants, which are in turn eaten by animals; thus all living things constantly take in both ordinary carbon— ^{12}C—and ^{14}C throughout their lifetimes. The proportion of ^{14}C to ^{12}C in an organism remains constant until its death. At that point, however, no further ^{14}C is taken in, and the amount of radioactive carbon present at that time undergoes its normal decrease through the process of radioactive decay. Thus measurement of the amount of ^{14}C

still present (and emitting radiation) in plant and animal remains enables us to determine the time elapsed since death. In other words, by calculating the difference between the amount originally present and that now present, and comparing that difference with the known rate of decay, we can compute the time passed in years. The radiocarbon decay rate is expressed in a half-life of about 5730 ± 40 years, and the amount of ^{14}C present in a fresh, contemporary organic specimen emits beta particles at a rate of about 15 particles per minute per gram of carbon (15 cpm/g). By comparison, a sample with an emission count of about 7.5 cpm/g would be about 5730 years old, since that is the amount of time necessary for one-half of the original radioactive material to disintegrate. After about 22,920 years, or four half-lives, the emission rate will be less than 1 cpm/g.

Any archaeological specimen of organic origin is potentially appropriate for direct radiocarbon dating. Charcoal from burned materials, such as that found in ancient hearths or fire pits, is most commonly used, but unburned organic material such as bone collagen, wood, seeds, shells, leather, and so forth—sometimes even the carbon in worked iron—can also be dated. Most of the latter materials require larger sample amounts because they contain a smaller proportion of carbon (Table 10.9).

Laboratories vary in the size of samples they can handle; the estimates listed are on the safe side for most laboratories. Any sample to be used for radiocarbon age determination should be kept free from contamination by modern carbon, which would cause an erroneous age measurement. To avoid contamination, excavators should refrain

Table 10.9

RECOMMENDED MINIMUM AMOUNTS OF SAMPLE
FOR RADIOCARBON DATING

Charcoal or wood	25 grams
Ivory	50 grams
Peat	50 to 200 grams
Organic/earth mixtures	50 to 300 grams
Shell	100 grams
Bone	Up to 300 grams

from excessive handling of the material to be dated, preferably touching it only with glass or metal tools, such as a trowel. Samples should be sealed immediately in clean protective containers. Of course, obvious impurities such as earth, roots, and twigs, should be removed; the technicians at the radiocarbon laboratory will remove other impurities before measuring the ^{14}C. The final step in preparing the sample for shipment to the laboratory is labeling with descriptive information, including when, where, and how the material was recovered as well as the excavator's estimate of probable age.

At the radiocarbon laboratory (Fig. 10.12), the sample is further cleaned and purified. It is finally placed in a shielded counting chamber, where the beta-particle emissions are measured, usually for a period of 24 hours. Results of the count are then converted to an age determination. Besides reporting the determinations to the original excavators, many laboratories also publish their "dates" in a specialized journal called *Radiocarbon*.

Radiocarbon age determination, developed in the late 1940s by Willard F. Libby, has revolutionized archaeological age determination. For both archaeology and geology, it provided the first means of relating dates and sequences on a worldwide basis, because unlike

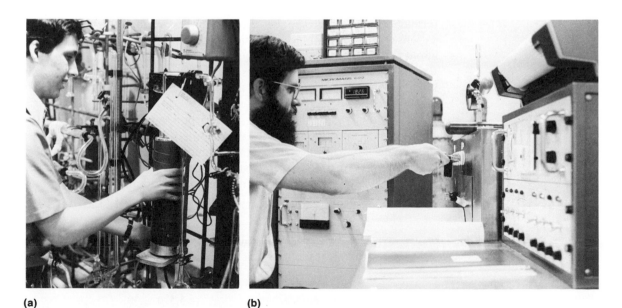

(a)   **(b)**

Figure 10.12 Determining age by radiocarbon analysis requires (a) facilities to purify and convert the sample into carbon dioxide (CO_2) and (b) a counter to measure its current radioactivity. (© Nicholas Hartmann, MASCA, University Museum, University of Pennsylvania.)

Table 10.10

PRESENT PROPORTIONS OF CARBON ISOTOPES ON EARTH

^{12}C	98.85%
^{13}C	1.15%
^{14}C	.000,000,000,107% $(1.07 \times 10^{-10}\%)$

varves, style dating, and other methods available at the time, it did not rely on local conditions. The great wave of enthusiasm led, however, to uncritical acceptance and overconfidence in the precision of radiocarbon "dates." Although radiocarbon age determination is still the most popular method and among the most useful of all dating techniques available to the archaeologist, it does have a number of limitations that must be clearly understood in order that the reliability of radiocarbon "dates" can be assessed.

The first limitation derives from the small amount of ^{14}C available for detection (see Table 10.10). For practical purposes, after seven half-life periods, or about 40,110 years, the beta particle emission rate is so low (about 0.1 cpm/g) that detection above normal background radioactivity has until recently been impossible. Thus most laboratories figure that 40,000 years is the upper limit to radiocarbon age determination. Under special circumstances (and at extraordinary expense) the time range of radiocarbon dating can be extended to about 70,000 years by a technique known as "isotopic enrichment." Currently, however, experiments with direct counting offer the possibility that without enrichment, dating can be carried back to about 100,000 years.

The second factor that limits radiocarbon age determination is the built-in uncertainty inherent in all radiometric techniques. The decay of a given atom of ^{14}C into ^{14}N is a random event, so both the beta particle emission rate of a measured carbon sample *and* the half-life by which its age is then calculated are no more than averages and estimates. As an illustration of this difficulty, Table 10.11 lists several

Table 10.11

SELECTED HALF-LIFE DETERMINATIONS FOR ^{14}C

Libby (1949)	$5{,}568 \pm 30$
Radiocarbon	$5{,}570 \pm 30$
Cambridge (1958)	$5{,}730 \pm 40$
New average (1961)	$5{,}735 \pm 45$

determinations for ^{14}C half-life. By international agreement, all dates published in *Radiocarbon* are calculated to the same half-life. Most authorities today, however, accept the Cambridge estimate of 5730 ± 40 years as more accurate; the Libby dates can easily be converted by multiplying them by 1.03. But any reported half-life and any calculated radiocarbon "age" expresses the built-in imprecision of the techniques by giving a time range rather than an exact "date." Thus a radiocarbon age of 3220 ± 50 years B.P. (Before Present—or, more accurately, before 1950) means *not* that the analyzed sample died 3220 years ago, but that there is a 67 percent probability—2 chances in 3— that the original organism died between 3170 and 3270 years before A.D. 1950. The probability that a reported range includes the right "date" can be improved to 97 percent by doubling the "±" range—in this case from 50 to 100 years on either side of the central date; but, for consistency, most reported dates use the 67 percent figure.

One consequence of these considerations is that a radiocarbon "date" is incomplete without a range figure and a statement of the particular half-life used in its calculation. Another implication is that an isolated age determination is weak evidence for chronological placement: any given date has 1 chance in 3 of being wrong. Clusters of mutually confirming dates give much stronger evidence that the indicated age is correct (Fig. 10.13).

A third limitation to the radiocarbon technique is the documented fluctuation of past levels of ^{14}C on earth. For instance, we know that the proportion of ^{12}C to ^{14}C has greatly increased since the nineteenth century, because of the release of large amounts of fossil carbon from the burning of coal, oil, and gas. And since the mid-twentieth century, the amount of ^{14}C has increased because of nuclear explosions. But neither of these effects should produce error in radiocarbon determinations if prior levels of ^{14}C remained constant. However, measurements of radiocarbon "dates" for wood samples whose ages were determined by dendrochronology have shown that fluctuations *did* occur in the past, probably because of differences in cosmic-ray bombardment rates. The result is that beyond about 1500 B.C., radiocarbon age determinations begin to furnish dates that are increasingly out of line (Fig. 10.14).

At 1500 B.C., radiocarbon age determinations are about 150 years too recent; by 4000 B.C. radiocarbon "dates" are about 700 years too young. The solution to this problem has emerged from the same source that exposed the error—dendrochronology. Extensive radiocarbon testing of known-age samples of wood, taken from the proper growth rings of trees, has enabled investigators to define a correction factor for radiocarbon dates (see Table 10.12). Use of a calibration

Depth (m)	Excavation levels	Ceramic complexes	Laboratory reference	Date B.P.	Date A.D./B.C.	Uncertainty ±	MASCA correction
0	1	Santana + Nuevo					
1	2						
	3	Cocos					
	5						
	6	Cocos + Lopez	Q-1158	2125	175 B.C.	65	390–70 B.C.
	8						
2	9	Lopez + Swasey					
	10						
	11						
			Q-1559	2680	730 B.C.	190	1100–750 B.C.
			Q-1476	2970	1020 B.C.	160	1500–1020 B.C.
			UCLA 1985a	3000	1050 B.C.	160	1540–1030 B.C.
3	19	Swasey					
	20						
	21–25		*UCLA 1985 b,c*	*1140*	*A.D. 810*	*100*	*A.D. 960–1170*
			UCLA 1985 d	*1700*	*A.D. 250*	*60*	*A.D. 180–360*
	27						
4	28		UCLA 1985e	4000	2050 B.C.	155	2910–2340 B.C.
	32						
4.7	33						
Bedrock							

Figure 10.13 This chart orders a series of radiocarbon age determinations from the site of Cuello, Belize, according to their stratigraphic provenience, and it provides indirect dates for associated ceramic complexes (periods). Note that most of the dated samples provided form an internally consistent series, but the two A.D. dates are obviously inconsistent. (Courtesy of Norman Hammond.)

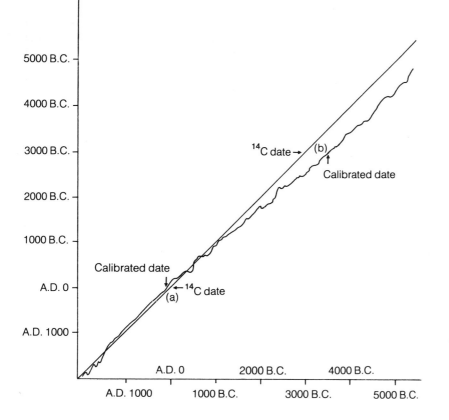

Figure 10.14 A representation of the discrepancy between the ideal ¹⁴C chronological scale (straight line) and a plotted series of samples, dated by radiocarbon analysis, whose age was independently determined by dendrochronology. The discrepancy is due to past fluctuations in the amount of ¹⁴C on earth. Note that in (a), a radiocarbon "date" of A.D. 0 must be corrected forward to A.D. 70, and in (b), a "date" of 3000 B.C. is corrected backward to 3640 B.C. (After Ralph, Michael, and Han 1973.)

Table 10.12

EXAMPLES OF ¹⁴C DATE CORRECTIONS

¹⁴C Date	Range or Midpoint for Corrected Date
A.D. 50	A.D. 130–110
A.D. 40	A.D. 130–110
A.D. 30	A.D. 110–90
A.D. 20	A.D. 100
A.D. 10	A.D. 90
A.D. 1/1 B.C.	A.D. 70
10 B.C.	A.D. 70
20 B.C.	A.D. 70
30 B.C.	A.D. 60
40 B.C.	A.D. 60
50 B.C.	A.D. 50

SOURCE: after Ralph, Michael, and Han 1973, Table 2.

formula allows a date given in radiocarbon years to be corrected to a more accurate time value. The correction tables are limited by our ability to secure known-age samples of wood; but use of the oldest living tree, the bristlecone pine found in southeastern California, has enabled scientists to extend the correction range back to 8200 years B.P.

The final limitation to radiocarbon dating lies with the archaeologist: any radiocarbon date is only as meaningful as the evaluation of the archaeological context from which it came. Charcoal from disturbed deposits—that is, from secondary contexts—will furnish dates, but these may have no bearing on the ages of associated materials. To use charcoal to date associated materials indirectly, the archaeologist must establish that all *were* deposited together.

These considerations are serious ones that must be kept in mind in assessing chronological frameworks based on radiocarbon age determinations. But they are meant only as cautions, not as discouragement: radiocarbon dating still provides archaeologists with one of their most valuable tools for establishing the age of archaeological materials. In fact, recent revisions and refinements in the radiocarbon technique have provided what Colin Renfrew has called the "second radiocarbon revolution." The first revolution was the development of a dating method that gave a uniform means to develop absolute chronologies applicable anywhere in the world; the second has been the realization of the archaeological implications, particularly in the Old World, of the dendrochronological calibrations that have revised many of the most ancient radiocarbon determinations, making them still older.

Before radiocarbon dating was available, Oscar Montelius, V. Gordon Childe, and others had used dating techniques based on stylistic and form comparisons to interrelate European and Near Eastern archaeological sequences. Whenever a question arose as to the source of an invention or innovation—such as copper metallurgy or the construction of megalithic (monumental stone) tombs—the usual assumption was that it had come from the "civilized" Near East to "barbaric" Europe. The first sets of radiocarbon dates seemed to support the chronological links based on these assumptions. Now, however, calibrated radiocarbon dates indicate that many of the interrelated elements, such as megalithic architecture, which had been thought to be the result of Near Eastern influence, actually occurred earlier in Europe! The traditional belief in a Near Eastern "monopoly" on innovation and cultural advance has been tossed aside, and archaeologists are now seriously re-examining interpretations of the long-distance communication in the Old World in the last few millennia B.C.

Radiocarbon calibration: Revision of Old World sequences

Potassium-Argon Age Determination

Although a variety of radiometric age-determination techniques have been developed (see Table 10.8), many of these are based on radioactive isotopes with half-lives that are too long to be of practical use to the archaeologist. However, one technique, potassium-argon (K-Ar) age determination, has been particularly helpful to archaeologists by yielding dates for the geological formations associated with fossil remains of early hominids.

The original potassium-argon technique is based on the radioactive decay of a rare isotope of potassium (^{40}K) to form argon (^{40}Ar) gas. The half-life of ^{40}K is 1.31 billion years, but the method can be used to date materials as recent as 100,000 years old. The technique is used principally to determine ages for geological formations that contain potassium. The basic principles of radiometric age determination, already described for the radiocarbon method, are used with a rock sample to measure the ratio of ^{40}K to ^{40}Ar. With this information, the original amount of ^{40}K present can be determined; this figure and the ^{40}K half-life enable the investigator to calculate the time interval that has passed since the rock was formed.

Obviously, this method can only be used with rocks that contained no argon gas when they were formed; otherwise the higher amount of ^{40}Ar would distort the calculations, producing a date far too old. For this reason, volcanic formations are best suited to the technique: the high temperatures characteristic of volcanism drive off accumulated argon in the process of forming the new rock. A complementary problem arises, however, in that some minerals naturally *lose* ^{40}Ar through time, again distorting the measurements and producing an age determination that would be too young. Examples include mica (which loses up to 20 percent of its ^{40}Ar) and feldspars (15–60 percent loss). As a result, only geological formations that retain ^{40}Ar can presently be used for reasonably accurate age determinations. Deposits of consolidated volcanic ash (tuff) are ideal candidates for this dating technique, because they contain no residual ^{40}Ar but do retain that produced by the decay of ^{40}K.

As noted above, the K-Ar technique has been particularly helpful in dating geological formations associated with the remains of fossil hominids and Lower Paleolithic tools. When Louis and Mary Leakey found the remains of *Zinjanthropus,* an early hominid now included in the genus *Australopithecus,* they were able to assign the bones an age of about 1.75 million years on the basis of potassium-argon dating of the volcanic tuff beds in which the remains were found. At the time (in the early 1960s), 1.75 million years was a much earlier date than most people were willing to accept for such a close evolutionary rela-

K-Ar dating: Olduvai Gorge, Tanzania

tive, so the Olduvai tuffs were subjected to another round of tests. These tests upheld the first set of dates, and thus an important chronological marker was set. More recently, potassium-argon dates have been determined for tuffs associated with early hominid finds in the Lake Rudolf/Omo Valley area on the border between Kenya and Ethiopia, extending the chronology of hominid existence back further than 2 million years.

A refinement of the potassium-argon technique has recently been developed, which uses the ratio of ^{40}Ar to ^{39}Ar to calculate the age of the rock sample. Although this procedure is more complicated and expensive than the original one, it allows several age determinations to be made from each sample, thus increasing the reliability of the "date."

Thermoluminescence

Many crystalline materials, such as ceramics or glass, "trap" electrons released by the natural radiation present in the material. These trapped electrons accumulate through time, to be released as light energy (*thermoluminescence* or TL) when the substance is heated above a critical temperature (400–500° C for ceramics). Thus, in theory at least, one can determine the time elapsed since a given material, such as pottery, was last heated above this critical temperature. One simply reheats the sample and measures the amount of energy that has accumulated (Fig. 10.15). The original heating of the pottery (during the firing process, for example) would have released all previously stored TL energy in the clay, thus "setting the clock at zero" and starting anew the process of trapping TL energy. The measured energy release can be converted into an age measurement by comparing it with a table of energy accumulation rates.

Note that the TL method does not necessarily measure the time elapsed since the pottery was fired—it just measures accumulated energy from the last time the pottery was heated above the critical temperature. If, for example, pottery was stored in a building that burned down, that blaze could reach the temperature required to reset the TL clock.

Unfortunately, use of this principle as an absolute dating method has encountered difficulties. In the first place, a specific rate of energy accumulation must be determined for each locale, and the capacity for given sample materials to retain that energy must also be established. Variables in the equation include both the site location— since background radiation is not constant from place to place—and the specific characteristics of the clay or other material being dated. These factors can be controlled by using a series of samples with dif-

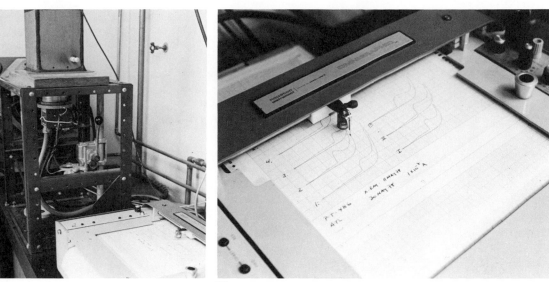

(a)   **(b)**

Figure 10.15 To determine age by thermoluminescence, (a) the sample is heated in a closed container and (b) the stored energy is released, measured, and recorded graphically. (© Nicholas Hartmann, MASCA, University Museum, University of Pennsylvania.)

ferent known ages, from a single site, to establish the accumulation rate and retention capabilities of the materials being analyzed. Once this is done, the method can assess the *relative* date of samples. In some cases, accurate *absolute* determinations have also been made.

The TL method is still experimental, but cross-checks with associated radiocarbon dates are being used to calibrate TL accumulation rates and help refine the method into a reliable means of acquiring absolute dates. As TL becomes a more trustworthy index of age, it may become a very important method of age determination: not only is it rapid and inexpensive, it also provides direct dates for one of the most common of all archaeological finds, pottery.

Fission Track Dating

This method determines ages by a process analogous to TL. The natural splitting (fission) of uranium-238 atoms present in obsidian and other glassy volcanic minerals leaves traces called *fission tracks*. These tracks can be detected by treating a prepared rock sample with hydrofluoric acid and then observing its surface under magnification (Fig. 10.16). Since fission tracks are erased if the mineral is heated above a critical temperature, the density of ^{238}U fission tracks is pro-

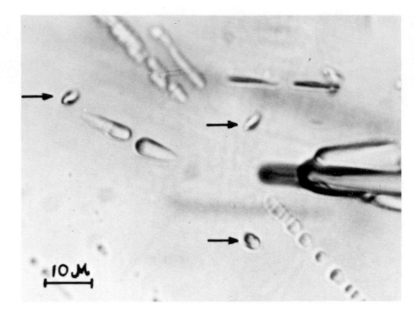

Figure 10.16   This photograph shows fission tracks in obsidian, indicated by arrows, after etching with hydrofluoric acid. The other marks are scratches and bubbles. (Reprinted from *Dating Techniques for the Archaeologist,* edited by H. N. Michael and E. K. Ralph, by permission of The MIT Press, Cambridge, Massachusetts; copyright © 1971 by the Massachusetts Institute of Technology.)

Fission track dating confirms Olduvai K-Ar dates

portional to the time elapsed since the sample was last heated above this temperature. To assign an actual date, however, the analyst must also know the ^{238}U content of the mineral; this is measured by bombarding the sample with a known dose of ^{238}U radiation. Once the ^{238}U content is known and the density of fission tracks determined, the analyst correlates the sample's fission track density with its estimated ^{238}U fission rate to assess its age. This age usually represents the time the rock was formed.

Like potassium-argon age determination, the fission track method is most suitable for samples of great age: a sample usually requires at least 100,000 years to accumulate tracks dense enough to be measurable. Fission track dating has, for instance, been applied to pumice samples from Bed I at Olduvai Gorge, Tanzania—the same geological formation discussed with regard to potassium-argon dating. Such dating by multiple methods is not redundant: independently determined but mutually confirming dates greatly increase the confidence the archaeologist can place in their reliability. At Olduvai, the fission track age determination for the pumice from Bed I was about 2 million years, well within the K-Ar range of 1.75 to 2.35 million years.

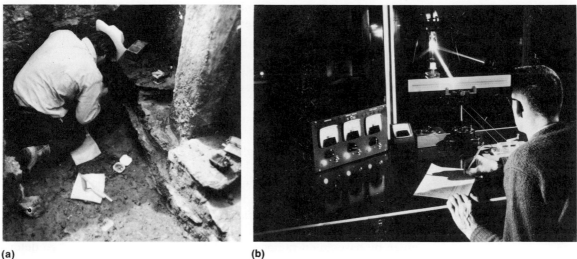

(a)   **(b)**

Figure 10.17 Age determinations based on archaeomagnetism require (a) careful collection and recording in the field in order to (b) analyze magnetic alignments later in the laboratory. (Photo (b), M. Leon Lopez and Helga Teiwes, © National Geographic Society.)

ARCHAEOMAGNETIC AGE DETERMINATION

This method relies upon the fact that the earth's magnetic field varies through time, and therefore the location of the magnetic north pole changes position. The location of magnetic north shifts in the horizontal plane, expressed as *declination* angle, as well as vertically, expressed by the *dip* angle; the course of these shifts over the past few hundred years has been determined from compass readings preserved in historical records. Certain mineral compounds, such as clay, contain iron particles that may align to magnetic north just as a compass does. This occurs most readily when clay is heated above its *curie* point—the critical temperature at which the particles lose their previous magnetic orientation. When the minerals cool again, the new magnetic alignment of the ferrous particles is "frozen" in the clay body. Thus if a sample of baked clay is not disturbed, it will preserve the angles of dip and declination from the time when it was heated. By using known-age samples of such fired clay, such as hearths dated by radiocarbon associations, archaeologists can trace the location of the magnetic pole into the past. Once enough cross-dated archaeomagnetic samples have been analyzed, the variations in angle of dip and declination can be matched to a time scale, thus allowing newly discovered fired clay samples to be dated directly, using the archaeomagnetic data alone (Fig. 10.17).

This method has proven most useful, but its reliability depends on two factors. First, the magnetic variation calibration must be worked out separately for different geographical areas, because declination and dip angles are a function of the magnetic sample's location in relation to the north magnetic pole. Such areal calibrations have been done in several regions, beginning with the southwestern United States, where the method was first developed. Other areas with archaeomagnetic calibrations now include Mesoamerica, Japan, Germany, France, and England.

Second, the successful application of the method relies on the availability of *undisturbed* fired clay samples: if the clay has been moved, its original declination and dip angles can no longer be measured and its archaeomagnetic value is lost. Thus features such as burned earth floors, hearths, and so on can be used, both to extend the archaeomagnetic sequence back in time (if their position in time can be given by associated radiocarbon dates) and as samples for age determination once a local calibration sequence exists. Pottery vessels, however, do not provide samples appropriate to archaeomagnetic dating unless they remain demonstrably in their original positions as fired.

Because of the importance of precise positional controls, archaeomagnetic samples must be collected by a specialist. First, the orientation of the burned surface is determined by accurate compass and level readings. Next, a series of samples is physically removed. Using the compass-and-level data, the undisturbed orientation of the samples is duplicated in the archaeomagnetic laboratory, where accurate measurements of the magnetic alignments are made.

CALENDRICAL AGE DETERMINATION

Any artifact or feature that bears a calendrical notation carries an obvious and direct date, and materials associated with such an artifact or feature can be dated indirectly. But the age determination provided in this way is not always an absolute date. Some systems lack a "zero point," consisting instead of recurring cycles that repeat endlessly through time. An illustration from our own calendar would be a notation such as "22 October '77," a date that recurs every 100 years. Such calendrical notations allow relative age determinations within the limits of the cycles used. Most ancient calendar systems, however, do provide absolute dates, for they have a fixed zero point similar to 0 A.D. in our calendar. These calendar systems yield absolute age determinations—provided, of course, that the notations can be deciphered and the calendar correlated to a known, standard system such as our own Gregorian calendar.

Because calendar notations are records, they are most often associated with cultures that used writing systems and that are therefore historically known. This is especially true in the Old World, where the calendrical records of civilizations such as ancient Egypt have greatly aided in constructing a basic chronology of past events. In the New World, cyclical calendrical systems based on a recurring cycle of 52 years were widespread within Mesoamerica at the time of the Spanish Conquest in the sixteenth century. These cyclical systems have allowed archaeologists to reconstruct short-term, relative calendrical chronologies for areas such as the Valley of Mexico and Oaxaca, in some places extending back from the Conquest for several hundred years. This is done by moving back in time from the date of the Conquest, which provides a link between European and Mesoamerican calendars. Successively older 52-year cycles can then be linked by keying on certain prominent individuals or events mentioned in accompanying "historical" texts recorded in pictographic writing.

In contrast, one Mesoamerican civilization—the Maya—possessed an absolute calendrical system based upon a fixed starting point, along with a true writing system using hieroglyphs. This calendrical system, known as the Maya "Long Count," was in use until about 600 years before the Spanish Conquest; it was used in the approximate period A.D. 0–900, and probably earlier as well. Unfortunately, the Long Count was not still in use when Europeans arrived, so direct correlation with the Gregorian calendar is impossible. Nevertheless, by working with the information available in the abbreviated (cyclical) system in use in the sixteenth century as well as with the ancient calendrical inscriptions, specialists in Maya calendrics deciphered the basic concepts of the Long Count by the beginning of the twentieth century, thus giving archaeologists a relative method of dating inscribed Maya monuments and associated materials.

Dates in the Maya Long Count are expressed in a *vigesimal* (base 20, in contrast to *decimal* or base 10) numerical notation system, with the notations recording the number of days elapsed from a fixed starting point. The number of days is written in five units:

Calendrical dating: The Maya correlation question

1 day = 1 *kin*

20 days = 1 *uinal*

360 days = 18 *uinals* = 1 *tun**

7,200 days = 20 *tuns* = 1 *katun*

144,000 days = 20 *katuns* = 1 *baktun*

*This is an alteration of the pure vigesimal system of multiples of 20, in order to approximate the length of the solar year of 365 days.

As an example of this system, the date inscribed on the earliest monument found at the site of Tikal is written as 8.12.14.8.15, or 8 baktuns, 12 katuns, 14 tuns, 8 uinals, and 15 kins. This notation refers to a period totalling 1,243,615 days (the sum of 8 × 144,000 plus 12 × 7200 plus 14 × 360 plus 8 × 20 plus 15 × 1) elapsed since the zero date.

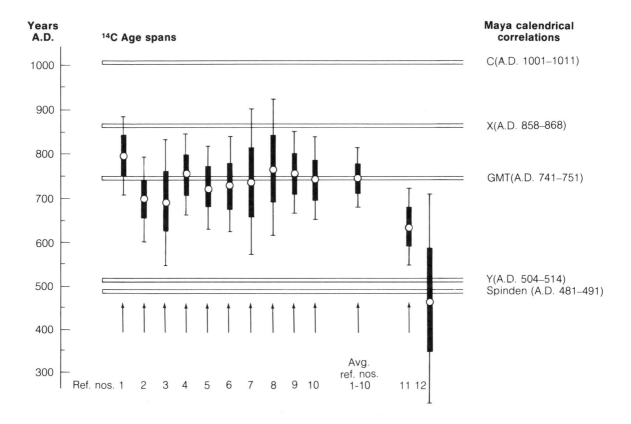

Figure 10.18 In this chart, the circles represent the midpoints of radiocarbon age ranges for 12 wood samples from Tikal, Guatemala, linked to Maya calendrical dates. The thick vertical lines indicate the single standard deviation for each "date" (67% probability that the actual date is within the range) and the fine lines, a double standard deviation (97% probability). The horizontal bars indicate where different correlations of Maya and Gregorian calendars predict the ¹⁴C dates to fall; these samples support strongly the GMT correlation. (After Satterthwaite and Ralph, reproduced by permission of The Society for American Archaeology, adapted from *American Antiquity* 26:176, 1960.)

Over the years, a number of attempts to correlate the Maya Long Count with the Gregorian calendar have been proposed. Until recently, two of these proposals appeared to be the best overall candidates, but scholarly opinion was divided as to which of these was, in fact, correct. The two correlations were named for their original proponents: the Goodman-Martinez-Thompson (or GMT) correlation and the Spinden correlation. Since the two systems differed by about 260 years, a significant disparity was involved in attempts to use them in converting the relative Maya chronology into an absolute one.

The archaeological excavations at Tikal, Guatemala—the largest known Maya site—presented an opportunity to test the competing correlations. Several of the stone temples at Tikal contain door lintels and roof beams made of *zapote,* a sturdy wood that has survived the ravages of time. Furthermore, the structures are associated with dates in the Maya Long Count system, some of them actually carved into the wooden lintels. It was proposed that a series of wood samples from the roof beams be subjected to radiocarbon age analysis. In selecting the samples, the archaeologists used the outermost rings of the wood in order to obtain dates as close as possible to the cutting date—and presumably to the construction date of the structure. The results of the radiocarbon analysis would thus provide evidence to decide between the Spinden and GMT correlations.

The radiocarbon age determinations for the Tikal wood samples cluster strongly in favor of the GMT correlation (see Fig. 10.18); as a result, the GMT correlation is the one generally used in Maya studies today. This determination has effectively converted the Maya calendrical system into a method of absolute dating. The zero point of the Long Count has been fixed at 3113 B.C., and the date given earlier for the earliest Tikal monument can be interpreted as A.D. 292 in the Gregorian system.

Ancient calendrical sytems are widely distributed among Old World civilizations, including Egypt, Mesopotamia, India, and China. It has even been claimed that Bronze Age European societies possessed sophisticated astronomical knowledge of the kind necessary to produce an accurate calendar based on the solar cycle. For example, Gerald Hawkins has proposed that Stonehenge functioned as an astronomical "computer," allowing its users to identify, record, and predict celestial events. Unfortunately, such a calendar was not associated with recorded dates and thus cannot be used by archaeologists to establish chronological controls.

SUMMARY

All the age determination methods discussed in this chapter, as well as new methods and those yet to be developed, benefit the archaeologist by aiding in the control of the temporal dimension of data. Yet all these methods retain inherent limitations that the archaeologist must take into account before applying them to structure data temporally with any degree of confidence. Some of these limitations are inherent in the archaeological data: demonstration of valid context of the sample being dated is always required, along with its association with the archaeological material that is being fixed in time. Other methods are so restricted in either time or space that their successful application is extremely limited. For instance, a calendrical correlation is good only for areas in which the given system was in use, and dendrochronology has been a prime dating tool only in the southwestern United States. And, as we have noted, most of the methods reviewed involve inherent inaccuracies that cannot be erased with our present capabilities. The prime example is that of the statistical probabilities inherent in radiometric methods and the time range or error factor in all age determinations by these techniques.

Because of the built-in inaccuracies of most (or all) methods of age determination, the archaeologist must be wary of temporal schemes that rely on a single method or on just a few individual dated samples. A sequence based on a dozen dated samples is obviously better than one based on three. A sequence based upon age determinations that are internally consistent is more likely to be valid than one with inconsistent results. The most obvious criterion here is that samples which can be arranged into a relative sequence on the basis of stratigraphic relationships should produce absolute age determinations that are consistent with the relative scheme.

The greatest degree of confidence in any chronological scheme arises from correspondence or agreement among results derived from many independent sources. If results from stratigraphic, seriational, radiocarbon, and thermoluminescent analyses all produce the same sequential arrangement, chances are good that the arrangement is accurate. As we have seen, archaeologists often check the results of one kind of age assessment against those from another source. Thus the potassium-argon date of Olduvai Bed I, which first appeared to be older than most researchers would accept, was subsequently supported by fission track analysis as well as by further potassium-argon tests.

Increasingly, comparisons among age determination methods are being used to improve the accuracy of the methods themselves. Archaeomagnetic dating has been developed by using known-age samples of baked clay surfaces; these surfaces are usually dated by radiocarbon determinations of associated charcoal samples. At least one major error inherent in the radiocarbon method has been corrected by using samples of trees, whose ages were determined by dendrochronology, to discover the correction factor for fluctuating ^{14}C levels in the past. And radiocarbon results have helped archaeologists to settle upon the best of competing calendrical correlations used in the Maya area of Mesoamerica.

The various methods of age determination now available can lead to accurate control of the time dimension for archaeological data—provided that the archaeologist is aware of each method's shortcomings, and that whenever possible two or more methods are used to cross-check the sequence to produce an internally consistent chronological order.

See p. 574 for "Suggestions for Further Reading."

House 11

House 12

N

House 13

These three cleared houses at the Neolithic site of Divostin, Yugoslavia, provide part of the framework for examining the spatial organization of activities in the prehistoric village. (Courtesy of Alan McPherron.)

Spatial Frameworks and Ancient Behavior

Because settlement patterns are, to a large extent, directly shaped by widely held cultural needs, they offer a strategic starting point for the functional interpretation of archaeological cultures.

(Gordon R. Willey,
Prehistoric Settlement
Patterns in the Virú Valley,
Peru, *1953*)

In Chapter 9 we examined the individual elements of archaeological data, and in Chapter 10 we discussed ways of arranging these in time. Now we are ready to examine the spatial distribution of data and to see how the spatial combinations of artifacts, ecofacts, and features may be used to reconstruct ancient behavior patterns. In a sense, spatial distributions and associations of archaeological data should be readily observable: plotting finds on plans and maps, for example, is an essential part of the data collection process. But until the artifacts, ecofacts, and features are described, individually analyzed, and then sorted in time, archaeologists do not know which parts of the observed spatial picture are remains of *related* activities. Past behavior cannot be reconstructed until the archaeologist knows which bits of evidence go together in time and which are from different periods: contemporaneous data clusters must be distinguished from sequential ones. The former give information about behavior and human interaction synchronically, at one point in time, while the latter allow the archaeologist to look diachronically at continuity and change in behavior.

Having established what the data are and how they are distributed in time, one can proceed to reconstruct the spatial aspect of the systemic structure preserved in the archaeological record. That is, by combining evidence from artifacts, ecofacts, and features, the archaeologist can infer how past societies functioned, both synchronically and diachronically.

In Chapter 1 we noted that Binford used three categories—technomic, sociotechnic, and ideotechnic—to classify the kinds of uses to which artifacts could be put. In this chapter we shall use a similar categorization to organize our discussion of the reconstruction of past culture and behavior. *Technology* is the means by which human societies interact most directly with the natural environment: technology consists of the set of techniques and the body of information that provide ways to convert raw materials into tools, to procure and process food, to construct or locate shelter, and so on. Because technology relates so closely to the natural environment, our discussion of technology will also examine the ways archaeologists reconstruct ancient environments. *Social systems* assign roles and define relationships among people: kinship organization, political structure, exchange networks and the like are all facets of the way people organize themselves and their social interactions. We shall consider settlement patterns and evidence of exchange systems as examples of frameworks for reconstructing ancient social systems. Finally, an *ideology* encompasses the belief and value systems held by a society. Religious beliefs come most readily to mind as examples of ideological systems, but art styles and other symbolic records also provide information about the ways human groups have codified their outlook on existence.

The divisions among these three categories of human activity should not be taken as strict or inflexible boundaries. For example, exchange systems serve to move tools and raw materials, thus acting as part of the technological system, as well as reflecting (and affecting) social relations. The categories simply represent broad distinctions among general kinds of cultural behavior: that relating people to the physical environment, that relating people to one another, and that relating people to ideas.

TECHNOLOGY AND ENVIRONMENT

One definition of culture commonly used by archaeologists today is that of Leslie White: culture is the extrasomatic (nonbiological) means by which people adapt to the physical and social environment. *Technology* is the part of culture most intimately linked with the physical environment, for it is the set of techniques and knowledge that allows people to convert natural resources into tools, food, clothing, shelter, and whatever other products and facilities they need and want. Specific techniques usually require for their execution a corollary set of specific tools. A simplistic but illustrative comparison can be made between a stone-tool technology, with its array of artifacts of stone, antler, and so on, and our contemporary technology involving computers, transistors, and an incredible diversity of equipment made of metals, plastics, and myriad other materials. Development and innovation in tools goes hand in hand with development and innovation in technical knowledge. Our landing on the moon in 1969 would not have been possible without sufficient prior elaboration in theories of aerodynamics since the time of the Wright brothers, along with increasing sophistication in knowledge of the physical properties of outer space and elaboration of materials capable of withstanding the special rigors of space travel. Technology, then, consists of the knowledge, techniques, and associated equipment that allow human societies to exploit their environment.

A related but cross-cutting term is *economy*, which refers to the provisioning of society. An economy is broader in scope than twentieth-century use of the term implies: prices, wages, international markets, capitalism, and so on are very specific characteristics of the present-day Western economy. In its broader sense, however, economy refers to the range of processes and mechanisms by which adequate food, clothing, and shelter are provided to all members of a society. Economic considerations include technological ones: How is food procured? How are houses built? But economy also includes social organizational aspects, such as controls exerted over the distribution of resources through the society. We will take up such social aspects of economy in the section on exchange systems later in this chapter.

Technology mediates human interaction with the environment in many ways. People build shelters and make clothing to protect them from heat, cold, rain, wind, and snow. They make baskets to help in plant collecting, fashion spears and arrows to kill food animals, and dig irrigation ditches to provide water for crops. The precise techniques and equipment used for a given task in a given time and place depend on past accumulation of technological knowledge. But they also depend on the nature of the environment and the raw materials it supplies. For example, one does not find wooden houses in a treeless area.

Chapter 2 mentioned that one of the current theoretical frameworks in anthropology is cultural ecology. First of all, human ecology includes interaction with a social environment—neighboring human groups—as well as the natural environment. Second, the relations between technology and environment are complex and interactive: for example, an innovation in technology may redefine the nature of the exploitable environment. The ecological questions asked by archaeologists center on which aspects of the range of environmental resources a prehistoric society exploited and which available resources it utilized. To answer these questions, archaeologists must reconstruct not only the nature of the techniques and equipment used by the past society, but also the nature of the environment that could be exploited. In terms of research, the most common meeting ground for these approaches is the issue of subsistence technology: What resources were available for food? What did the society choose to eat and how did it procure these resources? Here we shall discuss, first, some ways of reconstructing technology, then some means of reconstructing past environments, and finally the way information from both can be combined to outline prehistoric subsistence systems.

Technology

In Chapter 9, as part of the discussion of particular artifact industries, we presented specific information about the technologies involved in production and use of various kinds of artifacts. This information, focusing on the analysis of individual artifacts, enables the archaeologist to answer specific questions about how stone tools or pottery vessels were made. At this point we want to ask different questions. Most broadly, we want to know what technologies were available to a given group by which it could produce tools, facilities, and other manufactured products. In a specific research project, the question is usually phrased in more concrete terms; such as: Was metallurgy practiced by the occupants of this site (or region)? To answer such a question we must ask another: What is the evidence that indicates the presence of a given technology?

There are countless specific technologies that could be discussed; the survey in Chapter 9 touched only the most common products of tool and feature manufacture. Here we shall consider four categories of technology: food procurement, tool production, feature construction, and transportation.

Food procurement is obviously the most basic technology. Specific means of food procurement may be indicated by many kinds of archaeological data; we shall discuss only a few illustrative examples. To reconstruct food procurement and processing techniques, the archeologist begins with a knowledge of the procedures and equipment used in various systems. For example, hunting and gathering involve different kinds of knowledge and tools than does agriculture, and irrigated fields are technologically distinct from crop production that relies solely on rainfall. An archaeologist usually forms a working hypothesis about which subsistence technologies the prehistoric people being studied were likely to have used; this hypothesis is tested against the recovered evidence.

Projectile points, for instance, are usually taken as evidence of hunting; discovery of these points in association with slaughtered animals, as in the Olsen-Chubbuck, Lindenmeier or Folsom kill sites mentioned in previous chapters, clearly reveals the prehistoric subsistence technology. Other hunting technologies, however, leave little in the way of artifactual traces: hunting by means of trapping, for example, may involve digging a hole, putting upright sharpened stakes or other such lethal devices inside, and camouflaging the hole so the animal will fall through the surface cover to its death. Remains of such traps, or of snares or nets, are seldom preserved; the technology in such a case is usually reconstructed by analogy with modern hunting techniques used by inhabitants in the same area or a similar one.

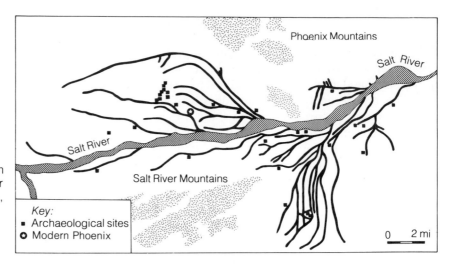

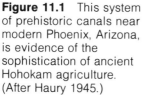

Figure 11.1 This system of prehistoric canals near modern Phoenix, Arizona, is evidence of the sophistication of ancient Hohokam agriculture. (After Haury 1945.)

Artifacts indicative of other food procurement or processing technologies include querns or grinding stones used to grind seeds and grain, and sickles and scythes used to harvest grains.

Ecofacts can provide direct evidence of ancient diets. As noted in Chapter 9, the only sure indication that a particular thing was consumed is its discovery in human coprolites or in the alimentary canal of preserved human remains. But bone and plant remains found in residential middens are also good—if not absolutely conclusive—clues to the kinds of foods eaten by the ancient occupants of a site. And the bones at the kill sites mentioned above provide convincing evidence of hunting and butchering practices.

Features sometimes yield information about ancient food procurement and food production systems. For example, some prehistoric animal pens have been tentatively identified in the archaeological record, and ancient granaries have been found at a variety of sites. Irrigation facilities, from simple ditches to elaborate canals (Fig. 11.1) and artificially constructed fields provide evidence of crop production and water management technologies.

We shall discuss food procurement and production technology later, in the context of a more detailed discussion of reconstruction of ancient subsistence systems.

Tool production technologies include the manufacture of all kinds of artifacts, from weapons to clothing, storage containers, and transport vehicles. Again, the archaeologist starts off with a working model of the way the ancient society may have functioned, and what tools and other artifacts it produced. Evidence for or against this preliminary view may come from several sources. The most direct evidence is the manufactured products themselves. Artifacts made by some techniques, especially those produced by subtractive industries such as stone-knapping, are more apt than others to preserve marks indicative of how they were made. Sometimes the archaeologist is fortunate enough to encounter art work or three-dimensional models that indicate graphically how certain products were made (Fig. 11.2). One extremely valuable form of technological evidence is provided by remains of workshops. These are particular, activity-specific clusters of artifacts, sometimes including specially constructed features such as kilns, that preserve a variety of details about manufacturing processes. Workshop features are of as many kinds as there are different manufacturing technologies; how formalized the area is depends on how specifically isolated the activity was. For example, flint-knapping might have been carried out at various locations over time, so that a number of casual chipping stations might be found in a given area of occupation. Activities that require specialized facilities, however, such as iron metallurgy with its need for intense and controlled heat, are more likely to have easily identifiable areas set aside as workshops. In a workshop, one would expect to find some or all of a variety of manufacturing remains, including raw materials, partially finished artifacts, mistakes (such as pottery vessels that cracked during firing), debris (such as stone debitage), and of course any special tools or facilities needed for production. For example, a pottery workshop might include lumps of unfired clay, pigment in bowls or on the grinding surfaces of small mortars, broken sherds or other tempering materials, molds and stamps used in forming or decorating the vessels, small pebbles for polishing vessel surfaces, and perhaps the remains of a kiln. Each kind of workshop may have its own specialized set of associated materials; the archaeologist specifies the particular elements expected for each kind, on the basis of a background knowledge of manufacturing technologies.

Evidence of the technology involved in the construction of features, from storage pits to houses to the pyramids of Egypt, is most readily gleaned from the constructed features themselves. In Chapter 9, we discussed, for example, the remains of a 300,000-year-old shelter unearthed at Terra Amata, at Nice, France. The archaeologists used the stone alignments, depressions in the ground, and other formal characteristics to infer the priorities and techniques involved in its construction. Similarly, other constructed features preserve information about the kinds of materials used and the engineering skills possessed by past societies.

Figure 11.2 This partially reconstructed ceramic vessel from Peru incorporates information on architectural form and construction through a three-dimensional model of a small thatched building, while the body of the vessel itself appears to represent a supporting platform. (Courtesy of the University Museum, University of Pennsylvania.)

The technology of transportation refers to the knowledge and techniques used for moving goods and persons. This is a direct interaction with the physical environment, because it affects the relative ease with which people can get about in the environment. For example, people can move more things farther and more easily if they have wheeled vehicles and beasts of burden than if they must walk and carry everything themselves. Transport in this sense obviously affects the range of territory (and resources) that a given group of people can conveniently exploit. Similarly, large bodies of water can be obstacles to transportation, but when boats or even rafts are available, water transport routes may be preferable to land routes.

Direct evidence of the transportation technologies available to ancient people may sometimes be found in artifacts, ranging from horse-trappings to actual wheeled vehicles to models or toys of boats and carts. Occasionally, pictorial representations are available, such as scenes of dignitaries being carried on litters. Frequently, however, evidence of transport is indirect. For example, Norman Hammond has used the distribution of obsidian artifacts from the Ixtepeque source in the highlands of Guatemala to infer that the goods, raw materials, or both were moved by canoe along the coast of the Yucatan peninsula (Fig. 11.3). Canoe travel was known to be important in this area at the time of Spanish contact in the sixteenth century, but evidence for its earlier occurrence is confined to such indirect inference.

Indirect evidence of transport: Norman Hammond and Maya obsidian trade

Environment

If technology is the means by which society interacts with the natural environment, how can the archaeologist discover what the ancient natural environment itself was like? Archaeologists seek two kinds of data in order to reconstruct ancient physical environments. The first is observations of the modern landscape, including topography and the range of biotic and mineral resources. The second is collection of ecofactual data, either from archaeological deposits or from other deposits within the zone under study. Such data give the archaeologist evidence as to whether—and how—the area may have been different, in terms of available resources, in ancient times from the way it is today. Combining these two approaches, the archaeologist, usually in consultation with other specialists, attempts to reconstruct the nature of the ancient environment in which the past society lived.

Observation of the modern environment involves recording the range of resources the archaeologist considers of potential use to local occupants. These resources include water supplies, game animals, edible plants, fertile soils for agriculture, suitable stone for tool produc-

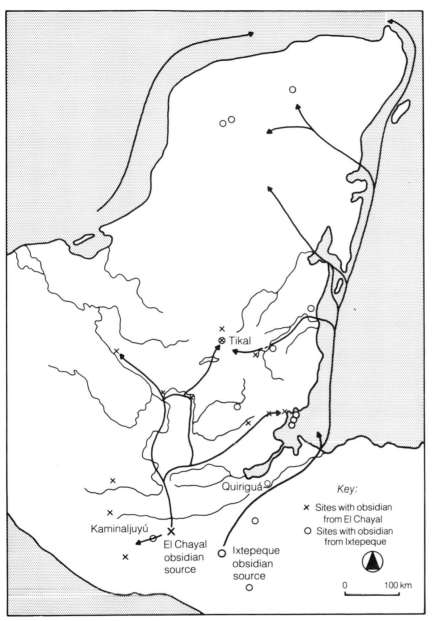

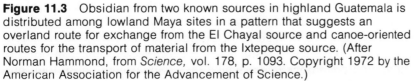

Figure 11.3 Obsidian from two known sources in highland Guatemala is distributed among lowland Maya sites in a pattern that suggests an overland route for exchange from the El Chayal source and canoe-oriented routes for the transport of material from the Ixtepeque source. (After Norman Hammond, from *Science,* vol. 178, p. 1093. Copyright 1972 by the American Association for the Advancement of Science.)

tion, wood or other materials for house construction, and so on. In describing observed resources, the archaeologist must note two kinds of distributional limits: seasonality and distance from occupation areas. That is, some of the resources, such as migratory game animals or intermittent streams, might be available only part of the year, and this fact limits their exploitation. In addition, resources are seldom spread evenly over the landscape: good chipping stone occurs in discrete, if sometimes large or abundant, deposits; edible plants may be restricted to certain elevations or distances from water sources. Various combinations of resources serve to define *microenvironments* which provide varying opportunities for exploitation. Although observations and descriptions of local resources are usually best made by the archaeologist or a specialist, quite detailed information can sometimes be obtained from existing published works, such as guides to local soils, flora, and fauna. Supplementary information can often be obtained from local inhabitants, who may know from personal experience when and where food and other resources are available.

The area to be observed may be defined in several ways. If the archaeological universe is a single site, the observations on the natural environment are usually made for a larger zone surrounding the site, on the assumption that people would sooner exploit resources closer to home. In studies taking a regional approach, such as a project focusing on occupation and exploitation of a valley, the resource area to be studied will usually coincide with the archaeological universe. In neither case can the archaeologist automatically assume that the observed area represents the zone exploited by prehistoric peoples, but if local supplies are preferred over those farther away, the observed zone should include at least part of the anciently exploited area. And paleoecological finds may substantiate the nature of local exploitation.

Defining micro-environments: MacNeish at Tehuacán, Mexico

Examples of various kinds of modern observational approaches are easy to find. For instance, in the Tehuacán Archaeological-Botanical Project, already described in Chapter 5, the resource area recorded was the same as that in which archaeological remains were recorded. The overall goal of the project was to trace the development of agriculture in the New World; the Tehuacán Valley, in the Mexican state of Puebla, was chosen as the research location partly because it contained a number of dry caves that seemed to promise the climatic conditions under which maize (corn) and other domesticated plants would be preserved. At the same time, however, Richard MacNeish and his colleagues needed to determine the range of food resources available to the ancient residents of the Tehuacán Valley, in order to outline the conditions under which they increasingly chose food production over food collection as their subsistence base. To get this information, the investigators surveyed the Tehuacán Valley and divided it into four microenvironmental types, each with its own set of seasonally or perennially available resources. Combining this information with analysis of ecofactual materials recovered from the various archaeological sites, MacNeish and his coworkers were able to reconstruct the subsistence-related migrations of ancient human populations within the valley, postulating their movements in search of shifting food resources as the seasons passed. In a later project, MacNeish and his colleagues were able to apply the same approach to study the ancient subsistence system in the Ayacucho Basin of Peru (Fig. 11.4).

A related approach was taken by Kent V. Flannery and Michael D. Coe in their study of the Ocós region of south coastal Guatemala. Instead of a nicely topographically circumscribed universe such as a valley, however, they were dealing with a broad expanse of coastal flood plain. To sample the range of resources in the vicinity of the site

Defining microenvironments: Coe and Flannery at Salinas la Blanca, Guatemala

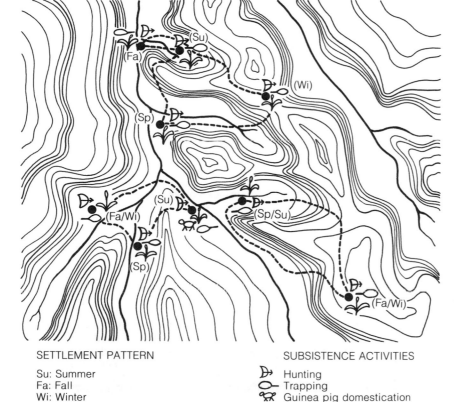

SETTLEMENT PATTERN

Su: Summer
Fa: Fall
Wi: Winter
Sp: Spring

SUBSISTENCE ACTIVITIES

Hunting
Trapping
Guinea pig domestication
Plant collecting

Figure 11.4 Synthesis of archaeological data from the Ayacucho Valley of Peru has led to postulation of seasonal population movements among sites to exploit different subsistence resources. (After MacNeish, Patterson, and Browman 1975.)

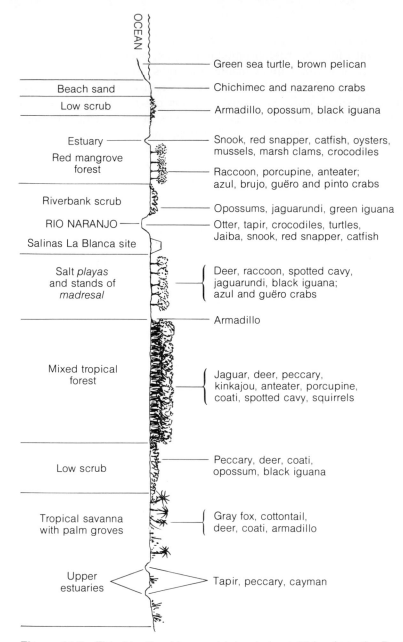

Figure 11.5 This idealized transect inland about 15 km from the Pacific Ocean shows the diversity of resources available to the prehistoric residents of Salinas la Blanca, Guatemala. (Redrawn and modified by permission of The Smithsonian Institution Press from *The Smithsonian Contributions to Anthropology,* vol. 3; *Early Cultures and Human Ecology in South Coastal Guatemala,* by Michael D. Coe and Kent V. Flannery, fig. 3, Washington, D.C. Government Printing Office, 1967.)

of Salinas la Blanca, they examined a transect of land extending inland from the Pacific Ocean, through Salinas la Blanca, over a linear distance of about 15 kilometers. This transect provided a cross-section through eight microenvironmental zones, each roughly parallel to the Pacific coast and each contributing different resources to the wealth available to local occupants (Fig. 11.5).

A third approach, developed by Claudio Vita-Finzi and Eric S. Higgs, is called *site-catchment analysis*. In reviewing studies of modern agriculturalists, Vita-Finzi and Higgs noted that exploitation areas tend to be limited to zones of 4 to 5 kilometers radius around the home base; for hunters and gatherers, the radius is about 10 kilometers. For purposes of data collection, however, and to adjust such straight-line distances to the vagaries of specific local topography, they defined their observation areas as those lying within one hour's walk of a site supposedly occupied by agriculturalists, or within two hours' walk of a hunter-gatherer camp. These zones are the site-catchment areas. Within a site-catchment area, distances are considered as insignificant in differentiating resources as more or less accessible; overall proportions or abundance of arable and nonarable land are recorded, as well as other resources. Examination of the site-catchment areas of a series of occupation sites in Israel—including Nahal Oren, El Wad, Kebarah, and Iraq el Baroud—led M. R. Jarman, Vita-Finzi, and Higgs to conclude, among other things, that the amount of arable land was too slight for agriculture to have played a significant part in the food procurement strategies of the ancient occupants.

The complementary perspective for reconstructing ancient environments is analysis of paleoecological data. In Chapter 9 we indicated some of the ways ecofacts in archaeological deposits could yield paleoecological information. For instance, pollen samples can indicate the variety of past local vegetation, which in turn indicates whether the surrounding area was open grassland or forested land with clearings, as was the case in the vicinity of Star Carr. Changes in vegetation cover can be determined from stratified pollen cores, as in the example from Chapter 10 in which changes through time in pollen profiles were used to trace the course of massive land clearing that is argued to be evidence of the spread of agricultural practices. Pollen and small animals such as snails are also useful and sensitive indices of climate: their presence or absence may indicate local change or continuity in temperature and humidity.

But paleoecological materials need not come from the archaeological deposits themselves. For example, in the Fenlands Research Project, of which the investigation of the Mesolithic site of Star Carr was a part, paleoenvironmental studies were conducted over a

Defining micro-environments: Vita-Finzi and Higgs in Israel

broader area as part of a coordinated effort between archaeologists and other scientists to reconstruct the natural history as well as the cultural prehistory for the fenlands area. We also noted in Chapter 10 that something of the paleoenvironment associated with Ertebölle sites in southern Finland was reconstructed by varve analysis, which elucidated the sequence of ancient shorelines and thereby indicated where the shore stood in relation to Ertebölle occupation (and vice versa). Recent analysis of sediment accumulations in the Aegean have similarly demonstrated that many "inland" sites, such as Pella in Macedonia (northern Greece), were much nearer the coast during their ancient occupation (Fig. 11.6): sedimentation has filled in many shallow bays, moving the shoreline away from sites that were once coastal.

Paleoecological data may indicate that local environmental conditions in ancient times were similar to those found today near the site or sites being studied, or they may suggest that resources were different from those available today. Either way, they define the environmental framework within which the past society functioned. Unless they come from archaeological contexts, however, these data tell us only what resources were *available* to be used, but not necessarily what choices the ancient inhabitants actually made about exploiting them. Whether past local occupants thought it appropriate—or had the technology—to smelt copper from ores or to grow crops on arable land can be determined only by combining data on paleoecological *potentials* with the technological and ecofactual data from archaeological contexts, indicating what resources were actually exploited and how they were used. To illustrate such reconstruction, we shall consider the study of subsistence systems.

Reconstructing Ancient Subsistence Systems

All organisms need water and nourishment to survive; no one need be reminded of that. All human societies, then, must have a set of customs—a part of the culture—that deals with the technology of supplying food and water to all the members of the society. The specific technology used will depend on two basic factors: the food and water resources potentially available in the environment and the choices the society makes about what it can or ought to consume. In most cases, many times more edible resources are available to a society than it will be able to or consider appropriate to eat. Our own society generally views insects as inedible, but in many parts of the world nutritious grubs and other insects are eaten with great gusto. In addition, a particular society may not have the technological capacity to exploit all food-resource potentials. For example, the "breadbasket" of the United States—the area of the Great Plains—was always fertile, but sowing crops was an arduous enterprise before the introduction of

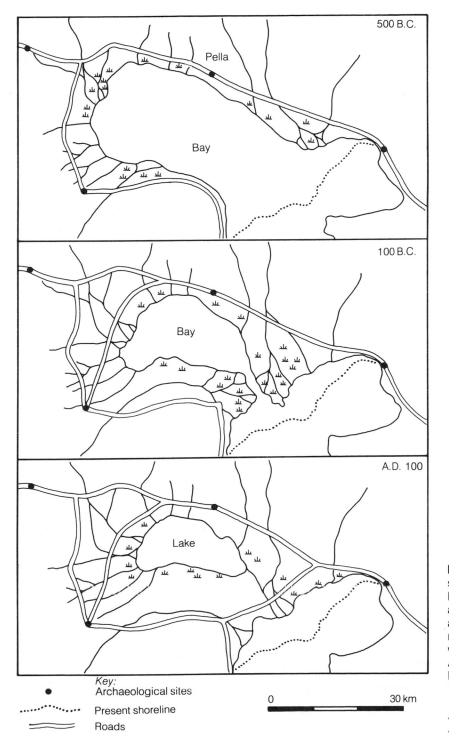

Figure 11.6 Gradual silting in of coastal bays has moved the shoreline away from sites such as Pella, Greece, originally founded near the water's edge. (After Kraft, Aschenbrenner, and Rapp, from *Science,* vol. 195, p. 943. Copyright 1977 by the American Association for the Advancement of Science.)

tools that could cut easily through the matted root system of the natural grass cover.

The point of these illustrations is that cultural adaptation to a given environment results from both the availability of resources and the ways people exploit those resources. Environment does not determine culture, even the subsistence aspect of it, but it provides a flexible framework within which a culture operates. Similarly, culture does not determine environment, but cultural values and technological capacity may serve to define the extent to which available resources are exploited.

Reconstructing ancient subsistence systems, then, requires knowledge of two reciprocal kinds of data. First, the archaeologist must be able to reconstruct the past environment, and be able to determine what the potential resources were. Second, he or she must reconstruct the technological capabilities of the society, and then determine which of the options made available by potential resources and technological abilities were actually, actively exploited in the past.

To specify the subsistence potentials of past environments, the archaeologist must go beyond a mere list of the edible plants and animals that were locally present or that could have been raised. The characteristics of these organisms must also be considered: the animals may migrate with the seasons, or fruits and nuts may be present only during parts of the year. Or local rainfall and soil fertility may be adequate to support one kind of crop and not another. More detailed analyses, taking these kinds of characteristics into account, are those that attempt to estimate the *carrying capacity* of a given area—the number and density of people it could sustain. Carrying capacity is *not* a fixed or magic number however; we shall discuss the flexibility of this calculation in a moment.

Carrying capacity calculations can include a number of considerations. For example, Bruce D. Smith and others have discussed ways of measuring how much meat is available in an area: such figures as annual productivity and biomass, calculated from modern wildlife studies, indicate the number of animals that can be expected per year within a given zone, and then how much meat could be obtained from them. And J. R. Harlan has measured experimentally the productivity of wild wheat stands in the Near East, in terms of the amount of effort required to supply a family with grain. Soil fertility has been tested under a number of conditions: for example, a number of researchers have planted experimental maize-growing plots in Mesoamerica, then measured the crop yields over a number of years as nutrients are progressively removed by successive crops. From these tests, maximum yields per unit of land are computed, as are the reserve lands that must be available to substitute for an exhausted plot

Carrying capacity: Bruce D. Smith on animal protein and J. R. Harlan on grain yields

while it lies fallow to recover nutrients and fertility. To calculate carrying capacity from such figures, one must first assess the amount of meat protein or grain each person would require per year; then one can determine how many people could be supported by the potential resources present.

As we noted above, however, carrying capacity is not a constant figure. If a resident group changes its definition of what is an acceptable (or desirable) food, it moves certain species into or out of the category of available food resources and thereby changes the carrying capacity of the area. Soil fertility and other measures of agricultural potential are particularly hard to control, for carrying capacity is also partly dependent upon the particular agricultural technology used. Shortening of the fallow period, even to the point of continuous cropping, and addition of fertilizers are among the ways crop yield can be increased or maintained.

Next let us consider the cultural-potential component in the problem—that of technology. We have already discussed some of the ways archaeologists reconstruct ancient food-procurement technologies. The archaeologist determines what alternatives were available and which ones were used by specifying what artifacts, ecofacts, and features should be indicative of particular subsistence strategies; the data actually recovered are then analyzed to see what strategies are indicated. For example, grinding stones do not in themselves unequivocally imply the deliberate growing of domesticated grain. But a complex of data including grinding equipment, grain storage facilities, and—preferably, of course—discovery of the remains of identifiable domesticates does indicate at least partial reliance on grain agriculture for subsistence.

Several other, indirect indices of subsistence strategies should be mentioned. For instance, evidence of seasonality of site residence attests to population movement in response to seasonal availability of food resources, as opposed to a sedentary population exploiting resources within a fixed, smaller area. Sedentism need not, however, imply agriculture: for example, the environment around the site of Salinas la Blanca, on the Pacific Coast of Guatemala, seems to have included such a diversity and abundance of nearby food resources that its residents could live in one place the year around and subsist by collecting wild food resources (see Fig. 11.5). The Pacific Coast of the northwestern United States seems to have provided a similarly generous habitat, especially in its fish resources, so that sedentism was easily feasible without agriculture.

Selectivity—food choices—can sometimes be reconstructed too. Bruce D. Smith has shown that the proportion of white-tailed deer, raccoon, and turkey represented in faunal assemblages of sites in the

Middle Mississippi Valley are out of line with the amounts that would be expected on the basis of their contributions to the potential biomass available for hunting. In other words, there are many more remains of these three kinds of animals, relative to other species, than there should be if the prehistoric hunters were simply killing prey indiscriminately to fill the quota of meat needed to eat. Smith therefore suggests that these three animals were actively sought and preferentially selected above other prey as food sources.

Finally, some aspects of the archaeological record (or inferences based on it) can serve as "checks" on reconstruction of subsistence

Figure 11.7 The discovery of ancient evidence of intensive agriculture, such as this complex of raised fields across the Candelaria River from the modern settlement of El Tigre, Campeche, Mexico, has helped spur a reevaluation of the Classic Lowland Maya subsistence base. (Reproduced by permission of Alfred H. Siemens and the Society for American Archaeology from *American Antiquity* 37: 235, 1972.)

systems. Specifically, reconstructions of population density can indicate whether the reconstructed subsistence pattern would have been feasible. Models of ancient Maya food production provide a case in point. Traditionally, the prehistoric Maya were believed to have subsisted primarily by slash-and-burn or swidden agriculture, growing maize and other crops in a rotating system of fields without fertilizers or irrigation. At the time of the Spanish Conquest, as today, the Maya relied on such a system to produce most of the food, and artifacts as well as symbolic representations of maize seemed to underscore its central importance in ancient life.

As we noted earlier, carrying capacity is a flexible figure. But in the 1960s, as more careful and more extensive surveys pieced together a picture of unexpectedly dense populations for the Classic Maya, archaeologists realized that maize swidden agriculture simply could not have supported these communities. During the last few years a reevaluation of the evidence for Maya subsistence has consequently taken place, including suggested alternatives and a search for new evidence (Fig. 11.7). It now appears that Classic Maya food production and procurement strategies varied greatly in time and space, and possibly as a function of social status. Maize remained a desirable crop but certainly not the most frequently eaten one. The search for new evidence and alternative subsistence models has led, among other things, to the discovery and recognition of irrigation features and artificially raised and enriched field systems. Dennis E. Puleston has argued repeatedly and forcefully that a significant part of the prehistoric Maya diet was supplied by fruit and nut trees and by the produce from kitchen gardens outside the houses. None of these new interpretations is contradicted by previous evidence of artifacts, ecofacts, and features, but scholars now see that the model into which they were previously incorporated was too narrow and simplified.

**Subsistence systems:
The Classic Maya**

SOCIAL SYSTEMS AND SPATIAL FRAMEWORKS

All societies distinguish among their members by assigning various roles and statuses. The most fundamental distinctions are those based on age and sex differences, but most human groups organize social interaction along a number of other lines as well. Kinship studies, a well-known part of anthropological research, have revealed the great variety of ways people have developed for naming relatives, reckoning descent, governing what family members one lives with, and so on. Principles of social organization extend beyond consideration of family organization, however, to include such other things as the ways power is channeled (political organization) and who controls production and distribution of wealth and other resources (economic organization).

As recorded by ethnographers and social anthropologists much of the evidence of social structure is intangible, such as attitudes of respect and deference or linguistic taxonomies of social relationships. But especially in recent years, archaeologists have tried to develop more sensitivity to aspects of material remains that may contain clues to past social organization. In this section we shall discuss three different approaches now in use to reconstruct past social relationships and social structure.

Ceramic Sociology

James R. Sackett coined the term "ceramic sociology" to describe an approach that is becoming increasingly popular in archaeology. Especially in the southwestern United States and the Near East, aspects of ceramic style have been subjected to analysis in order to define the different social groups within a community that were responsible for pottery production. To paraphrase Sackett, the underlying assumption is that, since standards and styles of pottery manufacture are socially transmitted, the social group within which such standards are taught should produce a consistent and recognizable style of pottery that can be distinguished from the styles produced by other, equivalent groups. In Chapter 9, in discussing the type-variety-mode approach to pottery classification, we noted that its chief proponent, James Gifford, argued a similar point: that the pottery types recognized by this classificatory method were believed to represent the products of discrete social groups. Most of what Sackett refers to as "ceramic sociology," however, has dealt not with pottery types (or more inclusive classificatory units), but with the distributional study of individual design elements or stylistic modes.

Ceramic sociology studies: Deetz, Longacre, and Hill

The most often-cited studies that come under this heading are the pioneer analyses of James Deetz, William A. Longacre, and James N. Hill. Deetz was working with sites and pottery from the Arikara area of South Dakota; Longacre and Hill both worked in Arizona, at the sites of Carter Ranch and Broken K, respectively. All three scholars studied associations and co-occurrences of pottery design motifs to define the existence of the pottery producing groups. In Deetz's study, the dissolution of recognizable styles through time was taken as indicative of the breakup of the (family) production units: the distinctive styles had dissolved because communication and mutual reinforcement among the potters had been disrupted. Robert Whallon has made a similar analysis of prehistoric pottery in the Iroquois area. In the Southwest, Hill and Longacre studied the distribution of motifs with regard to provenience units of the pottery. The potters were be-lieved, by ethnographic analogy, to have been groups of women; within these groups pottery technology and standards were passed down from mother to daughter. From this premise, the correlation of distinctive pottery styles with particular sectors of the site was argued to reflect residential divisions in which several generations of women would remain together throughout their lives. The residential pattern corresponding to this model is what anthropologists call matrilocal residence: women live with their mothers and aunts, and husbands become part of their wives' existing households. By the reasoning outlined above, then, archaeologists were able to use ceramic data to reconstruct part of social organization.

This approach has received many criticisms, both from archae-ologists and from sociocultural anthropologists. Specific critiques concern aspects ranging from the assumptions by which material data are connected to social attributes, to the methods of data collection and analysis, to consideration of the contexts from which the ana-lyzed sherds came. But few would suggest that the baby be thrown out with the bathwater: "ceramic sociology" is a new approach, and the studies done to date are still exploratory. Many refinements must yet be made in such an analytic approach, but it still offers a great po-tential for reconstructing aspects of prehistoric social organization.

Settlement Archaeology

Settlement archaeology is the study of the spatial distribution of an-cient human activities and occupation, ranging from the differential location of activities within a single room to the arrangement of sites in a region. Because they are concerned with locational information, settlement studies use features and sites as their principal data bases. This does not mean that individual artifacts and ecofacts are not con-sidered in such studies; however, since the focus is on understanding the distribution of ancient activities, the archaeologist doing set-tlement studies needs the locational information preserved by primary context, and features and sites retain such information intact.

The development of settlement archaeology has different roots in England and the United States, but in both cases it has involved at-tention to the way human occupation is distributed across the land-scape. In England, the work of Sir Cyril Fox in the second quarter of the twentieth century provided stimulus for relating the distribution of archaeological remains to the distribution of environmental features. In the United States, the inspiration for settlement studies can be traced most directly to Julian Steward's research in the Great Basin area in the 1930s. Steward recognized that patterns in the location of

Pioneering settlement studies: Sir Cyril Fox in England, Julian Stew-ard in the Great Basin, and Gordon Willey in the Virú Valley

household residence could be understood as a product of the interactions between environment and culture—especially, in the latter
case, the factors of technology and social organization. In other
words, the spatial patterning of archaeological features that represented ancient residences could be analyzed in order to reconstruct
past decisions regarding use of the environment, allocation of resources, social relationships, and the like. One of the first research
projects to apply Steward's ideas to strictly archaeological data was
Gordon R. Willey's study of changing regional patterns of settlement
in the Virú Valley of north coastal Peru. In 1954, the year after the
Virú research was published, Willey organized a symposium on prehistoric settlement patterns in the New World. At that time only
sketchy formulations could be offered for the various regions covered; in the ensuing quarter century, however, archaeological settlement research has greatly expanded, both in frequency and
sophistication, so that now archaeological research in most parts of
the world includes investigation of settlement distributions. In the
1970s, particularly, much effort has been expended to develop more
rigorous techniques for ferreting out structure in the spatial dimension
of archaeological data. Part of this new emphasis has resulted from a
theoretical reorientation to the view that the study of relations among
artifacts, ecofacts, and features is at least as important and informative as the study of artifacts, ecofacts, and features themselves. But
the change is due also to the increasing attention archaeologists now
pay to other social sciences, especially geography and regional planning, that study human behavior in a spatial framework. Related to
this is the growing adoption by archaeologists of statistical analytical
techniques and mathematically based models for describing and analyzing all the dimensions of archaeological data.

Clearly, by relating human occupation to the natural environment
and by placing sites and features in space, settlement studies have
much potential relevance for examining ancient evaluation and exploitation of that environment. This potential has certainly been recognized by archaeologists doing settlement research: for example, in
studying the subsistence systems used prehistorically in the Tehuacán
Valley, Richard MacNeish and his colleagues examined the distribution of occupational sites or base camps in order to reconstruct the
seasonal cycle of residence and food procurement. In this section,
however, we shall focus on the ways settlement archaeology can elu-
cidate past social systems.

The assumption underlying settlement archaeology is that the spatial patterning evident in the distributions of archaeological remains
results from and reflects spatial patterning in ancient human behavior.
In the growth of settlement studies, archaeologists have tended to analyze spatial patterns on three levels. The smallest level is that of ac-

tivities within a single structure or on a single occupation surface, such as a cave floor. The next or intermediate level concerns the arrangement of activities and features within a settlement or site. The largest-scale studies, in turn, examine the distribution of sites within a region. We shall consider some studies on each of these levels.

At the smallest level of human settlement, archaeologists reconstruct the spatial organization of activities within a single structure —be it a dwelling or some other kind of building—or within a comparably small unenclosed space. Such a study can consist of delineating areas in which various activities were carried out, such as distinguishing food preparation areas from other areas. The nature of the specific activities carried out in a given area is inferred by comparison of the archaeological remains with material remains of known activities. For example, hearths, fire-blackened jars, and grinding stones would indicate a cooking area. At this smallest level of settlement analysis, then, the archaeologist is attempting to understand how the prehistoric society divided up space into areas appropriate for particular activities.

A number of archaeologists, including Robert Whallon, John D. Speth, and Gregory A. Johnson, have used statistical analysis of activity areas to differentiate artifact clusters and thereby define distinct activity areas or "tool kits." These techniques have been used primarily on data from Paleolithic cave sites in the Old World, where tool kits are frequently difficult to sort out by visual inspection of artifact arrays as they are uncovered. The statistical approaches used in these studies go beyond impressionistic assessments of spatial clusterings of artifacts and other materials on occupation floors: rather, horizontal patterns and clusters are defined by statistical measures of spatial association. These techniques are still exploratory, but work is being done to make them more sensitive. For example, Robert K. Vierra and Richard L. Taylor have used imaginary or "dummy" data sets in which they make up proveniences for imaginary tool kits. Knowing which sets of artifacts *should* be distinguished, they test the adequacy of the statistical techniques for picking these out.

Statistical analysis of activity areas.

At this "microsettlement" level of analysis, the most frequently studied kind of feature is the dwelling. A number of scholars have examined the potential determinants for house form. Bruce G. Trigger's list of such factors includes subsistence regime (whether the society is sedentary or migratory); climate; available building materials; family structure; wealth; incorporation of special activities, such as craft production; ideology; security; and style. Although a number of these factors are related to environmental variables, several have to do with the social system of the culture being studied. For example, societies in which people live in extended families, with several generations of a family residing together, would have larger house structures than those in which nuclear families (parents plus children) are the usual household unit. Some studies have attempted to relate particular dwelling forms to particular kinship structures. By studying dwelling forms in a number of ethnographically known societies, for example, John W. M. Whiting and Barbara Ayres examined the extent to which such characteristics as number of rooms or curvilinear versus rectangular ground plans might be used to predict family organization. A frequently cited finding from their research is that curvilinear dwellings tend to occur in polygynous societies—that is, in societies in which a man may have more than one wife. This statistical association, though useful and suggestive for archaeological inference, should *not* be taken as an automatic predictor: round houses do not invariably indicate that the prehistoric society was polygynous.

Analysis of public buildings: Flannery and Marcus at Oaxaca, Mexico

Other buildings besides dwellings may be examined at this level: craft-production buildings and shrines are among the specific functional categories that may be identified. Kent Flannery and Joyce Marcus have traced the development of the "public building" in the Valley of Oaxaca, Mexico, during the last few millennia B.C. By public buildings they mean special structures to house communal rituals; they believe they can detect demarcation of public space as early as the fifth millennium B.C. at the site of Gheo-Shih (Fig. 11.8). The Gheo-Shih public space is a cleared lane, 20 m long and 7 m wide, whose cleanliness and lack of artifacts contrast markedly with the abundance of remains just outside its boulder-marked limits. By 1500 B.C. in Oaxaca, special buildings were constructed as public spaces; as time passed, these became larger, architecturally more elaborate, less accessible, and more diversified into recognizable types. Flannery and Marcus argue that this developmental record reflects, in part, the development of social relationships: the growth in size and elaboration and the tendency toward spatial segregation of these structures imply their association with a wealthy, elitist segment of society, and the increase in recognizable types attests to a diversification of social roles—perhaps of ritual specialists to manage and carry out the activities for which the buildings were constructed.

Although the examples just given have focused on structures, the archaeologist should also include outdoor areas in settlement analysis at this level. Although many activities do take place within buildings, many others, from stone-chipping to public dancing, can be performed as well outdoors. In hot climates, in fact, the majority of activities that do not require privacy may be carried out in the open air, often in patio areas adjacent to houses. Thus archaeologists who look only at structures may miss much of the overall picture of life in the prehistoric society.

Figure 11.8 This stone-bordered lane at the site of Gheo-Shih, Oaxaca, Mexico, is believed to be a local forerunner of "public spaces" later more formally defined by increasingly elaborate architecture. (From Flannery and Marcus 1976, by permission of the authors and Academic Press.)

Such a consideration leads us to the next level of settlement analysis: settlement layout. The site is the unit of analysis here, especially sites that are considered to be residential communities (as opposed to kill sites, for example). At this level, archaeologists consider the articulation of individual "micro-units" into the larger whole; this allows them to examine aspects of prehistoric social systems from a number of perspectives.

Social stratification, for example, is frequently inferred partly on the basis of evidence from settlement analysis. In the discussion of public buildings in Oaxaca just mentioned, structure size and architectural elaboration were interpreted as clues to differential wealth and/or power. At the Maya site of Tikal, Guatemala, archaeologists have found that houses are consistent in form throughout the site, but they range considerably in size, decoration, and the relative use of perishable versus stone construction materials. Larger, more substantial houses are assumed to house people who had more wealth or other means of controlling and acquiring goods and labor.

Aspects of social control can also be inferred from the regularity of settlement layouts. The site of Teotihuacán, Mexico, with its gridded streets and its orientation to the cardinal directions (see Fig. 6.1) is a striking example of imposed planning—which implies the presence of a powerful elite able to command and direct the placement of structures and facilities over this broad expanse of land. Ancient Chinese

Social organization: Keatinge and Day at Chan Chan, Peru

political centers were laid out according to a plan whose basis was partly religious, but whose execution required effective social control.

Concerns with privacy or security can also be detected. For instance, Richard W. Keatinge and Kent C. Day have described the complex urban center of Chan Chan, in the Moche Valley of Peru, as being divisible into three component parts: houses of the poor, intermediate buildings, and monumental structures. The three categories reflect differences both of complexity and of regularity of arrangement; the "monumental structures" are the most complex and regular of all. These comprise a set of 10 enclosures (see Fig. 11.9) that have been interpreted as elite residential compounds. Given this interpretation, the articulation of elite with nonelite people of the area can be partially examined by looking at how the residences relate—or were allowed to relate—in space: clearly the poorer areas were segregated even from the intermediate sections, but the monumental compounds were the most restrictive of all. Although they encompassed great amounts of space, each had only one or two entrances, allowing its occupants to control strictly with whom they would interact.

Besides social stratification, role differentiation and economic specialization can also be studied by using settlement data. For example, study of the distribution of workshop areas within a community might indicate whether these are associated with particular classes of people, whether they are segregated into specific quarters of the community, and so on. Some industries, such as flint-knapping, might be "cottage industries," carried out by every family (or other social unit) to supply its own needs; within the same community, other industries might be carried out by skilled specialists. In developmental studies of the rise of urbanism, the criteria used to define urban status often include not only population size and density but also the existence of specialized craft production of a number of commodities.

Some scholars have attempted to correlate settlement layouts with kinship structures. In a pioneering study of this kind, Kwang-Chih Chang suggested that segmented village plans might be associated with segmented lineage (descent group) social organization. This research—which was the direct inspiration for the Whiting and Ayres study on residence shape—is suggestive but cannot be used as a strictly predictive model for interpretation of archaeological settlement remains.

Kent V. Flannery has used house form and settlement layout to develop an hypothesis about the growth of village life and development of political organization. Specifically, he postulates that round houses and house compounds are less conducive than rectangular units to the addition of new units and the integration of larger numbers of people. He notes that in both Mesoamerica and the Near East, two major

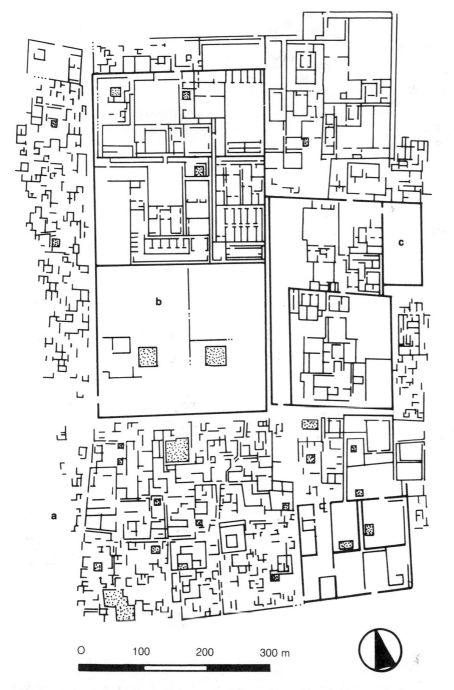

O   100   200   300 m

Figure 11.9 This portion of the map of Chan Chan, Peru, shows remains of (a) nonelite residential areas contrasting with (b, c) adjacent elite enclosures with restricted access from the outside. (After Moseley and Mackey 1974.)

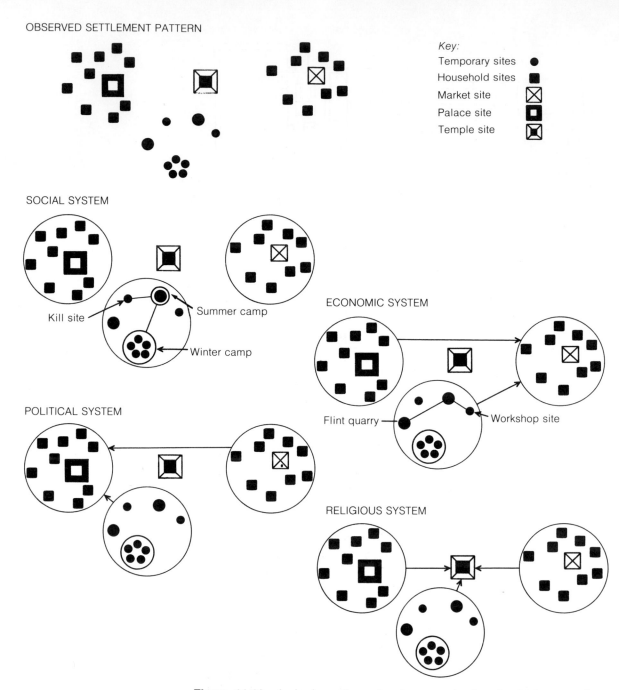

Figure 11.10 A single settlement pattern may be the physical expression of a number of systems of social relations. (Courtesy of K. C. Chang, *Settlement Patterns in Archaeology.* © 1972 by Addison-Wesley Publishing Company, Inc. Philippines copyright 1972 by Addison-Wesley Publishing Company, Inc.)

world centers in the development of agriculture and urbanism, the village of rectangular houses became stabilized as the "standard" community organization.

At the broadest level of settlement analysis, archaeologists consider the distribution of sites within a region. This can be approached in two ways. One is to reconstruct the function of each component in the settlement system and then to look at the various ways in which they may have been organized into an interacting social network. Chang rightly reminds archaeologists that the same settlement pattern can reflect a number of different systems of social relationships (Fig. 11.10). MacNeish's Tehuacán subsistence cycle is one example of a particular view of settlement systems. A different example is provided by analysis of Paleolithic sites, in France and elsewhere, having a Mousterian stone-tool assemblage. These sites have been categorized into a number of Mousterian "types"; François Bordes, a leader in delineating variation in Mousterian artifacts, has argued that the different sites reflect occupation of adjacent locales by contrasting social groups who used different styles of tool manufacture. Lewis and Sally Binford, however, have used statistical factor analysis of some of the tool assemblages to support their contention that the variability represents, not "ethnic" difference, but complementary sets of activities. The Binfords' analyses led them to posit that some of the occupations represent residential "base camps," while others represent hunting/butchering or other work camps. The contrast in the social interaction implied by the two interpretations is clear. In one view the Mousterian occupations represent contrasting human social groups doing similar things; in the other, an undifferentiable overall group was simply dividing up activities according to appropriate locales. Again, the nature of individual parts of the settlement system must be examined in order to reconstruct the social system involved.

An increasingly popular approach to multisite settlement studies involves analytic techniques borrowed from economic geographers. This approach is sometimes referred to as *regional analysis,* a name that emphasizes the scope of the investigation and its holistic point of view, focusing on interaction within the region. Many of the actual techniques, however, come under the term *locational analysis,* and a particularly important analytic model is that of *central place theory.* Underlying the latter theory—and other models derived from economic geography—is the assumption that efficiency and minimization of costs are among the most basic criteria involved in spatial organization of human activities. An individual settlement will be located in a position where a maximum number of resources can be exploited with the least effort; these resources will include not only aspects of the natural environment but also communication with neighboring

Social differentiation vs. complementary activities: Bordes and the Binfords on Mousterian artifacts

groups. As the landscape fills with people, settlements will tend to space themselves evenly across it, and the most efficient pattern for spacing of communities is a hexagonal lattice. This is all in theory, of course: in practice, landscape variables such as steep topography or presence of uninhabitable areas—swamps and the like—break up the predicted pattern. Still, a reasonably close approximation of the hexagonal-lattice pattern has been observed in a number of situations both modern and ancient, including Ian Hodder and Mark Hassall's study of Romano-British towns (Fig. 11.11).

Given this situation of an already populated landscape, Walter Christaller developed a model to describe the rise of cities; this is "classical" central place theory as first developed in Christaller's 1933 study of modern settlement in southern Germany. Briefly, the theory states that *central places* will develop within this lattice arrangement. These centers will provide a wider variety of goods and services than do surrounding smaller settlements. In fact, a hierarchy of central places will arise, with centers of equivalent level spaced equidistantly through the lattice (Fig. 11.11). Different lattices, reflecting different nesting patterns for the levels in the hierarchy, are more efficient for different goals; the three goals usually considered are movement of rurally produced goods, movement of centrally produced goods, and control of distribution patterns by centralized administration.

Central place theory has been of interest to archaeologists for describing regional settlement patterns; its primary application has been in studying the development of cities in the archaeological record. Although overall application of this model in anthropology has been made largely by social and cultural anthropologists, archaeologists studying areas of the world in which cities and civilizations emerged have also begun to explore the model's potentials. In so doing, they have brought forth variations on Christaller's basic model as well. For instance, Gregory Johnson's study of the settlement lattice on the Diyala Plains of Iraq at about 2800 B.C. shows that it fits Christaller's model but, probably because of the existence of a series of roughly parallel watercourses, the lattice there is composed of rhomboids rather than hexagons. Other work, such as Richard Blanton's interpretation of the rise of Teotihuacán, show what is called the primate pattern, in which the highest-order central place absorbs the function of intermediate centers, growing in size and importance at their expense and interacting directly with much smaller settlements. The value of central place theory and its variants is that, when an archaeological situation fits a particular variant, the theoretical model suggests the kinds of economic decision-making and organizational principles that may have been operating in the past society

Applications of central place theory: Johnson on the Diyala plain of Iraq, and Blanton on Teotihuacán, Mexico

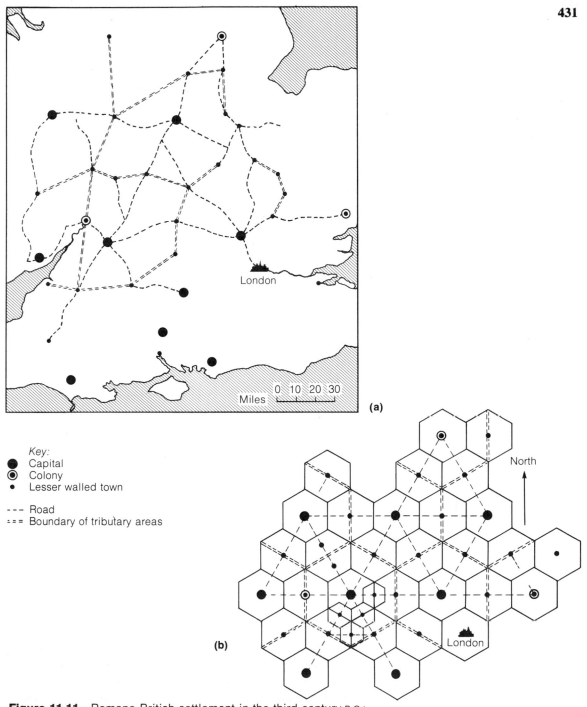

Figure 11.11 Romano-British settlement in the third century B.C.: (a) plotted on a conventional map and (b) fit to an idealized hexagonal lattice. (After Hodder and Hassall 1971, by permission of the Royal Anthropological Institute of Great Britain and Ireland.)

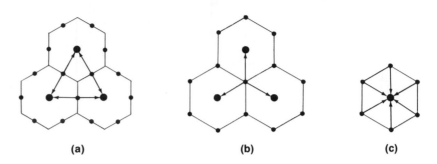

Figure 11.12   Central-place models of settlement are usually divided into three idealized variants. In all three, each large center has direct access to six smaller settlements. The difference is that in (a), the transport landscape, each smaller settlement relates to two larger centers; in (b), the marketing landscape, each smaller settlement is connected with three larger centers; and in (c), the administrative landscape, the smaller settlements interact with only one larger center.

(Fig. 11.12). The model does not in itself explain what actually went on in the past, but it helps to suggest explanatory hypotheses to be tested.

Other locational and spatial analyses have been or are being developed to describe, compare, and understand settlement distributions. These include such things as *network analyses* and use of *Thiesson polygons*. The former method examines routes of communication between settlements. The latter figures are imposed on a regional map by drawing perpendiculars at the midpoints between settlements; the areas included within the Thiesson polygons suggest the areas under the control of each settlement (in an approach different from but comparable to Vita-Finzi and Higgs' site-catchment analysis) as well as providing graphic indication of the equality or inequality of settlement spacing. This technique has been used in a variety of archaeological situations, including Hodder and Hassall's study of Romano-British walled towns and Norman Hammond's exploration of possible "realms" among the Classic Maya. A battery of techniques is now being tested for potential application to archaeological data; many of these involve use of statistics.

We shall consider one other, rather specific aspect of settlement archaeology here. That is the reconstruction of prehistoric population size and density. In previous contexts we have noted that population figures may be important indices of such things as degree of urbanization, or they may serve as a check on the feasibility of a reconstructed model of an ancient subsistence system. Population estimates are derived from archaeological data in a number of ways. One is by extrapolation from burial populations. The problem with this approach, however, is that excavated samples of human burials are seldom representative of the entire population, either statistically or demographically. And even if they were, burial populations constitute the *accumulation* of dead persons over the period of occupation of the settlement, not just a census of the living populace at one point in time. Another approach is to estimate possible population from carrying capacity figures. This gives an approximation of population size—but since it is based on carrying capacity estimates, the resulting figure *cannot* be used to "check" the feasibility of carrying capacity calculations.

Most reconstructions of population size and density have relied on settlement data. Specific approaches have included measures or counts of floor space, dwellings, middens, site areas, and available sleeping space. Perhaps the two most common approaches are dwelling counts and measurements of floor space. In the former, houses are identified and counted; then the archaeologist calculates the average family size per house and multiplies this figure by the number of houses to compute the population size. The figure for average family size is obtained from local ethnographic or historic descriptions. Although the method is simple, demonstrating the appropriateness of the household-size number presents a formidable difficulty.

One of the most frequently discussed means of estimating prehistoric population is Raoul Naroll's "floor space" formula. Compiling information from the Human Relations Area Files, an indexed compendium of ethnographic data from all over the world, Naroll found that, in his sample of 18 societies, roofed space averaged 10 m² per person. This figure has been used to reconstruct ancient population figures in a variety of archaeological situations, but it has not, of course, gone without criticism. For instance, Polly Wiessner has recently suggested that the appropriateness of this or any constant figure should be re-examined. Personal space requirements, she asserts, are not likely to be the same among hunters and gatherers as among urban dwellers, and roofed space may not adequately reflect the space needs of people who spend the majority of their time outdoors. Using data from modern !Kung Bushman camps, for example, she calculates about 5.9 m² per person within the camp area *as a whole;* thus the amount of roofed space per person would be a smaller figure yet.

A logical offshoot of Naroll's work has been the calculation of sleeping space, which is a portion of total roofed space. Richard E. W. Adams has used this approach to compute the size of elite populations at the Maya site of Uaxactún, Guatemala, and René Millon has used it in his population estimates for the urban site of Teotihuacán, Mexico. Whatever one's approach, the critical factors in population reconstruction are, first, how precisely the archaeologist can measure the physical population index—be it floor space, number of dwellings, or whatever—and second, how reliable a multiplier can be produced to convert the archaeological materials into counts of people.

Exchange Systems

Human societies establish exchange systems in order to acquire goods and services not normally available to them locally. As a result, trading ventures and institutions arise, involving cooperative and peaceful exchanges between two or more parties. Of course, there are other means to acquire nonlocal goods and services: foraging expeditions may be used to collect materials from distant sources, and raids or military conquests often serve to plunder foreign lands for wealth and slaves. The latter means present a contrast to trading systems in that they obviously do not involve either cooperation or two-way exchange. The archaeologist may have difficulty in distinguishing trade goods from those acquired by other means, but the distinction is important for at least two reasons. First, the recognition of trade in the archaeological record leads to the reconstruction of past economic systems, and since such systems are basic to all human societies, by extension this contributes to an understanding of the organization of entire ancient societies. Second, since cooperative exchange between individuals and between societies provides a primary means for the transmission of new ideas, recognition of trade leads the archaeologist to an understanding of culture change.

In this section we will discuss the ways in which archaeologists identify ancient trade goods and reconstruct exchange systems. Before doing this, however, we will briefly outline some of the characteristics of exchange systems as determined from ethnographic and historical examples.

Most anthropologists distinguish two basic forms of trade, which can often both be found within a single economic system. *Reciprocal exchange* refers to simple, direct trade between two parties; "payment" may be made through barter, in services, through indentured labor, or in monetary units. *Redistributive exchange* is more complex and indirect, involving a third party or an institution that collects goods or services, such as surpluses, tribute, duties or taxes, and reallocates the accumulated wealth to others. Reciprocal exchange is found in all human societies, but redistributive exchange is usually associated with more complex, socially stratified societies. In these societies, the allocating authority—be it chief, king, or centralized bureaucracy—usually has the right or power to retain a portion of the collected goods and services that pass through its hands. Colin Renfrew has outlined ten forms of resource acquisition. The simplest is

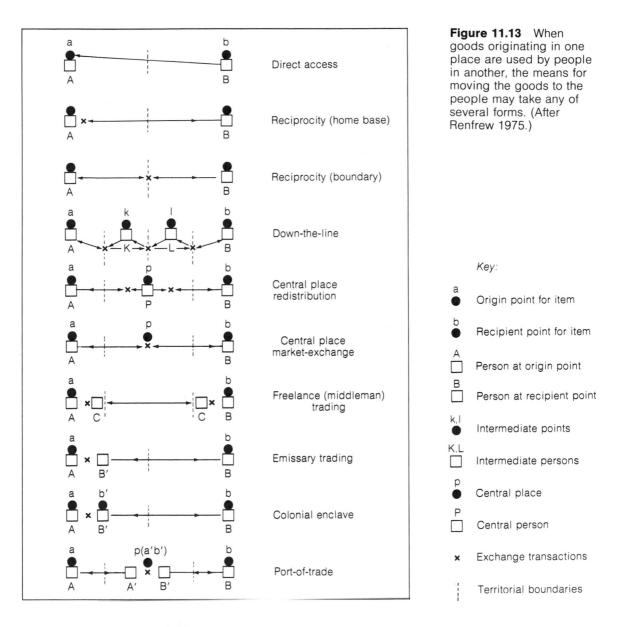

Figure 11.13 When goods originating in one place are used by people in another, the means for moving the goods to the people may take any of several forms. (After Renfrew 1975.)

direct access to resources; of the rest, two involve reciprocal exchange and the remaining seven involve redistribution (Fig. 11.13).

While human exchange systems involve transfer of goods, services, and ideas, by necessity archaeologists deal directly only with the tangible products of trade, usually recovered as artifacts and ecofacts. These data are traditionally divided into two classes. The first category, utilitarian items, refers to food items and tools for acquiring,

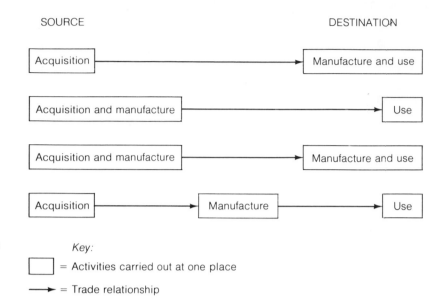

Figure 11.14 Exchange or trade may take place at any point during the behavioral cycle of acquisition, manufacture, and use of resources. The archaeologist attempts to determine the location of each of these activities.

storing, and processing food, as well as other materials such as weapons or clothing. The second category, nonutilitarian items, includes the remainder of exchanged commodities, including gifts and ritual and status goods.

By considering such distinctions, the archaeologist attempts to reconstruct both the inventory of trade goods and the mechanism of exchange, examining the relative amounts as well as the spatial distribution of recovered trade items. But before such interpretation can begin, the archaeologist must be able to separate trade goods from local goods in the archaeological record and to distinguish ancient acquisition, manufacture, and use behavior.

The identification of trade goods in archaeological situations is based upon a variety of classification procedures. The archaeologist must determine the source locations for the raw materials of both artifacts and ecofacts, the manufacturing place for artifacts, and areas of use for both artifacts and ecofacts. Area of use is inferred to be the site of discovery if the evidence is found in primary context. Places of manufacture are reconstructed directly by discovery of workshop sites, or indirectly from recovery of manufacturing debris in other associations, such as middens. Sources of raw materials are determined by identification of ancient quarries, mines, and other acquisition areas. Figure 11.14 presents the relationship of these identified activity areas to the reconstruction of ancient trade.

In dealing with ecofacts, such as floral and faunal remains, the archaeologist need identify only the source and use areas. For instance,

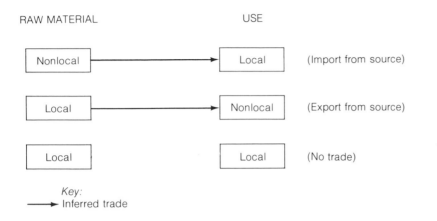

RAW MATERIAL   USE

| Nonlocal | → | Local | (Import from source) |

| Local | → | Nonlocal | (Export from source) |

| Local | | Local | (No trade) |

Key:
⟶ Inferred trade

Figure 11.15 Identification of trade in ecofacts depends on recognition of species that have been removed from their natural habitats.

marine materials may be recovered from a site located far inland, or bone of lowland-dwelling animals may be found at a site situated within a highland region. In both cases, the demonstration of trade rests upon the biological identification of plant and animal species, recognition that a recovered ecofact is nonlocal in origin, and subsequent identification of its probable source area (see Fig. 11.15).

Artifacts, on the other hand, often present a much more complex problem. Because artifacts are products of human manufacture or modification, the archaeologist must identify not only the source of raw materials and the location of use, but also the place of manufacture. Manufacture itself may involve several steps, each carried out at a different location (Fig. 11.16). For instance, mineral substances such as flint or obsidian are sometimes manufactured into tools right at the quarry site, and then traded as finished tools. In other cases, the raw material is traded first and then manufactured into tools at its destination. But manufacture may also be carried out at both source and destination: tool "blanks" may be roughed out at the quarry, traded, and converted into finished tools at the final destination. Other variations are also possible, such as manufacture at a point between source and destination (see Fig. 11.16). The archaeologist may also distinguish between original manufacture and reworking in the case of artifacts that were modified for secondary uses.

The identification of local versus imported artifacts may be made by either stylistic or technological (constituent) classification. Style types have traditionally been used to distinguish certain categories of traded artifacts, such as pottery. However, style attributes, such as surface color and decoration, may by themselves be unreliable criteria for differentiating local from nonlocal artifacts. This is because such stylistic attributes, along with most form attributes, can easily be copied by local manufacturers to mimic imported examples. This

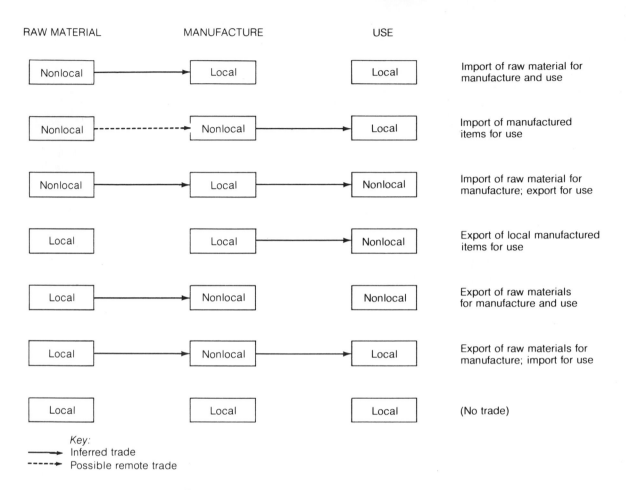

Figure 11.16 Trade in artifacts may involve exchange of raw materials, manufactured goods, partially manufactured goods, or some combination of these.

does not mean that either style or form types cannot contribute to the reconstruction of ancient exchange systems. The impact of trade relationships, as expressed in the exchange of *ideas,* can often be gauged by the extent to which foreign elements are accepted and integrated into local styles and forms, whether these are expressed by pottery, architecture, or other evidence.

The most reliable means of identifying trade goods is technological classification based upon constituent analysis. Constituent analysis identifies the chemical composition of the raw material (clay, metal, mineral, or whatever), using a variety of techniques ranging from microscopic visual inspection to sophisticated methods of analytic chemistry and physics, including optical spectroscopy, X-ray fluorescence, and neutron activation. The goal of these analyses is to identify characteristics unique or specific to material from a single source; this is often referred to as the "fingerprint" or the "signature" of the source. The choice of one analytic technique over another often depends upon such factors as cost, precision of the identification needed, and whether or not the artifact sample may be destroyed by the analysis.

Constituent identification of trade goods is usually applied within a regional archaeological strategy. The environmental survey of a given region should include the identification of potential sources of raw materials, such as mineral deposits, clay beds, metal ore deposits, and so forth. Samples of raw material from the potential sources are analyzed along with artifacts recovered archaeologically, using one or more of the techniques designed to reveal their chemical composition. The resulting characteristics of the samples are used to group the materials statistically according to their chemical "fingerprints." The artifact classes and the source classes are then compared to determine the probable sources of the raw materials for the artifacts under study (Fig. 11.17). Because the variability involved can be quite complex, the matches are often facilitated by a computer. Constituent analyses such as these have been done for a variety of materials in a number of areas, including turquoise in the southwestern United States and northern Mexico, and soapstone (steatite) in Virginia, but most of the emphasis has been placed on obsidian.

These data allow the archaeologist to reconstruct ancient trade and its accompanying social interaction by examining spatial patterning from several perspectives, including simple presence or absence of certain trade items as well as quantitative patterns in their occurrence. Simple presence/absence plots show the distributions for one or more categories of traded artifacts and their identified raw-material sources. Such maps may suggest quite readily the spatial range and even routes used in ancient trade systems (Fig. 11.18).

Colin Renfrew has discussed a number of mathematical models for studying quantitative patterning in distribution of trade items. These are *distance decay* functions: the traded item occurs in smaller quantities with increasing distance from the source. In his original studies of obsidian trade in the Near East, Renfrew posited a down-the-line social model to account for the quantitative distribution. According to this model, each town successively farther from the source passes along only a certain proportion of the total goods received. The result is an exponential decline in the amount of material moving down the line.

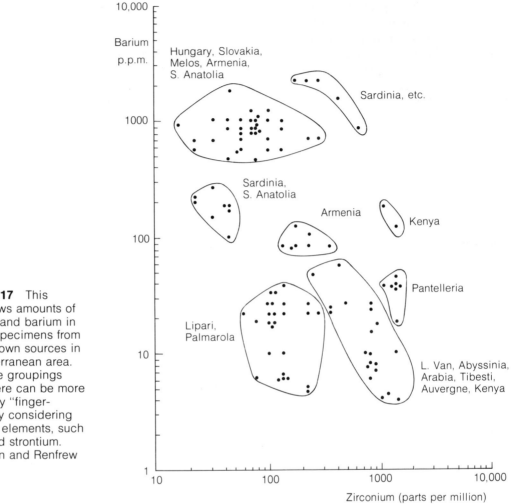

Figure 11.17 This graph shows amounts of zirconium and barium in obsidian specimens from several known sources in the Mediterranean area. The source groupings defined here can be more specifically "finger-printed" by considering additional elements, such as iron and strontium. (After Cann and Renfrew 1964.)

Detailed attention to refinement of trade models has pointed out a number of factors differentiating among trade systems. For instance, Ian Hodder has distinguished two categories of distance decay effects, which Renfrew discusses in terms of *network* or down-the-line trade as opposed to areally more limited *supply-zone* trade. The first category involves multiple trade transactions and/or movement over long distances; the second, apparently associated with common, bulky items such as roof tiles, seems to involve single transactions and short trips to supply a specified local area.

Central place theory also has a bearing on trade distributions: as central places arise, they produce bumps in the distance decay curves

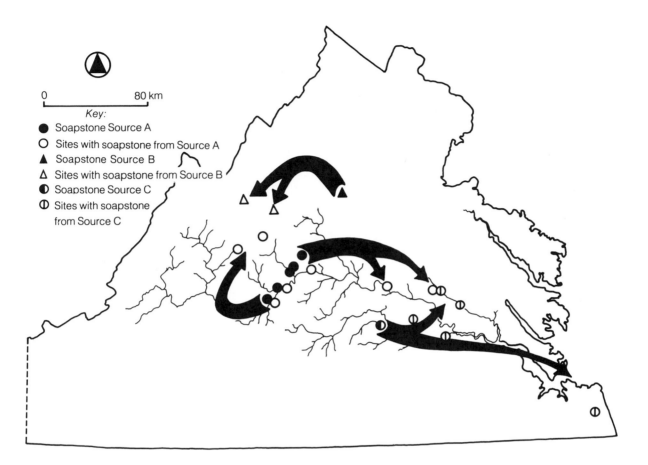

Figure 11.18 Matching sources and destinations in the prehistoric soapstone trade in eastern Virginia suggests that trade routes followed the drainage system of the James River. (After Luckenbach, Holland, and Allen, from *Science,* vol. 187, p. 58. Copyright 1975 by the American Association for the Advancement of Science.)

(Fig. 11.19). By serving as redistribution centers, they increase exchange interaction and accumulate more than their expected share of trade goods. For example, Raymond Sidrys has demonstrated that the quantities of obsidian found in Maya sites are a function both of distance from the source and of level of the site in a rough central-place hierarchy. As Renfrew notes, some of the increased accumulation in higher-order centers may result from the centers' role as marketplaces, but some may also be due to the greater personal wealth or prestige of residents of the central places, who are thus able to bring in more imported goods.

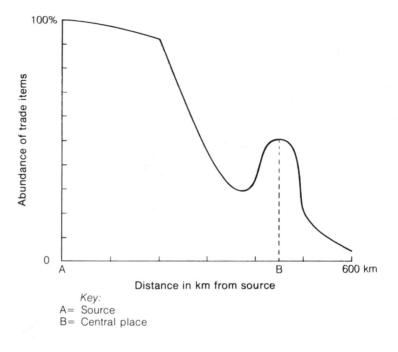

Figure 11.19 The amount of a trade item reaching a specific destination decreases with the distance of that destination from the source. But the rate of decrease is not completely constant, and the presence of redistribution centers in particular disrupts the distance decay curve. (After Renfrew 1975.)

Key:
A= Source
B= Central place

IDEOLOGICAL AND SYMBOL SYSTEMS

Ideological systems are the means by which human societies codify beliefs about both the natural and supernatural worlds. Through ideology, people structure their ideas about the order of the universe, their place in that universe, and their relationships with each other and with things and beings around them. Ancient ideologies are preserved through *symbols,* which are their material expression. The difficulty in reconstructing ideologies lies not in discovering symbolic representations, but in recognizing them as such and in assigning them an appropriate meaning. We have already mentioned that archaeologists commonly divide artifacts into "utilitarian" versus "ceremonial" classes. The latter category, although it appears to offer the kind of information needed to reconstruct ideologies, too often becomes simply a catch-all for forms whose utility is not immediately apparent.

It is one thing to discover a symbolic representation and another to intepret its intended meaning correctly. For example, figurines of human females occur abundantly in the archaeological record, beginning as early as the Upper Paleolithic in Europe. Traditionally, these have been interpreted as "mother goddesses" or as symbols for human fertility (Fig. 11.20). Peter J. Ucko, however, has argued that no

Variable functions: "Venus" figurines

grounds exist for assuming that *all* female figurines have served the same purpose or represented similar meanings. Some, especially those portrayed as pregnant, may indeed represent fertility symbols or mother goddesses, but others might simply be children's dolls. Similarly, ochre and other red pigments have been discovered in human burials in many prehistoric cultures, the oldest one associated with Neanderthal interments of the Middle Paleolithic. The common interpretation has been that the pigment was painted on the corpse to symbolize blood or warmth and was connected with beliefs about an afterlife for the deceased. These interpretations are not illogical, but we have no way of verifying them.

One of anthropology's most fundamental tenets is that there is no single, universal way of looking at the world. People of different cultures categorize their social and natural environment differently and hold different attitudes about raising children, burying the dead, respecting elders, extracting food from their surroundings, and so on. Through symbols, some of these beliefs are expressed concretely. If archaeologists are to interpret prehistoric symbols, they must have some working model of the ancient ideology into which the symbols

Figure 11.20 These two Upper Paleolithic figurines from Lespugue, France (left) and Willendorf, Austria (right) are usually seen as symbols of female fertility. (Photo of casts of originals, courtesy of the University Museum, University of Pennsylvania.)

fit. The most reliable interpretations, of course, can be made for situations in which ethnographic or historical records describe the symbols *and* their meanings; next best are situations in which the ancient
society is related to one for which there are such descriptions. For
example, since Egyptian hieroglyphic writing has been deciphered,
our understanding of the symbolism and meaning incorporated in
such items as funerary goods, the double crown of the pharaoh or a
sphinx have become richer and more reliable. The ancient civilization
of the Indus Valley was also a literate culture, but its script has not
been deciphered. Nonetheless, the continuity between many of the
symbols of Indus civilization of about 2000 B.C. and those of later
Hinduism seems clear enough to justify at least tentative interpretations of the former through the aid of Hindu documents.

Individual artifacts, ecofacts, and features may be symbols in and
of themselves. For example, pottery vessels and/or other artifacts
might be deposited as a dedicatory cache prior to a building's construction. Or a scepter and crown may symbolize a ruler's authority
and power derived from supernatural sanctions. Symbolic use of ecofacts includes such ancient behavior as placing food offerings for the
deceased, as provisions for an afterlife. Among the categories of archaeological data most frequently subject to symbolic interpretation
are burial practices and mortuary goods. We have already noted the
symbolic use of red ochre, and in Chapter 9 we described the use of
flowers in at least one Neanderthal burial at Shanidar cave. Much attention has recently been focused on funerary practices as indices of
social organization: among the social dimensions that have been so investigated are segregation of cemetery areas by rank or class, and
reflection of wealth or occupational differences in assemblages of
mortuary goods. Chiefs are often buried in areas separate from pau-

**Symbolic army buried
with Emperor Ch'in,
China**

pers, while grave goods in individual interments are frequently a
gauge of the kinds of possessions the deceased had in life. Emperor
Ch'in of China was buried with a full inventory of retainers, including
an armed force—made of pottery, to be sure, but life-size and complete down to horse trappings and weapons. These are seen to be
symbolic representations of his retinue in life, placed with his tomb to
accompany him after death. Interestingly, Emperor Ch'in was apparently the first ruler in China to break with the tradition of sacrificing
and burying human retainers; he appears to have chosen, rather, to be
accompanied by life-size pottery figures as symbolic substitutes (Fig.
1.2).

Although we have been discussing the symbolic use of artifacts,
ecofacts, and features themselves, archaeologists also look for symbol and meaning in the decorations of artifacts and features. From the
Paleolithic paintings in Lascaux cave to the abstractions of modern
art, scholars have looked for meaning behind the human penchant for

Figure 11.21 For over 100 years, scholars have sought the meanings that Upper Paleolithic cave paintings and sculptures may have had for the people who produced them. This view shows some of the beautiful paintings of Lascaux cave in southern France. (Reproduced from *Lascaux, A Commentary*, by Alan Houghton Brodrick, 1949, by permission of Ernest Benn Ltd., London.)

decorating things. Many of the cave paintings of the Upper Paleolithic have been interpreted as symbols used in sympathetic magic, whereby depicting the images of animals acted to increase the abundance of game (Fig. 11.21). In addition, it is argued, the depiction of spears and arrows piercing the same animals assured the ancient hunters' success. Recent observers have challenged the universality of this interpretation; Peter J. Ucko and Andrée Rosenfeld have summarized the conflicting interpretations of these prehistoric paintings. Their basic argument is that the paintings are too diverse and our links with Paleolithic peoples too tenuous for us to postulate a single framework for inferring meaning from cave art. Some of these paintings were obviously inaccessible, and thus may have been used for magic and ritual; but others may have been the casual doodles of either adults or children. Other pictorial symbols, closer to documented societies in time and space, are more readily susceptible to interpretation.

The most regularized codification of symbol systems is, of course, writing (Fig. 11.22). And it is with writing that archaeologists enter the realm of historical documentation, vastly increasing the wealth of their interpretive resources. Writing systems were developed by many peoples all over the world, and not all have yet been deciphered. We have already mentioned the script of the Indus civilization. Maya hieroglyphic inscriptions are only now beginning to be "read" with any facility. The earliest writing in the Near East dates to at least 3500 B.C., and people were carving inscriptions in stone in Mesoamerica in the first millenium B.C. In both cases, the earliest records archaeologists have unearthed pertain to counting—in the Near East, to accounting records for business transactions, and in Mesoamerica, to counts of time. It is interesting in this regard to examine the recent theories of Alexander Marshack. Marshack decided to take a closer—indeed, mircroscopic—look at scratches and marks on Upper Paleolithic artifacts (Fig. 11.23). These marks had usually been ignored by previous archaeologists; in fact they were sometimes left out of drawings of the artifacts because they were thought to be distracting! But Marshack was able to detect regularity in such characteristics as angle of nicking or spatial patterning of groups of marks, and he has argued that these works might represent the beginnings of notational systems—the precursors of writing.

Origins of symbolic notation: Alexander Marshack's theory

Figure 11.22 The earliest known written records are in cuneiform (wedge-shaped) characters, on clay tablets that first appeared in southwest Asia in the fourth millenium B.C. (Courtesy of the University Museum, University of Pennsylvania.)

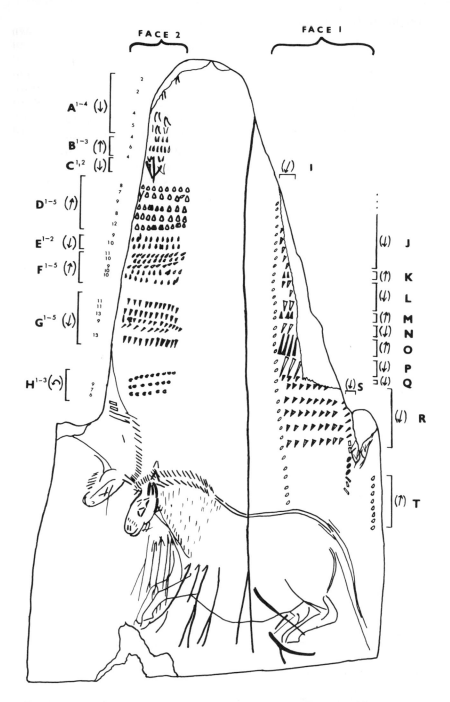

Figure 11.23 Alexander Marshack has postulated that some Upper Paleolithic engravings represent the precursors of writing. The notations on the La Marche bone, shown here, have been grouped (lettered brackets) according to differences in engraving tools and direction of engraving. (Marshack 1972, from *Science,* vol. 178, p. 822. Copyright 1972 by the American Association for the Advancement of Science.)

But writing is obviously useful for more than counting. It has been used to describe and record all aspects of human existence. Some of its other early uses were accounts of the origins of the world and of human society. The Bible and the Epic of Gilgamesh record ancient and venerated ideologies about the nature of creation. Both anthropologists and archaeologists have begun to appreciate the wealth of descriptive social data contained in such accounts, including many details of daily life and social relationships as well as attitudes toward people, animals, and deities.

SUMMARY

In this chapter we have examined various ways in which individual artifacts, ecofacts, and features may be reassembled into a whole system—that is, used to reconstruct prehistoric behavior. In previous chapters the emphasis was on individual aspects of archaeological data analysis—identification, classification, technical studies, and temporal order. But in this chapter we have turned to the ultimate goal of analysis—the reconstruction of ancient patterns of behavior.

First, we discussed technology and ancient environments. We considered these together because technology is the means by which people interact directly with the natural environment. In this regard we described both reconstruction of ancient technological capabilities and reconstruction of the nature of past environments. Then we combined these two perspectives in discussing how archaeologists reconstruct prehistoric subsistence systems.

Next, we turned to the reconstruction of social systems. There are a number of ways in which archaeologists can seek clues of ancient social organization; however, we singled out ceramic sociology, settlement archaeology, and exchange systems—all three based on the spatial patterning of archaeological data—as particularly useful approaches.

Finally, we considered the reconstruction of ideological and symbol systems. In many ways, these systems are the most difficult to interpret and the least accessible to the archaeologist. In particular, the problem in reconstructing ancient ideological behavior, or any kind of behavior, stems from the need to establish an appropriate interpretive framework. This brings us to our next section—and to a more detailed consideration of the way archaeologists establish the appropriateness of interpretations.

See p. 574 for ''Suggestions for Further Reading.''

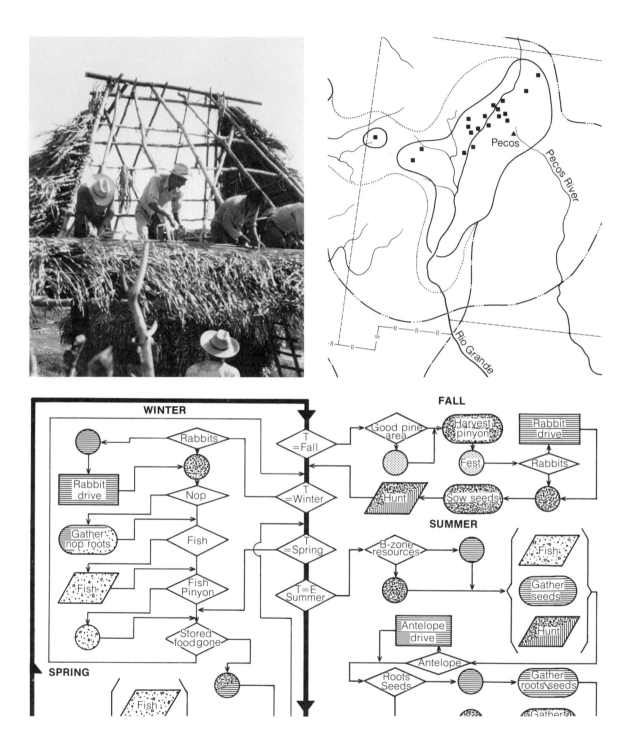

FALL

WINTER

T =Fall

Good pine area

Harvest pinyon

Rabbit drive

Rabbits

Fest

Rabbits

Rabbit drive

Nop

T =Winter

Hunt

Sow seeds

Fish

SUMMER

Gather nop roots

T =Spring

B-zone resources

Fish

Fish

Fish Pinyon

T=E Summer

Gather seeds

Stored food gone

Hunt

SPRING

Antelope drive

Antelope

Fish

Roots Seeds

Gather roots\seeds

Gather

Synthesis and Interpretation

Together, the synthesis and interpretation of archaeological data constitute the final stage in the research process. As we have seen, archaeological research begins with the formulation of a problem to be investigated. Next, the data relevant to this problem are collected and analyzed; that is, they are identified and examined as individual categories of evidence. In the past few chapters we have begun to see how these isolated data are pieced together again to provide spatial, temporal, and functional frameworks for reconstructing ancient behavior. The final chapters of this book will show how archaeological evidence is interpreted: by comparing the evidence with various models for human behavior, the archaeologist attempts to solve the problem that the research was designed to investigate: to reconstruct, describe, and explain events in the past.

Studies of contemporary human behavior provide analogies for interpreting archaeological data.

Analogy and Archaeological Interpretation

Analogy serves to provoke certain types of questions which can, on investigation, lead to the recognition of more comprehensive ranges of order in the archaeological data.

(Lewis R. Binford, "Smudge Pits and Hide Smoking: The Use of Analogy in Archaeological Reasoning," 1967)

Careful analysis . . . may lead to precise definition of significant and comparable technological elements. However, these techniques do not, by themselves, interpret prehistory. Such interpretation depends upon ethnographic analogy.

(Keith M. Anderson, "Ethnographic Analogy and Archaeological Interpretation," 1969)

In this chapter we move fully into the final step in archaeological research—the synthesis and interpretation of data. By *synthesis*, we mean the process of reassembling the data that have been isolated, described, and structured by analysis. We began turning toward synthesis in Chapters 10 and 11, when we discussed ways in which the temporal, spatial, and functional distributions of data may be established. In this chapter and those that follow, however, we shall consider how the archaeologist combines the analyses of different data categories (artifacts, ecofacts, and features) across dimensions of time, space, and function to interpret those data.

Interpretation is the meaning the archaeologist infers from analyzed and synthesized data. In its descriptive aspect, interpretation attempts to answer questions such as *what* happened in the past, *when* it happened, and *where* it happened. The explanatory aspect addresses the questions of *how* and *why* it happened.

Aspects of interpretation: James Deetz and the Arikara study

These various aspects of interpretation can be briefly illustrated by James Deetz's study of the eighteenth-century Arikara. In this case the archaeological data, once collected and analyzed, were used first to describe *what* took place in the past: changes in certain pottery styles were detected by classification methods. Specifically, the data showed an initial set of "standardized" pottery styles, or regular associations between attributes of form and decoration. This situation was followed in time by a more variable and less predictable assemblage, and then by a new "standardized" set of styles. *When* these changes took place was revealed by various methods of age determination, including such means as indirect dating by association with European trade goods of known age. *Where* the changes took place was identified by the spatial distribution of the sources of the pottery styles under study, in the middle Missouri River region of South Dakota.

Once the questions of *what, when,* and *where* had been answered, a correlation between Arikara residence patterns and mother-daughter transmission of pottery-making knowledge was used to explain *how* the changes took place. By using ethnographic data, Deetz postulated that residence in ancient Arikara families was matrilocal, with a husband coming to live in his wife's house, so that over time several generations of women would remain living in a single location. Pottery production was women's work, and a girl would learn from her mother and grandmother the proper ways of making vessels. Thus matrilocal residence would foster pottery styles that remained consistent and recognizable within a single residential area. A change in residence pattern, however, would tend to disrupt the consistency of pottery production by breaking up the women's groupings. Such a change in residential groups, Deetz argued, is exactly what accounted for the dissolution of eighteenth-century Arikara pottery styles. The reasons *why* these changes in pottery styles took place were postulated to be the factors that caused changes in residence rules, which in this case could be traced to disruptions brought about by contacts and conflicts with Europeans and other neighboring peoples— conflicts attested by documentary accounts as well as by archaeological evidence of fortifications.

In this case, the descriptive interpretation followed fairly directly from the data analysis: the artifacts were classified so as to reveal changes in time and space. The explanatory interpretation rested upon the application of analogy, which in this case could be at least partially supported by historical information. As we shall see, prehistoric archaeological interpretation is based on some kind of analogy. The rest of this chapter will be devoted to discussion of this vital interpretive tool.

ANALOGY

Because events in the prehistoric past cannot be directly observed, the archaeologist can only reconstruct them from the material evidence recovered. Such reconstruction is based on *analogy*—a form of reasoning whereby the identity of unknown items or relations may be inferred from those that are known. Reasoning by analogy is founded on the premise that if two classes of phenomena are alike in one respect, they may be alike in other respects as well. In archaeology, analogy is used to infer the identity of and relationships among archaeological data on the basis of comparison with similar phenomena documented in living human societies.

This is not to say that analogy underlies all archaeological reconstruction. Historical archaeology can often rely on documentary sources to identify archaeological remains. In protohistorical situations, later historical information is sometimes projected back in

Figure 12.1 Manufacture of chipped-stone tools in Ethiopia. Lithic technology survives today in several parts of the world, providing analogs for understanding similar technologies in the past. (Photo by James P. Gallagher.)

Analogy in interpretation: Binford's hide pits

time to assist archaeological reconstructions. Deetz's Arikara study is an example of this method (an application of the direct historical approach discussed in Chapter 2). But in clear-cut prehistoric situations, without direct links to historical information, the archaeologist must rely upon inferences based on analogy.

On the most basic level, it is analogy that allows the archaeologist to identify the remains of past human behavior as archaeological data. For example, the archaeologist does not observe the ancient human activity that produced an Acheulian hand-axe, a Paleolithic stone tool produced in Europe thousands of years ago. Hunters and gatherers in several remote parts of the world continue to make and use similar chipped-stone axes. The behavior associated with the manufacture and use of these tools has been recorded by ethnographers and other observers. Because of the similarity in form between the Paleolithic artifacts and the ethnographically observed examples, analogy has identified the Paleolithic hand-axes as ancient tools and, by extension, has allowed reconstruction of relevant manufacturing and use behavior associated with the ancient tools (Fig. 12.1).

Artifacts are not the only materials that are identified by use of analogy. Archaeological features, too, are recognized as the products of human behavior by use of such reasoning. In many cases, the archaeologist's use of analogy to identify a feature such as a building foundation or a burial is not a conscious process. This is because these features are so familiar that not even the professional archaeologist pauses to reflect that analogy is involved in recognizing a line of masonry as a building foundation. An automatic association takes place from everyday experience, where masonry foundations support modern buildings, to the archaeological feature; this process makes the identification. But often the archaeologist will encounter a feature or an artifact that is not familiar; it is in such cases that identification by analogy becomes most clearly a conscious, rational process.

A good example of detailed analogical reasoning is Lewis Binford's study of a certain category of pits encountered in sites of the middle and lower Mississippi River Valley and adjacent areas after A.D. 1000. The pits in question are always fairly small, averaging about 30 cm or less in length and width and slightly more than that in depth. They contain charred and carbonized twigs, bark, and corncobs, and they are found around houses and domestic storage areas, never near public buildings. The one sure interpretation concerning the nature of these pits was that the charred contents had been burned in place, in an oxygen-starved atmosphere that must have produced a lot of smoke. So the pits were labeled "smudge pits." Further interpretations offered for these features, however, included corncob "caches" or facilities for creating smoke to drive away mosquitoes!

In seeking a firmer interpretive base from which to establish the nature of these smudge pits, Binford went through the ethnographic literature on modern native American groups in that area. These accounts included descriptions of hide-smoking procedures in which an untanned deerskin was tied as a cover over a small hole. A smoldering, smoky fire was then set in the hole and allowed to burn until the hide was dried and toughened, ready to be sewn into clothing. Binford pointed out that whenever the ethnographic accounts offered details on the form and contents of the hide-smoking pits, these details corresponded well with equivalent attributes of the archaeological smudge-pits. Because there was a high degree of correspondence in *form* between ethnographic and archaeological examples, because the *geographical* areas involved were the same, and because a good case could be argued for the *continuity* of practices in that area from the archaeological past (after A.D. 1000) to the time of ethnographic observations (1700–1950), Binford argued—by analogy—that the archaeological smudge pits represented facilities for smoking animal skins.

More precisely, Binford offered the analogical interpretation as a hypothesis to be tested: if this identification is correct, other ethnographically described correlates of hide-smoking activities should also be found associated with the archaeological smudge pits. For example, since the ethnographic accounts describe tanning activities as occurring between, rather than during, peak hunting seasons, the sites with this kind of smudge-pits should be spring-summer camps, not hunting camps. The more correspondences that are found between the ethnographic and the archaeological data, and the more strictly the specific attributes identified refer to a *particular* kind of feature—in this case, hide-smoking pits rather than any other kind of smudging pits—the stronger the analogical interpretation.

The Use and Abuse of Analogy

How is analogy applied in interpreting archaeological data? This question is of crucial significance, since analogy has not always been used correctly, and since its improper use has led to erroneous reconstructions of the past. The smudge-pits example given above illustrates a proper use of analogy. But before examining in more detail the ways analogy *should* be used, we should first understand some of the errors that have resulted from its improper use in interpretation.

In the nineteenth century, when (as we saw in Chapter 2) anthropology was dominated by the theory of unilinear cultural evolution, living "primitive" societies were often equated directly with various postulated stages of the proposed evolutionary sequence (Fig. 12.2).

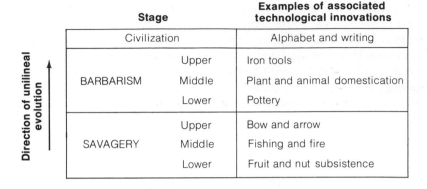

	Stage		Examples of associated technological innovations
Civilization			Alphabet and writing
BARBARISM		Upper	Iron tools
		Middle	Plant and animal domestication
		Lower	Pottery
SAVAGERY		Upper	Bow and arrow
		Middle	Fishing and fire
		Lower	Fruit and nut subsistence

Figure 12.2 Morgan's unilinear stages were used to equate past and present societies on a scale of evolutionary progress.

These stages were defined by technological attributes (Stone Age, Iron Age, and so on), and each stage had its own corresponding developmental level of social system, political organization, and religious beliefs. By means of these combined technological, social, and ideological attributes, living societies could be ranked as to their progress along the evolutionary scale.

Since technological attributes were weighted so heavily in this classification scheme, it was often relatively easy to link evidence of prehistoric technology gained from the archaeological record with the traits used to define the various evolutionary stages. Given their assumption that cultures everywhere had followed the same single course of development, the unilinearists found it easy to assign "appropriate" social and ideological traits to a particular prehistoric culture whose technological level was known. Living societies whose technology was similar to that inferred from archaeological evidence for a past culture were used as exact analogs for the reconstruction of the entire prehistoric culture. For instance, living societies still using stone-tool technologies, such as the Australian Aborigines, were used as analogs to reconstruct Paleolithic hunting societies that lived in Europe tens of thousands of years before. Technology simply provided a convenient, nonperishable link between the "known" world of today and the "unknown" of the prehistoric past.

It should be obvious that this kind of analogy is suspect, since it is founded upon only one criterion—technology—and ignores other variables such as time and space. In linking the Australian Aborigines with the European Paleolithic, for instance, the analogy disregards a temporal separation of more than 10,000 years and a spatial separation of over 10,000 miles. In a 1966 conference, 75 scholars spent four days discussing and debating the nature of cultures and societies that shared a single stated trait—hunting and gathering as the means of subsistence. The published report of that conference, a volume called *Man the Hunter,* makes it clear that although some regularities as social structure and cultural organization can certainly be recognized, one cannot use the single trait of "hunting" to predict the forms the rest of the culture will take. Yet this is essentially what the nineteenth-century unilinear evolutionists attempted to do.

Because of such simplistic reliance on limited criteria, usually technology, the wide-ranging analogies associated with the nineteenth-century unilinear cultural evolutionists are generally not accepted today. However, simplistic analogies are not confined to the literature of the nineteenth century; similar careless equations between living cultures and those of the past may be found in some archaeological publications of the twentieth century. And the general analogy between the hunters of the European Paleolithic and certain contemporary peoples still occurs—most recently in popular accounts of the discovery of the Tasaday tribe in the Philippines, which described this isolated society as a "stone-age tribe."

The obvious abuses of analogy in reconstructing the past have led to reactions, both by cultural anthropologists and by archaeologists, against the use of this method of reasoning. Much of the criticism of analogy has been concerned specifically with the use of ethnographic studies as analogs for archaeological interpretation. However, as we shall see below, the use of analogy in archaeology involves a wider range of analog sources, including historical accounts and modern experimental techniques. But we should examine this criticism of ethnographic analogy, since ethnography is perhaps the most common source of analogs for archaeological interpretation.

The most extreme critics of the use of analogy would completely eliminate ethnographic analogs as sources for the reconstruction of the past. The basis for their position is that all cultures are unique, and therefore no assurance is possible that any single trait from one society is equivalent to that from another society. Thus, according to this argument, the fact that small triangular chipped stones are used as projectile points in one culture does not mean that similar artifacts have the same function in another. Alternatively, it is argued, these artifacts might be used as articles of adornment, counters in a game, or even ritual symbols. As a result, the identification of an artifact or feature in an ethnographically observed culture cannot be used to identify any similar artifact or feature found archaeologically.

If archaeologists were to accept this position, they would not be able to interpret their data or reconstruct the events of the past. The archaeologist would merely collect and describe artifacts and features, without identifying how they were made or what they were used for. More importantly, the data could not be synthesized to reconstruct the past. Fortunately, this extreme argument against any use of analogy rests upon a false premise—that all cultures are completely unique. It is true that any given cultural trait, such as the projectile point mentioned above, may have many uses, and these uses may vary from society to society. However, to accept the position that the traits of one culture are *in no way* comparable to another is to deny the patterned regularities of human behavior described by countless ethnographers, historians, and other observers. Archaeologists can validly identify certain small triangular chipped stone artifacts as projectile points, because this identification is based on myriad cases of observed human behavior associated with objects possessing the same or similar characteristics. Furthermore, this identification is reinforced by archaeological evidence found in primary context—for instance, the discovery of such artifacts associated with the bones of game animals. This is not to say that the use of analogy in archaeological interpretation is not without the potential for error. But rather than rejecting analogy as a method, the archaeologist can minimize the error factor by following certain guidelines in the use of analogy.

Guidelines for Analogy

Some very general analogies—such as the identification of human bones in a pit as a human burial—require little defense. But for more detailed interpretations, the archaeologist must be prepared to defend the appropriateness of a given analog on three grounds: cultural continuity, comparability in environment, and similarity of cultural form. In the smudge-pits example described above, Binford was able to control all these factors in his analogy. We shall now examine each of these dimensions in more detail.

In the first place, the degree of cultural continuity between the prehistoric society and the society being used as an analog is an important and obvious factor. In most cases, the greater the degree of cultural continuity, the more reliable the analogy will be. In the southwestern United States, for instance, there is considerable evidence that the contemporary native American societies documented by ethnographic and historical accounts are the direct descendents, both culturally and biologically, of local prehistoric (pre-sixteenth century) occupants (Fig. 12.3). This link allows the archaeologist to draw frequent and reasonable analogies on the basis of living societies in order to interpret Southwestern prehistory. Studies by James Hill and William Longacre which, like Deetz's Arikara study, examine ceramic data as a reflection of prehistoric social organization, rely on this continuity of Southwestern occupation to support their analogical reconstructions of pottery production and residential patterns.

Figure 12.3   Cultural continuity, such as in the southwestern United States, is an important criterion for using ethnographic studies as analogs for understanding ancient societies. The photographs above were taken around the turn of the century and show (a) an overall view of Oraibi Pueblo, Arizona, and (b) a room with equipment for preparing meals. Compare (b) with the mealing bins in Fig. 9.27. (Courtesy, Field Museum of Natural History, Chicago.)

In the New World, such situations with maximum continuity fostered development of the *direct historical approach,* a method of reconstructing prehistoric societies by progressive extension of analogies back through time. This method, described in Chapter 2, first involves identification of sites occupied by documented groups: this step establishes the crucial link between prehistoric past and documented "present." Then earlier sites—either underlying the contact-period site or situated close to it—are located and examined. If similarity of material remains continue to be evident through the series of increasingly earlier settlements, then continuity of other aspects of culture is also posited. We will discuss the direct historical approach in more detail in Chapter 13 when we consider cultural historical reconstruction.

Consider, as a contrast, the degree of cultural continuity between contemporary English society and that of England's prehistoric past. The issue is not simply that the historic period is five times as long in England as in the southwestern United States, but during that history the known changes and upheavals in the local way of life make it difficult to justify analogies between contemporary industrialized society and Britain's *pre*historic past. On the other hand, analogs for prehistoric England *are* provided by historical documents that reduce the temporal separation between the present and the prehistoric past. The use of 2000-year-old Roman historical sources has been of great benefit in interpreting the archaeological evidence from Celtic sites of Iron Age England. A classic study in this regard is Sir Mortimer Wheeler's reconstruction of events at Maiden Castle, a first-century A.D. Celtic fortified settlement besieged and captured by an invading Roman army (Fig. 12.4). An account of the Roman conquest provided Wheeler with the means not only to interpret the archaeological evidence of the military action, but also to reconstruct aspects of daily life in Celtic England.

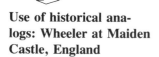

Use of historical analogs: Wheeler at Maiden Castle, England

But as the time span between the analog and the archaeological data increases, the chances for other variables to distort the reconstruction also increase. The Roman historical sources just mentioned have also been used in attempts to interpret aspects of the more distant past in England. However, conditions in Celtic England at the time of the Roman invasion may not be a reliable gauge of conditions several thousand years earlier. For instance, the popular (and erroneous) belief that Stonehenge was a center of druid worship is based on Roman accounts of Celtic religion, yet Stonehenge was built and used more than a thousand years before the Roman conquest.

Successful analogs also depend upon the control of another important variable, comparability of environment. The relationship between environment and culture was discussed in Chapter 11, but here we note that an analog drawn from a society living in an environment

Figure 12.4 Historic accounts complemented information from archaeological excavations to reconstruct ancient life and events at Maiden Castle, Dorset. Although protected by earthen fortifications, the settlement was stormed and sacked by Roman troops under Vespasian in about A.D. 47. (Ashmolean Museum, Oxford.)

different from that of the prehistoric society will be less reliable than one based on a society in a similar environment. It would obviously be difficult to maintain that Eskimo culture, which is adapted to an arctic environment, could be used to reconstruct Paleolithic societies in temperate Europe. Yet this was attempted during the heyday of the unilinear cultural evolutionists, on the basis of technological ("Stone-Age") criteria. A more valid application of analogy would be to use *aspects* of the Eskimo adaptation to the arctic environment in reconstructing prehistoric life along the northern coasts of Europe during the close of the last glacial period, when this area did possess an arctic environment. If we make the assumption that a given culture is adapted to its natural and social surroundings, then similar conditions of relative abundance or deficiency in natural resources—water, good soils, game animals, and so forth—will provide similar social opportunities and limitations. For example, desert-dwelling societies are generally best used as analogs for prehistoric communities that lived in arid environments, where the water supply is a constant and central concern. Likewise, groups living in tropical climates provide models for ancient societies in similar settings: archaeologists studying the Maya, whose civilization flourished in the tropics of Guatemala and adjacent areas in the first millennium A.D., have sought analogs in areas with like tropical settings, from modern Central America to West Africa and Southeast Asia.

Of course, the technological variable remains important too, despite its abuse in the nineteenth century. As we have pointed out before, the relationship between technology and environment is a fluid one. For example, similar environments encourage some similarities in technology: areas having fish as the primary food resource will foster development of fishing gear—hooks, spears, fishing boats, and so on. But technological changes can redefine environments. In Chapter 2, we cited the case of the Great Plains of the United States, where the European introduction of the horse as a means of transport increased the mobility and hunting range of the native American people in the area, effectively redefining the food resources available to them. The same innovation also affected their social organization—by increasing mobility—and the capacity to wage war on neighboring groups.

All of these factors enter into a final consideration, the question of cultural comparability. This factor includes a series of variables—some defined more objectively, others quite subjectively. The first criterion to consider is relative cultural complexity. To be successful, an analogy should involve a society that possesses the same degree of overall complexity as that indicated for the prehistoric situation. Cultural complexity is usually defined on the basis of the contemporary multilinear evolutionary scheme, discussed in Chapters 2 and 14. Thus, for example, the interpretation of data from prehistoric tribal societies should be based upon analogs drawn from documented tribal societies, rather than from examples that possess a greater or lesser degree of complexity. Other criteria of comparability should be considered also. For instance, some societies tend to resist change and to place a high value on preserving traditional ways. As a general rule, analogies based on such tradition-bound societies tend to be more useful in archaeology than those involving societies that have experienced rapid and drastic changes. For example, in Southeast Asia, conservative highland tribal groups provide more likely analogs for local prehistoric reconstructions than their urbanized neighbors in Bangkok. In a related way, some societies tend to isolate themselves from outside influences, whereas others are open and receptive to external influences. It is often preferable to choose analogs from societies that tend to be closed to external influences, since distortion due to change is less likely.

As long as the archaeologist is aware of these variables—cultural continuity, similarity of environment, and cultural comparability—and can isolate and control them in using analogy to deal with the prehistoric data, the resulting interpretation will be not only more complete but more accurate as well.

Sources for Analogs

The analogies used in archaeological interpretation come from three kinds of sources: historical accounts and documents that describe societies in the past, ethnographic studies that describe present-day societies, and experimental studies that attempt to duplicate conditions that existed in the past.

Historical sources include the full range of past records, including studies written by professional historians, and descriptions made by other observers such as travelers, merchants, soldiers, or missionaries. Since these sources have diverse origins and are usually not the product of trained anthropological perspective, the data they provide must be carefully assessed, and biased or inaccurate information tempered or disregarded. But with proper evaluation, historical data can be a prime source for analogs useful in the interpretation of archaeological data. We have already mentioned Wheeler's study of Maiden Castle based on Roman historical sources. In the New World, much of our understanding of the pre-Columbian cultures of Mesoamerica and the Andes rests upon documents from the Spanish Conquest in the sixteenth century (Fig. 12.5). Many of these were written by soldiers, missionaries, and administrators from Spain; they include accounts by such men as Fray Bernardino de Sahagún, Bernal Diaz del Castillo, and Hernando Cortés himself. Others were written by native chroniclers, trained by the Spanish to translate and record aspects of their vanishing way of life.

The use of historical sources may enable the archaeologist to identify *contact sites*—sites occupied by a prehistoric people at the time contact was made with a people possessing a historical tradition. Examples include Maiden Castle, England, documented in the Roman histories, and Cuzco, Peru, recorded in the Spanish Conquest accounts (Fig. 12.6). Contact sites such as these provide the archaeologist with a starting point for interpretation using the direct historical approach.

Ethnographic studies of living human societies are probably the most common source of archaeological analogs. Since they are written by professional anthropologists, ethnographies are generally more relevant and useful to the archaeologist than other sources. However, the overall quality of ethnographic accounts varies considerably.

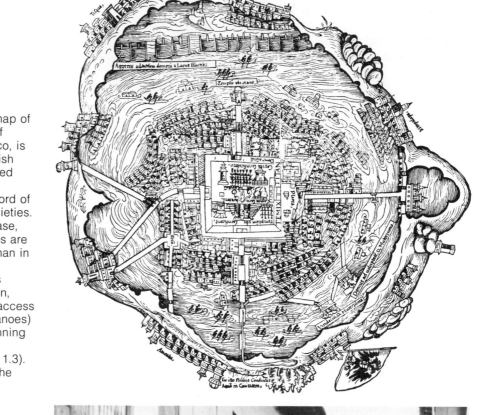

Figure 12.5 This sixteenth-century map of the Aztec capital of Tenochtitlán, Mexico, is illustrative of Spanish records that are used to complement the archaeological record of pre-Columbian societies. Although, in this case, spatial relationships are shown differently than in modern maps, the document provides valuable information, such as means of access (causeways and canoes) to the city and planning of its central plaza (compare with Fig. 1.3). (By permission of the British Library.)

Figure 12.6 Contact sites, such as Cuzco, Peru, offer a direct link between history and the prehistoric past. This photograph shows the incorporation of prehistoric buildings in modern structures along a street in Cuzco. (Courtesy of the University Museum, University of Pennsylvania.)

Usually there is some information of use to archaeologists, but since ethnographers pursue their studies for their own theoretical interests, the data are often not presented in ways that relate behavior to material remains—that is, in ways that facilitate archaeological analogy. Binford was able to find descriptive accounts that related hide-smoking behavior to smudge-pit features. But as Richard Gould points out in summarizing the ethnographic resources for the Australian Aborigines, the elaborateness of the kinship and ceremonial side of aboriginal life has so impressed most observers that, until recently, ethnographic descriptions of the Aborigines have focused on these particular aspects of culture, seldom relating them clearly to settlement patterns, subsistence behavior, and associated material remains.

Similar situations, in which ethnographic data cannot be related directly to the archaeological remains, are common enough that archaeologists are increasingly becoming trained to participate actively in ethnographic studies. Of particular concern in such projects are clear statements of relationships between those aspects of culture that are likely to be archaeologically preserved (durable material remains) and behavioral systems that are likely to be archaeologically "invisible." These studies, described by the terms *ethnoarchaeology, archaeological ethnography,* and *action archaeology,* have a variety of specific orientations. Many human ecological studies fall, at least in part, within this category. The studies by scholars such as Richard Lee and John Yellen of the !Kung Bushmen of Southwest Africa are oriented toward understanding the interrelationships among population size, social structure, subsistence system, and environment. Other research is more specific, such as Binford's examination of correlation between artifact variation and division into different social groups among Alaskan Eskimos, or Robert Wauchope's study of the construction and use of Maya houses.

A primary focus of ethnoarchaeological attention is the way material items enter the archaeological record: What gets thrown away, how often, and why? Nicholas David has presented detailed data on Fulani compounds in West Africa, including information on the average life expectancy of various types of pottery vessels. His figures indicate, for example, that vessel types that suffer more frequent breakage—and must more often be replaced—will be over-represented in any archaeological assemblage, relative to their numbers in a Fulani household during use. If specific forms reflect specific functions, then, this finding serves as a caution for direct analogical reconstruction: the *range* of pottery (and, indirectly, its uses) may be accurately recovered archaeologically, but archaeological frequency of form types should not be taken as a direct index of the relative emphasis placed on various activities (cooking, storage, or whatever).

Ethnoarchaeology: Nicholas David's study of Fulani pottery use

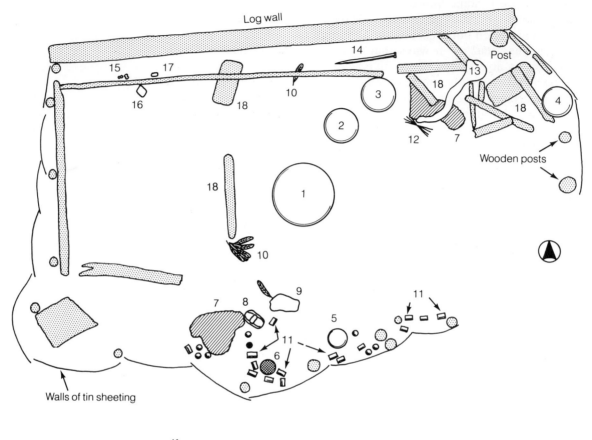

Key:

1	Wash tub over hearth	10	Turkey feathers
2	Wash basin	11	Tin cans
3	Enameled pail	12	Twigs
4	Milk can lid	13	Plastic sheeting
5	Tin can pail	14	Iron spike
6	Can of nails	15	Vertebrae
7	Burlap	16	Wallet
8	Grinding stones	17	Rawhide
9	Bread wrapper	18	Boards

Figure 12.7 Investigation of recently abandoned sites, such as this modern Apache *wickiup*, allows the archaeologist to test interpretation of the physical remains by interviewing informants who can describe the actual behavior associated with material remains. (After Longacre and Ayres 1968.)

Other studies treat occupied or recently abandoned settlements as archaeological sites, comparing what would be preserved archaeologically with what is present ethnographically. David's Fulani work includes this kind of consideration, as does Karl Heider's description of New Guinea settlements. A well-known example of "checking" archaeological observations and interpretations against ethnographic information is a study done by William Longacre and James Ayres. Taking a recently abandoned Apache *wickiup* (a small domestic structure) as an archaeological site, they recorded the visible artifacts, ecofacts, and features and their spatial relationships (Fig. 12.7). Then, using an Apache ethnographic analogy, they interpreted the material data as indicating the residence of a nuclear family—husband, wife, and unmarried children—in which there was a sexual division of labor, with female-associated activities predominating. The associations of distinct artifact and feature assemblages in different locations were also interpreted by analogy with modern Apache use of such assemblages: the *wickiup* structure itself had been a storage and food preparation facility, perhaps also serving as sleeping quarters during bad weather. Some cooking had also taken place outdoors, as attested by the hearths near the *wickiup*. After making these interpretations, Longacre and Ayres consulted a local Apache resident who was a friend of the former occupants, and thus were able to confirm the majority of their archaeological interpretations. Although the research was reported in order to give evidence for the behavioral structure reflected in spatial associations of archaeological data, it also serves as a reminder of the kinds of ethnographic observations that must be made—relating particular activities to the associated material remains—if ethnographic studies are to be maximally useful to archaeologists.

Several investigations have involved observation of "midden production," especially the accumulation and relative preservation of animal remains. Motivated at least in part by the controversy surrounding the bone assemblage from Makapansgat cave, discussed in Chapter 9, these studies have sought to determine the kinds of food-animal bones that wind up in and are preserved in trash deposits. At issue in the Makapansgat case is whether the array of non-human bones found in the cave represents elements selected by hominids for use as tools, or simply an accumulation of a carnivore's food refuse. As we noted in Chapter 9, Raymond Dart has argued that the set of elements found reflect deliberate hominid selection; using as illustrations some pieces whose original form had clearly been altered, he posited that the bones are the remains of an osteodontokeratic (bone-tooth-horn) toolmaking tradition. Many have

Ethnoarchaeology: Longacre and Ayres' Apache wickiup

Ethnoarchaeology: The Makapansgat controversy

taken issue with this position, arguing that Dart did not have the appropriate comparative base—the specific analogs from modern carnivore lairs and/or from modern cultural middens—to make his interpretation. Among the observational studies that have been done in response is Brain's study in Southwest Africa of what elements of goat bone survive in modern Hottentot middens after the goats are eaten by the local people and the bones have been exposed to scavenging dogs. More recently, Lewis Binford has studied "survivorship" of various sheep bone elements in Eskimo and Navajo camps of North America. The results of these studies have tended to contradict Dart's arguments, indicating instead that the Makapansgat assemblage could well be the remains of ancient food debris, in which the "selection" of parts preserved is a result of natural transformation processes.

The final source of archeological analogy is *experimental studies*. Although these have a long history in archaeology, only recently have they begun to reach their full potential as a fundamental source of interpretive analogy. Early experiments often involved using actual archaeological materials, such as cutting tools and musical instruments, in an attempt to discover their ancient functions. Such experiments continue, but in many cases experimental archaeology has been redefined, with the goal of providing analogs for a broader range of behavior—manufacture, use, and deposition—associated with archaeological materials.

Figure 12.8 Experimental knapping of chipped stone tools (here, direct percussion on flint using a hammer stone) provides analogs for the reconstruction of ancient manufacturing behavior.

Experimental work with stone artifacts is particularly well known. Don Crabtree and François Bordes have been leaders in reconstructing the techniques used to manufacture ancient stone tools, by experimental stone chipping or "knapping" designed to duplicate the archaeologically recovered forms (Fig. 12.8). S. A. Semenov has pioneered in studying the wear patterns produced on stone tools by various kinds of use (slicing, chopping, and so on). Some studies examine the relative efficiency of different technological systems, indicating how much time and effort each one requires to accomplish the same task; an example would be the experiments by Stephen Saraydar and Izumi Shimada comparing steel and stone tools for felling trees and planting crops. Similarly, archaeologists have fired pottery, smelted copper, caught fish, and done many other things in order to provide experimental analogs for interpreting past behavior associated with ancient artifacts.

Features, too, have been studied by experiment. For example, imposing structures such as the Egyptian pyramids or Stonehenge have inspired projects aimed at calculating the labor force needed for their construction. A famous Danish experiment at Roskilde reconstructed an Iron Age house, which was then burned and excavated. And at Overton Down, England, an earthwork has been built that duplicates prehistoric constructions (Fig. 12.9). While the building was in progress, the Overton Down project also enabled investigators to compare ancient and modern tool efficiency; ancient tools such as antler

Experimental archaeology: Production and use of artifacts

Experimental archaeology: Production and use of ancient features

Figure 12.9 The experimental earthwork at Overton Down, Wiltshire, was created to supply information on behavioral as well as transformational processes involved in the formation of similar archaeological features in England. (By permission of the British Association for the Advancement of Science.)

and bone pick and shovels were found to be nearly as productive as their modern counterparts. And a number of presumed storage features, from earthen pits in England to *chultun* chambers hollowed out of the limestone bedrock of northern Guatemala, have been filled with grain, water, and other such supplies to see how well they actually served their postulated function.

Possible environmental constraints on ancient cultures have been examined in a number of ways. For instance, experimental attempts to duplicate ancient agricultural practices have been made in a number of areas, from the Yucatan peninsula to the Negev desert of Israel. Energy spent in preparing, planting, and maintaining agricultural plots can be compared with final food yield, sometimes over a series of planting-harvesting cycles, to arrive at a more precise idea of how large a population a given area could have supported under that agricultural system. The influence of the sea on settlement of the Polynesian islands of the Pacific has also been examined experimentally. Best known is Thor Heyerdahl's dramatic trip aboard the raft *Kon-Tiki,* sailing westward to Polynesia from South America. More recently, Ben R. Finney has sailed in both directions between Hawaii and Tahiti—a distance of more than 5000 km each way—in reconstructed duplicates of traditional Polynesian canoes. Heyerdahl's voyages indicate that occasional ancient contacts between South America and the Pacific Islands were at least possible. Finney's more focused experiments, on the other hand, were aimed at discovering to what extent traditional craft could sail *into,* as well as *with,* the wind; the success of his canoes at doing both implies, by analogy, that prehistoric communication among people on the far-flung islands of Oceania was at least partly under human control, and not due solely to drifting canoes, sailing wherever the seas and the winds would take them.

The most elaborate experimental studies—and the least often manageable—involve reconstruction and maintenance of a community under ancient conditions. Archaeologists dealing with recent, historically documented periods are in a better position to do experiments of this kind. Plimouth Plantation in Massachusetts and Colonial Pennsylvania Plantation in eastern Pennsylvania are examples of "reconstituted" colonial American communities (Fig. 12.10); in these projects, crops have been raised, food cooked, buildings heated, and tools produced, all according to colonial customs. The experience provided by these cases is comparable to that of archaeological ethnography, for the archaeologist has the opportunity to observe and record the behavior associated with the material "remains." Granted, these reconstructed communities are somewhat more artificial than the communities studied by the ethnographer. But by putting the material remains back into a working social system, they do provide in-

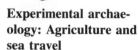

Experimental archaeology: Agriculture and sea travel

Experimental archaeology: Community living

Figure 12.10 The Colonial Pennsylvania Plantation is an example of experimental archaeology where past conditions and behavior are recreated to understand more fully what life was like in the past. (Courtesy of the Colonial Pennsylvania Plantation, Edgmont, Pa.)

sights and interpretive analogs not available from documents or other sources alone.

A last category of experimental archaeology involves study of what happens to archaeological materials upon deposition. These experiments consider the transformation processes discussed in Chapter 3. Although these processes do not always involve human behavior, they are relevant to the interpretation of human behavior. For example, Glynn Isaac and his colleagues have sought to outline details that will help in distinguishing whether stone-tool scatters in riverbank locations are intact sites or just the cumulative effects of artifacts being washed downstream from their original deposition points. To accomplish this, they set out a series of systematically arranged artifact scatters in the valley of a stream feeding into Lake Magadi, Kenya; then returned annually to chart the artifact positions in these experimental analogs. Archaeologists have also made controlled observations of various kinds of preservation and destruction, including burning experimental houses of various materials (sometimes by accident!), burial of hair under different soil conditions, and exposure of bones to weather and scavengers. Some of Binford's work on bone preservation, cited earlier, fits here, for it has crossed the line from ''detached'' ethnographic observation to the deliberately arranged and controlled situation of an experiment. The Overton Down earthwork construction can also be noted again here: during the construction, a series of organic and inorganic remains were incorporated in the earthwork. Sample excavations are scheduled to take place at predetermined intervals over the next century, in order to see how the processes of transformation have affected the preservation and recovery of archaeological data.

Experimental archaeology: Lake Magadi, Kenya

SUMMARY

Analogy provides the foundation for archaeological interpretation. Because past behavior can no longer be directly observed, the archaeologist must rely on analogy to interpret the behavioral significance of recovered material data. Reasoning by analogy has not always been correctly applied in archaeological situations, but one can follow a number of guidelines to keep its use within proper bounds. One must consider continuity of occupation, similarity of setting, and comparability of cultural forms between the archaeological situation and its proposed analog. The more links one can establish between the two situations in these respects, the stronger will be the case for using the analog to interpret the archaeological remains. Finally, we have examined and illustrated the three kinds of sources for archaeological analogs: historical documents, ethnographic observations, and archaeological experiments.

Analogy is the basis for both description and explanation of the past. The distinction between descriptive and explanatory interpretation is generally reflected in the distinction between *culture history* and *culture process.* The description of the *what, when,* and *where* of the past comprise the reconstruction of culture history, and the explanation of the *how* and *why* of the past delineate culture process.

In the development of archaeology as a scientific discipline, these two aspects of interpretation have taken on separate identities. However, both kinds of interpretation seek an understanding of culture process; that is, they seek to reveal the underlying causes of change within culture. Interpretation focusing on the reconstruction of culture history sees the understanding of process as a distant, ultimate goal, while interpretation based on culture process sees the understanding of process as the central, immediate goal of research. There are, of course, other differences, which will be explored in the next chapters; but we should consider the general distinctions before continuing.

The reconstruction of *culture history* is usually based on an inductive methodology. Thus the emphasis is upon the collection of sufficient archaeological data that can be classified and analyzed to derive broad generalizations that describe culture change in both time and space. Cultural historical interpretations usually assume a "normative" view of culture (see Chapter 2) and therefore rely on descriptive models involving general concepts such as trade, diffusion, and migration in their descriptions of culture change.

On the other hand, *cultural processual* interpretation is associated with a deductive methodology in which specific propositions are tested against archaeological data to delineate and attempt to explain the process of culture change. This approach usually assumes an "evolutionary" view of culture (see Chapter 2) and relies on specific concepts such as ecological adaptation, population dynamics, and systems theory to identify the causes and explain the processes of culture change.

With this introduction to archaeological interpretation, we shall now turn to detailed consideration of the final synthesis and interpretation of archaeological research, through the approaches of culture history and culture process.

See p. 575 for ''Suggestions for Further Reading.''

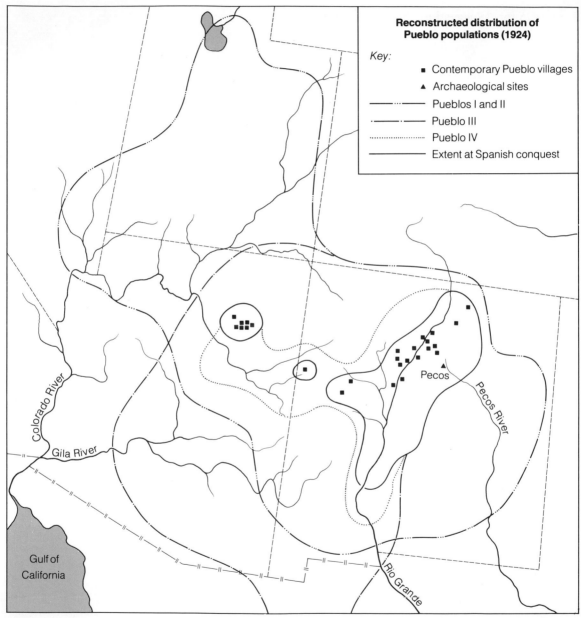

Reconstructed distribution of Pueblo populations (1924)

Key:

■ Contemporary Pueblo villages
▲ Archaeological sites
—··—·· Pueblos I and II
—·—·— Pueblo III
············ Pueblo IV
———— Extent at Spanish conquest

Colorado River

Gila River

Gulf of California

Pecos

Pecos River

Rio Grande

Map of the American Southwest showing distribution of prehistoric Pueblo culture through time as defined by the Cultural Historical approach to interpretation.

The Cultural Historical Approach

When the long task is finished . . . we must use our results for the solution of those general problems of anthropological science without . . . which we can never hope to arrive at valid conclusions as to the history of mankind as a whole.

> (A. V. Kidder, An Introduction to the
> Study of Southwestern Archaeology,
> *1924*)

Any attempt on the part of the archaeologist to contribute to the larger problems of cultural understanding was met with an astonishment like that in the classic case of the "talking dog"; it was not what the dog said that was so amazing but the fact that he could do it at all.

> (Gordon Willey and Jeremy Sabloff, A
> History of American Archaeology, *1974*)

In this chapter we will consider the first of two ways by which archaeologists synthesize and interpret their data: *cultural historical reconstruction*. Cultural historical interpretation is based on an inductive research methodology and a normative view of culture. Within these frameworks, the cultural historical approach emphasizes synthesis based upon chronological and spatial ordering of archaeological data. Thus the synthesis, from this perspective, is directed toward outlining the sequence and geographical distribution of past events. Once this is done, interpretation proceeds through use of either specific or general analogs as the basis for application of descriptive models, usually drawn from ethnography and history. The culmination of the interpretive process is a chronicle of events and general trends of cultural change and continuity in the prehistoric past.

ORIGINS OF CULTURAL HISTORICAL RECONSTRUCTION

Before we discuss either the research strategy or resulting syntheses associated with cultural historical reconstruction, we should briefly review the origin and development of the entire approach within the field of archaeology. A more thorough background discussion was given in Chapter 2.

Both the use of an overall inductive research methodology and reliance upon a normative view of culture are firmly rooted in the American school of anthropology founded by Franz Boas and his students at the beginning of the twentieth century. Boasian anthropology, often called "historical empiricism" or "historical particularism," was in part a reaction against the accumulated abuses of nineteenth-century cultural evolutionary theory. Unilinear evolutionary anthropology had used a generalized deductive research approach, in that it was oriented toward gathering data to support and refine the theory of unilinear cultural evolution. A critical flaw in the approach, however, was the lack of opportunity to actually test the model, to allow for its possible refutation. Reacting to this approach, Boas and his followers adopted a fundamentally inductive research methodology. Descriptive data were to be gathered first; models of change and continuity and specific problems for interpretation were not to be formulated until the data base was sufficient for such purposes.

Prehistoric archaeology in America, emerging at this time as part of the Boasian school of anthropology, inherited the inductive philosophy of its parent discipline. Thus the cultural historical approach to archaeological synthesis and interpretation is largely an American phenomenon. Although philosophically a product of the theoretical conditions prevailing within anthropology in the United States at the turn of the century, the cultural historical approach was also conditioned by the unique circumstances under which prehistoric archaeologists worked in the New World. Particularly important was the lack of historical records for periods before the sixteenth-century European conquest, a situation that contrasts markedly with the long historical tradition available in much of the Old World. There simply was no established framework into which to fit pre-Columbian archaeological data. Since archaeologists of the early twentieth century were unwilling to accept the model used in the Old World, they set out to collect the "hard data" from which they could reconstruct the events of American prehistory.

The cultural historical approach was forged by many individual scholars, using data collected in hundreds of separate archaeological investigations; as a result it is impossible even to mention most of these in our brief review. Several works on this subject are readily available for the student who wishes more detailed information. For present purposes, however, we can concentrate on the career of one American archaeologist who, more than any other individual, pioneered and refined the tenets of cultural historical interpretation in prehistoric archaeology: Alfred V. Kidder (1885–1963). So influential was Kidder, in fact, that his work was the principal focus of Walter Taylor's far-ranging critique of American archaeology published in 1948.

A. V. Kidder and the Cultural Historical Approach

Kidder's archaeological career began in 1907, while he was an undergraduate student at Harvard University. That summer, he and two other Harvard students joined Edgar L. Hewett's expedition to the southwestern United States. Kidder's actual initiation to the realities of archaeological fieldwork came as Hewett led his students to the top

Survey in the American Southwest: Hewett's field school

of a mesa in the Four Corners area of the Southwest. The view encompassed several hundred square miles—to Kidder it seemed "about half the world." Gazing out over this vast area, Hewett pointed out several principal landmarks and simply said, "I want you boys to make an archaeological survey of this country. I'll be back in six weeks. You'd better get some horses."

Kidder and his two companions went on to complete their first summer's fieldwork according to Hewett's rather terse instructions. After graduating from Harvard, Kidder traveled to Europe, and while in the Mediterranean area he visited several ongoing excavations. It was at this time that he was first exposed to stratigraphic excavation, as practiced by Egyptologist George A. Reisner. Returning to Harvard as an anthropology graduate student, Kidder took an archaeology course from Reisner and learned more about the latter's exacting standards for field research. Later, Kidder was among the first to apply the rigorous research techniques he had learned from Reisner and others at Harvard to archaeological work in the Americas.

Pioneering survey in northeastern Arizona: Kidder and Guernsey

In 1914, Kidder and Samuel J. Guernsey conducted an archaeological survey of northeastern Arizona. The results of this research, published in 1919, were the first to delineate separate cultural traditions in this region, on the basis of different spatial distributions of distinct artifact types and architectural styles.

Foundations of Southwest prehistory: Kidder at Pecos, New Mexico

In 1915 Kidder began investigations at Pecos, New Mexico. The site of Pecos was selected in order to document the sequence of prehistoric cultures in the Southwest, which was at that time almost completely unknown. Kidder chose Pecos for this work for a very good reason: it was a historic contact site, still occupied at the time of the first Spanish colonization in the sixteenth century, and it had thereafter become a Spanish mission center. Kidder hoped to discover and excavate stratified deposits through which, by applying the direct historical approach (discussed in Chapter 12), he could link the known historic Spanish period with successively earlier remains to reveal the full sequence of prehistoric occupation. The results of the Pecos excavations (Fig. 13.1)—which lasted until 1929—more than fulfilled this expectation. The data from stratified midden deposits at Pecos provided the basis for the first long-term chronology of human occupation in this part of the New World. And this sequence, in turn, provided the foundation for the first area synthesis in the Southwest. At Kidder's invitation, archaeologists from all over the Southwest met in 1927 at a conference at Pecos to pool their accumulated findings and reconstruct the temporal and spatial distributions and interconnections of their data. The resulting temporal and spatial synthesis still provides the basic framework for all South-

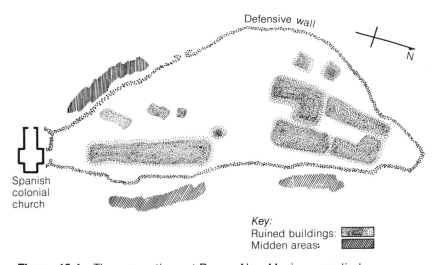

Figure 13.1 The excavations at Pecos, New Mexico, supplied a chronological sequence which served as a vital key for outlining the culture history of the southwestern United States. (After Kidder 1924.)

western archaeologists (Fig. 13.2); although subsequent research has refined the synthesis, the basic structure remains.

After 1929, Kidder's career took a new course. He became Director of the Division of Historical Research for the Carnegie Institution of Washington; in this position he was able to sponsor and oversee a multitude of anthropological and archaeological research projects during the next three decades. The focus of this research was in the Maya area of Mesoamerica. Kidder viewed the Maya as a unique, pristine laboratory for anthropological study. Contemporary Maya communities preserved many traditional (or non-European) aspects of culture; immediate ethnographic documentation was therefore needed to record this culture before it disappeared. Furthermore, contemporary Maya culture could provide analogs for the reconstruction of ancient Maya civilization. The direct study of past Maya civilization was Kidder's major interest, for in 1929 the temporal and spatial dimensions of ancient Maya life were largely unknown. In Kidder's view, the first priority was to gather archaeological data to establish the basic sequence and distribution of prehistoric Maya culture; these considerations were prerequisites for any attempt to answer such questions as the origins, development, and demise of Maya civilization. Accordingly, Kidder and the Carnegie Institution sponsored the first major archaeological investigations in the Maya area, selecting a site in each of the major environmental regions that promised, together, to cover the estimated time span of Maya occupation.

Foundations of Maya prehistory: Kidder with the Carnegie Institution

482

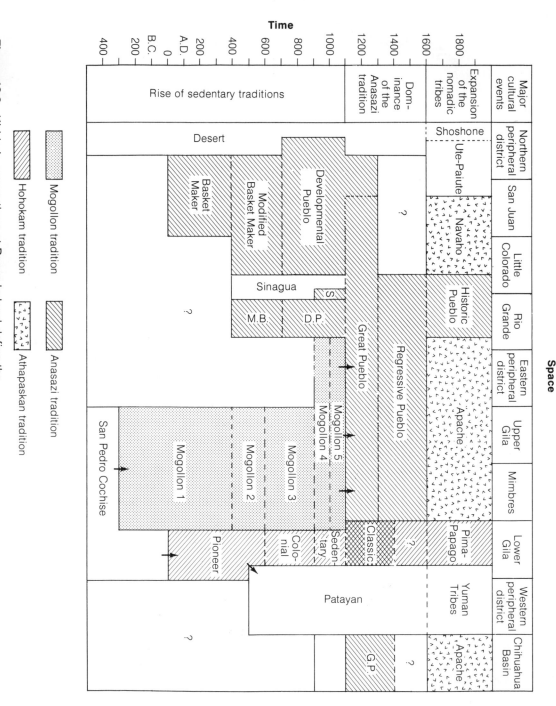

Figure 13.2 Kidder's excavations at Pecos helped define the chronological and spatial distributions of prehistoric societies in the southwestern United States. The cultural historical approach leads to the development of such time-space grids to summarize ancient events and cultural relationships. (After Rouse 1962.)

Projects at Uaxactún, in the Petén rain forest of Guatemala, and at Chichén Itzá, in arid Yucatan, were two of the major undertakings. In the Guatemalan highlands, the focus was the site of Kaminaljuyú —in Maya, the "hills of the dead." Work began at Kaminaljuyú in 1935, directed by Kidder himself. Its results were surprising. Although evidence was discovered of an occupation contemporary with the great lowland centers of the "Classic" period (ca. A.D. 200–900), much of the material culture from the Kaminaljuyú Classic period included obvious non-Maya attributes. In fact, some pottery and architectural styles found there were virtually identical to those from Central Mexico. This was the first indication that the Maya highlands, during the early portion of the Classic period at least, were intimately related to the political and economic power of Teotihuacán. An even more significant surprise emerged from the Kaminaljuyú excavations. Kidder and his colleague Edwin M. Shook discovered an earlier, "preclassic" civilization that appeared to have reached its peak several hundred years before the peak development of civilization in the Maya lowlands. Building on this research, Kidder hypothesized that Classic Maya civilization may have had substantial roots in the southern region of the highlands and Pacific coast of Guatemala—a hypothesis fully supported by subsequent archaeological investigations.

Kaminaljuyú excavations: Kidder and Shook

Kidder's archaeological research played a crucial role in the development of the cultural historical approach. His work was instrumental in establishing a rigorous inductive philosophy in archaeological research. And his emphasis on refinement of data gathering techniques, such as careful and detailed recording of excavations and the use of stratigraphic excavation, continues to influence contemporary archaeologists. Kidder's overall research strategy—as exemplified in his use of the direct historical approach at Pecos and in the building of site sequences into area syntheses in both the Southwest and the Maya area—shaped the entire cultural historical approach. But, as Kidder himself realized, this research method never realized its ultimate goal—an understanding of the processes of culture, the explanation of how and why civilizations such as that of the Maya rose and fell. Kidder felt that the Maya represented a potential key to this larger question: if one could use archaeology to unravel the important variables in the origin and demise of a single prehistoric civilization, such as that of the Maya, then cultural processes operating within all civilizations could be better understood.

As we shall see, a cultural historical approach can be used to outline the temporal, spatial, and even the functional dimensions of prehistory, but it is less suitable for documenting culture process or the specific causal factors operating in cultural development and change.

Before considering these larger issues, however, we shall describe exactly how the cultural historical approach provides temporal, spatial, and functional frameworks for chronicling the past.

THE CULTURAL HISTORICAL METHOD

The research method associated with the cultural historical approach is inductive, beginning with specific data from individual sites and combining these in increasing degrees of generalization and synthesis. The specific techniques used to collect, process, and analyze archaeological data have been discussed in previous chapters. Here we will briefly recount the steps normally followed in conducting inductive archaeological research in a previously uninvestigated area.

Once the zone of archaeological research has been selected, a reconnaissance program identifies archaeological sites and surface survey provides the initial round of data collections. From these collections, the archaeologist selects the traits that seem most sensitive to temporal change and that will therefore best allow the preliminary collections to be arranged in a tentative chronological sequence. The traits used may be attributes of features, such as architectural form or style; more commonly, however, they are attributes of pottery or of stone tools. Once the surface survey data are classified and analyzed, the archaeologist sets up a tentative chronological sequence, using seriation and/or the direct historical method. Incidentally, many of the basic artifact categories used in such classifications are divisions introduced by Kidder in his attempt to standardize procedures and to make chronological distinctions based upon typologies as uniform as possible. Kidder's artifactual categories were based primarily on substance; this distinction is still used, usually in combination with technology, thereby defining artifactual industries.

Once the preliminary chronological scheme is worked out, excavations are undertaken to test the sequence and to provide data for its refinement. Other goals may also be pursued in excavation, but the emphasis in the cultural historical approach usually lies in the discovery and investigation of stratified deposits that enable the archaeologist to document further or to rework the tentative time scheme. When the excavated data have been classified and analyzed in comparison with the initial collections, the changes observed between types are used to define broad chronological subdivisions, usually called *complexes,* for each artifact or feature category. Thus separate sequences of complexes are defined for pottery, chipped stone, houses, and so on. The selection of the defining criteria for each complex is arbitrary, but, as we have said before, it favors attributes and

types that are most sensitive to change through time; attributes and
types that continue relatively unchanged for long periods of time do
not provide sensitive time markers (Fig. 13.3).

Correlating sequences of complexes across data categories, the archaeologist next defines chronological *periods* or *phases* for the site
as a whole. Like complexes, phases have arbitrary boundaries, since
it is unlikely that all complexes will change simultaneously or at the

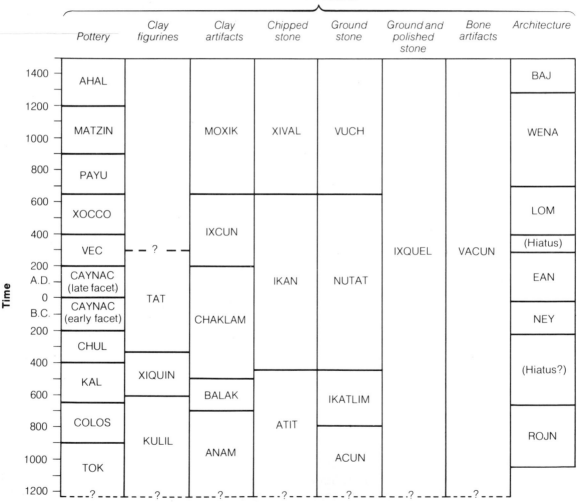

Figure 13.3 Changes in individual artifact and feature complexes are
correlated and compared to chart cultural-historical development of a site
or region. Note the contrast in rates of change between complexes in the
different industries.

same rate (Fig. 13.3). For example, pottery styles may change fairly rapidly, while house form may stay the same over a long time span. In many cases, artifact complexes that are most sensitive to change are emphasized and adopted as the principal criteria for defining site phases; this is one reason why pottery typologies are commonly the backbone of intrasite sequences.

The time scale for ordering both complexes and site periods may be either relative or absolute, depending on the nature of associated age determination evidence. Whether or not absolute dating is possible, however, the study gives maximum effort to securing the relative chronology, relying primarily on evidence recovered from stratified deposits to verify the typological sequence.

CULTURAL HISTORICAL SYNTHESIS

The synthesis of individual chronologies within a single site forms the foundation for cultural historical reconstruction. The next step in the procedure is to expand the synthesis beyond the individual site to encompass ever wider areas of geographical space. This enlargement of scope is accomplished by repeating the research procedures outlined above at sites adjacent to those already investigated. Newly acquired data can be compared to the sequences of complexes already defined, thus facilitating the task of chronological ordering at sites investigated later. Of course, not all of the artifacts and features found will duplicate previous finds, and so new types, complexes, and phases may be defined as new sites are studied. In this way, not only is the cultural chronology refined, but the archaeologist can also begin to plot the spatial distributions of artifact and feature types. As more and more sites are investigated and the number of known prehistoric cultural sequences grows, the process of temporal and spatial synthesis expands to cover ever larger geographic regions. These temporal and spatial syntheses, such as that worked out by Kidder and his collaborators at the 1927 Pecos conference, are often termed *time-space grids* (see Fig. 13.2).

As a rule, the working unit of cultural historical synthesis is the *culture area,* a conceptual unit originally based on ethnographically defined cultural similarities within a geographical area (Fig. 13.4). Various archaeologists working within a given culture area usually attempt to facilitate the process of temporal and spatial synthesis by using common terminology and classificatory concepts in order to make information from different sites comparable. The first cultural historical synthesis of an entire culture area in the New World was that of the Southwest, mentioned above. Since that time, other prehistoric culture area syntheses have been worked out, both in the New World

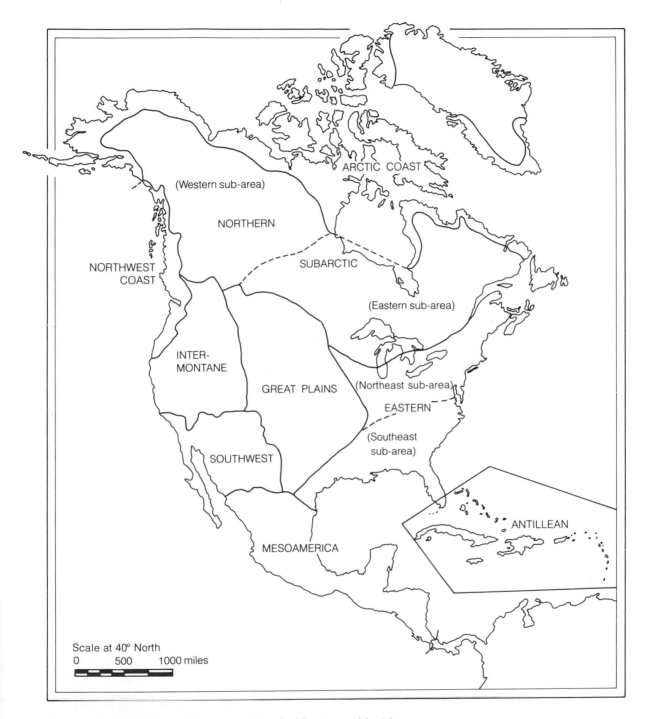

Figure 13.4 Cultural attributes combined with geographical factors are used to define culture areas, in this case, those of North America.

and in the Old. Some of these, however, have been based on terminology and concepts unique to a single culture area—McKern's Midwestern Taxonomic System (Fig. 13.5) is an important example. Variations in terminology and concepts have created difficulties when archaeologists have attempted wider syntheses, seeking to incorporate several culture areas or an entire continent within one time scheme. In order to bridge conceptual differences between culture areas, new and broader organizing models were needed.

As the next chapter will show, some archaeologists have been able to continue basing their area syntheses on evolutionary stages derived from the nineteenth-century unilinear theorists. Thus chronological

MIDWESTERN TAXONOMIC SYSTEM

Archaeological culture	Phase	Aspect	Focus	Component
Mississippi	Upper Mississippi	Nebraska	Omaha St. Helena	Rock Bluffs, Gates Saunders, Walker Gilmore II Butte, St. Helena, etc.
	Central Plains	Upper Republican	Lost Creek Sweetwater Medicine Creek North Platte	Lost Creek, Prairie Dog Creek, etc. Sweetwater, Munson Creek, etc. Medicine Creek Signal Butte, III, etc.
		Lower Loup (protohistoric Pawnee?)	Beaver Creek	Burkett, Schuyler, etc.
		Lower Platte (historic Pawnee)	Columbus Republican	Horse Creek, Fullterton, Linwood, etc. Hill, etc.
	Woodland	Iowa "Algonkian"	Sterns Creek	Walker Gilmore I
Great Plains	Early Hunting	Signal Butte II (?)	Signal Butte	Signal Butte II
		Signal Butte I	Signal Butte	Signal Butte I
		Folsom	Northern Colorado	Lindenmeier (Colo.)

Figure 13.5 This chart illustrates classification of prehistoric and historic cultures of the Plains area of the United States according to the Midwestern Taxonomic System. Note that chronology is not specified. (Adapted by permission of the Smithsonian Institution Press from *Smithsonian Miscellaneous Collections,* Volume 93, "An Introduction to Nebraska Archeology," Number 10, July 20, 1935, 323 pages, by Willian Duncan Strong: Table on page 2. Washington, D.C.: Smithsonian Institution, 1935.

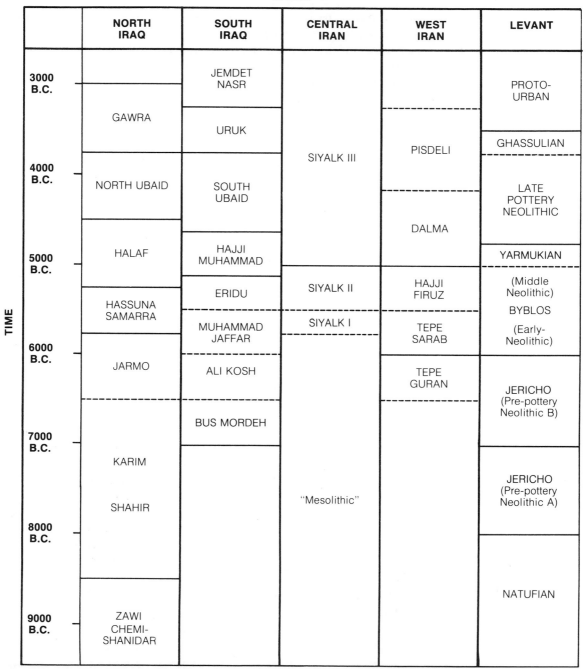

Figure 13.6   One version of the chronological and spatial distributions of prehistoric societies in the ancient Near East. (After Mellaart 1965.)

stages labeled Paleolithic, Mesolithic, Neolithic, and so forth still form a usable framework for prehistoric reconstructions in Europe, for this was the area for which the sequence was originally developed. Definitions of the divisions have been refined, of course, resulting in many detailed local chronological subdivisions for each stage (Fig. 13.6); but in much of the Old World, including Europe, the basic approach has continued to be broadly deductive, beginning with a generalized model and focusing research upon testing and refinement of that model. In the New World, on the other hand, prehistory has been reconstructed largely through an inductive approach, developed specifically to *avoid* using the nineteenth-century evolutionary model. As a consequence, the Paleolithic-Mesolithic-Neolithic scheme has never been successfully applied to New World prehistory, although these terms are occasionally used to note generalized similarities with Old World finds.

Somewhat ironically, as the explicitly inductive cultural historical approach began to be used to create broader and more general syntheses in the New World, archaeologists became increasingly aware that some kind of overriding scheme very much like the Old World evolutionary model would be necessary. Such a framework was worked out in the mid-twentieth century; it represents an inductively derived temporal-spatial synthesis for the entire New World. The terminology is distinct from that used in the Old World evolutionary model, and the resulting scheme is explicitly *not* founded on evolutionary theory. Yet the New World synthesis implicitly suggests a course of cultural development from simple to complex, certainly not identical with but clearly parallel to the course of Old World prehistory.

First New World cultural historical synthesis: Willey and Phillips

This New World model, developed in the late 1950s by Gordon R. Willey and Philip Phillips, is based on the complementary concepts of tradition and horizon. *Tradition* refers to cultural continuity through time, while *horizon* deals with ties and uniformity across space at a single point in time (Fig. 13.7). Applying these concepts to data from all areas of the Americas, Willey and Phillips defined a series of five developmental stages, or, as they have been more commonly applied, chronological periods. The exact temporal boundaries for each "stage" differ from area to area, but overall, Willey and Phillips' scheme represents a cultural historical synthesis for the entire New World.

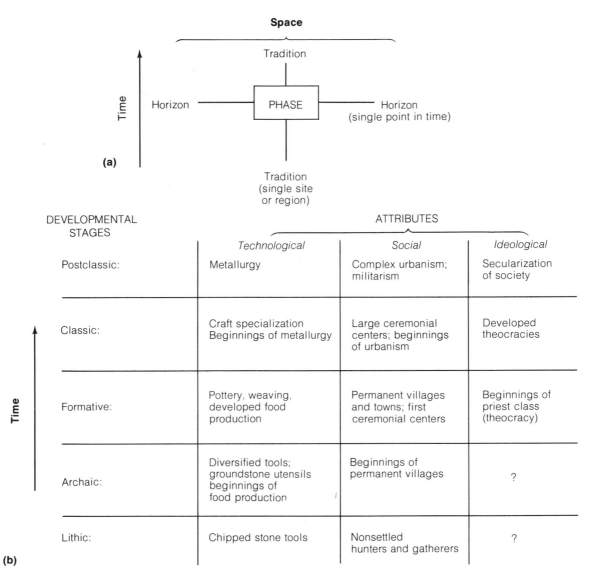

Figure 13.7 New World culture history was comprehensively outlined by Willey and Phillips, by (a) integrating the dimensions of time and space through the concepts of tradition and horizon, and (b) summarizing the inductively documented course of cultural development through five generalized stages. (After Willey and Phillips 1958, (a) copyright 1958 by The University of Chicago Press.)

CULTURAL HISTORICAL INTERPRETATION

The formal interpretation process follows the temporal and spatial synthesis of the archaeological data, and its scope is determined by the nature of that synthesis. If temporal and spatial distributions encompass only a single site, interpretation is obviously restricted to that site. If the scope of the synthesis includes many sites covering an entire region, the resulting synthesis will be similarly broadly based.

However large or small the area covered, the analogs used for cultural historical interpretation usually presuppose a normative view of culture (described in Chapter 2). Normative analogs describe idealized rules or "templates" for the ways things were done—how pottery was made, what house forms were prescribed, and so on. These models are primarily descriptive, not explanatory, in that they identify and describe the variables operating within situations of culture change, but do not attempt to describe the relationships among variables or identify the specific causes of change.

Some descriptive models used in archaeology are *synchronic,* identifying and describing what happened in the past at one point in time, or even irrespective of time (atemporal). Other descriptive models are *diachronic;* these identify and describe when past events occurred, emphasizing change through time. As an example of a synchronic descriptive model, we can recall McKern's Midwestern Taxonomic System referred to earlier in this chapter (Fig. 13.5). McKern's system allowed archaeological data to be identified and described rather precisely without referring to time or change. In contrast, Willey and Phillips' New World cultural stage model (Fig. 13.7) is diachronic and descriptive: it identifies and describes certain archaeological variables and their changes through time in order to define the posited "stages" of New World culture history.

Because the cultural historical approach emphasizes chronology and cultural change, most of the interpretive models used are diachronic, identifying and describing change in the archaeological record. However, some of these models also deal with situations involving cultural stability, or a lack of change through time. A more meaningful distinction, then, might be made between those diachronic models that emphasize the internal dynamics of culture and those that focus on external stimuli for change, whether cultural or noncultural in origin (Fig. 13.8). The principal internal cultural models include two sources of change (invention and revival) and three mechanisms to describe how change comes about (inevitable variation, cultural selection, and cultural drift). The primary external models include diffusion, trade, migration, invasion or conquest—all cultural sources— and environmental change, a noncultural source. In the remainder of

Two descriptive models: McKern, Willey and Phillips

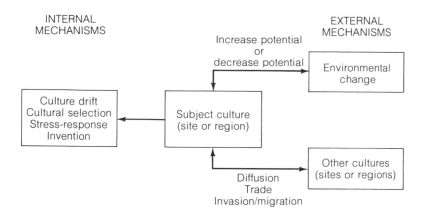

Figure 13.8 Cultural historical interpretation is based upon models that describe culture change as proceeding from either internal or external mechanisms.

this chapter we will consider these models and indicate how each is used in cultural historical interpretation.

Internal Cultural Models

The most general of the internal cultural models is often called the *inevitable variation* model. It is based on the simple premise that all cultures must change through time. One particular version of this model is the common thesis that all cultures experience growth and development analogous to that of a living organism: they grow, mature, and eventually die, a trajectory often referred to as the rise and fall of civilization. But the inevitable variation model is so simplistic and general that it is of little use in the interpretation of most archaeological situations. For instance, if we take a specific case of the collapse of a civilization, such as that of Rome or the Maya, applying the inevitable variation model adds nothing to our understanding. We do not increase our understanding by saying that a civilization fell apart because it was destined to collapse. Of greater benefit to archaeological interpretation are internal cultural models that identify specific variables with which to describe the mechanisms of culture change.

How does this change come about? The human species is inquisitive and innovative. *Cultural invention* is the result of these human qualities; the term refers to new ideas that originate within a culture, either by accident or by design. All new ideas have their ultimate origin in such invention, of course; but to attribute to invention the appearance of a given trait in the archaeological record at a particular place, the archaeologist must demonstrate that the trait was not introduced from outside by trade or some other external mechanism. A specific example is the controversy over the early occurrence of bronze metallurgy in southeast Asia. Proponents of an in-

Old World metallurgy: Independent invention or diffusion?

dependent invention model point out that cast bronze artifacts now being found in Thailand rival those of the Near East in age. The counterargument, however, is that the Near East exhibits a full range of evidence for the local development of metallurgical technology, including evidence of workshops as well as local sequential evidence of gradually increasing sophistication in metalworking techniques. In order to establish that southeast Asia was indeed an independent center for the invention of metallurgy, future archaeological research there must uncover evidence equivalent to that in the Near East, documenting the *local prototypes* and *developmental steps* leading up to the level of sophistication embodied in the artifact finds made to date.

To contribute to cultural change, an invention must be accepted in a culture. Two general models, both founded on loose analogies to biological evolution, have been offered to describe mechanisms of acceptance, perpetuation, or rejection of cultural traits (Fig. 13.9). The first, *cultural selection,* mirrors the biological concept of natural selection. According to the cultural selection model, those cultural traits that are advantageous to a society are accepted or retained, while those that are useless or actively harmful tend to be discarded. This tendency results in gradual and cumulative change through time. Selection can act on any cultural trait, whether in the technological, social, or ideological realm of culture. Whether a given trait is advantageous or not depends ultimately upon whether it contributes to—or hinders—the survival and well-being of the society. For example, investment of power in a central authority figure may increase a society's efficiency in food production, resolution of disputes, and management of interactions with neighboring societies. If such centralization of authority leads the society in question to prosper, the

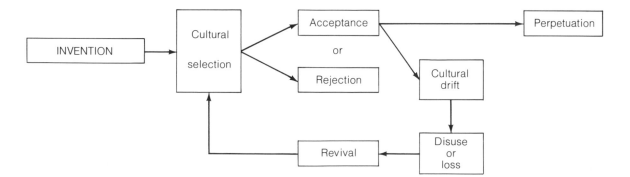

Selective mechanism: Acceptance or rejection of centralized leadership

Figure 13.9   Internally induced culture change is affected by the filtering mechanisms of cultural selection, cultural drift, and revival.

trait of power centralization is advantageous and selection will favor its perpetuation. If, however, the society falls on hard times as a result of power centralization—perhaps because of inept leadership—authority is likely to become more dispersed again.

Selection also acts against innovative traits that are inconsistent with prevailing cultural values or norms. Generally speaking, technological inventions are more likely to be accepted than social or ideological ones, because they are less likely to conflict with the value system. A new form of axe head, for instance, usually has an easier path to acceptance than does a revised authority hierarchy or an innovative religious belief.

A related model, often labeled *cultural drift* (Fig. 13.9), describes a mechanism complementary to that of cultural selection. In biological evolution, the term *genetic drift* describes a situation in which some genetic traits are lost because the few members of the population who have them do not produce offspring and so do not perpetuate the traits. Like selection, this process results in change through time. But this process is a random one; the reason for trait loss is chance alone rather than active selection against a characteristic. Although genetic traits are passed on by biological reproduction, cultural traits are transmitted from one generation to the next by learning. Cultural drift, then, results from the fact that cultural transmission is incomplete or imperfect: no individual ever learns all the information possessed by any other member of the society. Hence cultural changes through time have a random aspect. Sally Binford has suggested that cultural drift may be responsible for some of the variations in artifacts of early Paleolithic assemblages. That is, the accumulation of minor changes gives a superficial impression of deliberate stylistic innovation, but not until the Upper Paleolithic, or perhaps the Mousterian assemblages of the Middle Paleolithic, can definable zones of consistent and clustered stylistic types be discerned. Earlier variability (other than that related to artifact function and efficiency) may simply represent the cumulative effects of random cultural drift.

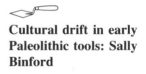

Cultural drift in early Paleolithic tools: Sally Binford

Another source for cultural change is *revival* of elements that have fallen into disuse. A number of stimuli may lead to revival of old forms, including chance discovery and reacceptance of old styles, reoccurrence of specific needs, and duplication of treasured heirlooms. One particular model relates revival to a coping response to stressful situations. Some kinds of stress elicit technological responses: for example, townspeople construct a fortification wall as a defense against seige. But sometimes societies deal with stress by social or ideological means. Cultural anthropologist Anthony F. C. Wallace has developed a model that describes rapid and radical cultural change in

Cultural revitalization: Wallace's model

**Prehistoric revital-
ization: Late Classic
Tikal**

the face of stress. This revitalization model refers to situations in which members of a society perceive their culture as falling apart—as unable to provide them with an adequate standard of living. In revitalization, a leader emerges who revives old symbols associated with earlier periods of well-being, squashes those identified with the stressful situation, inspires positive and prideful identification with the society, and promises renewed prosperity if people will adhere to the rules he sets down. The Ghost Dance phenomenon of 1890 was a revitalization response by native American groups to the dissolution and devaluation of their culture by Euro-American contacts; other examples include such different movements as the rise of Black Muslims in the United States in the mid-twentieth century and the Communist revolutions in Russia and China. Some archaeologists believe that a revitalization movement can be detected at the Maya site of Tikal, where the rise of rival power centers in the seventh century A.D. threatened Tikal's previous political supremacy. A powerful leader emerged shortly before A.D. 700 and rapidly galvanized his followers into reasserting their self-respect and Tikal's importance. Among the means he used in this effort were revival of symbols—including particular decorative motifs and specific genealogical reconstructions that recalled earlier heights of power and prosperity— and elaboration of previously minor symbols, such as a ceremonial architectural plan known as twin-pyramid groups, that were emblematic of Tikal itself. As noted in Chapter 11, interpretation of ideology and symbol systems is not easy; but a large and growing number of archaeologists argue that more attention should be given to reconstructing this aspect of ancient life.

External Cultural Models

Once a change, such as that resulting from the acceptance of an invention, has occurred within a society, its utility or prestige may allow it to spread far beyond its place of origin. The spread of new ideas and objects involves a complex set of variables, including time, distance, degree of utility or acceptance, and mode of dispersal. Various modes of dispersal are well documented by both history and ethnography; these are often used as models for cultural historical interpretation. These include the spread of ideas (diffusion), the dispersal of material objects by exchange or trade, and the movement of human populations through migration and invasion or conquest. The influences or changes within a given culture brought about by these external sources are collectively termed *acculturation* (Fig. 13.10).

Diffusion occurs under a variety of circumstances: any contact between individuals of different societies involves the potential trans-

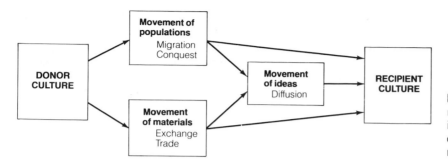

Figure 13.10 Externally induced culture change includes the mechanisms of diffusion, trade, migration, and conquest.

mission of new ideas from one culture to another. When a given society is exposed to a new idea, that idea may be accepted unchanged, reworked or modified to better fit the accepting culture, or completely rejected. A classic ethnographically documented case of diffusion is the spread of the Ghost Dance movement among native American groups in the late nineteenth century. Originating among the Paiute Indians in Nevada, the doctrine of the Ghost Dance of 1890 began primarily as a revival of traditional culture, brought about by the return of the "ghosts" of dead ancestors. As the movement spread east across the Great Plains, however, it was progressively modified by the various cultural groups that adopted it; finally it came to incorporate an active and hostile rejection of all things associated with the white culture. Adherents of the movement's altered doctrine argued that sufficient purification of native American culture (by purging the Euro-American traits) would increase the buffalo herds, restore ancestors to life, and drive away the whites—the source of troubles. Faith in the strength of the movement even led some to believe that the Ghost Dance shirts gave their wearers invincibility, a belief tragically disproven in the massacre at Wounded Knee. The Ghost Dance was not accepted by all native Americans, however. Some groups, such as the Navajo, rejected the pan-Indian movement altogether because of their strong avoidance of the dead and fear of "ghosts." The Ghost Dance, then, illustrates widespread diffusion of an idea, in which the idea is transmitted from one society to others, sometimes being accepted without modification, sometimes modified, and sometimes rejected because it conflicts with existing cultural values.

The archaeological record contains numerous examples of ideas that have diffused over varying distances with varying degrees of acceptance. The 260-day ritual calendar of Mesoamerica is found in a wide range of cultural contexts; although specific attributes such as day names vary from one culture to the next, the essential unity of this calendrical system bespeaks long-term, continuing exchange of calendrical ideas among its users. In the Old World, the distribution

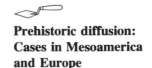

**Diffusion documented:
The Ghost Dance**

**Prehistoric diffusion:
Cases in Mesoamerica
and Europe**

of megalithic (large stone) tombs in Europe has traditionally been described as diffusion of an architectural idea westward from the cultures of the eastern Mediterranean in the third millennium B.C. As we
saw in Chapter 10, however, recent revisions of radiocarbon dating
techniques have indicated that the megalithic constructions in France
and Spain are earlier than those where the idea was supposed to have
originated. Spread of architectural ideas by diffusion may still describe the mechanism behind the observed spatial distribution, but the
specific model for spread clearly needs re-examination.

Diffusion is a well-documented, common mechanism of culture
change in historically and ethnographically known societies, even including the spread of nuclear technology today. Because diffusion is
so common, and because evidence of more specific mechanisms such
as trade, migration, invasion, and invention is sometimes difficult to
demonstrate, cultural historical interpretations have relied heavily on
diffusion as a model. All too often, however, the concept is used un-
critically, without consideration for the specific circumstances under
which ideas might have been transmitted. Thus any observed similarity between cultures may be attributed to diffusion. An extreme
example of abuse of this concept is found in the diffusionist school of
anthropology in the early twentieth century, especially the branch of
it that traced all civilizations of the world to roots in dynastic Egypt.
Proponents of this model, such as Sir Grafton Elliot Smith, argued
that the observed distribution of such widespread traits of civilization
as divine kingship and pyramid construction resulted from diffusion
from a single source culture: Egypt. Even when applied in less extreme ways, however, use of the concept of diffusion often raises the
further question as to why the cultures involved should have been in
communication in the first place.

A more recent, comprehensive diffusionist model is that presented
by James A. Ford to describe the course of cultural change and
spread of ideas in pre-Columbian America. On the basis of finds at
the Ecuadorian site of Valdivia, Betty J. Meggers, Clifford Evans,
and Emilio Estrada had argued that a series of early third millennium
innovations—including the oldest American occurrence of pottery—
were derived by trans-Pacific contacts from the contemporary
Japanese culture called Jomon. Ford accepted the Valdivia-Jomon
thesis and went further, tracing the spread of selected culture traits
throughout the Americas from 3000 B.C. onward. The ultimate origins of a number of culture traits, such as ring-shaped village plans in
Formative-period coastal settlements, were often assigned to Asiatic
sources, as were some of the human populations involved. Parts of
Ford's scheme may have validity, but much does not. The Jomon
question, for example, has been effectively refuted by the discovery
of earlier local prototypes for the Valdivia pottery. Unfortunately, the

**Abuse of diffusion:
Smith and "The Helio-
centric School"**

**Extreme diffusionism:
Proposed Old World–
New World links**

Ford model has become embroiled in a recurring philosophical stand-off between those who advocate independent invention as an over-riding mechanism of culture change and those who favor diffusion. Despite the polemics, each case must be examined individually; neither internal invention nor external contacts are likely alone to account for all instances of culture change.

Although diffusion is often an elusive mechanism, easy to invoke and difficult to substantiate, contact and communication via *trade* can frequently be concretely demonstrated. This is because trade involves the exchange of material objects; the less perishable of these may be recovered by the archaeologist as artifacts and ecofacts. In Chapter 11 we discussed the nature and detection of exchange systems in some detail; thus only a brief review will be given here.

Artifacts and ecofacts may be initially identified as imported goods either because they are infrequently occurring items, distinct from the bulk of items found in a site, or because they are made of raw materials known to be unavailable locally. Various technical analyses have been developed to identify sources of raw materials, including such widely traded stone materials as obsidian, jade, and steatite. In a number of cases, archaeologists have been able to plot both the distribution of sources of a particular material and the observed distribution of products from these sources, and to use this information to reconstruct ancient trade routes. The important implication of trade distributions for culture change is that archaeologists can use them to demonstrate contact between groups: when an obsidian trade route is reconstructed, for example, a minimal inference is that the obsidian was introduced to groups who could then add obsidian tools to their cultural inventory. But along with the obsidian, traders probably carried other goods, many of which would not survive in the archaeological record, along with information about ways of life in their home community. These traders also certainly acquired other goods and information, which they then introduced at home. The obsidian in this case is concrete evidence that attests to the means of transmitting a much broader array of materials and ideas.

Another mechanism of culture change is actual movement of populations, both as nonagressive *migrations* and as more agressive *invasions* and *conquests*. Cultural historical interpretations often cite these movements to account for evidence of widespread and rapid change. Numerous authors have discussed detection of population movements in the archaeological record; Emil W. Haury presents the requirements succinctly in his postulation of a migration from northern Arizona into the Point of Pines region of east central Arizona at the end of the thirteenth century. Haury sets forth four conditions that must be met for an archaeologist to argue that a migration has occurred. First, a number of new cultural traits must suddenly appear,

Evidence for prehistoric migration: Haury at Point of Pines, Arizona

too many to be feasibly accounted for by diffusion, invention, or trade, and none having earlier local prototypes. Second, some of the form or style of local materials should be modified or used in a different way by the newcomers. Third, a source for the immigrant population must be identified—a homeland where the intrusive cultural elements do have prototypes. Finally, the artifacts used as indices of population movement must exist in the same form at the same time level in both the homeland and the newly adopted home. At Point of Pines, Haury notes that new architectural styles, both sacred and secular, as well as very specific ceramic attributes appear suddenly in one particular sector of the site. At the same time level, some distinctively "foreign" design elements are found on locally made pottery vessels, also found in this one sector. These two conclusions supply the first two kinds of evidence needed to postulate a migration. Looking, then, for a source for these cultural traits, he finds the same elements in association at sites in northern Arizona, on an equivalent time level, and notes that independent evidence is available for a population decline in the proposed homeland at the appropriate time. His actual reconstructions are even more specific, for he presents additional evidence to suggest that the size of the migrating group was about 50 to 60 families, and to posit that the community into which they moved did not take kindly to the intrusion, ultimately setting fire to the newcomers' homes and driving them out again. The Point of Pines example, then, provides an outline of the basic conditions to be met in identifying evidence of migration in the archaeological record.

The concept of peaceful migration as one means of introducing new culture traits into an area can be contrasted with its more typically violent counterparts, invasion and conquest. These, too, involve population movements, but with presumably more drastic effects on the way of life of the recipient society. Elements cited as evidence of invasion or conquest include massive burning or other destruction of buildings in a settlement, usually accompanied by large-scale loss of human life. A famous instance of a reconstructed invasion involves human skeletons found in the upper levels at Mohenjo-daro, one of the great centers of the Indus Valley civilization around 2000 B.C. At Mohenjo-daro, the skeletal remains of numerous human corpses were found scattered in disarray in streets and alleys (Fig. 13.11), strongly suggesting that the victims were killed in short order, with no time to escape and no surviving relatives to dispose properly of their earthly remains.

The change brought about by conquest or invasion may, of course, be simple annihilation of the existing population, sometimes with no replacement by the intruders. In many cases, however, part of the original population survives and stays on, often under new political

Reconstructed invasion: Wheeler at Mohenjo-daro

Figure 13.11 Evidence of culture change through conquest can take dramatic forms. This photograph shows skeletal remains sprawled in a corner, as found in 1964, in the uppermost stratum of Mohenjo-daro. These and similar finds strongly suggest a raid after which the victims, along with the city, were abandoned. (Courtesy of George F. Dales.)

domination. The invaders may bring in new cultural elements, but some historically documented invasions show up rather inconsistently in the archaeological record. A case in point is the Spanish Conquest of the Americas in the sixteenth century. Both European and native chronicles of the period attest to the extent and severity of the changes wrought by the Spanish. Even so, archaeologists working in a number of the affected areas, including Mexico, Guatemala, and Peru, have sometimes had difficulty in actually identifying the dramatic onset of a Spanish presence. At some sites, distinctive features such as Catholic churches do appear, but pottery inventories often remain unchanged for long periods after the conquest. Numerous small communities, at varying distances from the civic and religious centers, must have undergone the change to Spanish rule without altering their tools, food, houses, or other material apsects of life. With reference to Haury's criteria, then, archaeologists can positively identify some prehistoric population movements, but the example just given argues rather strongly that not all such movements—violent or peaceful—can be detected in the archaeological record.

Archaeological evidence of conquest: The sixteenth-century Spanish

Environmental Change

Underlying cultural historical interpretation is also a general descriptive model that concerns the relationship between culture and the natural environment. Although this model has been very useful in identifying and describing some important effects of environmental variables on culture and culture change, the most common form of

Environmental impact: Martin at Tularosa Cave, New Mexico

Environmental impact: Sunset Crater, Arizona

the model identifies the environmental sources of culture change generally rather than specifically. In the next chapter we will discuss more specific, explanatory models that take the natural environment into account explicitly.

The usual cultural historical model of culture and environment interaction holds that each has the potential to modify the other. This relationship is diagramed in Figure 13.12. According to this model, environmental change may stimulate cultural change, or vice versa. For example, at Tularosa Cave, in the Mogollon area of western New Mexico, evidence indicates that maize and other cultivated plants generally increased in importance in the human diet over time. An exception, however, occurs between about A.D. 500 and A.D. 700; during this time maize consumption declined "almost to zero." This correlates with the period in which the total number of sites, as well as the area in square feet per house, reaches its lowest point. Paul S. Martin and his colleagues believe that a sustained series of short droughts may be at least partially responsible for this dietary change, by making agriculture difficult at best and leading to a renewed reliance on wild foods.

A more dramatic example of the cultural impact of an environmental change also comes from the southwestern United States—the effects of the eruption of Sunset Crater, near Flagstaff, Arizona, sometime in the middle of the eleventh century A.D. The initial effect of the eruption was to destroy or drive away all residents in the approximately 800 square miles blanketed by the black volcanic ash. A century later, however, the area was resettled by a diverse population

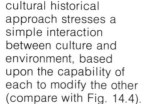

Figure 13.12 The cultural historical approach stresses a simple interaction between culture and environment, based upon the capability of each to modify the other (compare with Fig. 14.4).

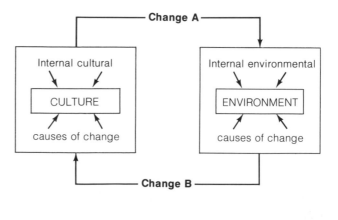

Key:
A: Environmental change caused by cultural factors
B: Culture change caused by environmental factors

who apparently took advantage of the rich mulching action of the volcanic soil. By A.D. 1300, however, the environment had changed again: wind had converted the ash cover to shifting dunes, exposing the original hard clay soil. The human settlers once again moved away.

In previous chapters we have given examples showing how culture changes environment. A change in technology may redefine the environment by increasing or decreasing the range of exploitable resources. Agricultural overuse may exhaust local soils; the clearing of trees on hillsides may foster erosion, landslides, and ultimately—by increasing the load deposited in a stream bed by erosional runoff—flooding. Alteration of the natural environment by cultural activities is not an exclusively modern phenomenon; the alterations today may be more extensive than before, but they are part of a long, global tradition of cultural impact on the state of the natural world.

SUMMARY

Cultural historical interpretation is built on the temporal and spatial synthesis of archaeological data. It emphasizes a chronicling of events, a demonstration of shifting cultural connections between sites, and an outline of relative change and stability of cultural forms within sites. The descriptive models used as the basis for interpretation are usually broad, general analogs founded in a normative concept of culture. Interpretation by means of these models attempts to account for the similarities and differences observed in the synthesized data. Differences between sites may be ascribed either to inevitable cultural variation or to processes of internal cultural change. Similarities, on the other hand, are interpreted as the result of mechanisms that lead to transfer of ideas between communities.

Most archaeologists recognize that observed cultural similarities, such as equivalent form or style attributes in the artifacts from two different sites, do not *in themselves* constitute sufficient evidence to distinguish among various mechanisms of prehistoric communication and contact—that is, to determine whether diffusion, trade, or migration accounts for the observed correspondences. Only detailed analysis can resolve this question; constituent analysis, for instance, may establish whether the raw materials of various artifacts have the same source.

The problem of interpreting observed similarities is compounded by documented examples of independent but parallel invention—a phenomenon that also leads to cultural similarity. For instance, the mathematical concept of zero is thought to have been invented at least twice—once in India at least as early as the sixth century A.D., and apparently even earlier by the ancient Maya of Mesoamerica. And the domestication of food plants is usually considered to be an independent but parallel cultural development in Old and New Worlds. Thus observed similarities in the data at two different sites may sometimes result from independent invention.

Deciding between internal and external sources for cultural change—and specifically settling the question of diffusion versus independent invention in interpreting observed cross-cultural similarities—has absorbed a great deal of intellectual energy. As we suggested in describing the controversy over James Ford's work, the debate has sometimes become acrimonious and polemical. The question of independence versus contact interpretations can be resolved by new evidence: the subsequent discovery of local prototypes for forms initially described as appearing "suddenly" was a strong refutation of Ford's (and Meggers', Evans', and Estrada's) trans-Pacific diffusion model. Discovery of local bronze tool prototypes would be evidence in favor of the postulated independent development of metallurgy in southeast Asia. Such models as these may originally arise as a result of inductive compilation of archaeological data in an unknown area. But to resolve the issues raised often requires further, deductively oriented research involving the testing of specific hypotheses.

We have seen that cultural historical interpretation is the result of a rational, scientific process of inquiry, by which an inductive strategy is used to gather and synthesize data. Models are subsequently adduced to account for observed variability in the data. Thus the cultural historical approach generates initial models and hypotheses about what happened in the past. In the next chapter we will consider the complementary aspect of the interpretive part of research—the means by which inductively derived hypotheses can be deductively tested.

See p. 575 for "Suggestions for Further Reading."

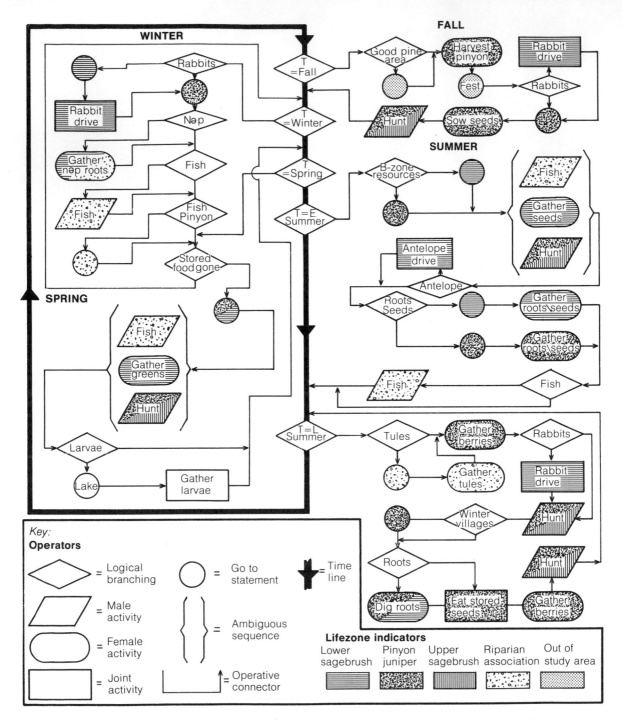

The outline of the Shoshonean subsistence system, as derived from Steward's ethnographic data and tested archaeologically by David Hurst Thomas, provides an excellent example of the cultural processual approach to interpretation. (After Thomas, reproduced by permission of The Society for American Archaeology, adapted from *American Antiquity* 38:159, 1973.)

The Cultural Processual Approach

We must continually work back and forth between the contexts of explaining the archaeological record and explaining the past; between the contexts of proposition formulation (induction) and proposition testing (deduction).

(Lewis R. Binford, "Some Comments on Historical versus Processual Archaeology," 1968)

The cultural processual approach is the second major way of conducting archaeological synthesis and interpretation. *Cultural process* refers to an understanding both of how the component parts of a culture work at one point in time (synchronic) and of how cultures change through time (diachronic). Although the cultural historical and cultural processual approaches are both concerned with the dynamics of culture, the former emphasizes *identification* of synchronic ties and of cultural change through description of a sequence of events, whereas the latter is concerned with discovering the *causes* of interactions and change. That is, the cultural processual approach seeks not only to identify and describe similarities and differences across time and space, but also to delineate the cause-effect relationships that explain the observed distributions. For example, change can be explained by understanding how and why an alteration in one variable, such as family structure, leads to adjustments and changes in other variables, such as pottery production.

How does the cultural processual approach attempt to identify the causes of change and thereby explain the processes involved in prehistoric cultural dynamics? In contrast to cultural historical reconstruction, the study of cultural process uses a deductive research methodology wherein hypotheses specify, at the outset of research, the working model of change (or interaction) and the kinds of data that will support or refute each hypothesis. Competing hypotheses are then tested against the archaeological data in order to eliminate those that are not supported by the evidence. Hypotheses that are supported in the first test are retested and refined by further research in order to isolate the factors involved in a given situation of prehistoric cultural change. In the cultural processual approach, synthesis corresponds to the assembly of archaeological data to test the hypotheses, while interpretation refers to the selection and refinement of specific hypotheses that best delineate cultural processes.

Of course the cultural processual approach is rooted, either directly or indirectly, in cultural historical reconstruction. A direct link may be apparent when the hypotheses tested by deductive procedures have been derived from the inductively developed cultural historical models. In an indirect way, however, *all* cultural processual interpretation is built on a cultural historical foundation, since the latter approach has provided the temporal and spatial frameworks of prehistory. These frameworks furnish the analytical controls without which cultural process cannot be discerned. The cultural processual approach represents the current culmination of the scientific method as applied to prehistoric archaeology; that is, initial inquiry based on the application of inductive reasoning allows the formulation of questions which may then be investigated deductively.

ORIGINS OF THE CULTURAL PROCESSUAL APPROACH

Like other theoretical perspectives cited in this text, the cultural processual approach can best be understood in the context of its origin and development within prehistoric archaeology and within anthropology generally (see Chapter 2). In reviewing the origin of the cultural processual approach, we will trace the development of both the deductive research method and the systemic-evolutionary concept of culture. These basic components of the cultural processual approach can both be traced to the rise of cultural anthropology in the late nineteenth century, for as we mentioned in Chapter 13, anthropology at that time was characterized by emphasis on the idea of cultural evolution and by a generally deductive research strategy.

The nineteenth-century concept of cultural evolution, usually labeled *unilinear,* treated all human societies, past and present, as part of a single evolutionary line (see again Fig. 12.2). The position of a society along this line was measured by its progress towards a "higher" society, as measured principally by development of an increasingly complex technology. As Chapter 13 discussed, the American school of anthropology rejected the idea of unilinear evolution in the early decades of the twentieth century. In Europe, however, the demise of this theory was neither as sudden nor as dramatic. Instead, European anthropologists and archaeologists, along with a few hardy American scholars, endeavored throughout the twentieth century to modify and redefine the theory of cultural evolution in light of the accumulated criticism and conflicting data that had made the old, over-simplified concept untenable.

An exception to this trend may be seen in the Soviet Union. Soviet archaeology, governed by political ideological considerations, has continued to use unilinear cultural evolution as an interpretive base. This is because the founders of modern Communism, Karl Marx and

Friedrich Engels, accepted many of the tenets of nineteenth-century unilinear theory, especially as set forth in the works of Lewis Henry Morgan. As a result, these early cultural evolutionary ideas have remained part of the theoretical underpinnings of archaeology in the Soviet Union.

In the West, however, a new concept of cultural evolution eventually emerged—a concept often labeled "cultural materialism" or, in the term we prefer here, *multilinear cultural evolution*. The multilinear concept has provided a tested, viable theory of culture dynamics that has been much more successful in accounting for long-term culture change than was the normative empirical approach of the Boasian school. We will discuss the details of multilinear evolutionary theory later in this chapter. At this point we shall trace the development of this theory by looking briefly at the work of some of the individuals who made important contributions to it.

One of the most influential scholars involved was V. Gordon Childe (1892–1957). Childe was born in Australia and educated in England; he devoted most of his archaeological career to the understanding of cultural development, especially that in the "cradle of civilization": the ancient Near East. His formulation of cultural evolution kept technology as the prime causal factor, holding that human societies evolved through the invention of new technological means for more efficient use of the environment. To Childe, some of these technological innovations were truly revolutionary, rapidly and radically transforming entire cultures. The first of these profound advances, the agricultural revolution, transformed wandering hunting-and-gathering societies into communities of settled farmers. The second was the urban revolution that gave rise to the earliest civilizations. The concept that revolutionary technological change was the prime mover in cultural evolution is not in itself a departure from the evolutionary ideas of the nineteenth century. What is important, however, is that after viewing the sum of the available archaeological evidence, Childe concluded that the specific courses followed by different societies have been distinct. Although there are parallels between cases, no single developmental trajectory can describe cultural evolution in detail.

The theme of separate but parallel cultural evolutionary paths has been expanded in the more recent work of Robert McC. Adams. Adams has outlined specific sequences of changes and cultural developments that culminated in the emergence of complex, urban civilization in the particular cases of Mesopotamia and Mesoamerica. In contrast to Childe, Adams argues against any single prime mover, asserting that changes in the realms of social and political organization generally took precedence in the evolution of civilization: devel-

Technological revolutions: Childe and the Near East

Organizational developments: Adams compares the Near East and Mesoamerica

opment of the social hierarchy and of managerial efficiency fostered changes in technological, subsistence, and ideological systems. All of these factors reinforced each other, leading to complex cultures of cities and civilization. Adams postulated a specific set of interrelated changes in social organization whose emergence could be tested by well-designed deductive archaeological investigation.

But the first detailed presentation of the concept of multilinear cultural evolution actually predated the work of both Childe and Adams. An American anthropologist, Julian H. Steward, is usually credited with originating the modern concept. Steward based his theory on ethnographic data concerning the adaptations of specific societies to specific environments; thus his concept of multilinear evolution focuses on the individual society's total environmental adaptation, or cultural ecology. This perspective attributes the observable regularities in the cultural evolutionary process to the finite number of environmental conditions under which human societies exist and the limited number of cultural responses or adaptations possible within each kind of environment. Certain environments provide more potential or flexibility for successful human exploitation than do others, but the cultural response is neither predetermined nor dictated by a particular environment: a range of adaptive choices are always open to any given society.

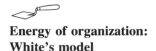

Cultural ecology: Steward's model

At the same time that Steward was putting forth his theory of multilinear, or specific, evolution, Leslie White was defending a modified version of general cultural evolution. While recognizing the problems involved with the nineteenth-century version of unilinear cultural evolution, White argued that broad, general stages could be defined to describe the overall trajectory of known cultural evolution. White's definition of culture as "man's extrasomatic (nonbiological) adaptation" has been widely adopted by archaeologists studying cultural process, as has his return to technological forms as the primary data sources for understanding cultural adaptation. The developmental model worked out by White and his students focuses on increases in efficiency in harnessing energy and organizing manpower.

Energy of organization: White's model

Another conceptual contribution came from the rise in the 1930s of the idea of functionalism in anthropology. This concept provides the background for study of culture as a system of inextricably interrelated parts. Each aspect of culture—whether part of the technological, social, or ideological realm—is a functional and useful part of the whole, and cannot be understood except as part of the overall system. The final explicit extension of this idea has been the incorporation of General Systems Theory, a theory for describing and interpreting the "behavior" of all kinds of systems, including living organisms and digital computers as well as cultures.

The foregoing theoretical contributions have become integrated in the current widespread concept of culture as a *system*—a complex entity composed of interrelated parts, in which the relationships among component parts are as important as are the component parts themselves. Such a conception is evolutionary in the sense that it views the sum of cultural change as analogous to cumulative changes seen in biological evolution: the system, whether cultural or biological, evolves, but not as part of a single uniform sequence. Rather, cultural evolution is a many-channeled process, governed by each society's ecological adaptation; specific societies adjust and change according to their own cultural and environmental circumstances.

The range of cultures and societies that result from this multilinear evolutionary process can be classified, and the cultural classification most used today combines criteria of technological and organizational complexity to define broad evolutionary stages. This classification is discussed in detail later on in this chapter; here we wish only to make clear that this revived cultural evolutionary model does *not* imply that the societies with the most complex organization and sophisticated technological adaptation represent the inevitable end product of cultural evolution. On the contrary, although multilinear evolution may lead toward increasing complexity, this is only one general alternative pattern of culture change. Other evolutionary routes may lead to stability—or no change—and still others may result in decreasing complexity and even extinction.

The second component of the cultural processual approach, the deductive research method, has a somewhat separate developmental career. The overall rationale of the original unilinear evolutionary theory involved a rather loose deductive research strategy. But the specific application of a rigorous, scientific deductive strategy to archaeological research has its roots in the first critiques of the inductive approach that is associated with cultural historical reconstruction.

Steward and Setzler's critique of archaeology

In 1938, Julian Steward and Frank M. Setzler took cultural historical archaeologists to task for placing such a heavy emphasis on description of the temporal and spatial distributions of prehistoric data. Steward and Setzler asserted that preoccupation with temporal and spatial description had become an end in itself: once all the time-space distributions had been worked out, archaeologists would be left with nothing to do. Instead, they argued, archaeologists should be asking fundamental anthropological questions about the process of culture change, and then using archaeological data to answer such questions.

Soon thereafter, a young graduate student named Walter W. Taylor wrote, as his doctoral dissertation, a critique of the prevailing practice of cultural historical reconstruction. This work, *A Study of Archeology,* was published in 1948; it represents the most thorough evaluation of the contributions and shortcomings of the descriptive emphasis then current in cultural historical archaeology. Taylor's fundamental criticism was not directed at the goals of cultural historical reconstruction, for these remain valid objectives for all archaeologists —that is, understanding of form, function, and process. Rather, Taylor pointed out the failure of these archaeologists to meet their stated goals—failure to integrate data into a picture more functionally and socially meaningful than, for example, noting artifactual similarities and differences between sites. And he found a complete lack of *any* worthwhile effort directed at understanding how and why cultures change. As a solution, Taylor called for what he termed a *conjunctive approach,* to reveal the interrelationships of archaeological data by considering them in their original social context rather than simply as interesting but isolated material finds. By looking at functional sets of archaeological data, one could reconstruct the ancient activities they represent and ultimately begin to understand the processes of cultural change. Although they do not explicitly espouse a deductive research strategy, Taylor's arguments imply—and have finally led to—the adoption of such an approach.

Walter Taylor's critique of archaeology

Lewis R. Binford made the first explicit, unmistakable call for an entirely new and scientific archaeological research strategy based on a deductive approach. The impact of Binford's critique of the prevailing practice of cultural historical archaeology, which had changed little since Taylor's original appeal some 15 years earlier, has been profound. Although Taylor had been largely ignored, the work of Binford and his students has been the single most important factor in the general acceptance of an explicitly deductive research method and of the cultural processual approach in general. With this in mind, let us now examine this approach more closely.

Lewis Binford's critique of archaeology

THE CULTURAL PROCESSUAL METHOD

The basic data gathering procedures used in the cultural processual approach are the same as those used for cultural historical reconstruction, but the orientation of research is critically different: the overall strategy is deductive rather than inductive. In practice, this means that research begins with the formulation of the propositions to be tested and the definition of relevant data—those kinds of data that provide appropriate tests for the propositions. As we have noted, in many cases previously achieved cultural historical reconstructions provide the source for propositions to be tested.

We shall consider two approaches to the delineation of prehistoric culture process. The first of these, based on formal scientific methodology, is the *deductive-nomological* approach. The second method, a less formal one, relies on the testing of *identification hypotheses*.

The Deductive-Nomological Approach

Deductive-nomological refers to a specific, formal scientific methodology advocated by such philosphers as Carl G. Hempel and Paul Oppenheim and such archaeologists as Lewis Binford, Patty Jo Watson, Steven A. LeBlanc, and Charles L. Redman. The approach relies on the philosophy of *logical positivism,* which holds that there is a real world composed of observable phenomena that behave in an orderly manner and that can be understood and explained by deductive inquiry. By observation, formulation of hypotheses, and testing of those hypotheses, one can (positively) understand how the world works.

Nomology is the science of general laws; thus deductive-nomological explanation refers to a method of explaining observable phenomena by deductive application of general laws. In this sense, "explanation" means indicating that the observed phenomenon is accounted for as a concrete case of an appropriate general law. In other words, deductive-nomological explanation is the same as prediction: a general law explains given phenomena if it accurately predicts their occurrence under a specified set of circumstances.

Law of evolutionary potential: Sahlins and Service

Most of the general laws used by archaeologists come from various branches of the social sciences; to cite one such law from cultural anthropology, we may rephrase Marshall Sahlins and Elman R. Service's "law of evolutionary potential" to read as follows: *The more specialized a culture's adaptation to a given environment, the more difficult will be its readaptation in the face of environmental change.* As this example shows, general laws are complex, abstract propositions. For this reason they are not directly testable. They can be tested indirectly, however, by deriving hypotheses from them which can then be applied to actual archaeological data. Such an *experimental hypothesis* restates the general law in specific terms, identifying a specific predicted relationship between two or more concretely defined variables and delineating the conditions under which the relationship is expected to hold. In logical terms, a hypothesis is stated as follows: given conditions *C,* if *A* occurs, then *B* will also occur.

Testing a hypothesis derived from a general law

In terms of the general law just cited, an archaeologist might hypothesize that the explanation behind the differential survival of two particular prehistoric communities was related to the degree of specialization of their adaptation to the local environment, and that when environmental conditions changed the less specialized culture was better able to cope with the change. To be more specific—but still keeping the example very simplified—suppose that the same region supported both a densely settled community that relied entirely on agricultural products for its food supply, and a nomadic group that subsisted on a wide variety of opportunistically gathered foods. In the face of, say a prolonged drought, the latter group would probably be more adept at procuring a food supply adequate to support its members. Rephrasing the general law as a hypothesis to fit this situation yields the following: *given a low degree of subsistence specialization, if environmental change occurs, a certain correspondingly high degree of adaptability (measured perhaps as survival or even prosperity) should be observed.*

If the observed data do not fit expectations, the researcher must reject the hypothesis. This may mean that the invoked law is invalid, or it may simply mean that its application in the particular case is inappropriate. A single test does not suffice to reject a *law.* Nor is a hypothesis found to be consistent with observed data "proven"; it is simply advanced as the best provisional explanation available, subject to further testing and refinement. It is possible, for example, that the same observed "results" can ensue from different causes under only slightly different conditions, such as an epidemic disease that affects only the settled society in the example above. Thus the more precisely a hypothesis is stated and the more specific the situations it can discriminate among, the stronger the inference that a supported hypothesis really presents the correct explanation.

Perhaps the most widely read argument in favor of the deductive-nomological approach in prehistoric archaeology was written by Patty Jo Watson, Steven A. LeBlanc, and Charles L. Redman. In their book *Explanation in Archeology,* Watson and her colleagues ask whether archaeologists can use prehistoric data to formulate and test hypotheses relevant both to the explanation of particular past situations and to the development of general laws about cultural process; they then reply affirmatively to this query—a response most archaeologists would agree with. Watson, LeBlanc, and Redman go on, however, to ask what precisely constitutes explanation of culture process. Their answer is that explanation refers strictly to the subsumption of past events and processes under general or *covering laws,* according to the deductive-nomological method just described.

However, this position does not appear to represent a consensus of archaeological opinion on the subject. In fact, though most archaeologists recognize the validity and utility of deductive research, few argue that a deductive-nomological approach is the only kind of explanation possible. Most archaeologists appear to question the appropriateness of such a specific deductive method, especially one derived from physical sciences such as physics and chemistry. This doubt

Archaeological explanations: Use of covering laws

stems from a central issue in the social and behavioral sciences: *are* there general laws that broadly govern human behavior and can thereby universally explain it? In the broadest sense, the answer must be yes; regularities and uniformities in human behavior must exist if we are to use analogy to interpret past behavior. But whether archaeologists (or other social scientists) can compile a set of specific formal rules or laws through which all behavior can theoretically be predicted—that is another question. This issue is not resolved, but those who would answer this question in the affirmative are actively pursuing their goal of establishing laws of human behavior.

Identification Hypotheses

Even when they do not use covering laws to explain past behavior, archaeologists often use a deductive approach to organize and orient their research. Particularly important in this regard are hypotheses that aid in the identification of archaeological data. In a cultural historical inductive research design, data are collected, analyzed, synthesized, and then interpreted. In a deductive approach, a research problem is first stated and the data that would be relevant to its solution are specified as concretely as possible; then these particular kinds of data are actively sought. Many other kinds of data, of course, are collected simultaneously. For example, in studying the island of Cozumel, off the coast of the Yucatan peninsula, Jeremy Sabloff and William Rathje postulated on documentary grounds that the island had served as an ancient Maya port-of-trade, where massive exchange operations were carried out. In order to investigate the exchange system specifically, they outlined the kinds of facilities they expected, such as warehouses, and even postulated the kinds of artifact style variability they would expect to find, assuming different sets of ancient political conditions. If the port were controlled by a single political authority, for example, the goods should show a preponderance of one style; if the place were a free port, with free exchange protected by mutual agreement of trading parties, the styles found in goods exchanged should show more diversity and closer to equal numerical representation. These predictions are deductive, but they are based on logical expectations for a specific situation rather than on general laws of human behavior.

Identification hypotheses can deal with data either synchronically or diachronically. Synchronic identification hypotheses predict the material forms that should be associated with particular activities at one point in time, or without regard to time; diachronic identifications specify the changes in material culture associated with changes in behavior through time. In general, this distinction corresponds to Mi-

Identification of prehistoric trade: Sabloff and Rathje on Cozumel Island, Mexico

chael Schiffer's categories of "correlation hypotheses" (synchronic) and "sociocultural change hypotheses" (diachronic). Schiffer also defines a third category, "transformation hypotheses," which involve definition of the processes affecting archaeological context and the formation of the archaeological record.

Following Schiffer, we can define three *sub*categories of identification hypotheses. Unlike Schiffer, however, who feels that these apply only to synchronic situations, we believe that the subcategories can be applied to diachronic data as well. The three subcategories are defined by the kinds of variables they deal with, but all may relate material remains to behavior at a single point in time or at several points in time, in order to reveal aspects of change. The first subcategory pertains to relationships between *artifacts* (or ecofacts) and ancient behavior, which is defined according to manufacturing, use, and disposal activities as discussed in Chapter 3. For instance, to identify a grain-grinding stone, one can specify the expected materials, wear pattern, surface residues, and so on, as well as the shape of the artifact and perhaps its association with other food preparation implements. The second subcategory refers to relationships between spatial distribution of *features and/or sites* and ancient behavior, where the latter is defined according to settlement patterns or other analytic approaches. The Cozumel port-of-trade hypothesis specifying that warehouses should be found is one example of this subcategory; similarly, at the Maya site of Nohmul, in Belize, Norman Hammond and Duncan Pring posited a port function and defined the position and form characteristics of a docking facility—which they then were able to locate and identify. The third subcategory pertains to *all three* kinds of variables—artifacts, sites or features—and ancient behavior. To cite an example mentioned in Chapter 13, archaeologists who suspect that a site was devastated by an invasion might seek specific kinds of artifacts and features, including evidence of destroyed buildings, unburied bodies, broken weapons, and so on.

Artifact-behavioral links

Spatial patterns–behavioral links

Artifact-spatial patterns–behavioral links

CULTURAL PROCESSUAL SYNTHESIS

In the cultural processual approach, synthesis involves assembling all the data relevant to rigorous testing of hypotheses under consideration. The testing of hypotheses in archaeology, as in any scientific discipline, must be by an explicit, fully documented procedure. In many sciences, from physics to psychology, hypotheses are tested by a repeatable *experiment*. For example, the hypothesis that explains how a barometer works holds that the weight of the earth's atmosphere—atmospheric pressure—supports the column of mercury.

Any change in atmospheric pressure should also change the height of the column supported. One such change is produced by variation in weather conditions; another, if the hypothesis is true, should result from variation in altitude. That is, much more atmosphere is located above a barometer at sea level than at, say, 5000 feet. If a barometer is moved from sea level to 5000 feet, the reduction in pressure should lead to a decrease in the column's height. An experiment to test this hypothesis would involve moving one barometer to a new altitude while a second remained at the first altitude as a check against change in weather conditions. This experiment is controlled, in that it rules out interference by other factors (in this case, weather). It is also repeatable: it can be performed any number of times.

Archaeology cannot rely upon controlled, repeatable experiments to test hypotheses. The archaeological record already exists, and archaeologists cannot manipulate variables or create special situations to test hypotheses. They can, however, provide rigorous tests by explicitly and clearly stating the conditions and expectations of their hypotheses and by adhering to certain principles governing nonexperimental research.

The testing procedure for archaeological hypotheses actually begins in the formulation stage, with the formulation of multiple hypotheses that make mutually exclusive predictions about the data. The use of *multiple working hypotheses* means that as many explanatory alternatives as possible are considered. This minimizes the opportunity for explanatory bias on the part of the investigator and maximizes the chance of finding the best available explanation. In the Cozumel example cited earlier, Sabloff and Rathje set forth two mutually contradictory hypotheses concerning the nature of political control at the ancient port: if authority were centralized, uniform artifact styles should be found, while decentralized authority would be reflected by diverse styles.

Multiple working hypotheses: Cozumel Island, Mexico

When the hypotheses are set forth and the relevant data assembled, the archaeologist checks the observed data against what was expected. The latter process usually begins with the test of *compatibility:* do the data agree or conflict with the expectations of a given hypothesis? In many cases, the compatibility test eliminates all but one hypothesis, which is advanced as the best available explanation. In other instances, however, several hypotheses may survive this test, and other criteria must be used to decide among them.

According to the deductive-nomological approach, *predictability* is the principal test of the validity of a hypothesis. According to this criterion, the hypothesis that allows the investigator to predict accurately other instances of the same phenomenon under the same conditions is upheld as the best explanation.

If two hypotheses account equally well for the observed data, the principle of *parsimony,* or Occam's razor, gives preference to the most economical, least complex explanation. A hypothesis that requires a complicated combination of circumstances is less likely to be accurate than one requiring only a few conditions. (Note that this principle can be used *only* to choose between explanations that otherwise account for the data equally well.) The criterion of *completeness* is also important: the more of the detailed observed data a given hypothesis accounts for, the stronger the evidence in favor of that explanation. Finally, the criterion of *symmetry* directs selection of the most internally unified, well-articulated hypothesis.

As we have seen, these criteria are applied with the goal of invalidating all but one hypothesis. The surviving hypothesis may then be advanced, not as proven, but as the best possible explanation given the present state of knowledge. All science involves the assumption that contemporary explanations will eventually be modified or completely replaced as new implications of them are tested by other data. It is also possible that the data base currently available may not be complete enough to allow the elimination of all but one hypothesis; two or more may survive all tests. In such cases both survivors will be retained, in the expectation that subsequent research may provide new data that will isolate the best explanation.

INTERPRETATION: CULTURAL PROCESSUAL MODELS

The models we discuss in this book are not necessarily restricted to either cultural historical or cultural processual interpretation. Although the descriptive models discussed in Chapter 13 are usually associated with cultural historical reconstruction, they may also be applied in cultural processual interpretations. As we have noted, cultural historical models often generate hypotheses that are tested, modified, and advanced as explanations for prehistoric cultural processes.

But just as some models are used more frequently in cultural historical reconstruction, certain others are primarily associated with cultural processual explanation. We shall discuss three such models, all of them based on fundamental concepts introduced in Chapter 2. The first—systems models—derives from the functional concept of culture, especially as it has been refined by application of General Systems Theory. The ecological concept of culture provides archaeologists with the second model, that based upon ecology; and the multilinear evolutionary concept furnishes the third model, founded on modern cultural evolutionary theory.

Systems Models

Descriptive studies of culture, such as those dealing with social organization of family units, kin groups, or whole communities, often focus on the individual constituent parts of the organization. But the dynamic qualities of any organization—how and why it survives and changes through time—can be understood only through examination of both its components and their interrelationships. Systems models recognize that an organization represents more than a simple sum of its parts; in fact they emphasize the study of the relations between these parts.

The systems models used in cultural processual interpretation are based on General Systems Theory as set forth in the work of Ludwig von Bertalanffy and others. This theory defines a system as a set of component parts and the relationships among the parts. Or, to quote Anatol Rapoport, "a whole which functions as a whole by virtue of the interdependence of its parts is a system." General Systems Theory also holds that any organization, from amoebae to cultures to computers, may be studied as a system, in order to examine how its components are related and how changes in some components or in their relations produce changes in the overall system. The term "environment," in a systems approach, refers to all factors that are external to the system being studied and that may cause change in the system or that are affected by the system. We introduced these concepts in Chapter 2 in defining the systemic view of culture.

Systems theorists distinguish two kinds of systems, open and closed. Closed systems receive no matter, energy, or information from the environment; all sources of change are internal. Open systems exchange matter, energy, and information with their environment; change can come either from within the system or from outside. Living organisms and sociocultural systems are both examples of open systems. In order to understand how systems operate, we will examine systems models that are often applied to cultural processual interpretation.

A closed system: Thermostats

We will begin with a simple closed systems model. As an example, consider the components and relationships within a self-regulated or *homeostatic* temperature control system, such as those found within many modern buildings (Fig. 14.1). The components in the system are the air in the room or building, the thermometer, the thermostat, and the heater or air conditioner. In this case, a change in the air temperature acts as a stimulus which is detected by a thermometer and transmitted to the thermostat. When the temperature rises above a predetermined level, the thermostat triggers the air conditioner. The cooling response acts as *feedback* by stimulating the same interdependent components to shut down the air conditioner once the temperature has gone below the critical level.

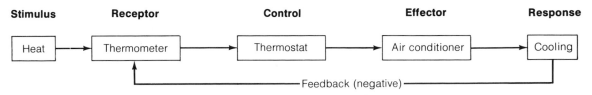

Figure 14.1 Diagram of a homeostatic temperature-control system, illustrating the operation of a closed system.

This closed system illustrates how certain systems operate to maintain a stable condition or *steady state*. When a specific change in one part of the system threatens the steady state, this stimulates a response from other component parts. When the steady state has been restored, a feedback loop shuts down the response. Feedback of this kind is *negative* in the sense that it dampens or cuts off the system's response and thus maintains a condition of *dynamic equilibrium* in which the system's components are active, but the overall system is stable and unchanging. Equilibrating systems such as that in the above example are characterized by regulatory or *deviation-counteracting processes* (Fig. 14.2). Although they are useful for illustrating the operation of systems, such models are applicable only to unchanging and stable aspects of human societies. Since archaeologists are at least as frequently concerned with processes of culture change, we must also consider dynamic systems models that can account for cumulative systemic change.

The most commonly applied model for this deals with *deviation-amplifying processes*. Some changes stimulate further changes through *positive feedback* (Fig. 14.3). An interesting application of these concepts to an archaeological situation is Kent Flannery's systems model for the development of food production in Mesoamerica. In setting forth the model, Flannery first describes the food procurement system used by peoples of highland Mexico between about 8000 and 5000 B.C. The components of this system were the people themselves, their technology—including knowledge and equipment—for obtaining food, and the plants and animals actually used for food. People in the highland valleys lived in small groups, periodically coming together into larger "macrobands" but never settling down in stationary villages. The subsistence technology available to them included knowledge of edible plants and animals that could be procured by gathering and hunting techniques; it also included the use of projectile points, baskets, storage pits, fiber shredders, and various other implements and facilities for collecting and processing the food. Among the food items actively used were cactus, avocado, white-tailed deer, rabbits, and so on. Wild grasses related to maize were sometimes eaten but did not form a very important part of the diet.

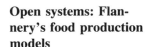

Open systems: Flannery's food production models

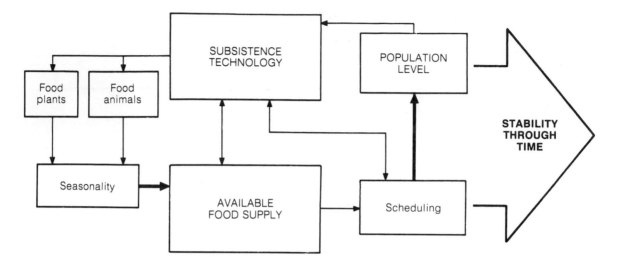

Figure 14.2 Simplified diagram of a system characterized by deviation-counteracting mechanisms (→) that lead to population and cultural stability through time; based upon data from prehistoric Mesoamerica (ca. 8000–5000 B.C.).

This food procurement system was regulated and maintained by two deviation-counteracting processes, which Flannery calls seasonality and scheduling. Seasonality refers to the characteristics of the food resources—some were available during only one season or another. To gather enough food, the people had to go where it was available; periodic abundance of particular resources allowed people to come together into the temporary macrobands, but the seasons of lean resources placed sharply defined limits on both total valley population and effective social group size. Scheduling, the other deviation-counteracting process Flannery posits, refers to the people's organizational response to seasonality: seasonal population movement and diet diversity prevented exhaustion of resources by overexploitation, but it also kept population levels low (see Fig. 14.2).

This stable system persisted for several thousand years. But eventually, a series of genetic changes in some of the wild grasses of the genus *Zea* stimulated a deviation-amplifying feedback system. Improved traits of the maize, such as larger cob size, induced people to reproduce the "improved" grass by sowing. As a result of this behavior, scheduling patterns were gradually altered. For instance, planting and harvesting requirements increased the time spent in spring and autumn camps, precisely where larger population gatherings had been feasible. The larger, more stable population groupings then invested more time and labor in improving the quality and quantity of crop yield; this positive feedback continued to induce change in the sub-

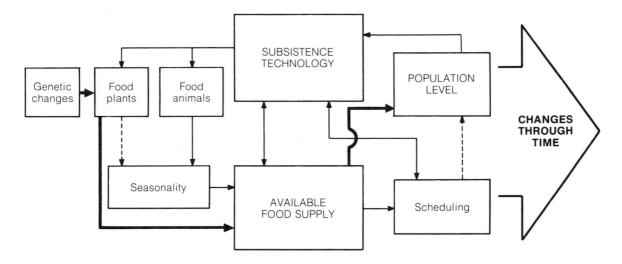

Figure 14.3 Simplified diagram of a system characterized by deviation-amplifying mechanisms that both weaken the deviation-counteracting mechanisms in Fig. 14.2 and lead to population growth and cultural change; based upon data from prehistoric Mesoamerica (after 5000 B.C.).

sistence system. For example, irrigation technology was developed to extend agriculture and settlement into more arid zones. As Flannery says, the "positive feedback following these initial genetic changes caused one minor [sub] system to grow out of all proportion to the others, and eventually to change the whole ecosystem of the Southern Mexican Highlands" (see Fig. 14.3).

Although some cultural systems may maintain a state of dynamic equilibrium for long periods of time, all cultures do change. Not all change involves growth, however. Sometimes deviation-amplifying processes result in cultural loss or decline, and ultimately in dissolution of the system. The modern case of the Ik of East Africa, as described by ethnographer Colin Turnbull, provides an example of such decline. Disruption of traditional behavior patterns by such factors as forced migration from preferred lands has led to apathy, intragroup hostility, a devaluation of human life, and population decline. The result in this case is as dramatically bleak as Flannery's is dramatically positive. Most cases of cultural change are less extreme, as cultural systems are affected simultaneously by both growth and decline of subsystems within them, in a gradual and cumulative course of change.

Dissolution of a system: The Ik of East Africa

Cultural Ecological Models

The second basic type of model used in cultural processual interpretation is provided by the perspective of cultural ecology. Although this conception derives from the wider field of ecology, its use within anthropology originated in the work of Julian Steward and others and has been developed in archaeology by such scholars as William Sanders. In its modern form, cultural ecology provides much more sophisticated models of the interaction between culture and environment than did the cultural historical model discussed in Chapter 13. The cultural ecological models are more sophisticated because they are both systemic and comprehensive. They are systemic in the sense that the overall approach of cultural ecology incorporates the tenets of General Systems Theory. They are comprehensive in that they partition the environment of a culture into three separate, complementary facets. Whereas the cultural historical approach often treated "environment" as a single entity, cultural ecology considers a given culture as interacting with an environmental system composed of three complex subsystems. These are the physical landscape (habitat), the biological environment (biome), and the cultural environment—other, adjacent human groups (Fig. 14.4).

This basic ecological system seems superficially simple, but in fact it is very complex. We can appreciate this by considering that each subsystem is composed of further subordinate systems, which in turn comprise smaller component systems, and so on. For example, the cultural subsystem combines three component systems: technological, social, and ideational (see Fig. 14.4). Each of these, in turn, can be broken down further; the social system, for example, includes such constituents as political, kinship, and economic systems.

For any given society, the sum of specific interactions contained within an overall cultural ecological system describes the nature of the society's *cultural adaptation*. Each society adapts to its environment primarily through its technological system, but also, secondarily, through the social and ideological systems. The technological system interacts directly with all three components of the environment—physical, biological, and cultural—by providing, for instance, the tools and techniques required for securing shelter, food, and defense from attack. The social system adapts by integrating and organizing society. The relation, described earlier, between band organization and seasonality and scheduling in preagricultural highland Mexican societies is an example of social system adaptation to the biological environment. And the ideological system is adaptive in that it reinforces the organization and integration of society by providing motivation, explanation, and confidence in the appropriateness of the technological and social adaptations.

Of course the full set of interactions within such a complex system is difficult to study all at once; as a result archaeologists often begin

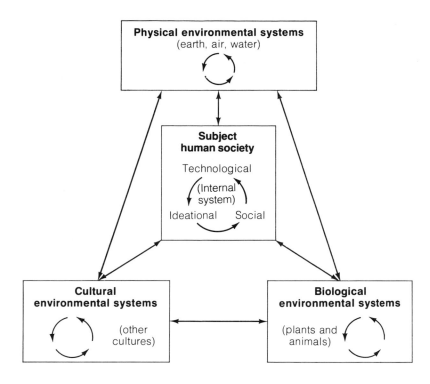

Figure 14.4   The cultural ecological system, illustrating the relationships between a given culture ("subject human society") and its environment, composed of physical, cultural, and biological subsystems (compare with Fig. 13.12).

by isolating one or more of the subordinate systems directly involved in cultural adaptation. The technological system is the obvious focus of studies seeking to understand the adaptive process. Fortunately for the prehistoric archaeologist, not only is the technological subsystem the principal agent of cultural adaptation, but the remains of ancient technology are also usually the fullest part of the archaeological record. These technological data may be used to reconstruct a particular aspect of the technological system, such as subsistence. Archaeologists then integrate their detailed models of different subsystems to create complex models of overall cultural adaptation.

Because of the mass of information involved in such models, computers are often used for information storage. Computers also enable the archaeologist to perform experimental manipulation of the models: after a hypothetical change is introduced in one component of the

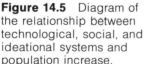

Computer simulation: Zubrow's projections of Southwest cultural development

stable hypothetical system, a *computer simulation* determines what deviation-amplifying or -counteracting reactions would be induced by the original change. For example, Ezra Zubrow has used computer simulations to examine relationships among human population size and structure, biological resources of the environment, and settlement location in the prehistoric Southwest; he finds that changing the characteristics of any of these system components produces different projected courses of growth and decline.

We should reiterate here that although many changes originate within the technological subsystem of culture, change may arise anywhere in the overall cultural ecological system. Technological development is important in cultural evolution, but it is not the only source of change.

In an analogy to biological adaptation, many archaeologists measure the effectiveness of cultural adaptation by the rate of population growth and resultant population size. In this sense, population growth and size are a measurable response to the overall cultural ecological system (see Fig. 14.5). Thus, with regard to population increase some societies exhibit the characteristics of deviation-amplifying systems possessing one or more positive feedback mechanisms. For example, changes in the technological system may provide more efficient food production and storage capabilities, resulting in an increase in population. Changes in the social or ideational systems will follow to accommodate the population growth; these in turn may allow more efficient food distribution or expansion via conquest or colonization to open new areas for food production and result in further population growth. This, in turn, may place new stress on the technology, which must respond with new changes to increase the food supply, and so forth. The result is an interrelated change-increase cycle, perhaps best illustrated by the phenomenon of recent world population growth.

However, some societies maintain their populations in dynamic equilibrium by negative feedback mechanisms. Such mechanisms include culturally acceptable population control methods (birth control,

Figure 14.5 Diagram of the relationship between technological, social, and ideational systems and population increase.

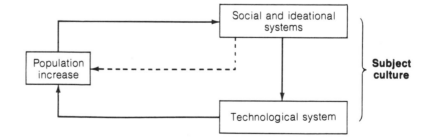

infanticide, warfare), migration, and social fission. Environmental mechanisms, including periodic famine or endemic disease, also contribute to the maintenance of deviation-counteracting systems.

The consideration of the dynamic consequences of cultural ecological models brings us to the final basic perspective on cultural processual interpretation—multilinear cultural evolution.

Multilinear Cultural Evolution Models

The systemic view of culture and the adaptation concept of cultural ecology are combined in the contemporary theory of multilinear cultural evolution. This theory sees the evolution of culture as the cumulative changes in a system resulting from the continuous process of cultural adaptation over extensive periods of time.

Unlike the nineteenth-century theory of unilinear cultural evolution, modern cultural evolutionary theory does not postulate any single inevitable course of change to be followed by all societies. Multilinear evolutionary theorists do, however, hold that certain recognizable regularities occur in the trajectory of culture change and differentiation through time. Building on the work of Leslie White and others, Sahlins and Service have distinguished between *specific* cultural evolution, which describes the unique course followed by a particular cultural system, and *general* cultural evolution, in which a series of broad developmental stages may be discerned. These stages or organizational levels—band, tribe, chiefdom, and state—are defined primarily by the related criteria of population size, social organizational complexity, and subsistence strategy. None of the categories is absolute or unvarying: intermediate or transitional versions can be found. We shall describe each of the four more concretely (Fig. 14.6).

Bands are small, egalitarian societies that meet their subsistence needs by hunting and gathering. Although they recognize a home territory, they do not live in settled communities but follow a seasonal migration pattern that corresponds to available food and water resources. Organizationally, a band consists of a single kin group, usually composed of related adult males, wives who have been brought in from other bands, and dependent children. There is no formal political organization, no economic specialization, and no social ranking other than that based on sex and relative age. Population size generally ranges from 25 to 100. Richard MacNeish, on whose work Flannery's highland Mexican agriculture model is based, has defined "macrobands" formed by coalescence of several regular bands ("microbands") during seasons of relative abundance of food resources. These macrobands may consist of as many as 500 individuals, but they usually represent only temporary social gatherings. Such tempo-

Band organizations: Tehuacán, Mexico

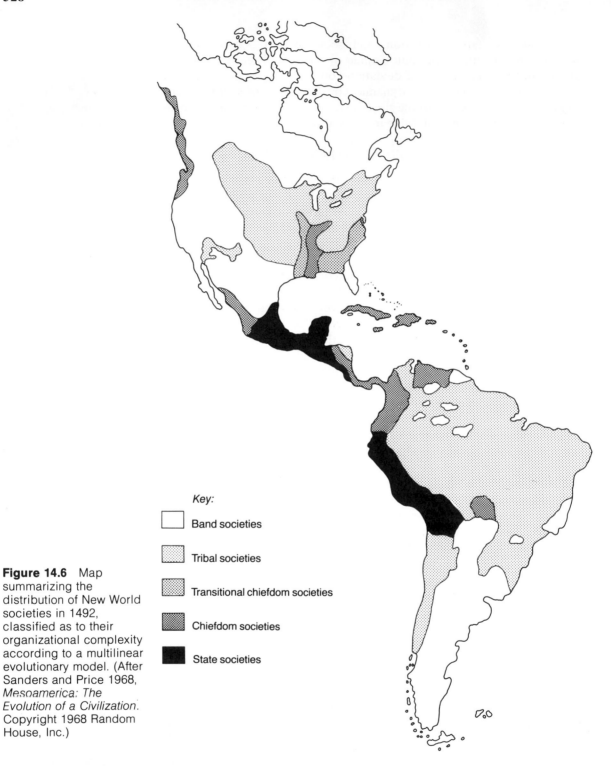

Figure 14.6 Map summarizing the distribution of New World societies in 1492, classified as to their organizational complexity according to a multilinear evolutionary model. (After Sanders and Price 1968, *Mesoamerica: The Evolution of a Civilization.* Copyright 1968 Random House, Inc.)

Key:

☐ Band societies

▫ Tribal societies

▪ Transitional chiefdom societies

▪ Chiefdom societies

■ State societies

rary gatherings are known from the ethnological literature; they may be represented archaeologically by short-lived occupation sites that are uncharacteristically large for their area. Examples may be found at Ipiutak, Alaska, as well as the posited macroband sites located by MacNeish's survey in the Tehuacán Valley of Mexico.

Tribes are also egalitarian societies, but they are usually larger in population size than bands, and they possess more efficient and stable subsistence strategies that allow permanent village settlement. Specific subsistence modes usually include some form of food production—agriculture or horticulture—but may also involve some hunting and gathering. Tribal systems have a variety of cross-cutting social institutions, beyond basic kinship ties, that integrate the members of the society; these include secret societies, age-grade groupings, and occupational groups, such as warrior or religious organizations. Permanent positions of leadership and authority do not exist, although some individuals may assume temporary leadership roles during times of stress, such as leaders of war parties. Tribal systems support populations ranging from about 500 up to several thousand individuals. Under unusual conditions, however, "composite tribes" with populations of more than 10,000 may be formed: an example is the congregation of tribes of the North American Great Plains when they were faced with serious military threat from Euro-American forces in the nineteenth century. The tribe level of organization can usually be recognized archaeologically by village settlements that show evidence of food-production subsistence practices but not of marked social status differentiation. Examples can be found the world over, from Pan P'o in central China to Basketmaker and early Pueblo sites in the southwestern United States.

Tribal organizations: Great Plains, central China, southwestern United States

Chiefdoms mark the appearance within age and sex groups of social rankings in which differential social status is conferred at birth. Kin groups such as lineages are often ranked, and the highest social status resides in a single permanent, hereditary position (the chief), who is normally the highest-ranked person within the highest-ranked lineage. The office and status of the chief are vital to the integration of society. Although the chief exercises authority primarily by economic power, often acting as the arbitrator in distribution of surplus wealth, his right to wield this authority is usually reinforced by religious sanctions as well as by the prestige vested in the office of chief. Chiefdoms are characterized by the existence of full-time economic and political specialists, as well as of permanent economic institutions such as markets and long-distance trade networks. Population size varies from less than 1000 to more than 10,000. Some well-developed chiefdoms, such as groups along the northwest coast of North America, are known to have supported populations approaching 100,000 by means of food-collecting subsistence systems—in this case, intensive

Chiefdom organizations: Northwest coast, Pueblo Bonito and Moundville

seacoast fishing and plant gathering. But such examples are exceptional; most chiefdoms rely on subsistence strategies that include efficient food-production systems, such as irrigation-based agriculture. Archaeological evidence of chiefdom systems is indicated by the material remains of the category's defining attributes—specified population size, marked social hierarchy, economic specialization, and so on. Examples include such sites as Pueblo Bonito, in Chaco Canyon, New Mexico, and—as argued by Christopher Peebles and Susan Kus —the site of Moundville, in Alabama.

State systems retain many characteristics of chiefdoms, at least in the initial period of their development. In many respects state systems merely elaborate and codify chiefdom-level institutions such as status ranking, occupational specialization, and market and trading institutions. State systems differ from chiefdoms in two crucial respects, however. In the first place, authority is based on true political power, sanctioned by the explicit threat of legitimized force in cases of deviant behavior. The means for carrying out the threat are usually manifested in permanent military, police, and judicial institutions. Second, states are too large and complex for the integrative functions of kin ties to be effective: social integration in states is facilitated and expressed by concepts of nationality and citizenship, usually defined with references to territorial boundaries. Thus membership in a state society is based less on genealogy and descent than on place of birth. A distinction is often made between urban and nonurban states, depending on relative size and density of major population centers. However, urbanism has proved to be a difficult concept to define ethnographically and sociologically, let alone for prehistoric situations; as a result, many archaeologists have come to disregard this distinction, focusing instead on attributes of organizational complexity. State systems are usually supported by intensive forms of agriculture, with agricultural technologies that include irrigation, fertilization, and so on. Populations range from about 10,000 up to the multimillions of modern nation states. State systems have emerged at various times in different parts of the world. In Mesopotamia, state organization was established in the fourth millennium B.C.; in Mesoamerica, the site of Teotihuacán represents the locus of power of a state system that arose in the last few centuries B.C.

State organizations: Mesopotamia and Mesoamerica

CAUSES OF PREHISTORIC CULTURAL CHANGE

By using any one of the interpretative models discussed above, or a combination of several, archaeologists attempt to understand the basic causes of prehistoric cultural change. But how does the archaeologist reveal these causes? Two schools of thought have emerged as to the best way to approach this question. The first emphasizes a general approach and concerns the identification of what are held to be the *prime movers* of cultural change. That is, this approach attempts to document the process of change in a universal context, revealing those primary causes that operate in all human societies. The second school is more particularistic, attempting to isolate and understand individual adaptive systems in order to explain particular instances of culture change. In this view there are no universal prime movers of change; rather, cultural change can only be understood by investigating each instance of the basic cultural adaptive process. At this point we will briefly examine each of these strategies.

Macrochange: The Prime Movers

This perspective emphasizes the identification of a few specific, primary factors that underlie the process of culture change and, ultimately, cultural evolution. It is based on the premise that the regularities and patterns in evolutionary change result from regularities of cause. Accordingly, without necessarily denying the validity of research focused on individual subsystems and microchange, this approach emphasizes the testing of broader hypotheses that seek the fundamental, far-reaching causes of all cultural change.

This approach is derived directly from the pioneering theories of Childe and Adams, discussed earlier in this chapter. Current workers in the field attempt to identify in more detail the workings of various prime movers in cultural change. Population growth is often proposed as a fundamental cause of cultural change. This prime mover has been applied in various regions to explain the course of cultural evolution. For example, Sanders and Price based their thesis for the evolution of pre-Columbian Mesoamerican culture upon population growth and its effects upon two secondary factors, competition and cooperation. Other universal causal factors have been proposed to explain specific evolutionary developments, such as the rise of complex state societies. Prime movers proposed for the development of state societies include environmental circumstriction and warfare, suggested by scholars such as Robert Carneiro and David Webster, and economic exchange systems, advanced by Malcolm Webb.

Population growth as prime mover: Sanders and Price in Meso-america

Microchange: The Multivariate Strategy

In this perspective, archaeologists attempt to delineate the basic processes of culture change by focusing their research on specific subsystems that are most directly involved in adaptation. In order to identify the focus of change, research of this kind may test hypotheses concerned, for example, with a variety of alternative subsistence modes, or with the acquisition and distribution of critical natural resources. Since each instance of change is unique, this view holds that no single factor or small group of "prime movers" cause cultural change. Cultural evolution, the overall product of change, is thus viewed as the product of a multitude of adaptive adjustments—each resulting in a microchange—that are a constant feature of all cultural systems. In basic terms, this is what has been called the "multivariate" model of cultural change. Specific models, such as Flannery's thesis bearing upon the transformation from hunting-and-gathering subsistence to food production build upon this premise and call for substantial cumulative cultural changes over a sufficient period of time.

The multivariate perspective sees cultural evolution operating through an interlocking, hierarchical systems model of culture, whose basic structure is common to all human societies, but whose details vary from culture to culture. These variations and unique features of certain systems produce the different patterns of cultural evolution in each society. These systemic variations account for the relative stability of some societies, characterized by deviation-counteracting relationships, while others characterized by deviation-amplifying relationships, change rapidly.

Thus the structure and operation of the multivariate concept of cultural evolution is based on the tenets of cultural ecological and systemic cultural models. This approach requires that the archaeologist identify the components, and understand the relationships, of those specific subsystems crucial to the cultural adaptive process. This is not an easy task, especially given the inherent limitations of archaeological data. The archaeologist must formulate and test a series of sophisticated hypotheses, using data that are often difficult to collect. Yet, when successful—as in the case of the transformation to food production in Mesoamerica described earlier in this chapter—such research may reveal multivariate causes to explain fundamental culture change.

SUMMARY AND CONCLUSION

Rather than simply summarizing the contents of this chapter, we shall consider the role of both the cultural historical and the cultural processual approaches within contemporary prehistoric archaeology. Archaeologists use both approaches, but the question remains as to whether these are alternative or mutually exclusive ways of interpreting the past. This is a fundamental concern, since each of these approaches has been defined as a *paradigm*—as an overall strategy with its own unique research methods, theory, and goals. Therefore, according to such a viewpoint, prehistoric archaeology consists of two research traditions, each defining its own problems for investigation and its own set of data considered relevant to such problems.

Competition between two or more paradigms is not unique to archaeology, but is inevitable in all scientific study. According to the rather popular view of one philosopher of science, Thomas Kuhn, the development of any scientific discipline through time is marked by periods of fairly tranquil acceptance of a single paradigm, interrupted by periods of conflict between the old paradigm and a newly emerged one that seeks to "revolutionize" the concepts and orientation of the discipline. This developmental view would appear to explain rather neatly the recent turmoil of the 1960s in archaeology—the conflict between the traditional cultural historical advocates and the followers of the newly emerged cultural processual approach, associated with the rise of the "new archaeology." In fact, some archaeologists, such as Mark Leone, have interpreted this as an explicit case of Kuhn's thesis. According to Kuhn's view of the development of science, however, the new paradigm does not necessarily provide the discipline with a better understanding of its subject matter than the previous one. Thus, according to Kuhn, science should "relinquish the notion, explicit or implicit, that changes of paradigm carry scientists . . . closer and closer to the truth."

Kuhn bases the latter point on the realization that the conflict between paradigms is not resolved solely by the cold logic of rational science, but by psychological and emotional factors as well. In other words, the replacement of one paradigm by another occurs only when scientists, as individuals, reject the old scheme and accept the new concepts. Interestingly, Kuhn speaks of this intellectual transfer process as a "conversion experience." In the case of prehistoric archaeology, Paul Martin, a former exponent of the culture history approach, wrote a now-famous article describing his acceptance of the "new archaeology" in terms comparable with those of a religious conversion. But, of course, not all the defenders of the old concepts convert to the new. Thus, according to Kuhn, full acceptance of the revolutionary view relies upon the emergence of a new generation of scientists trained in the new paradigm.

Kuhn's thesis holds that scientific disciplines develop by successive replacements of paradigms, but that these changes are strongly influenced by nonrational factors. The result is often the acceptance of a paradigm that is more psychologically satisfying but no better equipped than its predecessor to understand the real world. This tends to contradict the view held by many of the "new archaeologists" that their paradigm is superior to the culture history paradigm in gaining an understanding of the prehistoric past. According to this position, archaeologists still pursuing interpretations based upon cultural historical reconstructions are at best outmoded, or far worse, practicing invalid science.

But science does not progress only by the conflict between competing paradigms. Kuhn's thesis has been valuable in revealing the role of this aspect of scientific development, as well as the importance of nonrational factors in this process. However, science remains a logical enterprise which does advance on the basis of rational inquiry. And the foundation for scientific inquiry remains the scientific method, discussed at the beginning of this book. This method involves inquiry based on the generation, from inductive observations, of theories that can be used to derive, via deduction, hypotheses that are tested for their veracity. By this process new theories replace the old when they provide better or more efficient explanations.

If science relies on the combination of inductive and deductive methods to increase our understanding of the world, then archaeology, as a scientific discipline, should do no different. This means that the inductively-based cultural historical approach is not invalid, but rather serves as a necessary and vital basis for the deductively-oriented culture processual approach. Thus, rather than being mutually exclusive, these two approaches together form a coherent overall paradigm for prehistoric archaeology (Fig. 14.7).

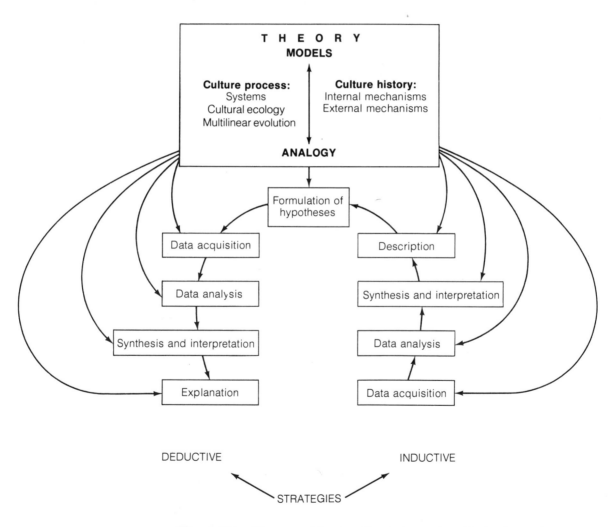

Figure 14.7   Diagram of the complementary roles of inductive and deductive research strategies in archaeology.

In this prehistoric archaeological paradigm, data are used inductively to generate temporal and spatial frameworks that define the past. In this way, cultural historical interpretations provide the foundation for deductive inquiry designed to identify specific causes of cultural change or stability. Variations within the cultural historical framework may be identified, and "normative" cultural concepts may be used to describe these changes. But only rigorously tested propositions can identify the causes of change and thereby begin to explain cultural process.

In summary, rather than being completely obsolete or invalid, cultural historical interpretations provide the necessary framework upon which cultural processual interpretations are made. The day may come when archaeologists complete the culture historical framework for all world areas and all prehistoric periods. Yet, given the tremendous diversity and time depth of human culture (and the toll from the destruction of archaeological remains), this day still seems far in the future. In the meantime, archaeology is pursuing the second aspect of its paradigm by generating and testing an increasing number of research questions designed to reveal the process of prehistoric cultural change.

See p. 575 for "Suggestions for Further Reading."

The Past in the Present and the Future

The foregoing chapters have defined archaeology and showed how it has developed and how the practice of archaeology is presently conducted. Although these discussions have necessarily abstracted and idealized the pursuit of archaeology, we have tried to remind the reader that archaeologists don't work in idealized situations— they are always working squarely within the larger context of the world around them. Archaeologists are certainly oriented to this larger world, in that their ultimate aim is to contribute to the general fund of knowledge about human behavior. But in this final chapter we would like to consider some problems the outside world has posed for archaeologists—problems that involve both preservation of physical archaeological remains and communication of archaeological interpretations about the past to the general public. These are challenges that all archaeologists must face now: challenges that must be met now and on whose solution rests the future of the study of the past.

Chapter 15: Challenges to Archaeology

A looted tomb, strewn with shattered pottery, is mute testimony to the accelerating destruction of archaeological evidence throughout the world, a situation presenting archaeology with one of its most difficult challenges. (Photo by Ian Graham, Peabody Museum.)

Challenges to Archaeology

We in the modern world have turned more stones, listened to more buried voices, than any culture before us. There should be a kind of pity that comes with time, when one grows truly conscious and looks behind as well as forward, for nothing is more brutally savage than the man who is not aware he is a shadow.

(Loren C. Eiseley, The Night Country, *1971*)

In this final chapter it seems appropriate to consider two challenging issues that face contemporary archaeologists. One is an intellectual challenge, posed by the growing popularity of what we term pseudo-archaeology. The other challenge represents a much more permanent and fundamental danger: the threat posed by the accelerating destruction of archaeological remains.

PSEUDO-ARCHAEOLOGY

The term *pseudo-archaeology* refers to a body of popularized accounts that use real or imaginary archaeological evidence to justify nonscientific and often overly dramatic reconstructions of prehistory. Pseudo-archaeology is really a specific case of the larger phenomenon of pseudo-science which plagues many branches of scientific study. Pseudo-scientists take dramatic stances on unconventional theories, attacking established scientific positions with highly selective data and accusing their proponents of narrow-mindedness and intellectual prejudice. In fact, the pseudo-scientists themselves are usually the ones who are guilty of such unscholarly sins.

Pseudo-archaeology has been with us for a long time. Included in the tradition are many of the accounts dealing with the "lost civilizations" of Atlantis and Mu, ancient mythical continents peopled with precociously sophisticated societies that have supposedly disappeared beneath the waves of the Atlantic and Pacific oceans. And every so often reports of mysterious hieroglyphs or symbols from pre-Columbian contexts revive the theory that Old World cultures were the source of native American civilizations. We noted in Chapter 2 that the debate over the identity of the "mound builders" of the ancient Americas grew quite heated in the nineteenth century, when peoples such as the Phoenicians, Assyrians, Romans, Chinese Buddhists, Norsemen, and Huns were suggested as the ones responsible for New World civilization. But archaeological research was then in its infancy, and to some extent the earliest proponents of those theories can be excused for a general lack of information. Today, however, pseudo-archaeology is characterized by ignorance or dismissal of accumulated evidence and of carefully reasoned archaeological interpretations, while the authors pick and choose those "facts" or bits of material evidence that seem to fit their case.

These fanciful arguments often have a widespread, romantic appeal. At present, the most popular theory in this category is that of Erich von Däniken, who seeks to explain a series of archaeological and historical "mysteries" by invoking visits from ancient astronauts. According to one report, von Däniken's books have sold more than 25 million copies in 32 languages; they have also spawned television programs and movies, as well as numerous imitative books by other authors. Some responses from professional archaeologists and scientifically oriented laymen have appeared: several books and articles are available, courses are being taught in a few colleges, and public television has produced a program in the *Nova* series that deals critically with von Däniken's propositions. But pseudo-archaeology continues to be more popular than scientific archaeology; and the public tends to regard the pseudo-archaeologist as more creative, imaginative, and open-minded, while the arguments of professional archaeologists appear stodgy and overly conservative. It would seem that the romantic speculations and the appeal to unsolved mysteries will always be more popular than the cold hard facts of science. If this is true, why should the archaeologist be concerned with the writings of pseudo-science? What is so harmful about these theories anyway?

At the beginning of this book we discussed the scientific method and the refinement of theories by testing hypotheses. A fair test of a hypothesis means that the scientist must consider all relevant data, allowing for possible disproof of the main hypothesis and support for alternative hypotheses. The pseudo-scientist does not do this. "Evidence" for hypotheses and "support" for theories is typically wrenched from its context: for example, von Däniken describes the sculptured scene on the sarcophagus lid from the famous tomb at the Maya site of Palenque, Mexico, as "obviously" representing an ancient astronaut at the controls of his ancient rocket (Fig. 15.1). But in making this statement, the author ignores all other evidence of Maya art and symbolism—the costume, the position of the figure, the representation of the maize plant, and ultimately, the hieroglyphic inscription that identifies the sculptured figure as one and the same as the buried ruler in the sarcophagus. The pseudo-archaeologist takes the data out of their larger context: other material remains of the Classic Maya indicate nothing about ancient astronauts, but because

Figure 15.1 Rubbing made from the sculptured sarcophagus lid found in the tomb beneath the Temple of the Inscriptions at Palenque, Mexico, representing the dead ruler surrounded by Maya supernatural symbols. (Rubbing, permission of Merle Greene.)

Fanciful vs. scientific interpretation: The Palenque sarcophagus lid

this single example has a superficial resemblance to the launch position of an astronaut, it is advanced as positive evidence for the "space visitor" theory.

A related problem is the ethnocentrism of such interpretations, in which everything is interpreted from the perspective of the observer's culture, rather than that of the culture from which the material comes. Such items as the Palenque sarcophagus lid, the rock art of Africa and northern Australia, or the carved figures in the "Gateway of the Sun" at Tiahuanaco in Bolivia are interpreted as evidence of astronauts or gods from outer space. But anyone who bothers to examine the rest of the local culture at any of these times and places finds that the figures depicted fit completely within gradually developed local traditions: they do not appear suddenly, they are not without parallels, and they are not followed by drastic changes in the archaeological record of the area. Details that look like antennae or bazookas to the pseudo-archaeologist do not convince those who have studied other artwork by the peoples in question. The record is there; but it does not speak for itself; it must be examined in its entirety, as responsible scholars examine it.

The problem of ethnocentrism (some would say racism) extends further. The basic questions underlying pseudo-archaeological theories is: How could ancient peoples possibly have built monuments such as the huge pyramids of Egypt? How could they have possessed the skills and the manpower to erect these and other awesome monuments before the advent of modern technology, without the aid of some extraterrestrial power? These rhetorical questions demand answers, but the pseudo-archaeologist phrases them in such a way as to suggest that ancient peoples could not have accomplished these feats, despite firm archaeological evidence to the contrary. For in fact, the accomplishments cited did not require superhuman skills or knowledge. Ancient Egyptians, for example, were quite able to move the huge and heavy stones of the pyramids—or entire obelisks—from the quarries by conventional water transport and by simple sledges and ramps; both methods are attested in written and pictorial Egyptian records. Certainly, we find the imposing accomplishments of the past awesome today. Perhaps, as William Rathje suggests, because the tasks involved are personally unfamiliar to us in our modern industrial culture, we find it difficult or impossible to accept that ancient preindustrial peoples could have accomplished such remarkable feats. One might well ask whether it is the archaeologist or the pseudo-archaeologist who is being narrow-minded.

Experiments refute von Däniken: Easter Island monuments

Significantly, pseudo-archaeologists reject relevant findings from experimental archaeology that demonstrate the capabilities of prehistorical peoples. For example, the great sculptures of Easter Island

Figure 15.2 View of the famous sculptured stone figures on Easter Island. Excavation and experiments indicate that these figures were quarried and transported by past inhabitants of the island, contrary to the speculations of pseudo-archaeologists. (Plate 12a from *The Art of Easter Island* by Thor Heyerdahl. Copyright © 1975 by Thor Heyerdahl. Reproduced by permission of Doubleday & Company, Inc., and George Allen & Unwin, Ltd.)

have impressed everyone who has seen them (Fig. 15.2). Von Dän-iken asserts, among other things, that the stone was too hard to be carved with the tools locally available, that the time required to carve the statues—and there are hundreds of these huge monolithic sculptures—implied an impossibly large population on the barren volcanic isle, and that the sculptures were far too heavy to have been moved from their quarry site to the platforms where they were set up. He therefore concludes that Easter Island presents a clear case of extraterrestrial intervention. But do von Däniken's claims hold up to critical examination? The stone statues are indeed steel-hard today, but experiments show that, when first quarried, the volcanic tuff involved is quite soft and can be cut with stone tools. After quarrying, this kind of stone becomes progressively harder by a common geological process called case-hardening. As for the time and labor involved, Thor Heyerdahl—whose transoceanic navigational experiments were mentioned in Chapter 12—set out to find some answers. First he recruited modern Easter Islanders, gave them stone tools like those found in the ancient quarries, and asked them to carve a statue like the ancient ones. This simple experiment indicated that a mere twenty workmen could finish one statue within a year. And since Easter Island is not nearly so barren as von Däniken would have us believe, during the 1200 years of known occupation it could have supported an ample population to provide the labor for the known sculptures. But what about the transport and placement of the idols? Von Däniken asserts there are no trees on the island for rollers or sledges. This is untrue—trees are not plentiful, but some do exist on the island. Heyerdahl conducted another experiment in which 150 local people, using wooden sledges, succeeded in moving a 10-ton idol. Larger monuments would have required more people and more sledges, but again, evidence in archaeological settlements on the island supports the contention that enough people were present in prehistoric times to do the job. Finally, Heyerdahl's experiments demonstrated that by using poles, ropes, and rocks, 12 men could raise a 25-ton statue from a horizontal to an upright position in just 18 days, by gradual leverage. As Peter White sums it up: Who needs ancient astronauts?

Who needs pseudo-archaeology? At first glance, the evidence cited in support of a theory such as von Däniken's may seem to fit together, but actually the pieces do not form a coherent whole. Each has been wrenched out of its original context and forced into an ill-suited new setting.

A disputed problem: The Nazca lines of Peru

Archaeologists, of course, don't claim to have all the answers. The famous lines marked on the Nazca plain in Peru are a case in point. Suggestions that the lines were used in astronomical observations have been contested, and there is no universally accepted explanation for the marks. But there is certainly no evidence to support their use as landing strips. And as for those examples that have elaborate shapes (constructed, according to von Däniken, to attract or please astronauts circling overhead!), Peter White points out that modern features such as Christian churches also have symbolic (in this case, cross-shaped) forms that are best viewed from above. He goes on to remind us that

> When men make designs that are best seen from the sky or take an interest in the stars it does not prove that there are astronauts. It proves that most people believe that gods are "up there" rather than down below us underground (though such beliefs are also known), or in the same world as we are but in some distant place.

(White 1974: 91)

What, then, is the challenge to professional archaeology? Archaeologists have too frequently failed to make themselves adequately heard in response to pseudo-archaeological ideas. But this is shirking a crucial responsibility—for if archaeologists do not point out the fallacies, who will? In the conclusion to a book surveying fantastic theories of the origin of American Indian culture, Robert Wauchope summarizes the problem and the challenge:

> It chagrins the professional scholar, whose books are usually subsidized because they find no popular market, that small fortunes are made by the publishers and authors of mystical nonsense . . . to the anthropologist, the Bering Strait hypothesis [of the peopling of the New World] and its implications embrace one of the greatest sagas of all human history. . . . Man was an essentially tropical animal and had to free himself from his southern habitat and economy; through perseverance, invention, and courage he

adapted himself to the forbiddingly different Inner Asiatic and north Siberian plains, steppes, and tundras, becoming a grasslands big-game hunter with his stone-tipped spears and throwing sticks.

This revolution was one of the most dramatic developments in the history of mankind, say the scientists, and the job of seeking the powerful motives that impelled Man, an essentially conservative creature, to move, a few miles here, a few more there, a generation here, a century there, until he found and populated an entire new pair of continents not discovered again for thousands of years, and built there some of the world's greatest ancient civilizations, should be to professional and amateur alike a thrilling detective story based on an imaginative plot, with dramatic as well as convincing actors. However, the scientist has not competed seriously for the reading public; the average professional anthropologist cannot or will not write the kind of book that people in any great numbers will want to read. For the most part he has surrendered this function, usually somewhat condescendingly, to the journalist, the travel-book writer, the sensationalist, and the devoted mystic, all of whom will prefer, any day, a lost continent, a lost tribe, or a lost city, to Lo the Poor Indian plodding through the snow and the centuries to his cultural destiny.

(Wauchope 1962: 135–137)

Prehistoric and preindustrial historic peoples were demonstrably capable of much more artistic, engineering, and other kinds of ingenuity than pseudo-archaeologists seem willing to allow them. Tales of extraterrestrial influences on cultural development make exciting science fiction, as anyone familiar with Arthur C. Clarke's *2001: A Space Odyssey* can well attest. But let these stories stay in the realm of fantasy where they belong, as good entertainment. Archaeology, as the science seeking to understand the human past, has a responsibility to prevent pseudo-archaeologists from robbing humanity of the real achievements of past cultures.

CONSERVING THE PAST

The most critical challenge to archaeology today is the accelerating destruction of the remains of past societies. As we saw at the beginning of this book, the processses of transformation affect all forms of archaeological data, whether by natural forces or the impact of later societies. However, in recent decades the toll of archaeological destruction has reached immense proportions; many archaeologists fear that unless immediate action is taken, critical information will be lost forever (Fig. 15.3).

During the past few years archaeologists have increasingly attempted to stimulate public awareness and concern over the threatened status of archaeological remains throughout the world. This new awakening is especially apparent in the United States, where public

Figure 15.3 The accelerating destruction of past cultural remains represents the single most critical threat to archaeology today; here, archaeologists attempt to salvage evidence from a site being destroyed by highway construction. (Courtesy of Hester Davis and the Florida Bureau of Archives and History.)

awareness and governmental protective action concerning archaeology have traditionally lagged behind other nations. There are encouraging signs that this situation is changing. A recent book by Charles McGimsey, a leading advocate of public and governmental support for archaeology in the United States, reviews the present situation and recommendations for future programs on both State and Federal governmental levels. McGimsey summarizes the basic issues as follows:

> The next fifty years—some would say twenty-five—are going to be the most critical in the history of American archaeology. What is recovered, what is preserved, and how these goals are accomplished during this period will largely determine *for all time* the knowledge available to subsequent generations of Americans concerning their heritage from the past. . . . The next generation cannot study or preserve what already has been destroyed.

> (McGimsey 1972: 3)

The destruction of archaeological evidence has two sources. On the one hand there is the looter who robs the remnants of ancient societies for artifacts or "art" that can be sold to collectors. On the other hand there are the constant destructive effects from expanding societies all over the world. Everyday activities such as farming and construction, though not intended to obliterate archaeological information, nevertheless take their toll. We will consider these threats in turn in the remainder of this chapter, together with some of the means archaeologists advocate to conserve the heritage of the past.

(a) **(b)**

Figure 15.4 Valuable archaeological evidence is often destroyed because it is sought by collectors and commands high prices on the commercial "art" market. In (a) we see Stela 1 from Jimbal, Guatemala, photographed shortly after its discovery in 1965. Less than 10 years later, (b) looters had sawed off the top panel in order to steal the sculpted figures, and in the process, destroyed the head of the Maya ruler and the top of the hieroglyphic inscription. ([a] courtesy of the Tikal Project, the University Museum, University of Pennsylvania; [b] courtesy of Joya Hairs.)

Looting and Antiquities Collecting

In discussing archaeological looting in the first part of this book, we concluded that the cause of the problem is economic. As long as collectors consider certain kinds of archaeological remains to be "art," the economics of supply and demand will lead to the plundering of sites to find those artifacts that have commercial value (Fig. 15.4). In this process, of course, information on the archaeological association and context of these objects is lost, and associated artifacts that lack commercial value are often destroyed.

Most archaeologists recognize that the looting of sites can never be stopped completely, except under the most repressive conditions (it is reported that in present-day China, long pillaged for its archaeological treasures, looting is now practically nonexistent). About all that can be done is to reduce the toll until it reaches insignificant proportions. New laws that restrict the international traffic in archaeological materials are needed, and present laws should be better enforced. International cooperation and standardization of import-export regulations would help, but customs laws alone cannot solve the problem.

The only effective way to reduce archaeological looting is to discourage the collector. If collectors no longer sought ''art'' from archaeological contexts, there would be no market for archaeological items and thus no incentive for the plundering of sites. Paintings, sculptures, or other works *produced for* the art market or art patrons are not included here. But the line must be drawn at any item that derives from an archaeological context, be it a Maya vase from a tomb or a Greek sculpture dragged from the bottom of the sea. The distinction is based on context; archaeological remains already ripped from their archaeological context have already lost their scientific value. Archaeologists must therefore direct their efforts to preventing further destruction of sites (Fig. 15.5).

When we speak of collectors we are referring to a diverse group that includes both individuals and institutions. Only a few decades ago, most museums acquired at least some of the objects in their archaeological collections by purchase, and thus encouraged (directly or indirectly) the looting of sites. Fortunately that situation has changed: most museums have signed or agreed to abide by a series of international agreements that prohibit commercial dealings in archaeological materials that lack documented ''pedigrees'' concerning the circumstances of their discovery. Unfortunately, some museums, including many art museums, have refused to abide by these agreements and continue to buy and sell archaeological ''art.''

Still, the individual collector remains the greatest problem, for although the museum acquisitions most often become public knowledge

Figure 15.5 Not all looting is motivated by the inflated prices typical of the commercial art market. Here we see the destruction of a prehistoric archaeological site by weekend artifact collectors. (Courtesy of Hester Davis and the Society for California Archaeologists.)

eventually, purchases of archaeological materials by private individuals usually take place privately and remain unknown to archaeologists. We do not mean to imply that collectors are evil. Many may not even be aware of the destruction of knowledge that continued collecting spawns. But they should be made aware, for as long as a market exists, looting will continue.

It is discouraging to note that some professional archaeologists retain close ties both to private collectors and to commercial dealers in antiquities. These archaeologists perform services such as authentication (distinguishing legitimate archaeological specimens from fakes) and evaluation (assessment of market value), often for a fee. These dealings are often defended on the grounds that they give the archaeologist the opportunity to observe and even record (photographs are sometimes permitted) objects that would otherwise remain closeted in a private collection and thus unknown. Yet the harsh fact is that any archaeologist who provides such services, whether to evaluate, authenticate, or merely record a looted object, *is engaged in an activity that encourages the further destruction of archaeological sites*. Obviously, any archaeological specimen that has been authenticated or evaluated by an archaeologist commands a greater price. But the mere fact that an object has been of interest to a professional archaeologist—especially if it was of sufficient interest to be photographed—will also increase that object's market value. The excuse of recording information otherwise lost is a delusion; the true archaeological information is already lost, destroyed when the object was robbed of its archaeological context. No person and no photograph can restore that loss of information. Here the authors take a firm stand favoring a uniform code of professional ethics that makes it clear that professional archaeologists should be committed to discouraging the destruction wrought by looting of sites, and therefore they must avoid any activity that fosters the plundering of the past, including interaction with dealers and encouragement of collectors. Severance of such interactions might contribute to the lowering of commercial values for antiquities, and thus begin to diminish the attractions of looting.

But the question still remains of how collectors are to be discouraged from seeking and purchasing looted archaeological materials. Various solutions have been offered. One promising line of legal action, already implemented by some governments, involves changes in the inheritance laws that do not permit an individual to bequeath archaeological collections to his or her heirs. One motive for maintaining private collections of antiquities is the fact that most antiquities, like legitimate art, increase in value over time and thus represent an investment. By excluding such a collection from the individual's estate, this kind of legislation makes it a much less desirable investment and thus removes one major incentive for collecting archaeological objects. Instead of being part of an inheritance, those items defined by law as archaeological materials pass to the state. Many collectors may think twice about purchasing "art" that will ultimately be taken by the government. Although it is promising, however, this kind of legal action is only partially effective, since some collectors avoid the law by moving their collections to other countries. Thus, once again, uniform international laws are needed.

The antiquities problem is as complex as it is urgent. In formulating antiquities legislation, considerations of politics and patronage often weigh more heavily than the security of archaeological materials. Archaeologists and interested persons alike must therefore fight to protect the past, or we shall lose it forever.

Destruction in the Name of Progress

Vandalism and looting are serious problems, but well-intentioned activity can also be harmful. Although they may be done in the name of progress, activities such as opening new lands to agriculture, construction of new roads and buildings, and creation of flood-control projects inevitably destroy countless remains of past human activity. Almost any action that affects the earth's surface is a threat to the archaeological record, and preserving all archaeological remains is clearly impossible. But much has already been destroyed, and the pace of destruction continues to accelerate in step with world population growth, so that only a small proportion of the archaeological record remains intact. In some areas of the world, entire regions have already been lost, entire ancient cities destroyed.

McGimsey's estimate, quoted earlier, is true not only for the United States but for the entire world. If the destructive forces are not controlled within a generation, so little may be left that further archaeological field research may well be futile. The loss will not be limited to the archaeologists (who will obviously no longer be able to conduct field research), but will extend to all of humanity. Under the best of circumstances we can never answer all our questions about past cultural development, but as the physical remains continue to be obliterated, our ability to ask any new questions at all is drastically curtailed.

Obviously we cannot simply stop population and construction growth, so a considerable number of sites are going to be destroyed. But an increasing number of archaeologists are adopting a conservationist attitude toward cultural remains. This attitude involves a heightened emphasis on planning and a restructuring of the relative roles of excavation and reconnaissance/survey in archaeological research. In the case of sites threatened with imminent destruction, the archaeologist's response has traditionally been to excavate quickly and recover as much data as possible—sometimes literally one step ahead of construction crews. Now, with the invaluable assistance of an increasing array of supportive legislation, archaeologists are more often able to take the time to assess the situation, to reconnoiter the area concerned, and then—if appropriate—to conduct excavations.

Since the excavation process itself destroys an archaeological site, it should be confined whenever possible to situations in which adequate planning, time, and money are available to ensure that a maximum of useful knowledge about the past is recovered. Archaeologists are thus becoming more actively concerned with ensuring that archaeological data are preserved in the ground, secure for future generations and future archaeologists. Of course, this philosophy applies to *un*threatened sites as well as immediately endangered ones. As we discussed in Chapter 3, archaeologists have a responsibility to the future, when greater resources and more sophisticated techniques may allow a more complete recovery of data. Therefore, unthreatened sites should never be completely excavated; a portion should always be left undisturbed for future archaeologists to investigate.

THE RESPONSE TO DESTRUCTION
OF ARCHAEOLOGICAL REMAINS

Archaeologists have always attempted to respond to the threat of destruction. Traditionally, as we have said, this response was to excavate whatever could be recovered before a site was destroyed. This kind of response is usually known as *salvage archaeology*. Often, such salvage work has been completely unforeseen and therefore unplanned. Almost every archaeologist has received an unexpected summons from a visitor or a telephone call reporting that archaeological materials have just been discovered by a farmer plowing his field, a houseowner digging a well, or some similar situation. The recent acceleration of looting activity throughout the world has greatly increased the incidence of salvage operations springing from reported discoveries made originally by illicit excavators. In many cases unexpected finds lead to hurried, emergency excavation in order to salvage at least some data before the feature or site is destroyed. In other cases, the discovery may be dramatic enough that the threat can be stopped, at least temporarily. Such a "stay of execution" may allow the archaeologist to plan an adequate salvage excavation, but seldom can the financial resources be gathered to support more than a few days or weeks of work. And even less frequently is any provision made for later analysis or publication of data gathered under such conditions.

In contrast to this kind of unexpected, emergency salvage work, archaeologists in many countries have conducted numerous planned projects by arrangement with land-clearing and construction enterprises. This kind of salvage project is often referred to as *contract archaeology,* since it is carried out under a legal contract between an archaeologist (or an archaeological institution) and the agency undertaking the construction project, often a governmental or private institution. Unfortunately, contract archaeology does not enjoy a uniformly good reputation among professional archaeologists. This stems from the fact that in the past many—though not all—contract projects were poorly funded, and almost all were rushed in order to meet deadlines imposed by the contracting agencies. These problems are well illustrated by the government-sponsored program of contract archaeology conducted in the United States during the Great Depression of the 1930s. During this period entire regions were transformed by dam-building programs, and archaeological contract work was used to salvage threatened historic and prehistoric sites. But neither time nor money was ever adequate, and these shortages were often compounded by the use of untrained labor, sometimes without adequate supervision. The Depression-era salvage projects had a secondary role—that of giving work to great numbers of unemployed people —in addition to investigating threatened archaeological sites. Unfortunately, the employment aspect often took on a greater importance than the archaeological investigations. In general, the archaeological work was subordinate to the priorities of the contracting agency, the flood-control engineer, or the dam builder, with predictably disastrous results as far as archaeology was concerned. When good research was done, as it was in some cases, it was due to the extraordinary efforts of individual archaeologists in the face of these obstacles.

Contract archaeology: Problems with Depression-era projects

Modern Contract Archaeology

Modern contract archaeology: Rescue of Abu Simbel

The lessons learned from Depression-era contract archaeology were not in vain. More recent work, both in the United States and in other countries, has benefited from this experience. In Egypt, the Aswan Dam salvage project conducted in the 1960s was well funded. Organized by UNESCO, the effort to save the site of Abu Simbel (Fig. 15.6) from the flood waters cost an estimated $40,000,000, of which the government of Egypt supplied more than half. The salvage program also included work in the less spectacular aspects of archaeology, such as locating prehistoric occupation sites. Although this work was less heavily funded, its inclusion was important in itself.

Figure 15.6 The spectacular remains of the temple of Abu Simbel were saved from the rising waters behind the Aswan dam by being cut apart, moved, and reassembled on higher ground at a cost of over $40,000,000. (Courtesy of David O'Connor.)

The overall quality of contract archaeology has vastly improved in recent years, due to both changing attitudes on the part of archaeologists and changing policies on the part of sponsoring agencies. One of the most significant changes, from both points of view, is that archaeological research is being given a new priority, usually more balanced with the demands of the sponsoring agency and less subject to its pressures. The incidence of contract archaeology is generally increasing in the climate of growing worldwide concern over the fate of the human heritage of the past. Most governments now require that archaeologists (or archaeological institutions) enter into legal agreements or contracts before permission is granted to conduct archaeological research within their boundaries. Thus the term *contract archaeology* is no longer appropriate only to salvage situations, but increasingly refers to many kinds of archaeological projects, whether concerned with threatened or unthreatened sites. As part of the contract, archaeologists undertaking nonsalvage archaeology, motivated entirely by their own theoretical interests, may find that their project will be supervised, and perhaps even modified, by agencies that represent the national interests of the country in which the site is located. Although legal requirements vary, many nations require that excavations be planned to minimize the destruction of sites, that visible features be restored or consolidated after excavation, that discovered artifacts remain the property of the host nation, and that copies of all research records and published reports be turned over to appropriate governmental agencies, such as national museums. In

some cases, contracts may require that final research reports be published in the appropriate governmental publication of the host
country.

The growth of contract archaeology in the context of protecting the
heritage of the past raises the possibility that nonsalvage investigations ("pure research") may be controlled or even dictated by government agencies granting contracts. The lesson here is the same as
that learned in earlier examples of salvage-oriented contract archaeology. If nonarchaeological priorities are placed before archaeological
needs, the result will be predictable: bad archaeology. The obvious
solution is a balance of priorities. Archaeologists must always expect
and demand that their research be conducted according to the principles of freedom of inquiry. They must also always expect and demand
that their research be conducted to ensure the maximum degree of
data conservation. And because the archaeological record is so vulnerable, and because each site represents a unique portion of that
record, every nation has the right to ensure that archaeological research within its boundaries is of the highest quality, that sites are
safeguarded during and after excavation, and that the results of research will be readily available to both the scholarly community and
the general public.

Cultural Resource Management and Conservation Archaeology

After many years of neglect and destruction, many nations have enacted firm protective legislation, based on the premise that the remains of the past, both historic and prehistoric, are a nonrenewable
national resource, analogous to such natural resources as petroleum
or mineral deposits. Unfortunately, some nations have been slow to
enact or enforce such legal conservation measures; but the worldwide
trend is clearly in this direction. The motives for such conservation
efforts are both humanistic and scientific, but they also have a very
practical basis. Knowledge of the past fosters self-esteem and national unity. It also fosters economic development; tourism, founded
at least in part upon a well-documented and spectacular past, is a
multi-million dollar business in some nations. Sites such as Teotihuacán in Mexico, Persepolis in Iran, and Williamsburg in the
United States not only serve as symbols of the national heritage, but
also attract millions of tourists every year (Fig. 15.7).

In the United States, a series of federal laws dating back to 1906
have been enacted to conserve archaeological sites. Until recently,
however, other countries, including many in Europe and several in
Latin America, were far ahead of the United States in providing legal
protection for their archaeological resources. Fortunately, a recent

Cultural and economic benefits: Teotihuacán, Persepolis, and Williamsburg

series of important legislative measures have helped the United States to catch up, and perhaps even to provide leadership in this area.

The most important of the new laws in the United States have been enacted by the federal government; these are sometimes reinforced by state and local laws designed to supplement the federal provisions. The National Environmental Policy Act (1969), along with the National Historic Preservation Act (1966) and Executive Order 11593 (1971), requires all United States governmental agencies to study and assess the effect of their programs upon the total environment, including archaeological sites, before those programs take effect. This means that any federal construction program, or any similar program requiring a federal permit must evaluate the impact of its project upon archaeological evidence and must take action to either avoid or mitigate any harmful effects to the archaeological record. As a result, a variety of governmental agencies, some of which—such as the National Park Service, the Department of Defense (Army Corps of Engineers), Federal Highway Administration, and the Department of Housing and Urban Development—have long been sponsors of "salvage archaeology," are now involved in a new kind of comprehensive cultural resource management that grants a high priority to archaeology. Archaeologists are now being contracted on an unprecedented scale, not only to locate sites and gather data, but also to develop the methods and policies that will conserve the archaeological resources of the United States for future generations.

During the 1970s, *cultural resource management archaeology* (some prefer the term *conservation archaeology*) has been the fastest-growing area within American professional archaeology. The federal government spent some $3 million in this area in 1971. This increased

Figure 15.7 Archaeological remains are recognized national symbols for many countries, as well as providing huge revenues from tourists. One of the most famous examples is Teotihuacán, Mexico.

over the next five years so that estimates for 1976 ranged from $10 to $25 million. This development has not been without growing pains, which have stemmed chiefly from several related issues. First of all, the sudden increase in both available funds and demand for archaeologists to conduct studies was not generally foreseen. Some of the results have been considerable confusion in dealing with the unfamiliar kinds of complexities of the federal laws, regulations, and bureaucratic procedures, and a shortage of qualified archaeologists interested in undertaking the flood of new contracts. Second, archaeologists have had to seriously re-examine the ethics and professional standards appropriate for this kind of contract work, in order to avoid the well-known mistakes of past salvage archaeology. And third, the priorities and policies needed to guide archaeologists in their attempts to conserve archaeological resources have also been subject to debate.

As far as federal law is concerned, cultural resource management is the responsibility of the Heritage Conservation and Recreation Service (HCRS), established by the Secretary of the Interior in January, 1978, with control over the natural, recreational, and cultural resources under federal jurisdiction. The responsibilities and archaeological programs of the Office of Archaeology and Historic Preservation, formerly part of the National Park Service, are now part of the cultural resource program of HCRS. Liaison between the professional archaeological community and HCRS, as well as with State and local agencies, has been established by the creation of the Coordinating Council of National Archaeological Societies. This coordinating council is composed of the presidents and vice-presidents of the six major national organizations of archaeology in the U.S.–American Society of Conservation Archaeologists, Association for Field Archaeology, Archaeological Institute of America, Society for American Archaeology, Society for Historical Archaeology, and Society of Professional Archeologists (see page 15). New legislation is still needed, both to facilitate the programs of HCRS and to insure that the cultural resources of the U.S. are conserved, but with increased communication and cooperation between government agencies and professional archaeologists there are good prospects for success.

Another encouraging development in this direction is the increasingly positive attitude of archaeologists toward contract archaeology and cultural resource management as areas in which creative research can be carried out. Traditional salvage archaeology programs earned the reputation of being carried out far too often without adequate planning, and with little attention to analysis and interpretation of the data collected. There was a common attitude that as long as sites were dug, the data would be used and useful somewhere, sometime. A growing number of archaeologists today, however, are engaged in efforts to coordinate with State Historic Preservation Officers in formulating broad regional research goals and priorities. Though flexible, such goals and priorities would increase the applicability of data collected under contract to questions of current cultural-historical, processual, and general theoretical interest. They would also provide guidelines for judging whether particular sites merited excavation or preservation. We cannot preserve or excavate all sites, and some sites have more to tell us than others. Clearly, then, increased attention should be paid to improving the means by which sites are evaluated for scientific importance and by which decisions are made between protection, immediate investigation, and sometimes-necessary sacrifice. The question is not whether the past should be protected, but how best to protect it in the context of a growing and changing world.

SUMMARY

In our final chapter we have considered two challenges that face contemporary archaeology. The first is posed by the popularization of pseudo-archaeology—reconstructions of past events based on unscholarly manipulation of archaeological data. The archaeologist has an obligation both to educate the public to discern fact from fiction, and to make sure that archaeological data are used in ways consistent with legitimate science.

The second challenge is more immediate and permanent, since it involves the irreversible destruction of archaeological data. This threat stems from two sources. The first is intentional destruction by looters, fostered by the market for archaeological "art" with its economic incentive for plundering archaeological sites. The second is nonintentional—the disruption of archaeological sites by everyday activities of our expanding world. Both problems point out the seriously endangered status of archaeological remains throughout the world. After reviewing some past responses and presently proposed solutions to these threats, we have outlined the contemporary trends within both archaeology and government in regard to the management of the world's archaeological resources. In this chapter the authors have indicated their opinion of the proper role and responsibilities of the archaeologist in order to ensure that there will be a future for the remains of the past.

See p. 576 for "Suggestions for Further Reading."

Glossary

Terms in italics are defined elsewhere in the glossary.

Absolute dating: Determination of age on a specific time-scale, as in years before present (B.P.) or according to a fixed calendrical system (compare with *relative dating*). (Chapter 10)

Acquisition: A stage in archaeological *research design* wherein data are gathered, normally by three basic procedures—*reconnaissance, surface survey* and *excavation*. (Chapters 4–7)

Adaptation: See *cultural adaptation*.

Aerial photographic map: A map of a *region* or *site* made through use of *aerial photography,* providing good control over distance and direction measurements but, unless made by professional cartographic equipment, little control over elevation. (Chapter 6)

Aerial photography: A technique of photographic recording, used principally in aerial reconnaissance, to record environmental conditions and surface and buried *sites;* may be vertical (camera at right angle to ground surface) or oblique (camera at less than a right angle to the ground). (Chapter 5)

Aerial reconnaissance: *Remote sensing* techniques, carried out from aerial platform (balloon, airplane, satellite, etc.); includes direct observation, as well as recording by photographic, thermographic and radar images. (Chapter 5)

Aerial thermography: A method of *aerial reconnaissance* that detects differential retention and radiation of heat from ground surfaces and thus aids in the identification of buried sites. (Chapter 5)

Alluvium: Soil deposited by running water. (Chapter 4)

Analogy: A process of reasoning where similarity between two entities in some characteristics is taken to imply similarity of other characteristics as well. (Chapter 12)

Analysis: A stage in archaeological *research design* wherein data are isolated, described and structured, usually via typological *classification,* along with chronometric, functional, technological and constituent determinations. (Chapters 4, 9–11)

Anthropology: The comprehensive study of the human species from biological, social and cultural perspectives using both *synchronic* and *diachronic* views; in North America, includes the subdisciplines of physical anthropology and cultural anthropology, the latter including *prehistoric archaeology*. (Chapter 1)

Antiquarian: A person with nonprofessional interests in the past, usually someone who studies the past for its artistic or cultural value (compare with *archaeologist* and *looter*). (Chapter 2)

Arbitrary levels: Excavation units defined metrically, as in the excavation of 5-, 10- or 20-cm levels (compare with *natural levels*). (Chapter 7)

Arbitrary sample unit: Subdivision of the *data universe* with no cultural relevance, such as sample units defined by a *site grid* (compare with *nonarbitrary sample unit*). (Chapter 3)

Archaeological culture: Maximum grouping of all *assemblages* assumed to represent the sum of human activities carried out within an ancient culture. (Chapter 8)

Archaeologist: A professional scholar who studies the human past through its physical remains (compare with *antiquarian* and *looter*). (Chapter 1, 2, 15)

Archaeology: The study of the social and cultural past through material remains with the aim of ordering and describing the events of the past and explaining the meaning of those events. (Chapter 1)

Archaeomagnetic age determination: Measurement of magnetic alignments, within undisturbed *features* such as hearths or kilns, which, when compared to known schedules of past magnetic alignments within a region, can yield an absolute age. (Chapter 10)

Archaic: New World chronological *period* characterized by permanent settlements and the transition from a hunting-and-gathering to an agricultural *economy*. (Chapter 13)

Area excavation: A type of *clearing excavation*

composed of large squares used to reveal the horizontal extent of data while preserving a stratigraphic record in the balks left between excavations (compare with *stripping excavations*). (Chapter 7)

Artifact: A discrete and portable object whose characteristics result wholly or in part from human activity; individually assignable to *ceramic, lithic, metal, organic* or other categories (see also *industry*). (Chapter 3 and 9)

Aspartic acid racemization: Process of cumulative change in form of amino acids, beginning at death of an organism; now being tested for use as a technique for *absolute dating* of bone tissue. (Chapter 10)

Aspect: A grouping of *foci,* defined by the *Midwestern taxonomic system* and used in North America. (Chapter 13)

Assemblage: Gross grouping of all *subassemblages* assumed to represent the sum of human activities carried out within an ancient community (see *archaeological culture*). (Chapter 8)

Association: Occurrence of an item of archaeological data adjacent to another and in or on the same matrix. (Chapter 3)

Attribute: Minimal characteristic used as criterion for grouping artifacts into classes; includes *stylistic, form* and *technological attributes* (also see *classification*). (Chapter 8)

Augering: A *subsurface detection* technique utilizing a drill run by either human or machine power to determine the depth and characteristics of archaeological or natural deposits. (Chapter 5)

Band: A small, egalitarian society subsisting by hunting and gathering, with no status distinctions other than those based upon age and sex; simplest *multilinear cultural evolutionary* stage. (Chapter 14)

Battleship-shaped curve: Lens-shaped graph representing changes in artifact type-frequencies through time, from origin to expanding popularity, decline and, finally, disappearance. (Chapter 10)

Behavioral processes: Human activities, including manufacturing, use and disposal behavior, that produce tangible archaeological remains (compare with *transformational processes*). (Chapter 3)

Bone age determination: Use of any of a variety of *relative dating* techniques applicable to bone material, including measurements of the depletion of nitrogen and the accumulation of fluorine and uranium. (Chapter 10)

Bowsing: A *subsurface detection* technique performed by striking the ground in order to locate buried features. (Chapter 5)

Calendrical age determination: Dating technique useable when objects are inscribed with calendrical dates, or are associated with calendrical inscriptions; an *absolute dating* technique, provided a correlation with a modern calendar exists. (Chapter 10)

Carrying capacity: Size and density of ancient populations that a given site or region can support under a specified subsistence technology. (Chapter 11)

Central place theory: Theory that human settlements will space themselves evenly across a landscape, depending upon the availability of resources and communication routes, and that these settlements will become differentiated forming a hierarchy of controlling centers called central places (see *locational analysis*). (Chapter 11)

Ceramic artifacts: *Artifacts* of fired clay, belonging to pottery, figurine or other ceramic *industries*. (Chapter 9)

Chiefdom: A large and complex society with differential social status, full-time occupational specializations and developed economic and political institutions headed by a hereditary authority, the chief; a *multilinear cultural evolutionary* stage. (Chapter 14)

Classic: New World chronological *period* marked by the appearance of initial urban *states* and limited to the Mesoamerican and Andean *culture areas*. (Chapter 13)

Classification: The ordering of phenomena into groups (classes), based upon the sharing of *attributes* (see *paradigmatic classification* and *taxonomic classification*). (Chapters 2, 8 and 9)

Clearing excavations: Excavations designed primarily to reveal the horizontal and, by inference, functional dimensions of archaeological *sites,* the extent, distribution and patterning of buried archaeological data (see *area* and *stripping excavations*). (Chapter 7)

Closed system: A *system* that receives no information, matter or energy from its environment; all sources of change are internal (compare with *open system*). (Chapter 14)

Cluster sampling: A sampling procedure whereby groups or *clusters* of *sample units,* rather than individual sample units, are selected. (Chapter 3)

Clusters: Groups of spatially proximate *sample units* whose internal variability is believed to be similar to that of the overall population. (Chapter 3)

Compass map: A map of a *region* or *site* made by using a compass to control geographical direction and, usually, pacing or tape measures to control distances, without control over elevation (compare with *sketch* and *instrument maps*). (Chapter 6)

Complex: Arbitrary chronological unit defined for data categories, such as artifact *industries,* and used in *cultural historical interpretation* (see *period, time-space grid*). (Chapter 13)

Composite data cluster: *Data clusters* that are internally heterogeneous and patterned in regard to activities other than those based upon age or sex differences, such as those reflecting status, occupational specializations or wealth distinctions. (Chapter 3)

Conjunctive approach: Pioneering approach to archaeological interpretation advocated by Walter Taylor (1948) involving the reconstruction of ancient behavior by defining functional sets of archaeological data. (Chapter 14)

Conquest (and invasion): Aggressive movement of human populations from one area to another, resulting in the subjugation of the indigenous society.

Conservation archaeology: See *cultural resource management.*

Constructed feature: A *feature* deliberately built to provide a setting for one or more activities, such as a house, storeroom or burial chamber (compare with *cumulative feature*). (Chapter 9)

Context: Characteristics of archaeological data that result from combined *behavioral* and *transformational processes,* evaluated by means of recorded *association, matrix* and *provenience* (see *primary context* and *secondary context*). (Chapter 3)

Contract archaeology: Archaeological research conducted under legal agreement with a governmental or private agency; in the U.S. usually carried out under authority of legislation designed to protect the nation's cultural resources (see *cultural resource management*). (Chapter 15)

Coprolites: Preserved ancient feces that provide food residues used to reconstruct ancient diet and subsistence activities. (Chapter 9)

Coring: A *subsurface detection* technique utilizing a hollow metal tube driven into the ground to lift a column of earth for stratigraphic study. (Chapter 5)

Cultural adaptation: The sum of the adjustments of a human society to its environment (see *cultural ecology*). (Chapter 14)

Cultural drift: Gradual cultural change due to the imperfect transmission of information between generations; analogous to genetic drift in biology. (Chapter 13)

Cultural ecology: The study of the dynamic interaction between human society and its environment, viewing *culture* as the primary adaptive mechanism in the relationship. (Chapters 2 and 14)

Cultural evolution: The theory that human societies change via a process analogous to the *evolution* of biological species (see *evolution, unilinear cultural evolution* and *multilinear cultural evolution*). (Chapters 2 and 14)

Cultural historical interpretation: An established and largely *inductive* approach to archaeological *interpretation* based upon temporal and spatial syntheses of data and the application of general descriptive *models* usually derived from a *normative concept of culture.* (Chapter 13)

Cultural invention: Origin of new cultural forms, within a society, by either accident or design. (Chapter 13)

Cultural processual interpretation: A recent and largely *deductive* approach to archaeological *interpretation* aimed at delineating the interactions and changes in cultural *systems* by the application of both descriptive and explanatory *models* based upon a *processual concept of culture.* (Chapter 14)

Cultural resource management (CRM): The conservation and selective investigation of prehistoric and historic remains; specifically, the development of ways and means, including legislation, to safeguard the past (see *contract archaeology*). (Chapter 15)

Cultural revival: Reacceptance of forms or ideas fallen into disuse. (Chapter 13)

Cultural selection: The process that leads to differential retention of cultural traits that increase a society's potential for successful *cultural adaptation,* while eliminating maladaptive traits (compare with *natural selection*). (Chapter 13)

Culture: The concept that both underlies and unites the discipline of *anthropology* and, in its various definitions, acts as a central *model* by which archaeological data are interpreted. A definition suited to archeology sees culture as the cumulative resource of human society that provides the means for nongenetic adaptation to the environment by regulating behavior in three areas— *technology, social systems* and *ideology.* (Chapter 1)

Culture area: A spatial unit defined by *ethnographically* observed cultural similarities within a given geographical area; used archaeologically to define spatial limits to *archaeological cultures* (see also *time-space grids*). (Chapter 13)

Cumulative feature: A *feature* without evidence of deliberate construction, resulting instead from accretion, as in a *midden,* or subtraction, as in a *quarry* (compare with *constructed feature*). (Chapter 9)

Cuneiform: Literally "wedge-shaped;" referring to the earliest known writing system, which developed in the ancient Near East (Mesopotamia). (Chapter 2)

Cybernetics: The study of *systems*. (Chapter 14)

Data cluster: Archaeological data found in *association* and in *primary context* and used to define areas and kinds of ancient activity; may be divided into *composite, differentiated, simple* and *unpatterned data clusters*. (Chapter 3)

Data pool: The archaeological evidence available within a given *data universe,* conditioned by both *behavioral* and *transformational processes*. (Chapter 3)

Data universe: Defined area of archaeological investigation, often a *region* or a *site,* bounded both in time and geographical space. (Chapter 3)

Debitage: The *lithic* debris, resulting from the manufacture of chipped-stone tools, that provides evidence for the reconstruction of ancient manufacturing behavior (see *technological attributes*). (Chapter 9)

Deduction: A process of reasoning by which one tests the validity of a generalization or law by deriving one or more hypotheses and applying these to specific observations (see *hypothesis testing;* compare with *induction*). (Chapters 1 and 14)

Deductive-nomological: A formal method of explaining observable phenomena by testing hypotheses derived from general ("cover") laws, advocated by some archaeologists as the proper approach for the explanation of culture processes (see also *identification hypotheses*). (Chapter 14)

Dendrochronology: The study of tree ring patterns which are linked to develop a continuous chronological sequence. (Chapter 10)

Deviation-amplifying system: A *system* that continues to change as a result of *positive feedback* (compare with *deviation-counteracting system*). (Chapter 14)

Deviation-counteracting system: A *system* that reaches equilibrium as a result of *negative feedback* (compare with *deviation-amplifying system*). (Chapter 14)

Diachronic: Pertaining to phenomena as they occur or change over a period of time; a chronological perspective (compare with *synchronic*). (Chapter 1)

Differentiated data cluster: Clustered data that are heterogeneous and patterned in regard to two or more activities reflective of age or sex differences; for example, a house floor with cooking utensils and hunting weapons in *primary context*. (Chapter 3)

Diffusion: Transmission of ideas from one culture to another. (Chapter 13)

Direct dating: Determination of age of archaeological data by analysis of an artifact, ecofact or feature (compare with *indirect dating*). (Chapter 10)

Direct historical approach: Method of chronological ordering based upon comparison of historically documented or contemporary artifacts with those recovered from archaeological contexts. (Chapters 2 and 13)

Discipline: A unified field of inquiry with an orderly methodology to recover data and a body of theory by which the data are interpreted. (Chapter 1)

Distance decay: Decline in a measurable phenomenon with distance from its source; used to describe the decreasing frequency of location of trade goods at destinations increasingly distant from their source. (Chapter 11)

Ecofact: Nonartifactual evidence from the past that has cultural relevance; includes both *inorganic* and *organic* (*faunal, floral* and *human*) *ecofacts*. (Chapters 7 and 9)

Economy: The provisioning of human society (food, water and shelter). (Chapter 11)

Elevation drawing: A two-dimensional rendering of a *feature,* viewed from the side, showing details of surface composition. (Chapter 7)

Ethnocentrism: Observational bias whereby other societies are evaluated by standards relevant to the observer's culture. (Chapters 2 and 15)

Ethnography: The description of contemporary cultures; part of the subdiscipline of cultural anthropology (see *anthropology*). (Chapter 1)

Ethnology: The comparative study of contemporary cultures; part of the subdiscipline of cultural anthropology (see *anthropology*). (Chapter 1)

Evolution: The process of gradual growth or change of one form into another, usually involving increasing complexity; in biology, the theory that all forms of life derive from a gradual process of change via *natural selection* (see *cultural evolution*). (Chapter 2)

Excavation: Removal of *matrix* in order to discover and retrieve archaeological data from beneath the ground, thereby revealing three-dimensional structure of the data and matrix, both vertically (see *penetrating excavations*) and horizontally (see *clearing excavations*). (Chapter 7)

Exchange systems: Systems for trade or transfer of goods, services and ideas between individuals and societies (see *reciprocal* and *redistributive exchange*). (Chapter 11)

Experimental hypothesis: A specific *hypothesis*, deduced from a generalization or general law, which can then be directly tested against data (see *hypothesis testing*). (Chapter 14)

Faunal ecofacts: *Ecofacts* derived from animals, including bone, teeth, antlers and so forth. (Chapter 9)

Feature: A nonportable *artifact,* not recoverable from its matrix without destroying its integrity (see *cumulative feature* and *constructed feature*). (Chapters 3 and 9)

Feedback: A response to stimulus that acts within a *system* (see *positive feedback* and *negative feedback*). (Chapter 14)

Fission track age determination: Technique similar to *thermoluminescence,* based upon the measure of traces of radioactivity (fission tracks) accumulated since a substance such as glass or obsidian was last heated above a critical temperature. (Chapter 10)

Floral ecofacts: *Ecofacts* derived from plants, including seeds, pollen, leaves and so forth. (Chapter 9)

Flotation: Placing excavated matrix in water to separate and recover small *ecofacts* and *artifacts*. (Chapter 7)

Focus: Minimal unit of the *Midwestern taxonomic system* representing an artifactual *assemblage* from a given site. (Chapter 13)

Form: Physical characteristics—arrangement, composition, size and shape—of any component of a *culture* or cultural *system*. In archaeological research the first objective is to describe and analyze the physical *attributes* (form) of data to determine distributions in time and space (see *function* and *process*). (Chapter 1)

Form attributes: *Attributes* based upon the physical characteristics of an artifact, including overall shape, the shape of parts, and measurable dimensions; leads to form *classifications*. (Chapter 8)

Form types: Artifact classes based upon *form attributes*. (Chapter 8)

Fossiles directeurs: "Type fossils" or particular classes of *lithic artifacts* associated with specific time *periods* and *archaeological cultures* of the European *paleolithic*. (Chapter 9)

Formative (or **Preclassic**): New World chronological *period* characterized by initial complex societies (*chiefdoms*) and long-distance trade networks. (Chapter 13)

Formulation: First stage in archaeological *research design,* involving definition of the research problem and goals, background investigations and feasibility studies. (Chapter 4)

Frequency seriation: A *relative dating* technique whereby artifacts or other archaeological data are chronologically ordered by ranking their relative frequencies to conform with *battleship-shaped curves* (see *seriation*). (Chapter 10)

Function: The purpose or use of a component of a *culture* or of a cultural *system*. The second goal of archaeological research involves the analysis of data and their relationships to determine function and thereby reconstruct ancient behavior (see *form* and *process*). (Chapter 1)

Functional concept of culture: A *model* of *culture* that is keyed to the *functions* of its various components united into a single network or structure. Used in archaeological *interpretation* for *synchronic* descriptions of ancient behavior. (Chapters 2 and 14)

General Systems Theory: Premise that any organization may be studied as a *system* to discover how its parts are related and how changes in either parts or their relationships produce changes in the overall system (see *cybernetics*). (Chapter 14)

Geochronology: Age determination by association with geological formations. (Chapter 10)

Geography: The descriptive study of the earth's surface and of its exploitation by life forms. (Chapter 11)

Geology: The study of the development of the earth, especially as preserved in its crust formations. (Chapters 2 and 7)

Geomorphology: That part of *geography* concerned with the form and development of the landscape. (Chapter 9)

Grid: See *Site grid*.

Ground reconnaissance: Traditional method for the discovery of archaeological *sites* by visual inspection from ground level. (Chapter 5)

Ground survey: *Surface survey* technique using direct observation in order to gather archaeological data present on the ground surface; specifically, mapping and surface collecting. (Chapter 6)

Ground truth: Determination of the causes of patterns revealed by *aerial reconnaissance,* such as by examining, on the ground, features identified by *aerial photography*. (Chapter 5)

Half-life: The period required for one-half of a radioactive isotope to decay and form a stable element. This rate, expressed as a statistical constant, provides the measurement scale for *radiometric age determination.* (Chapter 10)

Hieroglyphs: Literally "sacred carvings;" originally applied to the pictographic script of ancient Egypt, now commonly used to describe any pictographic writing system. (Chapter 2)

Historical archaeology: That area of *archaeology* concerned with literate societies, in contrast to *prehistoric archaeology,* although the distinction is not always clear-cut (see *protohistory*). For obvious reasons historical archaeology is often allied to the discipline of *history.* (Chapter 1)

History: The study of the past through written records which are compared, judged for veracity, placed in chronological sequence and interpreted in light of preceding, contemporary and subsequent events. (Chapter 1)

Horizon: Refers to cross-cultural regularities at one point in time; the spatial baseline of the New World *cultural historical* synthesis proposed by Willey and Phillips (1958) (compare with *tradition*). (Chapter 13)

Horizon marker: An item of data, such as an artifact type, with wide spatial distribution and a short temporal span (see *fossiles directeurs* and *horizon*). (Chapter 13)

Horizontal stratigraphy: Sometimes used to refer to chronological sequences based upon successive horizontal displacements, such as sequential beach terraces, and thus analogous to *stratigraphy.* (Chapter 10)

Human ecofacts: *Ecofacts* derived from human remains, including bone, teeth, *coprolites* and so forth. (Chapter 9)

Hypothesis: A proposition, often derived from a broader generalization or law, that postulates relationships between two or more variables, based upon specified assumptions. (Chapter 1)

Hypothesis testing: *Hypotheses* are tested against data to eliminate those found to be invalid and to identify those that best fit the observed phenomena. A successful hypothesis is not proved but found to be the best approximation of truth given the current state of knowledge. (Chapter 1)

Hypothesis-testing criteria: Archaeological *hypotheses* are tested by assessing their compatability with available data; other criteria include predictability, parsimony, completeness and symmetry. (Chapter 14)

Identification hypotheses: *Hypotheses* relating archaeological data to ancient behavior. (Chapter 14)

Ideofacts: Archaeological data resulting from past human ideological activities (see *ideology*). (Chapter 11)

Ideology: One of three components of *culture;* the knowledge or beliefs used by human societies to understand and cope with their existence (see also *technology* and *social systems*). (Chapters 2 and 11)

Implementation: Second stage in archaeological *research design;* involves obtaining permits, raising funds and making logistical arrangements. (Chapter 4)

Indirect dating: Determination of age of archaeological data by *association* with a *matrix* or object of known age (compare with *direct dating*). (Chapter 10)

Induction: A process of reasoning wherein one proceeds from a series of specific observations to derive a general conclusion (compare with *deduction*). (Chapter 1)

Industry: A gross *artifact* category defined by shared material and *technology,* such as a chipped-stone industry or a pottery industry. (Chapters 8 and 9)

Inevitable variation: Premise that all cultures vary and change through time without specific cause; a general and unsatisfactory descriptive *model* sometimes implied in *cultural historical interpretation.* (Chapter 13)

Infrared photography: Detection and recording on film of infrared radiation reflected from the sun (compare with *aerial thermography*). (Chapter 5)

Inorganic ecofacts: *Ecofacts* derived from non-biological remains, including soils, minerals and the like (compare with *organic ecofacts*). (Chapter 9)

Instrument map: An archaeological map made by use of surveyors' instruments, providing the most accurate control over distance, direction and elevation (compare with *compass* and *sketch maps*). (Chapter 6)

Interpretation: Stage in archaeological *research design* involving the *synthesis* of *analysis* results and the determination of their meaning in both descriptive and explanatory terms. (Chapters 4, 12–14)

Isometric drawing: Perspective (three-dimensional) rendering of a *feature* or *site,* often reconstructed to show what the subject may have looked like when in use. (Chapter 7)

LANDSAT: Refers to the Earth Resources Technology Satellites that produce small-scale images of vast areas of the earth's surface; used to study regional patterns of use of land and other resources (see *aerial reconnaissance* and *pixel*). (Chapter 5)

Lerici periscope: *Subsurface detection* probe fitted with a periscope or camera and light source used to examine subterranean chambers (most often Etruscan tombs). (Chapter 5)

Lithic: New World chronological *period* characterized by a lack of permanent settlements and a hunting and gathering *economy*. (Chapter 13)

Lithic artifacts: *Artifacts* made from stone, including chipped-stone and ground-stone *industries*. (Chapter 9)

Locational analysis: Techniques from *geography* used to study locations of human settlement and to infer the determinants of these locations (see *central place theory*). (Chapter 11)

Looter: An individual who plunders archaeological sites to find artifacts of commercial value, at the same time destroying the evidence that archaeologists rely upon to understand the past (compare with *antiquarian* and *archaeologist*). (Chapters 1 and 15)

Lot: See *provenience* lot.

Magnetometer: A device used in *subsurface detection* that measures minor variations in the earth's magnetic field, often revealing archaeological *features* as magnetic anomalies. (Chapter 5)

Matrix: The physical medium that surrounds, holds or supports archaeological data. (Chapter 3)

Mesolithic: Old World chronological *period* referring to the transition between the *paleolithic* and *neolithic*. (Chapters 9 and 13)

Metal artifacts: *Artifacts* made from metal, including copper, bronze and iron *industries*. (Chapter 9)

Midden: An accumulation of debris, resulting from human activities, removed from areas of manufacturing and use; may be the result of one-time refuse disposal or long-term disposal resulting in *stratification*. (Chapter 3)

Midwestern taxonomic system: Initial cultural historical synthesis for the Great Plains *culture area* of the U.S.; proposed by McKern (1939). (Chapter 13)

Migration: Movement of human populations from one area to another, usually resulting in cultural contact. (Chapter 13)

MNI: The Minimum Number of Individuals represented in a given faunal or human bone collection; determined from the number in the largest category of skeletal elements recovered. (Chapter 9)

Mode: An *attribute* with special significance because it distinguishes one *type* from another. (Chapter 8)

Model: A theoretical scheme constructed to understand a specific set of data or phenomena; descriptive models deal with the form and structure of phenomena, while explanatory models seek underlying causes for phenomena. Models may also be *diachronic* or *synchronic*. (Chapters 2, 13 and 14)

Multilinear cultural evolution: Theory of *cultural evolution* that sees each society pursuing an individual evolutionary career; often defined by four general levels of complexity (see *band, tribe, chiefdom* and *state*), rather than a single course (compare with *unilinear cultural evolution*). (Chapters 2 and 14)

Multiple working hypotheses: The testing of alternative *hypotheses* tested simultaneously to minimize bias and maximize the chances of finding the best available choice (see *hypothesis testing*). (Chapter 14)

Natural levels: Excavation units defined by *stratigraphy*, as opposed to *arbitrary levels*. (Chapter 7)

Natural secondary context: *Secondary context* resulting from natural transformational processes such as erosion, animal and plant activity (compare with *use-related secondary context*). (Chapter 3)

Natural selection: The mechanism that leads to differential survival and reproduction of those individuals suited to a given environment in contrast to others less well-adapted (compare with *cultural selection*). (Chapter 2)

Neolithic: Old World chronological *period* characterized by the development of agriculture and the use of ground-stone tool *industries*. (Chapters 9 and 13)

Negative feedback: A response to changing conditions that acts to dampen or stop a *system's* reaction (see *deviation-counteracting systems*).

Network analysis: Analysis of routes of communication among points such as human settlements. (Chapter 11)

Nonarbitrary sample unit: Subdivision of the *data universe* with cultural relevance, such as *sample units* defined by *data clusters* in remains of rooms or houses (compare with *arbitrary sample unit*). (Chapter 3)

Nonprobabilistic sampling: Sample data *acquisition* based upon informal criteria or personal judgment; does not allow evaluation of how representative the sample is with respect to the *data population* (compare with *probabilistic sampling*). (Chapter 3)

Normative concept of culture: A *model* of *culture* that is keyed to the abstracted set of rules (norms) that regulate and perpetuate human behavior; used in archaeological interpretation for both *synchronic* and *diachronic* descriptions of cultural *forms*. (Chapters 2 and 13)

Obsidian hydration: Absorption of water on exposed surfaces of obsidian, which, as long as the local hydration rate is known and constant, can be used as an absolute dating technique through measurement of the thickness of the hydration layer. (Chapter 10)

Open system: A *system* that receives information, matter or energy from its environment, and changes due to sources either internal or external to the system (compare with *closed system*). (Chapter 14)

Organic artifacts: *Artifacts* made of organic materials, including wood, bone, horn, ivory or hide *industries*. (Chapter 9)

Organic ecofacts: Ecofacts derived from living remains (see *floral, faunal* and *human ecofacts*). (Chapter 9)

Osteodontokeratic: Literally "bone-tooth-horn;" referring to the controversial tool *"technology"* of some early hominids. (Chapter 9)

Paleoanthropology: Sometimes used as a synonym for *prehistoric archaeology*. (Chapter 1)

Paleodemography: The study of ancient human populations. (Chapters 9 and 11)

Paleolithic: Old World chronological *period* characterized by the earliest known *lithic artifacts,* those of chipped stone, and by a hunting and gathering *economy*. (Chapters 9 and 13)

Paleontology: The study of past life forms from fossilized remains of plants and animals; includes human paleontology. (Chapter 1)

Palynology: The study of pollen (see *organic ecofacts*). (Chapter 9)

Paradigm: Conceptual framework for a scientific *discipline;* a strategy for integrating research method, theory and goals. (Chapter 14)

Paradigmatic classification: *Classification* based upon an equal weighting of *attributes,* so that each class is defined by a cluster of unique attributes and is not dependent upon the order in which the attributes were defined (compare with *taxonomic classification*). (Chapter 8)

Patination: Weathering reactions on the surfaces of minerals, including flint and other *lithic artifacts*. (Chapter 10)

Pedology: The study of soils. (Chapter 9)

Penetrating excavations: *Excavations* designed primarily to reveal the vertical and temporal dimensions within archaeological deposits; the depth, sequence and composition of buried data (see *sondage, test pit, trench* and *tunnel*). (Chapter 7)

Period: Broad and general chronological unit defined for a *site* or *region,* based upon combined data, such as defined *complexes* (see also *time-space grid*). (Chapter 13)

Periodicity: Occurrence of a phenomenon at regular intervals of regular patterns of equal spacing (compare *stratified systematic unaligned sampling*). (Chapter 3)

Petrology: Study of rocks; a branch of *geology*. (Chapter 9)

Phase: See *complex*.

Phase: A grouping of *aspects* in the *Midwestern taxonomic system*. (Chapter 13)

Physical structure: Positional relationships between archaeological data, described by *association, context* and *provenience* with reference to the vertical and horizontal dimensions of archaeological deposits (compare with *systemic structure*). (Chapters 3, 7, 10 and 11)

Pixel: Picture element, the minimum unit recorded electronically by the *LANDSAT* satellites. (Chapter 5)

Plan drawing: A two-dimensional rendering at a consistent scale, depicting the horizontal dimensions of archaeological data. (Chapter 7)

Planimetric maps: Archaeological maps that depict *sites* or *features* using nontopographic symbols (compare with *topographic maps*). (Chapter 6)

Pleistocene: Geological period characterized by successive glacial advances and retreats, ending about 11,500 years ago. (Chapter 10)

Population: The aggregate of all *sample units* within a *data universe*. (Chapter 3)

Positive feedback: A response to changing conditions that acts to stimulate further reactions within a *system* (see *deviation-amplifying systems*). (Chapter 14)

Postclassic: New World chronological *period* characterized by secular and militaristic emphases within societies found in both Mesoamerica and the Andean area. (Chapter 13)

Potassium-argon age determination: *Radiometric* dating technique based upon the *half-life* of the radioactive isotope of potassium (^{40}K) that decays to form argon (^{40}Ar). (Chapter 10)

Preclassic: See *formative*.

Prehistoric archaeology: The area of *archaeology*

concerned with preliterate or nonliterate societies, in contrast to *historical archaeology*. In North America prehistoric archaeology is considered a part of the discipline of *anthropology*. (Chapter 1)

Primary context: The condition where *provenience, association* and *matrix* have not been disturbed since original deposition of archaeological data (compare with *secondary context*). (Chapter 3)

Probabilistic sampling: Sample data acquisition based upon formal statistical criteria in selecting *sample units* to be investigated; allows evaluation of how representative the sample is with respect to the data *population* (compare with *nonprobabilistic sampling*). (Chapter 3)

Process: The cumulative effect of the interaction of components of a cultural *system* in time and space, resulting in either change or stability. The delineation of process is the ultimate goal of archaeological research in order to explain how and why cultures change (see *form* and *function*). (Chapters 1 and 14)

Processing: Stage in archaeological *research design* usually involving cleaning, conservation, numbering, inventory, cataloguing, photographing and initial sorting of archaeological data. (Chapters 4 and 8)

Processual concept of culture: A model of *culture* that is keyed to the systemic and dynamic relationships between the components of culture and between these components and the total environment; used in archaeological interpretation for *diachronic* descriptions and explanations of culture *process* (see also *cultural ecology* and *multilinear cultural evolution*). (Chapters 2 and 14)

Profile drawing: A two-dimensional rendering, similar to a *section drawing*, except that features are depicted in outline without showing their internal composition. (Chapter 7)

Protohistory: Transition between prehistoric and historic eras (see *prehistoric* and *historical archaeology*). (Chapter 2)

Provenience (provenance): Three-dimensional location of archaeological data within or on the *matrix* at the time of discovery. (Chapter 3)

Provenience lot: A defined spatial area, either in two dimensions (for surface data) or three dimensions (for excavated data), used as a minimal unit for *provenience* determination and recording. (Chapters 6 and 7)

Pseudo-archaeology: Use of real or imagined archaeological evidence to justify nonscientific accounts about the past. (Chapter 15)

Publication: The final stage of archaeological *research design*, providing reports of the data and interpretations resulting from archaeological research. (Chapter 4)

Quarry: A *cumulative feature* resulting from the mining of mineral resources. (Chapter 9)

Radar (pulse radar): An instrument used in *subsurface detection* that records differential reflection of radar pulses*rom buried *strata* and *features*. (Chapter 5)

Radar (side-looking airborne radar): An instrument used in *aerial reconnaissance* that can detect large archaeological *sites* using an oblique radar image; especially useful because it can penetrate cloud cover and, to a degree, vegetation. (Chapter 5)

Radiocarbon age determination: *Radiometric* dating technique based upon measuring the decay of the radioactive isotope of carbon (^{14}C) to stable nitrogen (^{14}N). (Chapter 10)

Radiometric age determination: A variety of *absolute dating* techniques based upon the transformation of unstable radioactive isotopes into stable elements (see *potassium-argon* and *radiocarbon age determination*). (Chapter 10)

Random sampling: See *simple random sampling*.

Reciprocal exchange: Simple and direct *trade* between two parties, involving the exchange of goods, services or monetary units (compare with *redistributive exchange*). (Chapter 11)

Reconnaissance: Systematic means of identifying archaeological remains, including both discovery and plotting of their location; often conducted along with *surface survey*. (Chapter 5)

Redistributive exchange: Complex and indirect *trade* involving a third party or institution that collects goods, services or monetary units and reallocates at least a portion to others (compare with *reciprocal exchange*). (Chapter 11)

Region: A geographically defined area containing a series of interrelated human communities sharing a single cultural-ecological *system*. (Chapter 3)

Regional maps: Maps designed to depict the distribution of archaeological *sites* within *regions*. (Chapter 6)

Relative dating: Determining chronological sequence without reference to a fixed time-scale (compare with *absolute dating*). (Chapter 10)

Remote sensing: *Reconnaissance* and *surface*

survey methods involving aerial or subsurface detection of archaeological data. (Chapter 5)

Research design: Systematic plan to coordinate archaeological research to insure the efficient use of resources and to guide the research according to the scientific method (see *formulation, implementation, acquisition, processing, analysis, interpretation* and *publication*). (Chapter 4)

Resistivity detector: An instrument used in *subsurface detection* that measures differences in the conductivity of electrical current, and thus may be used to identify archaeological *features*. (Chapter 5)

Salvage archaeology: Collection of archaeological data from a *site* or *region* in the face of the impending destruction of past remains. (Chapter 15)

Sample: A set of units selected from a *population*. (Chapter 3)

Sample data acquisition: Investigation of only a portion of the *sample units* in a *population*, either by *probabilistic* or *nonprobabilistic* means (compare with *total data acquisition*). (Chapter 3)

Sample unit: The basic unit of archaeological investigation; a subdivision of the *data universe*, defined by either *arbitrary* or *nonarbitrary* criteria. (Chapter 3)

Science: The systematic pursuit of knowledge about natural phenomena (in contrast to the nonnatural or supernatural) by a continually self-correcting method of testing and refining the conclusions resulting from observation (see *scientific method*). (Chapters 1 and 14)

Scientific method: The operational means of *science*, by which natural phenomena are observed and conclusions are drawn and tested using both *induction* and *deduction*. (Chapters 1 and 14)

Screening: Passing excavated *matrix* through a metal mesh to improve the recovery rate of *artifacts* and larger *ecofacts*. (Chapter 7)

Secondary context: The condition where *provenience, association* and *matrix* have been wholly or partially altered by *transformation processes* after original deposition of archaeological data (compare with *primary context*). (Chapter 3)

Section drawing: Two-dimensional rendering, at a consistant scale, depicting archaeological data and *matrix* as seen in the wall of an *excavation*. (Chapter 7)

Sequence dating: *Relative dating* technique based upon a *stylistic seriation* of Egyptian predynastic tomb pottery. (Chapter 10)

Seriation: Techniques used to order artifacts in a *relative dating* sequence, in such a way that adjacent items in the series are more similar to each other than to items further apart in the series (see *frequency* and *stylistic* seriation). (Chapter 10)

Settlement pattern: The distribution of *features* and *sites* across the landscape. (Chapter 11)

Simple data cluster: *Clustered* data that are internally homogeneous with regard to a single function, such as those from an obsidian tool workshop. (Chapter 3)

Simple random sampling: A *probabilistic sampling* technique whereby each *sample unit* has a statistically equal chance for selection. (Chapter 3)

Site: A spatial clustering of archaeological data, comprising *artifacts, ecofacts,* and *features* in any combination. (Chapter 3)

Site catchment analysis: Definition of available resources within a given distance of a site; determines an area within which distance is assumed to be insignificant in differential accessibility to these resources. (Chapter 11)

Site datum: A well-marked, permanent point of known elevation and geographical location, used as a control point for mapping and *provenience* control. (Chapter 6)

Site grid: A set of regularly spaced intersecting north-south and east-west lines, usually marked by stakes, providing the basic reference system for recording horizontal *provenience* (coordinates) within a site. (Chapter 6)

Site map: A map designed to depict the details of a *site*, usually by recording all observable surface *features*. (Chapter 6)

Site plan: A map designed to depict a specific detail within a *site*, usually a single *feature* or a group of features. (Chapter 6)

Sketch map: An impressionistic rendering of a *region, site* or *feature* made without instruments so that there is no control over geographical direction or elevation. Distances may be estimated by pacing. (compare with *compass* and *instrument maps*.) (Chapter 6)

SLAR: See *radar* (side-looking airborne radar).

Social systems: One of the three basic components of *culture;* the means by which human societies organize themselves and their interactions with other societies (see also *technology* and *ideology*). (Chapters 2 and 11)

Sociofacts: Archaeological data resulting from past human social activities (see *social systems*). (Chapter 2)

Sondage: A sounding pit; that is, an initial *test pit* placed so as to preview what lies beneath the ground. (Chapter 7)

State: A society retaining many *chiefdom* characteristics in elaborated form, but also including true political power sanctioned by legitimate force, and social integration through concepts of nationality and citizenship usually defined by territorial boundaries; the most complex *multilinear cultural evolutionary* stage. (Chapter 14)

Stereoscope: Apparatus for magnifying and viewing stereo pairs of *aerial photographs* that allows relief to appear in three dimensions. (Chapter 5)

Strata: The definable layers of archaeological *matrix* or *features* revealed by *excavation* (see *stratification*). (Chapter 7)

Strata (sampling): Divisions of a *population* based upon observed similarities (see *stratified sampling*). (Chapter 3)

Stratification: Multiple *strata* whose order of deposition reflects the law of superposition (lowest stratum having been deposited first, the uppermost last; see *stratigraphy*). (Chapter 7)

Stratified sampling: A *probabilistic sampling* technique whereby sample units are drawn from two or more sampling *strata*. (Chapter 3)

Stratified systematic unaligned sampling: A *probabilistic sampling* technique in which *periodicity* is avoided by varying the position of the *sample unit* within the specified interval (see *stratified* and *systematic sampling*). (Chapter 5)

Stratigraphy: The archaeological evaluation of the significance of *stratification* to determine the temporal sequence of data within stratified deposits by using both the law of superposition and *context* evaluations. (Chapter 7)

Stripping excavations: *Clearing excavations* wherein large areas of overburden are removed to reveal horizontal distributions of data without leaving balks (compare with *area excavations*). (Chapter 7)

Stylistic attributes: *Attributes* defined by the surface characteristics of *artifacts*—color, texture, decoration and so forth—leading to stylistic classifications. (Chapter 8)

Stylistic seriation: A *relative dating* technique whereby artifacts or other data are ordered chronologically according to stylistic similarities (see *seriation*). (Chapter 10)

Stylistic types: *Artifact* classes based upon *stylistic attributes*. (Chapter 8)

Subassemblage: Grouping of *artifacts* classes, based upon *form* and *functional* criteria, assumed to represent a single occupational group within an ancient community (see *assemblage* and *archaeological culture*). (Chapter 8)

Subsurface detection: *Remote sensing* techniques carried out from ground level, including *bowsing, augering, coring,* by use of the *Lerici periscope, magnetometer, resistivity detector, radar* and similar means. (Chapter 5)

Surface survey: Initial data gathering at, and evaluation of, archaeological *sites;* involves mapping and surface collection of *artifacts* and *ecofacts*. (Chapter 6)

Synchronic: Pertaining to phenomena at one point in time; a concurrent perspective (compare with *diachronic*). (Chapter 1)

Synthesis: The reassembling of analyzed data as the prelude to *interpretation*. (Chapter 12)

System: An organization that functions through the interdependence of its parts (see *General Systems Theory*). (Chapter 14)

Systematic sampling: A *probabilistic sampling* technique whereby the first *sample unit* is selected at random and all other units are selected by a predetermined interval from the first. (Chapter 3)

Systemic structure: The temporal and spatial relations among archaeological data, inferred from *physical structure* and data *analysis,* used to reconstruct ancient behavior. (Chapters 10 and 11)

Taxonomic classification: A *classification* based upon an unequal weighting of *attributes* that are imposed in a hierarchical order so that the attributes defining each class are dependent upon the order in which the attributes were considered (compare with *paradigmatic classification*). (Chapter 8)

Technofacts: Archaeological data resulting from past technological activities (see *technology*). (Chapter 2)

Technological attributes: *Attributes* comprised of the raw-material characteristics (constituents) and those resulting from manufacturing methods; leads to technological *classifications*. (Chapter 8)

Technological types: *Artifact* classes based upon *technological attributes*. (Chapter 8)

Technology: One of the three basic components of *culture;* the means used by human societies to interact directly with and adapt to the environment (see *ideology* and *social systems*). (Chapters 2 and 11)

Tell* or *tepe: Literally hill, term used in the Near East to refer to an archaeological *site*. (Chapter 3)

Test pit: *Penetrating excavation* used to probe the depth of archaeological *sites* within a very restricted area. (Chapter 7)

Thermoluminescence (TL): Age determination technique in which amount of light energy released in a pottery sample during heating gives a measure of time elapsed since the material was last heated to a critical temperature. (Chapter 10)

Thiesson polygons: Areas described by drawing perpendiculars midway between points, such as *sites* on a *regional map,* and connecting these lines to form polygons around each point; used in *locational analysis.* (Chapter 11)

Thin section: Prepared slice of stone or ceramic (ca. .03 mm thick) used by *petrologists* to identify constituents and thereby recognize *quarry* sources. (Chapter 9)

Three-age system: A traditional *diachronic model* describing the sequence of technological *periods* in the Old World, each period characterized by predominant use of stone, bronze or iron tools. (Chapter 2)

Time-space grid: *Synthesis* of temporal and spatial distributions of data used in *cultural historical interpretation,* based on *period* sequences within *culture areas.* (Chapter 13)

Topographic maps: Maps that depict topographic (landform) data in combination with representations of archaeological *sites* (compare with *planimetric maps*). (Chapter 6)

Total data acquisition: Investigation of all *sample units* in a *population* (compare with *sample data acquisition*). (Chapter 3)

Trade: Transmission of material objects from one society to another; descriptive cultural *model* used in *cultural historical interpretation* (see *exchange systems*). (Chapter 13)

Tradition: Cultural continuity through time; temporal baseline of the New World cultural historical synthesis proposed by Willey and Phillips in 1958 (compare with *horizon*). (Chapter 13)

Transformational processes: Conditions and events that affect archaeological data from the time of deposition to the time of recovery (compare with *behavioral processes*). (Chapter 3)

Transposed primary context: *Primary context* resulting from depositional activities, as in *midden* formation (compare with *use-related primary context*). (Chapter 3)

Trench: A long and narrow *penetrating excavation* used to reveal the vertical dimension of archaeological data, and to explore the horizontal dimension along one axis. (Chapter 7)

Tribe: An egalitarian society possessing a subsistence base stable enough to support permanent settlement, and social institutions such as age-grade groupings that supplement the kinship ties that integrate society; defines a *multilinear cultural evolutionary* stage. (Chapter 14)

Tunnel: A subsurface *penetrating excavation* that, instead of cutting through *strata* vertically, follows buried strata or *features* along one horizontal dimension. (Chapter 7)

Type: A class of data defined by a consistent clustering of *attributes* (see *classification*). (Chapter 8)

Type-variety-mode analysis: A standardized *taxonomic* pottery *classification* based upon *stylistic attributes* that defines a hierarchy of classes: *modes* and varieties (minimal units); *types,* groups, *complexes* and spheres (maximal units). (Chapter 9)

Unilinear cultural evolution: Nineteenth-century version of *cultural evolution* holding that all human societies change according to a single fixed evolutionary course, passing through the same stages (described as "savagery," "barbarism" and "civilization" by L. H. Morgan). (Chapter 2)

Union grid: Commonly used kind of *site grid,* infinitely expandable in all four cardinal directions. (Chapter 6)

Unpatterned data cluster: Refers to isolated archaeological data, or clustered data without patterning (see *data cluster*). (Chapter 3)

Use-related primary context: *Primary context* resulting from abandonment of materials during either manufacturing or use activities (compare with *transposed primary context*). (Chapter 3)

Use-related secondary context: *Secondary context* resulting from disturbance by human activity after original deposition of materials (compare with *natural secondary context*). (Chapter 3)

Varves: Fine layers of *alluvium* deposited in glacial lakes by retreating ice-sheets; used for age determination, based upon annual cycles of deposition. (Chapter 10)

Vector sampling: A sampling scheme using transects, the courses of which are plotted in a fashion analogous to the rebounding path of a ball on a billiard table. (Chapter 5)

Suggestions for Further Reading

CHAPTER 1

A View of the Past

Carter 1972; Coggins 1972; Diaz del Castillo 1956; Fagan 1975, 1978; Topping 1977

Archaeology: Method, Theory, and Goals

L. Binford 1968; Clarke 1972; Deetz 1967; Isaac 1971; Leone 1972; Martin 1971; Plog 1974; Schiffer 1976, 1978; Sterud 1978; Trigger 1970; Wheeler 1954; Willey and Phillips 1958

Archaeology As a Discipline

Daniel 1969; Deetz 1970; Hawkes 1968; Piggott 1959; Rowe 1961; Society of Professional Archeologists 1978; Wheeler 1954

Archaeology and History

Dymond 1974; Finley 1971; MacWhite 1956; Platt (ed.) 1976; South 1977; Wiseman 1964

Archaeology and Anthropology

L. Binford 1962; Chang 1967; Deetz 1970; Gumerman and Phillips 1978; Longacre 1970b; Taylor 1948; Tylor 1871; Willey and Phillips 1958

Archaeology and Science

Bayard 1969; L. Binford 1968; Flannery 1973; Fritz and Plog 1970; Levin 1973; MacNeish 1978; Morgan 1973, 1974; Read and LeBlanc 1978; Sabloff, Beale, and Kurland 1973; Salmon 1975, 1976; Spaulding 1968; Steward 1955; Thomas 1973; Watson 1973; Watson, LeBlanc, and Redman 1971; Watson 1976

CHAPTER 2

The Growth of Scientific Disciplines

Eiseley 1958; Kuhn 1970; Lovejoy 1936; Mayr 1972; Toulmin and Goodfield 1965

Antiquarians and the Origins of Archaeology

General Histories of Archaeology: Daniel 1962, 1967, 1976a; Fagan 1978; Heizer 1962

Old World: Issues and Personalities: Alcock 1971; Daniel 1943, 1971b, 1976b; Fagan 1975; Klindt-Jensen 1975; Lloyd 1955; Lynch and Lynch 1968; Poole and Poole 1966; Wheeler 1955

Old World: Classic Studies: Camden 1789; Frere 1800; Lubbock 1865

New World: Issues and Personalities: Brunhouse 1973; Fitting (ed.) 1973; Gorenstein 1977; Griffin 1959; Rowe 1954; Schuyler 1971; Thompson 1963; Wauchope 1965; Willey and Sabloff 1974; Wilmsen 1965

New World: Classic Studies: Cushing 1890; Gallatin 1836; Haven 1856; Koch and Peden (eds.) 1944; Squier and Davis 1848; Stephens 1841, 1843

Transition to Professional Archaeology; Origins and Influence of Anthropology

General Studies: J. Bennett 1976; Brew (ed.) 1968; Harris 1968; Kardiner and Preble 1961; Keesing 1974; Rowe 1965

Nineteenth-Century Classic Works: Darwin 1859; Lyell 1830–33; Morgan 1877; Spencer 1876; Tylor 1871

Emergence of Modern Archaeology: Historical and Anthropological Interpretations (See also Chapters 13 and 14)

General Studies: L. Binford 1968; Clarke 1973; Daniel 1971a; Deetz 1970; Flannery 1967; Ford 1977; Isaac 1971; Klejn 1977; Longacre 1970b; Martin 1971; Taylor 1972; Willey (ed.) 1974; Wilson 1975

Twentieth-Century Classic Works: Boas 1948; Childe 1954; Malinowski 1944; Steward 1955; Taylor 1948; White 1949

CHAPTER 3

The Forms of Archaeological Data

Bass 1966; Binford 1964; Deetz 1967; Flannery (ed.) 1976a; MacNeish 1964a; Parsons 1974; Spaulding 1960; Struever 1971; Willey 1953

The Determinants of Archaeological Data

Ascher 1968; David 1971; Fehon and Scholtz 1978; Heider 1967; Lange and Rydberg 1972; Schiffer 1972, 1976

The Structure of Archaeological Data

Ascher 1968; Flannery (ed.) 1976a; South 1978; Spaulding 1960

Approaches to Archaeological Data Acquisition

Binford 1964; Cowgill 1968, 1977; Doran and Hodson 1975; Hill 1966, 1967; Mueller 1974, 1975 (ed.); Ragir 1975; Redman 1973, 1974; Rowlett 1970; Thomas 1976, 1978

CHAPTER 4

Archaeology as Interdisciplinary Research

Brown and Struever 1973; Chang 1974; Gladfelter 1977; Gumerman and Phillips 1978; MacNeish 1967; Rapp 1975; Struever and Carlson 1977; Whittlesey 1977

Archaeological Research Projects

Alexander 1970; Cunningham 1974b; MacNeish 1967; Schiffer 1976; Shook and Coe 1961; A. Smith 1973; Wheeler 1954; Willey (ed.) 1974

Archaeological Research Design

Binford 1962, 1964; Brown and Struever 1973; Daniels 1972; Goodyear, Raab, and Klinger 1978; Grinsell, Rahtz, and Williams 1974; Gumerman 1973; Redman 1973; Struever 1968b; Taylor 1948; Thomas 1969; Tuggle, Townsend, and Riley 1972

A Case Study: The Quiriguá Project

Ashmore and Sharer 1978; Morley 1935; Sharer 1978a; Sharer and Coe 1978

CHAPTER 5

Objectives and Methods of Reconnaissance

Adams and Nissen 1972; Aitken 1974; Aston and Rowley 1974; Atkinson 1953; Breiner and Coe 1972; Coles 1972; Estes, Jensen, and Tinney 1977; Gumerman and Lyons 1971; Hamlin 1978; Harp (ed.) 1975; Kidder, Jennings, and Shook 1946; Linington 1970; MacNeish 1964b, 1974; Mueller 1974; Schorr 1974; Steponaitis and Brain 1976; Vogt (ed.) 1974

Approaches to Reconnaissance

Lovis 1976; Madeira 1931; Mueller 1974, 1975 (ed.), 1978; Plog 1976, 1978; Puleston 1974; Rice 1976; Schiffer, Sullivan, and Klinger 1978; Thomas 1978

Plotting the Location of Archaeological Sites

Adams 1965; Willey 1953

CHAPTER 6

Objectives and Methods of Surface Survey

Carr and Hazard 1961; Coles 1972; Cowgill 1974; Davis 1975; Dinsmoor 1977; Kamau 1977; Millon 1973, 1974; Napton 1975; Oleson 1977; Parsons 1971; Spier 1970

Approaches to Surface Survey

L. Binford and others 1970; Chartkoff 1978; Flannery 1976b; Fry 1972; Mueller (ed.) 1975; Redman and Watson 1970

Reliability of Surface Data

Baker 1978; L. Binford and others 1970; Flannery 1976b; Hanson and Schiffer 1975; Redman and Watson 1970; Sharer 1978b; Tolstoy 1958; Tolstoy and Fish 1975

CHAPTER 7

Stratification and Stratigraphy

Adams 1975; Casteel 1970; Drucker 1972; Harris 1975; Hawley 1937; Lloyd 1963; Movius 1977; Pyddoke 1961; Wilmsen 1974

Approaches to Excavation

L. Binford 1964; Flannery 1976c; Fry and Cox 1974; Hanson and Schiffer 1975; Hill 1967; Mueller (ed.) 1975; Redman 1974; Redman and Watson 1970; Winter 1976

Excavation Methodology

Alexander 1970; Bass 1966; Bass and Throckmorton 1961; Bird 1968; Bird and Ford 1956; Coe 1967; Coles 1972; Harp (ed.) 1975; Hester, Heizer, and Graham (eds.) 1975; Hole, Flannery, and Neely 1969; Hope-Taylor 1966, 1967; LeBlanc 1976; Limp 1974; Lloyd 1976; McIntosh 1977; MacNeish and others 1972; Movius 1974, 1977; Piggott 1965; Reed, Bennett, and Porter 1968; Sterud and Pratt 1975; Struever 1968a; Wheeler 1954

CHAPTER 8

Data Processing

Bennett and Bennett 1976; W. Bennett 1974; Chenhall 1975; Dowman 1970; Hope-Taylor 1966, 1967; LeBlanc 1976; Organ 1968; Plenderleith and Werner 1971; UNESCO 1968

Classification: Objectives, Kinds and Uses

Brew 1946; Clarke 1968; Doran and Hodson 1975; Dunnell 1971, 1978; Ford 1954; Gifford 1960; Hill 1978; Hill and Evans 1972; Hodson 1970; Krieger 1944, 1960; Rouse 1939, 1960; Sackett 1966; Schiffer 1976; Sokal and Sneath 1963; Spaulding 1953; Whallon 1972; Wheat, Gifford, and Wasley 1958

CHAPTER 9

Analysis of Artifacts

Brothwell and Higgs (eds.) 1970; Hodges 1964; Singer, Holmyard, and Hall (eds.) 1956; Tite 1972

Lithic Artifacts: Bordaz 1970; Bordes 1968; Clay 1976; Crabtree 1972; Hester and Heizer 1973; Jelinek 1976; Johnson 1978; Keeley 1974, 1977; Kidder 1932, 1947; Oakley 1956; Sackett 1966; Schiffer 1976; Semenov 1964; Sheets 1975; Swanson (ed.) 1975; Wilmsen 1968

Ceramic Artifacts: M. Bennett 1974; Ericson and Stickel 1973; Gifford 1960, 1976; Matson (ed.) 1965; Peacock 1970; Rice 1977; Sabloff and Smith 1969; Shepard 1971; Smith, Willey, and Gifford 1960; Whallon 1972

Metal Artifacts: Bayard 1972; Coghlan 1960; Lechtman 1976; Maddin, Muhly, and Wheeler 1977; Rowlands 1971; C. Smith 1973; Thompson 1970; Wertime 1973a, 1973b

Artifacts from Organic Materials: L. Binford and Bertram 1977; Brain 1969; Dart 1949, 1957; King 1978; Read-Martin and Read 1975; D. Thomas 1971

Artifacts and Sampling: Cowgill 1964; Kidder 1961; Mueller (ed.) 1975

Analysis of Ecofacts

Bray (ed.) 1976; Brothwell and Higgs (eds.) 1970; Callen 1970; Clark 1954, 1972; Higgs (ed.) 1972, 1975; Solecki 1975; Wheat 1972

Organic Remains (Flora): Dimbleby 1967, 1970; J. Iverson 1966; Gray and Smith 1962; Leroi-Gourhan 1975; Pickersgill 1972; Faegri and Renfrew 1973; Solecki 1975; Ucko and Dimbleby (eds.) 1969

Organic Remains (Fauna): L. Binford and Bertram 1977; Brain 1969; Casteel 1976; Chaplin 1971; Daly 1969; Gilbert 1973; Grayson 1973; Mori 1970; Olsen 1964, 1971; Perkins and Daly 1968; Read-Martin and Read 1975; B. Smith 1974; Speth and Davis 1976; D. Thomas 1971; von den Driesch 1976; Wheat 1972; White 1953; Zeuner 1964; Ziegler 1973

Organic Remains (Human): Anderson 1969; Angel 1969; Bass 1971; Brothwell 1963, 1971; Brothwell and Sandison (eds.) 1967; Cook 1972;

Deevey 1960; Haviland 1967; Petersen 1975; Ward and Weiss 1976; Weiss 1976; Zubrow (ed.) 1976

Inorganic Remains: Cornwall 1958, 1970; Doumas 1974; Gladfelter 1977; Limbrey 1972; Money 1973; Shackley 1975; Sheets 1971; Sjoberg 1976

Analysis of Features

Andrews 1975; Biddle (ed.) 1977; Dales 1966; Donnan 1964; Eddy 1974; Flannery 1972b; Flannery and Marcus 1976a; Forbes 1963; Hastings and Moseley 1975; Hawkins 1965; Hyslop 1977; Kopper and Rossello-Bordoy 1974; de Lumley 1969; Matheny 1976; Mendelssohn 1971; Moseley 1975; Movius 1966; Müller-Beck 1961; Potter 1977; Sharer 1978a; N. Smith 1978

CHAPTER 10

General References

Brothwell and Higgs (eds.) 1970; P. Hammond 1974; Michael and Ralph (eds.) 1971; Michels 1973; Oakley 1968; Taylor and Longworth (eds.) 1975; Zeuner 1958

Age Determination by Archaeological Classification

Stratigraphy: Harris 1975; Jennings 1957; Rowe 1961b

Seriation: Ascher and Ascher 1963; Brainerd 1951; Dempsey and Baumhoff 1963; Dethlefsen and Deetz 1966; Ford 1962; Hole and Shaw 1967; LeBlanc 1975; Meighan 1959; Petrie 1901; Robinson 1951

Sequence Comparison: Deetz and Dethlefsen 1965; Ehrich (ed.) 1965; Krieger 1946; Patterson 1963; Taylor and Meighan (eds.) 1978

Geological and Geochemical Age Determination

Geochronology: Giddings 1966; Salwen 1962; Smiley (ed.) 1955; Zeuner 1958

Varve Accumulation: Flint 1971; de Geer 1912; Zeuner 1958

Patination and Obsidian Hydration: Friedman and Smith 1960; Friedman and Trembour 1978; Goodwin 1960

Faunal and Floral Age Determination

Dendrochronology: Bannister 1962, 1970; Bannister and Smiley 1955; Stallings 1949

Bone Age Determination: McConnell 1962; Oakley 1948, 1970; Weiner 1955

Aspartic Acid Racemization: Bada and Helfman 1975; Bada, Schroeder, and Carter 1974

Radiometric Age Determination

Radiocarbon Age Determination: Arnold and Libby 1949; Bennett and others 1977; Deevey 1952; Grootes 1978; Libby 1955; Muller 1977; Nelson, Korteling, and Stott 1977; Ralph and Michael 1974; Ralph, Michael, and Han 1973; C. Renfrew 1971, 1973

Potassium-Argon Age Determination: Carr and Kulp 1957; Curtis 1975; Evernden and Curtis 1965

Thermoluminescence: Mazess and Zimmerman 1966; Ralph and Han 1966, 1969

Fission Track Dating: Watanabe and Suzuki 1969; Zimmerman 1971

Archaeomagnetic Age Determination

Aitken 1960; Tarling 1971

Calendrical Age Determination

Satterthwaite and Ralph 1960; Thompson 1972

CHAPTER 11

Technology and Environment

Clark 1952; Gabel 1967; Higgs (ed.) 1972, 1975; Netting 1977

Technology (See also Chapter 9): Hammond 1972; Klein 1973; Oakley 1956; Wheat 1967, 1972; Wilmsen 1970, 1974

Environment: Butzer 1964; Clark 1954; Coe and Flannery 1964; Jarman, Vita-Finzi, and Higgs 1972; MacNeish 1964a; MacNeish, Patterson, and Browman 1975; Vita-Finzi and Higgs 1970

Subsistence: Harlan 1967; Lee 1968; Roe (ed.) 1971; B. Smith 1974; P. Smith 1976; Struever 1968b, 1971; Ucko and Dimbleby (eds.) 1969

Social Systems and Spatial Frameworks

Binford and Binford (eds.) 1968; Hill and Gunn (eds.) 1977; Trigger and Longworth (eds.) 1974

Ceramic Sociology: Allen and Richardson 1971; Deetz 1965; Dumond 1977; Gifford 1960; Hill 1966, 1970; Longacre 1970a; Sackett 1977; Stanislawski 1973; Watson 1977; Whallon 1968

Settlement Archaeology: R. E. W. Adams 1974; L. Binford 1973; Binford and Binford 1966; Bordes and de Sonneville-Bordes 1970; Chang 1958, 1972; Christaller 1933; Clarke (ed.) 1977; Cunliffe (ed.) 1978; Flannery 1972b; Flannery and Marcus 1976a; Fox 1922; Haggett 1975; N. Hammond 1974; Hodder and Hassall 1971; Hodder and Orton 1976; Johnson 1972; Keatinge and Day 1974; MacNeish 1964a; Millon 1973; Naroll 1962; Parsons 1972; Speth and Johnson 1976; Steward 1938, 1955; Trigger 1968b; Ucko, Tringham, and Dimbleby (eds.) 1972; Vierra and Taylor 1977; Whallon 1973a, 1973b, 1974; Whiting and Ayres 1968; Wiessner 1974; Willey 1953, 1956 (ed.)

Exchange Systems: R. M. Adams 1974; Bray (ed.) 1973; Earle and Ericson (eds.) 1977; Johnson 1973; Polanyi, Arensburg, and Pearson (eds.) 1957; Renfrew 1969, 1975; Sabloff and Lamberg-Karlovsky (eds.) 1975; Sidrys 1977; Wilmsen (ed.) 1972

Ideological and Symbol Systems

Aveni (ed.) 1975; Baity 1973; Blanc 1961; Brown (ed.) 1971; Flannery 1976d; Flannery and Marcus 1976b; Kehoe and Kehoe 1973; Marshack 1972a, 1972b; Sears 1961; Thom 1971; Ucko 1968, 1969; Ucko and Rosenfeld 1967; Willey 1962

CHAPTER 12

Introduction and General

Ascher 1961a; Deetz 1965

Analogy: Uses, Guidelines, and Sources

K. Anderson 1969; Ascher 1961b; L. Binford 1967, 1972; L. Binford and Bertram 1977; Bonnichsen 1973; Bordes 1969; Callender 1976; Chang 1967; Coles 1973; Crabtree 1972; David 1971; Diaz del Castillo 1956; Finney 1977; Gould 1969, 1978 (ed.); Heider 1967; Hester and Heizer

1973; Heyerdahl 1950; Isaac 1967; Jewell 1963; Jewell and Dimbleby 1968; Johnson 1978; Lee and DeVore (eds.) 1968, 1976; Longacre and Ayres 1968; Longworth (ed.) 1971; McIntosh 1974; Munsen 1969; Puleston 1971; Saraydar and Shimada 1973; Semenov 1964; Steward 1942; Stiles 1977; Wauchope 1938; Wheeler 1943; Yellen 1977

CHAPTER 13

Origins of the Cultural Historical Approach

Fitting (ed.) 1973; Kidder 1962; Kidder and Guernsey 1919; Kidder, Jennings, and Shook 1946; Shook and Kidder 1952; Willey and Sabloff 1974; Woodbury 1973

The Cultural Historical Method

Flannery 1967; Kidder 1962; Rouse 1953; Taylor 1948; Trigger 1968a; Watson 1973

The Cultural Historical Synthesis

Ford 1969; Kroeber 1939; McKern 1939; Willey 1966, 1971; Willey and Phillips 1958

Cultural Historical Interpretation

W. Adams 1968; S. Binford 1968; Bischof and Viteri 1972; Ford 1969; Haury 1958; Jones 1977; Lathrap, Marcos, and Zeidler 1977; Martin and others 1952; Meggers, Evans, and Estrada 1965; Mooney 1965; Rowe 1966; G. Smith 1928; J. Smith 1974; Tschopik 1950; Wheeler 1966

CHAPTER 14

Origins of the Cultural Processual Approach

Adams 1966; L. Binford 1962; Childe 1954; Steward 1955; Steward and Setzler 1938; Taylor 1948; White 1949; Willey and Sabloff 1974

The Cultural Processual Method

L. Binford 1962, 1968; Hempel 1966; Hempel and Oppenheim 1948; Morgan 1973, 1974; Pring and Hammond 1975; Sabloff and Rathje 1973; Sahlins and Service (eds.) 1960; Schiffer 1976; Watson, LeBlanc, and Redman 1971

Cultural Processual Synthesis

Chamberlain 1897; Zubrow 1973

Interpretation: Cultural Processual Models

Systems Models: Bertalanffy 1968; Clarke 1968; Doran 1970; Flannery 1968; Hill (ed.) 1977; Plog 1975; Rapoport 1968; Salmon 1978

Cultural Ecological Models: Flannery 1965, 1969; Netting 1977; Sanders and Price 1968; Steward 1955, 1977; Thomas 1973; Zubrow 1975

Multilinear Cultural Evolution Models: Adams 1966; Flannery 1972a; Fried 1967; MacNeish 1964a; Peebles and Kus 1977; Sahlins and Service (eds.) 1960; Sanders and Price 1968; Service 1962; Steward 1955, 1977

CHAPTER 15

Pseudo-Archaeology

Heyerdahl (ed.) 1961, 1965; Rathje 1978; Story 1976; Stover and Harrison 1970; Von Däniken 1969, 1970; Wauchope 1962; White 1974

Destruction of the Past

Coggins 1972; Fagan 1975; McGimsey 1972; Meyer 1977; Nickerson 1972; Robertson 1972; Sheets 1973; R. Smith 1974

Response to Destruction of the Past: Modern Contract Archaeology and Cultural Resource Management/Conservation Archaeology

Burnham 1974; Cunningham 1974a; Davis 1972; Fowler 1974; Glassow 1977; King 1971; King, Hickman, and Berg 1977; Lipe 1974; Lipe and Lindsay (eds.) 1974; McGimsey 1972; McGimsey and Davis (eds.) 1977; Raab and Klinger 1977; Rahtz 1974; Schiffer and Gumerman (eds.) 1977; Schiffer and House 1977; R. Smith 1974; C. Thomas 1971; Wendorf 1973

Bibliography

Adams, R. E. W. 1974. A trial estimation of palace populations at Uaxactún. In *Meso-american Archaeology: New Approaches,* ed. N. Hammond, pp. 285–296. Austin: University of Texas Press.

———. 1975. Stratigraphy. In *Field Methods in Archaeology,* 6th ed., ed. T. R. Hester, R. F. Heizer, and J. A. Graham, pp. 147–162. Palo Alto, Calif.: Mayfield.

Adams, R. McC. 1965. *Land behind Baghdad: A History of Settlement on the Diyala Plains.* Chicago: University of Chicago Press.

———. 1966. *The Evolution of Urban Society.* Chicago: Aldine-Atherton.

———. 1972. A computer simulation model of Great Basin Shoshonean subsistence and settlement patterns. In *Models in Archaeology,* ed. D. L. Clarke, pp. 671–704. London: Methuen.

———. 1974. Anthropological perspectives on ancient trade. *Current Anthropology* 15:239–258.

Adams, R. McC., and H. Nissen. 1972. *The Uruk Countryside.* Chicago: University of Chicago Press.

Adams, W. Y. 1968. Invasion, diffusion, evolution? *Antiquity* 42:194–215.

Aitken, M. J. 1960. Magnetic dating. *Archaeometry* 3:41–44.

———. 1974. *Physics and Archaeology,* 2nd ed. Oxford: Clarendon Press.

Alcock, L. 1971. *Arthur's Britain: History and Archaeology, A.D.* pp. 367–634. Harmondsworth, England: Penguin.

Alexander, J. 1970. *The Directing of Archaeological Excavations.* London: John Baker.

Allen, W. L., and J. B. Richardson III. 1971. The reconstruction of kinship from archaeological data: The concepts, the methods, and the feasibility. *American Antiquity* 36:41–53.

Anderson, J. E. 1969. *The Human Skeleton: A Manual for Archeologists.* Ottawa: The National Museums of Canada.

Anderson, K. M. 1969. Ethnographic analogy and archaeological interpretation. *Science* 163:133–138.

Andrews, G. F. 1975. *Maya Cities: Urbanization and Placemaking.* Norman: University of Oklahoma Press.

Angel, J. L. 1969. The bases of paleodemography. *American Journal of Physical Anthropology* 30:427–438.

Arnold, J. R., and W. F. Libby. 1949. Age determinations by radiocarbon content: Checks with samples of known age. *Science* 110:678–680.

Ascher, M., and R. Ascher. 1963. Chronological ordering by computer. *American Anthropologist* 65:1045–1052.

Ascher, R. M. 1961a. Analogy in archaeological interpretation. *Southwestern Journal of Anthropology* 17:317–325.

———. 1961b. Experimental archaeology. *American Anthropologist* 63:793–816.

———. 1968. Time's arrow and the archaeology of a contemporary community. In *Settlement Archaeology,* ed. K. C. Chang, pp. 43–52. Palo Alto, Calif.: National Press.

Ashmore, W., and R. J. Sharer. 1978. Excavations at Quiriguá, Guatemala: The ascent of an elite Maya center. *Archaeology* 31(6):10–19.

Aston, M., and T. Rowley. 1974. *Landscape Archaeology: An Introduction to Fieldwork Techniques on Post-Roman Landscapes.* Newton Abbot, England: David and Charles.

Atkinson, R. J. C. 1953. *Field Archaeology,* 2nd ed. London: Methuen.

Aveni, A. F., ed. 1975. *Archaeoastronomy in Pre-Columbian America.* Austin: University of Texas Press.

Bada, J. L., and P. M. Helfman. 1975. Amino acid racemization dating of fossil bones. *World Archaeology* 7:160–173.

Bada, J. L., R. A. Schroeder, and G. F. Carter. 1974. New evidence for the antiquity of man in North America deduced from aspartic acid racemization. *Science* 184:791–793.

Baity, E. C. 1973. Archaeoastronomy and ethnoastronomy so far. *Current Anthropology* 14:389–449.

Baker, C. M. 1978. The size effect: An explanation of variability in surface artifact assemblage content. *American Antiquity* 43:288–293.

Bannister, B. 1962. The interpretation of tree-ring dates. *American Antiquity* 27:508–514.

———. 1970. Dendrochronology. In *Science in Archaeology,* 2nd ed., ed. D. Brothwell and E. S. Higgs, pp. 191–205. New York: Praeger.

Bannister, B., and T. L. Smiley. 1955. Dendrochronology. In *Geochronology,* ed. T. L. Smiley, pp. 177–195. University of Arizona Physical Science Bulletin No. 2.

Bass, G. F. 1966. *Archaeology Under Water.* London: Thames and Hudson.

Bass, G. F., and P. Throckmorton. 1961. Excavating a Bronze Age shipwreck. *Archaeology* 14:78–87.

Bass, W. M. 1971. *Human Osteology: A Laboratory and Field Manual of the Human Skeleton.* Columbia, Mo.: Missouri Archaeological Society.

Bayard, D. T. 1969. Science, theory and reality in the "new archaeology." *American Antiquity* 34:376–384.

———. 1972. Early Thai bronze: Analysis and new dates. *Science* 176:1411–1412.

Bennett, C. L., R. P. Beukens, M. R. Clover, H. E. Gove, R. B. Liebert, A. E. Litherland, K. H. Purser, and W. E. Sondheim. 1977. Radiocarbon dating using electrostatic accelerators: Negative ions provide the key. *Science* 198:508–510.

Bennett, J. W. 1976. Anticipation, adaptation and the concept of culture in anthropology. *Science* 192:847–853.

Bennett, M. A. 1974. *Basic Ceramic Analyses.* Eastern New Mexico University Contributions in Anthropology, 6 (1).

Bennett, M., and W. J. Bennett, Jr. 1976. The material culture registry at Tell el-Hesi. *Journal of Field Archaeology* 3:97–101.

Bennett, W. J., Jr. 1974. The field recording of ceramic data. *Journal of Field Archaeology* 1:209–214.

Bertalanffy, L. von. 1968. *General System Theory: Foundations, Development, Applications.* New York: George Braziller.

Biddle, M., ed. 1977. Architecture and archaeology. *World Archaeology* 9 (2).

Binford, L. R. 1962. Archaeology as anthropology. *American Antiquity* 28:217–225.

———. 1964. A consideration of archaeological research design. *American Antiquity* 29:425–441.

———. 1967. Smudge pits and hide smoking: The use of analogy in archaeological reasoning. *American Antiquity* 32:1–12.

———. 1968. Archeological perspectives. In *New Perspectives in Archeology,* ed. S. R. Binford and L. R. Binford, pp. 5–32. Chicago: Aldine.

———. 1972. Archaeological reasoning and smudge pits—revisited. In *An Archaeological Perspective,* L. R. Binford, pp. 52–58. New York: Seminar Press.

———. 1973. Interassemblage variability—the Mousterian and the "functional" argument. In *The Explanation of Culture Change: Models in Prehistory,* ed. C. Renfrew, pp. 227–254. Pittsburgh: University of Pittsburgh Press.

Binford, L. R., and J. B. Bertram. 1977. Bone frequencies—and attritional processes. In *For Theory Building in Archaeology,* ed. L. R. Binford, pp. 77–153. New York: Academic Press.

Binford, L. R., and S. R. Binford. 1966. A preliminary analysis of functional variability in the Mousterian of Levallois Facies. In *Recent Studies in Paleoanthropology,* ed. J. D. Clark and F. C. Howell, pp. 238–295, *American Anthropologist* 68 (2, Part 2).

Binford, L. R., S. R. Binford, R. Whallon, and M. A. Hardin. 1970. *Archaeology ,at Hatchery West.* Society for American Archaeology, Memoir 24.

Binford, S. R. 1968. Ethnographic data and understanding the Pleistocene. In *Man the Hunter,* ed. R. B. Lee and I. DeVore, pp. 274–275. Chicago: Aldine.

Binford, S. R., and L. R. Binford, eds. 1968. *New Perspectives in Archeology.* Chicago: Aldine.

Bird, J. B. 1968. More about earth-shaking equipment. *American Antiquity* 33:507–509.

Bird, J. B., and J. A. Ford. 1956. A new earth-shaking machine. *American Antiquity* 21:399–401.

Bischof, H., and J. Viteri G. 1972. Pre-Valdivia occupation on the southwest coast of Ecuador. *American Antiquity* 37:548–551.

Blakeley, R. L. 1971. Comparison of the mortality profiles of Archaic, Middle Woodland, and Middle Mississippian skeletal profiles. *American Journal of Physical Anthropology* 34:43–53.

Blanc, A. C. 1961. Some evidence for the ideologies of early man. In *Social Life of Early Man,* ed. Sherwood L. Washburn, pp. 119–136. Viking Fund Publications in Anthropology, no. 31.

Boas, F. 1948. *Race, Language and Culture.* New York: Macmillan.

Bonnichsen, R. 1973. Millie's camp: An experiment in archaeology. *World Archaeology* 4:277–291.

Bordaz, J. 1970. *Tools of the Old and New Stone Age.* Garden City: Natural History Press.

Bordes, F. 1968. *The Old Stone Age.* New York: McGraw-Hill.

———. 1969. Reflections on typology and techniques in the Palaeolithic. *Arctic Anthropology* 6:1–29.

Bordes, F., and D. de Sonneville-Bordes. 1970. The significance of variability in Palaeolithic assemblages. *World Archaeology* 2:61–73.

Brain, C. K. 1969. *The Contribution of Namib Desert Hottentots to an Understanding of Australopithecine Bone Accumulations.* Scientific Papers of the Namib Desert Research Station, 13.

Brainerd, G. W. 1951. The place of chronological ordering in archaeological analysis. *American Antiquity* 16:301–313.

Bray, W., ed. 1973. Trade. *World Archaeology* 5 (2).

———. ed. 1976. Climatic change. *World Archaeology* 8 (2).

Breiner, S., and M. D. Coe. 1972. Magnetic exploration of the Olmec civilization. *American Scientist* 60:566–575.

Brew, J. O. 1946. The use and abuse of taxonomy. In *The Archaeology of Alkali Ridge, Southern Utah,* J. O. Brew, pp. 44–66. Papers of the Peabody Museum, 21.

———. ed. 1968. *One Hundred Years of Anthropology.* Cambridge: Harvard University Press.

Brodrick, A. H. 1949. *Lascaux, A Commentary.* London: Ernest Benn, Ltd.

Brothwell, D. R. 1963. *Digging Up Bones.* London: British Museum.

———. 1971. Paleodemography. In *Biological Aspects of Demography,* ed. W. Brass, pp. 111–130. London: Taylor and Francis.

Brothwell, D., and E. S. Higgs, eds. 1970. *Science in Archaeology,* 2nd ed. New York: Praeger.

Brothwell, D. R., and A. T. Sandison, eds. 1967. *Diseases in Antiquity.* Springfield, Ill.: Thomas.

Brown, J. A. ed. 1971. *Approaches to the Social Dimensions of Mortuary Practices.* Society for American Archaeology, Memoir 25.

Brown, J. A., and S. Struever. 1973. The organization of archeological research: An Illinois example. In *Research and Theory in Current Archeology,* ed. Charles L. Redman, pp. 261–280. New York: Wiley-Interscience.

Brunhouse, R. L. 1973. *In Search of the Maya: The First Archaeologists.* Albuquerque: University of New Mexico Press.

Burnham, B., compiler. 1974. *The Protection of Cultural Property: Handbook of National Legislations.* Paris: The International Council of Museums, Tunisia.

Butzer, K. W. 1964. *Environment and Archaeology: An Introduction to Pleistocene Geography.* Chicago: Aldine.

Callen, E. O. 1970. Diet as revealed by coprolites. In *Science in Archaeology,* 2nd ed., ed. D. Brothwell and E. S. Higgs, pp. 235–243. New York: Praeger.

Callender, D. W., Jr. 1976. Reliving the past: Experimental archaeology in Pennsylvania. *Archaeology* 29:173–177.

Camden, W. 1789. *Britannia.* (Orig. pub. 1586), tr. R. Gough. London: J. Nichol (Sections reprinted 1977, annotated and edited by G. J. Copley. London: Hutchinson.)

Cann, J. R., and C. Renfrew. 1964. The characterization of obsidian and its application to the Mediterranean region. *Proceedings of the Prehistoric Society* 30:111–133.

Carlson, R. L. 1970. *White Mountain Redware.* Anthropological Papers of the University of Arizona, No. 19. Tucson: University of Arizona Press.

Carr, D. R., and J. L. Kulp. 1957. Potassium-argon method of geochronometry. *Bulletin of the Geological Society of America* 68:763–784.

Carr, R. F., and J. E. Hazard. 1961. *Map of the Ruins of Tikal, El Peten, Guatemala.* Tikal Reports, No. 11. Philadelphia: The University Museum.

Carter, H. 1972. *The Tomb of Tutankhamen.* (Orig. pub. 1922, 3 vols.) New York: Excalibur Books.

Casteel, R. W. 1970. Core and column sampling. *American Antiquity* 35:465–466.

————. 1976. *Fish Remains in Archaeology and Paleo-Environmental Studies.* New York: Academic Press.

Chamberlain, T. C. 1897. The method of multiple working hypotheses. *Journal of Geology* 39:155–165.

Chang, K. C. 1958. Study of the Neolithic social groupings: Examples from the New World. *American Anthropologist* 60:298–334.

————. 1967. Major aspects of the interrelationship of archaeology and ethnology. *Current Anthropology* 8:227–243.

————. 1972. *Settlement Patterns in Archaeology.* Addison-Wesley Modules in Anthropology, no. 24.

————. 1974. Man and land in central Taiwan: The first two years of an interdisciplinary project. *Journal of Field Archaeology* 1:264–275.

Chaplin, R. E. 1971. *The Study of Animal Bones from Archaeological Sites.* New York: Seminar Press.

Chartkoff, J. L. 1978. Transect interval sampling in forests. *American Antiquity* 43:46–53.

Chenhall, R. G. 1975. *Museum Cataloging in the Computer Age.* Nashville: American Association for State and Local History.

Childe, V. G. 1954. *What Happened in History.* Revised edition. Harmondsworth, England: Penguin.

Christaller, W. 1933. *Die zentralen Orte in Suddeutschland.* Jena: G. Fischer.

Clark, J. G. D. 1952. *Prehistoric Europe: The Economic Basis.* London: Methuen.
———. 1954. *Excavations at Star Carr.* Cambridge: Cambridge University Press. (Reprinted 1971.)
———. 1972. *Star Carr: A Case Study in Bioarchaeology.* Addison-Wesley Modules in Anthropology, no. 10.
Clarke, D. L. 1968. *Analytical Archaeology.* London: Methuen.
———. 1972. Models and paradigms in contemporary archaeology. In *Models in Archaeology,* ed. D. L. Clarke, pp. 1–60. London: Methuen.
———. 1973. Archaeology: the loss of innocence. *Antiquity* 47:6–18.
———. ed. 1977. *Spatial Archaeology.* New York: Academic Press.
Clay, R. B. 1976. Typological classification, attribute analysis, and lithic variability. *Journal of Field Archaeology* 3:303–311.
Coe, M. D., and K. V. Flannery. 1964. Microenvironments and Mesoamerican prehistory. *Science* 143:650–654.
Coe, W. R. 1967. *Tikal: A Handbook of the Ancient Maya Ruins.* Philadelphia: The University Museum.
Coggins, C. 1972. Archaeology and the art market. *Science* 175:263–266.
Coghlan, H. H. 1960. Metallurgical analysis of archaeological materials: I. In *The Application of Quantitative Methods in Archaeology,* ed. R. F. Heizer and S. F. Cook, pp. 1–20. Viking Fund Publications in Anthropology, 28.
Coles, J. 1972. *Field Archaeology in Britain.* London: Methuen.
———. 1973. *Archaeology by Experiment.* New York: Scribners.
Cook, S. F. 1972. *Prehistoric Demography.* Addison-Wesley Modules in Anthropology, no. 16.
Cornwall, I. W. 1958. *Soils for the Archaeologist.* London: Phoenix House.
———. 1970. Soil, stratification and environment. In *Science in Archaeology,* 2nd ed., ed. D. R. Brothwell and Eric S. Higgs, pp. 120–134. New York: Praeger.
Cowgill, G. L. 1964. The selection of samples from large sherd collections. *American Antiquity* 29:467–473.
———. 1968. Archaeological applications of factor, cluster and proximity analysis. *American Antiquity* 33:367–375.
———. 1974. Quantitative studies of urbanization at Teotihuacán. In *Mesoamerican Archaeology: New Approaches,* ed. N. Hammond, pp. 363–397. Austin: University of Texas Press.
———. 1977. The trouble with significance tests and what we can do about it. *American Antiquity* 42:350–368.
Crabtree, D. E. 1972. *An Introduction to Flintworking. Part I. An Introduction to the Technology of Stone Tools.* Occasional Papers of the Idaho State University, no. 28.
Cunliffe, B., ed. 1978. Landscape Archaeology. *World Archaeology* 9 (3).
Cunningham, R. D. 1974a. Impact of another new archaeology. *Journal of Field Archaeology* 1:365–369.
———. 1974b. Improve field research administration? How? *American Antiquity* 39:462–465.
Curtis, G. H. 1975. Improvements in potassium-argon dating: 1962–1975. *World Archaeology* 7:198–209.
Cushing, F. H. 1890. Preliminary notes on the origin, working hypotheses and primary researches of the Hemenway . . . Expedition. *Seventh International Congress of Americanists,* Berlin, pp. 151–194.

Dales, G. F. 1966. The decline of the Harappans. *Scientific American* 214 (5):92–100.
Daly, P. 1969. Approaches to faunal analysis in archaeology. *American Antiquity* 34:146–153.
Daniel, G. 1943. *The Three Ages: An Essay on Archaeological Method.* Cambridge: Cambridge University Press.

Daniel, G. 1962. *The Idea of Prehistory*. Baltimore: Penguin.

———. 1967. *The Origins and Growth of Archaeology*. Baltimore: Penguin.

———. 1969. Editorial. *Antiquity* 43:86–87.

———. 1971a. Editorial. *Antiquity* 45:246–249.

———. 1971b. From Worsaae to Childe: The models of prehistory. *Proceedings of the Prehistoric Society* 38:140–153.

———. 1976a. *A Hundred and Fifty Years of Archaeology*. Cambridge: Harvard University Press.

———. 1976b. Stone, bronze and iron. In *To Illustrate the Monuments: Essays on Archaeology Presented to Stuart Piggott*, ed. J. V. S. Megaw, pp. 35–42. London: Thames and Hudson.

Daniels, S. G. H. 1972. Research design models. In *Models in Archaeology*, ed. D. L. Clarke, pp. 201–229. London: Methuen.

Dart, R. A. 1949. The predatory implemental technique of the australopithecines. *American Journal of Physical Anthropology* 7:1–16.

———. 1957. *The Osteodontokeratic Culture of* Australopithecus prometheus. Transvaal Museum Memoirs, 18.

Darwin, C. R. 1859. *The Origin of Species*. London: J. Murray.

David, N. 1971. The Fulani compound and the archaeologist. *World Archaeology* 3:111–131.

Davis, E. L. 1975. The "exposed archaeology" of China Lake, California. *American Antiquity* 40:39–53.

Davis, H. A. 1972. The crisis in American archeology. *Science* 175:267–272.

Deetz, J. 1965. *The Dynamics of Stylistic Change in Arikara Ceramics*. Illinois Studies in Anthropology, No. 4. Urbana: University of Illinois Press.

———. 1967. *Invitation to Archaeology*. Garden City, N.Y.: Natural History Press.

———. 1968. The inference of residence and descent rules from archaeological data. In *New Perspectives in Archeology*, ed. S. R. Binford and L. R. Binford, pp. 41–48. Chicago: Aldine.

———. 1970. Archaeology as a social science. In *Current Directions in Anthropology*, ed. A. Fischer, pp. 115–125. American Anthropological Association, Bulletin 3, no. 3 (part 2).

Deetz, J., and E. Dethlefsen. 1965. The Doppler effect and archaeology: A consideration of the spatial aspects of seriation. *Southwestern Journal of Anthropology* 21:196–206.

———. 1967. Death's head, cherub, urn and willow. *Natural History* 76 (3):28–37.

Deevey, E. S., Jr. 1952. Radiocarbon dating. *Scientific American* 186 (2):24–28.

———. 1960. The human population. *Scientific American* 203 (3):195–205.

Dempsey, P., and M. A. Baumhoff. 1963. The statistical use of artifact distributions to establish chronological sequence. *American Antiquity* 28:496–509.

Dethlefsen, E., and J. Deetz. 1966. Death's heads, cherubs, and willow trees: Experimental archaeology in colonial cemeteries. *American Antiquity* 31:502–510.

Diaz del Castillo, B. 1956. *The Discovery and Conquest of Mexico, 1517–1521*. (Orig. pub. 1632), tr. A. P. Maudslay. New York: Grove Press.

Dimbleby, G. W. 1967. *Plants and Archaeology*. London: John Baker.

———. 1970. Pollen analysis. In *Science in Archaeology*, 2nd ed., ed. D. Brothwell and E. S. Higgs, pp. 167–177. New York: Praeger.

Dinsmoor, W. B., Jr. 1977. The archaeological field staff: The architect. *Journal of Field Archaeology* 4:309–328.

Donnan, C. B. 1964. An early house from Chilca, Peru. *American Antiquity* 30:137–144.

Doran, J. 1970. Systems theory, computer simulations and archacology. *World Archaeology* 1:289–298.

Doran, J. E., and F. R. Hodson. 1975. *Mathematics and Computers in Archaeology*. Cambridge: Harvard University Press.

Doumas, C. 1974. The Minoan eruption of the Santorini volcano. *Antiquity* 48:110–115.

Dowman, E. A. 1970. *Conservation in Field Archaeology*. London: Methuen.

Drucker, P. 1972. *Stratigraphy in Archaeology: An Introduction*. Addison-Wesley Modules in Anthropology, no. 30.

Dumond, D. E. 1977. Science in archaeology: The saints go marching in. *American Antiquity* 42:33–49.

Dunnell, R. C. 1971. *Systematics in Prehistory*. New York: Free Press.

————. 1978. Style and function: A fundamental dichotomy. *American Antiquity* +Sackett 43:192–202.

Dymond, D. P. 1974. *Archaeology and History: A Plea for Reconciliation*. London: Thames and Hudson.

Earle, T. K., and J. E. Ericson, eds. 1977. *Exchange Systems in Prehistory*. New York: Academic Press.

Eddy, J. A. 1974. Astronomical alignment of the Big Horn Medicine Wheel. *Science* 184:1035–1043.

Ehrich, R. W., ed. 1965. *Chronologies in Old World Archaeology*. Chicago: University of Chicago Press.

Eiseley, L. 1958. *Darwin's Century: Evolution and the Men Who Discovered It*. Garden City: Doubleday (Anchor).

Ericson, J. E., and E. G. Stickel. 1973. A proposed classification system for ceramics. *World Archaeology* 4:357–367.

Estes, J. E., J. R. Jensen, and L. R. Tinney. 1977. The use of historical photography for mapping archaeological sites. *Journal of Field Archaeology* 4:441–447.

Evernden, J. F., and G. H. Curtis. 1965. The potassium-argon dating of Late Cenozoic rocks in East Africa and Italy. *Current Anthropology* 6:343–385.

Faegri, K., and J. Iverson. 1966. *Textbook of Pollen Analysis*. New York: Hafner.

Fagan, B. M. 1975. *The Rape of the Nile*. New York: Scribners.

————. 1978. *Quest for the Past: Great Discoveries in Archaeology*. Reading, Mass.: Addison-Wesley.

Fehon, J. R., and S. C. Scholtz. 1978. A conceptual framework for the study of artifact loss. *American Antiquity* 43:271–273.

Finley, M. I. 1971. Archaeology and history. *Daedalus* 100:168–186.

Finney, B. R. 1977. Voyaging canoes and the settlement of Polynesia. *Science* 196:1277–1285.

Fitting, J. E., ed. 1973. *The Development of North American Archaeology: Essays in the History of Regional Traditions*. Garden City: Doubleday (Anchor).

Flannery, K. V. 1965. The ecology of early food production in Mesopotamia. *Science* 147:1247–1256.

————. 1967. Culture history vs. cultural process: A debate in American archaeology. *Scientific American* 217 (2):119–122.

————. 1968. Archeological systems theory and early Mesoamerica. In *Anthropological Archeology in the Americas,* ed. B. J. Meggers, pp. 67–87. Washington, D.C.: Anthropological Society of Washington.

————. 1969. Origins and ecological effects of early domestication in Iran and the Near East. In *The Domestication and Exploitation of Plants and Animals,* ed. P. J. Ucko and G. W. Dimbleby, pp. 73–100. Chicago: Aldine-Atherton.

————. 1972a. The cultural evolution of civilizations. *Annual Review of Ecology and Systematics* 2:399–426.

———. 1972b. The origins of the village as a settlement type in Mesoamerica and the Near East: A comparative study. In *Man, Settlement and Urbanism,* ed. P. J. Ucko, R. Tringham, and G. W. Dimbleby, pp. 23–53. London: Duckworth.

———. 1973. Archeology with a capital S. In *Research and Theory in Current Archeology,* ed. C. L. Redman, pp. 47–53. New York: Wiley-Interscience.

———. ed. 1976a. *The Early Mesoamerican Village.* New York: Academic Press.

———. 1976b. Sampling by intensive surface collecting. Ibid., pp. 51–62.

———. 1976c. Excavating deep communities by transect samples. Ibid., pp. 68–72.

———. 1976d. Contextual analysis of ritual paraphernalia from Formative Oaxaca. Ibid., pp. 333–345.

Flannery, K. V., and J. Marcus. 1976a. Evolution of the public building in Formative Oaxaca. In *Cultural Change and Continuity: Essays in Honor of James Bennett Griffin,* ed. C. E. Cleland, pp. 205–221. New York: Academic Press.

———. 1976b. Formative Oaxaca and the Zapotec cosmos. *American Scientist* 64:374–383.

Flint, R. N. 1971. *Glacial and Quaternary Geology.* New York: Wiley.

Forbes, R. J. 1963. *Studies in Ancient Technology,* vol. 7. Leiden: E. T. Brill.

Ford, J. A. 1954. The type concept revisited. *American Anthropologist* 56:42–53.

———. 1962. *A Quantitative Method for Deriving Cultural Chronology.* Pan American Union, Technical Manual 1.

———. 1969. *A Comparison of Formative Cultures in the Americas.* Smithsonian Contributions to Anthropology, vol. 11.

Ford, R. I. 1977. The state of the art in archaeology. In *Perspectives on Anthropology, 1976,* ed. A. F. C. Wallace, J. L. Angel, R. Fox, S. McLendon, R. Sady, and R. J. Sharer, pp. 101–115. American Anthropological Association, Special Publication 10.

Fowler, M. L. 1974. *Cahokia: Ancient Capital of the Midwest.* Addison-Wesley Modules in Anthropology, no. 48.

Fox, C. 1922. *The Archaeology of the Cambridge Region.* Cambridge: Cambridge University Press.

Frere, J. 1800. Account of flint weapons discovered at Hoxne in Suffolk. *Archaeologia* 13:204–205.

Fried, M. H. 1967. *The Evolution of Political Society.* New York: Random House.

Friedman, I., and R. L. Smith. 1960. A new dating method using obsidian: Part I, the development of the method. *American Antiquity* 25:476–493.

Friedman, I., and F. W. Trembour. 1978. Obsidian: The dating stone. *American Scientist* 66:44–51.

Fritz, J. M., and F. T. Plog. 1970. The nature of archaeological explanation. *American Antiquity* 35:405–412.

Fry, R. E. 1972. Manually operated post-hole diggers as sampling instruments. *American Antiquity* 37:259–262.

Fry, R. E., and S. C. Cox. 1974. The structure of ceramic exchange at Tikal, Guatemala. *World Archaeology* 6:209–225.

Gabel, C. 1967. *Analysis of Prehistoric Economic Patterns.* New York: Holt, Rinehart and Winston.

Gallatin, A. 1836. A synopsis of the Indian tribes within the United States east of the Rocky Mountains, in the British and Russian possessions in North America. *Archaeologia Americana* 2:1–422.

Geer, G. de. 1912. A geochronology of the last 12,000 years. *Comptes Rendus* (11th International Geological Congress, Stockholm, 1910) 1:241–258.

Giddings, J. L. 1964. *The Archeology of Cape Denbigh.* Providence, R.I.: Brown University Press.

———. 1966. Cross-dating the archaeology of northwestern Alaska. *Science* 153:127–135.

———. 1967. *Ancient Men of the Arctic.* New York: Knopf.

Gifford, J. C. 1960. The type-variety method of ceramic classification as an indicator of cultural phenomena. *American Antiquity* 25:341–347.

_____. 1976. *Prehistoric Pottery Analysis and the Ceramics of Barton Ramie in the Belize Valley.* Memoirs of the Peabody Museum, 18.

Gilbert, B. M. 1973. *Mammalian Osteoarchaeology.* Missouri Archaeological Society Special Publications.

Gladfelter, B. G. 1977. Geoarchaeology: The geomorphologist and archaeology. *American Antiquity* 42:519–538.

Glassow, M. A. 1977. Issues in evaluating the significance of archaeological resources. *American Antiquity* 42:413–420.

Glob, P. V. 1969. *The Bog People: Iron Age Man Preserved.* tr. R. Bruce-Mitford. Ithaca, N.Y.: Cornell University Press.

Goodwin, A. J. H. 1960. Chemical alteration (patination) of stone. In *The Application of Quantitative Methods in Archaeology,* ed. R. F. Heizer and S. F. Cook, pp. 300–312. Viking Fund Publications in Anthropology, no. 28.

Goodyear, A. C., L. M. Raab, and T. C. Klinger. 1978. The status of archaeological research design in cultural resource management. *American Antiquity* 43:159–173.

Gorenstein, S. 1977. History of American archaeology. In *Perspectives on Anthropology, 1976,* ed. A. F. C. Wallace, J. L. Angel, R. Fox, S. McLendon, R. Sady, and R. J. Sharer, pp. 86–100. American Anthropological Association, Special Publication 10.

Gould, R. A. 1969. Subsistence behavior among the Western Desert Aborigines of Australia. *Oceania* 39:251–274.

_____. ed. 1978. *Explorations in Ethnoarchaeology.* Albuquerque: University of New Mexico Press.

Gray, J., and W. Smith. 1962. Fossil pollen and archaeology. *Archaeology* 15:16–26.

Grayson, D. K. 1973. On the methodology of faunal analysis. *American Antiquity* 39:432–439.

Griffin, J. B. 1959. The pursuit of archaeology in the United States. *American Anthropologist* 61:379–388.

Grinsell, L., P. Rahtz, and D. P. Williams. 1974. *The Preparation of Archaeological Reports,* 2nd ed. London: John Baker.

Grootes, P. M. 1978. Carbon-14 time scale extended: Comparison of chronologies. *Science* 200:11–15.

Gumerman, G. J. 1973. The reconciliation of method and theory in archeology. In *Research and Theory in Current Archeology,* ed. C. L. Redman, pp. 261–280. New York: Wiley-Interscience.

Gumerman, G. J., and T. R. Lyons. 1971. Archaeological methodology and remote sensing. *Science* 172:126–132.

Gumerman, G. J., and D. A. Phillips, Jr. 1978. Archaeology beyond anthropology. *American Antiquity* 43:184–191.

Haggett, P. 1975. *Geography, A Modern Synthesis,* 2nd ed. New York: Harper and Row.

Hamlin, C. L. 1978. Machine processing of LANDSAT data: An introduction for anthropologists and archaeologists. *MASCA Newsletter* 13 (1/2):1–11.

Hammond, N. 1972. Obsidian trade routes in the Mayan area. *Science* 178:1092–1093.

_____. 1974. The distribution of Late Classic Maya major ceremonial centres in the Central Area. In *Mesoamerican Archaeology: New Approaches,* ed. N. Hammond, pp. 313–334. Austin: University of Texas Press.

_____. 1975. Maya settlement hierarchy in northern Belize. *Contributions of the University of California Archaeological Research Facility* 27:40–55.

Hammond, N., D. Pring, R. Berger, V. R. Switsur, and A. P. Ward. 1976. Radiocarbon chronology for early Maya occupation at Cuello, Belize. *Nature* 260:579–581.

Hammond, P. C. 1974. Archaeometry and time: A review. *Journal of Field Archaeology* 1:329–335.

Hanson, J. A., and M. B. Schiffer. 1975. The Joint Site—A preliminary report. In *Chapters in the Prehistory of Eastern Arizona, III: Fieldiana: Anthropology* 65:47–91.

Harlan, J. R. 1967. A wild wheat harvest in Turkey. *Antiquity* 20:197–201.

Harp, E., Jr., ed. 1975. *Photography in Archaeological Research.* Albuquerque: University of New Mexico Press. School of American Research Advanced Seminar Series.

Harris, E. C. 1975. The stratigraphic sequence: A question of time. *World Archaeology* 7:109–121.

Harris, M. 1968. *The Rise of Anthropological Theory: A History of Theories of Culture.* New York: Crowell.

Hastings, C. M., and M. E. Moseley. 1975. The adobes of Huaca del Sol and Huaca de la Luna. *American Antiquity* 40:196–203.

Haury, E. W. 1958. Evidence at Point of Pines for a prehistoric migration from northern Arizona. In *Migrations in New World Culture History,* ed. R. H. Thompson, pp. 1–6. University of Arizona Social Science Bulletin, no. 27.

Haven, S. F. 1856. *Archaeology of the United States.* Smithsonian Contributions to Knowledge 8 (article 2).

Haviland, W. A. 1967. Stature at Tikal, Guatemala: Implications for ancient demography and social organization. *American Antiquity* 32:316–325.

Hawkes, J. 1968. The proper study of mankind. *Antiquity* 42:255–262.

Hawkins, G. S. 1965. *Stonehenge Decoded.* New York: Doubleday.

Hawley, F. M. 1937. Reverse stratigraphy. *American Antiquity* 2:297–299.

Heider, K. G. 1967. Archaeological assumptions and ethnographical facts: A cautionary tale from New Guinea. *Southwestern Journal of Anthropology* 23:52–64.

Heizer, R. F. 1962. *Man's Discovery of His Past: Literary Landmarks in Archaeology.* Englewood Cliffs, N.J.: Prentice-Hall.

Hempel, C. G. 1966. *Philosophy of Natural Science.* Englewood Cliffs, N.J.: Prentice-Hall.

Hempel, C. G., and P. Oppenheim. 1948. Studies in the logic of explanation. *Philosophy of Science* 15:135–175.

Hester, T. A., and R. F. Heizer. 1973. *Bibliography of Archaeology I: Experiments, Lithic Technology, and Petrography.* Addison-Wesley Modules in Anthropology, no. 29.

Hester, T. A., R. F. Heizer, and J. A. Graham, eds. 1975. *Field Methods in Archaeology,* 6th ed. Palo Alto, Calif.: Mayfield.

Heyerdahl, T. 1950. *The Kon-Tiki Expedition: By Raft across the South Seas.* London: Allen and Unwin.

———. ed. 1961/1965. *Reports of the Norwegian Archaeological Expedition to Easter Island and the East Pacific.* 2 vols. London: Allen and Unwin.

———. 1975. *The Art of Easter Island.* London: Allen and Unwin.

Higgs, E. S., ed. 1972. *Papers in Economic Prehistory.* Cambridge: Cambridge University Press.

———. ed. 1975. *Palaeoeconomy.* Cambridge: Cambridge University Press.

Hill, J. N. 1966. A prehistoric community in eastern Arizona. *Southwestern Journal of Anthropology* 22:9–30.

———. 1967. The problem of sampling. In *Chapters in the Prehistory of Arizona, III: Fieldiana: Anthropology* 57:145–157.

———. 1968. Broken K Pueblo: patterns of form and function. In *New Perspectives in Archeology,* ed. S. R. Binford and L. R. Binford, pp. 103–142. Chicago: Aldine.

———. 1970. *Broken K Pueblo: Prehistoric Social Organization in the American Southwest.* Anthropological Papers of the University of Arizona, no. 18. Tucson: University of Arizona Press.

———. ed. 1977. *Explanation of Prehistoric Change.* Albuquerque: University of New Mexico Press, School of American Research Advanced Seminar Series.

———. 1978. Individuals and their artifacts: An experimental study in archaeology. *American Antiquity* 43:245–257.

Hill, J. N., and R. K. Evans. 1972. A model for classification and typology. In *Models in Archaeology,* ed. D. L. Clarke, pp. 231–273. London: Methuen.

Hill, J. N., and J. Gunn, eds. 1977. *The Individual in Prehistory.* New York: Academic Press.

Hodder, I. R., and M. Hassall. 1971. The non-random spacing of Romano-British walled towns. *Man* 6:391–407.

Hodder, I. R., and C. Orton. 1976. *Spatial Analysis in Archaeology*. Cambridge: Cambridge University Press.

Hodges, H. 1964. *Artifacts: An Introduction to Early Materials and Technology*. London: John Baker.

Hodson, F. R. 1970. Cluster analysis and archaeology: Some new developments and applications. *World Archaeology* 1:299–320.

Hole, F., K. V. Flannery, and J. A. Neely. 1969. *Prehistoric Human Ecology of the Deh Luran Plain: An Early Village Sequence from Khuzistan, Iran*. Memoirs of the Museum of Anthropology, University of Michigan, no. 1.

Hole, F., and M. Shaw. 1967. *Computer Analysis of Chronological Seriation*. Rice University Studies 53 (3).

Hope-Taylor, B. 1966. Archaeological draughtsmanship: Principles and practice. Part II: Ends and means. *Antiquity* 40:107–113.

––––––. 1967. Archaeological draughtsmanship: Principles and practice. Part III: Lines of communication. *Antiquity* 41:181–189.

Hyslop, J. 1977. Chulpas of the Lupaca zone of the Peruvian high plateau. *Journal of Field Archaeology* 4:149–170.

Isaac, G. L. 1967. Towards the interpretation of occupation debris. Some experiments and observations. *Kroeber Anthropological Society Papers* 37:371–375.

––––––. 1971. Whither archaeology? *Antiquity* 45:123–129.

Jarman, M. R., C. Vita-Finzi, and E. S. Higgs. 1972. Site catchment analysis in archaeology. In *Man, Settlement and Urbanism*, ed. P. J. Ucko, R. Tringham and G. W. Dimbleby, pp. 61–66. London: Duckworth.

Jelinek, A. J. 1976. Form, function, and style in lithic analysis. In *Cultural Change and Continuity*, ed. C. E. Cleland, pp. 19–34. New York: Academic Press.

Jennings, J. D. 1957. *Danger Cave*. Society for American Archaeology, Memoir 14.

Jewell, P. A. 1963. *The Experimental Earthwork on Overton Down, Wiltshire, 1960*. London: British Association for the Advancement of Science.

Jewell, P. A., and G. W. Dimbleby. 1968. The experimental earthwork on Overton Down, Wiltshire, England: The first four years. *Proceedings of the Prehistoric Society* 32:313–342.

Johnson, G. A. 1972. A test of the utility of central place theory in archaeology. In *Man, Settlement and Urbanism*, ed. P. J. Ucko, R. Tringham and G. W. Dimbleby, pp. 769–786. London: Duckworth.

––––––. 1973. *Local Exchange and Early State Development in Southwestern Iran*. University of Michigan Anthropological Papers, no. 51.

Johnson, L. L. 1978. A history of flint-knapping experimentation, 1838–1976. *Current Anthropology* 19:337–372.

Jones, C. 1977. Inauguration dates of three Late Classic rulers of Tikal, Guatemala. *American Antiquity* 42:28–60.

Kamau, C. K. 1977. Mapping of an archaeological site at Olduvai Gorge, Tanzania. *Journal of Field Archaeology* 4:415–422.

Kardiner, A., and E. Preble. 1961. *They Studied Man*. New York: World (and New American Library).

Keatinge, R. W., and K. C. Day. 1974. Chan Chan: A study of precolumbian urbanism and the management of land and water resources in Peru. *Archaeology* 27:228–235.

Keeley, L. H. 1974. Technique and methodology in microwear studies: A critical review. *World Archaeology* 5:323–336.

––––––. 1977. The functions of Paleolithic stone tools. *Scientific American* 237 (5):108–126.

Keesing, R. M. 1974. Theories of culture. *Annual Review of Anthropology* 3:71–97.

Kehoe, A. B., and T. F. Kehoe. 1973. Cognitive models for archaeological interepretation. *American Antiquity* 38:150–154.

Kidder, A. V. 1932. *The Artifacts of Pecos*. Papers of the Southwestern Expedition, Phillips Academy, Andover, Mass., No. 6.

———. 1947. *The Artifacts of Uaxactun, Guatemala*. Carnegie Institution of Washington, Publication 576.

———. 1961. Archaeological investigations at Kaminaljuyu, Guatemala. *Proceedings of the American Philosophical Society* 105:559–570.

———. 1962. *An Introduction to the Study of Southwestern Archaeology*. (Orig. pub. 1924; 1962 edition has an introduction, "Southwestern Archaeology Today," by I. Rouse.) New Haven: Yale University Press.

Kidder, A. V., and S. J. Guernsey. 1919. *Archaeological Explorations in Northeastern Arizona*. Bureau of American Ethnology, Bulletin 65.

Kidder, A. V., J. D. Jennings, and E. M. Shook. 1946. *Excavations at Kaminaljuyu, Guatemala*. Carnegie Institution of Washington, Publication 561.

King, M. E. 1978. Analytical methods and prehistoric textiles. *American Antiquity* 43:89–96.

King, T. F. 1971. A conflict of values in American archaeology. *American Antiquity* 36:255–262.

King, T. F., P. P. Hickman, and G. Berg. 1977. *Anthropology in Historic Preservation: Caring for Culture's Clutter*. New York: Academic Press.

Klein, R. G. 1973. *Ice-Age Hunters of the Ukraine*. Chicago: University of Chicago Press.

Klejn, L. S. 1977. A panorama of theoretical archaeology. *Current Anthropology* 18:1–42.

Klindt-Jensen, O. 1975. *A History of Scandinavian Archaeology*. London: Thames and Hudson.

Koch, A., and W. Peden, eds. 1944. *The Life and Selected Writings of Thomas Jefferson*. New York: Modern Library.

Kopper, J. S., and G. Rossello-Bordoy. 1974. Megalithic quarrying techniques and limestone technology in eastern Spain. *Journal of Field Archaeology* 1:161–170.

Kraft, J. C., S. E. Aschenbrenner, and G. Rapp, Jr. 1977. Paleogeographic reconstructions of coastal Aegean archaeological sites. *Science* 195:941–947.

Krieger, A. D. 1944. The typological concept. *American Antiquity* 9:271–288.

———. 1946. *Culture Complexes and Chronology in Northern Texas with Extension of Puebloan Datings to the Mississippi Valley*. University of Texas Publication 4640.

———. 1960. Archaeological typology in theory and practice. In *Selected Papers of the Fifth International Congress of Anthropological and Ethnological Sciences*, ed. A. F. C. Wallace, pp. 141–151. Philadelphia: University of Pennsylvania Press.

Kroeber, A. L. 1939. *Cultural and Natural Areas of Native North America*. Berkeley: University of California Press.

Kuhn, T. S. 1970. *The Structure of Scientific Revolutions*, 2nd ed. Chicago: University of Chicago Press.

Lange, F. W., and C. R. Rydberg. 1972. Abandonment and post-abandonment behavior at a rural Central American house-site. *American Antiquity* 37:419–432.

Lathrap, D. W., J. G. Marcos, and J. Zeidler. 1977. Real Alto: An ancient ceremonial center. *Archaeology* 30:2–13.

LeBlanc, S. A. 1975. Micro-seriation: A method for fine chronologic differentiation. *American Antiquity* 40:22–38.

———. 1976. Archaeological recording systems. *Journal of Field Archaeology* 3:159–168.

Lechtman, H. 1976. A metallurgical site survey in the Peruvian Andes. *Journal of Field Archaeology* 3:1–42.

Lee, R. B. 1968. What hunters do for a living, or, How to make out on scarce resources. In *Man the Hunter,* ed. R. B. Lee and I. DeVore, pp. 30–48. Chicago: Aldine.

Lee, R. B., and I. DeVore, eds. 1968. *Man the Hunter.* Chicago: Aldine.

———. eds. 1976. *Kalahari Hunter-Gatherers.* Cambridge: Harvard University Press.

Leone, M. P. 1972. Issues in anthropological archaeology. In *Contemporary Archaeology,* ed. M. P. Leone, pp. 14–27. Carbondale: Southern Illinois University Press.

Leroi-Gourhan, A. 1975. The flowers found with Shanidar IV, a Neanderthal burial in Iraq. *Science* 190:562–564.

Levin, M. E. 1973. On explanation in archaeology: A rebuttal to Fritz and Plog. *American Antiquity* 38:387–395.

Libby, W. F. 1955. *Radiocarbon Dating,* 2nd ed. Chicago: University of Chicago Press.

Limbrey, S. 1972. *Soil Science in Archaeology.* New York: Seminar Press.

Limp, W. F. 1974. Water separation and flotation processes. *Journal of Field Archaeology* 1:337–342.

Linington, R. E. 1970. Techniques used in archaeological field surveys. In *The Impact of the Natural Sciences on Archaeology,* ed. T. E. Allibone, pp. 89–108. London: Oxford University Press.

Lipe, W. D. 1974. A conservation model for American archaeology. *The Kiva* 39:213–245.

Lipe, W. D., and A. J. Lindsay, Jr., eds. 1974. *Proceedings of the 1974 Cultural Resource Management Conference.* Museum of Northern Arizona, Technical Paper no. 14.

Lloyd, S. 1955. *Foundations in the Dust: A Story of Mesopotamian Exploration.* Baltimore: Penguin.

———. 1963. *Mounds of the Near East.* Edinburgh: Edinburgh University Press.

———. 1976. Illustrating monuments: Drawn reconstructions of architecture. In *To Illustrate the Monuments: Essays on Archaeology Presented to Stuart Piggott,* ed. J. V. S. Megaw, pp. 27–34. London: Thames and Hudson.

Longacre, W. A. 1968. Some aspects of prehistoric society in east-central Arizona. In *New Perspectives in Archeology,* ed. S. R. Binford and L. R. Binford, pp. 89–102. Chicago: Aldine.

———. 1970a. *Archaeology as Anthropology: A Case Study.* Anthropological Papers of the University of Arizona, No. 17. Tucson: University of Arizona Press.

———. 1970b. Current thinking in American archaeology. In *Current Directions in Anthropology,* ed. A. Fischer, pp. 126–138. American Anthropological Association, Bulletin 3 (no. 3, part 2).

Longacre, W. A., and J. E. Ayres. 1968. Archeological lessons from an Apache wickiup. In *New Perspectives in Archeology,* ed. S. R. Binford and L. R. Binford, pp. 151–159. Chicago: Aldine.

Longworth, I., ed. 1971. Archaeology and ethnography. *World Archaeology* 3 (2).

Lovejoy, A. O. 1936. *The Great Chain of Being: A Study of the History of an Idea.* Cambridge: Harvard University Press. (Reprinted 1960. New York: Harper and Brothers.)

Lovis, W. A., Jr. 1976. Quarter sections and forests: An example of probability sampling in the northeastern woodlands. *American Antiquity* 41:364–372.

Lubbock, J. (Lord Avebury). 1865. *Prehistoric Times.* London: Williams and Norgate.

Luckenbach, A. H., C. G. Holland and R. O. Allen. 1975. Soapstone artifacts: Tracing prehistoric trade patterns in Virginia. *Science* 187:57–58.

Lumley, H. de. 1969. A Paleolithic camp at Nice. *Scientific American* 220 (5):42–50.

Lyell, Charles. 1830–1833. *Principles of Geology.* London: J. Murray.

Lynch, B. D., and T. F. Lynch. 1968. The beginnings of a scientific approach to prehistoric archaeology in 17th and 18th century Britain. *Southwestern Journal of Anthropology* 24:33–65.

McConnell, D. 1962. Dating of fossil bone by the fluorine method. *Science* 136:241–244.

McGimsey, C. R., III. 1972. *Public Archeology*. New York: Seminar Press.

McGimsey, C. R., III, and H. A. Davis, eds. 1977. *The Management of Archaeological Resources: The Airlie House Report*. Washington, D.C.: Society for American Archaeology.

McIntosh, R. J. 1974. Archaeology and mud wall decay in a West African village. *World Archaeology* 6:154–171.

———. 1977. The excavation of mud structures: An experiment from West Africa. *World Archaeology* 9:185–199.

McKern, W. C. 1939. The Midwestern Taxonomic Method as an aid to archaeological study. *American Antiquity* 4:301–313.

MacNeish, R. S. 1964a. Ancient Mesoamerican civilization. *Science* 143:531–537.

———. 1964b. The origins of New World civilization. *Scientific American* 211 (5):29–37.

———. 1967. An interdisciplinary approach to an archaeological problem. In *The Prehistory of the Tehuacan Valley, Volume I*, ed. D. S. Byers, pp. 14–24. Austin: University of Texas Press.

———. 1974. Reflections on my search for the beginnings of agriculture in Mexico. In *Archaeological Researches in Retrospect*, ed. G. R. Willey, pp. 207–234. Cambridge, Mass.: Winthrop.

———. 1978. *The Science of Archaeology?* North Scituate, Mass.: Duxbury Press.

MacNeish, R. S., M. L. Fowler, A. G. Cook, F. A. Peterson, A. Nelken-Terner, and J. A. Neely. 1972. *Excavations and Reconnaissance. The Prehistory of the Tehuacan Valley, Volume 5*. Austin: University of Texas Press.

MacNeish, R. S., T. C. Patterson, and D. L. Browman. 1975. *The Central Peruvian Prehistoric Interaction Sphere*. Andover, Mass.: Phillips Academy.

MacWhite, E. 1956. On the interpretation of archaeological evidence in historical and sociological terms. *American Anthropologist* 58:3–25.

Maddin, R., J. D. Muhly, and T. S. Wheeler. 1977. How the Iron Age began. *Scientific American* 237 (4):122–131.

Madeira, P. C. 1931. An aerial expedition to Central America. *Philadelphia Museum Journal* 22 (2).

Malinowski, B. 1944. *A Scientific Theory of Culture*. Chapel Hill: University of North Carolina Press.

Marshack, A. 1972a. Upper Paleolithic notation and symbol. *Science* 178:817–827.

———. 1972b. *The Roots of Civilization*. New York: McGraw-Hill.

Martin, P. S. 1971. The revolution in archaeology. *American Antiquity* 36:1–8.

Martin, P. S., J. B. Rinaldo, E. Bluhm, H. C. Cutler, and R. Grange, Jr. 1952. *Mogollon Cultural Continuity and Change; The Stratigraphic Analysis of Tularosa and Cordova Caves*. Fieldiana: Anthropology, Vol. 40.

Matheny, R. T. 1976. Maya lowland hydraulic systems. *Science* 193:639–646.

Matson, F. R., ed. 1965. *Ceramics and Man*. Chicago: Aldine.

Mayr, E. 1972. The nature of the Darwinian revolution. *Science* 176:981–989.

Mazess, R. B., and D. W. Zimmerman. 1966. Pottery dating from thermoluminescence. *Science* 152:347–348.

Meggers, B. J., C. Evans, and E. Estrada. 1965. *Early Formative Period of Coastal Ecuador: The Valdivia and Machalilla Phases*. Smithsonian Contributions to Anthropology, Vol. 1.

Meighan, C. W. 1959. A new method for the seriation of archaeological collections. *American Antiquity* 25:203–211.

Mellart, J. 1965. *Earliest Civilizations of the Near East*. New York: McGraw-Hill.

Mendelssohn, K. 1971. A scientist looks at the pyramids. *American Scientist* 59:210–220.

Meyer, K. E. 1977. *The Plundered Past*. New York: Atheneum.

Michael, H. N., and E. K. Ralph, eds. 1971. *Dating Techniques for the Archaeologist*. Cambridge, Mass.: MIT Press.

Michels, J. W. 1973. *Dating Methods in Archaeology*. New York: Academic Press.

Millon, R. 1973. *The Teotihuacán Map. Urbanization at Teotihuacán, Mexico, Volume 1*. Austin: University of Texas Press.

_____. 1974. The study of urbanism at Teotihuacán, Mexico. In *Mesoamerican Archaeology: New Approaches,* ed. N. Hammond, pp. 335–362. Austin: University of Texas Press.

Money, J. 1973. The destruction of Acrotiri. *Antiquity* 47:50–53.

Mooney, J. 1965. *The Ghost-Dance Religion and the Sioux Outbreak of 1890.* (Orig. pub. 1896). Abridged, with an introduction by A. F. C. Wallace. Chicago: University of Chicago Press (Phoenix).

Morgan, C. G. 1973. Archaeology and explanation. *World Archaeology* 4:259–276.

_____. 1974. Explanation and scientific archaeology. *World Archaeology* 6:133–137.

Morgan, L. H. 1877. *Ancient Society.* New York: Holt.

Mori, J. L. 1970. Procedures for establishing a faunal collection to aid in archaeological analysis. *American Antiquity* 35:387–389.

Morley, S. G. 1935. *Guide Book to the Ruins of Quiriguá.* Carnegie Institution of Washington, Supplementary Publication 16.

_____. 1937–1938. *The Inscriptions of Peten.* 5 vols. Carnegie Institution of Washington, Publication 437.

Moseley, M. E. 1975. Prehistoric principles of labor organization in the Moche valley, Peru. *American Antiquity* 40:190–196.

Moseley, M. E., and C. J. Mackey. 1974. *Twenty-four Architectural Plans of Chan Chan, Peru: Structure and Form at the Capital of Chimor.* Cambridge, Mass.: Peabody Museum Press.

Movius, H. L., Jr. 1966. The hearths of the Upper Perigordian and Aurignacian horizons at the Abri Pataud, Les Eyzies (Dordogne), and their possible significance. In *Recent Studies in Paleoanthropology,* ed. J. D. Clark and F. C. Howell, pp. 296–325. *American Anthropologist* 68 (2, part 2).

_____. 1974. The Abri Pataud Program of the French Upper Paleolithic in Retrospect. In *Archaeological Researches in Retrospect,* ed. G. R. Willey, pp. 87–116. Cambridge, Mass.: Winthrop.

_____. 1977. *Excavation of the Abri Pataud, Les Eyzies (Dordogne): Stratigraphy.* Cambridge, Mass.: American School of Prehistoric Research, Bulletin 31.

Mueller, J. W. 1974. *The Uses of Sampling in Archaeological Survey.* Society for American Archaeology, Memoir 28.

_____. ed. 1975. *Sampling in Archaeology.* Tucson: University of Arizona Press.

_____. 1978. A reply to Plog and Thomas. *American Antiquity* 43:286–287.

Muller, R. A. 1977. Radioisotope dating with a cyclotron. *Science* 196:489–494.

Müller-Beck, H. 1961. Prehistoric Swiss lake dwellers. *Scientific American* 205 (6):138–147.

Munsen, P. J. 1969. Comments on Binford's "Smudge pits and hide smoking: The use of analogy in archaeological reasoning." *American Antiquity* 34:83–85.

Napton, L. K. 1975. Site mapping and layout. In *Field Methods in Archaeology,* 6th ed., ed. T. R. Hester, R. F. Heizer, and J. A. Graham, pp. 37–63. Palo Alto, Calif.: Mayfield.

Naroll, R. 1962. Floor area and settlement population. *American Antiquity* 27:587–588.

Nelson, D. E., R. G. Korteling, and W. R. Stott. 1977. Carbon-14: Direct detection at natural concentrations. *Science* 198:507–508.

Netting, R. McC. 1977. *Cultural Ecology.* Menlo Park, Calif.: Cummings.

Nickerson, G. S. 1972. The implications of a self-fulfilling prophecy in American archaeology. *American Antiquity* 37:551–553.

Oakley, K. P. 1948. Fluorine and the relative dating of bones. *Advancement of Science* 4:336–337.

_____. 1956. *Man the Tool-Maker*. 3rd ed. London: British Museum.

_____. 1968. *Frameworks for Dating Fossil Man*. 3rd ed. Chicago: Aldine.

_____. 1970. Analytical methods of dating bones. In *Science in Archaeology,* 2nd ed., ed. D. Brothwell and E. S. Higgs, pp. 35–45. New York: Praeger.

Oleson, J. P. 1977. Underwater survey and excavation in the port (Santa Severa), 1974. *Journal of Field Archaeology* 4:297–308.

Olsen, S. J. 1964. *Mammal Remains from Archaeological Sites*. Papers of the Peabody Museum 56 (1).

_____. 1971. *Zooarchaeology: Animal Bones in Archaeology and Their Interpretation.* Addison-Wesley Modules in Anthropology, no. 2.

Organ, R. M. 1968. *Design for Scientific Conservation of Antiquities*. Washington: Smithsonian Institution Press.

Parsons, J. R. 1971. *Prehistoric Settlement Patterns in the Texcoco Region, Mexico.* Memoirs of the Museum of Anthropology, University of Michigan, No. 3.

_____. 1972. Archaeological settlement patterns. *Annual Review of Anthropology* 1:127–150.

_____. 1974. The development of a prehistoric complex society: A regional perspective from the Valley of Mexico. *Journal of Field Archaeology* 1:81–108.

Patterson, T. C. 1963. Contemporaneity and cross-dating in archaeological interpretation. *American Antiquity* 28:129–137.

Peacock, D. P. S. 1970. The scientific analysis of ancient ceramics: A review. *World Archaeology* 1:375–389.

Peebles, C. S., and S. M. Kus. 1977. Some archaeological correlates of ranked societies. *American Antiquity* 42:421–448.

Perkins, D., Jr., and P. Daly. 1968. A hunters' village in Neolithic Turkey. *Scientific American* 219 (5):96–106.

Petersen, W. 1975. A demographer's view of prehistoric demography. *Current Anthropology* 16:227–245.

Petrie, W. M. F. 1901. *Diospolis Parva*. London: Egyptian Exploration Fund Memoirs, No. 20.

Pickersgill. B. 1972. Cultivated plants as evidence for cultural contacts. *American Antiquity* 37:97–104.

Piggott, S. 1959. The discipline of archaeology. In *Approach to Archaeology,* S. Piggott. Cambridge: Harvard University Press.

_____. 1965. Archaeological draughtsmanship: Principles and practice. Part I: Principles and retrospect. *Antiquity* 39:165–176.

Platt, C., ed. 1976. Archaeology and history. *World Archaeology* 7 (3).

Plenderleith, H. J., and A. E. A. Werner. 1971. *The Conservation of Antiquities and Works of Art*. 2nd ed. London: Oxford University Press.

Plog, F. T. 1974. *The Study of Prehistoric Change*. New York: Academic Press.

_____. 1975. Systems theory in archaeological research. *Annual Review of Anthropology* 4:207–224.

Plog, S. 1976. Relative efficiencies of sampling techniques for archaeological surveys. In *The Early Mesoamerican Village,* ed. K. V. Flannery, pp. 136–158. New York: Academic Press.

_____. 1978. Sampling in archaeological surveys: A critique. *American Antiquity* 43:280–285.

Polanyi, K., C. M. Arensburg, and H. W. Pearson, eds. 1957. *Trade and Market in the Early Empires*. Glencoe, Ill.: Free Press.

Poole, L., and G. J. Poole. 1966. *One Passion, Two Loves: The Story of Heinrich and Sophia Schliemann, Discoverers of Troy*. New York: Crowell.

Potter, D. F. 1977. *Maya Architecture of the Central Yucatan Peninsula*. Middle American Research Institute, Publication 44.

Pring, D., and N. Hammond. 1975. Excavation of the possible river port at Nohmul. In *Archaeology in Northern Belize: British Museum–Cambridge University Corozal Project, 1974–75 Interim Report,* ed. N. Hammond. Cambridge: Centre of Latin American Studies, Cambridge University.

Puleston, D. E. 1971. An experimental approach to the function of Classic Maya chultuns. *American Antiquity* 36:322–335.

———. 1974. Intersite areas in the vicinity of Tikal and Uaxactun. In *Mesoamerican Archaeology: New Approaches,* ed. N. Hammond, pp. 303–311. Austin: University of Texas Press.

Pyddoke, E. 1961. *Stratification for the Archaeologist.* London: Phoenix House.

Raab, L. M., and T. C. Klinger. 1977. A critical appraisal of "significance" in contract archaeology. *American Antiquity* 42:629–634.

Ragir, S. 1975. A review of techniques for archaeological sampling. In *Field Methods in Archaeology,* 6th ed., ed. T. R. Hester, R. F. Heizer, and J. A. Graham, pp. 283–302. Palo Alto, Calif.: Mayfield.

Rahtz, P. A. 1974. *RESCUE Archaeology.* Harmondsworth, England: Penguin.

Ralph, E. K., and M. C. Han. 1966. Dating of pottery by thermoluminescence. *Nature* 210:245–247.

———. 1969. Potential of thermoluminescence in supplementing radiocarbon dating. *World Archaeology* 1:157–169.

Ralph, E. K., and H. N. Michael. 1974. Twenty-five years of radiocarbon dating. *American Scientist* 62:553–560.

Ralph, E. K., H. N. Michael, and M. C. Han. 1973. Radiocarbon dates and reality. *MASCA Newsletter* 9 (1).

Rapoport, A. 1968. Foreword. In *Modern Systems Research for the Behavioral Scientist,* ed. W. Buckley, pp. xiii–xxii. Chicago: Aldine.

Rapp, G., Jr. 1975. The archaeological field staff: The geologist. *Journal of Field Archaeology* 2:229–237.

Rathje, W. L. 1978. The ancient astronaut myth. *Archaeology* 31:4–7.

Read, D. W., and S. A. LeBlanc. 1978. Descriptive statements, covering laws, and theories in archaeology. *Current Anthropology* 19:307–335.

Read-Martin, C. E., and D. W. Read. 1975. Australopithecine scavenging and human evolution: An approach from faunal analysis. *Current Anthropology* 16:359–368.

Redman, C. L. 1973. Multistage fieldwork and analytical techniques. *American Antiquity* 38:61–79.

———. 1974. *Archaeological Sampling Strategies.* Addison-Wesley Modules in Anthropology, no. 55.

Redman, C. L., and P. J. Watson. 1970. Systematic, intensive surface collection. *American Antiquity* 35:279–291.

Reed, N. A., J. W. Bennett, and J. W. Porter. 1968. Solid core drilling of Monks Mound: Technique and findings. *American Antiquity* 33:137–148.

Renfrew, C. 1969. Trade and culture process in European prehistory. *Current Anthropology* 10:151–169.

———. 1971. Carbon 14 and the prehistory of Europe. *Scientific American* 225 (4):63–72.

———. 1973. *Before Civilization: The Radiocarbon Revolution and Prehistoric Europe.* New York: Knopf.

———. 1975. Trade as action at a distance: Questions of integration and communication. In *Ancient Civilization and Trade,* ed. J. A. Sabloff and C. C. Lamberg-Karlovsky, pp. 3–59. Albuquerque: University of New Mexico Press, School of American Research Advanced Seminar Series.

Renfrew, J. M. 1973. *Palaeoethnobotany.* New York: Columbia University Press.

Rice, D. S. 1976. Middle Preclassic Maya settlement in the central Maya lowlands. *Journal of Field Archaeology* 3:425–445.

Rice, P. M. 1977. Whiteware pottery production in the Valley of Guatemala: Specialization and resource utilization. *Journal of Field Archaeology* 4:221–233.

Robertson, M. G. 1972. Monument thievery in Mesoamerica. *American Antiquity* 37:147–155.

Robinson, W. S. 1951. A method for chronologically ordering archaeological deposits. *American Antiquity* 16:293–301.

Roe, D., ed. 1971. Subsistence. *World Archaeology* 2 (3).

Rouse, I. 1939. *Prehistory in Haiti: A Study in Method.* Yale University Publications in Anthropology, No. 21.

———. 1953. The strategy of culture history. In *Anthropology Today,* ed. A. L. Kroeber, pp. 57–76. Chicago: University of Chicago Press.

———. 1960. The classification of artifacts in archaeology. *American Antiquity* 25:313–323.

———. 1962. Summary of Southwestern archaeology today. In *An Introduction to the Study of Southwestern Archaeology,* (Reprint edition; orig. pub. 1924), A. V. Kidder. New Haven: Yale University Press.

Rowe, J. H. 1954. Max Uhle, 1856–1944: A memoir of the father of Peruvian archaeology. *University of California Publications in Archaeology and Ethnology* 46:1–134.

———. 1961a. Archaeology as a career. *Archaeology* 14:45–55.

———. 1961b. Stratigraphy and seriation. *American Antiquity* 26:324–330.

———. 1965. The Renaissance foundations of anthropology. *American Anthropologist* 67:1–20.

———. 1966. Diffusionism and archaeology. *American Antiquity* 31:334–338.

Rowlands, M. J. 1971. The archaeological interpretation of prehistoric metalworking. *World Archaeology* 3:210–224.

Rowlett, R. M. 1970. A random number generator for field use. *American Antiquity* 35:491.

Sabloff, J. A. 1975. *Excavations at Seibal: Ceramics.* Memoirs of the Peabody Museum, 13 (2).

Sabloff, J. A., T. W. Beale, and A. M. Kurland, Jr. 1973. Recent developments in archaeology. *Annals of the American Academy of Political and Social Science* 408:103–118.

Sabloff, J. A., and C. C. Lamberg-Karlovsky, eds. 1975. *Ancient Civilization and Trade.* Albuquerque: University of New Mexico Press, School of American Research Advanced Seminar Series.

Sabloff, J. A., and W. L. Rathje. 1973. Ancient Maya commercial systems: A research design for the island of Cozumel, Mexico. *World Archaeology* 5:221–231.

Sabloff, J. A., and R. E. Smith. 1969. The importance of both analytic and taxonomic classification in the type-variety system. *American Antiquity* 34:278–285.

Sackett, J. R. 1966. Quantitative analysis of Upper Paleolithic stone tools. In *Recent Studies in Paleoanthropology,* ed. J. D. Clark and F. C. Howell, pp. 356–394. *American Anthropologist* 68 (2, Part 2).

———. 1977. The meaning of style in archaeology: a general model. *American Antiquity* 42:369–380.

Sahlins, M. D., and E. R. Service, eds. 1960. *Evolution and Culture.* Ann Arbor: University of Michigan Press.

Salmon, M. 1975. Confirmation and explanation in archaeology. *American Antiquity* 40:459–464.

———. 1976. "Deductive" vs. "inductive" archaeology. *American Antiquity* 41:376–381.

———. 1978. What can Systems Theory do for archaeology? *American Antiquity* 43:174–183.

Salwen, B. 1962. Sea levels and archaeology in the Long Island Sound area. *American Antiquity* 28:46–55.

Sampson, C. G. 1974. *The Stone Age Archaeology of Southern Africa.* New York: Academic Press.

Sanders, W. T., and J. W. Michels. 1969. *Kaminaljuyu Project—1968 Season; Part I—The Excavations*. Occasional Papers in Anthropology, Department of Anthropology, Pennsylvania State University.

Sanders, W. T., and B. J. Price. 1968. *Mesoamerica: The Evolution of a Civilization*. New York: Random House.

Saraydar, S., and I. Shimada. 1973. Experimental archaeology: A new outlook. *American Antiquity* 38:344–350.

Satterthwaite, L., Jr., and E. K. Ralph. 1960. New radiocarbon dates and the Maya correlation problem. *American Antiquity* 26:165–184.

Schiffer, M. B. 1972. Archaeological context and systemic context. *American Antiquity* 37:156–165.

_____. 1976. *Behavioral Archeology*. New York: Academic Press.

_____. 1978. Taking the pulse of method and theory in American archaeology. *American Antiquity* 43:153–158.

Schiffer, M. B., and G. J. Gumerman, eds. 1977. *Conservation Archaeology: A Guide for Cultural Resource Management Studies*. New York: Academic Press.

Schiffer, M. B., and J. H. House. 1977. Cultural resource management and archaeological research: the Cache Project. *Current Anthropology* 18:43–68.

Schiffer, M. B., A. P. Sullivan, and T. C. Klinger. 1978. The design of archaeological surveys. *World Archaeology* 10:1–28.

Schliemann, H. 1881. *Ilios, the City and Country of the Trojans*. (Reissued 1968.) New York: Benjamin Blom.

Schorr, T. S. 1974. Aerial ethnography in regional studies: A reconnaissance of adaptive change in the Cauca Valley of Colombia. In *Aerial Photography in Anthropological Field Research*, ed. E. Z. Vogt, pp. 40–53. Cambridge: Harvard University Press.

Schuyler, R. L. 1971. The history of American archaeology: An examination of procedure. *American Antiquity* 36:383–409.

Sears, W. H. 1961. The study of social and religious systems in North American archaeology. *Current Anthropology* 2:223–246.

Semenov, S. A. 1964. *Prehistoric Technology*. New York: Barnes and Noble.

Service, E. R. 1962. *Primitive Social Organization: An Evolutionary Perspective*. New York: Random House.

Shackley, M. L. 1975. *Archaeological Sediments*. New York: Wiley (Halsted).

Sharer, R. J. 1978a. Archaeology and history at Quirigua, Guatemala. *Journal of Field Archaeology* 5:51–70.

_____. 1978b. The surface surveys. In *The Prehistory of Chalchuapa, El Salvador*, vol. 1, part 2, ed. Robert J. Sharer, pp. 15–26. Philadelphia: University of Pennsylvania Press.

Sharer, R. J., and W. R. Coe. 1978. *The Quirigua Project: Origins, Objectives and Research in 1973 and 1974*. Quirigua Reports, Paper No. 1. Philadelphia: The University Museum.

Sharp, L. 1952. Steel axes for Stone-Age Australians. *Human Organization* 11:17–22.

Sheets, P. D. 1971. An ancient natural disaster. *Expedition* 14(1):24–31.

_____. 1973. The pillage of prehistory. *American Antiquity* 38:317–320.

_____. 1975. Behavioral analysis and the structure of a prehistoric industry. *Current Anthropology* 16:369–391.

Shepard, A. O. 1971. *Ceramics for the Archaeologist*. 7th printing. Carnegie Institution of Washington, Publication 609.

Shook, E. M., and W. R. Coe. 1961. *Tikal: Numeration, Terminology and Objectives*. Tikal Report, No. 5. Philadelphia: The University Museum.

Shook, E. M., and A. V. Kidder. 1952. Mound E-III-3, Kaminaljuyu, Guatemala. *Contributions to American Anthropology and History* 11 (53):33–127. Carnegie Institution of Washington, Publication 596.

Sidrys, R. 1977. Mass-distance measures for the Maya obsidian trade. In *Exchange Systems in Prehistory*, ed. T. K. Earle and J. E. Ericson, pp. 71–90. New York: Academic Press.

Singer, C., E. J. Holmyard, and A. R. Hall, eds. 1956. *A History of Technology*. London: Oxford University Press.

Sjoberg, A. 1976. Phosphate analysis of anthropic soils. *Journal of Field Archaeology* 3:447–454.

Smiley, T. L., ed. 1955. *Geochronology*. University of Arizona Physical Science Bulletin No. 2.

Smith, A. L. 1973. *Uaxactún: A pioneering excavation in Guatemala*. Addison-Wesley Modules in Anthropology, no. 40.

Smith, B. D. 1974. Middle Mississippi exploitation of animal populations: A predictive model. *American Antiquity* 39:274–291.

Smith, C. S. 1973. Bronze technology in the East: A metallurgical study of early Thai bronzes, with some speculation on the cultural transmission of technology. In *Changing Perspectives in the History of Science,* ed. M. Teich and R. Young, pp. 21–32. London: Heinemann.

Smith, G. E. 1928. *In the Beginning: The Origin of Civilization*. New York: Morrow.

Smith, J. W. 1974. The Northeast Asian–Northwest American Microblade Tradition (NANAMT). *Journal of Field Archaeology* 1:347–364.

Smith, N. 1978. Roman hydraulic technology. *Scientific American* 238 (5):154–161.

Smith, P. E. L. 1976. *Food Production and Its Consequences*. Menlo Park, Calif.: Cummings.

Smith, R. E., G. R. Willey, and J. C. Gifford. 1960. The type-variety concept as a basis for the analysis of Maya pottery. *American Antiquity* 25:330–340.

Smith, R. H. 1974. Ethics in field archaeology. *Journal of Field Archaeology* 1:375–383.

Society of Professional Archeologists. 1978. Qualifications for recognition as a professional archeologist. *SOPADOPA: The Newsletter of the Society of Professional Archeologists* 2 (3).

Sokal, R. R., and P. H. A. Sneath. 1963. *Principles of Numerical Taxonomy*. San Francisco: W. H. Freeman.

Solecki, R. S. 1975. Shanidar IV, a Neanderthal flower burial in northern Iraq. *Science* 190:880–881.

South, S. A. 1977. *Method and Theory in Historical Archeology*. New York: Academic Press.

———. 1978. Pattern recognition in historical archaeology. *American Antiquity* 43:223–230.

Spaulding, A. C. 1953. Statistical techniques for the discovery of artifact types. *American Antiquity* 18:305–313.

———. 1960. The dimensions of archaeology. In *Essays in the Science of Culture in Honor of Leslie A. White,* ed. G. E. Dole and R. L. Carneiro, pp. 437–456. New York: Crowell.

———. 1968. Explanation in archeology. In *New Perspectives in Archeology,* ed. S. R. Binford and L. R. Binford, pp. 33–39. Chicago: Aldine.

Spencer, H. 1876. *Principles of Sociology*. New York: Appleton.

Speth, J. D., and D. D. Davis. 1976. Seasonal variability in early hominid predation. *Science* 192:441–445.

Speth, J. D., and G. A. Johnson. 1976. Problems in the use of correlation for the investigation of tool kits and activity areas. In *Cultural Change and Continuity: Essays in Honor of James Bennett Griffin,* ed. C. E. Cleland, pp. 35–57. New York: Academic Press.

Spier, R. F. G. 1970. *Surveying and Mapping: A Manual of Simplified Techniques*. New York: Holt, Rinehart and Winston.

Squier, E. G., and E. H. Davis. 1848. *Ancient Monuments of the Mississippi Valley*. Smithsonian Contributions to Knowledge 1.

Stallings, W. S., Jr. 1949. *Dating Prehistoric Ruins by Tree-Rings*. Rev. ed. Tucson: University of Arizona Laboratory of Tree-Ring Research.

Stanislawski, M. B. 1973. Review of *Archeology as Anthropology: A Case Study,* by W. A. Longacre. *American Antiquity* 38:117–121.

Stephens, J. L. 1841. *Incidents of Travel in Central America, Chiapas and Yucatan*. 2 vols. New York: Harper and Brothers. (Reprinted 1969. New York: Dover.)

———. 1843. *Incidents of Travel in Yucatan*. 2 vols. New York: Harper and Brothers. (Reprinted 1963. New York: Dover.)

Steponaitis, V. P., and J. P. Brain. 1976. A portable differential proton magnetometer. *Journal of Field Archaeology* 3:455–463.

Sterud, E. L. 1978. Changing aims of Americanist archaeology: A citations analysis of *American Antiquity*—1946–1975. *American Antiquity* 43:294–302.

Sterud, E. L., and P. P. Pratt. 1975. Archaeological intra-site recording with photography. *Journal of Field Archaeology* 2:151–167.

Steward, J. H. 1938. *Basin-Plateau Aboriginal Sociopolitical Groups*. Bureau of American Ethnology, Bulletin 120.

———. 1942. The direct historical approach to archaeology. *American Antiquity* 7:337–343.

———. 1955. *Theory of Culture Change*. Urbana: University of Illinois Press.

———. 1977. *Evolution and Ecology*. Ed. J. C. Steward and R. F. Murphy. Urbana: University of Illinois Press.

Steward, J. H., and F. M. Setzler. 1938. Function and configuration in archaeology. *American Antiquity* 1:4–10.

Stiles, D. 1977. Ethnoarchaeology: A discussion of methods and applications. *Man* 12:87–103.

Story, R. 1976. *The Space-Gods Revealed*. New York: Harper and Row.

Stover, L. E., and H. Harrison. 1970. *Apeman, Spaceman: Anthropological Science Fiction*. New York: Berkeley.

Strong, W. D. 1935. *An Introduction to Nebraska Archaeology*. Smithsonian Miscellaneous Collections, 93 (10).

Struever, S. 1968a. Flotation techniques for the recovery of small-scale archaeological remains. *American Antiquity* 33:353–362.

———. 1968b. Problems, methods and organization: A disparity in the growth of archeology. In *Anthropological Archeology in the Americas*, ed. B. J. Meggers, pp. 131–151. Washington, D.C.: Anthropological Society of Washington.

———. 1971. Comments on archaeological data requirements and research design. *American Antiquity* 36:9–19.

Struever, S., and J. Carlson. 1977. Koster site: The new archaeology in action. *Archaeology* 30:93–101.

Swanson, E., ed. 1975. *Lithic Technology: Making and Using Stone Tools*. Chicago: Aldine.

Tarling, D. H. 1971. *Principles and Applications of Palaeomagnetism*. London: Chapman and Hall.

Taylor, R. E., and I. Longworth, eds. 1975. Dating: New methods and new results. *World Archaeology* 7 (2).

Taylor, R. E., and C. W. Meighan, eds. 1978. *Chronologies in New World Archaeology*. New York: Academic Press.

Taylor, W. W. 1948. *A Study of Archeology*. American Anthropological Association, Memoir 69. (Reprinted 1964, 1967. Carbondale: Southern Illinois University Press.)

———. 1972. Old wine and new skins: A contemporary parable. In *Contemporary Archaeology*, ed. M. P. Leone, pp. 28–33. Carbondale: Southern Illinois University Press.

Thom, A. 1971. *Megalithic Lunar Observatories*. Oxford: Clarendon Press.

Thomas, C. 1971. Ethics in archaeology, 1971. *Antiquity* 45:268–274.

Thomas, D. H. 1969. Regional sampling in archaeology: A pilot Great Basin research design. *UCLA Archaeological Survey Annual Report* 11:87–100.

———. 1971. On distinguishing natural from cultural bone in archaeological sites. *American Antiquity* 36:366–371.

_____. 1973. An empirical test for Steward's model of Great Basin settlement patterns. *American Antiquity* 38:155–176.

_____. 1976. *Figuring Anthropology: First Principles of Probability and Statistics*. New York: Holt, Rinehart and Winston.

_____. 1978. The awful truth about statistics in archaeology. *American Antiquity* 43:231–244.

Thompson, F. C. 1970. Microscopic studies of ancient metals. In *Science in Archaeology*, ed. D. Brothwell and E. S. Higgs, pp. 555–563. New York: Praeger.

Thompson, J. E. S. 1963. *Maya Archaeologist*. Norman: University of Oklahoma Press.

_____. 1972. *Maya Hieroglyphs without Tears*. London: British Museum.

Tite, M. S. 1972. *Methods of Physical Examination in Archaeology*. New York: Academic Press.

Tolstoy, P. 1958. Surface survey of the northern Valley of Mexico: The Classic and Postclassic periods. *Transactions of the American Philosophical Society* 48 (5).

Tolstoy, P., and S. K. Fish. 1975. Surface and subsurface evidence for community size at Coapexco, Mexico. *Journal of Field Archaeology* 2:97–104.

Topping, A. 1977. Clay soldiers: The army of Emperor Ch'in. *Horizon* 19 (1):4–12.

Toulmin, S., and J. Goodfield. 1965. *The Discovery of Time*. New York: Harper and Row.

Trigger, B. G. 1968a. *Beyond History: The Methods of Prehistory*. New York: Holt, Rinehart and Winston.

_____. 1968b. The determinants of settlement patterns. In *Settlement Archaeology*, ed. K. C. Chang, pp. 53–78. Palo Alto, Calif.: National Press.

_____. 1970. Aims in prehistoric archaeology. *Antiquity* 44:26–37.

Trigger, B., and I. Longworth, eds. 1974. Political systems. *World Archaeology* 6 (1).

Tschopik, H., Jr. 1950. An Andean ceramic tradition in historical perspective. *American Antiquity* 15:196–218.

Tuggle, H. D., A. H. Townsend, and T. J. Riley. 1972. Laws, systems and research designs: A discussion of explanation in archaeology. *American Antiquity* 37:3–12.

Turnbull, C. M. 1972. *The Mountain People*. New York: Simon and Schuster.

Tylor, E. B. 1871. *Primitive Culture*. London: J. Murray.

Ucko, P. J. 1968. *Anthropomorphic Figurines of Predynastic Egypt and Neolithic Crete, with Comparative Material from the Prehistoric Near East and Mainland Greece*. Royal Anthropological Institute Occasional Paper 24. London: Andrew Szmidla.

_____. 1969. Ethnography and archaeological interpretation of funerary remains. *World Archaeology* 1:262–280.

Ucko, P. J., and G. W. Dimbleby, eds. 1969. *The Domestication and Exploitation of Plants and Animals*. London: Duckworth.

Ucko, P. J., and A. Rosenfeld. 1967. *Palaeolithic Cave Art*. New York: McGraw-Hill.

Ucko, P. J., R. Tringham, and G. W. Dimbleby, eds. 1972. *Man, Settlement and Urbanism*. London: Duckworth.

UNESCO. 1968. *The Conservation of Cultural Property*. UNESCO Press.

Vierra, R. K., and R. L. Taylor. 1977. Dummy data distributions and quantitative methods: An example applied to overlapping spatial distributions. In *For Theory Building in Archaeology*, ed. L. R. Binford, pp. 317–324. New York: Academic Press.

Vita-Finzi, C., and E. S. Higgs. 1970. Prehistoric economy in the Mount Carmel area of Palestine. *Proceedings of the Prehistoric Society* 36:1–37.

Vogt, E. Z., ed. 1974. *Aerial Photography in Anthropological Field Research*. Cambridge: Harvard University Press.

Von Däniken, E. 1969. *Chariots of the Gods?* New York: Bantam.

_____. 1970. *Gods from Outer Space.* New York: Bantam.

von den Driesch, A. 1976. *A Guide to the Measurement of Animal Bones from Archaeological Sites.* Peabody Museum Bulletin 1.

Ward, R. H., and K. M. Weiss. 1976. *The Demographic Evolution of Human Populations.* London: Academic Press.

Watanabe, N., and M. Suzuki. 1969. Fission-track dating of archaeological glass materials from Japan. *Nature* 222:1057–1058.

Watson, P. J. 1973. The future of archeology in anthropology: Cultural history and social science. In *Research and Theory in Current Archeology,* ed. C. L. Redman, pp. 113–124. New York: Wiley-Interscience.

_____. 1977. Design analysis of painted pottery. *American Antiquity* 42:381–393.

Watson, P. J., S. A. LeBlanc, and C. L. Redman. 1971. *Explanation in Archeology: An Explicitly Scientific Approach.* New York: Columbia University Press.

Watson, R. A. 1976. Inference in archaeology. *American Antiquity* 41:58–66.

Wauchope, R. 1938. *Modern Maya Houses.* Carnegie Institution of Washington, Publication 502.

_____. 1962. *Lost Tribes and Sunken Continents..* Chicago: University of Chicago Press.

_____. 1965. *They Found the Buried Cities.* Chicago: University of Chicago Press.

Weiner, J. S. 1955. *The Piltdown Forgery.* London: Oxford University Press.

Weiss, K. M. 1976. Demographic theory and anthropological inference. *Annual Review of Anthropology* 5:351–381.

Wendorf, F. 1973. "Rescue" archaeology along the Nile. In *In Search of Man: Readings in Archaeology,* ed. E. L. Green, pp. 39–42. Boston: Little, Brown.

Wertime, T. A. 1973a. The beginnings of metallurgy: A new look. *Science* 182:875–887.

_____. 1973b. Pyrotechnology: Man's first industrial uses of fire. *American Scientist* 61:670–682.

Whallon, R., Jr. 1968. Investigations of late prehistoric social organization in New York State. In *New Perspectives in Archeology,* ed. S. R. Binford and L. R. Binford, pp. 223–244. Chicago: Aldine.

_____. 1972. A new approach to pottery typology. *American Antiquity* 37:13–33.

_____. 1973a. Spatial analysis of occupation floors I: Application of dimensional analysis of variance. *American Antiquity* 38:266–278.

_____. 1973b. Spatial analysis of palaeolithic occupation areas. In *The Explanation of Culture Change: Models in Prehistory,* ed. C. Renfrew, pp. 115–130. Pittsburgh: University of Pittsburgh Press.

_____. 1974. Spatial analysis of occupation floors II: The application of nearest neighbor analysis. *American Antiquity* 39:16–34.

Wheat, J. B. 1967. A Paleo-Indian bison kill. *Scientific American* 216 (1):44–52.

_____. 1972. *The Olsen-Chubbuck Site: A Paleo-Indian Bison Kill.* Society for American Archaeology, Memoir 26.

Wheat, J. B., J. C. Gifford, and W. W. Wasley. 1958. Ceramic variety, type cluster, and ceramic system in Southwestern pottery analysis. *American Antiquity* 24:34–37.

Wheeler, M. 1943. *Maiden Castle, Dorset.* London: Society of Antiquaries of London.

_____. 1954. *Archaeology from the Earth.* Harmondsworth, England: Penguin.

_____. 1955. *Still Digging.* London: M. Joseph.

_____. 1966. *Civilizations of the Indus Valley and Beyond.* New York: McGraw-Hill.

White, L. A. 1949. *The Science of Culture.* New York: Grove Press.

White, P. 1974. *The Past is Human.* New York: Taplinger.

White, T. E. 1953. A method of calculating the dietary percentage of various food animals utilized by aboriginal peoples. *American Antiquity* 18:396–398.

Whiting, J. W. M., and B. Ayres. 1968. Inferences from the shape of dwellings. In *Settlement Archaeology,* ed. K. C. Chang, pp. 117–133. Palo Alto, Calif.: National Press.

Whittlesey, J. H. 1977. Interdisciplinary approach to archaeology. *Journal of Field Archaeology* 4:135–137.

Wiessner, P. 1974. A functional estimator of population from floor area. *American Antiquity* 39:343–350.

Willey, G. R. 1953. *Prehistoric Settlement Patterns in the Viru Valley, Peru*. Bureau of American Ethnology, Bulletin 155.

———, ed. 1956. *Prehistoric Settlement Patterns in the New World*. Viking Fund Publications in Anthropology 23.

———. 1962. The early great styles and the rise of the pre-Columbian civilizations. *American Anthropologist* 64:1–14.

———. 1966. *An Introduction to American Archaeology. Volume 1: North and Middle America*. Englewood Cliffs, N.J.: Prentice-Hall.

———. 1971. *An Introduction to American Archaeology. Volume 2: South America*. Englewood Cliffs, N.J.: Prentice-Hall.

———, ed. 1974. *Archaeological Researches in Retrospect*. Cambridge, Mass.: Winthrop.

Willey, G. R., and P. Phillips. 1958. *Method and Theory in American Archaeology*. Chicago: University of Chicago Press.

Willey, G. R., and J. A. Sabloff. 1974. *A History of American Archaeology*. San Francisco: W. H. Freeman.

Wilmsen, E. N. 1965. An outline of early man studies in the United States. *American Antiquity* 31:172–192.

———. 1968. Lithic analysis in paleoanthropology. *Science* 161:982–987.

———. 1970. *Lithic Analysis and Cultural Inference: A Paleo-Indian Case*. Anthropological Papers of the University of Arizona, No. 16. Tucson: University of Arizona Press.

———, ed. 1972. *Social Exchange and Interaction*. University of Michigan Anthropological Papers, no. 46.

———. 1974. *Lindenmeier: A Pleistocene Hunting Society*. New York: Harper and Row.

Wilson, D. 1975. *The New Archaeology*. New York: Knopf.

Winter, M. C. 1976. Excavating a shallow community by random sampling quadrats. In *The Early Mesoamerican Village*, ed. K. V. Flannery, pp. 62–67. New York: Academic Press.

Wiseman, J. 1964. Archaeology and the humanities. *Arion* 3:131–142.

Woodbury, R. B. 1973. *Alfred V. Kidder*. New York: Columbia University Press.

Woolley, C. L. 1934. *Ur Excavations, Volume II: The Royal Cemetery*. Oxford: British Museum and University Museum of the University of Pennsylvania.

Yellen, J. E. 1977. *Archaeological Approaches to the Present: Models for Reconstructing the Past*. New York: Academic Press.

Zeuner, F. E. 1958. *Dating the Past: An Introduction to Geochronology*. London: Methuen.

———. 1964. *A History of Domesticated Animals*. London: Hutchinson.

Ziegler, A. C. 1973. *Inference from Prehistoric Faunal Remains*. Addison-Wesley Modules in Anthropology, no. 43.

Zimmerman, D. W. 1971. Uranium distributions in archaeological ceramics: Dating of radioactive inclusions. *Science* 174:818–819.

Zubrow, E. 1973. Adequacy criteria and prediction in archeological models. In *Research and Theory in Current Archeology*, ed. C. L. Redman, pp. 239–255. New York: Wiley-Interscience.

———. 1975. *Prehistoric Carrying Capacity: A Model*. Menlo Park, Calif.: Cummings.

———, ed. 1976. *Demographic Anthropology: Quantitative Approaches*. Albuquerque: University of New Mexico Press, School of American Research Advanced Seminar Series.

Index